T0331860

Neutrosophic Sets in Decision Analysis and Operations Research

Mohamed Abdel-Basset
Zagazig University, Egypt

Florentin Smarandache
University of New Mexico, USA

A volume in the Advances in
Logistics, Operations, and
Management Science (ALOMS) Book
Series

Published in the United States of America by
   IGI Global
   Engineering Science Reference (an imprint of IGI Global)
   701 E. Chocolate Avenue
   Hershey PA, USA 17033
   Tel: 717-533-8845
   Fax: 717-533-8661
   E-mail: cust@igi-global.com
   Web site: http://www.igi-global.com

Library of Congress Cataloging-in-Publication Data

Names: Abdel-Basset, Mohamed, 1985- editor. | Smarandache, Florentin,
   editor.
Title: Neutrosophic sets in decision analysis and operations research /
   Mohamed Abdel-Basset and Florentin Smarandache, editors.
Description: Hershey, PA : Engineering Science Reference, [2020] | Includes
   bibliographical references and index. | Summary: "This book explores
   neutrosophic theory and its application in operations research and
   decision support"-- Provided by publisher.
Identifiers: LCCN 2019042038 (print) | LCCN 2019042039 (ebook) | ISBN
   9781799825555 (hardcover) | ISBN 9781799825562 (paperback) | ISBN
   9781799825579 (ebook)
Subjects: LCSH: Neutrosophic logic. | Decision making--Mathematical models.
Classification: LCC QA9.64 .N485 2020 (print) | LCC QA9.64 (ebook) | DDC
   511.3/13--dc23
LC record available at https://lccn.loc.gov/2019042038
LC ebook record available at https://lccn.loc.gov/2019042039

This book is published in the IGI Global book series Advances in Logistics, Operations, and Management Science (ALOMS) (ISSN: 2327-350X; eISSN: 2327-3518)

British Cataloguing in Publication Data
A Cataloguing in Publication record for this book is available from the British Library.

All work contributed to this book is new, previously-unpublished material.
The views expressed in this book are those of the authors, but not necessarily of the publisher.

For electronic access to this publication, please contact: eresources@igi-global.com.

Advances in Logistics, Operations, and Management Science (ALOMS) Book Series

ISSN:2327-350X
EISSN:2327-3518

Editor-in-Chief: John Wang, Montclair State University, USA

MISSION

Operations research and management science continue to influence business processes, administration, and management information systems, particularly in covering the application methods for decision-making processes. New case studies and applications on management science, operations management, social sciences, and other behavioral sciences have been incorporated into business and organizations real-world objectives.

The **Advances in Logistics, Operations, and Management Science** (ALOMS) Book Series provides a collection of reference publications on the current trends, applications, theories, and practices in the management science field. Providing relevant and current research, this series and its individual publications would be useful for academics, researchers, scholars, and practitioners interested in improving decision making models and business functions.

COVERAGE

- Decision analysis and decision support
- Marketing engineering
- Computing and information technologies
- Information Management
- Organizational Behavior
- Services management
- Risk Management
- Production Management
- Political Science
- Networks

IGI Global is currently accepting manuscripts for publication within this series. To submit a proposal for a volume in this series, please contact our Acquisition Editors at Acquisitions@igi-global.com or visit: http://www.igi-global.com/publish/.

Titles in this Series

For a list of additional titles in this series, please visit:
https://www.igi-global.com/book-series/advances-logistics-operations-management-science/37170

Multi-Criteria Decision Analysis in Management
Abhishek Behl (Indian Institute of Technology, Bombay, India)
Business Science Reference • © 2020 • 422pp • H/C (ISBN: 9781799822165) • US $245.00

Handbook of Research on Project Management Strategies and Tools for Organizational Success
Nelson Antonio Moreno-Monsalve (Universidad EAN, Colombia) H. Mauricio Diez-Silva (Universidad EAN, Colombia) Flor Nancy Diaz-Piraquive (Universidad Catolica de Colombia, Colombia) and Rafael Ignacio Perez-Uribe (Universidad EAN, Colombia)
Business Science Reference • © 2020 • 537pp • H/C (ISBN: 9781799819349) • US $285.00

Advancing Skill Development for Business Managers in Industry 4.0 Emerging Research and Opportunities
Sara Fazzin (H-Farm College, UK)
Business Science Reference • © 2020 • 168pp • H/C (ISBN: 9781799820369) • US $185.00

Management and Inter/Intra Organizational Relationships in the Textile and Apparel Industry
Vasilica-Maria Margalina (Technical University of Ambato, Ecuador) and José M. Lavín (CESINE University Centre, Spain)
Business Science Reference • © 2020 • 427pp • H/C (ISBN: 9781799818595) • US $215.00

Leadership, Management, and Adoption Techniques for Digital Service Innovation
Kamaljeet Sandhu (University of New England, Australia)
Business Science Reference • © 2020 • 342pp • H/C (ISBN: 9781799827993) • US $225.00

Global Perspectives on Green Business Administration and Sustainable Supply Chain Management
Syed Abdul Rehman Khan (Tsinghua University, China)
Business Science Reference • © 2020 • 362pp • H/C (ISBN: 9781799821731) • US $225.00

701 East Chocolate Avenue, Hershey, PA 17033, USA
Tel: 717-533-8845 x100 • Fax: 717-533-8661
E-Mail: cust@igi-global.com • www.igi-global.com

Editorial Advisory Board

Table of Contents

Detailed Table of Contents

Chapter 1
Yadigar Polat, Kilis 7 Aralık University, Kilis, Turkey
Irfan Deli, Kilis 7 Aralık University, Kilis, Turkey

Ranking of single valued trapezoidal neutrosophic numbers (SVTN-Numbers) plays a vital role in decision making and other single valued trapezoidal neutrosophic applications. In this chapter, the authors propose a new ranking method of SVTN-Numbers based on distance measure. Firstly, a new distance measure based on cut sets of SVTN-Numbers is developed. Secondly, some desired proportions and results of the distance measure are examined. Finally, the SVTN-Number method based on distance measure is given, and the effectiveness of our algorithm through a numerical example is illustrated.

Chapter 2
Sheng-Yi Ruan, Shaoxing University, China
Jun Ye, Shaoxing University, China
Wen-Hua Cui, Shaoxing University, China

This chapter introduces an improved proportional-integral-derivative (PID) adjusting method by applying a simulated annealing algorithm (SAA) and the cosine, tangent, exponential measures of single-valued neutrosophic sets (SvNSs). For the approach, characteristic values of the unit step response (rise time, peak time, settling time, undershoot ratio, overshoot ratio, and steady-state error) in the control system should be neutrosophicated by the neutrosophic membership functions. Next, one of cosine, tangent, and exponential measures is used to obtain the similarity measure of the ideal SvNS and the response SvNS to assess the control performance of the PID controller by the optimization values of the PID parameters Kp, Ki, and Kd searched by SAA. The results of the illustrative example obtained by these measures and SAA are better than the existing ones and indicate better PID controller performance. Comparative results can demonstrate the rationality and superiority of the improved PID adjusting method.

Chapter 3

In this study, the authors develop a new decision-making method on single-valued trapezoidal neutrosophic numbers (SVTN-Numbers) where all the decision information take the form of SVTN-Numbers. To construct the method, some new similarity measures between two SVTN-Numbers are presented. Then, concept of impact value on SVTN-Numbers by using the cut sets of SVTN-Numbers is proposed, and the corresponding properties are discussed. Finally, a real example is introduced and compared with different methods to show the applicability and feasibility of the proposed multi-attribute decision-making method.

Chapter 4

The neutrosophic relation equations are important elements of neutrosophic mathematics, and it can be widely applied in power systems, neutrosophic comprehensive evaluation. The aim of this chapter is to find the minimal solutions for the neutrosophic relation geometric programming having (V, Λ) operator. In this chapter, a max-min method has been built for finding an optimal solution in the neutrosophic relation equations, and a new characteristic matrix has been defined which is an important step to test the consistency of the system Aox=b and for finding all effective paths that lead to the set of all quasi-minimum solutions. The gained results are reasonable and harmonized with those results in Khalid's work. The method overcomes the problems of poor convergence efficiency inherited from the stochastic hill-climbing method or genetic algorithms. The suggested algorithm has the intersection column method which was proposed to find the effective paths that neglect the fallacious paths, and two new theorems were presented to deal with the optimal solution for (NREGP).

In this chapter, the authors present a new strategy for multi-attribute decision making in interval rough neutrosophic environment. They define Hamming distance and Euclidean distance between interval rough neutrosophic numbers. They also define interval rough neutrosophic relative positive ideal solution (IRNRPIS) and interval rough neutrosophic relative negative ideal solution (IRNRNIS). Then the ranking order of the alternatives is obtained by the technique for order preference by similarity to ideal solution (TOPSIS) strategy. Finally, a numerical example is provided to demonstrate the applicability and effectiveness of the proposed interval rough neutrosophic TOPSIS strategy.

The existing Rayleigh distribution under classical statistics has been widely applied for analyzing the data having all determined, certain, and precise observations. The neutrosophic statistics (NS) are the extension of classical statistics and applied under uncertainty environment. In this chapter, the authors introduce the neutrosophic Rayleigh distribution (NRD) under the NS. The proposed NRD is the generalization of the existing Rayleigh distribution. The authors give some basic properties of the proposed distribution. An application of the proposed distribution is discussed with the help of wind speed data.

#### Chapter 7

In this study, a new similarity measure for single valued neutrosophic numbers is defined. It is shown that this new similarity measure satisfies the conditions of similarity measure. This new similarity measure is used to assess professional proficiencies. In making this assessment, it is assumed that there is an imaginary ideal worker, and the authors determined the criteria of this ideal worker. Then, the rate of similarity of each worker to the ideal worker is determined with the new similarity measure. Thus, with the help of the new similarity measure, a more objective professional proficiency assessment is made.

Multi-attribute decision-making(MADM) strategy has been proposed to handle uncertain decision-making problems. The most extensively used models of grey system theory is grey relational analysis (GRA). This strategy was flourished by Chinese Professor J. Deng. This strategy also known as Deng's grey incidence analysis model. GRA uses a generic concept of intelligence. It describes any circumstance as no information as black and perfect information as white. Nevertheless, these idealized situations appear in real-world problems. In this chapter, the authors extend GRA strategy for multi-attribute decision making in trapezoidal neutrosophic number (TrNN) environment. To develop a GRA strategy in trapezoidal neutrosophic number (TrNN) environment, the authors use score function and accuracy function. Then Hamming distance for two trapezoidal neutrosophic number (TrNN) are also described. The authors solve a numerical problem to explain the pertinence of the proposed strategy. Lastly, they provide a comparison between VIKOR strategy with existing strategy.

#### Chapter 9

In this chapter, the concept of single valued neutrosophic number (SVN-Number) is presented in a generalized way. Using this notion, a crisp linear programming problem (LP-problem) is extended to a neutrosophic linear programming problem (NLP-problem). The coefficients of the objective function of a crisp LP-problem are considered as generalized single valued neutrosophic number (GSVN-Number). This modified form of LP-problem is here called an NLP-problem. An algorithm is developed to solve NLP-problem by simplex method. Finally, this simplex algorithm is applied to a real-life problem. The problem is illustrated and solved numerically.

Chapter 10

Interval-Valued Neutrosophic Subgroup Based on Interval-Valued Triple

Sudipta Gayen, National Institute of Technology, Jamshedpur, India
Florentin Smarandache, Department of Mathematics, University of New
Mexico, USA
Sripati Jha, National Institute of Technology, Jamshedpur, India
Ranjan Kumar, Jain University, Jayanagar, Bengaluru, India

Presently, interval-valued neutrosophic set theory has become an important research topic. It is widely used in various pure as well as applied fields. This chapter will provide some essential scopes to study interval-valued neutrosophic subgroup. Here the notion of interval-valued triple T-norm has been introduced, and based on that, interval-valued neutrosophic subgroup has been defined. Furthermore, some homomorphic characteristics of this notion have been studied. Additionally, based on interval-valued triple T-norm, interval-valued neutrosophic normal subgroup has been introduced and some of its homomorphic characteristics have been analyzed.

Chapter 11

New Unconventional Technique to Decipher MOTP in Neutrshopic

Krishna Prabha Sikkannan, PSNA College of Engineering and
Technology, India
Vimala Shanmugavel, Mother Terasa Womens University, India

Many papers have been proposed so far in the field of fuzzy and intuitionistic fuzzy multi-objective transportation problems. An innovative technique to unravel multi-objective neutroshopic (NS) transportation problem called mean method is proposed in this chapter. The objectives which have different units to membership values are aggregated by finding the mean of the values. A new algorithm is developed in order to solve the problems of this type is explained in this work. A numerical example is instigated to demonstrate the technique and the consequence is compared with VAM's method.

Chapter 12

Misturah Adunni Alaran, Moshood Abiola Polytechnic, Abeokuta,
Nigeria
AbdulAkeem Adesina Agboola, Federal University of Agriculture,
Nigeria
Adio Taofiki Akinwale, Federal University of Agriculture, Nigeria
Olusegun Folorunso, Federal University of Agriculture, Nigeria

The reality of human existence and their interactions with various things that surround them reveal that the world is imprecise, incomplete, vague, and even sometimes indeterminate. Neutrosophic logic is the only theory that attempts to unify all previous logics in the same global theoretical framework. Extracting data from a similar environment is becoming a problem as the volume of data keeps growing day-in and day-out. This chapter proposes a new neutrosophic string similarity measure based on the longest common subsequence (LCS) to address uncertainty in string information search. This new method has been compared with four other existing classical string similarity measure using wordlist as data set. The analyses show the performance of proposed neutrosophic similarity measure to be better than the existing in information retrieval task as the evaluation is based on precision, recall, highest false match, lowest true match, and separation.

Chapter 13

Said Broumi, Laboratory of Information Processing, Faculty of Science
Ben M'Sik, University Hassan II, Morocco
Selçuk Topal, Faculty of Science and Arts, Bitlis Eren University, Turkey
Assia Bakali, Ecole Royale Navale, Casablanca, Morocco
Mohamed Talea, Laboratory of Information Processing, Faculty of
Science Ben M'Sik, University Hassan II, Morocco
Florentin Smarandache, Department of Mathematics, University of New
Mexico, USA

Recently, single valued neutrosophic sets and interval valued neutrosophic sets have received great attention among the scholars and have been applied in many applications. These two concepts handle the indeterminacy and consistent information existing in real-life problems. In this chapter, a new Python toolbox is proposed under neutrosophic environment, which consists of some Python code for single valued neutrosophic matrices and interval valued neutrosophic matrices. Some definitions of interval neutrosophic vague set such as union, complement, and intersection are presented. Furthermore, the related examples are included.

Chapter 14

Mohanasundari M., Bannari Amman Institute of Technology, India
Mohana K., Nirmala College for Women, India

A correlation coefficient is one of the statistical measures that helps to find the degree of changes to the value of one variable predict change to the value of another. Quadripartitioned single valued neutrosophic sets is an improvization of Wang's single valued neutrosophic sets. This chapter deals the improved correlation coefficients of quadripartitioned single valued neutrosophic sets, interval quadripartitioned neutrosophic sets, and investigates its properties. And this concept is also applied in multiple-attribute decision-making methods with quadripartitioned single valued neutrosophic environment and interval quadripartitioned neutrosophic environment. Finally an illustrated example is given in the proposed method to the multiple-attribute decision-making problems.

Chapter 15

Siddhartha Sankar Biswas, Jamia Hamdard (Deemed), India

In this century the communication networks are expanding very fast in huge volumes in terms of their nodes and the connecting links. But for a given alive communication network, its complete core topology may not be always available to the concerned communication systems at a given real point of time. Thus, at any real-time instant the complete graph may not be available, but a subgraph of it to the system for executing its communication or transportation activities may be. In this chapter, the author introduces 'real-time neutrosophic graphs' (RTN-graphs) in which all real-time information (being updated every q quantum of time) are incorporated so that the communication/transportation system can serve very efficiently with optimal results. Although the style and philosophy of Dijkstra's algorithm is followed, the approach is completely new in the sense that the neutrosophic shortest path problem (NSPP) is solved with the real-time information of the network where most of the data are neutrosophic numbers.

    Elsayed Metwalli Badr, Benha University, Egypt
    Mustafa Abdul Salam, Benha University, Egypt
    Florentin Smarandache, University of New Mexico, USA

The neutrosophic primal simplex algorithm starts from a neutrosophic basic feasible solution. If there is no such a solution, we cannot apply the neutrosophic primal simplex method for solving the neutrosophic linear programming problem. In this chapter, the authors propose a neutrosophic two-phase method involving neutrosophic artificial variables to obtain an initial neutrosophic basic feasible solution to a slightly modified set of constraints. Then the neutrosophic primal simplex method is used to eliminate the neutrosophic artificial variables and to solve the original problem.

Preface

In the rising trends of information technology, the concepts of cost, time, delivery, space, quality, durability, and price have started gaining greater importance with time in solving managerial decision-making problems in supply chain model, transportation problem, or inventory control problems. Moreover, day by day competition is becoming tougher in imprecise environments. For instance, customer demand is often being affected by several varying factors like production price, income level, and the like. In these cases, the demand either remains unfulfilled or is difficult to obtain with certainty in the real-world market. Fuzzy sets are not always able to directly depict such uncertainties because they exhibit numeric only membership functions, whereas neutrosophic sets are found to be more suitable to accommodate inherent uncertainties. Neutrosophic sets and logic are generalizations of fuzzy and intuitionistic fuzzy sets and logic. These different uncertain systems can handle higher levels of uncertainty in more complex real world problems.

Neutrosophic sets and logic are gaining significant attention in solving many real life problems that involve uncertainty, impreciseness, vagueness, incompleteness, inconsistency, and indeterminacy. A number of new neutrosophic theories have been proposed and have been applied in computational intelligence, image processing, medical diagnosis, fault diagnosis, optimization design, and so on.

The main objective of this book is to understand the applicability of Multi-Criteria Decision Making (MCDM) and neutrosphic theory in operations research and also to know the various types of Neutrosophic Optimization and Neutrosoophic Mathematical Programming Models. This book will explore the possibilities and advantages created by Multi-Criteria Decision Making (MCDM) and neutrosophic methods, through both the presentation of thorough research and case studies. Once the material in this book has been mastered, the reader will be able to applying Multi-Criteria Decision Making (MCDM) and Neutrosophic Theories to his and her problem in operations research fields.

To facilitate this goal, in Chapter 1, Yadigar Polat and Irfan Deli propose a new ranking method of single valued trapezoidal neutrosophic numbers (SVTN) based on distance measure. Firstly, a new distance measure based on cut sets of

SVTN-Numbers is developed. Secondly, some desired proportions and results of the distance measure are examined. Finally, the SVTN-Number method based on distance measure is given, and the effectiveness of thie algorithm through a numerical example is illustrated.

This is followed by Chapter 2. Sheng-Yi Ruan, Jun Ye, and Wen-Hua Cui propose an improved proportional-integral-derivative (PID) adjusting method by applying a simulated annealing algorithm (SAA) and the cosine, tangent, exponential measures of single-valued neutrosophic sets (SvNSs). For this approach, characteristic values of the unit step response (rise time, peak time, settling time, undershoot ratio, overshoot ratio, and steady-state error) in the control system should be neutrosophicated by the neutrosophic membership functions. Next, one of cosine, tangent, and exponential measures is used to obtain the similarity measure of the ideal SvNS and the response SvNS to assess the control performance of the PID controller by the optimization values of the PID parameters. The results of the illustrative examples obtained by these measures and SAA are better than the existing ones and indicate better PID controller performance. Comparative results can demonstrate the rationality and superiority of the improved PID adjusting method.

In Chapter 3, Irfan Deli develops a new decision making method on single valued trapezoidal neutrosophic numbers (SVTN-numbers) - where all the decision information take the form of SVTN-numbers. To construct the method, some new similarity measures between two SVTN-numbers are presented. Then, the concept of impact value on SVTN-numbers by using the cut sets of SVTN-numbers is proposed, and the corresponding properties are discussed. Finally, a real example is introduced and compared with different methods to show the applicability and feasibility of the proposed multi-attribute decision making method.

Chapter 4 is written by Huda E. Khalid. The aim of this chapter is to find the minimal solutions for neutrosophic relation geometric programming model having operator in the objective function, subject to neutrosophic relation equations' constraints in their usual form. In this chapter, a max-min method has been built for finding an optimal solution in the neutrosophic relation equations of geometric programming (NREGP), a new characteristic matrix has been defined which is an important step to test the consistency of the system and for finding all effective paths that lead to the set of all quasi-minimum solutions.

In Chapter 5, Rumi Roy, Surapati Pramanik, and Tapan Kumar Roy present a new strategy for multi attribute decision making in interval rough neutrosophic environment. They define the Hamming distance and Euclidean distance between interval rough neutrosophic numbers; they also define the interval rough neutrosophic relative positive ideal solution (IRNRPIS) and interval rough neutrosophic relative negative ideal solution (IRNRNIS). Then the ranking order of the alternatives is obtained by the technique of order preference by similarity to ideal solution (TOPSIS) strategy. Finally, a numerical example is provided to demonstrate the applicability and effectiveness of the proposed interval rough neutrosophic TOPSIS strategy.

In Chapter 6, Muhammad Aslam introduces the Neutrosophic Rayleigh Distribution (NRD) under the Neutrosophic Statistics - which was introduced by Smarandache in 2014 and continued by Aslam in 2018. The proposed NRD is the generalization of the existing Rayleigh Distribution. An application of the proposed distribution is discussed with the help of wind speed data.

In Chapter 7, Memet Şahin and Abdullah Kargın propose a new similarity measure for single valued neutrosophic numbers. It is shown that this new similarity measure satisfies the conditions of similarity measure. This new similarity measure is used to assess the professional proficiencies. In making this assessment, it is assumed that there is an imaginary ideal worker and the authors determined the criteria of this ideal worker. Then, the rate of similarity of each worker to the ideal worker is determined with the newly similarity measure. With the help of this new similarity measure, a more objective professional proficiency assessment is introduced.

In Chapter 8, Surapati Pramanik and Rama Mallick introduced an improved Multi-Attribute Decision Making (MADM) strategy to handle the uncertain decision making problems. The most extensively used models of Grey system theory is the Grey Relational Analysis (GRA). This strategy was flourished by Chinese Professor J. Deng. This strategy is also known as Deng's Grey Incidence Analysis model. GRA uses a generic concept of intelligence. It describes any circumstance as follows: no information as black, and perfect information as white. Nevertheless, these idealized situations never appear in real world problem. In this chapter, GRA strategy is extended for multi attribute decision making in trapezoidal neutrosophic number (TrNN) environment. To develop a GRA strategy in trapezoidal neutrosophic number (TrNN) environment the authors defined an accuracy function for trapezoidal neutrosophic number (TrNN) environment in a new form. Then Hamming Distance for two trapezoidal neutrosophic numbers (TrNN) are also described. Lastly, a numerical problem is solved to explain the pertinence of the proposed strategy.

Chapter 9 is made by Nirmal Kumar Mahapatra and Tuhin Bera. In this chapter, the concept of single valued neutrosophic number (SVN-number) is presented in a generalized way. Using this notion, a crisp linear programming problem (LP-problem) is extended to a neutrosophic linear programming problem (NLP-problem). The coefficients of the objective function of a crisp LP-problem are considered as generalized single valued neutrosophic number (G_SVN-number). This modified form of LP-problem is here called an NLP-problem. An algorithm is developed to solve NLP-problem by simplex method. Finally, this simplex algorithm is applied to a real life problem. The problem is illustrated and solved numerically.

Chapter 10 is written by S. A. Edalatpanah and F. Smarandache. Data Envelopment Analysis (DEA) is one of the best mathematical methods to compute the overall performance of organizations which utilize similar sources to produce similar outputs. Original DEA schemes involve crisp information of inputs and outputs that may not always be accessible in real-world applications. Be that as it may, in some cases, the values of the data are information with indeterminacy, impreciseness, vagueness, inconsistency, and incompleteness. Furthermore, the conventional DEA models have been originally formulated solely for desirable outputs. However, undesirable outputs may additionally be present in the manufacturing system which wishes to be minimized. To tackle the above issues, this chapter presents a Neutrosophic DEA model with undesirable outputs. The proposed method is based on the weighted arithmetic average operator and has a simple structure. Finally, an example is given to illustrate the new model and ranking approach in details.

In Chapter 11, S. Krishna Prabha and S. Vimala propose an innovative technique to unravel Multi-Objective Neutrosophic Transportation Problem (MONTP). Trapezoidal neutrosophic numbers are defuzzified/deneutrosophicated by score function. The objectives which have different units to membership values are aggregated by finding the mean of the values. By applying the proposed algorithm the optimal solution is obtained. A numerical example is instigated to demonstrate the technique and the consequence is compared with Vogel's approximation method (VAM).

In Chapter 12, Misturah Adunni Alaran, Abdulakeem Adesina Agboola, and Adio Taofiki Akinwale propose a new neutrosophic string similarity measure based on the Longest Common Subsequence (LCS) to address uncertainty in string information search. The new method has been compared with four other existing classical string similarity measure using wordlist as data set. The analyses show the performance of proposed neutrosophic similarity measure to be better than the existing in information retrieval task as the evaluation is based on precision, recall, highest false match, lowest true match and separation.

In Chapter 13, Said Broumi, Selçuk Topal, Assia Bakali, Mohamed Talea, and Florentin Smarandache propose a new Python toolbox under neutrosophic environment, which consisting of some python code for single valued neutrosophic matrices and interval valued neutrosophic matrices. Some definitions of interval neutrosophic vague set such as union, complement and intersection are presented. Furthermore, the related examples are included.

In Chapter 14, M. Mohanasundari and K. Mohana talk about the correlation coefficient, which is one of the statistical measure which helps to find the degree of change of the value of one variable that predicts the change to the value of another. Quadripartitioned single valued neutrosophic sets is an improvement of Smarandache and Wang's single valued neutrosophic sets. The existing correlation coefficient between quadripartitioned single valued neutrosophic set has some drawbacks while dealing with decision making problems so that to overcome these disadvantages, an improved correlation coefficient of quadripartitioned single valued neutrosophic set and interval quadripartitioned neutrosophic set defined and also the authors investigate its properties. Further on, an example is illustrated in multiple attribute decision making methods with quadripartitioned single valued neutrosophic environment and interval quadripartitioned neutrosophic environment for the proposed method. Based on the weighted correlation coefficient between each alternative and the ideal alternative, the ranking order is obtained to select the best one. The suggested decision-making methods can efficiently deal with decision-making problems with the imperfect, undefined, and inconsistent information which occur frequently in real life situations.

Chapter 15 belongs to Siddhartha Sankar Biswas. In this century the communication networks are expanding very fast in huge volumes in terms of their nodes and the connecting links. But for a given alive communication network, its complete core topology may not be always available to fit to the concerned communication systems at a given real point in time. Thus, at any real time instant, the complete graph may not be available but a subgraph of it to the system for executing its communication or transportation activities. In this article the author introduces the 'Real Time Neutrosophic Graphs' (RTN-graphs) in which all real time information (being updated every q quantum of time) are incorporated so that the communication/transportation system can serve very efficiently with optimal results. Although the style and philosophy of Dijkstra's Algorithm is followed, author's approach is a completely new in the sense that the Neutrosophic Shortest Path Problem (NSPP) is solved with the real time information of the network where most of the data are neutrosophic numbers.

In Chapter 16, Elsayed Badr, Mustafa Abdul Salam, and Florentin Smarandache propose a neutrosophic two-phase method involving neutrosophic artificial variables, to obtain an initial neutrosophic basic feasible solution to a slightly modified set of constraints. the neutrosophic primal simplex method is used to eliminate the neutrosophic artificial variables and to solve the original problem.

Acknowledgment

The editors would like to acknowledge the help of all the people involved in this project and, more specifically, to the authors and reviewers that took part in the review process. Without their support, this book would not have become a reality.

We would like to thank each one of the authors for their contributions. The editors wish to acknowledge the valuable contributions of the reviewers regarding the improvement of quality, coherence, and content presentation of chapters. Most of the authors also served as referees; we highly appreciate their double task.

We are grateful to the series editor for his support. The editors would like to thank all members of IGI publishing house for their assistance and timely motivation in producing this book.

We hope the readers will share our excitement with this important scientific contribution of the body of knowledge about application multi-criteria decision making and neutrosophic theory in operations research.

Chapter 1
A TOPSIS Method Under SVTN-Numbers Based on Multi-Attribute Decision-Making Problems

Yadigar Polat
Kilis 7 Aralık University, Turkey

Irfan Deli
Kilis 7 Aralık University, Turkey

ABSTRACT

Ranking of single valued trapezoidal neutrosophic numbers (SVTN-Numbers) plays a vital role in decision making and other single valued trapezoidal neutrosophic applications. In this chapter, the authors propose a new ranking method of SVTN-Numbers based on distance measure. Firstly, a new distance measure based on cut sets of SVTN-Numbers is developed. Secondly, some desired proportions and results of the distance measure are examined. Finally, the SVTN-Number method based on distance measure is given, and the effectiveness of our algorithm through a numerical example is illustrated.

1 INTRODUCTİON

Multiple attribute decision making (MADM) is a research topic to modeling uncertainty and vagueness information in fuzzy set theory (Zadeh, 1965), intuitionistic fuzzy set theory (Atanassov, 1986) and neutrosophic set theory (Smarandache, 2005).

DOI: 10.4018/978-1-7998-2555-5.ch001

There are extensive literature about intuitionistic fuzzy set theory, for example; on logic programming language PROLOG (Atanassov, 1993), on entropy (Hung & Yang, 2006; Szmidt & Kacprzyk, 2001), on optimization (Angelov, 1997), on intuitionistic judgment matrix and interval-valued intuitionistic judgment matrices (Xu, 2007), on clustering algorithm of intuitionistic fuzzy sets (Xu, 2008), on distance measure between intuitionistic fuzzy sets (Wang & Xin, 2005; Burillo & Bustince, 1996; Szmidt & Kacprzyk, 2000), on strong intuitionistic fuzzy graphs (Akram & Davvaz, 2012), on intuitionistic fuzzy hypergraphs (Akram & Dudek, 2013), on intuitionistic fuzzy aggregation operators (Xu, 2010; Xu & Xia, 2011; Xu, 2007; Zeng, 2011; Beliakov et al., 2011; Zhou & Wu, 2008; Xu, & Chen, 2007; Xu, & Yager, 2006; Wei, 2010), on multi-attribute decision making problems where all the attribute values are expressed in intuitionistic fuzzy numbers (Xu & Yager, 2008; Hayat et al., 2018), on intuitionistic preference relation (Szmidt & Kacprzyk, 2003), on similarity measures (Dengfeng & Chuntian, 2002; Li et al., 2007; Hung & Yang, 2004; Liang & Shi, 2003), on intuitionistic fuzzy set to Hv-modules (Davvaz et al., 2006), on relations (Bustince & Burillo, 1996), on topological spaces (Grzegorzewski, 2002; Çoker, 1997; Alaca et al,, 2006; Saadati & Park, 2006; Lee & Lee, 2000), on correlation and correlation coefficient (Bustince & Burillo 1995; Hong & Hwang, 1995; Ye, 2010).

Neutrosophic set (Smarandache, 2005) is used to handle more uncertain and imprecise information than the ordinary fuzzy set and intuitionistic fuzzy set. Therefore; Smaradanche (Smarandache, 2004) presented a geometric interpretation of the neutrosophic set using the neutrosophic cube. Then, many researchers have studied on similarity measure on two single valued neutrosophic sets (Majumdar & Samanta,2013; Aydoğdu, 2015; Broumi & Smarandache, 2013), on projection and bidirectional projection measures (Jun, 2017), on neutrosophic cross entropy (Şahin & Küçük, 2014), on analytic hierarchy method (Alava et al., 2018), on WASPAS method (Zavadskas et el., 2015), on Transition Difficulties of IoT-Based Enterprises (Basset et al.,2019), on multi-attribute decision making (Karaaslan & Hayat, 2018; Jana et al., 2018; Karaaslan, 2018a; Karaaslan, 2018b; Karaaslan, 2019; Nabeeh et al., 2019b), on Shortest path problem (Broumi et al., 2019a; Broumi et al., 2019b), on TOPSIS method (Biswas et al., 2016; Nabeeh et al., 2019a) in single- valued neutrosophic environment.

Single valued trapezoidal neutrosophic numbers allow the concept of neutrosophic sets from the discrete values to the continuous values. Therefore, Deli and Subas (2014; 2015) and Ye (2015) introduced single valued trapezoidal neutrosophic number including some operational rules and operators. Tan and Zhang (2017) suggested two multiple attribute group decision making methods: one based on the trapezoidal fuzzy neutrosophic number hybrid averaging operator, and the other based on TOPSIS method. Deli and Subas (2017) developed values and ambiguities of single valued trapezoidal neutrosophic numbers by defining concepts of cut sets. Li et al. (2016) gave an improved generalized weighted Heronian mean operator and improved generalized weighted geometric Heronian mean (IGWGHM) operator based on crisp numbers. Pouresmaeil (Pouresmaeil 2016) developed a TOPSIS and a VIKOR method for determining the weights of decision makers with single valued neutrosophic information. Aal et al. (2018) proposed an Information Systems Quality (ISQ) evaluation model based on neutrosophic numbers. Sahin (2018) suggested a decision making method with new score functions based on the Hamming distance. Also, many researchers have developed and applied the theory in (Abdel-Basset et al., 2019; Broumi et al., 2016; Broumi et al., 2019c; Abdel-Basset et al., 2018; Biswas et al, 2015; Wu et al., 2018; Biswas et al., 2016; Broumi et al., 2017; Chakraborty et al., 2018; Wang et al., 2018).

The aim of the current research is to propose a new SVTN-Number method by using a new distance measure in MADM problems. It is evident from the previous studies, in the literature, that the method in this study has not yet been proposed at this extent. The remainder of the paper is constructed as follows. In section 2, some preliminaries of neutrosophic sets and SVTN-Numbers are introduced. In section 3, a new distance measure based on cut sets of SVTN-Numbers developed. Then, some deseired propertions and results of the distance measure are examined. In section 4, the SVTN-Number method based on distance measure is given, and the effectiveness of our algorithm through a numerical example is illustrated. In section 5, Concluding remarks are presented in the final section.

2 PRELIMINARY

This section presents the basic concepts, including fuzzy sets, intuitionistic fuzzy sets, spherical fuzzy sets, neutrosophic sets and SVTN-Numbers.

Definition 2.1 (Zadeh, 1965) Let E be a universe. Then a fuzzy set X over E is defined by

$$X = \{(\mu_x(x) / x) : x \in E\}$$

where μ_x is called membership function of X and defined by $\mu_x: E \to (0,1)$. For each $x \in E$, the value $\mu_x(x)$ represents the degree of x belonging to the fuzzy set X.

Definition 2.2 (Atanassov, 1986) Let E be a universe. An intuitionistic fuzzy set K over E is defined by

$$K = \{\langle x, \mu_K(x), \gamma_K(x)\rangle : x \in E\}$$

where $\mu_K: E \to (0,1)$ and $\gamma_K: E \to (0,1)$ such that $0 \le \mu K_{(x)} + \gamma K_{(x)} \le 1$ for any $x \in E$. For each $x \in E$, the values $\mu K_{(x)}$ and $\gamma K_{(x)}$ are the degree of membership and degree of non-membership of x. respectively.

Definition 2.3 (Gündoğdu & Kahraman, 2019) Let E.be a universe. A spherical fuzzy set A.over E.is defined by

$$A = \{\langle x, (\mu_A(x), v_A(x), \pi_A(x))\rangle : x \in E\}.$$

where μ_A, v_A and π_A are called membership function, nonmembership function and hesitancy function, respectively. They are respectively defined by

$$\mu_A : E \to (0,1), v_A : E \to (0,1), \pi_A : E \to (0,1)$$

such that $0 \le \mu_A^2(x) + v_A^2(x) + \pi_A^2(x) \le 1$.

Definition 2.4 (Gündoğdu & Kahraman, 2019) Let

$$A = \{\langle x, (\mu_A(x), v_A(x), \pi_A(x))\rangle : x \in E \quad \text{and} \quad B = \{\langle x, (\mu_B(x), v_B(x), \pi_B(x))\rangle : x \in E$$

be two spherical fuzzy sets. Then,

1. spherical distance between A and B, is denoted by dis (A,B). is defined as;

$$\text{Dis}(A,B) = \frac{2}{\pi} \sum_{j-1}^{n} \arccos(\mu_A(x_j)) + v_A(x_j) \cdot v_B(x_j) \cdot \pi_B(x_j).$$

2. spherical normalized distance between A and B, is denoted by $\text{dis}_n(A,B)$. is defined as;

$$\frac{2}{n\pi} \sum_{j-1}^{n} \arccos(\mu_A(x_j) \cdot \mu_B(x_j)) + v_A(x_j) \cdot v_B(x_j) + \pi_A(x_j) \cdot \pi_B(x_j).$$

Definition 2.5 (Smarandache, 1998) Let E.be a universe. A neutrosophic sets A. over E. is defined by

$$A = \{\langle x, (T_A(x), I_A(x), F_A(x)) \rangle : x \in E\}$$

where $T_A(x)$. $I_A(x)$.and $F_A(x)$.are called truth-membership function, indeterminacy-membership function and falsity-membership function, respectively. They are respectively defined by

$T_A: E \rightarrow {}^-0,1^+($, $I_A: E \rightarrow {}^-0,1^+($, $F_A: E \rightarrow {}^-0,1^+($.such that $0^- \leq T_A(x) + I_A(x) + F_A(x) \leq 3^+$.

Definition 2.6 (Deli & Şubaş, 2015) An SVTN-number $\tilde{a} = \langle (a, b, c, d); w_{\tilde{a}}, u_{\tilde{a}}, y_{\tilde{a}} \rangle$ on R, is characterized by a truth-membership function $T_{\tilde{a}} : R \rightarrow (0,1)$ an indeterminacy-membership function $I_{\tilde{a}} : R \rightarrow (0,1)$ and a falsity-membership function $F_{\tilde{a}} : R \rightarrow (0,1)$ is defined as;

$$\langle x, (T_{\tilde{a}}(x), I_{\tilde{a}}(x), F_{\tilde{a}}(x)) \rangle$$

$$= \begin{cases} \left\langle x, \left(\dfrac{(x-a)w_{\tilde{a}}}{b-a}, \dfrac{b-x+u_{\tilde{a}}(x-a)}{b-a}, \dfrac{b-x+y_{\tilde{a}}(x-a)}{b-a} \right) \right\rangle, & a \leq x < b \\[3mm] \langle x, (w_{\tilde{a}}, u_{\tilde{a}}, y_{\tilde{a}}) \rangle, & b \leq x \leq c \\[3mm] \left\langle x, \left(\dfrac{(d-x)w_{\tilde{a}}}{d-c}, \dfrac{x-c+u_{\tilde{a}}(d-x)}{d-c}, \dfrac{x-c+y_{\tilde{a}}(d-x)}{d-c} \right) \right\rangle, & c < x \leq d \\[3mm] \langle x, (0,1,1) \rangle, & otherwise \end{cases}$$

Note that the set of all SVTN-number-numbers on R will be denoted by Δ.

Definition 2.7 (Deli & Şubaş, 2015) Let

$$\tilde{a} = \langle (a_1, b_1, c_1, d_1); w_{\tilde{a}}, u_{\tilde{a}}, y_{\tilde{a}} \rangle \text{ and } \tilde{b} = \langle (a_2, b_2, c_2, d_2); w_{\tilde{b}}, u_{\tilde{b}}, y_{\tilde{b}} \rangle$$

be two SVTN-numbers and $\gamma \neq 0$ .be any real number. Then,

1. $\tilde{a} + \tilde{b} = \langle (a_1 + a_2, b_1 + h_2, c_1 + c_2, d_1 + d_2); w_{\tilde{a}} \wedge w_{\tilde{b}}, u_{\tilde{a}} \vee u_{\tilde{b}}, y_{\tilde{a}} \vee y_{\tilde{b}} \rangle$

2. $\tilde{a}\tilde{b} = \begin{cases} \langle (a_1 a_2, b_1 b_2, c_1 c_2, d_1 d_2); w_{\tilde{a}} \wedge w_{\tilde{b}}, u_{\tilde{a}} \vee u_{\tilde{b}}, y_{\tilde{a}} \vee y_{\tilde{b}} \rangle & (d_1 > 0, d_2 > 0) \\ \langle (a_1 d_2, b_1 c_2, c_1 b_2, d_1 a_2); w_{\tilde{a}} \wedge w_{\tilde{b}}, u_{\tilde{a}} \vee u_{\tilde{b}}, y_{\tilde{a}} \vee y_{\tilde{b}} \rangle & (d_1 < 0, d_2 > 0) \\ \langle (d_1 d_2, c_1 c_2, b_1 b_2, a_1 a_2); w_{\tilde{a}} \wedge w_{\tilde{b}}, u_{\tilde{a}} \vee u_{\tilde{b}}, y_{\tilde{a}} \vee y_{\tilde{b}} \rangle & (d_1 < 0, d_2 < 0) \end{cases}$

3. $\gamma\tilde{a} = \begin{cases} \langle (\gamma a_1, \gamma b_1, \gamma c_1, \gamma d_1); w_{\tilde{a}}, u_{\tilde{a}}, y_{\tilde{a}} \rangle (\gamma > 0) \\ \langle (\gamma d_1, \gamma c_1, \gamma b_1, \gamma a_1); w_{\tilde{a}}, u_{\tilde{a}}, y_{\tilde{a}} \rangle (\gamma < 0) \end{cases}$

Definition 2.8 (Deli & Şubaş, 2017) Let $\tilde{a} = \langle (a,b,c,d); w_{\tilde{a}}, u_{\tilde{a}}, y_{\tilde{a}} \rangle$ is an arbitrary SVTN-number. Then,

1. α-cut set of the SVTN-number $\tilde{a}$ for truth-membership is calculated as;

$$\tilde{a}_\alpha = (L_{\tilde{a}}(\alpha), R_{\tilde{a}}(\alpha)) = \left(\frac{w_{\tilde{a}} - \alpha)a + \alpha b}{w_a}, \frac{w_{\tilde{a}} - \alpha)d + \alpha c}{w_a} \right) \text{ where } \alpha \in (0, w_{\tilde{a}}).$$

2. β-cut set of the SVTN-number $\tilde{a}$ for indeterminacy-membership is calculated as;

$$\tilde{a}^\beta = (L'_{\tilde{a}}(\beta), R'_{\tilde{a}}(\beta)) = \left(\frac{(1-\beta)b + (\beta - u_{\tilde{a}})a}{1 - u_a}, \frac{(1-\beta)c + (\beta - u_{\tilde{a}})d}{1 - u_a} \right).$$

where $\beta \in (u_{\tilde{a}}, 1)$

3. γ-cut set of the SVTN-number $\tilde{a}$ for falsity-membership is calculated as;

$$\gamma_{\tilde{a}} = (L''_{\tilde{a}}(\gamma), R''_{\tilde{a}}(\gamma)) = \left(\frac{(1-\gamma)b + (\gamma - y_{\tilde{a}})a}{1 - y_{\tilde{a}}}, \frac{(1-\gamma)c + (\gamma - y_{\tilde{a}})d}{1 - y_a} \right).$$

where $\gamma \in (y_{\tilde{a}}, 1)$

3 A NEW DİSTANCE MEASURE BASED ON CUT SETS OF SVTN-NUMBERS

In this section, we define a new distance measure based on cut sets of SVTN-Numbers. Its adopted from ((Deli & Şubaş, 2015), (Deli & Şubaş, 2017), (Grzegorzewski, 2002), (Gündoğdu & Kahraman, 2019)).

Definition 3.1 Let

$$\tilde{a} = \left\langle (a_1, b_1, c_1, d_1); w_{\tilde{a}}, u_{\tilde{a}}, y_{\tilde{a}} \right\rangle \text{ and } \tilde{b} = \left\langle (a_2, b_2, c_2, d_2); w_{\tilde{b}}, u_{\tilde{b}}, y_{\tilde{b}} \right\rangle$$

be two arbitrary SVTN-numbers. Then, the distance measure based on cut sets of the SVTN-numbers between $\tilde{a}$ and $\tilde{b}$ denoted by $d(\tilde{a}, \tilde{b})$ .defined as;

$$d\left(\tilde{a}, \tilde{b}\right) = \frac{2}{\pi} \arccos(1 - \frac{1}{6}((\left|T_L(\alpha)\right| + \left|T_R(\alpha)\right| + \left|I_L(\beta)\right| + \left|I_R(\beta)\right| + \left|F_L(\gamma)\right| + \left|F_R(\gamma)\right|))$$

where

$$T_L(\alpha) = \int_0^{w_c} \left(L_L(\alpha) - L_R(\alpha)\right)^2 d\alpha, \quad T_R(\alpha) = \int_0^{w_c} \left(R_L(\alpha) - R_R(\alpha)\right)^2 d\alpha,$$

$$I_L(\beta) = \int_{u_c}^1 \left(L'_L(\beta) - L'_R(\beta)\right)^2 d\beta, \quad I_R(\beta) = \int_{u_c}^1 \left(R'_L(\beta) - R'_R(\beta)\right)^2 d\beta,$$

$$F_L(\gamma) = \int_{y_c}^1 \left(L''_L(\gamma) - L''_R(\gamma)\right)^2 d\gamma, \quad F_R(\gamma) = \int_{y_c}^1 \left(R''_L(\gamma) - R''_R(\gamma)\right)^2 d\gamma,$$

Theorem 3.2 Let

$$\tilde{a} = \left\langle (a_1, b_1, c_1, d_1); w_{\tilde{a}}, u_{\tilde{a}}, y_{\tilde{a}} \right\rangle \text{ and } \tilde{b} = \left\langle (a_2, b_2, c_2, d_2); w_{\tilde{b}}, u_{\tilde{b}}, y_{\tilde{b}} \right\rangle$$

be two arbitrary SVTN-number and $d\left(\tilde{a}, \tilde{b}\right)$ .be a the distance measure between $\tilde{a}$ and $\tilde{b}$ Then, $T_L(\alpha)$, $T_R(\alpha)$, $I_L(\alpha)$, $I_R(\alpha)$, $F_L(\alpha)$ and $F_R(\alpha)$ is computed as;

1. $T_L\left(\alpha\right) = \int_0^{w_c} \left(L_{\tilde{a}}\left(\alpha\right) - L_{\tilde{b}}\left(\alpha\right)\right)^2 d\alpha$

$$= \frac{w_c}{3}\left((a_1 - a_2)^2 + (b_1 - b_2)^2 + (a_1 - a_2)(b_1 - b_2)\right)$$

2. $T_R\left(\alpha\right) = \int_0^{w_c} \left(R_{\tilde{a}}\left(\alpha\right) - R_{\tilde{b}}\left(\alpha\right)\right)^2 d\alpha$

$$= \frac{w_c}{3}\left((c_1 - c_2)^2 + (d_1 - d_2)^2 + (c_1 - c_2)(d_1 - d_2)\right)$$

3. $$I_L(\beta) = \int_{u_c}^{1}\left(L'_L(\beta) - L'_R(\beta)\right)^2 d\beta$$

$$= \frac{1}{(1-u_c)^2}\left(\frac{1}{3} - u_c + u_c^2 - \frac{u_c^3}{3}\right)\left((a_1 - a_2)^2 + (b_1 - b_2)^2 + (a_1 - a_2)(b_1 - b_2)\right)$$

4. $$I_R(\beta) = \int_{u_c}^{1}\left(|R'_{\tilde{a}}(\beta) - R'_{\tilde{b}}(\beta)|^2\right)d\beta$$

$$= \frac{1}{(1-u_c)^2}\left(\frac{1}{3} - u_c + u_c^2 - \frac{u_c^3}{3}\right)\left((c_1 - c_2)^2 + (d_1 - d_2)^2 + (c_1 - c_2)(d_1 - d_2)\right)$$

5. $$F_L(\gamma) = \int_{y_c}^{1}\left(|L''_{\tilde{a}}(\gamma) - L''_{\tilde{b}}(\gamma)|^2\right)d\gamma$$

$$= \frac{1}{(1-y_c)^2}\left(\frac{1}{3} - y_c + y_c^2 - \frac{y_c^3}{3}\right)\left((a_1 - a_2)^2 + (b_1 - b_2)^2 + (a_1 - a_2)(b_1 - b_2)\right)$$

6. $$F_R(\gamma) = \int_{y_c}^{1}\left(|R''_{\tilde{a}}(\gamma) - R''_{\tilde{b}}(\gamma)|^2\right)d\gamma$$

$$= \frac{1}{(1-y_c)^2}\left(\frac{1}{3} - y_c + y_c^2 - \frac{y_c^3}{3}\right)\left((c_1 - c_2)^2 + (d_1 - d_2)^2 + (c_1 - c_2)(d_1 - d_2)\right)$$

Proof

1. Assume that $\tilde{a}_\alpha = (L_{\tilde{a}}(\alpha), R_{\tilde{a}}(\alpha))$ and $\tilde{b}_\alpha = (L_{\tilde{b}}(\alpha), R_{\tilde{b}}(\alpha))$ be α.cut set of the SVTN-number $\tilde{a}$ and $\tilde{b}$ respectively. Then,

$$T_L(\alpha) = \int_0^{w_c}\left(L_{\tilde{a}}(\alpha) - L_{\tilde{b}}(\alpha)\right)^2 d\alpha = \int_0^{w_c}\left(\frac{(w_c - \alpha)a_1 + \alpha b_1}{w_c} - \frac{(w_c - \alpha)a_2 + \alpha b_2}{w_c}\right)^2 d\alpha$$

$$= \int_0^{w_c} \left(\left(\frac{(w_c - \alpha)a_1 + \alpha b_1}{w_c} \right)^2 - 2\left(\frac{(w_c - \alpha)a_1 + \alpha b_1}{w_c} \right)\left(\frac{(w_c - \alpha)a_2 + \alpha b_2}{w_c} \right) \right.$$
$$\left. + \left(\frac{(w_c - \alpha)a_2 + \alpha b_2}{w_c} \right)^2 d\alpha \right)$$

$$= \int_0^{w_c} \left(\left(a_1 - \frac{a_1\alpha}{w_c} + \frac{b_1\alpha}{w_c} \right)^2 - 2\left(a_1 - \frac{a_1\alpha}{w_c} + \frac{b_1\alpha}{w_c} \right)\left(a_2 - \frac{a_2\alpha)}{w_c} + \frac{b_2\alpha}{w_c} \right) \right.$$
$$\left. + \left(a_2 - \frac{a_2\alpha)}{w_c} + \frac{b_2\alpha}{w_c} \right)^2 d\alpha \right)$$

$$= \int_0^{w_c} \left(a_1^2 - \frac{a_1^2\alpha}{w_c} + \frac{b_1 a_1\alpha}{w_c} - \frac{a_1^2\alpha}{w_c} + \frac{a_1^2\alpha^2}{w_c^2} - \frac{a_1 b_1\alpha^2}{w_c^2} + \frac{a_1 b_1\alpha}{w_c} - \frac{a_1 b_1\alpha^2}{w_c^2} + \frac{b_1^2\alpha^2}{w_c^2} \right.$$
$$- \frac{2\alpha^2 a_1 a_2}{w_c^2} + \frac{2\alpha^2 a_1 b_2}{w_c^2} - \frac{2b_1 a_2\alpha}{w_c} + \frac{2b_1 a_2\alpha^2}{w_c^2} - \frac{2b_1 b_2\alpha^2}{w_c^2} + 2a_2^2 - \frac{a_2^2\alpha}{w_c} + \frac{a_2 b_2\alpha}{w_c}$$
$$\left. - \frac{\alpha a_2^2}{w_c} + \frac{a_2^2\alpha^2}{w_c^2} - \frac{\alpha^2 a_2 b_2}{w_c^2} + \frac{b_2 a_2\alpha}{w_c} - \frac{a_2 b_2\alpha^2}{w_c^2} + \frac{b_2^2\alpha^2}{w_c^2} \right) d\alpha$$

$$= \left(\left[a_1^2\alpha - \frac{a_1^2\alpha^2}{2w_c} + \frac{a_1 b_1\alpha^2}{2w_c} - \frac{a_1^2\alpha^2}{2w_c} + \frac{a_1^2\alpha^3}{3w_c^2} - \frac{a_1 b_1\alpha^3}{3w_c^2} + \frac{a_1 b_1\alpha^2}{2w_c} - \frac{a_1 b_1\alpha^3}{3w_c^2} + \frac{b_1^2\alpha^3}{3w_c^2} \right.\right.$$
$$- 2a_1 a_2\alpha - \frac{2a_1 b_2\alpha^2}{2w_c} + \frac{2a_1 a_2\alpha^2}{2w_c} - \frac{2a_1 a_2\alpha^3}{3w_c^2} + \frac{2a_1 b_2\alpha^3}{3w_c^2} - \frac{2b_1 a_2\alpha^2}{2w_c} + \frac{2b_1 a_2\alpha^3}{3w_c^2}$$
$$\left.\left. - \frac{2b_1 b_2\alpha^3}{3w_c^2} + a_2^2\alpha - \frac{a_2^2\alpha^2}{2w_c} - \frac{a_2^2\alpha^2}{2w_c} + \frac{a_2^2\alpha^3}{3w_c^2} - \frac{a_2 b_2\alpha^3}{3w_c^2} + \frac{a_2 b_2\alpha^2}{2w_c} - \frac{a_2 b_2\alpha^3}{3w_c^2} + \frac{b_2^2\alpha^3}{3w_c^2} \right] \Big|_0^{w_c} \right)$$

9

$$= \left(\left[a_1^2 w_c - \frac{a_1^2 w_c^2}{2w_c} + \frac{a_1 b_1 w_c^2}{2w_c} - \frac{a_1^2 w_c^2}{2w_c} + \frac{a_1^2 w_c^3}{3w_c^2} - \frac{a_1 b_1 w_c^3}{3w_c^2} + \frac{a_1 b_1 w_c^2}{2w_c} - \frac{a_1 b_1 w_c^3}{3w_c^2} + \frac{b_1^2 w_c^3}{3w_c^2} \right. \right.$$

$$+ \frac{2a_1 a_2 w_c^2}{2w_c} - \frac{2a_1 b_2 w_c^2}{2w_c} + \frac{2a_1 a_2 w_c^2}{2w_c} - \frac{2a_1 a_2 w_c^3}{3w_c^2} + \frac{2a_1 b_2 w_c^3}{3w_c^2} - \frac{2b_1 a_2 w_c^2}{2w_c} + \frac{2b_1 a_2 w_c^3}{3w_c^2}$$

$$\left. \left. - \frac{2b_1 b_2 w_c^3}{3w_c^2} - \frac{a_2^2 w_c^2}{2w_c} + \frac{a_2 b_2 w_c^2}{2w_c} - \frac{a_2^2 w_c^2}{2w_c} + \frac{a_2^2 w_c^3}{3w_c^2} - \frac{a_2 b_2 w_c^3}{3w_c^2} + \frac{a_2 b_2 w_c^2}{2w_c} - \frac{a_2 b_2 w_c^3}{3w_c^2} + \frac{b_2^2 w_c^3}{3w_c^2} \right] \right)$$

$$= \left(\left[a_1^2 w_c - \frac{a_1^2 w_c}{2} + \frac{a_1 b_1 w_c}{2} - \frac{a_1^2 w_c}{2} + \frac{a_1^2 w_c}{3} - \frac{a_1 b_1 w_c}{3} + \frac{a_1 b_1 w_c}{2} - \frac{a_1 b_1 w_c}{3} + \frac{b_1^2 w_c}{3} \right. \right.$$

$$- 2a_1 a_2 w_c - 2a_1 b_2 w_c + 2a_1 a_2 w_c - \frac{2a_1 a_2 w_c}{3} + \frac{2a_1 b_2 w_c}{3} - 2b_1 a_2 w_c + \frac{2b_1 a_2 w_c}{3}$$

$$\left. \left. - \frac{2b_1 b_2 w_c}{3} + a_2^2 w_c + \frac{a_2 b_2 w_c}{2} - \frac{a_2^2 w_c}{2} + \frac{a_2^2 w_c}{3} - \frac{a_2 b_2 w_c}{3} + \frac{a_2 b_2 w_c}{2} - \frac{a_2 b_2 w_c}{3} + \frac{b_2^2 w_c}{3} \right] \right)$$

$$= w_c \left(a_1^2 - \frac{a_1^2}{2} - \frac{a_1^2}{2} + \frac{a_1^2}{3} \right) + \left(\frac{b_1^2}{3} \right) + \left(\frac{a_1 b_1}{2} - \frac{a_1 b_1}{3} + \frac{a_1 b_1}{2} - \frac{a_1 b_1}{3} \right) + \left(-2a_1 a_2 + a_1 a_2 \right.$$

$$+ a_1 a_2 + \left(-a_1 b_2 + \frac{2a_1 b_2}{3} \right) + \left(-b_1 a_2 + \frac{2b_1 a_2}{3} \right) + \left(\frac{a_2 b_2}{2} - \frac{a_2 b_2}{3} + \frac{a_2 b_2}{2} - \frac{a_2 b_2}{3} \right)$$

$$\left. + \left(\frac{b_2^2}{3} \right) - \frac{a_2^2}{2} - \frac{a_2^2}{2} \right)$$

$$= w_c \left(\frac{a_1^2}{3} + \frac{b_1^2}{3} + \frac{a_1 b_1}{3} - \frac{2a_1 a_2}{3} - \frac{a_1 b_2}{3} - \frac{b_1 a_2}{3} + \frac{a_2 b_2}{3} + \frac{b_2^2}{3} - \frac{2b_1 b_2}{3} + \frac{a_2^2}{3} \right)$$

$$= \frac{w_c}{3} \left(a_1^2 + b_1^2 + a_1 b_1 - 2a_1 a_2 - a_1 b_2 - b_1 a_2 + a_2 b_2 + b_2^2 - 2b_1 b_2 + a_2^2 \right).$$

$$= \left(\frac{w_c}{3} \left((a_1 - a_2)^2 + (b_1 - b_2)^2 + (a_1 - a_2)(b_1 - b_2) \right) \right).$$

2. Assume that $\tilde{a}_\alpha = (L_{\tilde{a}}(\alpha), R_{\tilde{a}}(\alpha))$ and $\tilde{b}_\alpha = (L_{\tilde{b}}(\alpha), R_{\tilde{b}}(\alpha))$ be α.cut set of the SVTN-number $\tilde{a}$ and $\tilde{b}$ respectively. Then,

$$T_R(\alpha) = \int_0^{w_c} \left(R_{\tilde{a}}(\alpha) - R_{\tilde{b}}(\alpha) \right)^2 d\alpha = \int_0^{w_c} \left(\frac{(w_c - \alpha)c_1 + \alpha d_1}{w_c} - \frac{(w_c - \alpha)c_2 + \alpha d_2}{w_c} \right)^2 d\alpha$$

$$= \int_0^{w_c} \left(\left(\frac{(w_c - \alpha)c_1 + \alpha d_1}{w_c} \right)^2 - 2\left(\frac{(w_c - \alpha)c_1 + \alpha d_1}{w_c} \right)\left(\frac{(w_c - \alpha)c_2 + \alpha d_2}{w_c} \right) \right.$$

$$\left. + \left(\frac{(w_c - \alpha)c_2 + \alpha d_2}{w_c} \right)^2 \right) d\alpha$$

$$= \int_0^{w_c} \left[c_1^2 - \frac{c_1^2 \alpha}{w_c} + \frac{d_1 c_1 \alpha}{w_c} - \frac{c_1^2 \alpha}{w_c} + \frac{c_1^2 \alpha^2}{w_c^2} - \frac{c_1 d_1 \alpha^2}{w_c^2} + \frac{c_1 d_1 \alpha}{w_c} - \frac{c_1 d_1 \alpha^2}{w_c^2} + \frac{d_1^2 \alpha^2}{w_c^2} - 2c_1 c_2 \right.$$

$$+ \frac{2c_1 c_2 \alpha}{w_c} - \frac{2c_1 \alpha d_2}{w_c} + \frac{2\alpha c_1 c_2}{w_c} - \frac{2\alpha^2 c_1 c_2}{w_c^2} + \frac{2\alpha^2 c_1 d_2}{w_c^2} - \frac{2d_1 c_2 \alpha}{w_c} + \frac{2d_1 c_2 \alpha^2}{w_c^2}$$

$$\left. - \frac{2d_1 d_2 \alpha^2}{w_c^2} + 2c_2^2 - \frac{c_2^2 \alpha}{w_c} + \frac{c_2 d_2 \alpha}{w_c} - \frac{\alpha c_2^2}{w_c} + \frac{c_2^2 \alpha^2}{w_c^2} - \frac{\alpha^2 c_2 d_2}{w_c^2} + \frac{d_2 c_2 \alpha}{w_c} - \frac{c_2 d_2 \alpha^2}{w_c^2} \right] d\alpha$$

$$= \left(\left[c_1^2 \alpha - \frac{c_1^2 \alpha^2}{2w_c} + \frac{c_1 d_1 \alpha^2}{2w_c} - \frac{c_1^2 \alpha^2}{2w_c} + \frac{c_1^2 \alpha^3}{3w_c^2} - \frac{c_1 d_1 \alpha^3}{3w_c^2} + \frac{c_1 d_1 \alpha^2}{2w_c} - \frac{c_1 d_1 \alpha^3}{3w_c^2} + \frac{d_1^2 \alpha^3}{3w_c^2} - 2c_1 c_2 \alpha \right. \right.$$

$$+ \frac{2c_1 c_2 \alpha^2}{2w_c} - \frac{2c_1 d_2 \alpha^2}{2w_c} + \frac{2c_1 c_2 \alpha^2}{2w_c} - \frac{2c_1 c_2 \alpha^3}{3w_c^2} + \frac{2c_1 d_2 \alpha^3}{3w_c^2} - \frac{2d_1 c_2 \alpha^2}{2w_c} + \frac{2d_1 c_2 \alpha^3}{3w_c^2} - \frac{2d_1 d_2 \alpha^3}{3w_c^2}$$

$$\left. \left. + c_2^2 \alpha - \frac{c_2^2 \alpha^2}{2w_c} + \frac{c_2 d_2 \alpha^2}{2w_c} - \frac{c_2^2 \alpha^2}{2w_c} + \frac{c_2^2 \alpha^3}{3w_c^2} - \frac{c_2 d_2 \alpha^3}{3w_c^2} + \frac{c_2 d_2 \alpha^2}{2w_c} - \frac{c_2 d_2 \alpha^3}{3w_c^2} + \frac{d_2^2 \alpha^3}{3w_c^2} \right] \right) \Big|_0^{w_c}$$

11

$$= \left(\left[c_1^2 w_c - \frac{c_1^2 w_c^2}{2w_c} + \frac{c_1 d_1 w_c^2}{2w_c} - \frac{c_1^2 w_c^2}{2w_c} + \frac{c_1^2 w_c^3}{3w_c^2} - \frac{c_1 d_1 w_c^3}{3w_c^2} + \frac{c_1 d_1 w_c^2}{2w_c} - \frac{c_1 d_1 w_c^3}{3w_c^2} + \frac{d_1^2 w_c^3}{3w_c^2} - 2c_1 c_2 w_c \right. \right.$$

$$+ \frac{2c_1 c_2 w_c^2}{2w_c} - \frac{2c_1 d_2 w_c^2}{2w_c} + \frac{2c_1 c_2 w_c^2}{2w_c} - \frac{2c_1 c_2 w_c^3}{3w_c^2} + \frac{2c_1 d_2 w_c^3}{3w_c^2} - \frac{2d_1 c_2 w_c^2}{2w_c} + \frac{2d_1 c_2 w_c^3}{3w_c^2} - \frac{2d_1 d_2 w_c^3}{3w_c^2}$$

$$\left. + c_2^2 w_c - \frac{c_2^2 w_c^2}{2w_c} + \frac{c_2 d_2 w_c^2}{2w_c} - \frac{c_2^2 w_c^2}{2w_c} + \frac{c_2^2 w_c^3}{3w_c^2} - \frac{c_2 d_2 w_c^3}{3w_c^2} + \frac{c_2 d_2 w_c^2}{2w_c} \right] \right)$$

$$= w_c \left[\left(c_1^2 - \frac{c_1^2}{2} - \frac{c_1^2}{2} + \frac{c_1^2}{3} \right) + \left(\frac{d_1^2}{3} \right) + \left(\frac{c_1 d_1}{2} - \frac{c_1 d_1}{3} + \frac{c_1 d_1}{2} - \frac{c_1 d_1}{3} \right) \right.$$

$$+ \left(-2c_1 c_2 + c_1 c_2 + c_1 c_2 - \frac{2c_1 c_2}{3} \right) + \left(-c_1 d_2 + \frac{2c_1 d_2}{3} \right) + \left(-d_1 c_2 + \frac{2d_1 c_2}{3} \right)$$

$$\left. + \left(\frac{c_2 d_2}{2} - \frac{c_2 d_2}{3} + \frac{c_2 d_2}{2} - \frac{c_2 d_2}{3} \right) + \left(\frac{d_2^2}{3} \right) + \left(\frac{-2d_1 d_2}{3} \right) + \left(\frac{c_2^2}{3} + c_2^2 - \frac{c_2^2}{2} - \frac{c_2^2}{2} \right) \right]$$

$$= w_c \left(\frac{c_1^2}{3} + \frac{d_1^2}{3} + \frac{c_1 d_1}{3} - \frac{2c_1 c_2}{3} - \frac{c_1 d_2}{3} - \frac{d_1 c_2}{3} + \frac{c_2 d_2}{3} + \frac{d_2^2}{3} - \frac{2d_1 d_2}{3} + \frac{c_2^2}{3} \right).$$

$$= \frac{w_c}{3} \left(c_1^2 + d_1^2 + c_1 d_1 - 2c_1 c_2 - c_1 d_2 - d_1 c_2 + c_2 d_2 + d_2^2 - 2d_1 d_2 + c_2^2 \right).$$

$$= \frac{w_c}{3} \left((c_1 - c_2)^2 + (d_1 - d_2)^2 + (c_1 - c_2)(d_1 - d_2) \right).$$

3.   Assume that $\tilde{a}_\beta = \left(L'_{\tilde{a}}(\beta), R'_{\tilde{a}}(\beta) \right)$ and $\tilde{b}_\beta = \left(L'_{\tilde{b}}(\beta), R'_{\tilde{b}}(\beta) \right)$ be β-cut set of the SVTN-number $\tilde{a}$ and $\tilde{b}$ respectively. Then,

$$I_L(\beta) = \int_{u_c}^{1} \left(\left| L'_{\tilde{a}}(\beta) - L'_{\tilde{b}}(\beta) \right|^2 \right) d\beta$$

$$= \int_{u_c}^{1} \left(\frac{(1-\beta)b_1 + (\beta - u_c)a_1}{1 - u_c} - \frac{(1-\beta)b_2 + (\beta - u_c)a_2}{1 - u_c} \right)^2 d\beta$$

$$= \int_{u_c}^{1} \left[\left(\frac{b_1}{1-u_c} - \frac{b_1\beta}{1-u_c} + \frac{a_1\beta}{1-u_c} - \frac{a_1u_c}{1-u_c} \right) \left(\frac{b_1}{1-u_c} - \frac{b_1\beta}{1-u_c} + \frac{a_1\beta}{1-u_c} - \frac{a_1u_c}{1-u_c} \right) \right.$$

$$-2 \left(\frac{b_1}{1-u_c} - \frac{b_1\beta}{1-u_c} + \frac{a_1\beta}{1-u_c} - \frac{a_1u_c}{1-u_c} \right) \left(\frac{b_2}{1-u_c} - \frac{b_2\beta}{1-u_c} + \frac{a_2\beta}{1-u_c} - \frac{a_2u_c}{1-u_c} \right)$$

$$\left. +\left(\frac{b_2}{1-u_c} - \frac{b_2\beta}{1-u_c} + \frac{a_2\beta}{1-u_c} - \frac{a_2u_c}{1-u_c} \right) \left(\frac{b_2}{1-u_c} - \frac{b_2\beta}{1-u_c} + \frac{a_2\beta}{1-u_c} - \frac{a_2u_c}{1-u_c} \right) \right] d\beta$$

$$\int_{u_c}^{1} \frac{1}{(1-u_c)^2} \left(b_1^2 - b_1^2\beta + a_1b_1\beta - a_1b_1u_c - b_1^2\beta + b_1^2\beta^2 - a_1b_1\beta^2 + a_1b_1u_c\beta + a_1b_1\beta \right.$$

$$\left. -a_1b_1\beta^2 + a_1^2\beta^2 - a_1^2u_c\beta - a_1b_1u_c + a_1b_1u_c\beta - a_1^2u_c\beta + a_1^2u_c^2 \right)$$

$$-\frac{2}{(1-u_c)^2} \left[b_1b_2 - b_1b_2\beta + b_1a_2\beta - b_1a_2u_c - b_1b_2\beta + b_1b_2\beta^2 - b_1a_2\beta^2 + b_1a_2u_c\beta + a_1b_2\beta \right.$$

$$\left. -a_1b_2\beta^2 + a_1a_2\beta^2 - a_1a_2u_c\beta - a_1b_2u_c + a_1b_2u_c\beta - a_1a_2u_c\beta + a_1a_2u_c^2 \right]$$

$$+\frac{1}{(1-u_c)^2} \left(b_2^2 - b_2^2\beta + a_2b_2\beta - a_2b_2u_c - b_2^2\beta + b_2^2\beta^2 - a_2b_2\beta^2 + a_2b_1u_c\beta + a_1b_1\beta - a_2b_2\beta^2 \right) \right] d\beta$$

$$= \frac{1}{(1-u_c)^2} \left[\left(b_1^2 - a_1b_1u_c - a_1b_1u_c + a_1^2u_c^2 \right) \beta + \left(-b_1^2 + a_1b_1 + a_1b_1u_c + a_1b_1 - b_1^2 \right. \right.$$

$$\left. -a_1^2u_c + a_1b_1u_c - a_1^2u_c \right) \frac{\beta^2}{2} + \left(b_1^2 - a_1b_1 - a_1b_1 + a_1^2 \right) \frac{\beta^3}{3} \right]$$

$$-\frac{2}{(1-u_c)^2} \left[\left(b_1b_2 - b_1a_2u_c - a_1b_2u_c + a_1a_2u_c^2 \right) \beta + \left(-b_1b_2 + b_1a_2 - b_1b_2 + b_1a_2u_c + a_1b_2 \right. \right.$$

$$\left. -a_1a_2u_c + a_1b_2u_c - a_1a_2u_c \right) \frac{\beta^2}{2} + \left(b_1b_2 - b_1a_2 - a_1b_2 + a_1a_2 \right) \frac{\beta^3}{3} \right]$$

$$+\frac{1}{(1-u_c)^2}\Bigg[\Big(b_2^2-a_2b_2u_c-a_2b_2u_c+a_2^2u_c^2\Big)\beta+\Big(-b_1^2+a_2b_2+a_2b_2u_c+a_2b_2-b_2^2-a_2^2u_c+a_2b_2u_c$$

$$-a_2^2u_c\Big)\frac{\beta^2}{2}+\Big(b_1^2-a_2b_2-a_2b_2+a_2^2\Big)\frac{\beta^3}{3}\Bigg]\Bigg|_{u_c}^1$$

$$=\frac{1}{(1-u_c)^2}\Bigg[\Big[\Big(b_1^2-a_1b_1u_c-a_1b_1u_c+a_1^2u_c^2\Big)+\Big(-b_1^2+a_1b_1+a_1b_1u_c+a_1b_1-b_1^2-a_1^2u_c$$

$$+a_1b_1u_c-a_1^2u_c\Big)\frac{1}{2}+\Big(b_1^2-a_1b_1-a_1b_1+a_1^2\Big)\frac{1}{3}\Big]-\Big[(b_1^2-a_1b_1u_c-a_1b_1u_c$$

$$+a_1^2u_c^2)u_c+(-b_1^2+a_1b_1+a_1b_1u_c+a_1b_1-b_1^2-a_1^2u_c+a_1b_1u_c-a_1^2u_c)\frac{u_c^2}{2}$$

$$+\Big(b_1^2-a_1b_1-a_1b_1+a_1^2\Big)\frac{u_c^3}{3}\Big]\Bigg]$$

$$-\frac{2}{(1-u_c)^2}\Bigg[(b_1b_2-b_1a_2u_c-a_1b_2u_c+a_1a_2u_c^2)+(-b_1b_2+b_1a_2-b_1b_2+b_1a_2u_c+a_1b_2$$

$$-a_1a_2u_c+a_1b_2u_c-a_1a_2u_c)\frac{1}{2}+(b_1b_2-b_1a_2-a_1b_2+a_1a_2)\frac{1}{3}\Big]-\Big[(b_1b_2$$

$$-b_1a_2u_c-a_1b_2u_c+a_1a_2u_c^2)u_c+(-b_1b_2+b_1a_2-b_1b_2+b_1a_2u_c+a_1b_2-a_1a_2u_c$$

$$+a_1b_2u_c-a_1a_2u_c)\frac{u_c^2}{2}+(b_1b_2-b_1a_2-a_1b_2+a_1a_2)\frac{u_c^3}{3}\Bigg]$$

$$+\frac{1}{(1-u_c)^2}\Bigg[\Big[(b_2^2-a_2b_2u_c-a_2b_2u_c+a_2^2u_c^2)+(-b_1^2+a_2b_2+a_2b_2u_c+a_2b_2-b_2^2-a_2^2u_c$$

$$+a_2b_2u_c-a_2^2u_c)\frac{1}{2}+(b_1^2-a_2b_2-a_2b_2+a_2^2)\frac{1}{3}\Big]-\Big[(b_2^2-a_2b_2u_c-a_2b_2u_c$$

$$+a_2^2u_c^2)u_c+(-b_1^2+a_2b_2+a_2b_2u_c+a_2b_2-b_2^2-a_2^2u_c+a_2b_2u_c-a_2^2u_c)\frac{u_c^2}{2}$$

$$+\Big(b_1^2-a_2b_2-a_2b_2+a_2^2\Big)\frac{u_c^3}{3}\Big]\Bigg]$$

$$= \frac{1}{(1-u_c)^2} \left[b_1^2 \left(1-1+\frac{1}{3}-u_c+u_c^2-\frac{u_c^3}{3} \right) + a_1 b_1 \left(+1-\frac{2}{3}-2u_c+u_c+2u_c^2-u_c^2 \right. \right.$$

$$\left. \left. -u_c^3+\frac{2u_c^3}{3} \right) + a_1^2 \left(\frac{1}{3}-u_c+u_c^2-u_c^3+u_c^3-\frac{u_c^3}{3} \right) \right]$$

$$-\frac{2}{(1-u_c)^2} \left[b_1 b_2 \left(1-\frac{1}{2}-\frac{1}{2}+\frac{1}{3}-u_c+\frac{u_c^2}{2}+\frac{u_c^2}{2}-\frac{u_c^3}{3} \right) + b_1 a_2 \left(\frac{1}{2}-\frac{1}{3}-u_c+\frac{u_c}{2}+u_c^2 \right. \right.$$

$$\left. -\frac{u_c^2}{2}+\frac{u_c^3}{3} \right) + a_1 b_2 \left(\frac{1}{2}-\frac{1}{3}-u_c+\frac{u_c}{2}+u_c^2-\frac{u_c^2}{2}-\frac{u_c^3}{3}+\frac{u_c^3}{3} \right) + a_1 a_2 \left(\frac{1}{3}-\frac{u_c}{2} \right.$$

$$\left. \left. -\frac{u_c}{2}+u_c^2-u_c^3+\frac{u_c^3}{2}+\frac{u_c^3}{2}-\frac{u_c^3}{3} \right) \right]$$

$$+\frac{1}{(1-u_c)^2} \left[b_2^2 \left(1-1+\frac{1}{3}-u_c+u_c^2-\frac{u_c^3}{3} \right) + a_2 b_2 \left(+1-\frac{2}{3}-2u_c+u_c+2u_c^2-u_c^2 \right. \right.$$

$$\left. \left. -u_c^3+\frac{2u_c^3}{3} \right) + a_1 b_2 \left(\frac{1}{3}-u_c+u_c^2-u_c^3+u_c^3-\frac{u_c^3}{3} \right) \right]$$

$$= \frac{1}{(1-u_c)^2} \left(\frac{1}{3}-u_c+u_c^2-\frac{u_c^3}{3} \right)$$

$$\left[\left(b_1^2+a_1 b_1+a_1^2 \right) + \left(b_2^2+a_2 b_2+a_2^2 \right) - \left(2b_1 b_2+2a_1 a_2 \right) - \left(b_1 a_2+a_1 b_2 \right) \right]$$

$$= \frac{1}{(1-u_c)^2} \left(\frac{1}{3}-u_c+u_c^2-\frac{u_c^3}{3} \right)$$

$$\left[b_1^2+a_1 b_1+a_1^2+b_2^2+a_2 b_2+a_2^2-2b_1 b_2-2a_1 a_2-b_1 a_2-a_1 b_2 \right]$$

$$= \frac{1}{(1-u_c)^2} \left(\frac{1}{3}-u_c+u_c^2-\frac{u_c^3}{3} \right) \left((a_1-a_2)^2+(b_1-b_2)^2+(a_1-a_2)(b_1-b_2) \right)$$

4. Assume that $\tilde{a}_\beta = \left(L'_{\tilde{a}}(\beta), R'_{\tilde{a}}(\beta) \right)$ and $\tilde{b}_\beta = \left(L'_{\tilde{b}}(\beta), R'_{\tilde{b}}(\beta) \right)$ be β-cut set of the SVTN-number $\tilde{a}$ and $\tilde{b}$, respectively. Then,

$$I_R(\beta) = \int_{u_c}^{1} \left(\left| R'_{\tilde{a}}(\beta) - R'_{\tilde{b}}(\beta) \right|^2 \right) d\beta$$

$$= \int_{u_c}^{1} \left(\frac{(1-\beta)d_1 + (\beta - u_c)c_1}{1 - u_c} - \frac{(1-\beta)d_2 + (\beta - u_c)c_2}{1 - u_c} \right)^2 d\beta$$

$$= \int_{u_c}^{1} \left[\left(\frac{d_1}{1-u_c} - \frac{d_1\beta}{1-u_c} + \frac{c_1\beta}{1-u_c} - \frac{c_1 u_c}{1-u_c} \right)\left(\frac{d_1}{1-u_c} - \frac{d_1\beta}{1-u_c} + \frac{c_1\beta}{1-u_c} - \frac{c_1 u_c}{1-u_c} \right) \right.$$

$$\left. -2 \left(\frac{d_1}{1-u_c} - \frac{d_1\beta}{1-u_c} + \frac{c_1\beta}{1-u_c} - \frac{c_1 u_c}{1-u_c} \right) \right]$$

$$= \int_{u_c}^{1} \frac{1}{(1-u_c)^2} (d_1^2 - d_1^2\beta + c_1 d_1\beta - c_1 d_1 u_c - d_1^2\beta + d_1^2\beta^2 - c_1 d_1\beta^2 + c_1 d_1 u_c\beta$$

$$+ c_1 d_1\beta - c_1 d_1\beta^2 + c_1^2\beta^2 - c_1^2 u_c\beta - c_1 d_1 u_c + c_1 d_1 u_c\beta - c_1^2 u_c\beta + c_1^2 u_c^2)$$

$$- \frac{2}{(1-u_c)^2} [d_1 d_2 - d_1 d_2\beta + d_1 c_2\beta - d_1 c_2 u_c - d_1 d_2\beta + d_1 d_2\beta^2 - d_1 c_2\beta^2 + d_1 c_2 u_c\beta + c_1 d_2\beta$$

$$- c_1 d_2\beta^2 + c_1 c_2\beta^2 - c_1 c_2 u_c\beta - c_1 d_2 u_c + c_1 d_2 u_c\beta - c_1 c_2 u_c\beta + c_1 c_2 u_c^2]$$

$$+ \frac{1}{(1-u_c)^2} (d_2^2 - d_2^2\beta + c_2 d_2\beta - c_2 d_2 u_c - d_2^2\beta + d_2^2\beta^2 - c_2 d_2\beta^2$$

$$+ c_2 d_1 u_c\beta + c_1 d_1\beta - c_2 d_2\beta^2) \Big] d\beta$$

$$= \frac{1}{(1-u_c)^2} \left[\left(d_1^2 - c_1 d_1 u_c - c_1 d_1 u_c + c_1^2 u_c^2 \right)\beta + (-d_1^2 + c_1 d_1 + c_1 d_1 u_c + c_1 d_1 - d_1^2 \right.$$

$$\left. - c_1^2 u_c + c_1 d_1 u_c - c_1^2 u_c)\frac{\beta^2}{2} + \left(d_1^2 - c_1 d_1 - c_1 d_1 + c_1^2 \right)\frac{\beta^3}{3} \right]$$

$$-\frac{2}{(1-u_c)^2}\Big[\big(d_1 d_2 - d_1 c_2 u_c - c_1 d_2 u_c + c_1 c_2 u_c^2\big)\beta + (-d_1 d_2 + d_1 c_2 - d_1 d_2 + d_1 c_2 u_c$$

$$+ c_1 d_2 - c_1 c_2 u_c + c_1 d_2 u_c - c_1 c_2 u_c)\frac{\beta^2}{2} + (d_1 d_2 - d_1 c_2 - c_1 d_2 + c_1 c_2)\frac{\beta^3}{3}\Big]$$

$$+\frac{1}{(1-u_c)^2}\Big[\big(d_2^2 - c_2 d_2 u_c - c_2 d_2 u_c + c_2^2 u_c^2\big)\beta + (-d_1^2 + c_2 d_2 + c_2 d_2 u_c + c_2 d_2 - d_2^2$$

$$-c_2^2 u_c + c_2 d_2 u_c - c_2^2 u_c)\frac{\beta^2}{2} + \big(d_1^2 - c_2 d_2 - c_2 d_2 + c_2^2\big)\frac{\beta^3}{3}\Big]\Big|_{u_c}^{1}$$

$$=\frac{1}{(1-u_c)^2}\Big[\Big[\big(d_1^2 - c_1 d_1 u_c - c_1 d_1 u_c + c_1^2 u_c^2\big) + (-d_1^2 + c_1 d_1 + c_1 d_1 u_c + c_1 d_1 - d_1^2 - c_1^2 u_c$$

$$+ c_1 d_1 u_c - c_1^2 u_c)\frac{1}{2} + \big(d_1^2 - c_1 d_1 - c_1 d_1 + c_1^2\big)\frac{1}{3}\Big] - \Big[\big(d_1^2 - c_1 d_1 u_c - c_1 d_1 u_c$$

$$+ c_1^2 u_c^2\big)u_c + (-d_1^2 + c_1 d_1 + c_1 d_1 u_c + c_1 d_1 - d_1^2 - c_1^2 u_c + c_1 d_1 u_c - c_1^2 u_c)\frac{u_c^2}{2}$$

$$+ \big(d_1^2 - c_1 d_1 - c_1 d_1 + c_1^2\big)\frac{u_c^3}{3}\Big]\Big]$$

$$-\frac{2}{(1-u_c)^2}\Big[\big(d_1 d_2 - d_1 c_2 u_c - c_1 d_2 u_c + c_1 c_2 u_c^2\big) + (-d_1 d_2 + d_1 c_2 - d_1 d_2 + d_1 c_2 u_c + c_1 d_2$$

$$-c_1 c_2 u_c + c_1 d_2 u_c - c_1 c_2 u_c)\frac{1}{2} + \big(d_1 d_2 - d_1 c_2 - c_1 d_2 + c_1 c_2\big)\frac{1}{3}\Big] - \Big[\big(d_1 d_2$$

$$-d_1 c_2 u_c - c_1 d_2 u_c + c_1 c_2 u_c^2\big)u_c + (-d_1 d_2 + d_1 c_2 - d_1 d_2 + d_1 c_2 u_c + c_1 d_2 - c_1 c_2 u_c$$

$$+ c_1 d_2 u_c - c_1 c_2 u_c)\frac{u_c^2}{2} + \big(d_1 d_2 - d_1 c_2 - c_1 d_2 + c_1 c_2\big)\frac{u_c^3}{3}\Big]$$

$$+\frac{1}{(1-u_c)^2}\left[\left[\left(d_2^2-c_2d_2u_c-c_2d_2u_c+c_2^2u_c^2\right)+\left(-d_1^2+c_2d_2+c_2d_2u_c+c_2d_2-d_2^2-c_2^2u_c\right.\right.\right.$$

$$\left.+c_2d_2u_c-c_2^2u_c^2\right)\frac{1}{2}+\left(d_1^2-c_2d_2-c_2d_2+c_2^2\right)\frac{1}{3}\right]-\left[\left(d_2^2-c_2d_2u_c-c_2d_2u_c\right.\right.$$

$$\left.+c_2^2u_c^2\right)u_c+\left(-d_1^2+c_2d_2+c_2d_2u_c+c_2d_2-d_2^2-c_2^2u_c+c_2d_2u_c-c_2^2u_c\right)\frac{u_c^2}{2}$$

$$\left.\left.+\left(d_1^2-c_2d_2-c_2d_2+c_2^2\right)\frac{u_c^3}{3}\right]\right]$$

$$=\frac{1}{(1-u_c)^2}\left[d_1^2\left(1-1+\frac{1}{3}-u_c+u_c^2-\frac{u_c^3}{3}\right)+c_1d_1\left(+1-\frac{2}{3}-2u_c+u_c+2u_c^2-u_c^2\right.\right.$$

$$\left.-u_c^3+\frac{2u_c^3}{3}\right)+c_1^2\left(\frac{1}{3}-u_c+u_c^2-u_c^3+u_c^3-\frac{u_c^3}{3}\right)\right]$$

$$-\frac{2}{(1-u_c)^2}\left[d_1d_2\left(1-\frac{1}{2}-\frac{1}{2}+\frac{1}{3}-u_c+\frac{u_c^2}{2}+\frac{u_c^2}{2}-\frac{u_c^3}{3}\right)+d_1c_2\left(\frac{1}{2}-\frac{1}{3}-u_c+\frac{u_c}{2}+u_c^2\right.\right.$$

$$\left.-\frac{u_c^2}{2}-\frac{u_c^3}{2}+\frac{u_c^3}{3}\right)+c_1d_2\left(\frac{1}{2}-\frac{1}{3}-u_c+\frac{u_c}{2}+u_c^2-\frac{u_c^2}{2}-\frac{u_c^3}{2}+\frac{u_c^3}{3}\right)$$

$$\left.+c_1c_2\left(\frac{1}{3}-\frac{u_c}{2}-\frac{u_c}{2}+u_c^2-u_c^3+\frac{u_c^3}{2}+\frac{u_c^3}{2}-\frac{u_c^3}{3}\right)\right]$$

$$+\frac{1}{(1-u_c)^2}\left[d_2^2\left(1-1+\frac{1}{3}-u_c+u_c^2-\frac{u_c^3}{3}\right)+c_2d_2\left(+1-\frac{2}{3}-2u_c+u_c+2u_c^2-u_c^2\right.\right.$$

$$\left.-u_c^3+\frac{2u_c^3}{3}\right)+c_2^2\left(\frac{1}{3}-u_c+u_c^2-u_c^3+u_c^3-\frac{u_c^3}{3}\right)\right]$$

$$= \frac{1}{(1-u_c)^2} \left[\left(d_1^2 + c_1 d_1 + c_1^2\right) \left(\frac{1}{3} - u_c + u_c^2 - \frac{u_c^3}{3}\right) \right]$$

$$- \frac{2}{(1-u_c)^2} \left[\left(d_1 d_2 + c_1 c_2\right) \left(\frac{1}{3} - u_c + u_c^2 - \frac{u_c^3}{3}\right) + \left(d_1 c_2 + c_1 d_2\right) \left(\frac{1}{6} - \frac{u_c}{2} + \frac{u_c^2}{2} - \frac{u_c^3}{6}\right) \right]$$

$$+ \frac{1}{(1-u_c)^2} \left[\left(d_2^2 + c_2 d_2 + c_2^2\right) \left(\frac{1}{3} - u_c + u_c^2 - \frac{u_c^3}{3}\right) \right]$$

$$= \frac{1}{(1-u_c)^2} \left(\frac{1}{3} - u_c + u_c^2 - \frac{u_c^3}{3}\right)$$

$$\left[\left(d_1^2 + c_1 d_1 + c_1^2\right) + \left(d_2^2 + c_2 d_2 + c_2^2\right) - \left(2 d_1 d_2 + 2 c_1 c_2\right) - \left(d_1 c_2 + c_1 d_2\right) \right]$$

$$= \frac{1}{(1-u_c)^2} \left(\frac{1}{3} - u_c + u_c^2 - \frac{u_c^3}{3}\right) (c_1 - c_2)^2 + \left((d_1 - d_2)^2 + (c_1 - c_2)\right)(d_1 - d_2)$$

5. Assume that $^\gamma \tilde{a} = \left(L''_{\tilde{a}}(\gamma), R''_{\tilde{a}}(\gamma)\right)$ and $^\gamma \tilde{b} = \left(L''_{\tilde{b}}(\gamma), R''_{\tilde{b}}(\gamma)\right)$ be γ-cut set of the SVTN-number $\tilde{a}$ and $\tilde{b}$, respectively. Then,

$$F_L(\gamma) = \int_{y_c}^1 \left(\left|L''_{\tilde{a}}(\gamma) - L''_{\tilde{b}}(\gamma)\right|^2\right) = \int_{y_c}^1 \left(\frac{(1-\gamma)b_1 + (\gamma - y_c)a_1}{1 - y_c} - \frac{(1-\gamma)b_2 + (\gamma - y_c)a_2}{1 - y_c}\right)^2 d\gamma$$

$$= \int_{y_c}^1 \left[\left(\frac{b_1}{1-y_c} - \frac{b_1 \gamma}{1-y_c} + \frac{a_1 \gamma}{1-y_c} - \frac{a_1 y_c}{1-y_c}\right) \left(\frac{b_1}{1-y_c} - \frac{b_1 \gamma}{1-y_c} + \frac{a_1 \gamma}{1-y_c} - \frac{a_1 y_c}{1-y_c}\right) \right.$$

$$- 2 \left(\frac{b_1}{1-y_c} - \frac{b_1 \gamma}{1-y_c} + \frac{a_1 \gamma}{1-y_c} - \frac{a_1 y_c}{1-y_c}\right) \left(\frac{b_2}{1-y_c} - \frac{b_2 \gamma}{1-y_c} + \frac{a_2 \gamma}{1-y_c} - \frac{a_2 y_c}{1-y_c}\right)$$

$$\left. + \left(\frac{b_2}{1-y_c} - \frac{b_2 \gamma}{1-y_c} + \frac{a_2 \gamma}{1-y_c} - \frac{a_2 y_c}{1-y_c}\right) \left(\frac{b_2}{1-y_c} - \frac{b_2 \gamma}{1-y_c} + \frac{a_2 \gamma}{1-y_c} - \frac{a_2 y_c}{1-y_c}\right) \right] d\gamma$$

$$= \int_{y_c}^{1} \frac{1}{(1-y_c)^2} (b_1^2 - b_1^2\gamma + a_1 b_1 \gamma - a_1 b_1 y_c - b_1^2 \gamma + b_1^2 \gamma^2 - a_1 b_1 \gamma^2 + a_1 b_1 y_c \gamma + a_1 b_1 \gamma$$

$$- a_1 b_1 \gamma^2 + a_1^2 \gamma^2 - a_1^2 y_c \gamma - a_1 b_1 y_c + a_1 b_1 y_c \gamma - a_1^2 y_c \gamma + a_1^2 y_c^2)$$

$$- \frac{2}{(1-y_c)^2} [b_1 b_2 - b_1 b_2 \gamma + b_1 a_2 \gamma - b_1 a_2 y_c - b_1 b_2 \gamma + b_1 b_2 \gamma^2 - b_1 a_2 \gamma^2 + b_1 a_2 y_c \gamma$$

$$+ a_1 b_2 \gamma - a_1 b_2 \gamma^2 + a_1 a_2 \gamma^2 - a_1 a_2 y_c \gamma - a_1 b_2 y_c + a_1 b_2 y_c \gamma - a_1 a_2 y_c \gamma + a_1 a_2 y_c^2]$$

$$+ \frac{1}{(1-y_c)^2}$$
$$(b_2^2 - b_2^2 \gamma + a_2 b_2 \gamma - a_2 b_2 y_c - b_2^2 \gamma + b_2^2 \gamma^2 - a_2 b_2 \gamma^2 + a_2 b_1 y_c \gamma + a_1 b_1 \gamma - a_2 b_2 \gamma^2)] d\gamma$$

$$= \frac{1}{(1-y_c)^2} \left[(b_1^2 - a_1 b_1 y_c - a_1 b_1 y_c + a_1^2 y_c^2)\gamma + (-b_1^2 + a_1 b_1 + a_1 b_1 y_c + a_1 b_1 - b_1^2 - a_1^2 y_c \right.$$

$$\left. + a_1 b_1 y_c - a_1^2 y_c) \frac{\gamma^2}{2} + \left(b_1^2 - a_1 b_1 - a_1 b_1 + a_1^2 \right) \frac{\gamma^3}{3} \right]$$

$$- \frac{2}{(1-y_c)^2} \left[(b_1 b_2 - b_1 a_2 y_c - a_1 b_2 y_c + a_1 a_2 y_c^2)\gamma + (-b_1 b_2 + b_1 a_2 - b_1 b_2 + b_1 a_2 y_c + a_1 b_2 \right.$$

$$\left. - a_1 a_2 y_c + a_1 b_2 y_c - a_1 a_2 y_c) \frac{\gamma^2}{2} + \left(b_1 b_2 - b_1 a_2 - a_1 b_2 + a_1 a_2 \right) \frac{\gamma^3}{3} \right]$$

$$+ \frac{1}{(1-y_c)^2} \left[(b_2^2 - a_2 b_2 y_c - a_2 b_2 y_c + a_2^2 y_c^2)\gamma + (-b_1^2 + a_2 b_2 + a_2 b_2 y_c + a_2 b_2 - b_2^2 - a_2^2 y_c \right.$$

$$\left. + a_2 b_2 y_c - a_2^2 y_c) \frac{\gamma^2}{2} + \left(b_1^2 - a_2 b_2 - a_2 b_2 + a_2^2 \right) \frac{\gamma^3}{3} \right]_{y_c}^{1}$$

$$= \frac{2}{(1-y_c)^2}\left[(b_1b_2 - b_1a_2y_c - a_1b_2y_c + a_1a_2y_c^2) + (-b_1b_2 + b_1a_2 - b_1b_2 + b_1a_2y_c + a_1b_2\right.$$

$$-a_1a_2y_c + a_1b_2y_c - a_1a_2y_c)\frac{1}{2} + (b_1b_2 - b_1a_2 - a_1b_2 + a_1a_2)\frac{1}{3}\Big] - \Big[(b_1b_2$$

$$-b_1a_2y_c - a_1b_2y_c + a_1a_2y_c^2)y_c + (-b_1b_2 + b_1a_2 - b_1b_2 + b_1a_2y_c + a_1b_2 - a_1a_2y_c$$

$$\left.+ a_1b_2y_c - a_1a_2y_c)\frac{y_c^2}{2} + (b_1b_2 - b_1a_2 - a_1b_2 + a_1a_2)\frac{y_c^3}{3}\right]$$

$$+ \frac{1}{(1-y_c)^2}\left[\left[(b_2^2 - a_2b_2y_c - a_2b_2y_c + a_2^2y_c^2) + (-b_1^2 + a_2b_2 + a_2b_2y_c + a_2b_2 - b_2^2 - a_2^2y_c\right.\right.$$

$$+ a_2b_2y_c - a_2^2y_c)\frac{1}{2} + (b_1^2 - a_2b_2 - a_2b_2 + a_2^2)\frac{1}{3}\Big] - \Big[(b_2^2 - a_2b_2y_c - a_2b_2y_c$$

$$+ a_2^2y_c^2)y_c + (-b_1^2 + a_2b_2 + a_2b_2y_c + a_2b_2 - b_2^2 - a_2^2y_c + a_2b_2y_c - a_2^2y_c)\frac{y_c^2}{2}$$

$$\left.\left.+ (b_1^2 - a_2b_2 - a_2b_2 + a_2^2)\frac{y_c^3}{3}\right]\right]$$

$$= \frac{1}{(1-y_c)^2}\left[b_1^2\left(1 - 1 + \frac{1}{3} - y_c + y_c^2 - \frac{y_c^3}{3}\right) + a_1b_1\left(+1 - \frac{2}{3} - 2y_c + y_c + 2y_c^2 - y_c^2\right.\right.$$

$$\left.\left.- y_c^3 + \frac{2y_c^3}{3}\right) + a_1^2\left(\frac{1}{3} - y_c + y_c^2 - y_c^3 + y_c^3 - \frac{y_c^3}{3}\right)\right]$$

$$- \frac{2}{(1-y_c)^2}\left[b_1b_2\left(1 - \frac{1}{2} - \frac{1}{2} + \frac{1}{3} - y_c + \frac{y_c^2}{2} + \frac{y_c^2}{2} - \frac{y_c^3}{3}\right) + b_1a_2\left(\frac{1}{2} - \frac{1}{3} - y_c + \frac{y_c}{2}\right.\right.$$

$$\left.+ y_c^2 - \frac{y_c^2}{2} - \frac{y_c^3}{2} + \frac{y_c^3}{3}\right) + a_1b_2\left(\frac{1}{2} - \frac{1}{3} - y_c + \frac{y_c}{2} + y_c^2 - \frac{y_c^2}{2} - \frac{y_c^3}{2} + \frac{y_c^3}{3}\right)$$

$$\left.+ a_1a_2\left(\frac{1}{3} - \frac{y_c}{2} - \frac{y_c}{2} + y_c^2 - y_c^3 + \frac{y_c^3}{2} + \frac{y_c^3}{2} - \frac{y_c^3}{3}\right)\right]$$

21

$$+\frac{1}{(1-y_c)^2}\left[b_2^2\left(1-1+\frac{1}{3}-y_c+y_c^2-\frac{y_c^3}{3}\right)+a_2b_2\left(+1-\frac{2}{3}-2y_c+y_c+2y_c^2-y_c^2\right.\right.$$

$$\left.\left.-y_c^3+\frac{2y_c^3}{3}\right)+a_2^2\left(\frac{1}{3}-y_c+y_c^2-y_c^3+y_c^3-\frac{y_c^3}{3}\right)\right]$$

$$=\frac{1}{(1-y_c)^2}\left[\left(b_1^2+a_1b_1+a_1^2\right)\left(\frac{1}{3}-y_c+y_c^2-\frac{y_c^3}{3}\right)\right]$$

$$-\frac{2}{(1-y_c)^2}\left[\left(b_1b_2+a_1a_2\right)\left(\frac{1}{3}-y_c+y_c^2-\frac{y_c^3}{3}\right)+\left(b_1a_2+a_1b_2\right)\left(\frac{1}{6}-\frac{y_c}{2}+\frac{y_c^2}{2}-\frac{y_c^3}{6}\right)\right]$$

$$+\frac{1}{(1-y_c)^2}\left[\left(b_2^2+a_2b_2+a_2^2\right)\left(\frac{1}{3}-y_c+y_c^2-\frac{y_c^3}{3}\right)\right]$$

$$=\frac{1}{(1-y_c)^2}\left(\frac{1}{3}-y_c+y_c^2-\frac{y_c^3}{3}\right)$$

$$\left(\left(b_1^2+a_1b_1+a_1^2\right)+\left(b_2^2+a_2b_2+a_2^2\right)-\left(2b_1b_2+2a_1a_2\right)-\left(b_1a_2+a_1b_2\right)\right)$$

$$=\frac{1}{(1-y_c)^2}\left(\frac{1}{3}-y_c+y_c^2-\frac{y_c^3}{3}\right)$$

$$\left(b_1^2+a_1b_1+a_1^2+b_2^2+a_2b_2+a_2^2-2b_1b_2-2a_1a_2-b_1a_2-a_1b_2\right)$$

$$=\frac{1}{(1-y_c)^2}\left(\frac{1}{3}-y_c+y_c^2-\frac{y_c^3}{3}\right)\left(\left(a_1-a_2\right)^2+\left(b_1-b_2\right)^2+\left(a_1-a_2\right)\left(b_1-b_2\right)\right)$$

6. Assume that $^\gamma\tilde{a}=\left(L''_{\tilde{a}}(\gamma),R''_{\tilde{a}}(\gamma)\right)$ and $^\gamma\tilde{b}=\left(L''_{\tilde{b}}(\gamma),R''_{\tilde{b}}(\gamma)\right)$ be γ-cut set of the SVTN-number $\tilde{a}$ and $\tilde{b}$, respectively. Then,

$$F_R(\gamma) = \int\limits_{y_c}^{1}\left(\left|R_{\tilde a}''(\gamma) - R_{\tilde b}''(\gamma)\right|^2\right)d\gamma$$

$$= \int\limits_{y_c}^{1}\left(\frac{(1-\gamma)d_1 + (\gamma - y_c)c_1}{1-y_c} - \frac{(1-\gamma)d_2 + (\gamma - y_c)c_2}{1-y_c}\right)^2 d\gamma$$

$$= \int\limits_{y_c}^{1}\left[\left(\frac{d_1}{1-y_c} - \frac{d_1\gamma}{1-y_c} + \frac{c_1\gamma}{1-y_c} - \frac{c_1 y_c}{1-y_c}\right)\left(\frac{d_1}{1-y_c} - \frac{d_1\gamma}{1-y_c} + \frac{c_1\gamma}{1-y_c} - \frac{c_1 y_c}{1-y_c}\right)\right.$$

$$-2\left(\frac{d_1}{1-y_c} - \frac{d_1\gamma}{1-y_c} + \frac{c_1\gamma}{1-y_c} - \frac{c_1 y_c}{1-y_c}\right)\left(\frac{d_2}{1-y_c} - \frac{d_2\gamma}{1-y_c} + \frac{c_2\gamma}{1-y_c} - \frac{c_2 y_c}{1-y_c}\right)$$

$$\left.+\left(\frac{d_2}{1-y_c} - \frac{d_2\gamma}{1-y_c} + \frac{c_2\gamma}{1-y_c} - \frac{c_2 y_c}{1-y_c}\right)\left(\frac{d_2}{1-y_c} - \frac{d_2\gamma}{1-y_c} + \frac{c_2\gamma}{1-y_c} - \frac{c_2 y_c}{1-y_c}\right)\right]d\gamma$$

$$= \int\limits_{y_c}^{1}\frac{1}{(1-y_c)^2}(d_1^2 - d_1^2\gamma + c_1 d_1\gamma - c_1 d_1 y_c - d_1^2\gamma + d_1^2\gamma^2 - c_1 d_1\gamma^2 + c_1 d_1 y_c\gamma + c_1 d_1\gamma$$

$$- c_1 d_1\gamma^2 + c_1^2\gamma^2 - c_1^2 y_c\gamma - c_1 d_1 y_c + c_1 d_1 y_c\gamma - c_1^2 y_c\gamma + c_1^2 y_c^2)$$

$$-\frac{2}{(1-y_c)^2}[d_1 d_2 - d_1 d_2\gamma + d_1 c_2\gamma - d_1 c_2 y_c - d_1 d_2\gamma + d_1 d_2\gamma^2 - d_1 c_2\gamma^2 + d_1 c_2 y_c\gamma$$

$$+ c_1 d_2\gamma - c_1 d_2\gamma^2 + c_1 c_2\gamma^2 - c_1 c_2 y_c\gamma - c_1 d_2 y_c + c_1 d_2 y_c\gamma - c_1 c_2 y_c\gamma + c_1 c_2 y_c^2]$$

$$+\frac{1}{(1-y_c)^2}$$
$$\left(d_2^2 - d_2^2\gamma + c_2 d_2\gamma - c_2 d_2 y_c - d_2^2\gamma + d_2^2\gamma^2 - c_2 d_2\gamma^2 + c_2 d_1 y_c\gamma + c_1 d_1\gamma - c_2 d_2\gamma^2\right)\Bigg]d\gamma$$

$$= \frac{1}{(1-y_c)^2}\left[\left(d_1^2 - c_1 d_1 y_c - c_1 d_1 y_c + c_1^2 y_c^2\right)\gamma + (-d_1^2 + c_1 d_1 + c_1 d_1 y_c + c_1 d_1 - d_1^2 - c_1^2 y_c\right.$$

$$\left.+ c_1 d_1 y_c - c_1^2 y_c)\frac{\gamma^2}{2} + \left(d_1^2 - c_1 d_1 - c_1 d_1 + c_1^2\right)\frac{\gamma^3}{3}\right]$$

$$-\frac{2}{(1-y_c)^2}\left[\left(d_1d_2-d_1c_2y_c-c_1d_2y_c+c_1c_2y_c^2\right)\gamma+\left(-d_1d_2+d_1c_2-d_1d_2+d_1c_2y_c\right.\right.$$

$$\left.+c_1d_2-c_1c_2y_c+c_1d_2y_c-c_1c_2y_c\right)\frac{\gamma^2}{2}+\left(d_1d_2-d_1c_2-c_1d_2+c_1c_2\right)\frac{\gamma^3}{3}\right]$$

$$+\frac{1}{(1-y_c)^2}\left[\left(d_2^2-c_2d_2y_c-c_2d_2y_c+c_2^2y_c^2\right)\gamma+\left(-d_1^2+c_2d_2+c_2d_2y_c+c_2d_2-d_2^2\right.\right.$$

$$\left.\left.-c_2^2y_c+c_2d_2y_c-c_2^2y_c\right)\frac{\gamma^2}{2}+\left(d_1^2-c_2d_2-c_2d_2+c_2^2\right)\frac{\gamma^3}{3}\right]\Bigg|_{y_c}^1$$

$$=\frac{1}{(1-y_c)^2}\left[\left[\left(d_1^2-c_1d_1y_c-c_1d_1y_c+c_1^2y_c^2\right)+\left(-d_1^2+c_1d_1+c_1d_1y_c+c_1d_1-d_1^2-c_1^2y_c\right.\right.\right.$$

$$\left.+c_1d_1y_c-c_1^2y_c\right)\frac{1}{2}+\left(d_1^2-c_1d_1-c_1d_1+c_1^2\right)\frac{1}{3}\right]-\left[\left(d_1^2-c_1d_1y_c-c_1d_1y_c\right.\right.$$

$$\left.+c_1^2y_c^2\right)y_c+\left(-d_1^2+c_1d_1+c_1d_1y_c+c_1d_1-d_1^2-c_1^2y_c+c_1d_1y_c-c_1^2y_c\right)\frac{y_c^2}{2}$$

$$\left.\left.+\left(d_1^2-c_1d_1-c_1d_1+c_1^2\right)\frac{y_c^3}{3}\right]\right]$$

$$-\frac{2}{(1-y_c)^2}\left[\left(d_1d_2-d_1c_2y_c-c_1d_2y_c+c_1c_2y_c^2\right)+\left(-d_1d_2+d_1c_2-d_1d_2+d_1c_2y_c+c_1d_2\right.\right.$$

$$\left.-c_1c_2y_c+c_1d_2y_c-c_1c_2y_c\right)\frac{1}{2}+\left(d_1d_2-d_1c_2-c_1d_2+c_1c_2\right)\frac{1}{3}\right]$$

$$-\left[\left(d_1d_2-d_1c_2y_c-c_1d_2y_c+c_1c_2y_c^2\right)y_c+\left(-d_1d_2+d_1c_2-d_1d_2+d_1c_2y_c\right.\right.$$

$$\left.\left.+c_1d_2-c_1c_2y_c+c_1d_2y_c-c_1c_2y_c\right)\frac{y_c^2}{2}+\left(d_1d_2-d_1c_2-c_1d_2+c_1c_2\right)\frac{y_c^3}{3}\right]$$

$$+\frac{1}{(1-y_c)^2}\left[\left[\left(d_2^2-c_2d_2y_c-c_2d_2y_c+c_2^2y_c^2\right)+\left(-d_1^2+c_2d_2+c_2d_2y_c+c_2d_2-d_2^2-c_2^2y_c\right.\right.\right.$$

$$+c_2d_2y_c-c_2^2y_c)\frac{1}{2}+\left(d_1^2-c_2d_2-c_2d_2+c_2^2\right)\frac{1}{3}\right]-\left[\left(d_2^2-c_2d_2y_c-c_2d_2y_c\right.\right.$$

$$+c_2^2y_c^2\big)y_c+(-d_1^2+c_2d_2+c_2d_2y_c+c_2d_2-d_2^2-c_2^2y_c+c_2d_2y_c-c_2^2y_c)\frac{y_c^2}{2}$$

$$+\left(d_1^2-c_2d_2-c_2d_2+c_2^2\right)\frac{y_c^3}{3}\bigg]\bigg]$$

$$=\frac{1}{(1-y_c)^2}\left[d_1^2\left(1-1+\frac{1}{3}-y_c+y_c^2-\frac{y_c^3}{3}\right)+c_1d_1\left(+1-\frac{2}{3}-2y_c+y_c+2y_c^2-y_c^2\right.\right.$$

$$\left.-y_c^3+\frac{2y_c^3}{3}\right)+c_1^2\left(\frac{1}{3}-y_c+y_c^2-y_c^3+y_c^3-\frac{y_c^3}{3}\right)\bigg]$$

$$-\frac{2}{(1-y_c)^2}\left[d_1d_2\left(1-\frac{1}{2}-\frac{1}{2}+\frac{1}{3}-y_c+\frac{y_c^2}{2}+\frac{y_c^2}{2}-\frac{y_c^3}{3}\right)+d_1c_2\left(\frac{1}{2}-\frac{1}{3}-y_c+\frac{y_c}{2}+y_c^2\right.\right.$$

$$\left.-\frac{y_c^2}{2}-\frac{y_c^3}{2}+\frac{y_c^3}{3}\right)+c_1d_2\left(\frac{1}{2}-\frac{1}{3}-y_c+\frac{y_c}{2}+y_c^2-\frac{y_c^2}{2}-\frac{y_c^3}{2}+\frac{y_c^3}{3}\right)$$

$$+c_1c_2\left(\frac{1}{3}-\frac{y_c}{2}-\frac{y_c}{2}+y_c^2-y_c^3+\frac{y_c^3}{2}+\frac{y_c^3}{2}-\frac{y_c^3}{3}\right)\bigg]$$

$$+\frac{1}{(1-y_c)^2}\left[d_2^2\left(1-1+\frac{1}{3}-y_c+y_c^2-\frac{y_c^3}{3}\right)+c_2d_2\left(+1-\frac{2}{3}-2y_c+y_c+2y_c^2-y_c^2\right.\right.$$

$$\left.-y_c^3+\frac{2y_c^3}{3}\right)+c_2^2\left(\frac{1}{3}-y_c+y_c^2-y_c^3+y_c^3-\frac{y_c^3}{3}\right)\bigg]$$

$$= \frac{1}{(1-y_c)^2}\left[\left(d_1^2+c_1d_1+c_1^2\right)\left(\frac{1}{3}-y_c+y_c^2-\frac{y_c^3}{3}\right)\right]$$

$$-\frac{2}{(1-y_c)^2}\left[\left(d_1d_2+c_1c_2\right)\left(\frac{1}{3}-y_c+y_c^2-\frac{y_c^3}{3}\right)+\left(d_1c_2+c_1d_2\right)\left(\frac{1}{6}-\frac{y_c}{2}+\frac{y_c^2}{2}-\frac{y_c^3}{6}\right)\right]$$

$$+\frac{1}{(1-y_c)^2}\left[\left(d_2^2+c_2d_2+c_2^2\right)\left(\frac{1}{3}-y_c+y_c^2-\frac{y_c^3}{3}\right)\right]$$

$$= \frac{1}{(1-y_c)^2}\left(\frac{1}{3}-y_c+y_c^2-\frac{y_c^3}{3}\right)$$

$$\left[\left(d_1^2+c_1d_1+c_1^2\right)+\left(d_2^2+c_2d_2+c_2^2\right)-\left(2d_1d_2-2c_1c_2\right)-\left(d_1c_2-c_1d_2\right)\right]$$

$$= \frac{1}{(1-y_c)^2}\left(\frac{1}{3}-y_c+y_c^2-\frac{y_c^3}{3}\right)$$

$$\left[d_1^2+c_1d_1+c_1^2+d_2^2+c_2d_2+c_2^2-2d_1d_2-2c_1c_2-d_1c_2-c_1d_2\right]$$

$$= \frac{1}{(1-y_c)^2}\left(\frac{1}{3}-y_c+y_c^2-\frac{y_c^3}{3}\right)\left((c_1-c_2)^2+(d_1-d_2)^2+(c_1-c_2)(d_1-d_2)\right)$$

Example 3.4 Let $\tilde{a}=(0.5,0.6,0.7,0.8;0.1,0.9,0.7)$ and $\tilde{b}=(0.1,0.3,0.7,0.9;0.7,0.3,0.2)$ be two SVTN-numbers. Then, the distance measure $d(\tilde{a},\tilde{b})$ between $\tilde{a}$ and $\tilde{b}$ is calculated as;

$$d(\tilde{a},\tilde{b})=\frac{2}{\pi}\arccos\left(1-\frac{1}{6}\left(|T_L(\alpha)|+|T_R(\alpha)|+|I_L(\beta)|+|I_R(\beta)|+|F_L(\gamma)|+|F_R(\gamma)|\right)\right)$$

$$=\frac{2}{\pi}\arccos\left(1-\frac{1}{6}\left(\int_0^{w_c}\left(\frac{(w_c-\alpha)a_1+\alpha b_1}{w_c}-\frac{(w_c-\alpha)a_2+\alpha b_2}{w_c}\right)^2 d\alpha\right)\right)$$

$$+\int_0^{w_c}\left(\frac{\left(w_c-\alpha\right)c_1+\alpha d_1}{w_c}-\frac{\left(w_c-\alpha\right)c_2+\alpha d_2}{w_c}\right)^2 d\alpha$$

$$+\int_{u_c}^1\left(\frac{\left(1-\beta\right)b_1+\left(\beta-u_c\right)a_1}{1-u_c}-\frac{\left(1-\beta\right)b_2+\left(\beta-u_c\right)a_2}{1-u_c}\right)^2 d\beta$$

$$+\int_{u_c}^1\left(\frac{\left(1-\beta\right)d_1+\left(\beta-u_c\right)c_1}{1-u_c}-\frac{\left(1-\beta\right)d_2+\left(\beta-u_c\right)c_2}{1-u_c}\right)^2 d\beta$$

$$+\int_{y_c}^1\left(\frac{\left(1-\gamma\right)b_1+\left(\gamma-y_c\right)a_1}{1-y_c}-\frac{\left(1-\gamma\right)b_2+\left(\gamma-y_c\right)a_2}{1-y_c}\right)^2 d\gamma$$

$$+\int_{y_c}^1\left(\frac{\left(1-\gamma\right)d_1+\left(\gamma-y_c\right)c_1}{1-y_c}-\frac{\left(1-\gamma\right)d_2+\left(\gamma-y_c\right)c_2}{1-y_c}\right)^2 d\gamma\right)$$

$$=\frac{2}{\pi}\arccos\left(1-\frac{1}{6}\left(\int_0^{0.1}\left(\frac{\left(0.1-\alpha\right)0.5+\alpha 0.6}{0.1}-\frac{\left(0.1-\alpha\right)0.1+\alpha 0.3}{0.1}\right)^2 d\alpha\right.\right.$$

$$+\int_0^{0.1}\left(\frac{\left(0.1-\alpha\right)0.7+\alpha 0.8}{0.1}-\frac{\left(0.1-\alpha\right)0.7+\alpha 0.9}{0.1}\right)^2 d\alpha$$

$$+\int_{0.9}^1\left(\frac{\left(1-\beta\right)0.6+\left(\beta-0.9\right)0.5}{1-0.9}-\frac{\left(1-\beta\right)0.3+\left(\beta-0.9\right)0.1}{1-0.9}\right)^2 d\beta$$

$$+\int_{0.9}^1\left(\frac{\left(1-\beta\right)0.8+\left(\beta-0.9\right)0.7}{1-0.9}-\frac{\left(1-\beta\right)0.9+\left(\beta-0.9\right)0.7}{1-0.9}\right)^2 d\beta$$

$$+\int_{0.7}^1\left(\frac{\left(1-\gamma\right)0.6+\left(\gamma-0.7\right)0.5}{1-0.7}-\frac{\left(1-\gamma\right)0.3+\left(\gamma-0.7\right)0.1}{1-0.7}\right)^2 d\gamma$$

$$+ \int_{0.7}^{1} \left(\frac{(1-\gamma)0.8 + (\gamma - 0.7)0.7}{1-0.7} - \frac{(1-\gamma)0.9 + (\gamma - 0.7)0.7}{1-0.7} \right)^2 d\gamma \Bigg)$$

$$= \frac{2}{\pi} \arccos\left(1 - \frac{1}{6}\right)$$

$$(0.012333 + 0.000333 + 0.012333 + 0.000333 + 0.03694702 + 0.000998)$$

$$= \frac{2}{\pi} \arccos\left(1 - \frac{1}{6}(0.063277)\right)$$

$$= \frac{2}{\pi} \arccos(0.98944)$$

$$= 0.92586$$

Remark 3.5 Let

$\tilde{a} = \langle (a_1, b_1, c_1, d_1); w_{\tilde{a}}, u_{\tilde{a}}, y_{\tilde{a}} \rangle$ and $\tilde{b} = \langle (a_2, b_2, c_2, d_2); w_{\tilde{b}}, u_{\tilde{b}}, y_{\tilde{b}} \rangle$

is an arbitrary SVTN-number. Then, the distance $d(\tilde{a}, \tilde{b})$ measure between $\tilde{a}$ and $\tilde{b}$, is computed as;

$$d(\tilde{a}, \tilde{b}) = \frac{2}{\pi} \arccos\left(1 - \frac{1}{6}\left(\left(\frac{w_c}{3} + \frac{1}{(1-u_c)^2}\left(\frac{1}{3} - u_c + u_c^2 - \frac{u_c^3}{3}\right) + \frac{1}{(1-y_c)^2}\left(\frac{1}{3} - y_c + y_c^2 - \frac{y_c^3}{3}\right)\right)\right.$$

$$\left. (a_1 - a_2)^2 + (b_1 - b_2)^2 + (a_1 - a_2)(b_1 - b_2) + (c_1 - c_2)^2 + (d_1 - d_2)^2 + (c_1 - c_2)(d_1 - d_2) \right)$$

Theorem 3.6 Let

$\tilde{a} = \langle (a_1, b_1, c_1, d_1); w_{\tilde{a}}, u_{\tilde{a}}, y_{\tilde{a}} \rangle$ and $\tilde{b} = \langle (a_2, b_2, c_2, d_2); w_{\tilde{b}}, u_{\tilde{b}}, y_{\tilde{b}} \rangle$

be two SVTN-number and $d(\tilde{a}, \tilde{b})$ be a the distance measure between $\tilde{a}$ and $\tilde{b}$.

Then, $d(\tilde{a}, \tilde{b})$ satisfies the following properties as

    1. $0 \leq d(\tilde{a}, \tilde{b}) \leq 1$

    2. $d(\tilde{a}, \tilde{b}) = d(\tilde{b}, \tilde{a})$

    3. $\tilde{a} = \tilde{b} \Rightarrow d(\tilde{a}, \tilde{b}) = 0$

4. $\quad d\left(\tilde{a},\tilde{b}\right)\le d\left(\tilde{a},\tilde{c}\right)+d\left(\tilde{c},\tilde{b}\right)$

Proof

1. It is obvious from the above Remark 2.8 that: $0\le d\left(\tilde{a},\tilde{b}\right)\le 1$ for all $\tilde{a},\tilde{b}\in$ SVTN-number

2. $\quad d\left(\tilde{a},\tilde{b}\right)$

$$=\frac{2}{\pi}\arccos\left(1-\frac{1}{6}\left(\frac{w_c}{3}+\frac{1}{(1-u_c)^2}\left(\frac{1}{3}-u_c+u_c^2-\frac{u_c^3}{3}\right)+\frac{1}{(1-y_c)^2}\left(\frac{1}{3}-y_c+y_c^2-\frac{y_c^3}{3}\right)\right.\right.$$
$$(a_1-a_2)^2+(b_1-b_2)^2+\left(a_1-a_2\right)\left(b_1-b_2\right)+(c_1-c_2)^2+(d_1-d_2)^2+(c_1-c_2)(d_1-d_2))$$

$$=\frac{2}{\pi}\arccos\left(1-\frac{1}{6}\left(\frac{w_c}{3}+\frac{1}{(1-u_c)^2}\left(\frac{1}{3}-u_c+u_c^2-\frac{u_c^3}{3}\right)+\frac{1}{(1-y_c)^2}\left(\frac{1}{3}-y_c+y_c^2-\frac{y_c^3}{3}\right)\right.\right.$$
$$(a_2-a_1)^2+(b_2-b_1)^2+\left(a_2-a_1\right)\left(b_2-b_1\right)+(c_2-c_1)^2+(d_2-d_1)^2+(c_2-c_1)(d_2-d_1))$$
$$=d\left(\tilde{b},\tilde{a}\right)$$

3. $\quad d\left(\tilde{a},\tilde{b}\right)$

$$=0\Leftrightarrow\frac{2}{\pi}\arccos\left(1-\frac{1}{6}\left(\frac{w_c}{3}+\frac{1}{(1-u_c)^2}\left(\frac{1}{3}-u_c+u_c^2-\frac{u_c^3}{3}\right)+\frac{1}{(1-y_c)^2}\left(\frac{1}{3}-y_c+y_c^2-\frac{y_c^3}{3}\right)\right.\right.$$
$$(a_1-a_2)^2+(b_1-b_2)^2+\left(a_1-a_2\right)\left(b_1-b_2\right)+(c_1-c_2)^2+\left(d_1-d_2\right)^2+\left(c_1-c_2\right)\left(d_1-d_2\right))$$

$$=0\Leftrightarrow\left(a_1-a_2\right)=0,\left(b_1-b_2\right)=0,\left(c_1-c_2\right)=0,\left(d_1-d_2\right)=0,$$
$$\Rightarrow a_1=a_2,b_1=b_2,c_1=c_2,d_1=d_2$$

$$\tilde{a}=\tilde{b}\Rightarrow\frac{2}{\pi}\arccos\left(1-\frac{1}{6}\left(\frac{w_c}{3}+\frac{1}{(1-u_c)^2}\left(\frac{1}{3}-u_c+u_c^2-\frac{u_c^3}{3}\right)+\frac{1}{(1-y_c)^2}\left(\frac{1}{3}-y_c+y_c^2-\frac{y_c^3}{3}\right)\right)\arcsin\theta\right.$$
$$(a_1-a_1)^2+(b_1-b_1)^2+(a_1-a_1)(b_1-b_1)+(c_1-c_1)^2+(d_1-d_1)^2+(c_1-c_1)(d_1-d_1))$$
$$=0\Leftrightarrow\left(a_1-a_1\right)=0,\left(b_1-b_1\right)=0,\left(c_1-c_1\right)=0,\left(d_1-d_1\right)=0$$

4. $\quad d\left(\tilde{a},\tilde{b}\right) \le d\left(\tilde{a},\tilde{c}\right) + d\left(\tilde{c},\tilde{b}\right)$

$$d\left(\tilde{a},\tilde{b}\right) = \frac{2}{\pi}\arccos\left(1-\frac{1}{6}\left(\frac{w_c}{3}+\frac{1}{(1-u_c)^2}\left(\frac{1}{3}-u_c+u_c^2-\frac{u_c^3}{3}\right)+\frac{1}{(1-y_c)^2}\left(\frac{1}{3}-y_c+y_c^2-\frac{y_c^3}{3}\right)\right)\right)$$

$$(a_1-a_2)^2+(b_1-b_2)^2+(a_1-a_2)(b_1-b_2)+(c_1-c_2)^2+(d_1-d_2)^2+(c_1-c_2)(d_1-d_2))$$

$$\le \frac{2}{\pi}\arccos\left(1-\frac{1}{6}\left(\frac{w_c}{3}+\frac{1}{(1-u_c)^2}\left(\frac{1}{3}-u_c+u_c^2-\frac{u_c^3}{3}\right)+\frac{1}{(1-y_c)^2}\left(\frac{1}{3}-y_c+y_c^2-\frac{y_c^3}{3}\right)\right)\right)$$

$$(a_1-a_3)^2+(b_1-b_3)^2+(a_1-a_3)(b_1-b_3)+(c_1-c_3)^2+(d_1-d_3)^2+(c_1-c_3)(d_1-d_3))$$

$$+\frac{2}{\pi}\arccos\left(1-\frac{1}{6}\left(\frac{w_c}{3}+\frac{1}{(1-u_c)^2}\left(\frac{1}{3}-u_c+u_c^2-\frac{u_c^3}{3}\right)+\frac{1}{(1-y_c)^2}\left(\frac{1}{3}-y_c+y_c^2-\frac{y_c^3}{3}\right)\right)\right)$$

$$(a_3-a_2)^2+(b_3-b_2)^2+(a_3-a_2)(b_3-b_2)+(c_3-c_2)^2+(d_3-d_2)^2+(c_3-c_2)(d_3-d_2))$$

$$= d\left(\tilde{a},\tilde{c}\right) + d\left(\tilde{c},\tilde{b}\right)$$

4 A MULTİ-ATTRİBUTE DECİSİON-MAKİNG METHOD WİTH SVTN-NUMBERS

In this section, we define a multi-criteria decision making method, so called SVTN-multi-criteria decision-making method. Its adopted from (Deli & Şubaş, 2015; Deli & Şubaş, 2017; Gündoğdu & Kahraman, 2018). From now on we use the weight of each attribute $u_i(i\in I_m)$ is ω_i which should satisfy the normalized conditions: $\omega_i\in(0,1)(i\in I_m)$ and $\sum_{i=1}^{m}\omega_i=1$.

Definition 4.1 (Deli & Şubaş, 2015) Let $X=\{x_1,x_2,\ldots,x_m\}$ be a set of alternatives, $A=\{a_1,a_2,\ldots,a_n\}$ be the set of attributes and

$$\left[\tilde{A}_{ij}\right] = \left\langle\left(a_{ij},b_{ij},c_{ij},d_{ij}\right);w_{\tilde{a}_{ij}},u_{\tilde{a}_{ij}},y_{\tilde{a}_{ij}}\right\rangle \text{ for } i\in I_m; j\in I_n \text{ be a SVTN-numbers. Then,}$$

$$(\tilde{A}_{ij})_{m\times n} = \begin{pmatrix} \langle(a_{11},b_{11},c_{11},d_{11});w_{\tilde{a}_{11}},u_{\tilde{a}_{11}},y_{\tilde{a}_{11}}\rangle & \langle(a_{12},b_{12},c_{12},d_{12});w_{\tilde{a}_{12}},u_{\tilde{a}_{12}},y_{\tilde{a}_{12}}\rangle \\ \langle(a_{21},b_{21},c_{21},d_{21});w_{\tilde{a}_{21}},u_{\tilde{a}_{21}},y_{\tilde{a}_{21}}\rangle & \langle(a_{22},b_{22},c_{22},d_{22});w_{\tilde{a}_{22}},u_{\tilde{a}_{22}},y_{\tilde{a}_{22}}\rangle \\ \vdots & \vdots \\ \langle(a_{m1},b_{m1},c_{m1},d_{m1});w_{\tilde{a}_{m1}},u_{\tilde{a}_{m1}},y_{\tilde{a}_{m1}}\rangle & \langle(a_{m2},b_{m2},c_{m2},d_{m2});w_{\tilde{a}_{m2}},u_{\tilde{a}_{m2}},y_{\tilde{a}_{m2}}\rangle \end{pmatrix}$$

$$\begin{pmatrix} \cdots & \langle(a_{1n},b_{1n},c_{1n},d_{1n});w_{\tilde{a}_{1n}},u_{\tilde{a}_{1n}},y_{\tilde{a}_{1n}}\rangle \\ \cdots & \langle(a_{2n},b_{2n},c_{2n},d_{2n});w_{\tilde{a}_{2n}},u_{\tilde{a}_{2n}},y_{\tilde{a}_{2n}}\rangle \\ \cdots & \vdots \\ \cdots & \langle(a_{mn},b_{mn},c_{mn},d_{mn});w_{\tilde{a}_{mn}},u_{\tilde{a}_{mn}},y_{\tilde{a}_{mn}}\rangle \end{pmatrix}$$

is called an SVTN-multi-criteria decision making matrix of the decision maker.

Now, we can give an algorithm of the SVTN multi-criteria decision-making method as follows,

Algorithm:

Step 1: Obtain the relative positive ideal solution $\alpha^+ = (\alpha_1^+, \alpha_2^+, ..., \alpha_n^+)$ and negative ideal solution $\alpha^- = (\alpha_1^-, \alpha_2^-, ...\alpha_n^-)$ of the attribute a_j for all $j \in I_n$ as respectively;

$$\alpha_j^+ = \langle a_{ij}^+, b_{ij}^+, c_{ij}^+, d_{ij}^+); w_{ij}^+, u_{ij}^+, y_{ij}^+\rangle$$
$$= \left\langle \min_i\{a_{ij}\}, \min_i\{b_{ij}\}, \max_i\{c_{ij}\}, \max_i\{d_{ij}\}); \max_i\{w_{ij}\}, \min_i\{u_{ij}\}, \min_i\{y_{ij}\} \right\rangle$$

And

$$\alpha_j^- = \langle a_{ij}^-, b_{ij}^-, c_{ij}^-, d_{ij}^-); w_{ij}^-, u_{ij}^-, y_{ij}^-\rangle$$
$$= \left\langle \min_i\{a_{ij}\}, \min_i\{b_{ij}\}, \max_i\{c_{ij}\}, \max_i\{d_{ij}\}); \min_i\{w_{ij}\}, \max_i\{u_{ij}\}, \max_i\{y_{ij}\} \right\rangle$$

for all $i \in I_m$

Step 2: Calculate the similarity degree between the evaluating result $\tilde{A}_{ij} = \left\langle (a_{ij}, b_{ij}, c_{ij}, d_{ij}); w_{\tilde{a}_{ij}}, u_{\tilde{a}_{ij}}, y_{\tilde{a}_{ij}} \right\rangle$ of alternative x_i with respect to attribute a_j

and the relative positive ideal value α_j^+ of attribute a_j, with $i=1,2,\ldots,m$ and $j=1,2,\ldots,n$ and construct the positive distance matrix $G^+ = (g_{ij}^+)_{m \times n} = d\left(\tilde{A}_{ij}, \alpha_j^+\right)$.

The similarity degree is expressed as:

$$d\left(\tilde{A}_{ij}, \alpha_j^+\right) = \frac{2}{\pi} \arccos\left(1 - \frac{1}{6}\left(\frac{w_c}{3} + \frac{1}{(1-u_c)^2}\left(\frac{1}{3} - u_c + u_c^2 - \frac{u_c^3}{3}\right) + \frac{1}{(1-y_c)^2}\left(\frac{1}{3} - y_c + y_c^2 - \frac{y_c^3}{3}\right)\right)\right.$$

$$\left. (a_{ij} - a_{ij}^+)^2 + (b_{ij} - b_{ij}^+)^2 + (a_{ij} - a_{ij}^+)(b_{ij} - b_{ij}^+) + (c_{ij} - c_{ij}^+)^2 + (d_{ij} - d_{ij}^+)^2 + (c_{ij} - c_{ij}^+)(d_{ij} - d_{ij}^+)\right)$$

Step 3: Calculate the similarity degree between the evaluating result $\tilde{A}_{ij} = \left\langle (a_{ij}, b_{ij}, c_{ij}, d_{ij}); w_{\tilde{a}_{ij}}, u_{\tilde{a}_{ij}}, y_{\tilde{a}_{ij}} \right\rangle$ of alternative x_i with respect to attribute a_j and the relative negative ideal value α_j^- of attribute a_j, with $i=1,2,\ldots,m$ and $j=1,2,\ldots,n$ and construct the negative distance matrix $G^- = (g_{ij}^-)_{m \times n} = d\left(\tilde{A}_{ij}, \alpha_j^-\right)$.

The similarity degree is expressed as:

$$(g_{ij}^-)_{m \cdot n} = \frac{2}{\pi} \arccos\left(1 - \frac{1}{6}\left(\frac{w_c}{3} + \frac{1}{(1-u_c)^2}\left(\frac{1}{3} - u_c + u_c^2 - \frac{u_c^3}{3}\right) + \frac{1}{(1-y_c)^2}\left(\frac{1}{3} - y_c + y_c^2 - \frac{y_c^3}{3}\right)\right)\right.$$

$$\left. (a_{ij} - a_{ij}^-)^2 + (b_{ij} - b_{ij}^-)^2 + (a_{ij} - a_{ij}^-)(b_{ij} - b_{ij}^-) + (c_{ij} - c_{ij}^-)^2 + (d_{ij} - d_{ij}^-)^2 + (c_{ij} - c_{ij}^-)(d_{ij} - d_{ij}^-)\right)$$

Step 4: Calculate the positive and negative scores based on the attribute weights $w_i(i \in I_m)$ and the distance matrices G^+ and G^- calculate the weighted positive score $S^+(x_i)(i \in I_m)$ and weighted negative score $S^-(x_i)(i \in I_m)$ for each alternative $x_i(i \in I_m)$ respectively as;

$$S^+\left(x_i\right) = \sum\nolimits_{j=1}^{n} w_j g_{ij}^+ \quad \text{and} \quad S^-\left(x_i\right) = \sum\nolimits_{j=1}^{n} w_j g_{ij}^-$$

Step 5: Obtain the relative closeness degree $c(x_i)$ of each alternative x_i as;

$$c\left(x_i\right) = \frac{S^+\left(x_i\right)}{\left(S^+\left(x_i\right) + S^-\left(x_i\right)\right)}, \left(i \in I_m\right)$$

Step 6: Get the preference order of all alternatives by comparing their relative closeness degree. Larger closeness degree indicates better preference order.

Example 4.2 A farmer want to invest some money to a project. There are five alternatives of farming to be assessed by a farmer. The decision maker evaluates these livestock companies with respect to four attributes to get the best option. Five alternative companies are given as:

(1) x_1 cattle breeding;
(2) x_2 goat breeding;
(3) x_3 sheep breeding;
(4) x_4 poultry breeding;
(5) x_5 bee breeding.

For attributes to be accounted are:

(1) a_1: the benefit rate;
(2) a_2: the risk of investment;
(3) a_3: the difficulty of investment; and
(4) a_4: the influence on environment.

The attribute weights of a_1, a_2, a_3 and a_4 are 0.3, 0.35, 0.10 and 0.25 respectively, i.e. $w = (0.30, 0.35, 0.10, 0.25)$. The decision matrix provided by decision maker is:

Algorithm:

Step 1: We obtained the relative positive ideal solution $\alpha^+ = \left(\alpha_1^+, \alpha_2^+, ..., \alpha_n^+ \right)$ and negative ideal solution $\alpha^- = \left(\alpha_1^-, \alpha_2^-, ... \alpha_n^- \right)$ of the attribute a_j for all $j \in I_n$ as;

$$\alpha^+ = \left(\alpha_1^+, \alpha_2^+, ..., \alpha_n^+ \right)$$

$$\left(\langle (0.1, 0.3, 0.7, 0.8); 0.3, 0.4, 0.5 \rangle, \langle (0.3, 0.5, 0.8, 0.1); 0.6, 0.3, 0.2 \rangle, \right.$$

$$\left. \langle (0.1, 0.3, 0.8, 0.9); 0.7, 0.4, 0.3 \rangle, \langle (0.2, 0.4, 0.8, 0.9); 0.8, 0.4, 0.5 \rangle \right)$$

and

$$\alpha^- = \left(\alpha_1^-, \alpha_2^-, ..., \alpha_n^- \right)$$

$$\left(\langle (0.1, 0.3, 0.7, 0.8); 0.1, 0.9, 0.7 \rangle, \langle (0.3, 0.5, 0.8, 0.1); 0.2, 0.6, 0.8 \rangle, \right.$$

$$\left. \langle (0.1, 0.3, 0.8, 0.9); 0.3, 0.8, 0.8 \rangle, \langle (0.2, 0.4, 0.8, 0.9); 0.2, 0.7, 0.8 \rangle \right)$$

Step 2: We calculated the similarity degree between the evaluating result $\tilde{A}_{ij} = \left\langle \left(a_{ij}, b_{ij}, c_{ij}, d_{ij} \right); w_{\tilde{a}_{ij}}, u_{\tilde{a}_{ij}}, y_{\tilde{a}_{ij}} \right\rangle$ of alternative x_i with respect to attribute a_j

and the relative positive ideal value α_j^+ of attribute a_j with $i=1,2,\ldots,m$ and $j=1,2,\ldots$ $,n$ and we construct the positive distance matrix $G^+ = (g_{ij}^+)_{m\times n} = d\left(\tilde{A}_{ij}, \alpha_j^+\right)$ as:

$$G^+ = \begin{pmatrix} 0.9673 & 0.9529 & 0.9286 & 0.9765 \\ 0.9689 & 0.9291 & 0.9708 & 0.9968 \\ 0.9788 & 0.9915 & 0.9517 & 0.9827 \\ 0.9915 & 0.9766 & 0.8920 & 0.9494 \\ 0.9766 & 0.9952 & 0.9639 & 0.9378 \end{pmatrix}$$

Step 3: We calculated the similarity degree between the evaluating result $\tilde{A}_{ij} = \left\langle \left(a_{ij}, b_{ij}, c_{ij}, d_{ij}\right); w_{\tilde{a}_{ij}}, u_{\tilde{a}_{ij}}, y_{\tilde{a}_{ij}} \right\rangle$ of alternative x_i with respect to attribute a_j and the relative negative ideal value α_j^- of attribute a_j with $i=1,2,\ldots,m$ and $j=1,2,\ldots$ $,n$ and we constructed the negative distance matrix $G^- = (g_{ij}^-)_{m\times n} = d\left(\tilde{A}_{ij}, \alpha_j^-\right)$ as:

$$G^- = \begin{pmatrix} 0.9673 & 0.9731 & 0.9616 & 0.9913 \\ 0.9805 & 0.9717 & 0.9814 & 0.9975 \\ 0.9894 & 0.9943 & 0.9740 & 0.9913 \\ 0.9965 & 0.9830 & 0.9529 & 0.9728 \\ 0.9894 & 0.9958 & 0.9851 & 0.9666 \end{pmatrix}$$

Step 4: We calculated the weighted positive score $S^+(x_i)(i \in I_m)$ and weighted negative score $S^-(x_i)(i \in I_m)$ for each alternative $x_i(i \in I_m)$ respectively as;

$$S^+\left(x_1\right) = 0.9607, S^+\left(x_2\right) = 0.9621,$$
$$S^+\left(x_3\right) = 0.9815, S^+\left(x_4\right) = 0.9658, S^+\left(x_5\right) = 0.9722$$

and

$$S^-\left(x_1\right) = 0.9748, S^-\left(x_2\right) = 0.9818,$$
$$S^-\left(x_3\right) = 0.9901, S^-\left(x_4\right) = 0.9815, S^-\left(x_5\right) = 0.9855$$

Step 5: We obtain the relative closeness degree $c(x_i)$ of each alternative x_i as;

$$c(x_1) = 0.4964, c(x_2) = 0.4949, c(x_3) = 0.4978, c(x_4) = 0.4960, c(x_5) = 0.4966$$

Step 6: Since $T(x_3) > T(x_5) > T(x_1) > T(x_4) > T(x_2)$, we can rank five alternatives x_1, x_2, x_3, x_4 and x_5 in the preference order: $x_2 \succ x_4 \succ x_1 \succ x_5 \succ x_3$.

The better preference is x_3.

5 CONCLUSİON

Ranking of single valued trapezoidal neutrosophic numbers (SVTN-Numbers) plays a vital role in decision making and other single valued trapezoidal neutrosophic applications. In this paper, we propose a new ranking method of SVTN-Numbers based on distance measure. Firstly, a new distance measure based on cut sets of SVTN-Numbers developed. Secondly, some deseired propertions and results of the distance measure are examined. Finally, the SVTN-Number method based on distance measure is given, and the effectiveness of our algorithm through a numerical example is illustrated. We will focus on the following problems: single valued trapezoidal neutrosophic methods with analytic hierarchy method, WASPAS method and TOPSIS method and applications in artificial intelligence and general systems.

REFERENCES

Aal, S. I. A., Ellatif, M. M. A. A., & Hassan, M. M. (2018). Proposed Model for Evaluating Information Systems Quality Based on Single Valued Triangular Neutrosophic Numbers. I.J. *Mathematical Sciences and Computing, 1*, 1–14.

Abdel-Basset, M., Mohamed, M., & Sangaiah, A. K. (2018). Neutrosophic AHP-Delphi Group decision making model based on trapezoidal neutrosophic numbers. *Journal of Ambient Intelligence and Humanized Computing, 9*(5), 1427–1443. doi:10.100712652-017-0548-7

Abdel-Basset, M., Saleh, M., Gamal, A., & Smarandache, F. (2019). An approach of TOPSIS technique for developing supplier selection with group decision making under type-2 neutrosophic number. *Applied Soft Computing, 77*, 438–452. doi:10.1016/j.asoc.2019.01.035

Akram, M., & Davvaz, B. (2012). Strong intuitionistic fuzzy graphs. Faculty of Sciences and Mathematics, University of Nis. *Serbia Filomat, 26*(1), 177–196. doi:10.2298/FIL1201177A

Akram, M., & Dudek, W. A. (2013). Intuitionistic fuzzy hypergraphs with applications. *Information Sciences*, *218*, 182–193. doi:10.1016/j.ins.2012.06.024

Alaca, C., Türkoğlu, D., & Yıldız, C. (2006). Fixed points in intuitionistic fuzzy metric spaces. *Chaos, Solitons, and Fractals*, *29*(5), 1073–1078. doi:10.1016/j.chaos.2005.08.066

Alava,, M.V., Figueroa,, S.P.D., & Alcivar,, H.M.B., & Vã¡zquez, M.L. (2018). Single Valued Neutrosophic Numbers and Analytic Hierarchy Process for Project Selection. *Neutrosophic Sets and Systems*, *21*, 122–130.

Angelov, P. P. (1997). Optimization in an intuitionistic fuzzy environment. *Fuzzy Sets and Systems*, *86*(3), 299–306. doi:10.1016/S0165-0114(96)00009-7

Atanassov, K. (1986). Intuitionistic fuzzy sets. *Fuzzy Sets and Systems*, *20*(1), 87–96. doi:10.1016/S0165-0114(86)80034-3

Atanassov, K., & Georgiev, C. (1993). Intuitionistic fuzzy Prolog. *Fuzzy Sets and Systems*, *53*(2), 121–128. doi:10.1016/0165-0114(93)90166-F

Atanassov, K. T. (1999). *Intuitionistic Fuzzy Sets*. New York: Pysica-Verlag A Springer-Verlag Company. doi:10.1007/978-3-7908-1870-3

Aydoğdu, A. (2015). On Similarity and Entropy of Single Valued Neutrosophic Sets. *Gen. Math. Notes*, *29*(1), 67–74.

Basset, M. A., Nabeeh, N. A., El-Ghareeb, H. A., & Aboelfetouh, A. (2019). *Utilizing Neutrosophic Theory to Solve Transition Difficulties of IoT-Based Enterprises*. Enterprise Information Systems, 2017 Impact Factor: 2.1. doi:10.1080/17517575.2019.1633690

Beliakov, G., Bustince, H., Goswami, D. P., Mukherjee, U. K., & Pal, N. R. (2011). On averaging operators for Atanassov's intuitionistic fuzzy sets. *Information Sciences*, *181*(6), 1116–1124. doi:10.1016/j.ins.2010.11.024

Biswas. P., Pramanik. S., & Giri, B.C. (2015). Multi-attribute group decision making based on expected value of neutrosophic trapezoidal numbers. *New Math. Natural Comput*.

Biswas, P., Pramanik, S., & Giri, B. C. (2016). Value and ambiguity index based ranking method of single-valued trapezoidal neutrosophic numbers and its application to multi-attribute decision making. *Neutrosophic Sets and Systems*, *12*, 127–138.

Broumi, S., Bakali, A., Talea, M., & Smarandache, F. (2016). Computation of Shortest Path Problem in a Network with SV-Trapezoidal Neutrosophic Numbers. *Proceedings of the 2016 International Conference on Advanced Mechatronic Systems*, 417-422. 10.1109/ICAMechS.2016.7813484

Broumi, S., Bakali, A., Talea, M., Smarandache, F., & Vladareanu, L. (2017). Computation of Shortest Path Problem in a Network with SV-Triangular Neutrosophic Numbers. *2017 IEEE International Conference on innovations in Intelligent Systems and Applications (INISTA)*, 426-431.

Broumi, S., Dey, A., Talea, M., Bakali, A., Smarandache, F., Nagarajan, D., ... Kumar, R. (2019a). *Shortest Path Problem using Bellman Algorithm under Neutrosophic Environment*. Complex & Intelligent Systems. doi:10.100740747-019-0101-8

Broumi, S., Nagarajan, D., Bakali, A., Talea, M., Smarandache, F., & Lathamaheswari, M. (2019c). *The shortest path problem in interval valued trapezoidal and triangular neutrosophic environment*. Complex & Intelligent Systems. doi:10.100740747-019-0092-5

Broumi, S., & Smarandache, F. (2013). Several similarity measures of neutrosophic sets. *Neutrosophic Sets Syst, 1*(1), 54–62.

Broumi, S., Talea, M., Bakali, A., Smarandache, F., Nagarajan, D., Lathamaheswari, M., & Parimala, M. (2019b). *Shortest path problem in fuzzy, intuitionistic fuzzy and neutrosophic environment: an overview*. Complex & Intelligent Systems. doi:10.100740747-019-0098-z

Burillo, P., & Bustince, H. (1996). Entropy on intuitionistic fuzzy sets and on interval-valued fuzzy sets. *Fuzzy Sets and Systems, 78*(3), 305–316. doi:10.1016/0165-0114(96)84611-2

Bustince, H., & Burillo, P. (1995). Correlation of interval-valued intuitionistic fuzzy sets. *Fuzzy Sets and Systems, 74*(2), 237–244. doi:10.1016/0165-0114(94)00343-6

Bustince, H., & Burillo, P. (1996). Structures on intuitionistic fuzzy relations. *Fuzzy Sets and Systems, 78*(3), 293–303. doi:10.1016/0165-0114(96)84610-0

Chakraborty, A., Mondal, S. P., Ahmadian, A., Senu, N., Alam, S., & Salahshour, S. (2018). Ahmadian A., Senu N., Alam S., Salahshour S., Different Forms of Triangular Neutrosophic Numbers, De-Neutrosophication Techniques, and their Applications. *Symmetry, 10*(8), 327. doi:10.3390ym10080327

Çoker, D. (1997). An introduction to intuitionistic fuzzy topological spaces. *Fuzzy Sets and Systems, 88*(1), 81–89. doi:10.1016/S0165-0114(96)00076-0

Das, S., & Guha, D. (2013). Ranking of Intuitionistic Fuzzy Number by Centroid Point. *Journal of Industrial and Intelligent Information, 1*(2), 107–110. doi:10.12720/jiii.1.2.107-110

Davvaz, B., Dudek, W. A., & Jun, Y. B. (2006). Intuitionistic fuzzy Hv-submodules. *Information Sciences, 176*(3), 285–300. doi:10.1016/j.ins.2004.10.009

Deli, I., & Şubaş, Y. (2014). Single valued neutrosophic numbers and their applications to multicriteria decision making problem. *Neutrosophic Sets Syst., 2*, 1–13.

Deli, I., & Şubaş, Y. (2015). Some weighted geometric operators with SVTrN-numbers and their application to multi-criteria decision making problems. *Journal of Intelligent & Fuzzy Systems.* doi:10.3233/jifs-151677

Deli, I., & Şubaş, Y. (2017). A ranking method of single valued neutrosophic numbers and its applications to multi-attribute decision making problems. *International Journal of Machine Learning and Cybernetics, 8*(4), 1309–1322. doi:10.100713042-016-0505-3

Dengfeng, L., & Chuntian, C. (2002). *New Similarity Measures of Intuitionistic Fuzzy Sets and Application to Pattern Recognitions. Pattern Recognition Letters, 23*, 221–225.

Grzegorzewski, P. (2002). Nearest interval approximation of a fuzzy number. *Fuzzy Sets and Systems, 130*(3), 321–330. doi:10.1016/S0165-0114(02)00098-2

Gündoğdu, F. K., & Kahraman, C. (2019). Spherical fuzzy sets and spherical fuzzy TOPSIS method. *Journal of Intelligent & Fuzzy Systems.* doi:10.3233/JIFS-181401

Hayat, K., Ali, M. I., Cao, B. Y., Karaaslan, F., & Yang, X. P. (2018). Another view of group-based generalized intuitionistic fuzzy soft sets: Aggregation operators and multiattribute decision making. *Symmetry, 10*(12), 25–32. doi:10.3390ym10120753

Hong, D. H., & Hwang, S. Y. (1995). Correlation of intuitionistic fuzzy sets in probability spaces. *Fuzzy Sets and Systems, 75*(1), 77–81. doi:10.1016/0165-0114(94)00330-A

Hung, W. L., & Yang, M. S. (2004). Similarity measures of intuitionistic fuzzy sets based on Hausdorff distance. *Pattern Recognition Letters, 25*(14), 1603–1611. doi:10.1016/j.patrec.2004.06.006

Hung, W.L., & Yang, M.S. (2006). Fuzzy Entropy on Intuitionistic Fuzzy Sets. *International Journal of Intelligent Systems, 21*, 443-451.

Jana, C., Pal, M., Karaaslan, F., & Wang, J. Q. (2018). Trapezoidal neutrosophic aggregation operators and its application in multiple attribute decision-making process. *Scientia Iranica*, *5*. doi:10.24200/SCI.2018.51136.2024

Jun, Y. (n.d.). Projection and bidirectional projection measures of singlevalued neutrosophic sets and their decision-making method for mechanical design schemes. *Journal of Experimental & Theoretical Artificial Intelligence*, *29*(4), 731–740.

Karaaslan, F. (2018a). Multi-criteria decision-making method based on similarity measures under single-valued neutrosophic refined and interval neutrosophic refined environments. *International Journal of Intelligent Systems*, *33*(5), 928–952. doi:10.1002/int.21906

Karaaslan, F. (2018b). Gaussian Single-valued neutrosophic number and its application in multi-attribute decision making. *Neutrosophic Sets and Systems*, *22*, 101–117.

Karaaslan, F. (2019). Correlation Coefficient of Neutrosophic Sets and Its Applications in Decision-Making. *Springer Nature Switzerland AG*, 369.

Lee, S. J., & Lee, E. P. (2000). The Category Of Intuitionistic Fuzzy Topologcal Spaces. *Bulletin of the Korean Mathematical Society*, *37*(1), 63–76.

Li, Y., Liu, P., & Chen, Y. (2016). Some Single Valued Neutrosophic Number Heronian Mean Operators and Their Application in Multiple Attribute Group Decision Making. *INFORMATICA*, *27*(1), 85–110. doi:10.15388/Informatica.2016.78

Li, Y., Olson, D. L., & Qin, Z. (2007). Similarity measures between intuitionistic fuzzy (vague) sets: A comparative analysis. *Pattern Recognition Letters*, *28*(2), 278–285. doi:10.1016/j.patrec.2006.07.009

Liang, Z., & Shi, P. (2003). Similarity measures on intuitionistic fuzzy sets. *Pattern Recognition Letters*, *24*(15), 2687–2693. doi:10.1016/S0167-8655(03)00111-9

Majumdar, P., & Samanta, S. K. (2013). On similarity and entropy of neutrosophic sets. *Journal of Intelligent & Fuzzy Systems*. doi:10.3233/IFS-130810

Nabeeh, N. A., Basset, M. A., El-Ghareeb, H. A., & Aboelfetouh, A. (2019b). *Neutrosophic Multi-Criteria Decision Making Approach for IoT-Based Enterprises*. IEEE Access. doi:10.1109/ACCESS.2019.2908919

Nabeeh, N. A., Smarandache, F., Basset, M. A., El-Ghareeb, H. A., & Aboelfetouh, A. (2019a). *An Integrated Neutrosophic-TOPSIS Approach and its Application to Personnel Selection: A New Trend in Brain Processing and Analysis*. IEEE Access. doi:10.1109/ACCESS.2019.2899841

Pouresmaeil, H., Shivanian, E., Khorram, E., & Fathabadi, H. S. 2016. An Extended Method Using TOPSIS And Vikor For Multiple Attribute Decision Making With Multiple Decision Makers And Single Valued Neutrosophic Numbers. Advances and Applications in Statistics 2016. Pushpa Publishing House.

Saadati, R., & Park, J. H. (2006). On the intuitionistic fuzzy topological spaces. *Chaos, Solitons, and Fractals*, *27*(2), 332–344. doi:10.1016/j.chaos.2005.03.019

Şahin, M., Kargın, A., & Smarandache, F. (2018). Generalized Single Valued Triangular Neutrosophic Numbers and Aggregation Operators for Application to Multi-attribute Group Decision Making. New Trends in Neutrosophic Theory and Applications. *Quai du Batelage, 2*, 51-84.

Şahin, R., & Kucuk, A. (2014). Subsethood measure for single valued neutrosophic sets. *Journal of Intelligent & Fuzzy Systems*. doi:10.3233/IFS-141304

Smarandache, F. (1998). *A Unifying Field in Logics Neutrosophy: Neutrosophic Probability, Set and Logic*. Rehoboth: American Research Press.

Smarandache, F. (2005). Neutrosophic set, a generalisation of the intuitionistic fuzzy sets. *International Journal of Pure and Applied Mathematics*, *24*, 287–297.

Smarandache, F. (2004). *A Geometric Interpretation of the Neutrosophic Set, A Generalization of the Intuitionistic Fuzzy Set Set*. arXiv preprint math/0404520

Szmidt, E., & Kacprzyk, J. (2000). Distances between intuitionistic fuzzy sets. *Fuzzy Sets and Systems*, *114*(3), 505–518. doi:10.1016/S0165-0114(98)00244-9

Szmidt, E., & Kacprzyk, J. (2001). Entropy for intuitionistic fuzzy sets. *Fuzzy Sets and Systems*, *118*(3), 467–477. doi:10.1016/S0165-0114(98)00402-3

Szmidt, E., & Kacprzyk, J. (2003). A Consensus-Reaching Process Under Intuitionistic Fuzzy Preference Relations. *International Journal Of Intelligent Systems, 18*, 837-852.

Tan, R., & Zhang, W. (2017). Multiple attribute group decision making methods based on trapezoidal fuzzy neutrosophic numbers. *Journal of Intelligent & Fuzzy Systems*, *33*(4), 2547–2564. doi:10.3233/JIFS-161984

Wang, J., Wei, G., & Wei, Y. (2018). Models for Green Supplier Selection with Some 2-Tuple Linguistic Neutrosophic Number Bonferroni Mean Operators. *Symmetry*, *10*(5), 131. doi:10.3390ym10050131

Wang, W., & Xin, X. (2005). Distance measure between intuitionistic fuzzy sets. *Pattern Recognition Letters*, *26*(13), 2063–2069. doi:10.1016/j.patrec.2005.03.018

Wei, G. (2010). Some Arithmetic Aggregation Operators with Intuitionistic Trapezoidal Fuzzy Numbers and Their Application to Group Decision Making. *Journal of Computers, 5*(3), 345–351. doi:10.4304/jcp.5.3.345-351

Wu, X., Qian, J., Peng, J., & Xue, C. (2018). A Multi-Criteria Group Decision-Making Method with Possibility Degree and Power Aggregation Operators of Single Trapezoidal Neutrosophic Numbers. *Symmetry, 10*(11), 590. doi:10.3390ym10110590

Xu, Z. (2007). Intuitionistic Fuzzy Aggregation Operators. *IEEE Transactions On Fuzzy Systems, 15*(6), 1179-1187.

Xu, Z. (2010). Choquet integrals of weighted intuitionistic fuzzy information. *Information Sciences, 180*(5), 726–736. doi:10.1016/j.ins.2009.11.011

Xu, Z., & Chen, J. (2007). On Geometric Aggregation Over Interval-Valued Intuitionistic Fuzzy Information. *Fourth International Conference on Fuzzy Systems and Knowledge Discovery (FSKD)*. 10.1109/FSKD.2007.427

Xu, Z., & Xia, M. (2011). Induced generalized intuitionistic fuzzy operators. *Knowledge-Based Systems, 24*(2), 197–209. doi:10.1016/j.knosys.2010.04.010

Xu, Z., & Yager, R. R. (2006). Some geometric aggregation operators based on intuitionistic fuzzy sets. *International Journal of General Systems, 35*(4), 417–433. doi:10.1080/03081070600574353

Xu, Z., & Yager, R. R. (2008). Dynamic intuitionistic fuzzy multi-attribute decision making. *International Journal of Approximate Reasoning, 48*(1), 246–262. doi:10.1016/j.ijar.2007.08.008

Xu, Z. S. (2007). Intuitionistic fuzzy aggregation operators. *IEEE Transactions on Fuzzy Systems, 15*(6), 1179–1187. doi:10.1109/TFUZZ.2006.890678

Xu, Z. S., Chen, J., & Wu, J. (2008). Clustering algorithm for intuitionistic fuzzy sets. *Information Sciences, 178*(19), 3775–3790. doi:10.1016/j.ins.2008.06.008

Ye, F. (2010). An extended TOPSIS method with interval-valued intuitionistic fuzzy numbers for virtual enterprise partner selection. *Expert Systems with Applications, 37*(10), 7050–7055. doi:10.1016/j.eswa.2010.03.013

Ye, J. (2015). Multiple attribute decision-making method based on the possibility degree ranking method and ordered weighted aggregation operators of interval neutrosophic numbers. *Journal of Intelligent & Fuzzy Systems, 28*, 1307–1317.

Zadeh, L. A. (1965). Fuzzy Sets. *Information and Control, 8*(3), 338–353. doi:10.1016/S0019-9958(65)90241-X

Zavadskas, E. K., Bauiys, R., & Lazauskas, M. (2015). Sustainable Assessment of Alternative Sites for the Construction of aWaste Incineration Plant by Applying WASPAS Method with Single-Valued Neutrosophic Set. *Sustainability*, *7*(12), 15923–15936. doi:10.3390u71215792

Zeng, S., & Su, W. (2011). Intuitionistic fuzzy ordered weighted distance operator. *Knowledge-Based Systems*, *24*(8), 1224–1232. doi:10.1016/j.knosys.2011.05.013

Zhou, L., & Wu, W. Z. (2008). On generalized intuitionistic fuzzy rough approximation operators. *Information Sciences*, *178*, 2448–2465.

Chapter 2
An Improved PID Tuning Method by Applying Single-Valued Neutrosophic Cosine, Tangent, and Exponential Measures and a Simulated Annealing Algorithm

Sheng-Yi Ruan
Shaoxing University, China

Jun Ye
ⓘ https://orcid.org/0000-0003-2841-6529
Shaoxing University, China

Wen-Hua Cui
Shaoxing University, China

ABSTRACT

This chapter introduces an improved proportional-integral-derivative (PID) adjusting method by applying a simulated annealing algorithm (SAA) and the cosine, tangent, exponential measures of single-valued neutrosophic sets (SvNSs). For the approach, characteristic values of the unit step response (rise time, peak time, settling time, undershoot ratio, overshoot ratio, and steady-state error) in the control system should be neutrosophicated by the neutrosophic membership functions. Next, one of cosine, tangent, and exponential measures is used to obtain the similarity measure of the ideal SvNS and the response SvNS to assess the control performance of the PID

DOI: 10.4018/978-1-7998-2555-5.ch002

controller by the optimization values of the PID parameters Kp, Ki, and Kd searched by SAA. The results of the illustrative example obtained by these measures and SAA are better than the existing ones and indicate better PID controller performance. Comparative results can demonstrate the rationality and superiority of the improved PID adjusting method.

1. INTRODUCTION

The proportional-integral-derivative (PID) control algorithm is widely utilized in control engineering areas at present. Its advantage is a simple model and less information needed for the controlled plant, so it is very easy to realize its control systems. Then determining the PID parameters called K_p, K_i and K_d is a cumbersome process. Hence, a high precision, a fast algorithm is urgently needed to find PID parameters. There exist mainly open-loop and closed-loop methods for PID tuning, like the Cohen–Coon and Ziegler–Nichols experience methods. Among the software-based PID tuning methods, particle swarm optimization (PSO) (Gaing,2004;Solihin et al., 2011; Monika et al., 2019), genetic algorithm (GA) (Bagis,2007;Neath et al.,2014), simulated annealing algorithm (SAA) (Kwok & Sheng, 1994; Gupta et al., 2017), and fuzzy logic method (Malleham & Rajani,2006; Khodadadi & Ghadiri, 2018; Dettori et al. 2018; Tripathy et al. 2019; Rohan et al., 2018; Bai & Roth, 2019; Eltag, 2019) are commonly used in the PID tuning research at present.

Extended from a fuzzy set (FS) (Zadeh, 1965), an interval-valued FS (Grattan-Guiness, 1976), an intuitionistic FS (Wang et al., 2013) and an interval-value intuitionistic FS (Tan, 2011), a neutrosophic set (NS) (Smarandache, 1998) was proposed to cope with uncertain and inconsistent information, and then the single-valued NS (SvNS) (Wang, 2010) was presented as a branch of NS to solve practical engineering problems such as group decision making (Ye, 2014; Ye & Cui, 2018), fault diagnosis (Ye, 2017; Ye, 2018), and medical diagnosis (Ye, 2015; Fu & Ye, 2017).

For designing a control system, its unit step response characteristics (USRCs) are often examined to evaluate whether a control system is good or bad. But sometimes the response of a control system contains indeterminacy. Hence, Can and Ozguven designed neutrosophic PID controllers for the angular speed control of a direct current (DC) motor (Can & Ozguven, 2016) and the position tracking control of a robot arm (Can & Ozguven, 2018). Based on the neutrosophic similarity measures, Can and Ozguven (Can & Ozguven, 2017) also put forward a PID adjusting method by the time-domain USRC values of the control system. In this PID tuning process, one first needs to use the Ziegler–Nichols tuning method to get the approximate range of K_p, K_i, K_d parameters, and further determine their specific values by the increasing step algorithm, where by the defined neutrosophic membership functions, the USRC values of the control system are transformed into a response SvNS and then the similarity measure between the response SvNS and the ideal SvNS realizes the performance evaluation of the PID controller. However, the increasing step algorithm results in either low control precision or long time-consuming. To solve this problem, Ye [30] (Ye, 2019) applied the genetic algorithm and cosine measure of SvNSs for PID tuning, but the designed PID controller indicates its general control performance. So far, these PID tuning methods have lacked the investigations of the tangent and exponential similarity measures of SvNSs. Hence, an improved PID tuning approach is presented by applying the cosine, tangent, and exponential measures of SvNSs (Fu & Ye, 2017; Ye, 2019; Ye & Fu, 2016) and SAA (Kwok & Sheng, 1994) as the complement and improvement of the existing ones. Then,the contribution of this chapter is that the improved one will be more convenient to find more suitable three parameters of a PID controller for obtaining better PID control performance.

For the rest of this paper, cosine, tangent, and exponential similarity measures of SvNSs are briefly described in Section 2. Then an improved PID tuning approach is presented based on the three SvNS similarity measures mentioned above and SAA in Section 3. After that, a comparative analysis is presented with illustrative examples in Section 4. Conclusions and further study are shown in Section 5.

2. SIMILARITY MEASURES BETWEEN SvNSs

This section describes that Wang et al. (Wang et al., 2010) defined a SvNS as a branch of NS (Smarandache, 1998) and Ye and Fu (Fu & Ye, 2017; Ye, 2019; Ye & Fu, 2016) presented the cosine, tangent and exponential similarity measures of SvNSs.

Definition 1 (Wang et al., 2010). Suppose $\gamma = \{z, T_\gamma(z), U_\gamma(z), F_\gamma(z) | z \in Z\}$ is a SvNS in a universe of discourse Z, where $T_\gamma(z)$, $U_\gamma(z)$ and $F_\gamma(z)$ denote the membership functions of truth, indeterminacy, and falsity respectively, with the conditions of $T_\gamma(z)$, $U_\gamma(z)$, $F_\gamma(z) \in [0,1]$ and $0 \leq T_\gamma(z) + U_\gamma(z) + F_\gamma(z) \leq 3$ for each z in Z. For convenience, $x = (T, U, F)$ can be denoted by a single-valued neutrosophic number (SvNN) in γ.

Let $\mu = (T_\mu, U_\mu, F_\mu)$ and $v = (T_v, U_v, F_v)$ be two SvNNs. Then there exit the relations [20]:

(1)   Complement: $\mu^c = (F_\mu, 1-U_\mu, T_\mu)$;
(2)   Inclusion: $\mu \subseteq v \Leftrightarrow T_\mu \leq T_v$, $U_\mu \geq U_v$ and $F_\mu \geq F_v$;
(3)   Equality: $\mu = v \Leftrightarrow \mu \subseteq v$ and $v \subseteq \mu$.

Regarding cosine function, Ye (Ye, 2019) defined a cosine measure between SvNSs below.

Definition 2 (Ye, 2019). Suppose $\mu = \{z, T_\mu(z_i), U_\mu(z_i), F_\mu(z_i) | z_i \in Z\}$ and $v = \{z, T_v(z_i), U_v(z_i), F_v(z_i) | z_i \in Z\}$ are two SvNSs in the universe set $Z = \{z_1, z_2, \ldots, z_n\}$. Thus, a cosine measure between μ and v can be given by

$$Cs(\mu, v) = \frac{1}{n} \sum_{i=1}^{n} \cos\left\{\frac{\pi}{6} \left[\left| T_\mu(z_i) - T_v(z_i) \right| + \left| U_\mu(z_i) - U_v(z_i) \right| + \left| F_\mu(z_i) - F_v(z_i) \right| \right]\right\}.$$
(1)

Thus, the cosine measure indicates the properties [30]:

(1) $0 \leq Cs(\mu, v) \leq 1$;
(2) $Cs(\mu, v) = 1 \leftrightarrow \mu = v$;
(3) $Cs(\mu, v) = Cs(v, \mu)$;
(4) If γ is a SvNS in Z and $\mu \subseteq v \subseteq \gamma$, then $Cs(\mu, \gamma) \leq Cs(\mu, v)$ and $Cs(\mu, \gamma) \leq Cs(v, \gamma)$.

Regarding tangent function, Ye and Fu (Ye & Fu, 2016) defined a tangent measure between SvNSs below.

Definition 3 (Ye & Fu, 2016). Suppose $\mu = \{z, T_\mu(z_i), U_\mu(z_i), F_\mu(z_i) | z_i \in Z\}$ and $v = \{z, T_v(z_i), U_v(z_i), F_v(z_i) | z_i \in Z\}$ are two SvNSs in the universe of discourse $Z = \{z_1, z_2, \ldots, z_n\}$. Thus, a tangent measure between μ and v can be expressed by

$$Ts(\mu, v) = 1 - \frac{1}{n} \sum_{i=1}^{n} \tan\left\{\frac{\pi}{12} \left[\left| T_\mu(z_i) - T_v(z_i) \right| + \left| U_\mu(z_i) - U_v(z_i) \right| + \left| F_\mu(z_i) - F_v(z_i) \right| \right]\right\}.$$
(2)

Then, the tangent measure contains the following properties [31]:

(1) $Ts(\mu, v) \in [0, 1]$;
(2) $Ts(\mu, v) = 1 \leftrightarrow \mu = v$;
(3) $Ts(\mu, v) = Ts(v, \mu)$;
(4) If γ is a SvNS in Z and $\mu \subseteq v \subseteq \gamma$, then $Ts(\mu, \gamma) \leq Ts(\mu, v)$ and $Ts(\mu, \gamma) \leq Ts(v, \gamma)$.

Based on an exponential function, Fu and Ye [26] proposed an exponential measure between SvNSs and gave the following definition.

Definition 4 (Fu & Ye, 2017). Suppose $\mu = \{z_i, T_\mu(z_i), U_\mu(z_i), F_\mu(z_i) | z_i \in Z\}$ and $v = \{z_i, T_v(z_i), U_v(z_i), F_v(z_i) | z_i \in Z\}$ are two SvNSs in the universe set $Z = \{z_1, z_2, \ldots, z_n\}$. Thus, an exponential measure between μ and v is

$$\text{Es}(\mu, v) = \frac{1}{n} \sum_{i=1}^{n} \frac{\exp\left\{-\frac{1}{3}\begin{bmatrix} |T_\mu(z_i) - T_v(z_i)| + \\ |U_\mu(z_i) - U_v(z_i)| + \\ |F_\mu(z_i) - F_v(z_i)| \end{bmatrix}\right\} - \exp(-1)}{1 - \exp(-1)}. \tag{3}$$

Then, the exponential measure contains the following properties [26]:

(1) $0 \le \text{Es}(\mu, v) \le 1$;
(2) $\text{Es}(\mu, v) = 1 \leftrightarrow \mu = v$;
(3) $\text{Es}(\mu, v) = \text{Es}(v, \mu)$;
(4) If γ is a SVNS in Z and $\mu \subseteq v \subseteq \gamma$, then $\text{Es}(\mu, \gamma) \le \text{Es}(\mu, v)$ and $\text{Es}(\mu, \gamma) \le \text{Es}(v, \gamma)$.

3. PID TUNING APPROACH USING THE SIMILARITY MEASURES AND SIMULATED ANNEALING ALGORITHM

To improve the existing PID tuning methods (Can & Ozguven, 2017; Ye, 2019), an improved PID tuning approach is introduced by applying SAA and the cosine, tangent and exponential similarity measures of SvNSs in this section.

3.1 PID Control System

As a typical PID control system given in Figure 1, the output of the PID controller in the time domain is

$$u(t) = K_p e(t) + K_i \int_0^t e(t) \, dt + K_d \frac{de(t)}{dt}, \tag{4}$$

where the error $e(t)$ is the error of the input $r(t)$ minus the output $y(t)$ and K_p, K_i, and K_d are the parameters of the PID controller.

Then the PID output in the s domain is obtained by the Laplace transform of Eq. (4) as follows:

Figure 1. Typical PID control system

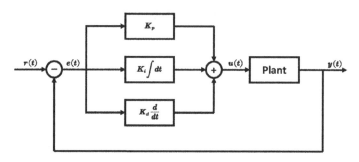

$$u(s) = E(s)\left(K_P + \frac{K_i}{s} + K_d s \right). \tag{5}$$

3.2 Neutrosophic Membership Functions and Neutrosophication

In a netrosophication process (Can & Ozguven, 2017), six transient state characteristics including rise time, peak time, settling time, undershoot ratio, overshoot ratio, and steady-state error are selected in the control system and can be yielded by the "stepinfo" function built-in MATLAB. Then the USRCs are converted into the membership degrees of truth, falsity and indeterminacy by their membership degree functions. Finally, one of three similarity measures is used to calculate the measure value between the system transient characteristics (the response SvNS) and the ideal response characteristics (the ideal SvNS).

Similar to some fuzzification process (Can & Ozguven, 2017), the process of netrosophication also uses triangle and trapezoid membership functions. Hence, the authors regard the six USRCs: (a) S_1: rise time (s), (b) S_2: settling time (s), (c) S_3: peak time (s), (d) S_4: overshoot ratio (%), (e) S_5: undershoot ratio (%) and (f) S_6: stead-state error, as a feature set $S=\{S_1,S_2,S_3,S_4,S_5,S_6\}$. Then, the membership functions and the range values of T_i, U_i, and F_i ($i=1,2,\ldots,6$) in a SvNS γ are determined from living examples. According to the membership functions in Figure 2, the SvNS γ is obtained by the following form:

$$\gamma = \left\{ S_1,T_1,U_1,F_1,S_2,T_2,U_2,F_2,S_3,T_3,U_3,F_3,S_4,T_4,U_4,F_4,S_5,T_5,U_5,F_5,S_6,T_6,U_6,F_6 \right\}.$$

Then the ideal SvNS γ^* can be determined as

Figure 2. Membership functions of six USRCs

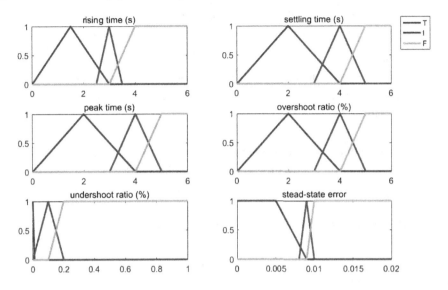

$$\gamma^* = \left\{\left\langle S_1,1,0,0\right\rangle\left\langle S_2,1,0,0\right\rangle\left\langle S_3,1,0,0\right\rangle\left\langle S_4,1,0,0\right\rangle\left\langle S_5,1,0,0\right\rangle\left\langle S_6,1,0,0\right\rangle\right\}.$$

3.3 Simulated Annealing Algorithm

SAA (Kwok & Sheng, 1994) is a general algorithm to solve the optimization problem by a simple heuristic search, and then the advantage can abandon the local optimal solution probabilistically and eventually obtain the global optimal solution. It is very suitable for solving the optimization parameters in the PID controller design. The parameters K_p, K_i and K_d are considered as their design variables and constrained in the specified range of them. Then, the optimization object is to maximize the similarity measure between the system response result (response SvNS) and the ideal response result (ideal SvNS). Since the general SAA can find the problem of the minimum value, the object function can be modified as:

$$f(\omega)=1-\mathrm{Cs}(\gamma,\gamma^*) \text{ or } f(\omega)=1-Ts(\gamma,\gamma^*) \text{ or } f(\omega)=1-Es(\gamma,\gamma^*),$$

(6)

where $\omega = (K_p, K_i, K_d)$. The general algorithm steps of SAA are given below:

Step 1. Generate the initial temperature T_0 and $T=T_0$ and an initial solution ω and calculate $f(\omega)$.

Step 2. Decrease the temperature T.

Step 3. Perturb the present solution and make a new solution ω'.

Step 4. If $\Delta f = f(\omega') - f(\omega) < 0$, then $\omega = \omega'$, else accept it with a certain probability.

Step 5. Perform Step 3 and Step 4 till the iteration number is reached.

Step 6. Determine whether the temperature reaches the minimum setting, then quit the algorithm, otherwise continue Step 2.

It should be noted that the optimal solution in history should be recorded in this algorithm. Then Figure 3 shows the general flow chart of SAA.

4. EXAMPLES AND COMPARATIVE ANALYSIS

To display the superiority of the presented approach, an illustrate example is adapted from the references (Can & Ozguven, 2017; Ye, 2019) for convenient comparison, and a speed control system of DC motor is designed.

4.1. PID Tuning Methods Using the Cosine Measures and SAA and the Relative Comparison

The effectiveness of the PID adjusting method applying the SAA and cosine measure is verified by the open-loop transfer function (Can & Ozguven, 2017) as follows:

$$G(s) = \frac{1}{(s+1)(s+4)}. \tag{7}$$

Then, Figure 4 indicates the step response curves obtained by using both the cosine measure and the SAA, increasing step algorithm, and GA. Table 1 further illustrates their relative results for the convenient comparison.

Obviously, the results obtained by using both the cosine measure and SAA are much better than the existing algorithms and indicate the improvement of control performance in the control system.

Figure 3. Flow chart of simulated annealing algorithm

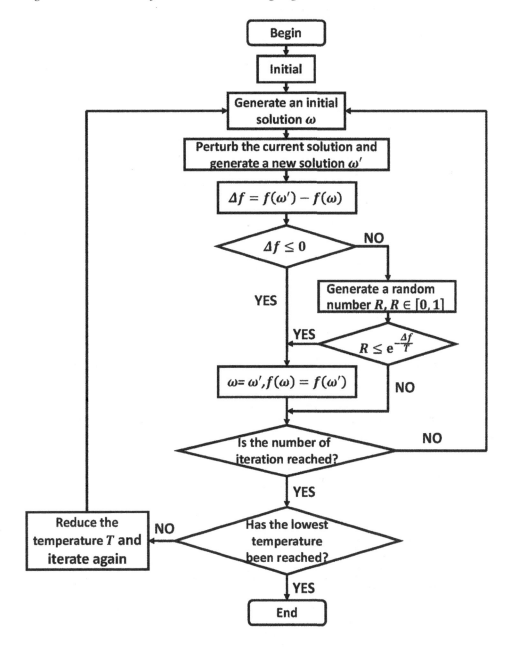

Figure 4. The response curves obtained by using both the cosine measure and the SAA, increasing step algorithm, and GA

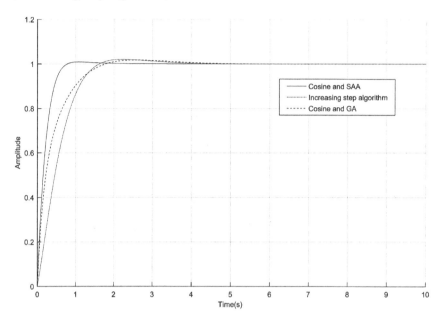

Table 1. The results obtained by using both the cosine measure and the SAA, increasing step algorithm, and GA

Result	Cosine and SAA	Cosine and GA	Increasing step
K_p	25.0080	12.4693	8
K_i	21.5868	11.7133	8
K_d	4.4639	3.8330	1
Settling time (s)	0.6433	1.5095	2.3000
Rise time (s)	0.4160	0.9597	1.0027
Peak time (s)	1.0770	2.5716	2.2295
Undershoot (%)	0	0	0
Over shoot (%)	0.8752	1.7056	2.0152
Steady-state error	0	0	0

4.2. PID Tuning Methods Using the Cosine, Tangent, and Exponential Measures, and SAA

By using the same transfer function of the example above, the results obtained by using the cosine, tangent and exponential measures and SAA are shown in Figure 5 and Table 2.

For Figure 5, the three response curves are so close that their difference is difficult to be seen. The response characteristics and three parameters K_p, K_i and K_d in the control system are similar in Table 2. It is obvious that using different measure algorithms scarcely affect control performance regarding the PID tuning method applying SAA. This case shows the robustness of the SAA optimization method

Figure 5. The response curves obtained by using the cosine, tangent, and exponential measures, and SAA

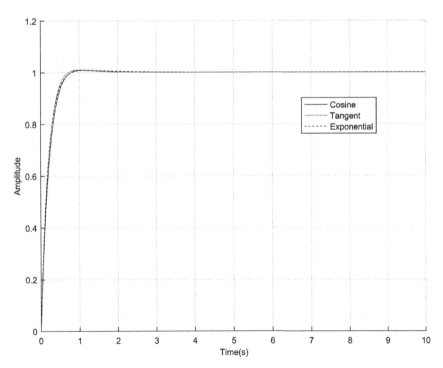

Table 2. The results obtained by using the cosine, tangent and exponential measures, and SAA

Result	Cosine	Tangent	Exponential
K_p	25.0080	27.4318	26.9137
K_i	21.5868	23.8285	23.9488
K_d	4.4639	4.9140	5.2366
Settling time (s)	0.6433	0.5884	0.6345
Rise time (s)	0.4160	0.3815	0.3944
Peak time (s)	1.0770	1.0098	1.1705
Undershoot (%)	0	0	0
Over shoot (%)	0.8752	0.9796	0.9188
Steady-state error	0	0	0

4.3. Application Example

For a DC motor, the steady speed of 1200 r/min is obtained by adding a certain voltage of 10V to the armature, and the time to reach the value of 63.2% is 1.4s. Then, by the time domain analysis method, the open-loop transfer function of the DC motor can be obtained as

$$G(s) = \frac{4.119}{s(s+0.328)}.$$

Based on the obtained transfer function, the control system of the DC motor can be further designed using the proposed PID tuning method. Since the different similarity measures of this method have similar effects on the control performance, only the results obtained by using the tangent measurement and SAA are shown in Figure 6 and Table 3 for the comparison with the original system.

From the results, it is manifest that all the performance indicators of the system corrected by applying the proposed PID tuning method are significantly improved.

6. CONCLUSION

The contribution of this study is that the PID tuning approach is improved by using both the cosine, tangent and exponential measures and the SAA to search the optimization parameters of a PID controller. The results of the illustrative examples obtained by

Figure 6. The response curves obtained by using the tangent measures and SAA

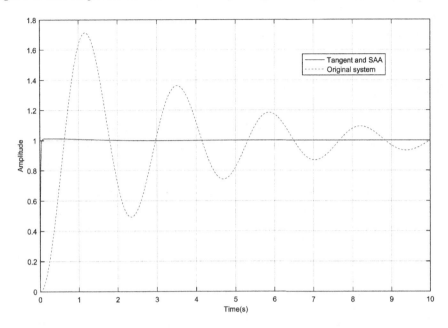

Table 3. The results obtained by using the tangent measure and SAA

Result	Tangent and SAA	Original system
K_p	16.8673	1
K_i	22.1254	0
K_d	11.5471	0
Settling time (s)	0.0421	13.1192
Rise time (s)	0.0254	0.4208
Peak time (s)	0.0827	1.1661
Undershoot (%)	0	0
Over shoot (%)	0.9980	71.2570
Steady-state error	0	0.0014

these measures and SAA are better than the existing ones (Can & Ozguven, 2017; Ye, 2019) and indicate better PID controller performance. Comparative results can illustrate the advantage and effectiveness of the PID adjusting method applying the three similarity measures and SAA. In the future, the authors will further promote the existing PID adjusting approach and extend it to the neutrosophic control system.

ACKNOWLEDGMENT

Conflicts of Interest: The authors declare no conflict of interest.

REFERENCES

Bagis, A. (2007). Determination of the PID controller parameters by modified genetic algorithm for improved performance. *Journal of Information Science and Engineering*, *23*, 1469–1480.

Bai, Y., & Roth, Z. S. (2019). Interval Type-2 Fuzzy Logic Controllers. In *Classical and Modern Controls with Microcontrollers* (pp. 549–579). Cham: Springer. doi:10.1007/978-3-030-01382-0_9

Can, M. S., & Ozguven, O. F. (2016). Design of the neutronsophic membership valued fuzzy-PID controller and rotation angle control of a permanent magnet direct current motor. *Journal of New Results in Science*, *5*, 126–138.

Can, M. S., & Ozguven, O. F. (2017). PID tuning with neutrosophic similarity measure. *International Journal of Fuzzy Systems*, *19*(2), 489–503. doi:10.100740815-015-0136-y

Can, M. S., & Ozguven, O. F. (2018). Fuzzy PID Control by Grouping of Membership Functions of Fuzzy Antecedent Variables with Neutrosophic Set Approach and 3-D Position Tracking Control of a Robot Manipulator. *Journal of Electrical Engineering & Technology*, *13*, 969–980.

Dettori, S., Iannino, V., Colla, V., & Signorini, A. (2018). An adaptive fuzzy logic-based approach to PID control of steam turbines in solar applications. *Applied Energy*, *227*, 655–664. doi:10.1016/j.apenergy.2017.08.145

Eltag, K., Aslamx, M. S., & Ullah, R. (2019). Dynamic Stability Enhancement Using Fuzzy PID Control Technology for Power System. *International Journal of Control, Automation, and Systems*, *17*(1), 234–242. doi:10.100712555-018-0109-7

Fu, J., & Ye, J. (2017). Simplified neutrosophic exponential similarity measures for the initial evaluation/diagnosis of benign prostatic hyperplasia symptoms. *Symmetry*, *9*(8), 154. doi:10.3390ym9080154

Gaing, Z. L. (2004). A particle swarm optimization approach for optimum design of PID controller in AVR system. *IEEE Transactions on Energy Conversion*, *19*(2), 384–391. doi:10.1109/TEC.2003.821821

Grattan-Guiness, I. (1976). Fuzzy membership mapped onto intervals and many-valued quantities. *Mathematical Logic Quarterly, 22*(1), 149–160. doi:10.1002/malq.19760220120

Gupta, A., Goindi, S., Singh, G., Saini, H., & Kumar, R. (2017). Optimal design of PID controllers for time delay systems using genetic algorithm and simulated annealing. *The 2017 International Conference on Innovative Mechanisms for Industry Applications (ICIMIA)*, 66-69. 10.1109/ICIMIA.2017.7975554

Khodadadi, H., & Ghadiri, H. (2018). Self-tuning PID controller design using fuzzy logic for half car active suspension system. *International Journal of Dynamics and Control, 6*(1), 224–232. doi:10.100740435-016-0291-5

Kwok, D. P., & Sheng, F. (1994). Genetic algorithm and simulated annealing for optimal robot arm PID control. *Proceedings of the First IEEE Conference on Evolutionary Computation*, 707-713. 10.1109/ICEC.1994.349971

Malleham, G., & Rajani, A. (2006). Automatic tuning of PID controller using fuzy logic. *The 8th International Conference on Development and Application Systems*, 120-127.

Monika, R., Sasireka, M., Prasad, S. S., & Senthilkumar, A. (2019). Multi-objective particle swarm optimization based PID tuning of ball and beam system. *Journal of Control & Instrumentation, 7*, 35–40.

Neath, M. J., Swain, A. K., Madawala, U. K., & Thrimawithana, D. J. (2014). An optimal PID controller for a bidirectional inductive power transfer system using multiobjective genetic algorithm. *IEEE Transactions on Power Electronics, 29*(3), 1523–1531. doi:10.1109/TPEL.2013.2262953

Rohan, A., Asghar, F., & Kim, S. H. (2018). Design of fuzzy logic tuned PID controller for electric vehicle based on IPMSM using flux-weakening. *Journal of Electrical Engineering & Technology, 13*, 451–459.

Smarandache, F. (1998). *Neutrosophy*. Rehoboth: Neutrosophic Probability, Set, and Logic, Amer. Res. Press.

Solihin, M. I., Tack, L. F., & Kean, M. L. (2011). Tuning of PID controller using particle swarm optimization (PSO). *Proceeding of the International Conference on Advanced Science, Engineering and Information Technology 2011*, 458-461.

Tan, C. Q. (2011). A multi-criteria interval-valued intuitionistic fuzzy group decision making with Choquet integral-based TOPSIS. *Expert Systems with Applications, 38*(4), 3023–3033. doi:10.1016/j.eswa.2010.08.092

Tripathy, D., Barik, A. K., Choudhury, N. B. D., & Sahu, B. K. (2019). Performance comparison of SMO-based fuzzy PID controller for load frequency control. In *Soft computing for problem solving* (pp. 879–892). Singapore: Springer. doi:10.1007/978-981-13-1595-4_70

Wang, H., Smarandache, F., Zhang, Y. Q., & Sunderraman, R. (2010). Single valued neutrosophic sets. *Multispace Multistruct*, *4*, 410–413.

Wang, J. Q., Nie, R. R., Zhang, H. Y., & Chen, X. H. (2013). Intuitionistic fuzzy multi-criteria decision-making method based on evidential reasoning. *Applied Soft Computing*, *13*(4), 1823–1831. doi:10.1016/j.asoc.2012.12.019

Ye, J. (2014). Vector similarity measures of simplified neutrosophic sets and their application in multicriteria decision making. *International Journal of Fuzzy Systems*, *16*(2), 204–211.

Ye, J. (2015). Improved cosine similarity measures of simplified neutrosophic sets for medical diagnoses. *Artificial Intelligence in Medicine*, *63*(3), 171–179. doi:10.1016/j.artmed.2014.12.007 PMID:25704111

Ye, J. (2017). Single valued neutrosophic similarity measures based on cotangent function and their application in the fault diagnosis of steam turbine. *Soft Computing*, *21*(3), 817–825. doi:10.100700500-015-1818-y

Ye, J. (2018). Fault diagnoses of hydraulic turbine using the dimension root similarity measure of single-valued neutrosophic sets. *Intelligent Automation & Soft Computing*, *24*(1), 1–8. doi:10.1080/10798587.2016.1261955

Ye, J. (2019). PID tuning method using single-valued neutrosophic cosine measure and genetic algorithm. *Intelligent Automation & Soft Computing*, *25*, 15–23.

Ye, J., & Cui, W. H. (2018). Exponential entropy for simplified neutrosophic sets and its application in decision making. *Entropy (Basel, Switzerland)*, *20*(5), 357. doi:10.3390/e20050357

Ye, J., & Fu, J. (2016). Multi-period medical diagnosis method using a single valued neutrosophic similarity measure based on tangent function. *Computer Methods and Programs in Biomedicine*, *123*, 142–149. doi:10.1016/j.cmpb.2015.10.002 PMID:26506531

Zadeh, L. A. (1965). Fuzzy Sets. *Information and Control*, *8*(3), 338–353. doi:10.1016/S0019-9958(65)90241-X

Chapter 3
A New Multi–Attribute Decision–Making Method Based on Similarity Measures of SVTN–Numbers

Irfan Deli
Kilis 7 Aralık University, Turkey

ABSTRACT

In this study, the authors develop a new decision-making method on single-valued trapezoidal neutrosophic numbers (SVTN-Numbers) where all the decision information take the form of SVTN-Numbers. To construct the method, some new similarity measures between two SVTN-Numbers are presented. Then, concept of impact value on SVTN-Numbers by using the cut sets of SVTN-Numbers is proposed, and the corresponding properties are discussed. Finally, a real example is introduced and compared with different methods to show the applicability and feasibility of the proposed multi-attribute decision-making method.

1 INTRODUCTION

In real decision making to select the best alternative from all the feasible set of alternatives, multi-attribute decision making problems and solution methods are the important branches of modern decision sciences to deal with incomplete, indeterminate and inconsistent information. To modeling the multi-attribute decision making problems, theory of fuzzy sets initiated by (Zadeh, 1965) is an effective theory to describe uncertain information. Since the theory only has a membership and cannot

DOI: 10.4018/978-1-7998-2555-5.ch003

express non-membership, (Atanassov, 1999) defined theory of intuitionistic fuzzy sets which has both membership and non-membership such that $0 \leq$ membership value $+$ non-membership ≤ 1 where $0 \leq$ membership value ≤ 1 and $0 \leq$ non-membership ≤ 1. The fuzzy sets and intuitionistic fuzzy sets, have been studied and applied in different fields in decision making problems including multi-attribute decision making(MADM) problems in (Ban, 2008; Chen & Li, 2011; Li, 2014; Li, 2010; Peng et al. 2014; Pramanik et al., 2015; Wang & Zhang, 2009).

Sometimes the theories can not handle incomplete information indeterminate information and inconsistent information. To handle this type of information, Smarandache (Smarandache, 1998; Smarandache, 2005) gave theory of neutrosophic sets which contains truth-membership function, indeterminacy membership function and false-membership function are completely independent. After Smarandache, (Wang et al., 2010) gave the theory of single-valued neutrosophic sets which is a particular case of the neutrosophic set which presents more reasonable mathematical tools to deal with indeterminate data. The theories have studied in various areas such as (Cao et al. 2016; Deli & Broumi, 2015; Farhadinia & Ban, 2013; Ji et al. 2018; Hayat et al., 2018; Karaaslan & Hayat, 2018; Karaaslan 2018; Karaaslan 2019; Kumar & Kaur, 2013; Li, 2014; Li et al., 2010; Liu et al.,2002; Liang et al., 2018; Liang et al.,2017; Liu et al.,2012; Liu et al.,2011; Li et al., 2016; Liu et al.,2016; Liu & Liu, 2014; Liu & Shi, 2015; Peng et al., 2016; Peng et al., 2014; Shenify & Mazarbhuiya, 2015; Tian et al., 2016a; Tian et al., 2016b; Tian et al., 2016c; Wu et al., 2016; Wang & Wang, 2016; Ye, 2010; Ye, 2012; Ye, 2014a; Ye, 2014b).

In some real applications and related fields, the researcher uses some similarity measure that is an important mathematical tool. For example, Ye (2015a) defined cosine function can overcome the shortcomings of the existing cosine similarity measures between two vectors in some cases. Also, he proposed two cotangent similarities measures for single-valued neutroophic sets based on a cotangent function in Ye (2015c). Pramanik et al. (2015) introduced new vector similarity measures on both single-valued neutrosophic sets and interval neutrosophic sets based on Dice and Cosine similarity measures. Ye (2014b) developed three vector similarity measures between two single-valued neutrosophic set as a generalization of the Jaccard, Dice, and cosine similarity measures. The other similarity measures are developed in Biswas et al (2014), Can & Özgüven, (2016), Chatterjee et al. (2016), and Ye, (2014c). Moreover, since the correlation coefficient is an important tool for judging the relationship between two objects based on neutrosophic information, correlation coefficients of neutrosophic sets including inteval neutrosophic sets have been studied many authors in Broumi and Smarandache (2013), Farhadinia and Ban (2013), Ye (2013), Ye, (2014c), and Zhang et al. (2015).

By combining trapezoidal fuzzy numbers and a single-valued neutrosophic set, it introduces single valued trapezoidal neutrosophic numbers (SVTN-numbers) with relating definitions based on multiple attribute decision making problems (Ye, 2015b; Ye, 2016). Also, Şubaş (2015), generalized the definition of Ye's by using generalized trapezoidal intuitionistic fuzzy number (Li, 2014). Then, Şimşek and Deli (2015) proposed expected value of SVTN-numbers and applied to MADM problems. Deli et al. (2015) developed some new operation based on Einstein operations of SVTN-numbers. Jana et al. (2018) proposed Trapezoidal neutrosophic aggregation operators. Karaaslan (2018) defined Gaussian Single-valued neutrosophic number and gave its application in multi-attribute decision making. Deli and Şubaş (2017) proposed a method for solving MADM problems with SVTN-numbers by introducing values and ambiguities of SVTN-numbers. In this paper, the similarity measure of single-valued neutrosophic sets is extended to SVTN-numbers by using the α, β and γ-cut values, to construct a MADM method. To do this, in Section 2, some basic definitions and results of single valued neutrosophic sets and single valued trapezoidal neutrosophic numbers (SVTN-numbers) are given. In Section 3, some similarity measures based on SVTN-numbers are proposed. In section 4, a novel decision making method on single valued trapezoidal neutrosophic numbers (SVTN-numbers) are developed, where all the decision information takes the form of SVTN-numbers. Also, a numerical example is presented based on the proposed similarity measure to show the applicability and feasibility of the proposed MADM method. In Section 5 we discussed the influence of parameters and similarity measures on the final ranking. In Section 6, the conclusion is introduced. The present expository paper is a generalization of the conference presentation in (Deli, 2016).

2 BACKGROUND

This section reviews some basic concepts of neutrosophic sets, single-valued trapezoidal neutrosophic numbers, which will be utilized in the rest of this paper.

Definition 2.1 (Wang et al, 2010) Let X be a space of points (objects) with a generic element in X, denoted by x. A single valued neutrosophic set A in X is characterized by a truth-membership function $T_A: X \to [0,1]$, an indeterminacy-membership function $I_A: X \to [0,1]$ and a falsity-membership function $F_A: X \to [0,1]$ as;

$$A = \left\{ \left\langle x, \left(T_A\left(x\right), I_A\left(x\right), F_A\left(x\right) \right) \right\rangle : x \in X \right\}.$$

Definition 2.2 (Ye, 2014b) Let $A = \langle T_A(x_i), I_A(x_i), F_A(x_i) \rangle$ and $B = \langle T_B(x_i), I_B(x_i), F_B(x_i) \rangle$ be two SVN-sets in a universe of X= $(x_1,$ $x_2,...,x_n)$. Then

1. Jaccard similarity measure between SVN-sets A and B in the vector space is defined as follows:

$$J(A,B) = \frac{1}{n}\sum_{i=1}^{n} \times \left(\frac{T_A(x_i)T_B(x_i) + I_A(x_i)I_B(x_i) + F_A(x_i)F_B(x_i)}{\left[\begin{array}{c} ((T_A)^2(x_i) + (I_A)^2(x_i) + (F_A)^2(x_i)) + ((T_B)^2(x_i) + (I_B)^2(x_i) \\ + (F_B)^2(x_i)) - (T_A(x_i)T_B(x_i) + I_A(x_i)I_B(x_i) + F_A(x_i)F_B(x_i)) \end{array} \right]} \right)$$

Then, this similarity measure satisfies the following properties:

    i. $0 \leq J(A,B) \leq 1$;

    ii. $J(A,B) = J(B,A)$;

    iii. $J(A,B) = 1$ for A=B i.e.

$T_A(x_i) = T_B(x_i), I_A(x_i) = I_B(x_i), F_A(x_i) = F_B(x_i)(i = 1,2...,n)$ $\forall x_i(i = 1,2,...,n) \in X.$

2. Dice similarity measure between SVN-sets A and B in the vector space is defined as follows:

$$D(A,B) = \frac{1}{n}\sum_{i=1}^{n} \times \left(\frac{2(T_A(x_i)T_B(x_i) + I_A(x_i)I_B(x_i) + F_A(x_i)F_B(x_i))}{\left[((T_A)^2(x_i) + (I_A)^2(x_i) + (F_A)^2(x_i)) + ((T_B)^2(x_i) + (I_B)^2(x_i) + (F_B)^2(x_i)) \right]} \right)$$

It satisfies the following properties:

    i. $0 \leq D(A,B) \leq 1$;

    ii. $D(A,B) = D(B,A)$;

    iii. $D(A,B) = 1$ for A=B i.e.

$T_A(x_i) = T_B(x_i), I_A(x_i) = I_B(x_i), F_A(x_i) = F_B(x_i)(i = 1,2...,n)$ $\forall x_i(i = 1,2,...,n) \in X.$

3. Cosine similarity measure between SVN-sets A and B in the vector space is defined as follows:

$$C(A,B) = \frac{1}{n}\sum_{i=1}^{n} \times \left(\frac{T_A(x_i)T_B(x_i) + I_A(x_i)I_B(x_i) + F_A(x_i)F_B(x_i)}{\left[\sqrt{((T_A)^2(x_i) + (I_A)^2(x_i) + (F_A)^2(x_i))} \cdot \sqrt{((T_B)^2(x_i) + (I_B)^2(x_i) + (F_B)^2(x_i))} \right]} \right)$$

It satisfies the following properties:

    i. $0 \leq C(A,B) \leq 1$;
    ii. $C(A,B) = C(B,A)$
    iii. $C(A,B) = 1$ for $A = B$ i.e.

$$T_A(x_i) = T_B(x_i), I_A(x_i) = I_B(x_i), F_A(x_i) = F_B(x_i)(i = 1, 2..., n) \quad \forall x_i (i = 1, 2, ..., n) \in X.$$

Definition 2.3 (Pramanik et al., 2015) Let $A = \langle T_A(x_i), I_A(x_i), F_A(x_i) \rangle$ and $B = \langle T_B(x_i), I_B(x_i), F_B(x_i) \rangle$ be two SVN-sets in a universe of discourse $X = (x_1, x_2, ..., x_n)$. Then, Hybrid similarity measure between SVN-sets A and B in the vector space is defined as follows:

$$E(A,B) = \lambda \left(\frac{2(T_A(x_i)T_B(x_i) + I_A(x_i)I_B(x_i) + F_A(x_i)F_B(x_i))}{\left[((T_A)^2(x_i) + (I_A)^2(x_i) + (F_A)^2(x_i)) + ((T_B)^2(x_i) + (I_B)^2(x_i) + (F_B)^2(x_i)) \right]} \right)$$

$$+ (1 - \lambda) \left(\frac{T_A(x_i)T_B(x_i) + I_A(x_i)I_B(x_i) + F_A(x_i)F_B(x_i)}{\left[\sqrt{((T_A)^2(x_i) + (I_A)^2(x_i) + (x_i))} \cdot \sqrt{((T_B)^2(x_i) + (I_B)^2(x_i) + (F_B)^2(x_i))} \right]} \right).$$

It satisfies the following properties:

    i. $0 \leq E(A,B) \leq 1$;
    ii. $E(A,B) = E(B,A)$
    iii. $E(A,B) = 1$ for $A = B$.

Definition 2.4 (Şubaş, 2015) A SVTN-number $\tilde{a} = \langle (a, b, c, d); w_{\tilde{a}}, u_{\tilde{a}}, y_{\tilde{a}} \rangle$ on $X \subseteq R$ is characterized by a truth-membership function $T_A: X \rightarrow [0,1]$, an indeterminacy-membership function $I_A: X \to [0,1]$ and a falsity-membership function $F_A: X \to [0,1]$ as;

$$\mu_{\tilde{a}}(x) = \begin{cases} (x-a)w_{\tilde{a}}/(b-a) & (a \le x < b) \\ w_{\tilde{a}} & (b \le x \le c) \\ (d-x)w_{\tilde{a}}/(d-c) & (c < x \le d) \\ 0 & \text{otherwise,} \end{cases}$$

$$v_{\tilde{a}}(x) = \begin{cases} (b-x+u_{\tilde{a}}(x-a))/(b-a) & (a \le x < b) \\ u_{\tilde{a}} & (b \le x \le c) \\ (x-c+u_{\tilde{a}}(d-x))/(d-c) & (c < x \le d) \\ 1 & \text{otherwise} \end{cases}$$

and

$$\lambda_{\tilde{a}}(x) = \begin{cases} (b-x+y_{\tilde{a}}(x-a))/(b-a) & (a \le x < b) \\ y_{\tilde{a}} & (b \le x \le c) \\ (x-c+y_{\tilde{a}}(d-x))/(d-c) & (c < x \le d) \\ 1 & \text{otherwise} \end{cases}$$

respectively.

For any $\tilde{a} = \langle (a_1, b_1, c_1, d_1); w_{\tilde{a}}, u_{\tilde{a}}, y_{\tilde{a}} \rangle$ and $\tilde{b} = \langle (a_2, b_2, c_2, d_2); w_{\tilde{b}}, u_{\tilde{b}}, y_{\tilde{b}} \rangle$;

$$\tilde{a} + \tilde{b} = \langle (a_1 + a_2, b_1 + b_2, c_1 + c_2, d_1 + d_2); w_{\tilde{a}} \wedge w_{\tilde{b}}, u_{\tilde{a}} \vee u_{\tilde{b}}, y_{\tilde{a}} \vee y_{\tilde{b}} \rangle$$

$$\tilde{a} - \tilde{b} = \langle (a_1 - d_2, b_1 - c_2, c_1 - b_2, d_1 - a_2); w_{\tilde{a}} \wedge w_{\tilde{b}}, u_{\tilde{a}} \vee u_{\tilde{b}}, y_{\tilde{b}} \vee y_{\tilde{b}} \rangle$$

i.

$$\tilde{a}\tilde{b} = \begin{cases} \langle (a_1a_2, b_1b_2, c_1c_2, d_1d_2); w_{\tilde{a}} \wedge w_{\tilde{b}}, u_{\tilde{a}} \vee u_{\tilde{b}}, y_{\tilde{a}} \vee y_{\tilde{b}} \rangle & (c_1 > 0, c_2 > 0) \\ \langle (a_1d_2, b_1c_2, c_1b_2, d_1a_2); w_{\tilde{a}} \wedge w_{\tilde{b}}, u_{\tilde{a}} \vee u_{\tilde{b}}, y_{\tilde{a}} \vee y_{\tilde{b}} \rangle & (c_1 < 0, c_2 > 0). \\ \langle (d_1d_2, c_1c_2, b_1b_2, a_1a_2); w_{\tilde{a}} \wedge w_{\tilde{b}}, u_{\tilde{a}} \vee u_{\tilde{b}}, y_{\tilde{a}} \vee y_{\tilde{b}} \rangle & (c_1 < 0, c_2 < 0) \end{cases}$$

$$
\text{ii.} \quad \gamma \tilde{a} = \begin{cases} \langle (\gamma a_1, \gamma b_1, \gamma c_1, \gamma d_1); w_{\tilde{a}}, u_{\tilde{a}}, y_{\tilde{a}} \rangle & (\gamma > 0) \\ \langle (\gamma d_1, \gamma c_1, \gamma b_1, \gamma a_1); w_{\tilde{a}}, u_{\tilde{a}}, y_{\tilde{a}} \rangle & (\gamma < 0) \end{cases}
$$

$$
\text{iii.} \quad \tilde{a}^{\gamma} = \begin{cases} \langle (a_1^{\gamma}, b_1^{\gamma}, c_1^{\gamma}, d_1^{\gamma}); w_{\tilde{a}}, u_{\tilde{a}}, y_{\tilde{a}} \rangle & (\gamma > 0) \\ \langle (d_1^{\gamma}, c_1^{\gamma}, b_1^{\gamma}, a_1^{\gamma}); w_{\tilde{a}}, u_{\tilde{a}}, y_{\tilde{a}} \rangle & (\gamma < 0) \end{cases}
$$

Definition 2.5 (Deli & Şubaş, 2017) Let $\tilde{a} = \langle (a_1, b_1, c_1, d_1); w_{\tilde{a}}, u_{\tilde{a}}, y_{\tilde{a}} \rangle$ be a SVTN-number and $\alpha \in [0, w_{\tilde{a}}]$, $\beta \in [u_{\tilde{a}}, 1]$ and $\gamma \in [y_{\tilde{a}}, 1]$. Then, α, β and γ-cut set of the SVTN-number $\tilde{a}$, is defined as;

$$
\tilde{a}_{\alpha} = \{x \mid \mu_{\tilde{a}}(x) \geq \alpha, \ x \in R\} = \left[L_{\tilde{a}}(\alpha), R_{\tilde{a}}(\alpha) \right],
$$

$$
\tilde{a}^{\beta} = \{x \mid v_{\tilde{a}}(x) \leq \beta, \ x \in R\} = \left[L'_{\tilde{a}}(\beta), R'_{\tilde{a}}(\beta) \right]
$$

and

$$
{}^{\gamma}\tilde{a} = \{x \mid \lambda_{\tilde{a}}(x) \leq \gamma, \ x \in R\} = \left[L''_{\tilde{a}}(\gamma), R''_{\tilde{a}}(\gamma) \right],
$$

respectively.

Definition 2.6 (Deli & Şubaş, 2017) Let $\tilde{a} = \langle (a_1, b_1, c_1, d_1); w_{\tilde{a}}, u_{\tilde{a}}, y_{\tilde{a}} \rangle$ be a SVTN-number with α-cut, β-cut and γ-cut set representations. Then, the values of the SVTN-number $\tilde{a}$ for
i. α-cut set is defined as;

$$
V_{\mu}(\tilde{a}) = \int_0^{w_{\tilde{a}}} \left(L_{\tilde{a}}(\alpha) + R_{\tilde{a}}(\alpha) \right) \alpha \, d\alpha \tag{1}
$$

ii. β-cut set is defined as;

$$
V_{v}(\tilde{a}) = \int_{u_{\tilde{a}}}^1 \left(L'_{\tilde{a}}(\beta) + R'_{\tilde{a}}(\beta) \right) (1 - \beta) \, d\beta \tag{2}
$$

iii. γ-cut set is defined as;

$$V_{\lambda}\left(\tilde{a}\right) = \int_{y_{\tilde{a}}}^{1}\left(L''_{\tilde{a}}\left(\gamma\right)+R''_{\tilde{a}}\left(\gamma\right)\right)\left(1-\gamma\right)d\gamma \qquad (3)$$

where $\alpha \in [0, w_{\tilde{a}}])$, $\beta \in [u_{\tilde{a}}, 1])$, $\gamma \in [y_{\tilde{a}}, 1])$.

Definition 2.7 (Şubaş, 2015) Let $\tilde{a}_j = \left\langle (a_j, b_j, c_j, d_j); w_{\tilde{a}_j}, u_{\tilde{a}_j}, y_{\tilde{a}_j} \right\rangle \in (j \in I_n)$ be SVTN-numbers. Then

i. SVTN weighted arithmetic operator, denoted by G_{ao}, is defined as;

$$G_{ao}: \Delta^n \to \Delta, \quad G_{ao}\left(\tilde{a}_1, \tilde{a}_2, ..., \tilde{a}_n\right) = \sum_{i=1}^{n}\tilde{a}_i^{w_i}$$

ii. SVTN weighted geometric operator, denoted by G_{go}, is defined as;

$$G_{go}: \Delta^n \to \Delta, \quad G_{go}\left(\tilde{a}_1, \tilde{a}_2, ..., \tilde{a}_n\right) = \prod_{i=1}^{n}\tilde{a}_i^{w_i}$$

where, $w = (w_1, w_2, ..., w_n)^T$ is a weight vector associated with the G_{go} operator, for every $j \in I_n$ such that, $w_j \in [0,1]$ and $\sum_{j=1}^{n}w_j = 1$.

3 SIMILARITY MEASURES AND IMPACT FACTOR BASED ON SVTN-NUMBERS

In this section, some similarity measures by extending the similarity measure of single-valued neutrosophic sets to SVTN-numbers are proposed. Some of it is quoted from [(Biswas et al., 2014), (Deli, 2016), (Li, 2014), (Pramanik, 2015), (Şimşek & Deli, 2015), (Şubaş, 2015), (Ye, 2011), (Ye, 2014a), (Ye, 2014b), (Ye, 2014c)].

Definition 3.1 Let $\tilde{a}$ and $\tilde{b}$ be two SVTN-numbers with α-cut, β-cut and γ-cut set representations. Then,

i. Jaccard similarity similarity measure $S_J\left(\tilde{a}, \tilde{b}\right)$ between $\tilde{a}$ and $\tilde{b}$ is defined as,

$$S_J\left(\tilde{a},\tilde{b}\right)=\frac{V_\mu\left(\tilde{a}\right)V_\mu\left(\tilde{b}\right)+V_\nu\left(\tilde{a}\right)V_\nu\left(\tilde{b}\right)+V_\lambda\left(\tilde{a}\right)V_\lambda\left(\tilde{b}\right)}{V_\mu^2\left(\tilde{a}\right)+V_\mu^2\left(\tilde{b}\right)+V_\nu^2\left(\tilde{a}\right)+V_\nu^2\left(\tilde{b}\right)+V_\lambda^2\left(\tilde{a}\right)+V_\lambda^2\left(\tilde{b}\right)-V_\mu\left(\tilde{a}\right)V_\mu\left(\tilde{b}\right)-V_\nu\left(\tilde{a}\right)V_\nu\left(\tilde{b}\right)-V_\lambda\left(\tilde{a}\right)V_\lambda\left(\tilde{b}\right)}$$

ii. Dice similarity similarity measure $S_E\left(\tilde{a},\tilde{b}\right)$ between $\tilde{a}$ and $\tilde{b}$ is defined as,

$$S_E\left(\tilde{a},\tilde{b}\right)=2\frac{V_\mu\left(\tilde{a}\right)V_\mu\left(\tilde{b}\right)+V_\nu\left(\tilde{a}\right)V_\nu\left(\tilde{b}\right)+V_\lambda\left(\tilde{a}\right)V_\lambda\left(\tilde{b}\right)}{V_\mu^2\left(\tilde{a}\right)+V_\mu^2\left(\tilde{b}\right)+V_\nu^2\left(\tilde{a}\right)+V_\nu^2\left(\tilde{b}\right)+V_\lambda^2\left(\tilde{a}\right)+V_\lambda^2\left(\tilde{b}\right)}$$

iii. Cosine similarity similarity measure $S_C\left(\tilde{a},\tilde{b}\right)$ between $\tilde{a}$ and $\tilde{b}$ is defined as,

$$S_C\left(\tilde{a},\tilde{b}\right)=\frac{V_\mu\left(\tilde{a}\right)V_\mu\left(\tilde{b}\right)+V_\nu\left(\tilde{a}\right)V_\nu\left(\tilde{b}\right)+V_\lambda\left(\tilde{a}\right)V_\lambda\left(\tilde{b}\right)}{\sqrt{V_\mu^2\left(\tilde{a}\right)+V_\nu^2\left(\tilde{a}\right)+V_\lambda^2\left(\tilde{a}\right)}\sqrt{V_\mu^2\left(\tilde{b}\right)+V_\nu^2\left(\tilde{b}\right)+V_\lambda^2\left(\tilde{b}\right)}}$$

iv. Hybrid similarity similarity measure $S_H\left(\tilde{a},\tilde{b}\right)$ between $\tilde{a}$ and $\tilde{b}$ is defined as,

$$S_H\left(\tilde{a},\tilde{b}\right)=2\lambda\frac{V_\mu\left(\tilde{a}\right)V_\mu\left(\tilde{b}\right)+V_\nu\left(\tilde{a}\right)V_\nu\left(\tilde{b}\right)+V_\lambda\left(\tilde{a}\right)V_\lambda\left(\tilde{b}\right)}{V_\mu^2\left(\tilde{a}\right)+V_\mu^2\left(\tilde{b}\right)+V_\nu^2\left(\tilde{a}\right)+V_\nu^2\left(\tilde{b}\right)+V_\lambda^2\left(\tilde{a}\right)+V_\lambda^2\left(\tilde{b}\right)}$$
$$+\left(1-\lambda\right)\frac{V_\mu\left(\tilde{a}\right)V_\mu\left(\tilde{b}\right)+V_\nu\left(\tilde{a}\right)V_\nu\left(\tilde{b}\right)+V_\lambda\left(\tilde{a}\right)V_\lambda\left(\tilde{b}\right)}{\sqrt{V_\mu^2\left(\tilde{a}\right)+V_\nu^2\left(\tilde{a}\right)+V_\lambda^2\left(\tilde{a}\right)}\sqrt{V_\mu^2\left(\tilde{b}\right)+V_\nu^2\left(\tilde{b}\right)+V_\lambda^2\left(\tilde{b}\right)}}$$

Theorem 3.2 Let $\tilde{a}$, $\tilde{b}$ be two SVTN-numbers. Then, $S_i\left(\tilde{a},\tilde{b}\right)$, for $i\in\{J,E,C,H\}$, similarity measures satisfies the following properties,

i. $0\leq S_i\left(\tilde{a},\tilde{b}\right)\leq1$

ii. $S_i\left(\tilde{a},\tilde{b}\right)=S_i\left(\tilde{b},\tilde{a}\right)$

iii. $S_i\left(\tilde{a},\tilde{a}\right)=1$

Proof:

    i.   It is obvious that the property is true according to the inequality $x^2+y^2 \geq 2xy$ for $S_i\left(\tilde{a},\tilde{b}\right)$, $i \in \{J,E,C,H\}$

    ii.   It is obvious that the property is true according to the equalities $x^2+y^2=y^2+x^2$ and $xy=yx$ for $S_i\left(\tilde{a},\tilde{b}\right)$, $i \in \{J,E,C,H\}$

    iii.   When $\tilde{a}=\tilde{b}$, there are $V_\mu\left(\tilde{a}\right)=V_\mu\left(\tilde{b}\right)$, $V_v\left(\tilde{a}\right)=V_v\left(\tilde{b}\right)$ and $V_\lambda\left(\tilde{a}\right)=V_\lambda\left(\tilde{b}\right)$. So there are $S_i\left(\tilde{a},\tilde{a}\right)=1$, $i \in \{J,E,C,H\}$.

However, $S_i\left(\tilde{a},\tilde{a}\right)=1$, $i \in \{J,E,C,H\}$ is undefined if

$$V_\mu\left(\tilde{a}\right)=V_v\left(\tilde{a}\right)=V_\lambda\left(\tilde{a}\right)=0 \text{ and } V_\mu\left(\tilde{b}\right)=V_v\left(\tilde{b}\right)=V_\lambda\left(\tilde{b}\right)=0.$$

In this case, let the measure value $S_i\left(\tilde{a},\tilde{a}\right)=0$, $i \in \{J,E,C,H\}$. It is easy from Definition 3.1.

Definition 3.3 Let $\tilde{a}_j = \left\langle (a_j,b_j,c_j,d_j); w_{\tilde{a}_j}, u_{\tilde{a}_j}, y_{\tilde{a}_j} \right\rangle \in \Gamma\left(j \in \{1,2,...,n\}\right)$. Then,

    i.   impact value of $\tilde{a}_j$ is denoted by $IV\left(\tilde{a}_j\right)$, is defined as;

$$IV\left(\tilde{a}_j\right) = \frac{V_\mu\left(\tilde{a}_j\right)+V_v\left(\tilde{a}_j\right)+V_\lambda\left(\tilde{a}_j\right)}{3}$$

    ii.   normalized impact value of $\tilde{a}_j$ is denoted by $IV_N\left(\tilde{a}_j\right)$, is defined as;

$$IV_N\left(\tilde{a}_j\right) = \frac{V_\mu\left(\tilde{a}_j\right)+V_{\frac{1}{2}}\left(\tilde{a}_j\right)+V_\lambda\left(\tilde{a}_j\right)}{3\sum_{i=1}^{n}\left(V_\mu\left(\tilde{a}_i\right)+V_{\frac{1}{2}}\left(\tilde{a}_i\right)+V_\lambda\left(\tilde{a}_i\right)\right)}$$

Theorem 3.4 Let $\tilde{a} = \langle (a,b,c,d); w_{\tilde{a}}, u_{\tilde{a}}, y_{\tilde{a}} \rangle$ is an SVTN-number. Then, impact value of $\tilde{a}$ is

$$IV\left(\tilde{a}\right) = \frac{\left(a+2b+2c+d\right)w_{\tilde{a}}^2+\left(a+2b+2c+d\right)(1-u_{\tilde{a}})^2+\left(a+2b+2c+d\right)(1-y_{\tilde{a}})^2}{18}$$

Proof: It is easy from Definition 2.6 and Definition 3.3

Example 3.5 Let $\tilde{a}_1 = \langle (2,3,4,5); 0.4, 0.6, 0.7 \rangle$ and $\tilde{a}_2 = \langle (1,3,5,7); 0.9, 0.8, 0.1 \rangle$ be two SVTN-numbers. Then

    i.   impact value of $\tilde{a}_j$ (j=1,2) is computed as;

$$IV(\tilde{a}_1) = 0,463 \text{ and } I(\tilde{a}_2) = 2,078$$

    ii.   normalized impact value of $\tilde{a}_j$ (j=1,2) is computed as;

$$IV_N(\tilde{a}_1) = 0.182 \text{ and } I_N(\tilde{a}_2) = 0.817$$

4. A SUPERIOR MADM METHOD WITH SVTN-NUMBERS

In this section, a decision making method based on MADM with SVTN-numbers is defined. (It's adopted from [(Biswas et al., 2014), (Deli, 2016), (Li, 2014), (Pramanik, 2015), (Şimşek & Deli, 2015), (Şubaş, 2015), (Ye, 2011), (Ye, 2014a), (Ye, 2014b), (Ye, 2014c)].

Definition 4.1 (Şubaş, 2015) Let X= $(x_1, x_2, \ldots, x_n)$ be a set of alternatives, U= $(u_1, u_2, \ldots, u_m)$ be the set of attributes and $\left[\tilde{A}_{ij} \right] = \left\langle (a_{ij}, b_{ij}, c_{ij}, d_{ij}); w_{\tilde{a}_{ij}}, u_{\tilde{a}_{ij}}, y_{\tilde{a}_{ij}} \right\rangle$ (for $i \in I_m$; $j \in I_n$) be a SVTN-numbers. Then,

$$
[\tilde{A}_{ij}]_{m \times n} =
\begin{array}{c}
\\
u_1 \\
u_2 \\
\vdots \\
u_m
\end{array}
\begin{array}{cccc}
x_1 & x_2 & \cdots & x_n \\
\left(\begin{array}{cccc}
\tilde{A}_{11} & \tilde{A}_{12} & \cdots & \tilde{A}_{1n} \\
\tilde{A}_{21} & \tilde{A}_{22} & \cdots & \tilde{A}_{2n} \\
\vdots & \vdots & \vdots & \vdots \\
\tilde{A}_{m1} & \tilde{A}_{m2} & \cdots & \tilde{A}_{mn}
\end{array}\right)
\end{array}
$$

is decision matrix.

Now, we can present an algorithm as;

Algorithm:

    Step 1. Give the decision matrix $A = (\tilde{A}_{ij})_{m \times n}$ based on the characteristic of each alternative and attribute by the linguistic values of SVTN-numbers according to Table 1.

Step 2. Give weight value of criterions is represented by SVTN-numbers according to Table 1.

Step 3. Present normalized impact value of weight value of criterions and get the weight vector.

Step 4. Give an ideal alternative a^+ for decision according to Table 1.

Step 5. Compute $a_j = G_{go}\left(\tilde{a}_{1j}, \tilde{a}_{2j}, ..., \tilde{a}_{mj}\right)$ for $j \in I_n$;

Step 6. Compute the similarity values between a_j and a^+ for $j \in I_n$ and ranked the alternatives.

Example 4.2 Suppose that us consider a MADM problem from Ref. [(Biswas et al., 2014)] in which a customer intends to buy a tablet from the set of primarily chosen three alternatives A= $\{x_1, x_2, x_3\}$.

There are five evaluation attributes, including:

1. u_1 is features;
2. u_2 is hardware;
3. u_3 is affordable price
4. u_4 is customer care;
5. u_5 is comfortable use

The three possible alternatives are to be evaluated under the above five attributes by corresponding to linguistic values of SVTN-numbers for linguistic terms (adapted from Şubaş, 2015), as shown in Table 1.

Step 1. The decision maker give the decision-making matrix $A = (\tilde{A}_{ij})_{m \times n}$; for decision as shown in box 1.

Box 1. The decision-making matrix A

	x_1	x_2	x_3
u_1	$\langle(0.9,0.8,0.9,1.0);0.4,0.5,0.6\rangle$	$\langle(0.0,0.2,0.3,0.4);0.9,0.0,0.5\rangle$	$\langle(0.5,0.6,0.6,0.7);0.4,0.4,0.5\rangle$
u_2	$\langle(0.6,0.7,0.8,0.9);0.2,0.5,0.5\rangle$	$\langle(0.1,0.2,0.5,0.7);0.3,0.2,0.1\rangle$	$\langle(0.1,0.3,0.4,0.5);0.4,0.7,0.7\rangle$
u_3	$\langle(0.5,0.6,0.8,0.9);0.8,0.8,0.8\rangle$	$\langle(0.4,0.5,0.6,0.7);0.7,0.8,0.8\rangle$	$\langle(0.1,0.3,0.4,0.6);0.9,0.5,0.8\rangle$
u_4	$\langle(0.4,0.5,0.6,0.7);0.7,0.8,0.8\rangle$	$\langle(0.5,0.6,0.8,0.9);0.8,0.8,0.8\rangle$	$\langle(0.1,0.3,0.4,0.6);0.9,0.5,0.8\rangle$
u_5	$\langle(0.5,0.6,0.6,0.7);0.4,0.4,0.5\rangle$	$\langle(0.6,0.7,0.8,0.9);0.2,0.5,0.5\rangle$	$\langle(0.1,0.3,0.4,0.5);0.4,0.7,0.7\rangle$

Table 1. Linguistic values of SVTN-numbers

Linguistic terms	Linguistic values
Low	$\langle(0.0, 0.2, 0.3, 0.4); 0.9, 0.0, 0.5\rangle$
very low	$\langle(0.1, 0.3, 0.4, 0.5); 0.4, 0.7, 0.7\rangle$
very very low	$\langle(0.1, 0.3, 0.4, 0.6); 0.9, 0.5, 0.8\rangle$
essentially low	$\langle(0.1, 0.2, 0.5, 0.7); 0.3, 0.2, 0.1\rangle$
neither low nor high	$\langle(0.4, 0.5, 0.6, 0.7); 0.7, 0.8, 0.8\rangle$
high	$\langle(0.5, 0.6, 0.6, 0.7); 0.4, 0.4, 0.5\rangle$
very high	$\langle(0.5, 0.6, 0.8, 0.9); 0.8, 0.8, 0.8\rangle$
very very high	$\langle(0.6, 0.7, 0.8, 0.9); 0.2, 0.5, 0.5\rangle$
essentially high	$\langle(0.9, 0.8, 0.9, 1.0); 0.4, 0.5, 0.6\rangle$

Step 2. The decision maker propose the weighted vector as;

$$W = \{w_1 = \langle(0.0, 0.2, 0.3, 0.4); 0.9, 0.0, 0.5\rangle, w_2 = \langle(0.5, 0.6, 0.6, 0.7); 0.4, 0.4, 0.5\rangle,$$
$$w_3 = \langle(0.4, 0.5, 0.6, 0.7); 0.7, 0.8, 0.8\rangle, w_4 = \langle(0.1, 0.3, 0.4, 0.5); 0.4, 0.7, 0.7\rangle,$$
$$w_5 = \langle(0.6, 0.7, 0.8, 0.9); 0.2, 0.5, 0.5\rangle\}$$

Step 3. We calculated the normalized weighted vector by using impact value as;

w= (0.268244203, 0.248177946, 0.176147657, 0.093989588, 0.213440606)

Step 4. The decision maker introduce an ideal alternative according to ref. (Chen & Li, 2011) as

$$a^+ = \langle(1,1,1,1); 1, 0, 0\rangle$$

Step 5. We compute $a_j = G_{go}\left(\tilde{a}_{1j}, \tilde{a}_{2j}, ..., \tilde{a}_{mj}\right)$ for $j \in I_n$;

$$a_1 = \langle\left(0.599774339, 0.661969296, 0.755790475, 0.85696362\right); 0.2, 0.8, 0.8\rangle$$

$$a_2 = \langle\left(0, 0.340484103, 0.520188324, 0.650816864\right); 0.2, 0.8, 0.8\rangle$$

$$a_3 = \langle\left(0.153990756, 0.361302366, 0.445959532, 0.5748543290, 40, 70, 8\right); 0.4, 0.7, 0.8\rangle$$

Step 6. We computed the similarity values and ranked the alternatives as shown in Table 2.

Table 2. Results of Jaccard similarity measure

Similarity measure	Measure value	Ranking order
$S_J(a^+, a_t)$	$S_J(a^+, a_1) = 0.08169325$	$x_3 \succ x_1 \succ x_2$
	$S_J(a^+, a_2) = 0.073093316$	
	$S_J(a^+, a_3) = 0.136476523$	

5. COMPARISON AND ANALYSIS DISCUSSION

In this section, a comparative analysis aiming was conducted with two other methods based on the same illustrative example to certify the feasibility of the method with other methods. The comparison analysis consists of three cases:

Case 1: The method 1 by using Jaccard similarity measure between SVNSs, method 2 by using Dice similarity measure between SVNSs and method 3 by using Cosine similarity measure between SVNSs are compared. The Example 4.2 resolved with different similarity measures. (It is shown in Table 3.)

The worst alternative is different but the best one is same.

Case 2: A comparative study is presented with different values of by using Hybrid similarity measure between SVNSs. The different values of λ used to resolve the multi-attribute decision making problem in Example 4.2 are shown in Table 4. As presented in Table 4, the similarity values of alternatives and final rankings

Table 3. Results for difference similarity measures

Similarity measure	Measure value	Ranking order
$S_J(a^+, a_i)$	$S_J(a^+, A_1) = 0.08169325$	$x_3 \succ x_1 \succ x_2$
	$S_J(a^+, A_2) = 0.073093316$	
	$S_J(a^+, A_3) = 0.136476523$	
$S_E(a^+, a_i)$	$S_E(a^+, A_1) = 0.151046981$	$x_3 \succ x_1 \succ x_2$
	$S_E(a^+, A_2) = 0.136229188$	
	$S_E(a^+, A_3) = 0.240174822$	
$S_C(a^+, a_i)$	$S_C(a^+, A_1) = 0.749268649$	$x_3 \succ x_2 \succ x_1$
	$S_C(a^+, A_2) = 0.878458592$	
	$S_C(a^+, A_3) = 0.886476924$	

are different, but the best alternatives are same when the corresponding values of λ, Also, for λ < 0.9 both final rankings and the best alternatives are same.

Case 3: A comparative study is presented with different methods used to solve the multi-attribute decision making problem in Example 4.2 by using score functions is given by (Ye, 2016) and (Şubaş, 2015). It is shown in Table 4.

As presented in Table 4, the final rankings of alternatives are same. Generally, the worst one in Dice similarity measure, Jaccard similarity measure (Table 3) and in Ye (2016) and Şubaş (2015) (Table 4) is x_2. There are a number of reasons why differences exist between the final rankings of the methods such as; the authors use a score and accurate function in Ye's method (Ye, 2016) and (Şubaş, 2015). Finally, the best alternatives generally are x_3 and the worst one generally is x_1 in all methods except for Jaccard similarity measure, Dice similarity measure, Hybrid similarity measure for λ < 0.9 and in Ye (2016) and Şubaş (2015). Therefore, the main advantages of the method developed in this paper are not only its ability to effectively deal with the preference information SVTN-numbers but also its consideration that the attribute weights are in the form of SVTN-numbers. At the same time, the proposed method for SVTN-numbers is different from those existing methods which always involve different similarity measures whose impact on the final solution may be considerable, as was discussed earlier, as it can overcome these shortcomings. Therefore, the proposed method is effective and feasible.

Table 4. Results by using score function in Ye (2016) and Subas (2015)

	Score value	Ranking order
$In\,(Subas, 2015)$	$S(a_1) = 0.107793665$	$x_1 \succ x_3 \succ x_2$
	$S(a_2) = 0.056680848$	
	$S(a_3) = 0.086406018$	
$In\,(Ye, 2016)$	$S(a_1) = 0.143724887$	$x_1 \succ x_3 \succ x_2$
	$S(a_2) = 0.075574465$	
	$S(a_3) = 0.115208024$	

6. CONCLUSION

SVTN-numbers can exibly express uncertain, imprecise, incomplete and inconsistent information that widely exist in MADM problems. In this paper, the basis definitions related to SVTN-numbers are proposed and the useful operational laws and properties are given in detail. Then, a novel decision making method on SVTN-numbers is firstly developed to select the best alternative, where all the decision information takes the form of SVTN-numbers. Also, a numerical example is introduced to show the applicability and feasibility of the proposed MADM method. Moreover, comparison analysis with the other methods is introduced. Furthermore, the methods given in this paper extend existing some other methods which contain uncertain, imprecise, incomplete and inconsistent information.

ACKNOWLEDGMENT

The author would like to express appreciation to the anonymous reviewers and Editors for their very helpful comments that improved the paper.

Compliance With Ethical Standards

Conflict of interest: The author declares that I have no conict of interest regarding the publication of this paper.

REFERENCES

Atanassov, K. T. (1999). Intuitionistic Fuzzy Sets. Pysica-Verlag. doi:10.1007/978-3-7908-1870-3

Ban, A. (2008). Trapezoidal approximations of intuitionistic fuzzy numbers expressed by value, ambiguity, width and weighted expected value. *Int. Conf. on IFSs, Sofia, NIFS, 14*(1), 38-47.

Biswas, P., Pramanik, S., & Giri, B. C. (2014). Cosine Similarity Measure Based Multi-attribute Decision making with Trapezoidal Fuzzy Neutrosophic Numbers. *Neutrosophic Sets and Systems, 8*, 47–57.

Broumi, S., & Smarandache, F. (2013). Correlation coeffcient of interval neutrosophic set. *Mechanical Engineering and Manufacturing, 436*, 511–517.

Can, M. S., & Ozguven, O. F. (2016). PID Tuning with Neutrosophic Similarity Measure. *International Journal of Fuzzy Systems*. doi:10.100740815-015-0136-y

Cao, Y. X., Zhou, H., & Wang, J. Q. (2016). An approach to interval-valued intuitionistic stochastic multicriteria decision-making using set pair analysis. *International Journal of Machine Learning and Cybernetics*. doi:10.100713042-016-0589-9

Chatterjee, R., Majumdar, P., & Samanta, S. K. (2016). On some similarity measures and entropy on quadripartitioned single valued neutrosophic sets. *Journal of Intelligent & Fuzzy Systems, 30*(4), 2475–2485. doi:10.3233/IFS-152017

Chen, Y., & Li, B. (2011). Dynamic multi-attribute decision making model based on triangular intuitionistic fuzzy number. *Scientia Iranica B, 18*(2), 268–274. doi:10.1016/j.scient.2011.03.022

Deli, I. (2016). *A new multi attribute decision making model based on single valued trapezoidal neutrosophic numbers*. International Conference on Mathematics and Mathematics Education (ICMME-2016), Elazıg.

Deli, I., & Broumi, S. (2015). Neutrosophic Soft Matrices and NSM-decision Making. *Journal of Intelligent & Fuzzy Systems, 28*(5), 2233–2241. doi:10.3233/IFS-141505

Deli, I., Simsek, I., & Cagman, N. (2015). A Multiple Criteria Group Decision Making Methods on Single Valued Trapezoidal Neutrosophic Numbers Based on Einstein Operations. In *The 4th Intern. Fuzzy Systems Symp. (FUZZYSS'15)*. Yildiz Technical University.

Deli, I., & Subas, Y. (2017). A ranking method of single valued neutrosophic numbers and its applications to multi attribute decision making problems. *International Journal of Machine Learning and Cybernetics, 8*(4), 1309–1322. doi:10.100713042-016-0505-3

Farhadinia, B., & Ban, A. I. (2013). Developing new similarity measures of generalized intuitionistic fuzzy numbers and generalized interval-valued fuzzy numbers from similarity measures of generalized fuzzy numbers. *Mathematical and Computer Modelling, 57*(3-4), 812–825. doi:10.1016/j.mcm.2012.09.010

Hanafy, I. M., Salama, A. A., & Mahfouz, K. M. (2013). Correlation Coeffcients of Neutrosophic Sets by Centroid Method. *International Journal of Probability and Statistics, 2*(1), 9–12.

Hayat, K., Ali, M. I., Cao, B. Y., Karaaslan, F., & Yang, X. P. (2018). Another view of group-based generalized intuitionistic fuzzy soft sets: Aggregation operators and multiattribute decision making. *Symmetry, 10*(12), 25–32. doi:10.3390ym10120753

Jana, C., Pal, M., Karaaslan, F., & Wang, J. Q. (2018). Trapezoidal neutrosophic aggregation operators and its application in multiple attribute decision-making process. *Scientia Iranica, 5*. doi:10.24200/SCI.2018.51136.2024

Ji, P., Zhang, H. Y., & Wang, J. Q. (2018). A fuzzy decision support model with sentiment analysis for items comparison in e-commerce: The case study of PConline. com. *IEEE Transactions on Systems, Man, and Cybernetics. Systems.* doi:10.1109/TSMC.2018.2875163

Karaaslan, F. (2018). Multi-criteria decision-making method based on similarity measures under single-valued neutrosophic refined and interval neutrosophic refined environments. *International Journal of Intelligent Systems, 33*(5), 928–952. doi:10.1002/int.21906

Karaaslan, F. (2018). Gaussian Single-valued neutrosophic number and its application in multi-attribute decision making. *Neutrosophic Sets and Systems, 22*, 101–117.

Karaaslan, F., & Hayat, K. (2018). Some new operations on single-valued neutrosophic matrices and their applications in multi-criteria group decision making. *Applied Intelligence, 48*(2), 4594–4614. doi:10.100710489-018-1226-y

Karaaslan, F. (2019). Correlation Coefficient of Neutrosophic Sets and Its Applications in Decision-Making. *Springer Nature Switzerland AG*, 369.

Kumar, A., & Kaur, M. (2013). A Ranking Approach for Intuitionistic Fuzzy Numbers and its Application. *Journal of Applied Research and Technology, 11*(3), 381–396. doi:10.1016/S1665-6423(13)71548-7

Li, D. F. (2010). A ratio ranking method of triangular intuitionistic fuzzy numbers and its application to MADM problems. *Computers & Mathematics with Applications (Oxford, England), 60*(6), 1557–1570. doi:10.1016/j.camwa.2010.06.039

Li, D. F. (2014). *Decision and Game Theory in Management With Intuitionistic Fuzzy Sets. Studies in Fuzziness and Soft Computing, 308.* Springer. doi:10.1007/978-3-642-40712-3

Li, D. F., Nan, J. X., & Zhang, M. J. (2010). A ranking method of triangular intuitionistic fuzzy numbers and application to decision making. *Int J. Comput. Intell. Syst., 3*(5), 522–530. doi:10.2991/ijcis.2010.3.5.2

Li, P., Zhang, H. Y., & Wang, J. Q. (2016). A projection-based TODIM method under multi-valued neutrosophic environments and its application in personnel selection. *Neural Computing & Applications.* doi:10.100700521-016-2436-z

Liang, R. X., Wang, J. Q., & Li, L. (2018). Multi-criteria group decision making method based on interdependent inputs of single valued trapezoidal neutrosophic information. *Neural Computing & Applications, 30*(1), 241–260. doi:10.100700521-016-2672-2

Liang, R. X., Wang, J. Q., & Zhang, H. Y. (2017). Evaluation of e-commerce websites: An integrated approach under a single-valued trapezoidal neutrosophic environment. *Knowledge-Based Systems, 135*, 44–59. doi:10.1016/j.knosys.2017.08.002

Liu, B., & Member, S. (2002). Expected Value of Fuzzy Variable and Fuzzy Expected Value Models IEEE. *Transactons on Fuzzy Systems, 10*(4), 445–450. doi:10.1109/TFUZZ.2002.800692

Liu, P., Jin, F., Zhang, X., Su, Y., & Wang, M. (2011). Research on the multi-attribute decision-making under risk with interval probability based on prospect theory and the uncertain linguistic variables. *Knowledge-Based Systems, 24*(4), 554–561. doi:10.1016/j.knosys.2011.01.010

Liu, P., Zhang, X., & Jin, F. (2012). A multi-attribute group decision-making method based on interval valued trapezoidal fuzzy numbers hybrid harmonic averaging operators. *Journal of Intelligent & Fuzzy Systems, 23*(5), 159–168.

Liu, P. D., He, L., & Yu, X. C. (2016). Generalized Hybrid Aggregation Operators Based on the 2-Dimension Uncertain Linguistic Information for Multiple Attribute Group Decision Making. *Group Decision and Negotiation*, *25*(1), 103–126. doi:10.100710726-015-9434-x

Liu, P. D., & Liu, Y. (2014). An approach to multiple attribute group decision making based on intuitionistic trapezoidal fuzzy power generalized aggregation operator. *International Journal of Computational Intelligence Systems*, *7*(2), 291–304. doi:10.1080/18756891.2013.862357

Liu, P. D., & Shi, L. L. (2015). The Generalized Hybrid Weighted Average Operator Based on Interval Neutrosophic Hesitant Set and Its Application to Multiple Attribute Decision Making. *Neural Computing & Applications*, *26*(2), 457–471. doi:10.100700521-014-1736-4

Peng, J. J., Wang, J., & Yang, W. (2016). A multi-valued neutrosophic qualitative exible approach based on likelihood for multi-criteria decision-making problems. *International Journal of Systems Science*. doi:10.1080/00207721.2016.1218975

Peng, J. J., Wang, J. Q., Wu, X. H., Wang, J., & Chen, X. H. (2014). Multi-valued Neutrosophic Sets and Power Aggregation Operators with Their Applications in Multi-criteria Group Decision-making Problems. *International Journal of Computational Intelligence Systems*, *8*(2), 345–363. doi:10.1080/18756891.2015.1001957

Peng, J. J., Wang, J. Q., Zhang, H. Y., & Chen, X. H. (2014). An outranking approach for multi-criteria decision-making problems with simplified neutrosophic sets. *Applied Soft Computing*, *25*, 336–346. doi:10.1016/j.asoc.2014.08.070

Pramanik, S., Biswas, P., & Giri, B. C. (2015). Hybrid vector similarity measures and their applications to multi-attribute decision making under neutrosophic environment. *Neural Comput and Applic*. DOI 00521-015-2125-3 doi:10.1007

Shenify, M., & Mazarbhuiya, F. (2015). The Expected Value of a Fuzzy Number. *International Journal of Intelligence Science*, *5*(1), 1–5. doi:10.4236/ijis.2015.51001

Simsek, I., & Deli, I. (2015). Expected Value of SV-Trapezoidal Neutrosophic Numbers and its Applications to Multi-Attribute Decision Making Problems. In *The 4th International Fuzzy Systems Symposium (FUZZYSS'15)*. Yildiz Technical University.

Smarandache, F. (1998). *A Unifying Field in Logics Neutrosophy: Neutrosophic Probability, Set and Logic*. Rehoboth: American Research Press.

Smarandache, F. (2005). Neutrosophic set, a generalisation of the intuitionistic fuzzy sets. *International Journal of Pure and Applied Mathematics, 24*, 287–297.

Subas, Y. (2015). *Neutrosophic numbers and their application to Multi-attribute decision making problems* (Masters Thesis). Kilis 7 Aralık University, Graduate School of Natural and Applied Science. (in Turkish)

Tian, Z. P., Wang, J., Wang, J. Q., & Zhang, H. Y. (2016a). Simplified neutrosophic linguistic multi-criteria group decision-making approach to green product development. *Group Decision and Negotiation*. doi:10.100710726-016-9479-5

Tian, Z. P., Wang, J., Zhang, H. Y., & Wang, J. Q. (2016b). An improved MULTIMOORA approach for multicriteria decision-making based on interdependent inputs of simplified neutrosophic linguistic information. *Neural Computing & Applications*. doi:10.100700521-016-2378-5

Tian, Z. P., Wang, J., Zhang, H. Y., & Wang, J. Q. (2016c). Multi-criteria decision-making based on generalized prioritized aggregation operators under simplified neutrosophic uncertain linguistic environment. *International Journal of Machine Learning and Cybernetics*. doi:10.100713042-016-0552-9

Wan, S. P. (2013). Power average operators of trapezoidal intuitionistic fuzzy numbers and application to multi-attribute group decision making. *Applied Mathematical Modelling, 37*(6), 4112–4126. doi:10.1016/j.apm.2012.09.017

Wan, S. P., Wanga, Q. Y., & Dong, J. Y. (2013). The extended VIKOR method for multi-attribute group decision making with triangular intuitionistic fuzzy numbers. *Knowledge-Based Systems, 52*, 65–77. doi:10.1016/j.knosys.2013.06.019

Wang, C. H., & Wang, J. Q. (2016). A multi-criteria decision-making method based on triangular intuitionistic fuzzy preference information. *Intelligent Automation and Soft Computing, 22*(3), 473–482. doi:10.1080/10798587.2015.1095418

Wang, H., Smarandache, F., Zhang, Y. Q., & Sunderraman, R. (2010). Single valued neutrosophic sets. *Multispace and Multistructure, 4*, 410–413.

Wang, J. Q., & Zhang, Z. (2009). Aggregation operators on intuitionistic trapezoidal fuzzy number and its application to multi-criteria decision making problems. *Journal of Systems Engineering and Electronics, 20*(2), 321–326.

Wei, G. (2010). Some Arithmetic Aggregation Operators with Intuitionistic Trapezoidal Fuzzy Numbers and Their Application to Group Decision Making. *Journal of Computers, 5*(3), 345–351. doi:10.4304/jcp.5.3.345-351

Wu, J., & Liu, Y. (2013). An approach for multiple attribute group decision making problems with interval valued intuitionistic trapezoidal fuzzy numbers. *Computers & Industrial Engineering, 66*(2), 311–324. doi:10.1016/j.cie.2013.07.001

Wu, X. H., Wang, J. Q., Peng, J. J., & Chen, X. H. (2016). Cross-entropy and prioritized aggregation operatör with simplified neutrosophic sets and their application in multi-criteria decision-making problems. *International Journal of Fuzzy Systems, 18*(6), 1104–1116. doi:10.100740815-016-0180-2

Ye, F. (2010). An extended TOPSIS method with interval-valued intuitionistic fuzzy numbers for virtual enterprise partner selection. *Expert Systems with Applications, 37*(10), 7050–7055. doi:10.1016/j.eswa.2010.03.013

Ye, J. (2011). Expected value method for intuitionistic trapezoidal fuzzy multicriteria decision-making problems. *Expert Systems with Applications, 38*(9), 11730–11734. doi:10.1016/j.eswa.2011.03.059

Ye, J. (2012). The Dice similarity measure between generalized trapezoidal fuzzy numbers based on the expected interval and its multicriteria group decision-making method. *Journal of the Chinese Institute of Industrial Engineers, 29*(6), 375–382. doi:10.1080/10170669.2012.710879

Ye, J. (2013). Multicriteria decision-making method using the correlation coefficient under single-valued neutrosophic environment. *International Journal of General Systems, 42*(4), 386–394. doi:10.1080/03081079.2012.761609

Ye, J. (2014). Improved correlation coeffcients of single valued neutrosophic sets and interval neutrosophic sets for multiple attribute decision making. *Journal of Intelligent & Fuzzy Systems, 27*, 2453–2462.

Ye, J. (2014a). A multicriteria decision-making method using aggregation operators for simplified neutrosophic sets. *Journal of Intelligent & Fuzzy Systems, 26*, 2459–2466.

Ye, J. (2014b). Vector Similarity Measures of Simplified Neutrosophic Sets and Their Application in Multicriteria Decision Making. *International Journal of Fuzzy Systems, 16*(2), 204–211.

Ye, J. (2014c). Clustering Methods Using Distance-Based Similarity Measures of Single-Valued Neutrosophic Sets. *Journal of Intelligent Systems, 23*(4), 379–389. doi:10.1515/jisys-2013-0091

Ye, J. (2015a). Improved cosine similarity measures of simplified neutrosophic sets for medical•diagnoses. *Artificial Intelligence in Medicine, 63*(3), 171–179. doi:10.1016/j.artmed.2014.12.007 PMID:25704111

Ye, J. (2015b). Trapezoidal neutrosophic set and its application to multiple attribute decision-making. *Neural Computing & Applications*, *26*(5), 1157–1166. doi:10.100700521-014-1787-6

Ye, J. (2015c). Single-valued neutrosophic similarity measures based on cotangent function and their application in the fault diagnosis of steam turbine. *Soft Computing*. doi:10.100700500- 015-1818-y

Ye, J. (2016). *Some Weighted Aggregation Operators of Trapezoidal Neutrosophic Numbers and Their Multiple Attribute Decision Making Method*. Retrieved from http://vixra.org/abs/1508.0403

Zadeh, L. A. (1965). Fuzzy Sets. *Information and Control*, *8*(3), 338–353. doi:10.1016/S0019-9958(65)90241-X

Zhang, H., Ji, P., Wang, J., & Chen, X. (2015). Improved Weighted Correlation Coefficient based on Integrated Weight for Interval Neutrosophic Sets and its Application in Multi-criteria Decision Making Problems. *International Journal of Computational Intelligence Systems*, *8*(6), 1027–1043. doi:10.1080/18756891.2015.1099917

Chapter 4
Geometric Programming Dealing With Neutrosophic Relational Equations Under the (Max–Min) Operation

Huda E. Khalid

ⓘ https://orcid.org/0000-0002-0968-5611

Department of Scientific Affairs and Cultural Relations, Telafer University, Iraq

ABSTRACT

The neutrosophic relation equations are important elements of neutrosophic mathematics, and it can be widely applied in power systems, neutrosophic comprehensive evaluation. The aim of this chapter is to find the minimal solutions for the neutrosophic relation geometric programming having (V, Λ) operator. In this chapter, a max-min method has been built for finding an optimal solution in the neutrosophic relation equations, and a new characteristic matrix has been defined which is an important step to test the consistency of the system Aox=b and for finding all effective paths that lead to the set of all quasi-minimum solutions. The gained results are reasonable and harmonized with those results in Khalid's work. The method overcomes the problems of poor convergence efficiency inherited from the stochastic hill-climbing method or genetic algorithms. The suggested algorithm has the intersection column method which was proposed to find the effective paths that neglect the fallacious paths, and two new theorems were presented to deal with the optimal solution for (NREGP).

DOI: 10.4018/978-1-7998-2555-5.ch004

1. THE NEUTRALITY CONCEPT SEEDS AT THE THOUGHT OF ANCIENT ARAB SCHOLARS

1.1. Neutrality in the Idiomatic Concept (Al-Baghdadi, 1928)

Neutrality is an expression that joins many fields: political, economic, social religious and scientific. Opinions and concepts varied according to each jurisdiction. Therefore, the Arab ancient scholars defined it as follow: If meant are individuals, then it means that the persons who adopt the average attitude between two conflicting parties and did not tend to one of the sides without the other. As an example the neutral countries are Not- Aligned to any of the Warring States, also the neutral school is against the sectarian school.

Neutrality in the conventional Concept, if the neutral has been fired to the one of the basic science, as an example in physics, it will be meaning that particle does not hold a negative or positive charge, while in the chemistry science the neutral matter means neither acid material nor basal.

1.2. Al-Muʿtazilah and Neutrality (Altai, 2016)

Muʿtazila (in Arabic: المعتزلة) is a rationalist school of Islamic theology that flourished in the cities of Basra and Baghdad, both in Iraq, appeared at the beginning of the second century AH when Wāṣil ibn ʿAṭāʾ (d. 131 AH/748 AD) left the teaching lessons of Hasan al-Basri after a theological dispute regarding the issue of a position between two positions.

The name Muʿtazili is derived from the reflexive of the root "separate, segregate", "separate to withdraw from". The name is derived from the founder's school of Al-Muʿtazilah when he withdrew from the studying circle of Hasan Al- Basri the wake of theological disagreement between them, Wāṣil ibn ʿAṭāʾ asked about the legal state of a person who has committed a serious sin, is he a believer or an unbeliever? Hasan answered the person remains a Muslim. Wasil dissented, suggesting that a sinner was neither a believer nor an unbeliever and withdrew from the study circle. Others followed Hasan to form a new circle, including ʿAmr ibn ʿUbayd. Hasan's remark, "Wāṣil has withdrawn from us", is said to be the origin of the movement's name.

There are five basic tenets make up the Mu'tazilite creed:

1. Justice and unity (monotheism).
2. The inevitability of the threats and promises of God (or "the warning and the promise").

3. The intermediary position (i.e. Muslims who die without repentance after committing a grave sin are neither mu'mineen (believers), nor kuffar (non-believers), but in an intermediate position).
4. The injunction of right.
5. Promotion of Virtue and Prevention of Vice.

In this section, we will focus on the third tenet of their creed (Al-manzilah bayna al-manzilatayn) the intermediate position, that is, Muslims who commit grave sins and die without repentance are not considered as mu'mins (believers), nor considered as kafirs (non-believers), but in an intermediate position between the two. The reason behind this that a mu'min is a person who has faith and conviction in and about God, and who has his/her faith reflected in his/her deeds and moral choices. Any lacking on any of these two fronts makes him/ her not a mu'min. On the other hand, one does not become a kafir (i.e. rejecter; non-believer), for this entails, inter alia, denying the Creator's mercy full, something not necessarily done by a committer of a grave sin. The fate of those who commit grave sins and die without repentance is Hell. Hell is not considered a monolithic state of affairs but as encompassing many degrees to accommodate the wide spectrum of human works and choices, and the lack of comprehension associated to the Ultimate Judge (Al-Hakam is one of the other names of God in Islam). Consequently, those in the intermediate position, though in Hell, would have a lesser punishment because of their belief and other good deeds. Al-Muʿtazilah adopted this position as a middle ground between Kharijites and Murjites. In the words of ʿAbd al-Jabbar, the doctrine of the intermediate position is the knowledge that whoever murders, or commit adultery (Zina), or commits serious sins is a grave sinner (fasiq) and not a believer, nor in the same case of believers with respect to praise and attributing greatness, since he has to be cursed and disregarded. Nonetheless, he is not an unbeliever who cannot be buried in our Muslim cemetery or be prayed on him after died, or marry a Muslim. Rather, he has an intermediate position, in contrast to Kharijites sect who say that he is an unbeliever or the Delaying sect (Murjites) who say that he is a believer.

2. INTRODUCTION

The biological mathematician Sanchez (1976) took the lead in putting forward the concept of fuzzy relation equation by describing in details its structure; he also gave the formula of the maximal solution. Cao (1987) set up the mathematical fundamentals of fuzzy geometric programming, and he introduced it at the second IFSA conference, in Tokyo.

The neutrosophic logic was first introduced at 1995 by Smarandache (1998). Khalid (2015) established a new branch of the geometric programming, called neutrosophic geometric programming where the formula of the maximum solution for neutrosophic relational equations in the problems of geometric programming has been presented. The novel method to find the minimum solution set of neutrosophic relational geometric programming with (max, min) composition was the second work in this scope by Khalid (2016). Later many basic concepts regarded to neutrosophic geometric programming were created and established by Khalid and Smarandache (2016 & 2018).

A system of neutrosophic relation equation with max-min composition is of the form

$$V_{j=1}^{n}\left(a_{ij} \wedge x_{j}\right) = b_{i} \quad \left(1 \le i \le m\right) \tag{1}$$

The notations V and $\wedge$ denote the maximum and minimum operators, respectively. In the matrix form, a system of max-min equation can be represented by Aox=b where "o" denotes the max-min composite operation.

We call

$$\min f\left(x\right) = \left(c_{1} \wedge x_{1}^{\gamma_{1}}\right) V\left(c_{2} \wedge x_{2}^{\gamma_{2}}\right), \dots, V\left(c_{n} \wedge x_{n}^{\gamma_{n}}\right) \tag{2}$$

s.t. Aox=b $\tag{3}$

$$x_{j} \in \left[0,1\right] \cup I \quad \left(1 \le j \le n\right).$$

A max-min $(V, \wedge)$ neutrosophic relation geometric programming (NRGP), where $A = (a_{ij}) \left(a_{ij} \in \left[0,1\right] \cup I\right)$ is an (m×n)-dimensional neutrosophic matrix, x= $(x_1, x_2, \dots, x_n)^T$ n-dimensional variable vector, b= $(b_1, b_2, \dots, b_m)^T$ $\left(b_i \in \left[0,1\right] \cup I\right)$ and c= $(c_1, c_2, \dots, c_n)$ $c_j \in \left[0,1\right] \cup I$ are (m & n)-dimensional constants respectively, γ_j are arbitrary real numbers. Without loss of generality, suppose $1 \ge b_1 \ge b_2 \ge, \dots, b_m \ge 0$ and the elements of the matrix A is corresponding rearranged. When the solution set of the system of equations (3) is not empty, it's in general, a non-convex set that can be completely determined by unique maximum solution and a finite number of minimal solutions.

The structure of this chapter consists of six basic sections; the upcoming section goes for preliminaries, while section 3 contains two new theorems discussing the optimal solutions of equations (1, 2&3). The intersection column method that was presented in section 4 was necessarily established to filter the conservative paths. Depending on the concepts that presented in the previous sections, it is necessary to construct an algorithm for finding the minimum solution that has been discussed in section 5, finally, a numerical example was given in section 6 to demonstrate that the suggested procedure is feasible.

3. PRELIMINARIES

This section consists of two subsections which will shed lights on the basic definitions of (NREGP) as the essential theoretical concepts of the work should be recognized. Of course, un-cited definitions, un-cited theorems, and methods, indicates that they are originally written by the author.

3.1 Basic Definitions

The fundamental definitions of this subsection are either recalled or newly constructed, as they are necessary for studying the structure of solution for Eq.(3).

Definition (3.1.1) Suppose that

$$X(A,b) = \{(x_1, x_2, \cdots, x_n)^T \in [0,1]^n \cup I | Aox = b, \ x_j \in [0,1] \cup I\}$$

is the whole solution set to Eq. (3). $\forall x', x'' \in X(A,b)$ we define $x' \leq x'' \leftrightarrow x_j' \leq x_j'' (1 \leq j \leq n)$. Such a definition "$\leq$." is a partial ordered defined relation on X(A,b). If there exists a solution to Eq. (3), it is called compatible.

For any partial ordered relation in neutrosophic numbers, ones should take in consideration the following rules:

$$\max\{x, I\} = I \ \forall x \in [0,1) \cup I, \max\{0, I\} = I, \max\{1, I\} = 1$$

$$\min\{x, I\} = I \ \forall x \in (0,1] \cup I, \min\{0, I\} = 0, \min\{1, I\} = I$$

Definition (3.1.2) (Yang & Cao, 2007). If $\exists \hat{x} \in X(A,b)$ such that $x \leq \hat{x}, \ \forall x \in X(A,b)$, then $\hat{x}$ is called the greatest solution to Eq. (3). If

$\exists \breve{x} \in X(A,b)$, such that $\breve{x} \leq x, \quad \forall x \in X(A,b)$, then $\breve{x}$ is called a minimal solution to Eq. (3).

Definition (3.1.3) (Khalid, 2015) If $X(A,b) \neq \varnothing$, it can be completely determined by a unique maximum solution and a finite number of minimal solutions. The maximum solution can be obtained by applying the following operation:

$$\hat{x}_j = \Lambda \begin{cases} 1 & a_{ij} \leq b_i \text{ or } a_{ij} = b_i = I \\ b_i & a_{ij} > b_i \\ 0 & a_{ij} = I \text{ and } b_i = [0,1] \\ I & b_i = I \text{ and } a_{ij} = (0,1] \\ \text{not compatible} & a_{ij} = 0 \text{ and } b_i = I \end{cases} \tag{4}$$

If $\hat{x}(\hat{x}_1, \hat{x}_2, \ldots, \hat{x}_n)$ is a solution to Eq. (3), then $\hat{x}$ must be the greatest solution.

As the characteristic matrix is the only way to test the consistency of the system Aox=b the following definition for the characteristic neutrosophic matrix is well defined and successfully find the effective paths, this matrix has been presented for the first time in this chapter and originated to appropriate for NREGP problems.

Definition (3.1.4) the characteristic neutrosophic matrix $\tilde{Q} = \left(\tilde{q}_{ij} \right)_{m \times n}$ of Aox=b is defined by

$$\tilde{q}_{ij} = \begin{cases} \left[b_i, \hat{x}_j \right] & \text{if} \quad a_{ij} \Lambda \hat{x}_j = b_i \\ I & \text{if} \quad a_{ij} \Lambda \hat{x}_j = b_i = I \\ 1 & \text{if} \quad a_{ij} \Lambda \hat{x}_j = b_i = 1 \\ \left[\hat{x}_j, b_i \right] & \text{if} \quad a_{ij} \Lambda \hat{x}_j < b_i \text{ and with } \hat{x}_j \leq b_i \\ \varnothing & \text{otherwise} \end{cases} \tag{5}$$

Note that $\tilde{q}_{ij}$ indicates all the possible values for neutrosophic variable x_j satisfy the i-th equation without violating other equations from the upper side. Consequently, a system Aox=b is consistent if and only if each row of $\tilde{Q}$ contains at least one nonempty neutrosophic element.

Definition (3.1.5) (Yang & Cao, 2007) Let Q be a Boolean matrix. The sequence road$^-$= (road$_1$ road$_2$ ... road$_m$)$\in$G is called a path to $\tilde{Q}$. For each, road$^-$= (road$_1$ road$_2$ ... road$_m$)$\in$Glet

$$x_j^{road^-} = V\left\{b_i \middle| k_i = j\right\} \quad \left(1 \le j \le n\right) \tag{6}$$

where k_i is the element of road$^-$ regarded as a position of b_i in the vector b and suppose that $\{\varnothing V\varnothing...V\varnothing=0\}$. Then $x^{road^-} = \left(x_1^{road^-}, x_2^{road^-}, ..., x_n^{road^-}\right)^T$ is a solution to Eq. (3), and x^{road^-} is called a quasi-minimal solution to Eq. (3).

Definition (3.1.6) (Yang & Cao, 2007) Let road$^-$= (road$_1$ road$_2$ ... road$_m$)$\in$G road$^-$ be called an effective path of Q when $\left(road_1\ road_2\ ...\ road_{k-1}\right) \cap G_k \ne \varnothing$. If road$_i$ is an element among $\{road_1\ road_2\ ...\ road_{k-1}$ that first comes into G_k then there is road$_k$=road$_i$, $\forall k \in \{2,3,...m\}$. When m=1 every path of $\tilde{Q}$ is effective one.

Remark (3.1.7)

1. $\breve{X}^*\left(A, b\right)$ denotes all quasi-minimal solution sets of Eq.(3).

2. $\breve{X}\left(A, b\right)\left(A, b\right)$ was obtained after deleting the duplicates and non-minimal solutions in $\breve{X}^*\left(A, b\right)$.

3. For finding all paths to any characteristic matrix $\tilde{Q}$ let $G_i = \left\{j \middle| q_{ij} \ne \varnothing, 1 \le j \le n\right\}$ $\left(1 \le i \le m\right)$ and G= $G_1 \times ... \times G_m$.

4. Aox=b is compatible if and only if $G \ne \varnothing$.

3.2 The Theoretical Concepts of the Work

Definition (3.2.1) Let Aox=b be a system of max-min equations with a potential maximum solution $\hat{x}$ and a characteristic neutrosophic matrix $\tilde{Q}$. We can define a (0-1) matrix $Q = \left(q_{ij}\right)_{m \times n}$ induced with the characteristic $\tilde{Q}$ defined in formula (5):

$$q_{ij} = \begin{cases} 1, & \text{if } \tilde{q}_{ij} \ne \varnothing \\ 0, & \text{otherwise} \end{cases} \tag{7}$$

Clearly, the induced matrix Q is a Boolean matrix. If Q has no zero rows, then Aox=b is consistent and each equation can be satisfied by a neutrosophic variable, say x_j at a unique value $\hat{x}_j$. Hence we say a system Aox=b is "simple" if all nonempty neutrosophic elements of its characteristic matrix are singletons. It is clear that Aox=b is simple if for each $1 \leq i \leq m$. $b_i \neq a_{ij}$ holds for all $1 \leq j \leq n$. The consistency of Aox=b can be verified by constructing and checking the potential maximum solution in a time complexity of O(mn). Once the maximum solution is obtained, the neutrosophic characteristic matrix $\tilde{Q}$ can be constructed in a time complexity of O(mn). However, the detection of all minimal solutions is a complicated and challenging issue for investigation.

Lemma (3.2.2) (Yang & Cao, 2007) Aox=b is compatible if and only if the greatest solution $\hat{x}$ to Eq. (1) exists.

4. SOME NEW IMPORTANT IMPLICATIONS

In this section, we present two new theorems that dealt and for the first time with the optimal solutions for the neutrosophic relational equations in geometric programming problems (NREGP).

Theorem (4.1) If $\gamma_j < 0$ ($1 \leq j \leq n$) then the greatest solution to equation (1) is optimal for equations (2) &(3).

Proof Since $\gamma_j < 0$ ($1 \leq j \leq n$) with $x_j \in [0,1] \cup I$. then $\dfrac{d\left(x_j^{\gamma_j}\right)}{dx_j} = \gamma_j x_j^{\gamma_j - 1} < 0$ for each

$x_j \in [0,1] \cup I$ implies that $x_j^{\gamma_j}$ is monotone decreasing function of x_j, so is $V_{j=1}^n \left(a_{ij} \Lambda x_j^{\gamma_j}\right)$ of x_j. Moreover, $\forall x \in X(A,b)$ when $x \leq \hat{x}$ then $V_{j=1}^n \left(a_{ij} \Lambda x_j^{\gamma_j}\right) \geq V_{j=1}^n \left(a_{ij} \Lambda \hat{x}_j^{\gamma_j}\right)$. Consequently, $f(x) \geq f\left(\hat{x}\right)$. Hence $\hat{x}$ is an optimal solution to equations (2) &(3).

It remains to study the case that if $\gamma_j < 0$ with x_j in $\hat{x}$ equal to I we know that I^n is undefined for $n \leq 0$, at this case the component $x_j = I$ that has $\gamma_j < 0$ will be replaced by that corresponding x_j in the quasi-minimal solution $\check{x}$.

Finally, for the special case that has $\gamma_j < 0$ with $x_j = I$ of $\hat{x}$ .simultaneously with $x_j = I$ at all corresponding x_j's in quasi-minimum points $\check{x}$ the problem is not compatible as both maximal and quasi-minimal were failed to find the optimal solution.

Theorem (4.2) At $\gamma_j > 0$ $(1 \leq j \leq n)$ a minimal solution to equation (1) must be an optimal solution for the equations (2)&(3).

Proof Since $\gamma_j > 0$ $(1 \leq j \leq n)$, then $\dfrac{d\left(x_j^{\gamma_j}\right)}{dx_j} = \gamma_j x_j^{\gamma_j - 1} > 0$ for each $x_j \in [0,1] \cup I$

implies that $x_j^{\gamma_j}$ is monotone increasing function of x_j, so is $V_{j=1}^{n}\left(a_{ij} \wedge x_j^{\gamma_j}\right)$

of x_j. Moreover, there exist $\breve{x} \in \breve{X}(A,b)$. where $\forall x \in X(A,b)$. $x \geq \breve{x}$ that is,

$x_j \geq \breve{x}_j$ then $V_{j=1}^{n}\left(a_{ij} \wedge x_j^{\gamma_j}\right) \geq V_{j=1}^{n}\left(a_{ij} \wedge \breve{x}_j^{\gamma_j}\right)$. This means that, the optimal

solution to Aox=b. must be exist in $\breve{X}(A,b)$. Suppose that

$\left(\breve{x}^*\right) = \min\left\{f\left(\breve{x}\right) \mid \breve{x} \in \breve{X}(A,b)\right\}$, where $\breve{x}^* \in \breve{X}(A,b)$. Consequently,

$f(x) \geq f\left(\breve{x}^*\right)$ for all $x \in X(A,b)$. Hence $\breve{x}^*$ is an optimal solution to equations (2) & (3).

To filter all effective paths, based on definition (3.1.6) and theorems (4.1) & (4.2), the author proposed the following intersection column method for finding the effective paths to candidate the minimal solutions.

5. THE INTERSECTION COLUMN METHOD

Depending upon the characteristic matrix $\tilde{Q} = \tilde{q}_{ij}$ and the induced matrix Q the author proposed an easy method to filter all effective paths which leads to the set of all quasi-minimum solutions.

1. Determine all non-zero elements in the matrix Q.
2. The following steps must be done.
   a. Let Sr_i the set of all columns values for those non-zero elements in the i-th row of Q.
   b. Let $S_{r1} = \{z_1, z_2, \ldots, z_n\}$, $S_{r2} = \left\{\tilde{z_1}, \tilde{z_2}, \ldots, \tilde{z_n}\right\}$. If $z_1 \cap S_{r2} \neq \varnothing$ connect between z_1 and the least element in S_{r2}. unless many paths will be drawn from z_1 of all elements in S_{r2} [i.e. this case hold at $z_1 \cap S_{r2} = \varnothing$].
   c. Let S_{r1r2} be the set of all sub paths $z_1 \tilde{z_j}$ where j's are some of columns values in the second row of Q.

3. Note that S_{r1r2} contains parts of an effective path.
4. Repeat the ideas in (c-d) steps for S_{r1r2} and S_{r3} to get S_{r1r2r3} and so on for all rows of Q.
5. Again do the same progresses stated in (c-d-e) for z_2 and repeat it for all elements of S_{r1}.
6. The final set will be $S_{r1r2.....rm} = \{road\tilde{\ }_1, road\tilde{\ }_2, ...\}$. which represents the set of all effective paths and $x^{road\tilde{\ }_i}$. is a minimal solution.

6. ALGORITHM

1. Without loss of generality, rearrange the components of b (i.e. b_i in descending order, and following to this rearranging, the matrices A and x will be adjusted.
2. Using the formula (4) to find the maximum solution $\hat{x}$ .of the NREGP defined in problem (2,3).
3. If all the exponents of x_j's are negative (i.e. $\gamma_j < 0$, stipulate that $\hat{x}$ .is the optimal solution ; print $f(\hat{x})$ .and stop.
4. If the sign of $\gamma_j > 0$ for some j's and negative for others, then participate the objective function $f(x)$ into two sub functions, $f_1(x)$ for those terms having $\gamma_j < 0$ and $f_2(x)$ for those terms having $\gamma_j > 0$.
5. Find the characteristic matrix $\tilde{Q} = \left[\tilde{q}_{ij} \right]_{m \times n}$ .that defined by formula (5) and find the Boolean matrix Q.
6. Use the intersection column method to find all effective paths in the matrix Q.that leads to the quasi -minimum.
7. Evaluate $x^{road\tilde{\ }_i}$. for all paths that resulting from step (6).
8. Compute $f_2(x)$ for all $x^{road\tilde{\ }_i}$, and take in consideration the minimum one is the optimal one.
9. To find x^* check the sign of γ_j by using theorems (4.1), (4.2).
10. Print $f(x^*)$ and stop.

Notes

1- All the duplicate solutions in $\breve{X}^*(A,b)$ must be deleted.
2- If the duplicated and non-minimal solution in $\breve{X}^*(A,b)$ had been deleted, then $\breve{X}^*(A,b)$ will be obtained.
3- Denote the set of all effective paths of Q by $S_{r1r2...rm}$.

4- $x^{road^-_i}$ is called a quasi-minimal solution to Eq.(1).

7. NUMERICAL EXAMPLE

Solve the following (NREGP) problem

$$\text{Min} f\left(x\right)=\left(1.5\Lambda x_1^{.5}\right) V\left(I\Lambda x_2\right) V\left(.8\Lambda x_3^{.5}\right) V\left(.9\Lambda x_4^{-2}\right) V\left(.7\Lambda x_5^{-4}\right) V\left(I\Lambda x_6^{-1}\right)$$

s. t. Aox=b, where

$$A = \begin{bmatrix} I & .8 & .9 & .3 & .85 & .4 \\ .2 & .2 & .1 & .95 & I & .8 \\ .8 & .8 & .4 & .1 & .1 & .1 \\ .1 & .1 & .1 & .1 & .1 & 0 \end{bmatrix}_{46} \text{ and b=(.85, .6, .5, .1).}$$

It is clear that b is arranged in decreasing order.

Depending on formula (4), the maximum solution is $\hat{x} = \left(0, .5, .85, .6, 0, .6\right)$.

Table 1 is required to conclude the elements of the characteristic matrix $\tilde{Q}$.

$$\tilde{Q} = \begin{bmatrix} [0,.85] & [.5,.85] & .85 & [.6,.85] & [0,.85] & [.6,.85] \\ [0,.6] & [.5,.6] & \varnothing & .6 & [0,.6] & .6 \\ [0,.5] & .5 & \varnothing & \varnothing & [0,.5] & \varnothing \\ [0,.1] & [.1,.5] & [.1,.85] & [.1,1.6] & [0,.1] & \varnothing \end{bmatrix}.$$

The Boolean matrix Q induced with $\tilde{Q}$ is

$$Q = \begin{bmatrix} 1 & 1 & 1 & 1 & 1 & 1 \\ 1 & 1 & 0 & 1 & 1 & 1 \\ 1 & 1 & 0 & 0 & 1 & 0 \\ 1 & 1 & 1 & 1 & 1 & 0 \end{bmatrix}.$$

$G_1=\{1,2,3,4,5,6\}$, $G_2=\{1,2,4,5,6\}$, $G_3=\{1,2,5\}$, $G_4\{1,2,3,4,5\}$,

Table 1. Internal elements of $\tilde{Q}$.matrix

q_{ij}	a_{ij}	$\hat{x}_j$	b_i
$q_{11}=[0, .85]$	I	0	.85
$q_{21}=[0, .6]$	.2	0	.6
$q_{31}=[0, .5]$	.8	0	.5
$q_{41}=[0, .1]$	.1	0	.1
$q_{12}=[.5, .85]$	.8	.5	.85
$q_{22}=[.5, .6]$	.2	.5	.6
$q_{32}=.5$	.8	.5	.5
$q_{42}=[.1, .5]$	.1	.5	.1
$q_{13}=.85$	.9	.85	.85
$q_{23}=\varnothing$	.1	.85	.6
$q_{33}=\varnothing$	.4	.85	.5
$q_{43}=[.1, .85]$	.1	.85	.1
$q_{14}=[.6, .85]$	.3	.6	.85
$q_{24}=.6$	.95	.6	.6
$q_{34}=\varnothing$	.1	.6	.5
$q_{44}=[.1, .6]$	.1	.6	.1
$q_{15}=[0, .85]$	.85	0	.85
$q_{25}=[0, .6]$	I	0	.6
$q_{35}=[0, .5]$	.1	0	.5
$q_{45}=[0, .1]$	.1	0	.1
$q_{16}=[.6, .85]$	.4	.6	.85
$q_{26}=.6$	.8	.6	.6
$q_{36}=\varnothing$	.1	.6	.5
$q_{46}=\varnothing$	0	.6	.1

$G_1 \times G_2 = \{11,12,14,15,16,21,22,24,25,26,31,32,34,35,36,41,42,44,45,46,51,52,54,$
$55,56,61,62,64,65,66\}$

It is of 90 elements, $G_1 \times G_2 \times G_3 = \{111,121,141,\ldots,665\}$
It is of 450 elements, $G = G_1 \times G_2 \times G_3 \times G_4 = \{1111,1211,\ldots,6655\}$
Now, to filter the conservative paths from all above 450 elements of G the author used the intersection column method as follow:
Let $S_{r1} = \{1\ 2\ 3\ 4\ 5\ 6\}$, $S_{r2} = \{1\ 2\ 4\ 5\ 6\}$, $S_{r3} = \{1\ 2\ 5\}$, $S_{r4} = \{1\ 2\ 3\ 4\ 5\}$

So, $1\Lambda S_{r2}=\varnothing$, $2\Lambda S_{r2}=\varnothing$, $3\Lambda S_{r2}=\varnothing$, $4\Lambda S_{r2}=\varnothing$, $5\Lambda S_{r2}=\varnothing$, $6\Lambda S_{r2}=\varnothing$
Therefore, $S_{r1r2}=\{11,21,31,41,51,61\}$.

$11\Lambda S_{r3}=\varnothing$, $21\Lambda S_{r3}=\varnothing$, $31\Lambda S_{r3}=\varnothing$, $41\Lambda S_{r3}=\varnothing$, $51\Lambda S_{r3}=\varnothing$, $61\Lambda S_{r3}=\varnothing$

Consequently, $S_{r1r2r3}=\{111,211,311,411,511,611\}$.

$111\Lambda S_{r4}=\varnothing$, $211\Lambda S_{r4}=\varnothing$, $311\Lambda S_{r4}=\varnothing$, $411\Lambda S_{r4}=\varnothing$, $511\Lambda S_{r4}=\varnothing$, $611\Lambda S_{r4}=\varnothing$

$\therefore S_{r1r2r3r4}=\{1111,2111,3111,4111,5111,6111\}$.

$$x_1^{road_1} = V(.85,.6,.5,.1) = .85$$

$$x_2^{road_1} = V(\varnothing) = 0$$

$$x_3^{road_1} = V(\varnothing) = 0$$

$$x_4^{road_1} = V(\varnothing) = 0$$

$$x_5^{road_1} = V(\varnothing) = 0$$

$$x_6^{road_1} = V(\varnothing) = 0$$

$$x^{road_1} = (.85,0,0,0,0,0).$$

By the same way, the remain quasi-minimum points can be concluded,

$$x^{road_2} = (.6,.85,0,0,0,0)$$

$$x^{road_3} = (.6,0,.85,0,0,0)$$

$$x^{road_4} = (.6,0,0,.85,0,0)$$

$$x^{road_5} = (.6,0,0,0,.85,0)$$

$$x^{road_6} = (.6,0,0,0,0,.85)$$

We will divide the objective function f(x)into two sub objective functions $f_1(x)$ having those terms of negative powers, and $f_2(x)$ having those terms of positive exponents,

$$f_1(x) = \left(.9 \wedge x_4^{-2}\right) V\left(.7 \wedge x_5^{-4}\right) V\left(I \wedge x_6^{-1}\right)$$

$f_1(x) = (.9 \wedge .6^{-2})V(.7 \wedge 0^{-4})V(I \wedge .6^{-1})$

$f_1(x) = (.9 \wedge 2.77)V(.7 \wedge \infty)V(I \wedge 1.666)$

$f_1(x) = (.9)V(.7)V(I)$

$f_1(x) = I$

$$f_2(x) = \left(1.5 \wedge x_1^{.5}\right) V\left(I \wedge x_2\right) V\left(.8 \wedge x_3^{.5}\right)$$

$$f_2\left(x^{road^\sim_4}\right) = f_2\left(x^{road^\sim_5}\right) = f_2\left(x^{road^\sim_6}\right) = .775$$

$$f_2\left(x^{road^\sim_1}\right) = .92195$$

$$f_2\left(x^{road^\sim_2}\right) = I$$

$$f_2\left(x^{road^\sim_3}\right) = .8 \,.$$

The minimum values of $f_2\left(x^{road^\sim_1}\right), f_2\left(x^{road^\sim_2}\right), \ldots, f_2\left(x^{road^\sim_6}\right)$ is $f_2\left(x^{road^\sim_2}\right) = I$.

$$x^* = \left(\underbrace{.6, .5, 0}_{\text{from quasi minimum } x^{road\tilde{2}}} \,, \underbrace{.6, 0, .6}_{\text{from maximum } sol} \right).$$

$$\min f(x) = \left(1.5 \wedge x_1^{.5}\right)V\left(I \wedge x_2\right)V\left(.8 \wedge x_3^{.5}\right)V\left(.9 \wedge x_4^{-2}\right)V\left(.7 \wedge x_5^{-4}\right)V\left(I \wedge x_6^{-1}\right)$$

min f(x)=$f_1(x)$ V $f_2(x)$

min f(x)=I V I=I

It is important to notice that the final result in this example is congruous to the result of the same example was solved by Khalid (2016).

CONCLUSION

In view of the importance of geometric programming with the neutrosophic relation equations, in this chapter, a new definition of a characteristic matrix has been originated, as well as, a max-min method has been built for finding an optimal solution to neutrosophic relation equation of geometric programming based on $(\vee,\wedge)$ composition. The author proposed an easy way to find the effective paths; new theorems were presented to deal with the optimal solution of special problems. Neutrosophic geometric programming has wide applications in the fields of optimal design, transportation problems, management, electronics, chemical plants, biology, the study of labor problems, and automation control. As an Arabic researcher, it was essential to connect the scientific production of the ancient Arab scholars with the modern paradox school belonging to its founder Smarandache F. by presenting the neutrality in the Al-Muʿtazilah thought.

REFERENCES

Al-Baghdadi, A. Q. (1928). Usul al Din. Istanbul: Academic Press.

Altai, M. B. (2016). *God, Nature, and the Cause: Essays on Islam and Science*. John Templeton Foundation.

Khalid, H. E. (2015). An Original Notion to Find Maximal Solution in the Fuzzy Neutrosophic Relation Equations (FNRE) with Geometric Programming (GP). *Neutrosophic Sets and Systems*, *7*, 3–7.

Khalid, H. E. (2016). The Novel Attempt for Finding Minimum Solution in Fuzzy Neutrosophic Relational Geometric Programming (FNRGP) with (max, min) Composition. *Neutrosophic Sets and Systems*, *11*, 107–111.

Khalid, H. E., Smarandache, F., & Essa, A. K. (2018). The Basic Notions for (over, off, under) Neutrosophic Geometric Programming Problems. *Neutrosophic Sets and Systems*, *22*, 50–62.

Sanchez, E. (1976). Resolution of Composite Fuzzy Relation Equations. *Information and Control*, *30*(1), 38–48. doi:10.1016/S0019-9958(76)90446-0 .

Smarandache, F. (1998). *Neutrosophy, neutrosophic probability, set and logic.* Rehoboth: Amer. Res. Press.

Smarandache, F., Khalid, H. E., & Essa, A. K. (2018). Neutrosophic Logic: the Revolutionary Logic in Science and Philosophy. In *Proceedings of the National Symposium*. EuropaNova.

Smarandache, F., Khalid, H. E., Essa, A. K., & Ali, M. (2016). The Concept of Neutrosophic Less Than or Equal To: A New Insight in Unconstrained Geometric Programming. *Critical Review, XII*, 72–80.

Yang, J. H., & Cao, B. Y. (2007). Monomial Geometric Programming with Fuzzy Relation Equation Constraints. *Fuzzy Optimization and Decision Making*, 6(4), 337–349. doi:10.100710700-007-9017-7

Chapter 5
Interval Rough Neutrosophic TOPSIS Strategy for Multi-Attribute Decision Making

Rumi Roy
Indian Institute of Engineering Science and Technology, Shibpur, India

Surapati Pramanik
 https://orcid.org/0000-0002-8167-7026
Nandalal Ghosh B. T. College, Panpur, India

Tapan Kumar Roy
Indian Institute of Engineering Science and Technology, Shibpur, India

ABSTRACT

In this chapter, the authors present a new strategy for multi-attribute decision making in interval rough neutrosophic environment. They define Hamming distance and Euclidean distance between interval rough neutrosophic numbers. They also define interval rough neutrosophic relative positive ideal solution (IRNRPIS) and interval rough neutrosophic relative negative ideal solution (IRNRNIS). Then the ranking order of the alternatives is obtained by the technique for order preference by similarity to ideal solution (TOPSIS) strategy. Finally, a numerical example is provided to demonstrate the applicability and effectiveness of the proposed interval rough neutrosophic TOPSIS strategy.

DOI: 10.4018/978-1-7998-2555-5.ch005

1. INTRODUCTION

Broumi et al. (2014) introduced rough neutrosophic set by combining the concept of rough set (Pawlak et al., 1982) and neutrosophic set (Smarandache et al., 1998). Neutrosophic sets have been widely applied in decision making problems (Biswas et la, 2014). So there is enormous chance of success of rough neutrosophic set in decision making. Several studies of rough neutrosophic sets have been reported in the literature. Mondal and Pramanik (2015) applied the concept of rough neutrosophic set in multi-attribute decision making (MADM) based on grey relational analysis. Pramanik and Mondal (2015) presented cosine similarity measure of rough neutrosophic sets and its application in medical diagnosis. Pramanik and Mondal (2015) also proposed some rough neutrosophic similarity measures namely Dice and Jaccard similarity measures of rough neutrosophic environment. Mondal and Pramanik (2015) proposed rough neutrosophic MADM based on rough score accuracy function. Pramanik and Mondal (2015) presented cotangent similarity measure of rough neutrosophic sets and its application to medical diagnosis. Pramanik and Mondal (2015) presented trigonometric Hamming similarity measure of rough neutrosophic sets. Mondal et al. (2019) presented rough neutrosophic aggregation operators for MADM.

Broumi and Smarandache defined interval rough neutrosophic set (IRNS) (Broumi et al., 2015) by combining the concept of rough set and interval neutrosophic set (Broumi et al., 2015). Pramanik et al. (2018) presented an MADM based on projection and bidirectional projection measures under IRNS environment. Pramanik et al. (2018) proposed an MADM based on trigonometric Hamming similarity measures in IRNS environment.

Hwang and Yoon (1981) introduced a technique for order preference by similarity to ideal solution(TOPSIS). Biswas et al. (2015) proposed TOPSIS strategy for MAGDM for under single valued neutrosophic environment. Chai and Liu (2013) developed TOPSIS strategy for MADM with interval neutrosophic set. Broumi et al. (Broumi et al., 2015) presented extended TOPSIS strategy for multiple attribute decision making based on interval neutrosophic uncertain linguistic variables. Pramanik et al. (2015) presented TOPSIS for singled valued soft expert set based MADM problems. Dey et al. (2015) presented TOPSIS for generalized neutrosophic soft MADM. Dey et al. (2016) proposed TOPSIS for solving MADM problems under bi-polar neutrosophic environment. Sahin et al.(2016) proposed another approach of TOPSIS strategy for supplier selection in neutrosophic environment. Elhassouny and Smarandache (Elhassouny e tal, 2016) briefly provided a survey on neutrosophic TOPSIS applications and its methodologies. Mondal et al. (2016) studied TOPSIS in rough neutrosophic environment. Interval rough TOPSIS is yet to appear in the literature. To fill the research gap, we extend the TOPSIS strategy in IRNS environment.

Research Gap

MADM strategy using TOPSIS strategy in IRNS environment. The objectives of the paper are:

- To define Hamming distance measure and Euclidean distance measure between interval rough neutrosophic sets.
- To develop a new MADM strategy based on the TOPSIS in IRNS environment.

Contributions

- In this paper, we propose Hamming distance measure and Euclidean distance measure under IRNS environment.
- In this paper, we develop a new MADM strategy based on the TOPSIS method under IRNS environment.
- We also present a numerical example to show the effectiveness and applicability of the proposed strategy.

Rest of the paper is organized as follows: Section 2 describes preliminaries of neutrosophic number, SVNS, RNS and IRNS. Section 3 presents definitions and properties of proposed Hamming distance measure and Euclidean distance measure between IRNSs. Section 4 describes the MADM strategy based on TOPSIS strategy in IRNS environment. In section 5 we describe a numerical example. In section 6 we present the comparison analysis between the proposed strategy and the existing strategies. Finally, in section 7 we present the conclusion and future scope of research.

2. PRELIMINARIES

In this section, we provide some basic definitions regarding SVNSs, IRNSs which are useful in the paper.

2.1. Neutrosophic Set

In 1999, Smarandache gave the following definition of neutrosophic set(NS) (Smarandache, 1998).

Definition 2.1.1 Let X be a space of points (objects) with generic element in X denoted by x. A NS A in X is characterized by a truth-membership function T_A, an indeterminacy membership function I_A and a falsity membership function

F_A. The functions T_A, I_A and F_A are real standard or non-standard subsets of $({}^-0,1^+)$ that is $T_A{:}X \rightarrow ({}^-0, 1^+)$, $I_A{:}X \rightarrow ({}^-0, 1^+)$ and $F_A{:}X \rightarrow ({}^-0, 1^+)$. It should be noted that there is no restriction on the sum of $T_A(x)$, $I_A(x)$ and $F_A(x)$ i.e. $0^- \leq T_A(X) + I_A(X) + F_A(X) \leq 3^+$.

Definition 2.1.2: The complement of a neutrosophic set (Smarandache, 1998). A is denoted by $C(A)$ and is defined by $T_{C(A)}(x) = \{1^+\}\text{-}T_A(x)$, $I_{C(A)}(x)=\{1^+\}\text{-}I_A(x)$, $F_{C(A)}(x)=\{1^+\}\text{-}F_A(x)$.

Definition 2.1.3: A neutrosophic set A (Smarandache, 1998) is contained in the other neutrosophic set B, denoted by $A \subseteq B$ iff

$$\inf T_A(x) \leq \inf T_B(x),\ \sup T_A(x) \leq \sup T_B(x)$$

$$\inf I_A(x) \geq \inf I_B(x),\ \sup I_A(x) \geq \sup I_B(x)$$

$$\inf F_A(x) \geq \inf F_B(x),\ \sup F_A(x) \geq \sup F_B(x)\ \forall x \in X$$

Definition 2.1.4: Single-valued neutrosophic set (SVNS)

Let X be a universal space of points (objects) with a generic element of X denoted by x. An SVNS (Wang et al, 2010) A is characterized by a truth membership function $T_A(x)$, a falsity membership function $F_A(x)$ and indeterminacy function $I_A(x)$ with $T_A(x)$, $I_A(x)$, and $F_A(x) \in [0,1]\ \forall x$ in X.

When X is continuous, an SNVS S can be written as follows

$$A = \int_x \langle T_A(x), F_A(x), I_A(x) \rangle / x \forall x \in X$$

and when X is discrete, an SVNS S can be written as follows

$$A = \sum \langle T_A(x), F_A(x), I_A(x) \rangle / x \forall x \in X$$

For an SVNS S, $0 \leq \sup T_A(x) + \sup I_A(x) + \sup F_A(x) \leq 3$.

Definition 2.1.5: The complement of an SVNS A is denoted by $c(A)$ and is defined by $T_{c(A)}(x) = F_A(x)$, $I_{c(A)}(x) = 1\text{-}I_A(x)$, $F_{c(A)}(x) = T_A(x)$.

Definition 2.1.6: An SVNS A is contained in the other SVNS B, denoted as $A \subseteq B$ iff, $T_A(x) \leq T_B(x)$, $I_A(x) \geq I_B(x)$, and $F_A(x) \geq F_B(x)\ \forall x \in X$.

2.2. Rough Neutrosophic Set

Definition 2.2.1: Let Y be a non-null set and R be an equivalence relation on Y. Let P be neutrosophic set in Y with the membership function T_p, indeterminacy function I_p and non-membership function F_p. The lower and the upper approximations of P in the approximation (Y, R) denoted by are respectively defined as:

$$\underline{N(P)} = \left\langle \left\langle x, T_{\underline{N(P)}}(x), I_{\underline{N(P)}}(x), F_{\underline{N(P)}}(x) \right\rangle / y \in [x]_R, x \in Y \right\rangle$$

and

$$\overline{N(P)} = \left\langle \left\langle x, T_{\overline{N(P)}}(x), I_{\overline{N(P)}}(x), F_{\overline{N(P)}}(x) \right\rangle / y \in [x]_R, x \in Y \right\rangle$$

where,

$$T_{\underline{N(P)}}(x) = \wedge z \in [x]_R T_P(Y), \qquad T_{\overline{N(P)}}(x) = \vee z \in [x]_R T_P(Y),$$

$$I_{\underline{N(P)}}(x) = \wedge z \in [x]_R I_P(Y), \quad \text{and} \quad I_{\overline{N(P)}}(x) = \vee z \in [x]_R I_P(Y),$$

$$F_{\underline{N(P)}}(x) = \wedge z \in [x]_R F_P(Y). \qquad F_{\overline{N(P)}}(x) = \vee z \in [x]_R F_P(Y).$$

So,

$$0 \leq T_{\underline{N(P)}}(x) + I_{\underline{N(P)}}(x) + F_{\underline{N(P)}}(x) \leq 3$$

and

$$0 \leq T_{\overline{N(P)}}(x) + I_{\overline{N(P)}}(x) + F_{\overline{N(P)}}(x) \leq 3$$

Here $\vee$ and $\wedge$ denote "max" and "min" operators respectively, $T_p(y), I_p(y)$ and $F_p(y)$ are the membership, indeterminacy and non-membership of Y with respect to P.

Thus NS mapping, $\underline{N}, \overline{N} : N(Y) \to N(Y)$ are, respectively, referred to as the lower and upper rough NS approximation operators, and the pair $(\underline{N(P)}, \overline{N(P)})$ is called the rough neutrosophic set (Broumi et al, 2014).

2.3. Interval Rough Neutrosophic Set

Interval neutrosophic rough set is the hybrid structure of rough sets and interval neutrosophic sets. According to Broumi and Smarandache (2015) interval neutrosophic rough set is the generalizations of interval valued intuitionistic fuzzy rough set.

Definition 2.3.1 Let R be an equivalence relation on the universal set U. Then the pair (U, R) is called a Pawlak approximation space. An equivalence class of R containing x will be denoted by $[x]_R$ for $X \in U$, the lower and upper approximations of X subset U with respect to (U, R) are denoted by respectively, $\underline{R}X$ and $\overline{R}X$ are defined by

$$\underline{R}X = \{x \in U : [x]_R \subseteq X\}, \ \overline{R}X = \{x \in U : [x]_R \cap X \neq \emptyset\}.$$

Now if $\underline{R}X = \overline{R}X$, then X is called definable; otherwise X is called a rough set.

Definition 2.3.2: Let U be a universe and X be a rough set in U. An intuitionistic fuzzy rough set A in U is characterized by a membership function $\mu_A : U \rightarrow [0, 1]$ and non-membership function $\nu_A: U \rightarrow [0, 1]$ such that $\mu_A(\underline{R}X) = 1$ and $\nu_A(\underline{R}X) = 0$

i.e., $[\mu_A(x), \nu_A(x)] = [1,0]$ if $x \in (\underline{R}X)$ and $\mu_A(U - \overline{R}X) = 0$, $\nu_A(U - \overline{R}X) = 1$

i.e., $0 \leq \mu_A(\overline{R}X - \underline{R}X) + \nu_A(\overline{R}X - \underline{R}X) \leq 1$

Definition 2.3.3: Assume that, (U, R) be a Pawlak approximation space, for an interval neutrosophic set

$A = \{<x, [T_A{}^L(x), T_A{}^U(x)], [I_A{}^L(x), I_A{}^U(x)], [F_A{}^L(x), F_A{}^U(x)]> : x \in U\}$

The lower approximation $\underline{A_R}$ and the upper approximation $\overline{A_R}$ of A in the Pawlak approximation space (U, R) are expressed as follows:

$$\underline{A_R} = \left\{ \left\langle x, [\wedge_{y \in [x]_R} \{T_A^L(y)\}, \wedge_{y \in [x]_R} \{T_A^U(y)\}], [\vee_{y \in [x]_R} \{I_A^L(y)\}, \vee_{y \in [x]_R} \{I_A^U(y)\}], \right. \right.$$
$$\left. \left. [\vee_{y \in [x]_R} \{F_A^L(y)\}, \vee_{y \in [x]_R} \{F_A^U(y)\}] \right\rangle : x \in U \right\},$$
$$\overline{A_R} = \left\{ \left\langle x, [\vee_{y \in [x]_R} \{T_A^L(y)\}, \vee_{y \in [x]_R} \{T_A^U(y)\}], [\wedge_{y \in [x]_R} \{I_A^L(y)\}, \wedge_{y \in [x]_R} \{I_A^U(y)\}], \right. \right.$$
$$\left. \left. [\wedge_{y \in [x]_R} \{F_A^L(y)\}, \wedge_{y \in [x]_R} \{F_A^U(y)\}] \right\rangle : x \in U \right\}.$$

The symbols $^\wedge$ and $^\vee$ indicate "min" and "max" operators respectively. R denotes an equivalence relation for interval neutrosophic set A. Here $[x]_R$ is the equivalence class of the element x. It is obvious that

$$[\wedge_{y\in[x]_R} \{T_A^U(y)\}, \wedge_{y\in[x]_R} \{T_A^L(y)\}] \subset [0,1],$$

$$[\vee_{y\in[x]_R} \{I_A^U(y)\}, \vee_{y\in[x]_R} \{I_A^L(y)\}] \subset [0,1],$$

$$[\vee_{y\in[x]_R} \{F_A^U(y)\}, \vee_{y\in[x]_R} \{F_A^L(y)\}] \subset [0,1].$$

and $0 \le \wedge_{y\in[x]_R} \{T_A^U(y)\} + \vee_{y\in[x]_R} \{I_A^U(y)\} + \vee_{y\in[x]_R} \{F_A^U(y)\} \le 3.$

Then $\underline{A_R}$ is an interval neutrosophic set (INS). Similarly we have

$$[\vee_{y\in[x]_R} \{T_A^L(y)\}, \vee_{y\in[x]_R} \{T_A^U(y)\}] \subset [0,1],$$

$$[\wedge_{y\in[x]_R} \{I_A^L(y)\}, \wedge_{y\in[x]_R} \{I_A^U(y)\}] \subset [0,1],$$

$$[\wedge_{y\in[x]_R} \{F_A^L(y)\}, \wedge_{y\in[x]_R} \{F_A^U(y)\}] \subset [0,1].$$

and $0 \le \vee_{y\in[x]_R} \{T_A^L(y)\} + \wedge_{y\in[x]_R} \{I_A^L(y)\} + \wedge_{y\in[x]_R} \{F_A^L(y)\} \le 3.$

Then $\overline{A_R}$ is an interval neutrosophic set. If $\underline{A_R} = \overline{A_R}$ then A is a definable set, otherwise A is an interval valued neutrosophic rough set [48]. Here, $\underline{A_R}$ and $\overline{A_R}$ are called the lower and upper approximations of interval neutrosophic set with respect to approximation space *(U,R)*, respectively. $\underline{A_R}$ and $\overline{A_R}$ are simply denoted by $\underline{A}$ and $\overline{A}$ respectively.

3. THE DISTANCE BETWEEN IRNS

In this section we propose the distance between IRNSs. Let,

$$M_{ij} = \left\langle \left(\left[\underline{T_{iM}^-}, \underline{T_{iM}^+}\right], \left[\underline{I_{iM}^-}, \underline{I_{iM}^+}\right], \left[\underline{F_{iM}^-}, \underline{F_{iM}^+}\right], \left[\overline{T_{iM}^-}, \overline{T_{iM}^+}\right], \left[\overline{I_{iM}^-}, \overline{I_{iM}^+}\right], \left[\overline{F_{iM}^-}, \overline{F_{iM}^+}\right] \right) \right\rangle$$

and

$$N_{ij} = \left\langle \left(\left[\underline{T_{iN}^-}, \underline{T_{iN}^+}\right], \left[\underline{I_{iN}^-}, \underline{I_{iN}^+}\right], \left[\underline{F_{iN}^-}, \underline{F_{iN}^+}\right], \left[\overline{T_{iN}^-}, \overline{T_{iN}^+}\right], \left[\overline{I_{iN}^-}, \overline{I_{iN}^+}\right], \left[\overline{F_{iN}^-}, \overline{F_{iN}^+}\right] \right) \right\rangle$$

be two IRNSs. Then,

1.   1. The Euclidean distance between M and N is:

$$
E(M,N) = \left[\sum_{i=1}^{n} \{ (T_{iM}^{-} - T_{iN}^{-})^2 + (T_{iM}^{+} - T_{iN}^{+})^2 + (I_{iM}^{-} - I_{iN}^{-})^2 + (I_{iM}^{+} - I_{iN}^{+})^2 + (F_{iM}^{-} - F_{iN}^{-})^2 \right.
$$
$$
+ (F_{iM}^{+} - F_{iN}^{+})^2 + (\overline{T_{iM}^{-}} - \overline{T_{iN}^{-}})^2 + (\overline{T_{iM}^{+}} - \overline{T_{iN}^{+}})^2 + (\overline{I_{iM}^{-}} - \overline{I_{iN}^{-}})^2 + (\overline{I_{iM}^{+}} - \overline{I_{iN}^{+}})^2
$$
$$
\left. + (\overline{F_{iM}^{-}} - \overline{F_{iN}^{-}})^2 + (\overline{F_{iM}^{+}} - \overline{F_{iN}^{+}})^2 \} \right]^{\frac{1}{2}}
$$

(1)

2.   2. The normalized Euclidean distance between M and N is:

$$
E(M,N) = \left(\frac{1}{12n} \left[\sum_{i=1}^{n} \{ (T_{iM}^{-} - T_{iN}^{-})^2 + (T_{iM}^{+} - T_{iN}^{+})^2 + (I_{iM}^{-} - I_{iN}^{-})^2 + (I_{iM}^{+} - I_{iN}^{+})^2 \right. \right.
$$
$$
+ (F_{iM}^{-} - F_{iN}^{-})^2 + (F_{iM}^{+} - F_{iN}^{+})^2 + (\overline{T_{iM}^{-}} - \overline{T_{iN}^{-}})^2 + (\overline{T_{iM}^{+}} - \overline{T_{iN}^{+}})^2 + (\overline{I_{iM}^{-}} - \overline{I_{iN}^{-}})^2 \cdots
$$
$$
\left. \left. + (\overline{I_{iM}^{+}} - \overline{I_{iN}^{+}})^2 + (\overline{F_{iM}^{-}} - \overline{F_{iN}^{-}})^2 + (\overline{F_{iM}^{+}} - \overline{F_{iN}^{+}})^2 \} \right] \right)^{\frac{1}{2}}
$$

(2)

4. TOPSIS METHOD FOR SOLVING MADM PROBLEM WITH INTERVAL ROUGH NEUTROSOPHIC INFORMATION

In this section, we present a strategy for MADM problem by using the TOPSIS measure of interval rough neutrosophic numbers.

Consider $C = \{ C_1, \ldots, C_m \}$ be the set of attributes and $A = \{ A_1, \ldots, A_n \}$ be a set of alternatives. Now we provide an algorithm for MADM problems involving interval rough neutrosophic information.

Algorithm

Step 1: *Construction of the decision matrix with interval rough neutrosophic number.* Decision maker considers the decision matrix with respect to m attributes and n alternatives in terms of interval rough neutrosophic numbers as follows:

Interval Rough neutrosophic decision matrix

$$D = \left\langle Z_{ij} \right\rangle_{nxm} = \begin{bmatrix} Z_{11} & Z_{12} & \dots & \dots & Z_{1m} \\ Z_{21} & Z_{22} & \dots & \dots & Z_{2m} \\ \dots & \dots & \dots & \dots & \dots & \dots \\ \dots & \dots & \dots & \dots & \dots & \dots \\ \dots & \dots & \dots & \dots & \dots & \dots \\ Z_{n1} & Z_{n2} & \dots & \dots & Z_{nm} \end{bmatrix}$$

where

$$Z_{ij} = \left\langle \left(\left[\underline{T_{iM}^-}, \underline{T_{iM}^+}\right], \left[\underline{I_{iM}^-}, \underline{I_{iM}^+}\right], \left[\underline{F_{iM}^-}, \underline{F_{iM}^+}\right], \left[\overline{T_{iM}^-}, \overline{T_{iM}^+}\right], \left[\overline{I_{iM}^-}, \overline{I_{iM}^+}\right], \left[\overline{F_{iM}^-}, \overline{F_{iM}^+}\right] \right) \right\rangle$$

with

$$0 \leq \vee_{y \in [x]_R} \{T_A^U(y)\} + \wedge_{y \in [x]_R} \{I_A^U(y)\} + \wedge_{y \in [x]_R} \{F_A^U(y)\} \leq 3.$$

for $i = 1, 2, ..., n$ and $j = 1, 2, ..., m$.

Step 2: *Construction of weighted decision matrix.* Assume that the weighting vector of the attributes is $W = (w_1, w_2, ..., w_n)^T$. Then the weighted decision matrix is obtained by multiplying weights of the attributes. The weighted decision matrix is as follows:

Interval Rough neutrosophic weighted decision matrix

$$D = <r_{ij}>_{nxm} = \begin{bmatrix} r_{11} & r_{12} & \dots & \dots & r_{1m} \\ r_{21} & r_{22} & \dots & \dots & r_{2m} \\ \dots & \dots & \dots & \dots & \dots & \dots \\ \dots & \dots & \dots & \dots & \dots & \dots \\ \dots & \dots & \dots & \dots & \dots & \dots \\ r_{n1} & r_{n2} & \dots & \dots & r_{nm} \end{bmatrix}$$

where $r_{ij} = w_j * Z_{ij}$ for $i = 1, 2, ..., n$ and $j = 1, 2, ..., m$.

Step 3: Determination of the positive ideal alternative and the negative ideal alternative. We define the positive ideal alternative (PIS) as

$$Q^+ = \left\{ \left(\max_i \underline{T_{ij}}, \min_i \underline{I_{ij}}, \min_i \underline{F_{ij}} \right), \left(\min_i \overline{T_{ij}}, \max_i \overline{I_{ij}}, \max_i \overline{F_{ij}} \right) \right\} \tag{3}$$

and the negative ideal alternative(NIS) as

$$Q^- = \left\{ \left(\min_i \underline{T_{ij}}, \max_i \underline{I_{ij}}, \max_i \underline{F_{ij}} \right), \left(\max_i \overline{T_{ij}}, \min_i \overline{I_{ij}}, \min_i \overline{F_{ij}} \right) \right\} \tag{4}$$

Step 4: Calculation of distance of each alternative from PIS and NIS. The normalized Euclidean distance of each alternative $A_i (i = 1, 2, ..., n)$ from the PIS and the NIS can be calculated by using (2).

Step 5: Calculate the relative closeness coefficient. The relative closeness coefficient δ_i of each alternative $A_i (i = 1, 2, ..., n)$ can be calculated by using the formula

$$\delta_i = \frac{E(A, Q^-)}{E(A, Q^-) + E(A, Q^+)} \tag{5}$$

Step 6: *Ranking the alternatives*. Using the relative closeness coefficient of each alternative, the ranking order of all alternatives can be determined and the best alternative can be selected with the highest relative closeness coefficient value.

Step 7: End.

5. A NUMERICAL EXAMPLE

Assume that a decision maker intends to select the most suitable laptop for random use from the three initially chosen laptops (A_1, A_2, A_3) by considering four attributes namely: features C_1, reasonable price C_2, customer care C_3 and risk factor C_4. Based on the proposed approach discussed in section 5, the considered problem is solved by the following steps:

Figure 1. A flowchart of the proposed decision making method

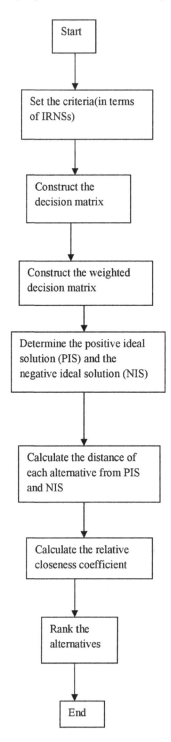

Step1: *Construct the decision matrix with interval rough neutrosophic number.* The decision maker construct the decision matrix with respect to the three alternatives and four attributes in terms of interval rough neutrosophic number.

Table 1. The Interval rough neutrosophic decision matrix

	C_1	C_2	C_3	C_4
A_1	⟨([.6, .7], [.3, .5], [.3, .4]), ([.8, .9], [.1, .3], [.1, .2])⟩	⟨([.5, .7], [.3, .4], [.1, .2]), ([.7, .9], [.3, .5], [.3, .4])⟩	⟨([.5, .6], [.4, .5], [.4, .6]), ([.7, .8], [.2, .4], [.3, .4])⟩	⟨([.8, .9], [.3, .4], [.5, .6]), ([.7, .8], [.3, .5], [.3, .5])⟩
A_2	⟨([.7, .8], [.2, .3], [.0, .2]), ([.7, .9], [.1, .2], [.1, .2]) ⟩	⟨([.6, .7], [.1, .2], [.0, .2]), ([.6, .7], [.1, .3], [.1, .3])⟩	⟨([.5, .7], [.2, .3], [.1, .2]), ([.6, .9], [.3, .5], [.2, .4])⟩	⟨([.7, .8], [.3, .5], [.1, .3]), ([.5, .7], [.5, .6], [.2, .3])⟩
A_3	⟨([.6, .7], [.3, .4], [.0, .3]), ([.6, .9], [.1, .2], [.1, .2])⟩	⟨([.5, .7], [.2, .4], [.2, .4]), ([.6, .8], [.1, .3], [.1, .2])⟩	⟨([.6, .8], [.2, .4], [.3, .4]), ([.6, .8], [.2, .5], [.3, .5])⟩	⟨([.4, .7], [.2, .4], [.4, .5]), ([.5, .8], [.2, .5], [.0, .2])⟩

Step 2: *Construction of weighted decision matrix.* The weight vectors considered by the decision maker are *0.35, 0.25, 0.25* and *0.15* respectively. The weighted decision matrix is:

Table 2. The weighted decision matrix

	C_1	C_2	C_3	C_4
S_1	⟨([0.21,0.245], [0.105,0.175], [0.105,0.14]), ([0.28,0.315], [0.035,0.105], [0.035,0.07])⟩	⟨([0.125,0.175], [0.075,0.1], [0.025,0.05]), ([0.175,0.225], [0.075,0.125], [0.075,0.1])⟩	⟨([0.125,0.15], [0.1,0.125], [0.1,0.15]), ([0.175,0.2], [0.05,0.1], [0.075,0.1])⟩	⟨([0.12,0.135], [0.045,0.06], [0.075,0.09]), ([0.105,0.12], [0.045,0.075], [0.045,0.75])⟩
S_2	⟨([0.245,0.28], [0.07,0.105], [0.0,0.07]), ([0.245,0.315], [0.035,0.07], [0.035,0.07])⟩	⟨([0.15,0.175], [0.025,0.05], [0.0,0.05]), ([0.15,0.175], [0.025,0.075], [0.025,0.075])⟩	⟨([0.125,0.175], [0.05,0.075], [0.025,0.05]), ([0.15,0.225], [0.075,0.125], [0.05,0.1])⟩	⟨([0.105,0.12], [0.045,0.75], [0.015,0.045]), ([0.075,0.105], [0.075,0.09], [0.03,0.045])⟩
S_3	⟨([0.21,0.245], [0.105,0.14], [0.0,0.105]), ([0.21,0.315], [0.035,0.7], [0.035,0.7])⟩	⟨([0.125,0.175], [0.05,0.1], [0.05,0.1]), ([0.15,0.2], [0.025,0.075], [0.025,0.05])⟩	⟨([0.15,0.2], [0.05,0.1], [0.075,0.1]), ([0.15,0.2], [0.05,0.125], [0.075,0.125])⟩	⟨([0.06,0.105], [0.03,0.06], [0.06,0.075]), ([0.075,0.12], [0.03,0.075], [0.0,0.03])⟩

Step 3: *Determination of the positive ideal alternative and the negative ideal alternative.* The positive ideal alternative and the negative ideal alternative can be calculated using (3) and (4) respectively.

The positive ideal alternative(PIS) is:

Q^+ = {⟨(([0.245, 0.28], [0.07, 0.105], [0.0, 0.07]), ([0.21, 0.315], [0.035, 0.105], [0.035, 0.07])ñ á([0.15, 0.175], [0.025, 0.05], [0.0, 0.05]), ([0.15, 0.175], [0.075, 0.125], [0.075, 0.1])ñ á([0.15, 0.2], [0.05, 0.075], [0.025, 0.05]), ([0.15, 0.2], [0.075, 0.125], [0.075, 0.125])ñ á([0.12, 0.135], [0.03, 0.06], [0.015, 0.045]), ([0.075, 0.105], [0.075, 0.09], [0.045, 0.075])⟩}

The negative ideal alternative(NIS) is:

Q^- = {⟨(([0.21, 0.245], [0.105, 0.175], [0.105, 0.140]), ([0.28, 0.315], [0.035, 0.07], [0.035, 0.07])ñ ([0.125, 0.175], [0.075, 0.1], [0.05, 0.1]), ([0.175, 0.225], [0.025, 0.075], [0.025, 0.05])ñ á([0.125, 0.15], [0.1, 0.125], [0.1, 0.15]), ([0.175, 0.225], [0.05, 0.1], [0.05, 0.1])ñ á([0.06, 0.105], [0.045, 0.075], [0.075, 0.09]), ([0.105, 0.12], [0.03, 0.075], [0.0, 0.03])⟩

Step 4: *Calculation of distance of each alternative from PIS and NIS.* The distance of each alternative from PIS and NIS can be calculated using (2).

The distance of each alternative from PIS are:

$E(A_1, Q^+)$ = 0.039031, $E(A_2, Q^+)$ = 0.01809, $E(A_3, Q^+)$ = 0.028979

The distance of each alternative from NIS are:

$E(A_1, Q^-)$ = 0.022535, $E(A_2, Q^-)$ = 0.03968, $E(A_3, Q^-)$ = 0.026829

Step 5: *Calculate the relative closeness coefficient.* The relative closeness coefficient can be calculated using (5). The relative closeness coefficient of alternative A_1, A_2, A_3 are $RC_1 = 0.366025$, $RC_2 = 0.686779$, $R C_3 = 0.480735$ respectively.

Step 6: *Ranking the alternatives.* The best alternative can be selected with the highest relative closeness coefficient value. The ranking order of all alternatives can be determined using the relative closeness coefficient of each alternative.

As from Step 5, $C_2 > C_3 > C_1$, So $A_2 > A_3 > A_1$.

Figure 2. A flowchart of the proposed decision making method for laptop selection

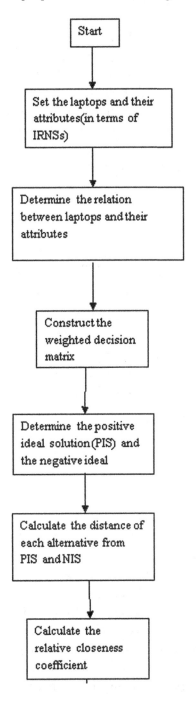

6. COMPARATIVE ANALYSIS

In this section, we compare our results with the results of the other existing decision making method for interval rough nutrosophic sets i.e. with the projection and bidirectional projection measure (Pramanik et al, 2018) and trigonometric Hamming similarity measure (Pamanik et al, 2018).

According to projection and bidirectional projection measure and trigonometric Hamming similarity measure A_1 is the best alternative. But in TOPSIS method A_2 is the best alternative.

The ranking results obtained from proposed strategies and the existing strategy is furnished in Table 3.

Table 3. Comparison analysis

Strategies	Laptops	Ranking order
Proposed strategy (based on TOPSIS)	A_1	
	A_2	$A_2 > A_3 > A_1$
	A_3	
Trigonometric Hamming similarity measure strategy[51]	A_1	
	A_2	$A_1 > A_3 > A_2$
	A_3	
Projection and Bidirectional projection measure[50]	A_1	
	A_2	$A_1 > A_2 > A_3$
	A_3	

7. CONCLUSION

In this chapter, we develop a TOPSIS strategy for solving MADM problems in IRNS environment. For this we also propose the Euclidean distance and Normalized Euclidean distance between two IRNSs. Interval rough neutrosophic positive ideal solution (PIS) and interval rough neutrosophic negative ideal solution (NIS) are also defined. Using this, we develop an algorithm and also demonstrate the algorithm by making flowcharts. An illustrative example is also provided to demonstrate the applicability and effectiveness of the developed strategy. In the decision making process, the rankings of each alternatives are presented. In the future work, the developed TOPSIS strategy can be applied to other practical problems such as brick-selection, teacher selection, weaver selection, various problems (Mondal et al, 2014; Mondal et al, 2015; Dey et al, 2015; Smarandache et al, 2018).

REFERENCES

Abdel-Basset, M., Mohamed, M., & Smarandache, F. (2018). An extension of neutrosophic AHP–SWOT analysis for strategic planning and decision-making. *Symmetry, 10*(4), 116. doi:10.3390ym10040116

Biswas, P., Pramanik, S., & Giri, B. C. (2014). Entropy based grey relational analysis method for multi-attribute decision making under single valued neutrosophic assessments. *Neutrosophic Sets and Systems, 2*, 102–110.

Biswas, P., Pramanik, S., & Giri, B. C. (2014). A new methodology for neutrosophic multi-attribute decision-making with unknown weight information. *Neutrosophic Sets and Systems, 3*, 42–50.

Biswas, P., Pramanik, S., & Giri, B. C. (2015). TOPSIS method for multi-attribute group decision-making under single valued neutrosophic environment. *Neural Computing & Applications*. doi:10.100700521-015-1891-2

Biswas, P., Pramanik, S., & Giri, B. C. (2016). Aggregation of triangular fuzzy neutrosophic set information and its application to multi-attribute decision making. *Neutrosophic Sets and Systems, 12*, 20–40.

9. Biswas, P., Pramanik, S., & Giri, B. C. (2016). Value and ambiguity index based ranking method of single-valued trapezoidal neutrosophic numbers and its application to multi-attribute decision making. *Neutrosophic Sets and Systems, 12*, 127–138.

Biswas, P., Pramanik, S., & Giri, B. C. (2018). *Multi-attribute group decision making based on expected value of neutrosophic trapezoidal numbers. In New trends in neutrosophic theory and applications* (vol. 2, pp. 103–124). Pons Editions.

Biswas, P., Pramanik, S., & Giri, B. C. (2018). Non-linear programming approach for single-valued neutrosophic TOPSIS method. *New Mathematics and Natural Computation.*

Biswas, P., Pramanik, S., & Giri, B. C. (2019). Neutrosophic TOPSIS with group decision making. In C. Kahraman & I. Otay (Eds.), Fuzzy Multicriteria Decision Making Using Neutrosophic Sets, Studies in Fuzziness and Soft Computing (vol. 369, pp. 543-585). Academic Press. doi:10.1007/978-3-030-00045-5_21

Broumi, S., & Smarandache, F. (2015). Interval neutrosophic rough sets. *Neutrosophic Sets and Systems, 7*, 23–31.

Broumi, S., Smarandache, F., & Dhar, M. (2014a). Rough neutrosophic sets. *International Journal of Pure and Applied Mathematics, 32*, 493–502.

Broumi, S., Smarandache, F., & Dhar, M. (2014b). Rough neutrosophic sets. *Neutrosophic Sets and Systems*, *3*, 60–66.

Broumi, S., Ye, J., & Smarandache, F. (2015). An extended TOPSIS method for multiple attribute decision making based on interval neutrosophic uncertain linguistic variables. *Neutrosophic Sets and Systems*, *8*, 22–31.

Chi, P., & Liu, P. (2013). An extended TOPSIS method for multi-attribute decision making problems on interval neutrosophic set. *Neutrosophic Sets and Systems*, *1*, 63–70.

Dalapati, S., Pramanik, S., Alam, S., Smarandache, S., & Roy, T. K. (2017). IN-cross entropy based MAGDM strategy under interval neutrosophic set environment. *Neutrosophic Sets and Systems*, *18*, 43–57. doi:10.5281/zenodo.1175162

Deli, I., & Subas, Y. (2016). A ranking method of single valued neutrosophic numbers and its applications to multi-attribute decision making problems. *International Journal of Machine Learning and Cybernetics*. doi:10.100713042016-0505-3

Dey, P. P., Pramanik, S., & Giri, B. C. (2015). Generalized neutrosophic soft multi-attribute group decision making basedon TOPSIS. *Critical Review*, *11*, 41–55.

Dey, P. P., Pramanik, S., & Giri, B. C. (2015). Multi-criteria group decision making in intuitionistic fuzzy environment based on grey relational analysis for weaver selection in Khadi institution. *Journal of Applied Quantitative Methods*, *10*(4), 1–14.

Dey, P. P., Pramanik, S., & Giri, B. C. (2016). Extended projection-based models for solving multiple attribute decision making problems with interval –valued neutrosophic information. In F. Smarandache & S. Pramanik (Eds.), *New trends in neutrosophic theory and applications* (pp. 127–140). Brussels: Pons Editions.

Dey, P.P., Pramanik, S., & Giri, B.C. (2016). TOPSIS for solving multi-attribute decision making problems under bipolar neutrosophic environment. *New Trends in Neutrosophic Theories and Applications*, 65-77.

Elhassouny, A., & Smarandache, F. (2016). Neutrosophic-simplified-TOPSIS multi-criteria decision-making using combined simplified-TOPSIS method and Neutrosophics. *IEEE Int. Conf. Fuzzy Syst.* 10.1109/FUZZ-IEEE.2016.7738003

Hwang, C. L., & Yoon, K. (1981). *Multiple attribute decision making: methods and applications*. New York: Springer. doi:10.1007/978-3-642-48318-9

Ji, P., Wang, J. Q., & Zhang, H. Y. (2016). Frank prioritized Bonferroni mean operator with single-valued neutrosophic sets and its application in selecting third-party logistics providers. *Neural Computing & Applications*. doi:10.100700521-016-2660-6

Kharal, A. (2014). A neutrosophic multi-criteria decision making method. *New Mathematics and Natural Computation, 10*(02), 143–162. doi:10.1142/S1793005714500070

Liang, R. X., Wang, J. Q., & Zhang, H. Y. (2017). A multi-criteria decision-making method based on single-valued trapezoidal neutrosophic preference relations with complete weight information. *Neural Computing & Applications*. doi:10.100700521-017-2925-8

Liu, P., Chu, Y., Li, Y., & Chen, Y. (2014). Some generalized neutrosophic number Hamacher aggregation operators and their application to group decision making. *International Journal of Fuzzy Systems, 16*(2), 242–255.

Liu, P., & Wang, Y. (2014). Multiple attribute decision-making method based on single-valued neutrosophic normalized weighted Bonferroni mean. *Neural Computing & Applications, 25*(7), 2001–2010. doi:10.100700521-014-1688-8

Liu, P. D., & Li, H. G. (2017). Multiple attribute decision-making method based on some normal neutrosophic Bonferroni mean operators. *Neural Computing & Applications, 28*(1), 179–194. doi:10.100700521-015-2048-z

Mondal, K., & Pramanik, S. (2014). Multi-criteria group decision making approach for teacher recruitment in higher education under simplified Neutrosophic environment. *Neutrosophic Sets and Systems, 6*, 28–34.

Mondal, K., & Pramanik, S. (2014). Intuitionistic fuzzy multicriteria group decision making approach to quality-brick selection problem. *Journal of Applied Quantitative Methods, 9*(2), 35–50.

Mondal, K., & Pramanik, S. (2015). Neutrosophic decision making model of school choice. *Neutrosophic Sets and Systems, 7*, 62–68.

Mondal, K., & Pramanik, S. (2015). Neutrosophic tangent similarity measure and its application to multiple attribute decision making. *Neutrosophic Sets and Systems, 9*, 85–92.

Mondal, K., & Pramanik, S. (2015). Rough neutrosophic multi-attribute decision-making based on grey relational analysis. *Neutrosophic Sets and Systems, 7*, 8–17.

Mondal, K., & Pramanik, S. (2015). Rough neutrosophic multi-attribute decision-making based on rough accuracy score function. *Neutrosophic Sets and Systems, 8*, 16–22.

Mondal, K., & Pramanik, S. (2015). Neutrosophic decision making model for clay-brick selection in construction field based on grey relational analysis. *Neutrosophic Sets and Systems.*, *9*, 64–71.

Mondal, K., Pramanik, S., & Giri, B. C. (2018). Single valued neutrosophic hyperbolic sine similarity measure based MADM strategy. *Neutrosophic Sets and Systems*, *20*, 3–11. doi:10.5281/zenodo.1235383

Mondal, K., Pramanik, S., & Giri, B. C. (2018). Hybrid binary logarithm similarity measure for MAGDM problems under SVNS assessments. *Neutrosophic Sets and Systems*, *20*, 12–25. doi:10.5281/zenodo.1235365

Mondal, K., Pramanik, S., & Giri, B. C. (2018). Interval neutrosophic tangent similarity measure based MADM strategy and its application to MADM problems. *Neutrosophic Sets and Systems*, *19*, 47–56.

Mondal, K., Pramanik, S., & Giri, B. C. (2019). Rough neutrosophic aggregation operators for multi-criteria decision-making. In C. Kahraman & I. Otay (Eds.), Fuzzy Multicriteria Decision Making Using Neutrosophic Sets, Studies in Fuzziness and Soft Computing (vol. 369, pp.79-105). Academic Press. doi:10.1007/978-3-030-00045-5_5

Mondal, K., Pramanik, S., & Smarandache, F. (2016). Role of neutrosophic logic in data mining. In F. Smarandache & S. Pramanik (Eds.), *New trends in neutrosophic theory and application* (pp. 15–23). Brussels, Belgium: Pons Editions.

Mondal, K., Pramanik, S., & Smarandache, F. (2016). Several trigonometric Hamming similarity measures of rough neutrosophic sets and their applications in decision making. *New Trends in Neutrosophic Theory and Applications, 1*, 93-103.

Mondal, K., Pramanik, S., & Smarandache, F. (2016). TOPSIS in rough neutrosophic environment. *Neutrosophic Sets and Systems*, *13*, 105–117.

Pawlak, Z. (1982). Rough sets. *International Journal of Information and Computer Sciences*, *11*(5), 341–356. doi:10.1007/BF01001956

Pramanik, S., Banerjee, D., & Giri, B. C. (2016). TOPSIS approach for Multi-Attribute Decision Making in Neutrosophic Environment. In F. Smarandache & S. Pramanik (Eds.), *New trends in neutrosophic theory and applications* (pp. 79–92). Brussels: Pons Editions.

Pramanik, S., Biswas, P., & Giri, B. C. (2017). Hybrid vector similarity measures and their applications to multi-attribute decision making under neutrosophic environment. *Neural Computing & Applications*, *28*(5), 1163–1176. doi:10.100700521-015-2125-3

Pramanik, S., Dalapati, S., Alam, S., Smarandache, S., & Roy, T. K. (2018). NS-cross entropy-based MAGDM under single-valued neutrosophic set environment. *Information*, *9*(2), 37. doi:10.3390/info9020037

Pramanik, S., Dalapati, S., & Roy, T. K. (2016). Logistics center location selection approach based on neutrosophic multi-criteria decision making. In F. Smarandache & S. Pramanik (Eds.), *New trends in neutrosophic theory and applications* (pp. 161–174). Brussels: Pons Editions.

Pramanik, S., Dalapati, S., & Roy, T. K. (2016). Neutrosophic multi-attribute group decision making strategy for logistics center location selection. In F. Smarandache, M. A. Basset, & V. Chang (Eds), Neutrosophic Operational Research Volume III (pp. 13-32). Brussels: Pons asbl.

Pramanik, S., Dey, P. P., & Giri, B. C. (2015). TOPSIS for singled valued soft expert set based multi-attribute decision making problems. *Neutrosophic Sets and Systems*, *10*, 88–95.

Pramanik, S., Mallick, R., & Dasgupta, A. (2018). Contributions of selected Indian researchers to multi-attribute decision making in neutrosophic environment. *Neutrosophic Sets and Systems*, *20*, 108–131.

Pramanik, S., & Mondal, K. (2015). Cosine similarity measure of rough neutrosophic sets and its application in medical diagnosis. *Global Journal of Advanced Research*, *2*(1), 212–220.

Pramanik, S., & Mondal, K. (2015). Some rough neutrosophic similarity measure and their application to multiattribute decision making. *Global Journal of Engineering Science and Research Management*, *2*(7), 61–74.

Pramanik, S., & Mondal, K. (2015). Cotangent similarity measure of rough neutrosophic sets and its application to medical diagnosis. *Journal of New Theory*, *4*, 90–102.

Pramanik, S., & Mukhopadhyaya, D. (2011). Grey relational analysis based intuitionistic fuzzy multi-criteria group decision-making approach for teacher selection in higher education. *International Journal of Computers and Applications*, *34*, 21–29.

Pramanik, S., Roy, R., & Roy, T. K. (2018). Multi criteria decision making based on projection and bidirectional projection measures of rough neutrosophic sets. In F. Smarandache & S. Pramanik (Eds.), *New trends in neutrosophic theory and applications-Vol-II* (pp. 175–187). Brussels: Pons Editions.

Pramanik, S., Roy, R., Roy, T. K., & Smarandache, F. (2018). Multi attribute decision making strategy on projection and bidirectional projection measures of interval rough neutrosophic sets. *Neutrosophic Sets and Systems*, *19*, 101–109.

Pramanik, S., Roy, R., Roy, T. K., & Smarandache, F. (2018). Multi attribute decision making based on several trigonometric hamming similarity measures under interval rough neutrosophic environment. *Neutrosophic Sets and Systems*, *19*, 110–118.

Sahin, R., & Kucuk, A. (2014). Subsethood measure for single valued neutrosophic sets. *Journal of Intelligent & Fuzzy Systems*. doi:10.3233/IFS-141304

Sahin, R., & Yigider, M. A. (2016). Multi-Criteria Neutrosophic Group Decision Making Method Based TOPSIS for Supplier Selection. *Applied Mathematics & Information Sciences*, *10*(5), 1843–1852. doi:10.18576/amis/100525

Smarandache, F. (1998). *A unifying field in logics, neutrosophy: neutrosophic probability, set and logic*. Rehoboth: AmericanResearch Press.

Smarandache, F., & Pramanik, S. (Eds.). (2018). *New trends in neutrosophic theory and applications* (Vol. 2). Brussels: Pons Editions.

Wang, H., Smarandache, F., Zhang, Y., & Sunderraman, R. (2010). Single valued neutrosophic sets. *Multi-space and Multi-structure*, *4*, 410–413.

Wang, H., Smarandache, F., Zhang, Y. Q., & Sunderraman, R. (2005). *Interval neutrosophic sets and logic: theory and applications in computing*. Phoenix, AZ: Hexis.

Ye, J. (2013). Multicriteria decision-making method using the correlation coefficient under single-valued neutrosophic environment. *International Journal of General Systems*, *42*(4), 386–394. doi:10.1080/03081079.2012.761609

Ye, J. (2013). Single valued neutrosophic cross-entropy for multi criteria decision making problems. *Applied Mathematical Modelling*, *38*(3), 1170–1175. doi:10.1016/j.apm.2013.07.020

Ye, J. (2016). Projection and bidirectional projection measures of single valued neutrosophic sets and their decision – making method for mechanical design scheme. Journal of Experimental & Theoretical Artificial Intelligence. doi:10.1080/0952813X.2016.1259263

Chapter 6
Neutrosophic Rayleigh Distribution With Some Basic Properties and Application

Muhammad Aslam
King Abdulaziz University, Saudi Arabia

ABSTRACT

The existing Rayleigh distribution under classical statistics has been widely applied for analyzing the data having all determined, certain, and precise observations. The neutrosophic statistics (NS) are the extension of classical statistics and applied under uncertainty environment. In this chapter, the authors introduce the neutrosophic Rayleigh distribution (NRD) under the NS. The proposed NRD is the generalization of the existing Rayleigh distribution. The authors give some basic properties of the proposed distribution. An application of the proposed distribution is discussed with the help of wind speed data.

INTRODUCTION

The Rayleigh distribution was originally introduced by Lord Rayleigh to study acoustics problems in Physics. Now days, this distribution has been widely used to analyze the positively skewed data in the areas of quality, reliability and engineering. Balakrishnan (1989) estimated the parameters of this distribution for the censoring data. Johnson et al. (1994) discussed the applications of the Rayleigh distribution in the reliability problems. Best et al. (2010) used the Rayleigh distribution to model the wind speed data. More applications of the Rayleigh distribution can be seen in Dhaundiyal and Singh (2016).

DOI: 10.4018/978-1-7998-2555-5.ch006

The Rayleigh distribution under classical statistics is applied when all observations or parameters are determined. As mentioned by Zadeh (1978) "when the complexity of a system increases, our aptitude to formulate precision and meaningful statements decrease up to a threshold beyond which precision and significance became mutually exclusive characteristics. The real question is whether replacing stubbornly imprecise data by fixed ones will influence our investigation or not. If you replace arbitrarily imprecise data by the fixed values in a model, you will leave no other chance to the model but churn out meaningless outcomes sometime". Therefore, when some observations or the parameters are not precise, the statistical distributions based on fuzzy logic can be applied for the estimation purpose. Pak et al. (2014b) studied the fuzzy Rayleigh distribution for the reliability analysis. Dhaundiyal and Singh (2016) used the Fuzzy Rayleigh distribution in biomass pyrolysis. Van Hecke (2018) discussed the estimation of fuzzy Rayleigh distribution. Pak et al. (2014a) provided a detailed study of the estimation of parameter of Rayleigh distribution for fuzzy lifetime data. Shafiq et al.(2017) presented a detailed work on reliability issues of distribution using the fuzzy approach. Chaturvedi et al. (2018) focused on analyzing hybrid censored data using the fuzzy approach.

The fuzzy logic considers the measure of truth and false in the analysis. The neutrosophic logic considers additional measure is called the measure of indeterminacy. The neutrosophic logic is considered as the generalized form of the fuzzy logic which measure indeterminacy, see Smarandache (2010). More information about neutrosophic logic can be seen in Nabeeh et al. (2019), Nabeeh et al. (2019) and Abdel-Basset et al. (2019). Smarandache (2014) gave the idea of descriptive neutrosophic statistics using the neutrosophic logic. The neutrosophic statistics (NS), which is the extension of classical statistics and has been widely used under uncertainty, see Smarandache (2014) and Aslam (2018b), Chen et al. (2017) and Chen et al. (2017) used neutrosophic numbers to study rock measuring problems. Alhabib et al. (2018) presented some distributions based on NS. Aslam (2018b) introduced the NS in the area of neutrosophic statistical quality control (NSQC). More applications in the areas of process control and quality control can be seen in Aslam (2018a) and Aslam (2019a).

Aslam and Arif (2018) and Aslam (2019b) introduced the neutrosophic Weibull distribution and applied them for the testing of the product purpose. They did not study the properties of the Weibull distribution. In this chapter, we will introduce the neutrosophic Rayleigh distribution. The existing Rayleigh distribution under classical statistics cannot be applied under uncertainty environment. In the reliability analysis, it is not possible to have the precise or the determined observations always. Therefore, there is a need to derive the neutrosophic Rayleigh distribution (NRD) for the estimation of such data. In this chapter, we will originally derive the NRD.

We will discuss some basic properties of the proposed NRD distribution. We will apply the proposed distribution on the wind speed data.

METHODOLOGY

In this section, we will first discuss the Rayleigh distribution under classical statistics and then we will introduce the Rayleigh distribution under neutrosophic statistics.

Suppose that a random variable X follows the Rayleigh distribution. The probability density function (pdf) and cumulative distribution function (cdf) of Rayleigh distribution under classical statistics are given by

$$f(x) = \frac{x}{\beta^2} \exp\left(-\frac{1}{2}\right)\left(\frac{x}{\beta}\right)^2 ; x \geq 0$$

$$F(x) = \left(1 - \exp-\frac{1}{2}\left(\frac{x}{\beta}\right)^2\right)$$

Suppose that $X_N = s + uI$; $X_N \in [X_L, X_L]$ where X_L and X_U are lower and upper values of the NRD be a neutrosophic Rayleigh random variable having determined part s and indeterminate part uI; $I \in [\inf I, \sup I]$. Note here that the $X_N \in [X_L, X_U]$ reduces to Rayleigh random variable under classical statistics when $X_L = X_U$. Therefore, the proposed NRD will be the generalization of the traditional Rayleigh distribution under classical Statistics (CS). The neutrosophic cumulative distribution function (ncdf) of NRD having neutrosophic scale parameter $\beta_N \in [\beta_L, \beta_U]$ is defined by

$$F(x_L, x_U) = \left[\left(1 - \exp-\frac{1}{2}\left(\frac{x_L}{\beta_L}\right)^2\right), \left(1 - \exp-\frac{1}{2}\left(\frac{x_U}{\beta_U}\right)^2\right)\right]; F(x_N) \in \left[F(x_L), F(x_U)\right]$$

$$(1)$$

It is important to note that the ncdf of NRD reduces to the Rayleigh distribution under classical statistics when $x_L = x_U$ and $\beta_L = \beta_U$.

The corresponding neutrosophic probability density function (npdf) of the NRD can be obtained as follows

$$f(x_N) = \frac{d}{dx_N} F(x_N); F(x_N) \in \left[F(x_L), F(x_U) \right] \tag{2}$$

By following (Balakrishnan, 1989), the npdf using Eq. (2) can be obtained as follows

$$f(x_L, x_U) = \left[\left(\frac{x_L}{\beta_L^2} \exp\left(-\frac{1}{2} \right) \left(\frac{x_L}{\beta_L} \right)^2 \right), \left(\left(\frac{x_U}{\beta_U^2} \exp\left(-\frac{1}{2} \right) \left(\frac{x_U}{\beta_U} \right)^2 \right) \right) \right]; f(x_N) \in \left[f(x_L), f(x_U) \right] \tag{3}$$

SOME BASIC PROPERTIES OF NRD

In this section, some basic properties of the NRD distribution given in Eq. (1) and Eq. (3) are discussed. Let $X_N \sim R_N(x_N, \beta_N)$ be the neutrosophic Rayleigh random variable.

The Neutrosophic Expected Value

The neutrosophic expected value, which is also known as, the neutrosophic average of NRD is given by

$$E(X_L, X_U) = \left[\left(\int_0^\infty x_L f(x_L) dx_L \right), \left(\int_0^\infty x_U f(x_U) dx_U \right) \right]; E(X_N) \in \left[E(X_L), E(X_U) \right] \tag{4}$$

or

$$E(X_N) = \left[\left(\int_0^\infty x_L \left(\frac{x_L}{\beta_L^2} \exp\left(-\frac{1}{2} \right) \left(\frac{x_L}{\beta_L} \right)^2 \right) dx_L \right), \left(\int_0^\infty x_U \left(\frac{x_U}{\beta_U^2} \exp\left(-\frac{1}{2} \right) \left(\frac{x_U}{\beta_U} \right)^2 \right) dx_U \right) \right] \tag{5}$$

After some simplification of Eq. (5), we have

$$E(X_N) = \left[\left(\beta_L \sqrt{\frac{\pi}{2}} \right), \left(\beta_U \sqrt{\frac{\pi}{2}} \right) \right]; E(X_N) \in \left[E(X_L), E(X_U) \right] \tag{6}$$

The Neutrosophic Variance

Using Eq. (4) and Eq. (6), the neutrosophic variance of the proposed NRD can be derived as follows

$$V(X_N) = E(X_N^2) - (E(X_N))^2 ; \ V(X_N) \epsilon \left[V(X_L), V(X_U) \right] \tag{7}$$

$$V(X_N) = \beta_N^2 \left(2 - \frac{\pi}{2} \right) \tag{8}$$

Parameters Estimation

Although several methods of estimations such as the method of moments and local frequency ratio methods are available in the literature the method of maximum likelihood estimation (MLE) is simple, see Venkatesh and Manikandan (2016). Let $x_{1N}, x_{2N}, \ldots, x_{nN}$ be a neutrosophic Rayleigh random variable. By following Venkatesh and Manikandan (2016), the neutrosophic maximum likelihood estimation (NMLE) is given as

$$f(x_N) = \frac{x_N}{\beta_N^2} \exp\left(-\frac{1}{2} \right)\left(\frac{x_N}{\beta_N} \right)^2 ; x_N \in [x_L, x_U] > 0; \beta_N \in [\beta_L, \beta_U] \tag{9}$$

The neutrosophic likelihood function is given by

$$L_N = \prod_{i=1}^{x_{nN}} f(x_N) = \prod_{i=1}^{x_{nN}} \frac{x_N}{\beta_N^2} \exp\left(-\frac{1}{2} \right)\left(\frac{x_N}{\beta_N} \right)^2 ; \beta_N \in [\beta_L, \beta_U]$$

$$\log L_N = \log\left(\prod_{i=1}^{x_{nN}} x_{nNi} \right) - 2n_N \log \beta_N - \frac{1}{2} \sum_{i=1}^{n_N} \left(\frac{x_N}{\beta_N} \right)^2 ; \beta_N \in [\beta_L, \beta_U] \tag{10}$$

Partially differentiate Eq. (10) with respect to $\beta_N \in [\beta_L, \beta_U]$, we have

$$-\frac{2n_N}{\beta_N} + \frac{\sum_{i=1}^{n_N} x_N^2}{\beta_N^3} = 0 \Rightarrow \hat{\beta}_N = \sqrt{\frac{\sum_{i=1}^{n_N} x_N^2}{2n}}; \ \hat{\beta}_N \in \left[\hat{\beta}_L, \hat{\beta}_U\right]$$ (11)

APPLICATION

In this section, we will discuss the application of the proposed distribution using wind speed data. The wind turbines are the alternative sources to produce electricity. As mentioned by Best et al. (2010) "The distribution of average daily wind speed is important in examining the feasibility of installing wind turbines and the Rayleigh distribution is a possible candidate distribution". Due to the complexity in measuring the wind speed data, it may not possible to record all observations in the data in the determined form. Therefore, while measuring the wind speed data, some imprecise observations are noted. These observations are in an interval rather than the exact value. The neutrosophic wind speed data is shown in Table 1. The neutrosophic maximum likelihood estimates (NMLE) of wind speed data is $\sigma \in [3.3272, 3.3899]$. Some neutrosophic descriptive statistics of the wind speed data are shown in Table 2. The neutrosophic Kolmogorov-Smirnov (N-KS) test is applied on wind speed data to see whether it can be modelled using the neutrosophic Rayleigh distribution. The null hypothesis is that the given neutrosophic wind speed data follows the neutrosophic Rayleigh distribution vs the alternative hypothesis that it does not follow the neutrosophic Rayleigh distribution. The neutrosophic p-value that is $p_N \in [0.14012, 0.65123]$ from the N-KS test. We note that $p_N > \alpha$, where α is the level of significance. These results show that the neutrosophic wind speed data is well fitted to the neutrosophic Rayleigh distribution with $\sigma \in [3.3272, 3.3899]$. Best et al. (2010) presented the wind speed data under classical statistics. We extended Best et al. (2010) wind speed data under neutrosophic statistics. The npdf and ncdf of the show that the wind speed data follows the neutrosophic Rayleigh distribution. The npdf and ncdf of the neutrosophic Rayleigh distribution for the wind speed data are shown in Figures 1-2.

Table 1. The neutrosophic wind speed data

[2.7,2.9]	[2.1,2.1]	[7.6,7.7]	[4.2,4.2]	[2.9,2.91]
[4.6,4.6]	[4.3,4.5]	[3.7,3.7]	[4.9,4.10]	[7.7,7.9]
[5.2,5.3]	[4.2,4.2]	[2.5,2.55]	[3.1,3.1]	[2.8,2.9]
[3.2,3.3]	[4.8,4.9]	[4.7,4.7]	[4.0,4.1]	[2.9,2.9]
[4.8,4.8]	[4.6,4.6]	[2.4,2.6]	[4.0,4.0]	[10.0,11.0]
[2.6,2.7]	[3.6,3.7]	[3.3,3.5]	[3.7,3.8]	[4.0,4.2]

Table 2. The neutrosophic descriptive statistics of wind speed data

Statistic	Value		Percentile	Value
Sample Size	[30,30]		Min	[2.1,2.1]
Range	[7.9,8.9]		5%	[2.265, 2.3475]
Mean	[4.17, 4.2487]		10%	[2.51, 2.61]
Variance	[2.9277, 3.3357]		25% (Q1)	[2.9, 2.9075]
Std. Deviation	[1.711, 1.8264]		50% (Median)	[4, 4.05]
Coef. of Variation	[0.41032, 0.42987]		75% (Q3)	[4.725, 4.625]
Std. Error	[0.31239, 0.33345]		90%	[7.36, 7.46]
Skewness	[1.8349, 2.2033]		95%	[8.735, 9.295]
Excess Kurtosis	[4.1317, 6.0326]		Max	[10, 11]

Figure 1. The npdf for the wind speed data

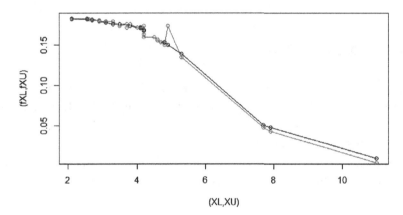

Figure 2. The ncdf for the wind speed data

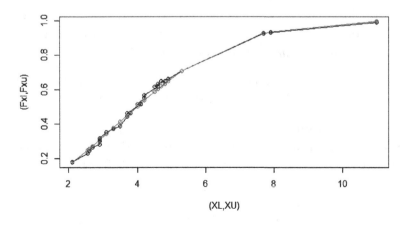

DISCUSSION AND COMPARISON

As mentioned above, the NS is the extension of CS. The descriptive neutrosophic statistics for wind speed data is shown in Table 2. From Table 2, we note that under uncertainty the mean can be from 4.17 to 4.24, the range can be from 7.9 to 8.9, the variance can be from 2.92 to 3.33 and skewness can be expected from 1.83 to 2.20. The 50% percentile shows that 50% values are above and 50% values are below from 4 to 4.05. Similarly, NMLE for $\sigma \in [3.3272, 3.3899]$ shows that under uncertainty, the unknown value of σ can be from 3.32 to 3.38. These neutrosophic descriptive statistics reduces to traditional descriptive statistics when no fuzzy or vogues observations are recorded. For example, when all observations are determined the MLE of the wind speed data is 3.32. By comparing the results of the proposed neutrosophic Rayleigh distribution with Rayleigh distribution under classical statistics, we conclude that the proposed NRD is more flexible, informative and adequate to be applied under uncertainty.

CONCLUDING REMARKS

In this paper, we introduced the neutrosophic Rayleigh distribution (NRD) under the NS. The proposed NRD is the generalization of the existing Rayleigh distribution. We discussed some basic properties of the proposed distribution. From the comparison, we conclude that the proposed neutrosophic Rayleigh distribution is an effective and adequate model for uncertainty environment. We will work for other distribution such as the Weibull distribution and generalized exponential distribution as future work.

REFERENCES

Abdel-Basset, M., Nabeeh, N. A., El-Ghareeb, H. A., & Aboelfetouh, A. (2019). Utilising neutrosophic theory to solve transition difficulties of IoT-based enterprises. *Enterprise Information Systems*, 1–21. doi:10.1080/17517575.2019.1633690

Alhabib, R., Ranna, M. M., Farah, H., & Salama, A. (2018). Some Neutrosophic Probability Distributions. *Neutrosophic Sets and Systems*, 30.

Aslam, M. (2018a). Design of Sampling Plan for Exponential Distribution under Neutrosophic Statistical Interval Method. *IEEE Access: Practical Innovations, Open Solutions*, 6, 64153–64158. doi:10.1109/ACCESS.2018.2877923

Aslam, M. (2018b). A New Sampling Plan Using Neutrosophic Process Loss Consideration. *Symmetry*, *10*(5), 132. doi:10.3390ym10050132

Aslam, M. (2019a). Attribute Control Chart Using the Repetitive Sampling under Neutrosophic System. *IEEE Access: Practical Innovations, Open Solutions*.

Aslam, M. (2019b). A new failure-censored reliability test using neutrosophic statistical interval method. *International Journal of Fuzzy Systems*, *21*(4), 1214–1220. doi:10.100740815-018-0588-y

Aslam, M., & Arif, O. (2018). Testing of Grouped Product for the Weibull Distribution Using Neutrosophic Statistics. *Symmetry*, *10*(9), 403. doi:10.3390ym10090403

Balakrishnan, N. (1989). Approximate MLE of the scale parameter of the Rayleigh distribution with censoring. *IEEE Transactions on Reliability*, *38*(3), 355–357. doi:10.1109/24.44181

Best, D. J., Rayner, J. C., & Thas, O. (2010). Easily applied tests of fit for the Rayleigh distribution. *Sankhya B*, *72*(2), 254–263. doi:10.100713571-011-0011-2

Chaturvedi, A., Singh, S. K., & Singh, U. (2018). Statistical Inferences of Type-II Progressively Hybrid Censored Fuzzy Data with Rayleigh Distribution. *Austrian Journal of Statistics*, *47*(3), 40–62. doi:10.17713/ajs.v47i3.752

Chen, J., Ye, J., & Du, S. (2017). Scale effect and anisotropy analyzed for neutrosophic numbers of rock joint roughness coefficient based on neutrosophic statistics. *Symmetry*, *9*(10), 208. doi:10.3390ym9100208

Chen, J., Ye, J., Du, S., & Yong, R. (2017). Expressions of rock joint roughness coefficient using neutrosophic interval statistical numbers. *Symmetry*, *9*(7), 123. doi:10.3390ym9070123

Dhaundiyal, A., & Singh, S. B. (2016). Application of Fuzzy Rayleigh Distribution in the Nonisothermal Pyrolysis of Loose Biomass. *Acta Environmentalica Universitatis Comenianae*, *24*(2), 14–22. doi:10.1515/aeuc-2016-0008

Johnson, N. L., Kotz, S., & Balakrishnan, N. (1994). Continuous univariate distributions (Vol. 1). Academic Press.

Nabeeh, N. A., Abdel-Basset, M., El-Ghareeb, H. A., & Aboelfetouh, A. (2019). Neutrosophic multi-criteria decision making approach for iot-based enterprises. *IEEE Access: Practical Innovations, Open Solutions*, *7*, 59559–59574. doi:10.1109/ACCESS.2019.2908919

Nabeeh, N. A., Smarandache, F., Abdel-Basset, M., El-Ghareeb, H. A., & Aboelfetouh, A. (2019). An integrated neutrosophic-topsis approach and its application to personnel selection: A new trend in brain processing and analysis. *IEEE Access: Practical Innovations, Open Solutions, 7*, 29734–29744. doi:10.1109/ACCESS.2019.2899841

Pak, A., Parham, G. A., & Saraj, M. (2014a). Inference for the Rayleigh distribution based on progressive Type-II fuzzy censored data. *Journal of Modern Applied Statistical Methods; JMASM, 13*(1), 19. doi:10.22237/jmasm/1398917880

Pak, A., Parham, G. A., & Saraj, M. (2014b). Reliability estimation in Rayleigh distribution based on fuzzy lifetime data. *International Journal of System Assurance Engineering and Management, 5*(4), 487–494. doi:10.100713198-013-0190-5

Shafiq, M., Atif, M., & Viertl, R. (2017). Parameter and reliability estimation of three-parameter lifetime distributions for fuzzy life times. *Advances in Mechanical Engineering, 9*(8), 1687814017716887. doi:10.1177/1687814017716887

Smarandache, F. (2010). Neutrosophic Logic-A Generalization of the Intuitionistic Fuzzy Logic. *Multispace & Multistructure. Neutrosophic Transdisciplinarity, 4*, 396.

Smarandache, F. (2014). *Introduction to neutrosophic statistics*. Infinite Study.

Van Hecke, T. (2018). Fuzzy parameter estimation of the Rayleigh distribution. *Journal of Statistics and Management Systems, 21*(7), 1391–1400. doi:10.1080/0 9720510.2018.1519162

Zadeh, L. A. (1978). Fuzzy sets as a basis for a theory of possibility. *Fuzzy Sets and Systems, 1*(1), 3–28. doi:10.1016/0165-0114(78)90029-5

Chapter 7

New Similarity Measure Between Single-Valued Neutrosophic Sets and Decision-Making Applications in Professional Proficiencies

Memet Şahin
Gaziantep University, Turkey

Abdullah Kargın
Gaziantep University, Turkey

ABSTRACT

In this study, a new similarity measure for single valued neutrosophic numbers is defined. It is shown that this new similarity measure satisfies the conditions of similarity measure. This new similarity measure is used to assess professional proficiencies. In making this assessment, it is assumed that there is an imaginary ideal worker, and the authors determined the criteria of this ideal worker. Then, the rate of similarity of each worker to the ideal worker is determined with the new similarity measure. Thus, with the help of the new similarity measure, a more objective professional proficiency assessment is made.

DOI: 10.4018/978-1-7998-2555-5.ch007

1 INTRODUCTION

There are many uncertainties in daily life. The logic of classical mathematics is often insufficient to explain these uncertainties. Because it is not always possible to call a situation or event absolutely right or wrong. For example, we cannot always call the weather cold or hot. It can be hot for some, cold for some and cool for others. Similar situations in which we remain indecisive may appear in the professional proficiency assessment. It is often difficult to determine whether a work done or a product produced is always definite good or definite bad. Such a situation reduces the reliability of evaluating professional proficiencies. In order to cope with these uncertainties, Smarandache (1999) defined the concept of neutrosophic logic and neutrosophic set. In the concept of neutrosophic logic and neutrosophic sets, there is T degree of membership, I degree of undeterminacy and F degree of non-membership. These degrees are defined independently of each other. A neutrosophic value is shown by (T, I, F). In other words, a condition is handled according to both its accuracy and its inaccuracy and its uncertainty. Therefore, neutrosophic logic and neutrosophic set help us to explain many uncertainties in our lives. In addition, many researchers have made studies on this theory (Şahin M., Kargın A., 2019a; Olgun N., Çelik M., 2019; Şahin M., Kargın A, 2019b; Şahin M., Kargın A., 2019c; Smarandache F., Ali M., 2016; Şahin M., Kargın A., 2019d; Şahin M., Kargın A., 2019e; Uluçay V., Şahin M., Hassan N., 2018; Uluçay V., Kiliç A., Yildiz I., Sahin M. 2018; Ulucay V., Şahin M., Olgun N. 2018; Şahin M., Olgun N., Kargın A., Uluçay V. 2018; Liu P., Shi L. 2015a; Liu P., Shi L. 2015b; Liu P., Tang G. 2016a; Liu P., Tang G. 2016b; Liu P., Wang Y. 2016; Liu P., Teng F. 2015; Liu P., Zhang L., Liu X., Wang P. 2016; Sahin M., Deli I., Ulucay V., 2016; Şahin M., Kargın A., 2017; Smarandache F., Şahin M., Kargın A., 2018; Hassan N., Uluçay, V., Şahin M. 2018; Şahin M., Kargın A., Çoban M. A., 2018; Şahin M., Kargın A., 2018; Şahin, M., Uluçay, V., Olgun, N., & Kilicman A., 2017). In fact, in the concept of fuzzy logic and fuzzy sets (Zadeh A. L., 1965), there is only a degree of membership. In addition, the concept of intuitionistic fuzzy logic and intuitionistic fuzzy set (Atanassov T. K., 1986) includes membership degree, degree of undeterminacy and degree of non-membership. But these degrees are defined dependently of each other. Therefore, neutrosophic set is a generalized state of fuzzy and intuitionistic fuzzy set. Also, single valued neutrosophic set (Wang H., Smarandache F., Zhang Y. Q., Sunderraman R., 2010) is a special set of neutrosophic sets. In single valued neutrosophic set, values of membership, indeterminacy and non – membership are in the [0, 1] closed interval. Similarity measure is a measure of how similar other entities look to an asset whose properties are known. The performance of a human being, a cancer cell, a machine can be an example of the entities we are talking about. For example, by comparing the properties of a tissue known to carry definite disease to other tissues suspected to be disease, it can be found which tissue is similar to the diseased tissue. Thus, a decision can be made as to whether the suspicious tissues carry this disease. Furthermore, many researchers have made studies on similarity measure. Recently; a new similarity measure on single valued neutrosophic sets and applications to pattern recognition (Şahin M., Olgun N., Uluçay V., Kargın A., Smarandache F., 2017); some new generalized aggregation operators based on centroid single valued triangular neutrosophic numbers and their applications (Şahin M., Ecemiş O., Uluçay V., Kargın A., 2017); similarity measures in neutrosophic sets-I (Chatterjee R., Majumdar P., Samanta S. K. 2019); similarity measures of single valued neutrosophic rough sets (Mohana K., Mohanasundari M. 2019); word-level neutrosophic sentiment similarity (Smarandache F., et al., 2019) and similarity measures between interval neutrosophic sets and their applications (Ye J., 2014) were obtained.

In this study, we compared the flawless characteristics of an imaginary ideal worker with the proficiency of the workers with a measure of similarity and determine how similar the workers are to the ideal worker.

2. PRELIMINARIES

Definition 2.1: (Smarandache F., 1999) Let U be a universe of discourse. The neutrosophic set A is an object having the farm $A = \{(x: T_{A(x)}, I_{A(x)}, F_{A(x)}), x \in U\}$. Where the functions $T:U \rightarrow]0^-,1^+[$, $I:U \rightarrow]0^-,1^+[$ and $F:U \rightarrow]0^-,1^+[$ respectively the degree of membership, the degree of indeterminacy and degree of non-membership of the element $x \in U$ to the set A with the condition $0^- \leq T_{A(x)} + I_{A(x)} + F_{A(x)} \leq 3^+$.

Definition 2.2: (Wang H., Smarandache F., Zhang Y. Q., Sunderraman R., 2010) Let U be a universe of discourse. The single neutrosophic set A is an object having the farm $A = \{(x: T_{A(x)}, I_{A(x)}, F_{A(x)}), x \in U\}$. Where the functions $T:U \rightarrow [0, 1]$, $I:U \rightarrow [0, 1]$ and $F:U \rightarrow [0, 1]$ respectively the degree of membership, the degree of indeterminacy and degree of non-membership of the element $x \in U$ to the set A with the condition $0 \leq T_{A(x)} + I_{A(x)} + F_{A(x)} \leq 0$.

For convenience we can simply use x = (T, I, F) to represent an element x in SVNS, and element x can be called a single valued neutrosophic number.

Definition 2.3: (Wang H., Smarandache F., Zhang Y. Q., Sunderraman R., 2010) Let $A = \{(x: \langle T_{A(x)}, I_{A(x)}, F_{A(x)} \rangle)\}$ and $B = \{(x: \langle T_{B(x)}, I_{B(x)}, F_{B(x)} \rangle)\}$ be two single valued neutrosophic sets. If $A = B$, then $T_{A(x)} < T_{B(x)}$, $I_{A(x)} < I_{B(x)}$, $F_{A(x)} < F_{B(x)}$.

Definition 2.4: (Wang H., Smarandache F., Zhang Y. Q., Sunderraman R., 2010)
Let A={ (x: $\langle T_{A(x)}, I_{A(x)}, F_{A(x)} \rangle$)} and B={ (x: $\langle T_{B(x)}, I_{B(x)}, F_{B(x)} \rangle$)} be two single valued neutrosophic sets. If A<B, then $T_{A(x)} < T_{B(x)}$, $I_{A(x)} < I_{B(x)}$, $F_{A(x)}$ $F_{B(x)}$.

Property 2.5: (Ye J., 2014) Let A={ (x: $\langle T_{A(x)}, I_{A(x)}, F_{A(x)} \rangle$)} and B={ (x: $\langle T_{B(x)}, I_{B(x)}, F_{B(x)} \rangle$)} be two single valued neutrosophic sets and S(A, B) be a similarity measure for single valued neutrosophic sets. S(A, B) is satisfies the following properties.

i) $0 \leq SN(A_1, A_2) \leq 1$

ii) $SN(A_1, A_2) = SN(A_1, A_2)$

iii) $S_N(A_1, A_2) = 1$ if and only if $A_1 = A_2$.

iv)   If $A_1 \leq A_2 \leq A_3$, then $S_N(A_1, A_3) \leq S_N(A_2, A_3)$.

3. A NEW SIMILARITY MEASURE FOR SINGLE VALUED NEUTROSOPHIC NUMBERS

Definition 3.1: Let $A_1 = \langle T_1, I_1, F_1 \rangle$ and $A_2 = \langle T_2, I_2, F_2 \rangle$ two single valued neutrosophic numbers.

$$S_N(A_1, A_2) =$$

$$1 - 2/3 \left\{ \frac{min\left\{ \left| 3(T_1 - T_2) - 2(F_1 - F_2) \right|, \left| F_1 - F_2 \right| \right\}}{\left\{ max\left\{ \left| 3(T_1 - T_2) - 2(F_1 - F_2) \right|, \left| F_1 - F_2 \right| \right\} / 5 \right\} + 1} \right.$$

$$+ \frac{min\left\{ \left| 4(T_1 - T_2) - 3(I_1 - I_2) \right|, \left| I_1 - I_2 \right| \right\}}{\left\{ max\left\{ \left| 4(T_1 - T_2) - 3(I_1 - I_2) \right|, \left| I_1 - I_2 \right| \right\} / 7 \right\} + 1}$$

$$\left. + \frac{min\left\{ \left| 5(T_1 - T_2) - 2(F_1 - F_2) - 3(I_1 - I_2) \right|, \left| T_1 - T_2 \right| \right\}}{\left\{ max\left\{ \left| 5(T_1 - T_2) - 2(F_1 - F_2) - 3(I_1 - I_2) \right|, \left| T_1 - T_2 \right| \right\} / 10 \right\} + 1} \right\}$$

is a similarity measure for single valued neutrosophic numbers.

Theorem 3.2: Let S_N be a similarity measure for single valued neutrosophic numbers. S_N is satisfies the following properties in Properties 2.5.

i) $0 \leq S_N(A_1, A_2) \leq 1$

ii) $S_N(A_1, A_2) = S_N(A_2, A_1)$

iii) $S_N(A_1, A_2) = 1$ if and only if $A_1 = A_2$.

iv)   If $A_1 \leq A_2 \leq A_3$, then $S_N(A_1, A_3) \leq S_N(A_2, A_3)$.

Proof: i) Since A_1 and A_2 are single valued neutrosophic numbers, we obtain

$$\max\left\{\frac{\min\left\{\left|3(T_1-T_2)-2\left(F_1-F_2\right)\right|,\left|F_1-F_2\right|\right\}}{\left\{\max\left\{\left|3(T_1-T_2)-2\left(F_1-F_2\right)\right|,\left|F_1-F_2\right|\right\}/5\right\}+1}\right\}=\tfrac{1}{2},$$

$$\min\left\{\frac{\min\left\{\left|3(T_1-T_2)-2\left(F_1-F_2\right)\right|,\left|F_1-F_2\right|\right\}}{\left\{\max\left\{\left|3(T_1-T_2)-2\left(F_1-F_2\right)\right|,\left|F_1-F_2\right|\right\}/5\right\}+1}\right\}=0,$$

$$\max\left\{\frac{\min\left\{\left|4(T_1-T_2)-3\left(I_1-I_2\right)\right|,\left|I_1-I_2\right|\right\}}{\left\{\max\left\{\left|4(T_1-T_2)-3\left(I_1-I_2\right)\right|,\left|I_1-I_2\right|\right\}/7\right\}+1}\right\}=\tfrac{1}{2},$$

$$\min\left\{\frac{\min\left\{\left|4(T_1-T_2)-3\left(I_1-I_2\right)\right|,\left|I_1-I_2\right|\right\}}{\left\{\max\left\{\left|4(T_1-T_2)-3\left(I_1-I_2\right)\right|,\left|I_1-I_2\right|\right\}/7\right\}+1}\right\}=0,$$

$$\max\left\{\frac{\min\left\{\left|5(T_1-T_2)-2\left(F_1-F_2\right)-3\left(I_1-I_2\right)\right|,\left|T_1-T_2\right|\right\}}{\left\{\max\left\{\left|5(T_1-T_2)-2\left(F_1-F_2\right)-3\left(I_1-I_2\right)\right|,\left|T_1-T_2\right|\right\}/10\right\}+1}\right\}=1/2,$$

$$\min\left\{\frac{\min\left\{\left|5(T_1-T_2)-2\left(F_1-F_2\right)-3\left(I_1-I_2\right)\right|,\left|T_1-T_2\right|\right\}}{\left\{\max\left\{\left|5(T_1-T_2)-2\left(F_1-F_2\right)-3\left(I_1-I_2\right)\right|,\left|T_1-T_2\right|\right\}/10\right\}+1}\right\}=0.$$

Thus, it is clear that

$\min\{S_N(A_1,A_2)\} = 1 - 2/3(1/2 + 1/2 + 1/2) = 1- 1 = 0.$

$\max\{S_N(A_1,A_2)\} = 1 - 2/3(0+0+0) = 1- 0 = 1.$

Therefore, we obtain $0 \leq S_N(A_1,A_2) \leq 1$.

ii) $S_N(A_1, A_2)$

$=1\text{-}2/3$

$$\left\{ \frac{min\left\{\left|3(T_1-T_2)-2\left(F_1-F_2\right)\right|,\left|F_1-F_2\right|\right\}}{\left\{max\left\{\left|3(T_1-T_2)-2\left(F_1-F_2\right)\right|,\left|F_1-F_2\right|\right\}/5\right\}+1} + \frac{min\left\{\left|4(T_1-T_2)-3\left(I_1-I_2\right)\right|,\left|I_1-I_2\right|\right\}}{\left\{max\left\{\left|4(T_1-T_2)-3\left(I_1-I_2\right)\right|,\left|I_1-I_2\right|\right\}/7\right\}+1} \right.$$

$$\left. + \frac{min\left\{\left|5(T_1-T_2)-2\left(F_1-F_2\right)-3\left(I_1-I_2\right)\right|,\left|T_1-T_2\right|\right\}}{\left\{max\left\{\left|5(T_1-T_2)-2\left(F_1-F_2\right)-3\left(I_1-I_2\right)\right|,\left|T_1-T_2\right|\right\}/10\right\}+1} \right\}$$

$= 1\text{-}2/3$

$$\left\{ \frac{min\left\{\left|-[3(T_1-T_2)-2\left(F_1-F_2\right)]\right|,\left|-(F_1-F_2)\right|\right\}}{\left\{max\left\{\left|-[3(T_1-T_2)-2\left(F_1-F_2\right)]\right|,\left|-(F_1-F_2)\right|\right\}/5\right\}+1} \right.$$

$$+ \frac{min\left\{\left|-[4(T_1-T_2)-3\left(I_1-I_2\right)]\right|,\left|-(I_1-I_2)\right|\right\}}{\left\{max\left\{\left|-[4(T_1-T_2)-3\left(I_1-I_2\right)]\right|,\left|-(I_1-I_2)\right|\right\}/7\right\}+1}$$

$$\left. + \frac{min\left\{\left|-[5(T_1-T_2)-2\left(F_1-F_2\right)-3\left(I_1-I_2\right)]\right|,\left|-(T_1-T_2)\right|\right\}}{\left\{max\left\{\left|-[5(T_1-T_2)-2\left(F_1-F_2\right)-3\left(I_1-I_2\right)]\right|,\left|-(T_1-T_2)\right|\right\}/10\right\}+1} \right\}$$

$= 1\text{-}2/3$

$$\left\{ \frac{min\left\{\left|3(T_2-T_1)-2\left(F_2-F_1\right)\right|,\left|F_2-F_1\right|\right\}}{\left\{max\left\{\left|3(T_2-T_1)-2\left(F_2-F_1\right)\right|,\left|F_2-F_1\right|\right\}/5\right\}+1} + \frac{min\left\{\left|4(T_2-T_1)-3\left(I_2-I_1\right)\right|,\left|I_2-I_1\right|\right\}}{\left\{max\left\{\left|4(T_2-T_1)-3\left(I_2-I_1\right)\right|,\left|I_2-I_1\right|\right\}/7\right\}+1} \right.$$

$$\left. + \frac{min\left\{\left|5(T_2-T_1)-2\left(F_2-F_1\right)-3\left(I_2-I_1\right)\right|,\left|T_2-T_1\right|\right\}}{\left\{max\left\{\left|5(T_2-1)-2\left(F_2-F_1\right)-3\left(I_2-I_1\right)\right|,\left|T_2-T_1\right|\right\}/10\right\}+1} \right\}$$

$= S_N\left(A_2, A_1\right).$

iii) $\Rightarrow$: Since $S_N\left(A_1, A_2\right)$

$= 1\text{-}2/3$

$$\left\{ \frac{min\left\{\left|3(T_1-T_2)-2\left(F_1-F_2\right)\right|,\left|F_1-F_2\right|\right\}}{\left\{max\left\{\left|3(T_1-T_2)-2\left(F_1-F_2\right)\right|,\left|F_1-F_2\right|\right\}/5\right\}+1} + \frac{min\left\{\left|4(T_1-T_2)-3\left(I_1-I_2\right)\right|,\left|I_1-I_2\right|\right\}}{\left\{max\left\{\left|4(T_1-T_2)-3\left(I_1-I_2\right)\right|,\left|I_1-I_2\right|\right\}/7\right\}+1} \right.$$

$$\left. + \frac{min\left\{\left|5(T_1-T_2)-2\left(F_1-F_2\right)-3\left(I_1-I_2\right)\right|,\left|T_1-T_2\right|\right\}}{\left\{max\left\{\left|5(T_1-T_2)-2\left(F_1-F_2\right)-3\left(I_1-I_2\right)\right|,\left|T_1-T_2\right|\right\}/10\right\}+1} \right\} = 1$$

it is clear that

$$\left\{ \frac{min\left\{\left|3(T_1 - T_2) - 2(F_1 - F_2)\right|, \left|F_1 - F_2\right|\right\}}{\left\{max\left\{\left|3(T_1 - T_2) - 2(F_1 - F_2)\right|, \left|F_1 - F_2\right|\right\} / 5\right\} + 1} + \frac{min\left\{\left|4(T_1 - T_2) - 3(I_1 - I_2)\right|, \left|I_1 - I_2\right|\right\}}{\left\{max\left\{\left|4(T_1 - T_2) - 3(I_1 - I_2)\right|, \left|I_1 - I_2\right|\right\} / 7\right\} + 1} \right.$$

$$\left. + \frac{min\left\{\left|5(T_1 - T_2) - 2(F_1 - F_2) - 3(I_1 - I_2)\right|, \left|T_1 - T_2\right|\right\}}{\left\{max\left\{\left|5(T_1 - T_2) - 2(F_1 - F_2) - 3(I_1 - I_2)\right|, \left|T_1 - T_2\right|\right\} / 10\right\} + 1} \right\} = 0$$

Thus, we obtain

$$\frac{min\left\{\left|3(T_1 - T_2) - 2(F_1 - F_2)\right|, \left|F_1 - F_2\right|\right\}}{\left\{max\left\{\left|3(T_1 - T_2) - 2(F_1 - F_2)\right|, \left|F_1 - F_2\right|\right\} / 5\right\} + 1} = 0,$$

$$\frac{min\left\{\left|4(T_1 - T_2) - 3(I_1 - I_2)\right|, \left|I_1 - I_2\right|\right\}}{\left\{max\left\{\left|4(T_1 - T_2) - 3(I_1 - I_2)\right|, \left|I_1 - I_2\right|\right\} / 7\right\} + 1} = 0,$$

$$\frac{min\left\{\left|5(T_1 - T_2) - 2(F_1 - F_2) - 3(I_1 - I_2)\right|, \left|T_1 - T_2\right|\right\}}{\left\{max\left\{\left|5(T_1 - T_2) - 2(F_1 - F_2) - 3(I_1 - I_2)\right|, \left|T_1 - T_2\right|\right\} / 10\right\} + 1} = 0.$$

Therefore, we can take

$$min\left\{\left|3(T_1 - T_2) - 2(F_1 - F_2)\right|, \left|F_1 - F_2\right|\right\} = 0,$$

$$min\left\{\left|4(T_1 - T_2) - 3(I_1 - I_2)\right|, \left|I_1 - I_2\right|\right\} = 0,$$

$$min\left\{\left|5(T_1 - T_2) - 2(F_1 - F_2) - 3(I_1 - I_2)\right|, \left|T_1 - T_2\right|\right\} = 0.$$

Now, let's write all the cases that can make these statements 0 separately.

a) We take the following equalities

$$3(T_1 - T_2) - 2(F_1 - F_2) = 0, \tag{1}$$

135

$$4(T_1 - T_2) - 3(I_1 - I_2) = 0, \tag{2}$$

$$5(T_1 - T_2) - 2(F_1 - F_2) - 3(I_1 - I_2) = 0. \tag{3}$$

From (1), we obtain $3(T_1 - T_2) = 2(F_1 - F_2)$. Thus, from (3), we can take $2(T_1 - T_2) - 3(I_1 - I_2) = 0$. Finally, from (2), we obtain $(T_1 - T_2) = (I_1 - I_2) = 0$ and $(F_1 - F_2) = 0$. Thus, $T_1 = T_2$, $I_1 = I_2$ and $F_1 = F_2$. Also, from Definition 2.3, we obtain $A_1 = A_2$.

b)   We take the following equalities

$$T_1 - T_2 = 0, \tag{4}$$

$$I_1 - I_2 = 0, \tag{5}$$

$$F_1 - F_2 = 0. \tag{6}$$

From (4), (5) and (6); we obtain $T_1 = T_2$, $I_1 = I_2$ and $F_1 = F_2$. From Definition 2.3, we obtain $A_1 = A_2$.

c)   We take the following equalities

$$3(T_1 - T_2) - 2(F_1 - F_2) = 0, \tag{7}$$

$$4(T_1 - T_2) - 3(I_1 - I_2) = 0, \tag{8}$$

$$T_1 - T_2 = 0. \tag{9}$$

It is clear that $T_1 - T_2 = (I_1 - I_2) = (F_1 - F_2) = 0$, from (7), (8) and (9). Thus, we obtain $T_1 = T_2$, $I_1 = I_2$ and $F_1 = F_2$. Also, from Definition 2.3, we obtain $A_1 = A_2$.

d)   We take the following equalities

$$3(T_1 - T_2) - 2(F_1 - F_2) = 0, \tag{10}$$

$$I_1 - I_2 = 0, \tag{11}$$

$$5(T_1 - T_2) - 2(F_1 - F_2) - 3(I_1 - I_2) = 0. \tag{12}$$

Since $(I_1-I_2) = 0$ in (11), we can take $4(T_1-T_2) - 2(F_1-F_2) = 0$ in (12). Thus, we obtain $(T_1-T_2) = (F_1-F_2) = 0$ from (10). Therefore, we can take $T_1=T_2$, $I_1=I_2$ and $F_1=F_2$. Also, from Definition 2.3, we obtain $A_1=A_2$.

e)   We take the following equalities

$$F_1-F_2 = 0, \tag{13}$$

$$4(T_1-T_2) - 3(I_1-I_2) = 0, \tag{14}$$

$$5(T_1-T_2) - 2(F_1-F_2) - 3(I_1-I_2) = 0. \tag{15}$$

Since $(F_1-F_2) = 0$ in (13), we can take $5(T_1-T_2) - 3(I_1-I_2) = 0$. Thus, from (14), we obtain $(T_1-T_2) = (I_1-I_2) = 0$. Therefore, we can take $T_1=T_2$, $I_1=I_2$ and $F_1=F_2$. Also, from Definition 2.3, we obtain $A_1=A_2$.

f)   We take the following equalities

$$(F_1-F_2) = 0, \tag{16}$$

$$(I_1-I_2) = 0, \tag{17}$$

$$5(T_1-T_2) - 2(F_1-F_2) - 3(I_1-I_2) = 0. \tag{18}$$

From (16) and (17), we obtain $I_1-I_2=F_1-F_2 = 0$. Thus, we can take $5(T_1-T_2) = 0$ in (18). Therefore, we can take $T_1=T_2$, $I_1=I_2$ and $F_1=F_2$. Also, from Definition 2.3, we obtain $A_1=A_2$.

g)   We take the following equalities

$$(F_1-F_2) = 0, \tag{19}$$

$$4(T_1-T_2) - 3(I_1-I_2) = 0, \tag{20}$$

$$(T_1-T_2) = 0. \tag{21}$$

From (19) and (21), we obtain $F_1-F_2=T_1-T_2 = 0$. Thus, we can take $3(I_1-I_2) = 0$ in (20). Therefore, we can take $T_1=T_2$, $I_1=I_2$ and $F_1=F_2$. Also, from Definition 2.3, we obtain $A_1=A_2$.

h)   We take the following equalities

$$3(T_1-T_2) - 2(F_1-F_2) = 0, \tag{22}$$

$$(I_1-I_2) = 0, \tag{23}$$

$$(T_1-T_2) = 0. \tag{24}$$

From (23) and (24), we obtain $(T_1-T_2) = (I_1-I_2) = 0$. Thus, we can take $2(F_1-F_2) = 0$ in (22). Therefore, we can take $T_1=T_2$, $I_1=I_2$ and $F_1=F_2$. Also, from Definition 2.3, we obtain $A_1=A_2$.

$\Leftarrow$: Let $A_1=A_2$. From Definition 2.3, we obtain $T_1=T_2$, $I_1=I_2$ and $F_1=F_2$. Thus, we can take $S_N (A_1, A_2)$

$=1-2/3$

$$\left\{ \frac{min\left\{\left|3(T_1 - T_1) - 2\left(F_1 - F_1\right)\right|, \left|F_1 - F_1\right|\right\}}{\left\{max\left\{\left|3(T_1 - T_2) - 2\left(F_1 - F_2\right)\right|, \left|F_1 - F_2\right|\right\}/5\right\}+1} + \frac{min\left\{\left|4(T_1 - T_1) - 3\left(I_1 - I_1\right)\right|, \left|I_1 - I_1\right|\right\}}{\left\{max\left\{\left|4(T_1 - T_1) - 3\left(I_1 - I_1\right)\right|, \left|I_1 - I_1\right|\right\}/7\right\}+1} \right.$$
$$\left. + \frac{min\left\{\left|5(T_1 - T_1) - 2\left(F_1 - F_1\right) - 3\left(I_1 - I_1\right)\right|, \left|T_1 - T_1\right|\right\}}{\left\{max\left\{\left|5(T_1 - T_1) - 2\left(F_1 - F_1\right) - 3\left(I_1 - I_1\right)\right|, \left|T_1 - T_1\right|\right\}/10\right\}+1} \right\} = 0$$

iv) Let $A_1\leq A_2\leq A_3$. From Definition 2.4, we can take $T_1\leq T_2\leq T_3$, $I_1\geq I_2\geq I_3$ and $F_1\geq F_2\geq F_3$. Thus,

$$min\left\{\left|3(T_1 - T_3) - 2\left(F_1 - F_3\right)\right|, \left|F_1 - F_3\right|\right\} \leq 1,$$

$$\left\{max\left\{\left|3(T_1 - T_3) - 2\left(F_1 - F_3\right)\right|, \left|F_1 - F_3\right|\right\}/5\right\} \leq 1,$$

$$min\left\{\left|3(T_2 - T_3) - 2\left(F_2 - F_3\right)\right|, \left|F_2 - F_3\right|\right\} \leq 1,$$

$$\left\{max\left\{\left|3(T_2 - T_3) - 2\left(F_2 - F_3\right)\right|, \left|F_2 - F_3\right|\right\}/5\right\} \leq 1$$

and

138

$$\min\left\{\left|3(T_1-T_3)-2\left(F_1-F_3\right)\right|,\left|F_1-F_3\right|\right\} \geq \min\left\{\left|3(T_2-T_3)-2\left(F_2-F_3\right)\right|,\left|F_2-F_3\right|\right\},$$

$$\left\{\max\left\{\left|3(T_1-T_3)-2\left(F_1-F_3\right)\right|,\left|F_1-F_3\right|\right\}/5\right\} \geq \left\{max\left\{\left|3(T_2-T_3)-2\left(F_2-F_3\right)\right|,\left|F_2-F_3\right|\right\}/5\right\}.$$

Therefore, we obtain

$$\frac{min\left\{\left|3(T_1-T_3)-2\left(F_1-F_3\right)\right|,\left|F_1-F_3\right|\right\}}{\left\{max\left\{\left|3(T_1-T_3)-2\left(F_1-F_3\right)\right|,\left|F_1-F_3\right|\right\}/5\right\}+1} \geq \frac{min\left\{\left|3(T_2-T_3)-2\left(F_2-F_3\right)\right|,\left|F_2-F_3\right|\right\}}{\left\{max\left\{\left|3(T_2-T_3)-2\left(F_2-F_3\right)\right|,\left|F_2-F_3\right|\right\}/5\right\}+1}$$

$$(25)$$

Similarly,

$$min\left\{\left|4(T_1-T_3)-3\left(I_1-I_3\right)\right|,\left|I_1-I_3\right|\right\} \leq 1,$$

$$\left\{max\left\{\left|4(T_1-T_3)-3\left(I_1-I_3\right)\right|,\left|I_1-I_3\right|\right\}/7\right\} \leq 1,$$

$$min\left\{\left|4(T_2-T_3)-3\left(I_2-I_3\right)\right|,\left|I_2-I_3\right|\right\} \leq 1,$$

$$\left\{max\left\{\left|4(T_2-T_3)-3\left(I_2-I_3\right)\right|,\left|I_2-I_3\right|\right\}/7\right\} \leq 1$$

and

$$\min\left\{\left|4(T_1-T_3)-3\left(I_1-I_3\right)\right|,\left|I_1-I_3\right|\right\} \geq \min\left\{\left|4(T_2-T_3)-3\left(I_2-I_3\right)\right|,\left|I_2-I_3\right|\right\},$$

$$\left\{max\left\{\left|4(T_1-T_3)-3\left(I_1-I_3\right)\right|,\left|I_1-I_3\right|\right\}/7\right\} \geq max\left\{\left|4(T_2-T_3)-3\left(I_2-I_3\right)\right|,\left|I_2-I_3\right|\right\}/7\}.$$

Thus, we obtain

$$\frac{min\left\{\left|4(T_1-T_3)-3\left(I_1-I_3\right)\right|,\left|I_1-I_3\right|\right\}}{\left\{max\left\{\left|4(T_1-T_3)-3\left(I_1-I_3\right)\right|,\left|I_1-I_3\right|\right\}/7\right\}+1} \geq \frac{min\left\{\left|4(T_2-T_3)-3\left(I_2-I_3\right)\right|,\left|I_2-I_3\right|\right\}}{\left\{max\left\{\left|4(T_2-T_3)-3\left(I_2-I_3\right)\right|,\left|I_2-I_3\right|\right\}/7\right\}+1}$$

(26)

Similarly,

$$min\left\{\left|5(T_1-T_3)-2\left(F_1-F_3\right)-3\left(I_1-I_3\right)\right|,\left|T_1-T_3\right|\right\} \leq 1,$$

$$min\left\{\left|5(T_2-T_3)-2\left(F_2-F_3\right)-3\left(I_2-I_3\right)\right|,\left|T_2-T_3\right|\right\} \leq 1,$$

$$\left\{max\left\{\left|5(T_1-T_3)-2\left(F_1-F_3\right)-3\left(I_1-I_3\right)\right|,\left|T_1-T_3\right|\right\}/10\right\} \leq 1,$$

$$\left\{max\left\{\left|45(T_2-T_3)-2\left(F_2-F_3\right)-3\left(I_2-I_3\right)\right|,\left|T_2-T_3\right|\right\}/10\right\} \leq 1,$$

and

$$min\left\{\left|5(T_1-T_3)-2\left(F_1-F_3\right)-3\left(I_1-I_3\right)\right|,\left|T_1-T_3\right|\right\}$$
$$\geq min\left\{\left|5(T_2-T_3)-2\left(F_2-F_3\right)-3\left(I_2-I_3\right)\right|,\left|T_2-T_3\right|\right\},$$

$$\left\{max\left\{\left|5(T_1-T_3)-2\left(F_1-F_3\right)-3\left(I_1-I_3\right)\right|,\left|T_1-T_3\right|\right\}/10\right\}$$
$$\geq \left\{max\left\{\left|5(T_2-T_3)-2\left(F_2-F_3\right)-3\left(I_2-I_3\right)\right|,\left|T_2-T_3\right|\right\}/10\right\}.$$

Thus, we obtain

$$\frac{min\left\{\left|5(T_1-T_3)-2\left(F_1-F_3\right)-3\left(I_1-I_3\right)\right|,\left|T_1-T_3\right|\right\}}{\left\{max\left\{\left|5(T_1-T_3)-2\left(F_1-F_3\right)-3\left(I_1-I_3\right)\right|,\left|T_1-T_3\right|\right\}/10\right\}+1}$$
$$\geq \frac{min\left\{\left|5(T_2-T_3)-2\left(F_2-F_3\right)-3\left(I_2-I_3\right)\right|,\left|T_2-T_3\right|\right\}}{\left\{max\left\{\left|5(T_2-T_3)-2\left(F_2-F_3\right)-3\left(I_2-I_3\right)\right|,\left|T_2-T_3\right|\right\}/10\right\}+1}.$$

(27)

From (25), (26) and (27), we can take

$$1-2/3\left\{\frac{min\left\{\left|3(T_1-T_3)-2\left(F_1-F_3\right)\right|,\left|F_1-F_3\right|\right\}}{\left\{max\left\{\left|3(T_1-T_3)-2\left(F_1-F_3\right)\right|,\left|F_1-F_3\right|\right\}/5\right\}+1}\right.$$

$$+\frac{min\left\{\left|4(T_1-T_3)-3\left(I_1-I_3\right)\right|,\left|I_1-I_3\right|\right\}}{\left\{max\left\{\left|4(T_1-T_3)-3\left(I_1-I_3\right)\right|,\left|I_1-I_3\right|\right\}/7\right\}+1}$$

$$\left.+\frac{min\left\{\left|5(T_1-T_3)-2\left(F_1-F_3\right)-3\left(I_1-I_3\right)\right|,\left|T_1-T_3\right|\right\}}{\left\{max\left\{\left|5(T_1-T_3)-2\left(F_1-F_3\right)-3\left(I_1-I_3\right)\right|,\left|T_1-T_3\right|\right\}/10\right\}+1}\right\}$$

$$\geq 1-2/3\left\{\frac{min\left\{\left|3(T_2-T_3)-2\left(F_2-F_3\right)\right|,\left|F_2-F_3\right|\right\}}{\left\{max\left\{\left|3(T_2-T_3)-2\left(F_2-F_3\right)\right|,\left|F_2-F_3\right|\right\}/5\right\}+1}\right.$$

$$+\frac{min\left\{\left|4(T_2-T_3)-3\left(I_2-I_3\right)\right|,\left|I_2-I_3\right|\right\}}{\left\{max\left\{\left|4(T_2-T_3)-3\left(I_2-I_3\right)\right|,\left|I_2-I_3\right|\right\}/7\right\}+1}$$

$$\left.+\frac{min\left\{\left|5(T_2-T_3)-2\left(F_2-F_3\right)-3\left(I_2-I_3\right)\right|,\left|T_2-T_3\right|\right\}}{\left\{max\left\{\left|5(T_2-T_3)-2\left(F_2-F_3\right)-3\left(I_2-I_3\right)\right|,\left|T_2-T_3\right|\right\}/10\right\}+1}\right\}$$

Thus, we obtain $S_N(A_1,A_3)\leq S_N(A_2,A_3)$.

4. DECISION MAKING APPLICATIONS IN PROFESSIONAL PROFICIENCIES

Now, let us give the necessary algorithm steps to evaluate the professional proficiencies with the help of a new measure of similarity for a single valued neutrosophic number.

Algorithm 4.1

Step 1: Criteria to be considered in the assessment of professional proficiency are determined. Let $C = \{c_1, c_2, ..., c_m\}$ be set of criteria.

Step 2: The weight values of the criteria to be considered in the assessment of professional proficiency are determined. Let $W = \{w_1, w_2, ..., w_m\}$ be set of weight values of criteria. For example,

weight value of the criteria c_1 is w_1,

weight value of the criteria c_2 is w_2,

weight value of the criteria c_3 is w_3,

weight value of the criteria c_m is w_m,

Also, it is satisfied that $\displaystyle\sum_{i=1}^{m} w_i = 1$.

Step 3: Each worker to be assessed for qualification is assessed by the experts according to each criterion. Each criterion is determined as a single valued neutrosophic number. Let $T = \{t_1, t_2, ..., t_n\}$ be set of workers. Also, each worker is defined such

$$t_1 = \{c_1 : \left\langle T_{t_1(c_1)}, I_{t_1(c_1)}, F_{t_1(c_1)} \right\rangle, c_2 : \left\langle T_{t_1(c_2)}, I_{t_1(c_2)}, F_{t_1(c_2)} \right\rangle, ..., c_m : \left\langle T_{t_1(c_m)}, I_{t_1(c_m)}, F_{t_1(c_m)} \right\rangle;$$
$$c_i \in C \ (i = 1, 2, ..., m)\},$$

$$t_2 = \{c_1 : \left\langle T_{t_2(c_1)}, I_{t_2(c_1)}, F_{t_2(c_1)} \right\rangle, c_2 : \left\langle T_{t_2(c_2)}, I_{t_2(c_2)}, F_{t_2(c_2)} \right\rangle, ..., c_m : \left\langle T_{t_2(c_m)}, I_{t_2(c_m)}, F_{t_2(c_m)} \right\rangle;$$
$$c_i \in C \ (i = 1, 2, ..., m)\},$$

$$t_3 = \{c_1 : \left\langle T_{t_3(c_1)}, I_{t_3(c_1)}, F_{t_3(c_1)} \right\rangle, c_2 : \left\langle T_{t_3(c_2)}, I_{t_3(c_2)}, F_{t_3(c_2)} \right\rangle, ..., c_m : \left\langle T_{t_3(c_m)}, I_{t_3(c_m)}, F_{t_3(c_m)} \right\rangle;$$
$$c_i \in C \ (i = 1, 2, ..., m)\},$$

$$\vdots$$

$$t_n = \{c_1 : \left\langle T_{t_n(c_1)}, I_{t_n(c_1)}, F_{t_n(c_1)} \right\rangle, c_2 : \left\langle T_{t_n(c_2)}, I_{t_n(c_2)}, F_{t_n(c_2)} \right\rangle, ..., c_m : \left\langle T_{t_n(c_m)}, I_{t_n(c_m)}, F_{t_n(c_m)} \right\rangle;$$
$$c_i \in C \ (i = 1, 2, ..., m)\}.$$

where, $c_1, c_2, ..., c_m$ are criterias in Step 1.

Step 4: A fictitious ideal worker is determined by which workers will be compared according to their qualifications. Let fictitious ideal worker be I such that

$$I = \{c_1 : \langle 1, 0, 0\rangle, c_2 : \langle 1, 0, 0\rangle, ..., c_m : \langle 1, 0, 0\rangle; c_i \in C \ (i = 1, 2, ..., m)\}.$$

Step 5: Let us express the workers given in Step 3 as a single valued neutrosophic set in a matrix according to their criteria. Assuming that there are n workers and m criteria, we obtain the matrix of type nxm in Table 1.

Step 6: We will compare the individual criterion values given for each worker in Table 1 and the individual criterion values of the ideal I worker in Step 4 with the measure of similarity in Chapter 3. So we will get a matrix of type nxm again. In this calculation, we will calculate the similarity measure $S_N(I_{c_j}, t_{i_{c_j}})$ for the a_{ij} element of the matrix. It is clear that $t_{i_{c_j}} = a_{ij}$ in Table 1. Thus, we obtain Table 2.

Step 7: The similarity values of the criteria in Table 2 are multiplied by the weight values of the criteria in Step 2. When doing this, k. each similarity value in column k. multiplied by the k. each weight value (k = 1, 2,..., m). Thus, we obtain the weighted similarity matrix in Table 3.

Step 8: In this last step, the weighted similarity values obtained for each worker in Table 3 will be added and the final similarity values of the workers will be revealed. Here, the similarity value of the k. worker to the I ideal worker will be obtained by the operation $S_{Nk}(t_k, I) = \sum_{i=1}^{n} w_i \cdot S_N\left(I_{c_i}, t_{k_{c_i}}\right)$. That is, the similarity value of a worker is the sum of the values in the row of that worker. Thus, we obtain the matrix in Table 4. Also, appropriate workers will be selected according to the similarity values.

Table 1. Criteria matrix of workers

	c_1	c_2	$\cdots$	c_m
t_1	$\left\langle T_{t_1(c_1)}, I_{t_1(c_1)}, F_{t_1(c_1)} \right\rangle$	$\left\langle T_{t_1(c_2)}, I_{t_1(c_2)}, F_{t_1(c_2)} \right\rangle$	$\cdots$	$\left\langle T_{t_1(c_m)}, I_{t_1(c_m)}, F_{t_1(c_m)} \right\rangle$
t_2	$\left\langle T_{t_2(c_1)}, I_{t_2(c_1)}, F_{t_2(c_1)} \right\rangle$	$\left\langle T_{t_2(c_2)}, I_{t_2(c_2)}, F_{t_2(c_2)} \right\rangle$	$\cdots$	$\left\langle T_{t_2(c_m)}, I_{t_2(c_m)}, F_{t_2(c_m)} \right\rangle$
$\vdots$	$\vdots$	$\vdots$	$\cdots \atop \vdots$	$\vdots$
t_n	$\left\langle T_{t_n(c_1)}, I_{t_n(c_1)}, F_{t_n(c_1)} \right\rangle$	$\left\langle T_{t_n(c_2)}, I_{t_n(c_2)}, F_{t_n(c_2)} \right\rangle$	$\cdots$	$\left\langle T_{t_n(c_m)}, I_{t_n(c_m)}, F_{t_n(c_m)} \right\rangle$

Table 2. Matrix of similarity of workers' criteria to ideal worker's criteria

	c_1	c_2	$\cdots$	c_m
t_1	$S_N(I_{c_1}, t_{1_{c_1}})$	$S_N(I_{c_2}, t_{1_{c_2}})$	$\cdots$	$S_N(I_{c_m}, t_{1_{c_m}})$
t_2	$S_N(I_{c_1}, t_{2_{c_1}})$	$S_N(I_{c_2}, t_{2_{c_2}})$	$\cdots$	$S_N(I_{c_m}, t_{2_{c_m}})$
$\vdots$	$\vdots$	$\vdots$	$\cdots$ $\vdots$	$\vdots$
t_n	$S_N(I_{c_1}, t_{n_{c_1}})$	$S_N(I_{c_2}, t_{n_{c_2}})$	$\cdots$	$S_N(I_{c_m}, t_{n_{c_m}})$

Table 3. Matrix of weighted similarity of workers' criteria to ideal worker's criteria

	w_1c_1	w_2c_2	$\cdots$	w_mc_m
t_1	$w_1.S_N(I_{c_1}, t_{1_{c_1}})$	$w_2.S_N(I_{c_2}, t_{1_{c_2}})$	$\cdots$	$w_m.S_N(I_{c_m}, t_{1_{c_m}})$
t_2	$w_1.S_N(I_{c_1}, t_{2_{c_1}})$	$w_2.S_N(I_{c_2}, t_{2_{c_2}})$	$\cdots$	$w_m.S_N(I_{c_m}, t_{2_{c_m}})$
$\vdots$	$\vdots$	$\vdots$	$\cdots$ $\vdots$	$\vdots$
t_n	$w_1.S_N(I_{c_1}, t_{n_{c_1}})$	$w_2.S_N(I_{c_2}, t_{n_{c_2}})$	$\cdots$	$w_m.S_N(I_{c_m}, t_{n_{c_m}})$

Table 4. Matrix of workers' similarity to the ideal worker

	Similarity Values
t_1	$S_{N1}(t_1, I)$
t_2	$S_{N2}(t_2, I)$
$\vdots$	$\vdots$
t_n	$S_{Nn}(t_n, I)$

Example 4.2: Using the steps in Algorithm 4.1, let us identify the most suitable workers among the four workers who apply for two workers to be admitted to a textile factory.

Step 1: Let C = $\{c_1, c_2, c_3\}$ be set of criterias such that
c_1 = Work experience (as years)
c_2 = technical knowledge level
c_3 = application skill

Step 2: Let

weight value of the criteria c_1 is 0,2,

weight value of the criteria c_2 is 0.3,

weight value of the criteria c_3 is 0.5.

Step 3: Let $T = \{t_1, t_2, t_3, t_4\}$ be set of workers such that

$t_1 = \{c_1:\langle 0.4, 0, 0\rangle, c_2:\langle 0.6, 0.3, 0.2\rangle, c_3:\langle 0.7, 0.2, 0.3\rangle\}$

$t_2 = \{ c_1:\langle 0.5, 0, 0\rangle, c_2:\langle 0.5, 0.3, 0.4\rangle, c_3:\langle 0.7, 0.4, 0.2\rangle\}$

$t_3 = \{ c_1:\langle 0.3, 0, 0\rangle, c_2:\langle 0.7, 0.2, 0.1\rangle, c_3:\langle 0.8, 0.2, 0.2\rangle\}$

$t_4 = \{ c_1:\langle 0.5, 0, 0\rangle, c_2:\langle 0.7, 0.2, 0.3\rangle, c_3:\langle 6, 0.3, 0.3\rangle\}.$

Step 4: Let I be fictitious ideal worker such that

$I = \{c_1: \langle 1, 0, 0\rangle, c_2: \langle 1, 0, 0\rangle, c_3: \langle 1, 0, 0\rangle\}.$

Step 5: From Step 3, we obtain criteria matrix of workers in Table 5.

Step 6: From Step 4, we obtain matrix of similarity of workers' criteria to ideal worker's criteria in Table 6.

Step 7: From Step 6, we obtain matrix of weighted similarity of workers' criteria to ideal worker's criteria in Table 7.

Step 8: From Step 7, we obtain matrix of workers' similarity to the ideal worker in Table 8.

Table 5. criteria matrix of workers

	c_1	c_2	c_3
t_1	$\langle 0.4, 0, 0\rangle$	$\langle 0.6, 0.3, 0.2\rangle$	$\langle 0.7, 0.2, 0.3\rangle$
t_2	$\langle 0.5, 0, 0\rangle$	$\langle 0.5, 0.3, 0.4\rangle$	$\langle 0.7, 0.4, 0.2\rangle$
t_3	$\langle 0.3, 0, 0\rangle$	$\langle 0.7, 0.2, 0.1\rangle$	$\langle 0.8, 0.2, 0.2\rangle$
t_4	$\langle 0.5, 0, 0\rangle$	$\langle 0.7, 0.2, 0.3\rangle$	$\langle 0.6, 0.3, 0.3\rangle$

Table 6. matrix of similarity of workers' criteria to ideal worker's criteria

	c_1	c_2	c_3
t_1	0.6923	0.5511	0.6281
t_2	0.7333	0.4411	0.5429
t_3	0.6543	0.6766	0.6666
t_4	0,7333	0.5826	0.5080

145

Table 7. Matrix of weighted similarity of workers' criteria to ideal worker's criteria

	$0.2c_1$	$0.3c_2$	$0.5c_3$
t_1	0.1384	0.1653	0.3140
t_2	0.1466	0.1323	0.2714
t_3	0.1308	0.2029	0.3333
t_4	0.1466	0.1747	0.2540

Table 8. Matrix of workers' similarity to the ideal worker

	Similarity Values
t_1	$S_{N1}(t_1, I) = 0.6177$
t_2	$S_{N2}(t_2, I) = 0.5503$
t_3	$S_{N3}(t_3, I) = 0.6670$
t_4	$S_{N4}(t_4, I) = 0.5703$

In Table 8, we obtain $S_{N3} > S_{N1} > S_{N4} > S_{N2}$. Thus, the two workers to be selected from four workers are t_3 and t_1 respectively.

CONCLUSION

In this study, we defined a new measure of similarity for single valued neutrosophic numbers. We have shown that this measure satisfies the conditions of similarity measure. In addition, using this similarity measure, we have developed an algorithm that can evaluate professional competencies and give an example of the algorithm. In this algorithm and example, we tried to eliminate the uncertainties by using single valued neutrosophic numbers. Thus, with the help of a new similarity measure, we have made a more objective professional competence assessment. Moreover, this measurement and algorithm can be made not only for textile workers, but also for any profession. For example, teacher competence assessment, athlete competence assessment, manager competence assessment can be done with this algorithm. In addition, more than one expert opinion can be obtained and different weight values can be created for each expert.

ACKNOWLEDGMENT

This chapter is supported by the Gaziantep University Scientific Research Projects Governing Unit (BAPYB)".

REFERENCES

Atanassov, T. K. (1986). Intuitionistic fuzzy sets. *Fuzzy Sets and Systems, 20*(1), 87–96. doi:10.1016/S0165-0114(86)80034-3

Chatterjee, R., Majumdar, P., & Samanta, S. K. (2019). *Similarity Measures in Neutrosophic Sets-I. In Fuzzy Multi-criteria Decision-Making Using Neutrosophic Sets* (pp. 249–294). Cham: Springer. doi:10.1007/978-3-030-00045-5_11

Hassan, N., Uluçay, V., & Şahin, M. (2018). Q-neutrosophic soft expert set and its application in decision making. *International Journal of Fuzzy System Applications, 7*(4), 37–61. doi:10.4018/IJFSA.2018100103

Liu, P., & Shi, L. (2015a). The Generalized Hybrid Weighted Average Operator Based on Interval Neutrosophic Hesitant Set and Its Application to Multiple Attribute Decision Making. *Neural Computing & Applications, 26*(2), 457–471. doi:10.100700521-014-1736-4

Liu, P., & Tang, G. (2016a). Some power generalized aggregation operators based on the interval neutrosophic numbers and their application to decision making. *Journal of Intelligent & Fuzzy Systems, 30*(5), 2517–2528. doi:10.3233/IFS-151782

Mohana, K., & Mohanasundari, M. (2019). On Some Similarity Measures of Single Valued Neutrosophic Rough Sets. *Neutrosophic Sets and Systems, 24*, 10–22.

Olgun, N., & Çelik, M. (2019). Neutrosophic triplet R - module. *Neutrosophic Triplet Research, 1*, 35–42.

P., & L. (2015b). Some Neutrosophic Uncertain Linguistic Number Heronian Mean Operators and Their Application to Multi-attribute Group Decision making. *Neural Computing & Applications*. doi:10.100700521-015-2122-6

P., & Tang, G. (2016b). Multi-criteria group decision-making based on interval neutrosophic uncertain linguistic variables and Choquet integral. *Cognitive Computation, 8*(6), 1036-1056.

P., & Teng, F. (2015). Multiple attribute decision making method based on normal neutrosophic generalized weighted power averaging operator. *Internal Journal of Machine Learning and Cybernetics*. doi:10.100713042-015-0385-y

P., & Wang, Y. (2016). Interval neutrosophic prioritized OWA operator and its application to multiple attribute decision making. *Journal of Systems Science & Complexity, 29*(3), 681-697.

P., Zhang, L., Liu, X., & Wang, P. (2016). Multi-valued Neutrosophic Number Bonferroni mean Operators and Their Application in Multiple Attribute Group Decision Making. *Internal Journal of Information Technology & Decision Making, 15*(5), 1181-1210.

Sahin, M., Deli, I., & Ulucay, V. (2016). Similarity measure of bipolar neutrosophic sets and their application to multiple criteria decision making. *Neural Comput & Applic.* DOI 10.1007/S00521

Şahin, M., Ecemiş, O., Uluçay, V., & Kargın, A. (2017). Some new generalized aggregation operators based on centroid single valued triangular neutrosophic numbers and their applications in multi-attribute decision making. *Asian Journal of Mathematics and Computer Research., 16*(2), 63–84.

Şahin, M., & Kargın, A. (2017). Neutrosophic triplet inner product space. *Neutrosophic Operational Research*, 2, 193–215.

Şahin, M., & Kargın, A. (2018). Neutrosophic triplet v – generalized metric space. *Axioms – MDPI, 7*, 67.

Şahin, M., & Kargın, A. (2019b). Neutrosophic triplet partial v – generalized metric space. *Neutrosophic Triplet Research, 1*, 22–34.

Şahin, M., & Kargın, A. (2019c). Neutrosophic triplet Lie Algebra. *Neutrosophic Triplet Research, 1*, 68–78.

Şahin, M., & Kargın, A. (2019d). Neutrosophic triplet partial v – generalized metric space. *Neutrosophic Triplet Research, 1*, 22–34.

Şahin, M., & Kargın, A. (2019e). Neutrosophic triplet Lie Algebra. *Neutrosophic Triplet Research, 1*, 68–78.

Şahin, M., Kargın, A., & Çoban, M. A. (2018). Fixed point theorem for neutrosophic triplet partial metric space. *Symmetry – MDP, 10*, 240.

Şahin, M., Olgun, N., Kargın, A., & Uluçay, V. (2018). *Isomorphism theorems for soft G -modules*. Afrika Matematika; doi:10.100713370-018-0621-1

Şahin, M., Olgun, N., Uluçay, V., Kargın, A., & Smarandache, F. (2017). A new similarity measure on falsity value between single valued neutrosophic sets based on the centroid points of transformed single valued neutrosophic numbers with applications to pattern recognition. *Neutrosophic Sets and Systems*, *15*, 31-48. doi:10.5281/zenodo570934

Şahin, M., Uluçay, V., Olgun, N., & Kilicman, A. (2017). On neutrosophic soft lattices. *Afrika Matematika*, *28*(3-4), 379–388. doi:10.100713370-016-0447-7

Smarandache, F. (1999). Neutrosophy: Neutrosophic Probability, Set and Logic. Rehoboth: Amer. Research Press.

Smarandache, F., & Ali, M. (2016). Neutrosophic triplet group. *Neural Computing & Applications*, *29*(7), 595–601. doi:10.100700521-016-2535-x

Smarandache, F., Colhon, M., Vlăduţescu, Ş., & Negrea, X. (2019). Word-level neutrosophic sentiment similarity. *Applied Soft Computing*, *80*, 167–176. doi:10.1016/j.asoc.2019.03.034

Smarandache, F., Şahin, M., & Kargın, A. (2018). Neutrosophic Triplet G- Module. *Mathematics – MDPI*, *6*, 53.

Smarandache, F., Şahin, M., & Kargın, A. (2019a). Neutrosophic triplet partial inner product space. *Neutrosophic Triplet Research*, *1*, 10–21.

Uluçay, V., Kiliç, A., Yildiz, I., & Sahin, M. (2018). A new approach for multi-attribute decision-making problems in bipolar neutrosophic sets. *Neutrosophic Sets and Systems*, *23*(1), 142–159.

Uluçay, V., Şahin, M., & Hassan, N. (2018). Generalized neutrosophic soft expert set for multiple-criteria decision-making. *Symmetry*, *10*(10), 437. doi:10.3390ym10100437

Ulucay, V., Şahin, M., & Olgun, N. (2018). Time-Neutrosophic Soft Expert Sets and Its Decision Making Problem. *Afrika Matematika*, *34*(2), 246–260.

Wang, H., Smarandache, F., Zhang, Y. Q., & Sunderraman, R. (2010). Single valued neutrosophic sets. *Multispace Multistructure*, *4*, 410–413.

Ye, J. (2014). Similarity measures between interval neutrosophic sets and their applications in multicriteria decision – making. *Journal of Intelligent & Fuzzy Systems*, *26*(1), 165–172.

Zadeh, A. L. (1965). Fuzzy sets. *Information and Control*, *8*(3), 338–353. doi:10.1016/S0019-9958(65)90241-X

Chapter 8
Extended GRA–Based MADM Strategy With Single–Valued Trapezoidal Neutrosophic Numbers

Surapati Pramanik
Umeschandra College, India

Rama Mallick
Umeschandra College, India

ABSTRACT

Multi-attribute decision-making(MADM) strategy has been proposed to handle uncertain decision-making problems. The most extensively used models of grey system theory is grey relational analysis (GRA). This strategy was flourished by Chinese Professor J. Deng. This strategy also known as Deng's grey incidence analysis model. GRA uses a generic concept of intelligence. It describes any circumstance as no information as black and perfect information as white. Nevertheless, these idealized situations appear in real-world problems. In this chapter, the authors extend GRA strategy for multi-attribute decision making in trapezoidal neutrosophic number (TrNN) environment. To develop a GRA strategy in trapezoidal neutrosophic number (TrNN) environment, the authors use score function and accuracy function. Then Hamming distance for two trapezoidal neutrosophic number (TrNN) are also described. The authors solve a numerical problem to explain the pertinence of the proposed strategy. Lastly, they provide a comparison between VIKOR strategy with existing strategy.

DOI: 10.4018/978-1-7998-2555-5.ch008

1. INTRODUCTION

In 1998, Smarandache (Smarandache, 1998) consecrated the notion of neutrosophic set by incorporating the philosophy of neutrosophy (Smarandache, 1998) in mathematical arena. Thereafter, Wang et al. (Wang et al., 2010) defined single valued neutrosophic set. Neutrosophic set and its various extensions and neutrosophic hybrid sets have been widely employed in decision making problems such as single valued neutrosophic set environment (Biswas, Pramanik, & Giri, 2014, Biswas, Pramanik, & Giri, 2015, Mondal, & Pramanik, 2015, Pramanik, Dalapati, & Roy, 2016, Smarandache, & Pramanik, 2016, Biswas, Pramanik, & Giri, 2017, Pramanik, Mallick, & Dasgupta, 2018, Mondal, Pramanik, & Giri, 2018, Mondal, Pramanik, & Giri, 2018, Biswas, Pramanik, & Giri, 2018, Biswas, Pramanik, & Giri 2019, Abdel-Basset, Manogaran, Gamal, & Smarandache, 2018, Abdel-Basset, Mohamed, Zhou, Hezam, 2017, Abdel-Basset, Gunasekaran, Mohamed, Chilamkurti, 2018, Abdel-Basset, Mohamed, & Smarandache, 2018a, Abdel-Basset, Mohamed, & Smarandache, 2018b, Abdel-Basset, Zhou, Mohamed, Chang, 2018, Abdel-Basset, & Mohamed, 2018, Abdel-Basset, Mohamed, Sangaiah, & Jain, 2018, Abdel-Basset, Chang, Gamal, & Smarandache, 2019, Abdel-Baset, Chang, & Gamal, 2019, Abdel-Basset, Manogaran, Gamal, & Smarandache, 2019, Abdel-Basset, Gamal, Manogaran, Son, & Long, 2019, Biswas, Pramanik, & Giri, 2019), interval neutrosophic set environment (Pramanik, Dey, & Giri, 2015, Dey, Pramanik, & Giri, 2016, Dalapati, Pramanik, Alam, Smarandache, & Roy, 2017, Mondal, Pramanik, & Giri, 2018), neutrosophic single valued soft expert set environment (Pramanik, Dey, & Giri, 2015, Pramanik, Dey, & Giri, 2016a, Pramanik, Dey, & Giri 2016b, Pramanik, & Dalapati, 2016), rough neutrosophic set environment (Mondal, & Pramanik, 2015, Mondal, & Pramanik, 2015, Mondal, & Pramanik, 2015, Mondal, Pramanik, & Smarandache 2016a, Mondal, Pramanik, & Smarandache 2016b, Mondal, Pramanik, & Smarandache 2016c, Pramanik, Roy, Roy, & Smarandache, 2017, Pramanik, Roy, & Roy, 2018, Mondal, Pramanik, & Giri, 2018, Mondal, Pramanik, 2015, Pramanik, Roy, Roy, & Smarandache, 2018, Pramanik, Roy, Roy, & Smarandache, 2018), neutrosophic refined set environment (Mondal, & Pramanik, 2015, Mondal, & Pramanik, 2015, Mondal, Pramanik, & Giri, 2018), neutrosophic hesitant fuzzy set environment (Biswas, Pramanik, & Giri, 2016a, Biswas, Pramanik, & Giri, 2016b, Biswas, Pramanik, & Giri, 2019), bipolar neutrosophic set environment (Dey, Pramanik, & Giri, 2016, Dey, Pramanik, & Giri, Smarandache, 2017, Pramanik, Dalapati, Alam, & Roy, 2018, Pramanik, Dalapati, Alam, & Roy, 2018, Pramanik, Dey, Smarandache, & Ye, 2018, Pramanik, Dey, & Smarandache, 2018, Pramanik, Dalapati, Alam, & Roy, 2018), neutrosophic cubic set environment (Pramanik, Dalapati, Alam, & Roy, 2017, Pramanik, Dalapati, Alam, Roy, & Smarandache, 2017, Pramanik, Dey, & Smarandache, 2017, Pramanik, Dalapati, Alam, & Roy,

2018, Dalapati, & Pramanik, 2018), triangular and trapezoidal neutrosophic set environment (Biswas, Pramanik, & Giri, 2016, Giri, Molla, & Biswas, 2018, Abdel-Basset, Mohamed, Hussien, Sangaiah, 2018, Biswas, Pramanik, & Giri, 2015, Biswas, Pramanik, & Giri, 2018), neutrosophic number environment (Pramanik, Roy, & Roy, 2016, Pramanik, & Dey, 2018, Mondal, Pramanik, & Smarandache, 2018, Pramanik, & Banerjee, 2018), conflict resolution (Pramanik, & Roy, 2014), image processing (Xu, Wang, Yang, & Jiang, 2018), medical diagnosis (Mondal, & Pramanik, 2015), social science (Pramanik, & Chackrabarti, 2013) etc.

Ye (Ye, 2017) introduced trapezoidal neutrosophic number (TrNN) in 2017. The TrNN and the single valued neutrosophic set (SVNS)(Wang et al. 2010) are very effective mathematical tools to deal with indeterminacy, incomplete, and inconsistent information. Single valued trapezoidal neutrosophic number (SVTrNN) (Deli, & Subas, 2016) is an extension of SVNS. Each element of SVTrNN is distinguished by trapezoidal number with truth membership degree, indeterminacy membership degree and falsity membership degree. In 2018, Liang et al. (Liang et al. 2018) defined score function, accuracy function and certainty function in SVTrNN environment, using center of gravity (COG). Biswas et al. (Biswas, Pramanik, & Giri, 2016) documented value and ambiguity based ranking strategy for SVTrNN and employed the strategy to handle multi-attribute decision making (MADM) problem. Biswas et al. (Biswas, Pramanik, & Giri, 2018a) developed a technique for order of preference by similarity to ideal solution (TOPSIS) strategy for MADM with TrNNs. In this article they defined Hamming distance for TrNNs. Biswas et al. (Biswas, Pramanik, & Giri, 2018b) also developed distance measure based MADM strategy with interval trapezoidal neutrosophic numbers (ITrNNs). Pramanik and Mallick (Pramanik, & Mallick, 2018) developed a VIKOR strategy to deal with multi attribute group decision making (MAGDM) in trapezoidal neutrosophic number environment. To develop this strategy, they used trapezoidal neutrosophic weighted arithmetic averaging operator (TNWAA). In this paper, they discussed a numerical problem. At the end, they present a sensitivity analysis of decision making mechanism coefficient for different values on ranking order of the alternative. Pramanik and Mallick (Pramanik, & Mallick, 2019) also developed TODIM strategy to deal with MAGDM for the same environment. In this paper they used score function and accuracy function for TrNN. They also give a comparative analysis for decay factor of loss.

In 1982, Deng (Deng, 1989, Deng, 2005) introduced a grey relation analysis (GRA) to deal with uncertainty. Rao and Singh (Rao, & Singh, 2010) introduced modified GRA strategy for decision making in manufacturing situation. In 2011, Pramanik and Mukhopadhayaya (Pramanik, & Mukhopadhyaya, 2011) studied a GRA based MCGDM strategy for teacher selection in intuitionistic fuzzy set environment. In 2011, Wei (Wei, 2011) introduced a GRA strategy for intuitionistic fuzzy MADM. Zhang et al. (Zhang, Jin, & Liu, 2013) developed a grey relation projection strategy for MADM in intuitionistic trapezoidal fuzzy environment in 2013. Biswas et al. (Biswas, Pramanik, & Giri, 2014) discussed an entropy related GRA for MADM strategy in SVNS environment. Dey et al. (Dey, Pramanik, & Giri, 2015) developed a GRA based MCGDM strategy for weaver selection in Khadi institutions in intuitionistic fuzzy environment in 2015. In 2015, Pramanik and Mondal (Pramanik, & Mondal, 2015) proposed a GRA for MADM strategy in an interval neutrosophic set environment. Dey et al. (Dey, Pramanik, & Giri, 2016) studied an extended GRA for neutrosophic MADM strategy in interval uncertain linguistic setting. Banerjee et al. (Banerjee, Pramanik, & Giri, 2017) constructed an MADM model via GRA for neutrosophic cubic set environment.

Till now GRA based TrNN-MADM strategy is not proposed in the literature. To fill the research gap, we propose an extended GRA based MADM strategy to deal decision making problems in TrNN environment. Contributions of the chapter are stated as follows:

- We develop a new GRA based MADM strategy in TrNN environment.
- We provide a numerical example to show the applicability and effectiveness of the proposed strategy.
- We also compare proposed strategy with VIKOR strategy.

This chapter is organized as follows: In section 2, we introduce some definitions relating to neutrosophic set and trapezoidal neutrosophic number. In section 3, we describe the standardize process of decision matrix. In section 4, we describe GRA strategy. In section 5, we develop an extended GRA strategy for MADM. In section 6, an illustrative example is discussed to demonstrate the applicability of the proposed strategy. We give a comparative study between GRA strategy and VIKOR strategy in section 7. In section 8 we discuss future direction of research. Lastly, section 9 represents the concluding remarks.

2. PRELIMINARIES

In this section, we recall some basic definitions related to fuzzy set, trapezoidal fuzzy number, neutrosophic sets, trapezoidal neutrosophic set, score function, accuracy function and Hamming distance.

Definition 2.1. A fuzzy set (Zadeh, 1965) F in a universal set Z is defined by

$$F = \{\langle z, v_F(z) \rangle | z \subset Z\} \tag{1}$$

where $v_F(z)$: $Z \rightarrow [0,1]$ is known as membership function of F and value of $v_F(z)$ is called the degree of membership.

Example 1: A real estate broker wants to classify the house he offers to his clients. One indicator of comfort of these houses is the number of bedrooms in it. Let Z = {1, 2, …,6} be the set of available types of houses described by z = number of bedrooms on a house. Then the fuzzy set "comfortable type of house for a four-person family" may be described as

F = {(1,.2), (2,.5), (3,.8), (4,1), (5,.7), (6,.3)}

Figure 1. Graphical representation of trapezoidal fuzzy number

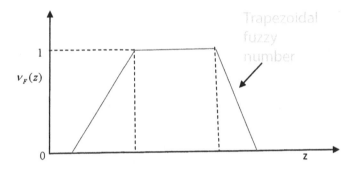

Definition 2.2. A fuzzy number F is called trapezoidal fuzzy number (TrFN) (Dubois, & Prade, 1983, Heilpern, 1992) (see Figure 1) if its membership function is defined by

$$v_F(z) = \begin{cases} \dfrac{z-e}{f-e}, & e \leq z < f \\ 1, & f \leq z \leq g \\ \dfrac{h-z}{h-g}, & g < z \leq h \\ 0, & otherwise \end{cases} \tag{2}$$

The TrFN F is denoted by $F=(e,f,g,h)$ where e, f, g, h are real number and $e \leq f \leq g \leq h$.

Definition 2. 3. Let Z be a universal set. A single-valued neutrosophic set (SVNS) (Wang et al. 2010) (see Figure 2) Y in Z is given by

$$Y = \{z, \langle T_Y(z), I_Y(z), F_Y(z) \rangle | z \in Z\} \tag{3}$$

where $T_Y(z)$: $Z \rightarrow [0,1]$, $I_Y(z)$: $Z \rightarrow [0,1]$ and $F_Y(z)$: $Z \rightarrow [0,1]$ with the condition $0 \leq T_Y(z) + I_Y(z) + F_Y(z) \leq 3$ for all $z \in Z$. The functions $T_Y(z), I_Y(z)$ and $F_Y(z)$ are respectively, the truth membership function, the indeterminacy membership function and the falsity membership function of the element z to the set.

Figure 2. Graphical representation of neutrosophic set

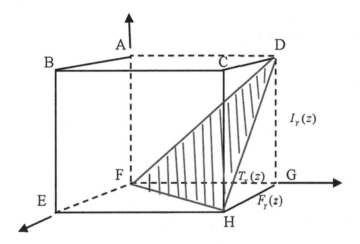

Example 2: Assume that, there is a possibility p such that tomorrow will be rainy day. One person can put the truth degree of p as 45%, the falsity degree of p as 38% and the indeterminacy degree of p as 20% in independently. The situation can be expressed in neutrosophic sense as p <0.45,0.2,0.38>.

Definition 2.4. Let X be a single valued trapezoidal neutrosophic number (SVTrNN) (Deli, & Subas, 2016). Then, its truth membership function is

$$T_X(z) = \begin{cases} \dfrac{(z-e)t_X}{(f-e)}, e \leq z < f \\ t_X, f \leq z \leq g \\ \dfrac{(h-z)t_X}{(h-g)}, g < z \leq h \\ 0, otherwise \end{cases} \tag{4}$$

Its indeterminacy membership function is

$$I_X(z) = \begin{cases} \dfrac{(f-z)+(z-e')i_X}{(f-e')}, e' \le z < f \\ i_X, f \le z \le g \\ \dfrac{z-g+(h'-z)i_X}{h'-g}, g < z \le h' \\ 0, otherwise \end{cases} \quad (5)$$

And its falsity membership function is

$$F_X(z) = \begin{cases} \dfrac{f-z+(z-e'')f_X}{f-e''}, e'' \le z < f \\ f_X, f \le z \le g \\ \dfrac{z-g+(h''-z)f_X}{h''-g}, g < z \le h'' \\ 0, otherwise \end{cases} \quad (6)$$

where $0 \le T_X(z) \le 1$, $0 \le I_X(z) \le 1$ and $0 \le F_X(z) \le 1$ and $0 \le T_X(z)+I_X(z)+F_X(z) \le 3$; $e, f, g, h \in R$. Then $X = ([e, f, g, h]; t_X, i_X, f_X)$ is called a neutrosophic trapezoidal number.

If $0 \le e \le f \le g \le h$, then m is called a positive TrNN. If $e \le f \le g \le h \le 0$, then X is called a negative TrNN. If $0 \le e \le f \le g \le h \le 1$ and $T_X, I_X, F_X \in [0,1]$, then X is called a normalized TrNN.

Figure 3. Graphical representation of single valued trapezoidal neutrosophic set

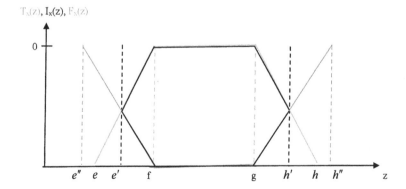

Example: A company wants to invest a large amount of money in a best option. They have three alternative car company, arm company and food company. They assign value for the alternative, car company is $\langle(0.5,0.6,0.7,0.7); 0.3,0.2,0.1\rangle$, for arm company is $\langle(0.3,0.4,0.5,0.7); 0.5,0.3,0.1\rangle$ and lastly for food company is $\langle(0.7,0.7,0.8,0.8); 0.4,0.2,0.2\rangle$.

Table 1. Comparative table between fuzzy sets, Intuitionistic fuzzy sets, single valued neutrosophic set, and single valued trapezoidal neutrosophic number (SVTrNN) including advantages and disadvantages

Name of the set	Advantage	Disadvantage
Fuzzy set	■ We can differentiate different type of uncertainty using fuzzy set. It is very useful in a wide range of domains in which information is incomplete.	■ In fuzzy set it has only one membership degree. Sometime the grade of membership itself is uncertain and hard to find crisp value. ■ When degree of indeterminacy involves as independent component, fuzzy set cannot deal with the situation.
Intuitionistic fuzzy set	■ When degree of non-membership is independent of degree of membership, fuzzy set cannot deal this situation, but intuitionistic fuzzy set can deal this situation. ■ An intuitionistic fuzzy set can be viewed as an alternative approach when available information is not sufficient to define the impreciseness by the conventional fuzzy set. ■ Since intuitionistic fuzzy set is an extension of the standard fuzzy set, its range of applications are wide than fuzzy sets.	■ When degree of indeterminacy involves as independent component, intuitionistic fuzzy set cannot deal with the situation.
Single valued neutrosophic set	■ A neutrosophic set is a general framework which generalizes the concept of fuzzy set, and intuitionistic fuzzy set. ■ It can deal the situation where degree of non-membership and degree of indeterminacy are independent. ■ It can deal with incomplete and inconsistent information.	■ Sometimes it is difficult to assign degree of indeterminacy explicitly.
Single valued trapezoidal neutrosophic number	■ SVTrNN is an extended concept of single valued neutrosophic number (SVNN), trapezoidal fuzzy number, and intuitionistic trapezoidal fuzzy number. ■ It has wide range of applications as it is the generalization of trapezoidal fuzzy number, and intuitionistic trapezoidal fuzzy number.	■ Literature of SVTrNN is very poor. ■ Few applications are available in the literature.

Definition 2.5. (Liang et al. 2018) Let $A=[e,f,g,h]$ be a trapezoidal fuzzy number on R, and $e \leq f \leq g \leq h$; then, the centre of gravity (COG) of X defined by:

$$COG(A) = \begin{cases} A & \text{if } e = f = g = h = A \\ \dfrac{1}{3}\left[e + f + g + h - \dfrac{gh - ef}{g + h - e - f} \right] & \text{otherwise} \end{cases}$$

(7)

Definition 2.6. (Liang et al. 2018) Let $X=([e,f,g,h]; T_X, I_X, F_X)$ $g = \langle (k,l,m,n); T_g, I_g, F_g \rangle$ be a TrNN. Then the score function $Sc(X)$, accuracy function (X) and certainty function $E(X)$ of TrNN is defined by

$$Sc(X) = COG(A) \times \frac{(2 + T_X - I_X - F_X)}{3}$$

(8)

$$Ac(X) = COG(X) \times (T_X - F_X)$$

(9)

$$E(X) = COG(A) \times T_X$$

(10)

Here COG(A) is defined in (7).

Definition 2. 7. Comparison of two TrNNs: Let $K_1 = \langle (e_1, f_1, g_1, h_1); T_{K_1}, I_{K_1}, F_{K_1} \rangle$ and $K_2 = \langle (e_2, f_2, g_2, h_2); T_{K_2}, I_{K_2}, F_{K_2} \rangle$ be any two TrNN. The comparison between the two TrNNs K_1 and K_2 is stated as follows:
1. If $Sc(K_1) > Sc(K_2)$, then $K_1 > K_2$
2. If $Sc(K_1) = Sc(K_2)$ and $Ac(K_1) > Ac(K_2)$, then $K_1 > K_2$
3. If $Sc(K_1) = Sc(K_2)$ and $Ac(K_1) < Ac(K_2)$, then $K_1 < K_2$ and
4. If $Sc(K_1) = Sc(K_2)$ and $Ac(K_1) = Ac(K_2)$, and $E(K_1) > E(K_2)$, $K_1 > K_2$ and when $E(K_1) < E(K_2)$, then $K_1 < K_2$ and $K_1 = K_2$ when $E(K_1) = E(K_2)$.
5. If $Sc(K_1) = Sc(K_2)$ and $Ac(K_1) = Ac(K_2)$, then $K_1 = K_2$

Definition 2.8. Let $K_1 = ([e_1, f_1, g_1, g_1]; t_{K_1}, i_{K_1}, f_{K_1})$ and $K_2 = ([e_2, f_2, g_2, h_2]; t_{K_2}, i_{K_2}, f_{K_2})$ be two neutrosophic trapezoidal fuzzy numbers, its Hamming distance (Biswas et al. (2018a)) between K_1 and K_2 is defined as follows:

$$d(K_1, K_2) = \frac{1}{12}\left(\left| e_1(2 + t_{K_1} - i_{K_1} - f_{K_1}) - e_2(2 + t_{K_2} - i_{K_2} - f_{K_2}) \right| + \left| f_1(2 + t_{K_1} - i_{K_1} - f_{K_1}) - f_2(2 + t_{K_2} - i_{K_2} - f_{K_2}) \right| \right.$$
$$\left. + \left| g_1(2 + t_{K_1} - i_{K_1} - f_{K_1}) - g_2(2 + t_{K_2} - i_{K_2} - f_{K_2}) \right| + \left| h_1(2 + t_{K_1} - i_{K_1} - f_{K_1}) - h_2(2 + t_{K_2} - i_{K_2} - f_{K_2}) \right| \right)$$

(11)

3. STANDARDIZE THE DECISION MATRIX

We consider the decision matrix $D = (c_{ij})_{p \times q}$ as a neutrosophic decision matrix, where the SVTrNN $\tilde{c}_{ij} = ([c_{ij}^1, c_{ij}^2, c_{ij}^3, c_{ij}^4]; t_{\tilde{c}_{ij}}, i_{\tilde{c}_{ij}}, f_{\tilde{c}_{ij}})$ is the rating value of alternative Y_i w.r.t. attribute Z_j. Now to eliminate the effect from different physical dimension into decision making process, we should standardize the decision matrix $(c_{ij})_{p \times q}$ based on two common types of attribute such as benefit and cost type attribute. We consider the following technique to obtain the standardized decision matrix $Z^* = (\tilde{z}_{ij})_{p \times q}$, in which the component z_{ij}^k of the entry $\tilde{z}_{ij} = ([z_{ij}^1, z_{ij}^2, z_{ij}^3, z_{ij}^4]; t_{\tilde{z}_{ij}}, i_{\tilde{z}_{ij}}, f_{\tilde{z}_{ij}})$ in the matrix Z are considered as:

i. For benefit types attribute:

$$\tilde{z}_{ij} = ([\frac{c_{ij}^1}{q_j^+}, \frac{c_{ij}^2}{q_j^+}, \frac{c_{ij}^3}{q_j^+}, \frac{c_{ij}^4}{q_j^+}]; t_{\tilde{z}_{ij}}, i_{\tilde{z}_{ij}}, f_{\tilde{z}_{ij}})\} \tag{12}$$

ii. For cost type attribute:

$$\tilde{z}_{ij} = ([\frac{q_j^-}{c_{ij}^4}, \frac{q_j^-}{c_{ij}^3}, \frac{q_j^-}{c_{ij}^2}, \frac{q_j^-}{c_{ij}^1}]; t_{\tilde{z}_{ij}}, i_{\tilde{z}_{ij}}, f_{\tilde{z}_{ij}}) \tag{13}$$

where $q_j^+ = \max\{c_{ij}^4 | i = 1, 2, ..., p\}$ and $q_j^- = \min\{c_{ij}^1 | i = 1, 2, ..., p\}$ for j=1,2,….,q.

Then we obtain the following standardized decision matrix:

$$Z = (\tilde{z}_{ij})_{m \times n} = \begin{pmatrix} z_{11} & z_{12} & z_{1n} \\ z_{21} & z_{22} \cdots & z_{2n} \\ \vdots & \ddots & \vdots \\ z_{m1} & z_{m2} \cdots & z_{mn} \end{pmatrix} \tag{14}$$

4. GREY RELATIONAL ANALYSIS

Chinese mathematician Prof. Deng Julong (Deng, 1989, Deng, 2005) grounded grey system theory (GST) that complies with principles of normality, symmetry, entirety, and proximity. A grey system refers to a system in which part of information is known and part of information is unknown. Since uncertainty is inevitable, a human being always lies somewhere in middle, between the extremes, in the grey area.

Grey analysis presents a set of statements regarding system solution. At one extreme, grey analysis states that no solution can be defined for a system having no information. At the other extreme, grey analysis states that a system having perfect information bears a unique solution. In the middle, grey systems offer a variety of available solution. For real life problem, no attempt is made to seek the best solution, but grey analysis offers techniques for obtaining a good solution, an appropriate solution.

GRA is one of the most widely employed models of GST. GRA utilizes a specific concept of information. GRA defines situations having perfect information as white and situations having no information as black. We do not usually come in contact with these idealized situations in our daily life. Situations between the white and black having partial information are described as being grey.

Assume that $Y'' = \{Y_0'', Y_1''...., Y_n''\}$ be a set of grey relation (Rao, & Singh, 2010). Referential sequence and comparative sequence are denoted by Y_0'' and Y_i'' respectively, where $i = 1, 2, ..., n$. Y_0'' and Y_i'' both comprise of p elements and they can be represented as follows:

$$Y_0'' = \{Y_0''(1), Y_0''(2),...., Y_0''(h),...., Y_0''(p)\} \text{ and } Y_i'' = \{Y_i''(1), Y_i''(2),...., Y_i''(h),...., Y_i''(p)\}$$

where $i = 1, 2, ..., n$; $h = 1, 2, ..., p$; $p \in P$, $Y_0''(h)$ and $Y_i''(h)$ are the numbers of referential sequence and comparative sequence at point h, respectively. In real life application, the referential sequence can be an ideal objective and the comparative sequences are alternatives. The highest degree of grey relation reflects the best alternative. At point h, $\chi(y_0''(h), y_i''(h))$ is the grey relation coefficient of the referential sequence and comparative sequence. Then grey relation coefficient $\chi(y_0''(h), y_i''(h))$ satisfies the following four conditions:

1.   Normal interval:

$0 < \chi(y_0'', y_i'') \leq 1$.

If $\chi(y_0'', y_i'') = 1$ $<=>$ $y_0'' = y_i''$

If $\chi(y_0'', y_i'') = 0$ $<=>$ $y_0'', y_i'' \in \phi$, f is empty set.

2.   Dual symmetry:

$y_0'', y_i'' \in Y''$

$\chi(y_0'', y_i'') = \chi(y_i'', y_0'') \quad <=> \quad Y'' = \{y_0'', y_i''\}$

3.   Wholeness:

Often $\chi(y_0'', y_i'') \neq \chi(y_i'', y_0'')$

4.   Approachability:

$\chi(y_0''(h), y_i''(h))$ becomes smaller when $\left| y_0''(h) - y_i''(h) \right|$ is bigger.

At the point h, grey relational coefficient $\chi(y_0''(h), y_i''(h))$ of the referential sequence and comparative sequence can be presented by as follow:

$$\chi(y_0''(h), y_i''(h)) = \frac{\min\limits_i \min\limits_h \left| y_0''(h) - y_i''(h) \right| + \rho \max\limits_i \max\limits_h \left| y_0''(h) - y_i''(h) \right|}{\left| y_0''(h) - y_i''(h) \right| + \rho \max\limits_i \max\limits_h \left| y_0''(h) - y_i''(h) \right|} \tag{15}$$

where ρ is termed as "contrast control" or "environmental coefficient" or "distinguishing coefficient" or "identification coefficient".

Its value, over a broad appropriate range of values, does not affect the ordering of the grey relational grade values, but a good value of the contrast control is needed for clear identification of key system factors.

Generally, in broad range ρ does not affect ranking of grey relational grade values. But for a standard solution ρ needed a clear identification of the system factor. Comparison environment is unaltered when $\rho=1$ and comparison environment disappears when $\rho=0$. In general, we take $\rho=0.5$.

5. GRA STRATEGY FOR SOLVING MADM PROBLEM UNDER TRAPEZOIDAL NEUTROSOPHIC NUMBER ENVIRONMENT

Assume that $\tilde{B} = \{\tilde{B}_1, \tilde{B}_2, ..., \tilde{B}_p\}$ be the p alternatives and $R' = \{R_1', R_2', ..., R_q'\}$ be the set of q attributes. Also assume that the rating values each of the alternative corresponding to each of the attribute are expressed in the form of $m_{ij} = ([b_1, b_2, b_3, b_4]; t_{m_{ij}}, i_{m_{ij}}, f_{m_{ij}})$. Here, we describe GRA strategy for TrNN by considering the weight vector $\tilde{w} = \{\tilde{w}_1, \tilde{w}_2, ..., \tilde{w}_q\}^T$ of attributes where $\tilde{w}_b \in [0,1]$ and $\sum_{b=1}^{q} \tilde{w}_b = 1$ using the following steps.

Step-1: First we define decision matrix as follows:

$$Q = \begin{pmatrix} & R'_1 & R'_2 & .... & R'_q \\ \tilde{B}_1 & m_{11} & m_{12} & .... & m_{1q} \\ \tilde{B}_2 & m_{21} & m_{22} & .... & m_{2q} \\ .... & .... & .... & .... & ..... \\ \tilde{B}_P & m_{p1} & m_{p2} & .... & m_{pq} \end{pmatrix} \qquad (16)$$

Step-2: Generally, decision making problem consists of cost and benefit attribute. So we need to standardize the decision matrix. To standardize the benefit criterion, we use the equation (12) and for cost criterion we use (13). After standardizing, the decision matrix reduces to

$$Q' = \begin{pmatrix} & R'_1 & R'_2 & .... & R'_q \\ \tilde{B}_1 & m'_{11} & m'_{12} & .... & m'_{1q} \\ \tilde{B}_2 & m'_{21} & m'_{22} & .... & m'_{2q} \\ .... & .... & .... & .... & ..... \\ \tilde{B}_P & m'_{p1} & m'_{p2} & .... & m'_{pq} \end{pmatrix} \qquad (17)$$

Step-3: In this step we calculate score value and accuracy value using equation (8) and (9).

Step-4: Here, we describe the positive ideal solution (PIS) and negative ideal solution (NIS) for TrNN.

$$T^+ = ([b_1^+, b_2^+, b_3^+, b_4^+]; \max t_{m_{ij}}, \min i_{m_{ij}}, \min f_{m_{ij}}) \qquad (18)$$

$$T^- = ([b_1^-, b_2^-, b_3^-, b_4^-]; \min t_{m_{ij}}, \max i_{m_{ij}}, \max f_{m_{ij}}) \qquad (19)$$

Step-5: Determine the grey relation coefficient of each alternative from T$^+$ and T$^-$ by the following equations:

$$\chi_{bc}^{+} = \frac{\min\limits_{1 \leq b \leq p}\min\limits_{1 \leq b \leq p} D(x_{bc}, T_c^{+}) + \rho \max\limits_{1 \leq b \leq p}\max\limits_{1 \leq b \leq p} D(x_{bc}, T_c^{+})}{D(x_{bc}, T_c^{-}) + \rho \max\limits_{1 \leq b \leq p}\max\limits_{1 \leq b \leq p} D(x_{bc}, T_c^{+})} \tag{20}$$

$$\chi_{bc}^{-} = \frac{\min\limits_{1 \leq b \leq p}\min\limits_{1 \leq b \leq p} D(x_{bc}, T_c^{-}) + \rho \max\limits_{1 \leq b \leq p}\max\limits_{1 \leq b \leq p} D(x_{bc}, T_c^{-})}{D(x_{bc}, T_c^{-}) + \rho \max\limits_{1 \leq b \leq p}\max\limits_{1 \leq b \leq p} D(x_{bc}, T_c^{-})} \tag{21}$$

where the identification coefficient is considered as $\rho = 0.5$.

Step-6: In this step, we employ the pre-determined weight vector of attributes as $w = \{w_1, w_2, \ldots, w_q\}$ and $\sum\limits_{c=1}^{q} w_c = 1$

Step-7: In this step, we determine the degree of grey relation coefficient of each alternative $\tilde{B}_b$ (b=1,2,..., p) from χ_{bc}^{+} and χ_{bc}^{-} by the following equations:

$$\vartheta_b^{+} = \sum_{c=1}^{q} w_c \chi_{bc}^{+} \tag{22}$$

$$\vartheta_b^{-} = \sum_{c=1}^{q} w_c \chi_{bc}^{-} \tag{23}$$

Step-8: Evaluating the relative closeness coefficient ϑ_b for each alternative $\tilde{B}_b$ (b=1,2,..., p) w.r.t. the positive ideal solution T^{+} as

$$\vartheta_b = \frac{\vartheta_b^{+}}{\vartheta_b^{+} + \vartheta_b^{-}} \tag{24}$$

For b=1,2, ..., p.

Step-9: Ranking the alternative according to the relative closeness coefficient ϑ_b (b=1,2,..., p). Greater value of ϑ_b implies the best alternative.

Figure 4. GRA based MADM strategy in trapezoidal neutrosophic number environment

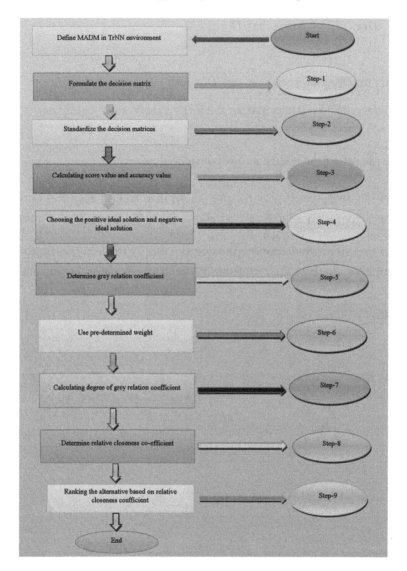

6. NUMERICAL EXAMPLE

Here, we describe trapezoidal neutrosophic number MADM to illustrate the applicability and effectiveness of the proposed strategy. We solve a decision making problem adapted from (Abdel-Basset, Saleh, Gamal, & Smarandache, 2019) which is stated as follows. Recently in India people seek for choosing the best bank to operate banking transactions such as deposit their money, withdraw financial loans, transfer of money, change currencies, etc. This section presents a numerical case to select the best bank for citizens and investors. There are four alternatives $\tilde{B}_1, \tilde{B}_2, \tilde{B}_3$ and $\tilde{B}_4$, five criteria are considered as selection factor Reputation and elegance (R'_1), Customer service (R'_2), Offers (R'_3), Place of the bank and its branches (R'_4), Fees (R'_5). The alternatives $\tilde{B}_i$ (i = 1,2,3,4) with respect to criterion R'_i (i = 1,2,3,4,5) are expressed with SVTrNN as follows. We assume that weight of the criteria R'_i (i = 1,2,3,4,5) are w= (0.20, 0.25, 0.30, 0.15, 0.10).

Step-1: Here we defined decision matrix

$$Q = \begin{pmatrix} & R'_1 & R'_2 \\ \tilde{B}_1 & ([0.5,0.6,0.7,0.8];0.65,0.25,0.20) & ([0.7,0.8,0.8,0.9];0.60,0.35,0.30) \\ \tilde{B}_2 & ([0.7,0.8,0.8,0.9];0.80,0.20,0.15) & ([0.6,0.7,0.8,0.9];0.50,0.40,0.35) \\ \tilde{B}_3 & ([0.4,0.5,0.6,0.7];0.50,0.40,0.30) & ([0.7,0.8,0.9,0.9];0.85,0.30,0.25) \\ \tilde{B}_4 & ([0.6,0.7,0.7,0.8];0.70,0.35,0.25) & ([0.5,0.6,0.6,0.7];0.65,0.35,0.30) \end{pmatrix}$$

R'_3	R'_4	R'_5
([0.4,0.5,0.5,0.6];0.48,0.26,0.20)	([0.4,0.5,0.6,0.7];0.55,0.32,0.10)	([0.5,0.5,0.6,0.7];0.50,0.20,0.10)
([0.3,0.4,0.5,0.6];0.50,0.45,0.35)	([0.5,0.5,0.6,0.7];0.70,0.40,0.15)	([0.3,0.4,0.4,0.5];0.40,0.20,0.10)
([0.6,0.6,0.7,0.7];0.65,0.22,0.18)	([0.6,0.6,0.7,0.7];0.85,0.40,0.20)	([0.6,0.6,0.6,0.7];0.75,0.30,0.25)
([0.5,0.6,0.6,0.7];0.60,0.40,0.30)	([0.5,0.6,0.7,0.7];0.70,0.40,0.20)	([0.5,0.6,0.6,0.7];0.60,0.25,0.15)

Step-2: Among the selected five attribute first three attribute are benefit type attribute and last two attribute are cost type attribute. Thus we can standardized the decision matrix $\left(Q_{ij}\right)_{4X4}$ to $\left(Q'_{ij}\right)_{4X4}$ by using equation (12) and (13). The standardized decision matrix represented as follow.

$$Q' = \begin{pmatrix} & R'_1 & R'_2 \\ \tilde{B}_1 & ([0.62,0.75,0.88,1];0.65,0.25,0.20) & ([0.78,0.89,0.89,1];0.60,0.35,0.30) \\ \tilde{B}_2 & ([0.78,0.89,0.89,1];0.80,0.20,0.15) & ([0.67,0.78,0.89,1];0.50,0.40,0.35) \\ \tilde{B}_3 & ([0.57,0.71,0.86,1];0.50,0.40,0.30) & ([0.78,0.89,1,1];0.85,0.30,0.25) \\ \tilde{B}_4 & ([0.75,0.88,0.88,1];0.70,0.35,0.25) & ([0.71,0.86,0.86,1];0.65,0.35,0.30) \end{pmatrix}$$

R'_3	R'_4	R'_5
([0.67,0.83,0.83,1];0.48,0.26,0.20)	([0.57,0.71,0.80,1];0.55,0.32,0.10)	([0.71,0.83,1,1];0.50,0.20,0.10)
([0.50,0.67,0.83,1];0.50,0.45,0.35)	([0.71,0.83,1,1];0.70,0.40,0.15)	([0.6,0.75,0.75,1];0.40,0.20,0.10)
([0.86,0.86,1,1];0.65,0.22,0.18)	([0.85,0.85,1,1];0.85,0.40,0.20)	([0.85,1,1,1];0.75,0.30,0.25)
([0.71,0.86,0.86,1];0.60,0.40,0.30)	([0.71,0.71,0.83,1];0.70,0.40,0.20)	([0.71,0.83,0.83.1];0.60,0.25,0.15)

Step-3: Calculating score value and accuracy value by using equation (8) and (9).

$$Sc(Q') = \begin{pmatrix} & R_1' & R_2' & R_3' & R_4' & R_5' \\ \tilde{B}_1 & 0.59 & 0.58 & 0.56 & 0.54 & 0.64 \\ \tilde{B}_2 & 0.73 & 0.49 & 0.50 & 0.64 & 0.55 \\ \tilde{B}_3 & 0.47 & 0.70 & 0.70 & 0.69 & 0.70 \\ \tilde{B}_4 & 0.62 & 0.57 & 0.54 & 0.67 & 0.62 \end{pmatrix}$$

$$Ac(Q') = \begin{pmatrix} & R_1' & R_2' & R_3' & R_4' & R_5' \\ \tilde{B}_1 & 0.36 & 0.27 & 0.23 & 0.27 & 0.35 \\ \tilde{B}_2 & 0.58 & 0.13 & 0.13 & 0.50 & 0.16 \\ \tilde{B}_3 & 0.16 & 0.55 & 0.44 & 0.64 & 0.48 \\ \tilde{B}_4 & 0.40 & 0.30 & 0.26 & 0.48 & 0.38 \end{pmatrix}$$

Step-4: Identifying positive ideal solution (PIS) T^+ and negative ideal solution (NIS) T^- using equation (18) and (19)

$$T^+ = \left(\begin{matrix} R_1' & R_2' \\ ([0.78,0.89,0.89,1];0.80,0.20,0.15) & ([0.78,0.89,1,1];0.85,0.30,0.25) \end{matrix} \right.$$
$$\begin{matrix} R_3' & R_4' & R_5' \\ ([0.86,0.86,1,1];0.65,0.22,0.18) & ([0.57,0.67,0.8,1];0.55,0.42,0.20) & ([0.6,0.75,0.75,1];0.40,0.20,0.10) \end{matrix} \right)$$

$$T^- = \left(\begin{matrix} R_1' & R_2' \\ ([0.57,0.71,0.86,1];0.50,0.40,0.30) & ([0.67,0.78,0.89,1];0.50,0.40,0.35) \end{matrix} \right.$$
$$\begin{matrix} R_3' & R_4' & R_5' \\ ([0.50,0.67,0.83,1];0.50,0.45,0.35) & ([0.85,0.85,1,1];0.85,0.40,0.20) & ([0.85,1,1,1];0.75,0.30,0.25) \end{matrix} \right)$$

Step-5: Using (20) and (21) we calculate grey relation coefficient:

$$\chi^+ = \begin{pmatrix} 0.51 & 0.52 & 0.49 & 1 & 0.56 \\ 1 & 0.39 & 0.33 & 0.56 & 1 \\ 0.347 & 1 & 1 & 0.49 & 0.45 \\ 0.55 & 0.51 & 0.47 & 0.8 & 0.64 \end{pmatrix}$$

$$\chi^{-} = \begin{pmatrix} 0.52 & 0.60 & 0.5 & 0.49 & 0.70 \\ 0.35 & 1 & 1 & 0.69 & 0.45 \\ 1 & 0.52 & 0.33 & 1 & 1 \\ 0.59 & 0.62 & 0.54 & 0.52 & 0.61 \end{pmatrix}$$

Step-6: In this step, we assume the weights are

$w_1 = 0.20$, $w_2 = 0.25$, $w_3 = 0.30$, $w_4 = 0.15$, $w_5 = 0.10$

Step-7: Calculate the degree of grey relation coefficient by equation (22) and (23)

$\vartheta_1^{+} = 0.585, \vartheta_2^{+} = 0.580, \vartheta_3^{+} = 0.74, \vartheta_4^{+} = 0.562 \quad \vartheta_1^{-} = 0.548, \vartheta_2^{-} = 0.768, \vartheta_3^{-} = 0.679, \vartheta_4^{-} = 0.574$

Step-8: Using equation (24) we evaluate the relative closeness co-efficient

$\vartheta_1 = 0.516$, $\vartheta_2 = 0.430$, $\vartheta_3 = 0.521$, $\vartheta_4 = 0.495$

Step-9: The ranking of the alternative based on relative closeness co-efficient is

$$\tilde{B}_3 > \tilde{B}_1 > \tilde{B}_4 > \tilde{B}_2$$

We see that $\tilde{B}_3$ has highest value. Therefore, $\tilde{B}_3$ is the best solution.

7. COMPARATIVE STUDIES

In the literature VIKOR strategy (Pramanik, & Mallick, 2018) has been proposed in SVTrNN environment. So we present the comparison with VIKOR strategy with the proposed GRA strategy in SVTrNN environment. The ranking order of alternatives using VIKOR strategy and the proposed strategy is shown in Table 2. Ranking order differs for VIKOR and GRA strategies and we observe that the best alternative for GRA strategy is alternative three and for VIKOR strategy best alternative is first one.

8. FUTURE RESEARCH DIRECTIONS

In future, the developed strategy can be applied to real-world problems such as teacher selection (Mondal, & Pramanik, 2014), brick selection (Mondal, & Pramanik, 2014,

Table 2. Comparison of GRA and VIKOR strategy

Strategy	Rank of the alternative
GRA strategy	$\tilde{B}_3 > \tilde{B}_1 > \tilde{B}_4 > \tilde{B}_2$
VIKOR strategy	$\tilde{B}_1 < \tilde{B}_3 < \tilde{B}_4 < \tilde{B}_2$

Mondal, & Pramanik, 2015), pattern recognition (Alia, Delib, & Smarandache, 2016), clustering analysis (Qiaoyan, Yingcang, Smarandache, & Shauangwu, 2018), image processing (Zhang, Zhang, & Cheng, 2010, Sengur, & Guo, 2011, Koundal, Gupta, & Singh, 2018), medical diagnosis (Edward Samuel & Narmadhagnanam, 2017, Ajitha Priyadharshini, & Selvakumari, 2017, Ye, Fu, & Ye, 2015), various problems (Smarandache, & Pramanik, 2018) etc.

9. CONCLUSION

Literature dealing with the development of single valued trapezoidal neutrosophic number is very rare (Biswas, et al. 2018a, Pramanik, & Mallick, 2018, Pramanik, & Mallick, 2019). Research on applications involving single valued trapezoidal neutrosophic number is few (Biswas, et al. 2018a, Pramanik, & Mallick, 2018, Pramanik, & Mallick, 2019). This chapter takes the challenge to explore single valued neutrosophic number in multi attribute decision making. This chapter integrates grey relational analysis and single valued trapezoidal neutrosophic number for multi attribute decision making strategy. In this chapter, we have explored multi attribute decision making strategy in single valued trapezoidal neutrosophic number environment. We have developed an extended grey relational analysis based multi attribute decision making strategy to deal with multi attribute decision making problems in trapezoidal neutrosophic number environment. An illustrative numerical example has been solved to show the applicability and effectiveness of the proposed single valued trapezoidal neutrosophic number strategy.

REFERENCES

Abdel-Baset, M., Chang, V., & Gamal, A. (2019). Evaluation of the green supply chain management practices: A novel neutrosophic approach. *Computers in Industry*, *108*, 210–220. doi:10.1016/j.compind.2019.02.013

Abdel-Baset, M., Chang, V., Gamal, A., & Smarandache, F. (2019). An integrated neutrosophic ANP and VIKOR method for achieving sustainable supplier selection: A case study in importing field. *Computers in Industry, 106*, 94–110. doi:10.1016/j.compind.2018.12.017

Abdel-Basset, M., Gamal, A., Manogaran, G., Son, L. H., & Long, H. V. (2019). A novel group decision making model based on neutrosophic sets for heart disease diagnosis. *Multimedia Tools and Applications*, 1–26. doi:10.100711042-019-07742-7

Abdel-Basset, M., Gunasekaran, M., Mohamed, M., & Chilamkurti, N. (2018). Three-way decisions based on neutrosophic sets and AHP-QFD framework for supplier selection problem. *Future Generation Computer Systems, 89*, 19–30. doi:10.1016/j.future.2018.06.024

Abdel-Basset, M., Manogaran, G., Gamal, A., & Smarandache, F. (2018). A hybrid approach of neutrosophic sets and DEMATEL method for developing supplier selection criteria. *Design Automation for Embedded Systems, 22*(3), 257–287. doi:10.100710617-018-9203-6

Abdel-Basset, M., Manogaran, G., Gamal, A., & Smarandache, F. (2019). A Group Decision Making Framework Based on Neutrosophic TOPSIS Approach for Smart Medical Device Selection. *Journal of Medical Systems, 43*(2), 1–13. doi:10.100710916-019-1156-1 PMID:30627801

Abdel-Basset, M., & Mohamed, M. (2018). The role of single valued neutrosophic sets and rough sets in smart city: Imperfect and incomplete information systems. *Measurement, 124*, 47–55. doi:10.1016/j.measurement.2018.04.001

Abdel-Basset, M., Mohamed, M., Hussien, A. N., & Sangaiah, A. K. (2018). A novel group decision-making model based on triangular neutrosophic numbers. *Soft Computing, 22*(20), 6629–6643. doi:10.100700500-017-2758-5

Abdel-Basset, M., Mohamed, M., Sangaiah, A. K., & Jain, V. (2018). An integrated neutrosophic AHP and SWOT method for strategic planning methodology selection. *Benchmarking: An International Journal, 25*(7), 2546–2564. doi:10.1108/BIJ-08-2017-0232

Abdel-Basset, M., Mohamed, M., & Smarandache, F. (2018a). An extension of neutrosophic AHP–SWOT analysis for strategic planning and decision-making. *Symmetry, 10*(4), 116. doi:10.3390ym10040116

Abdel-Basset, M., Mohamed, M., & Smarandache, F. (2018b). A Hybrid Neutrosophic Group ANP-TOPSIS Framework for Supplier Selection Problems. *Symmetry, 10*(6), 226. doi:10.3390ym10060226

Abdel-Basset, M., Mohamed, M., Zhou, Y. M., & Hezam, I. (2017). Multi-criteria group decision making based on neutrosophic analytic hierarchy process. *Journal of Intelligent & Fuzzy Systems*, *33*(6), 4055–4066. doi:10.3233/JIFS-17981

Abdel-Basset, M., Saleh, M., Gamal, A., & Smarandache, F. (2019). An approach of TOPSIS technique for developing supplier selection with group decision making under type-2 neutrosophic number. *Applied Soft Computing*, *77*, 438–452. doi:10.1016/j. asoc.2019.01.035

Abdel-Basset, M., Zhou, Y., Mohamed, M., & Chang, V. (2018). A group decision making framework based on neutrosophic VIKOR approach for e-government website evaluation. *Journal of Intelligent & Fuzzy Systems*, *34*(6), 4213–4224. doi:10.3233/JIFS-171952

Ajitha Priyadharshini, M., & Selvakumari, K. (2017). VIKOR Method For Medical Diagnosis Problem Using Triangular Neutrosophic Soft Matrix. *International Journal of Pure and Applied Mathematics*, *114*(16), 169–176.

Alia, M., Delib, I., & Smarandachec, F. (2016). The theory of neutrosophic cubic sets and their applications in pattern recognition. *Journal of Intelligent & Fuzzy Systems*, *16*, 1064–1246.

Banerjee, D., Pramanik, S., & Giri, B. C. (2017). GRA for multi attribute decision making in neutrosophic cubic set environment. *Neutrosophic Sets and Systems*, *15*, 60–69. doi:10.5281/zenodo.570938

Biswas, P., Pramanik, S., & Giri, B. C. (2014). A new methodology for neutrosophic multi-attribute decision making with unknown weight information. *Neutrosophic Sets and Systems*, *3*, 42–52. doi:10.5281/zenodo.571212

Biswas, P., Pramanik, S., & Giri, B. C. (2014). Entropy based grey relational analysis method for multi-attribute decision – making under single valued neutrosophic assessments. *Neutrosophic Sets and Systems*, *2*, 102–110.

Biswas, P., Pramanik, S., & Giri, B. C. (2015). TOPSIS method for multi-attribute group decision making under single-valued neutrosophic environment. *Neural Computing & Applications*, *27*(3), 727–737. doi:10.100700521-015-1891-2

Biswas, P., Pramanik, S., & Giri, B. C. (2015). Cosine similarity measure based multi-attribute decision-making with trapezoidal fuzzy neutrosophic numbers. *Neutrosophic Sets and Systems*, *8*, 46-56. doi.org/10.5281/zenodo.571274

Biswas, P., Pramanik, S., & Giri, B. C. (2016). Aggregation of triangular fuzzy neutrosophic set information and its application to multi-attribute decision making. *Neutrosophic Sets and Systems*, *12*, 20–40. doi:10.5281/zenodo.571125

Biswas, P., Pramanik, S., & Giri, B. C. (2016). Value and ambiguity index based ranking method of single-valued trapezoidal neutrosophic numbers and its application to multi-attribute decision making. *Neutrosophic Sets and Systems*, *12*, 127–138. doi.org/10.5281/zenodo.571154

Biswas, P., Pramanik, S., & Giri, B. C. (2016a). Some distance measures of single valued neutrosophic hesitant fuzzy sets and their applications to multiple attribute decision making. In F. Smarandache & S. Pramanik (Eds.), *New Trends In Neutrosophic Theory And Applications*. Pons Editions.

Biswas, P., Pramanik, S., & Giri, B. C. (2016b). GRA method of multiple attribute decision making with single valued neutrosophic hesitant fuzzy set information. In F. Smarandache & S. Pramanik (Eds.), *New Trends In Neutrosophic Theory And Applications*. Pons Editions.

Biswas, P., Pramanik, S., & Giri, B. C. (2017). Hybrid vector similarity measures and their applications to multi-attribute decision making under neutrosophic environment. *Neural Computing & Applications*, *28*(5), 1163–1176. doi:10.100700521-015-2125-3

Biswas, P., Pramanik, S., & Giri, B. C. (2018). Neutrosophic TOPSIS with group decision making. In Fuzzy Multicriteria Decision Making Using Neutrosophic Sets. Studies in Fuzziness and Soft Computing, (pp. 543–585). Academic Press. doi:10.1007/978-3-030-00045-5_21

Biswas, P., Pramanik, S., & Giri, B. C. (2018). Multi-attribute group decision making based on expected value of neutrosophic trapezoidal numbers. In F. Smarandache & S. Pramanik (Eds.), *New Trends In Neutrosophic Theory And Applications* (Vol. 2, pp. 103–124). Brussels: Pons Editions.

Biswas, P., Pramanik, S., & Giri, B. C. (2018a). TOPSIS strategy for multi-attribute decision making with trapezoidal numbers. *Neutrosophic Sets and Systems*, *19*, 29–39. doi:10.5281/zenodo.1235335

Biswas, P., Pramanik, S., & Giri, B. C. (2018b). Distance measure based MADM strategy with interval trapezoidal neutrosophic numbers. *Neutrosophic Sets and Systems*, *19*, 40–46. doi:10.5281/zenodo.1235165

Biswas, P., Pramanik, S., & Giri, B. C. (2019). *Non-linear programming approach for single-valued neutrosophic TOPSIS method*. New Mathematics and Natural Computation. doi:10.1142/S1793005719500169

Biswas, P., Pramanik, S., & Giri, B. C. (2019). Non-linear programming approach for single-valued neutrosophic TOPSIS method. *New Mathematics and Natural Computation, 15*(2), 1–20. doi:10.1142/S1793005719500169

Biswas, P., Pramanik, S., & Giri, B. C. (2019). NH-MADM Strategy in neutrosophic hesitant fuzzy set environment based on extended GRA. *Informatica, 30*(2), 213–242. doi:10.15388/Informatica.2019.204

Dalapati, S., & Pramanik, S. (2018). A revisit to NC-VIKOR based MAGDM strategy in neutrosophic cubic set environment. *Neutrosophic Sets and Systems, 21*, 131–141. doi:10.5281/zenodo.1408665

Dalapati, S., Pramanik, S., Alam, S., Smarandache, F., & Roy, T. K. (2017). IN-cross entropy based MAGDM strategy under interval neutrosophic set environment. *Neutrosophic Sets and Systems, 18*, 43–57. doi:10.5281/zenodo.1175162

Deli, I., & Subas, Y. (2016). A ranking method of single valued neutrosophic numbers and its applications to multi-attribute decision making problems. *International Journal of Machine Learning and Cybernetics, 8*(4), 1309–1322. doi:10.100713042-016-0505-3

Deng, J. L. (1989). Introduction to grey system theory. *Journal of Grey System, 1*(1), 1–24.

Deng, J. L. (2005). *The primary methods of grey system theory*. Wuhan, China: Huazhong University of Science and Technology Press.

Dey, P. P., Pramanik, S., & Giri, B. C. (2015). Multi-criteria group decision making in intuitionistic fuzzy environment based on grey relational analysis for weaver selection in Khadi institution. *Journal of Applied Quantitative Methods, 10*(4), 1–14.

Dey, P. P., Pramanik, S., & Giri, B. C. (2016). Extended projection based models for solving multiple attribute decision making problems with interval valued neutrosophic information. In F. Smarandache & S. Pramanik (Eds.), *New trends in neutrosophic theory and applications* (pp. 127–140). Brussels: Pons Editions.

Dey, P. P., Pramanik, S., & Giri, B. C. (2016). TOPSIS for solving multi-attribute decision making problems under bi-polar neutrosophic environment. In F. Smarandache & S. Pramanik (Eds.), *New Trends In Neutrosophic Theory And Applications* (pp. 65–77). Brussels: Pons Editions.

Dey, P. P., Pramanik, S., & Giri, B. C. (2016). An extended grey relational analysis based multiple attribute decision making in interval neutrosophic uncertain linguistic setting. *Neutrosophic Sets and Systems, 11*, 21–30.

Dey, P. P., Pramanik, S., Giri, B. C. & Smarandache, F. (2017). Bipolar neutrosophic projection based models for solving multi-attribute decision-making problems. *Neutrosophic Sets and Systems*, *15*, 70-79. doi.org/10.5281/zenodo.570936

Dubois, D., & Prade, H. (1983). Ranking fuzzy numbers in the setting of possibility theory. *Information Sciences*, *30*(3), 183–224. doi:10.1016/0020-0255(83)90025-7

Edward Samuel, A., & Narmadhagnanam, R. (2017). Neutrosophic Refined Sets in Medical Diagnosis. *International Journal of Fuzzy Mathematical Archive*, *14*(1), 117-123.

Giri, B. C., Molla, M. U., & Biswas, P. (2018). TOPSIS method for MADM based on interval trapezoidal neutrosophic numbers. *Neutrosophic Sets and Systems*, *22*, 151–167. doi:10.5281/zenodo.2160749

Heilpern, S. (1992). The expected value of fuzzy number. *Fuzzy Sets and Systems*, *47*(1), 81–86. doi:10.1016/0165-0114(92)90062-9

Koundal, D., Gupta, S., & Singh, S. (2018). Computer aided thyroid nodule detection system using medical ultrasound images. *Biomedical Signal Processing and Control*, *40*, 117–130. doi:10.1016/j.bspc.2017.08.025

Liang, R. X., Wang, J. Q., & Zhang, H. Y. (2018). A multi-criteria decision making method based on single valued trapezoidal neutrosophic preference relation with complete weight information. *Neural Computing & Applications*, *30*(11), 3383–3398. doi:10.100700521-017-2925-8

Mondal, K., & Pramanik, S. (2014). Multi-criteria group decision making approach for teacher recruitment in higher education under simplified Neutrosophic environment. *Neutrosophic Sets and Systems*, *6*, 28–34. doi:10.5281/zenodo.571479

Mondal, K., & Pramanik, S. (2014). Intuitionistic fuzzy multicriteria group decision making approach to quality-brick selection problem. *Journal of Applied Quantitative Methods*, *9*(2), 35–50.

Mondal, K., & Pramanik, S. (2015). Neutrosophic tangent similarity measure and its application to multiple attribute decision making. *Neutrosophic Sets and Systems*, *9*, 80-87. doi.org/10.5281/zenodo.571578.

Mondal, K., & Pramanik, S. (2015). Rough neutrosophic multi-attribute decision-making based on grey relational analysis. *Neutrosophic Sets and Systems*, *7*, 8-17. doi.org/10.5281/zenodo.571603

Mondal, K., & Pramanik, S. (2015). Rough neutrosophic multi-attribute decision-making based on rough accuracy score function. *Neutrosophic Sets and Systems*, *8*, 14-21. doi.org/10.5281/zenodo.571604

Mondal, K., & Pramanik, S. (2015). Tri-complex rough neutrosophic similarity measure and its application in multi-attribute decision making. *Critical Review*, *11*, 26–40.

Mondal, K., & Pramanik, S. (2015). Decision making based on some similarity measures under interval rough neutrosophic environment. *Neutrosophic Sets and Systems, 10*, 46-57. doi.org/10.5281/zenodo.571358

Mondal, K., & Pramanik, S. (2015). Neutrosophic refined similarity measure based on tangent function and its application to multi attribute decision making. *Journal of New Theory*, *8*, 41–50. doi:10.5281/zenodo.23176

Mondal, K., & Pramanik, S. (2015). Neutrosophic refined similarity measure based on cotangent function and its application to multi-attribute decision making. *Global Journal of Advanced Research, 2*(2), 486-494.

Mondal, K., & Pramanik, S. (2015). Cosine similarity measure of rough neutrosophic sets and its application in medical diagnosis. *Global Journal of Advanced Research*, *2*(1), 212–220.

Mondal, K., & Pramanik, S. (2015). Neutrosophic decision making model for clay-brick selection in construction field based on grey relational analysis. *Neutrosophic Sets and Systems*, *9*, 64–71. doi:10.5281/zenodo.34864

Mondal, K., Pramanik, S., & Giri, B. C. (2018). Single valued neutrosophic hyperbolic sine similarity measure based MADM strategy. *Neutrosophic Sets and Systems*, *20*, 3–11. doi:10.5281/zenodo.1235383

Mondal, K., Pramanik, S., & Giri, B. C. (2018). Hybrid binary logarithm similarity measure for MAGDM problems under SVNS assessments. *Neutrosophic Sets and Systems*, *20*, 12–25. doi:10.5281/zenodo.1235365

Mondal, K., Pramanik, S., & Giri, B. C. (2018). Interval neutrosophic tangent similarity measure based MADM strategy and its application to MADM problems. *Neutrosophic Sets and Systems*, *19*, 47–56. doi:10.5281/zenodo.1235201

Mondal, K., Pramanik, S., & Giri, B. C. (2018). Rough neutrosophic aggregation operators for multi-criteria decision-making. In C. Kahraman & I. Otay (Eds.), Fuzzy Multicriteria Decision Making Using Neutrosophic Sets, Studies in Fuzziness and Soft Computing. Academic Press. doi:10.1007/978-3-030-00045-5_5

Mondal, K., Pramanik, S., & Giri, B. C. (2018). Multi-criteria group decision making based on linguistic refined neutrosophic strategy. In F. Smarandache & S. Pramanik (Eds.), *New trends in neutrosophic theory and applications* (Vol. 2). Pons Editions.

Mondal, K., Pramanik, S., & Smarandache F. (2016a). Rough neutrosophic TOPSIS for multi-attribute group decision making. *Neutrosophic Sets and Systems, 13*, 105-117. doi.org/10.5281/zenodo.570866

Mondal, K., Pramanik, S., & Smarandache, F. (2016b). Multi-attribute decision making based on rough neutrosophic variational coefficient similarity measure. *Neutrosophic Sets and Systems, 13*, 3–17. doi:10.5281/zenodo.570854

Mondal, K., Pramanik, S., & Smarandache, F. (2016c). Rough neutrosophic hyper-complex set and its application to multiattribute decision making. *Critical Review, 13*, 111–126.

Mondal, K., Pramanik, S., & Smarandache, F. (2018). NN-harmonic mean aggregation operators-based MCGDM strategy in a neutrosophic number environment. *Axioms, 7*(12). doi:10.3390/axioms7010012

(2016). New Trends. InSmarandache, F., & Pramanik, S. (Eds.), *Neutrosophic Theory And Applications*. Brussels: Pons Editions.

Pramanik, S., & Banerjee, D. (2018). Neutrosophic number goal programming for multi-objective linear programming problem in neutrosophic number environment. *MOJ Current Research & Review, 1*(3), 135–141. doi:10.15406/mojcrr.2018.01.00021

Pramanik, S., & Chackrabarti, S. N. (2013). A study on problems of construction workers in West Bengal based on neutrosophic cognitive maps. *International Journal of Innovative Research in Science. Engineering and Technology, 2*(11), 6387–6394.

Pramanik, S., & Dalapati, S. (2016). GRA based multi criteria decision making in generalized neutrosophic soft set environment. *Global Journal of Engineering Science and Research Management, 3*(5), 153–169. doi:10.5281/zenodo.53753

Pramanik, S., Dalapati, S., Alam, S., & Roy, T. K. (2017). NC-TODIM-based MAGDM under a neutrosophic cubic set environment. *Information, 8*(4), 149. doi:10.3390/info8040149

Pramanik, S., Dalapati, S., Alam, S., & Roy, T. K. (2018). VIKOR based MAGDM strategy under bipolar neutrosophic set environment. *Neutrosophic Sets and Systems, 19*, 57–69. doi:10.5281/zenodo.1235341

Pramanik, S., Dalapati, S., Alam, S., & Roy, T. K. (2018). TODIM method for group decision making under bipolar neutrosophic set environment. In F. Smarandache & S. Pramanik (Eds.), *New Trends In Neutrosophic Theory And Applications* (pp. 140–155). Brussels: Pons Editions.

Pramanik, S., Dalapati, S., Alam, S., & Roy, T. K. (2018). TODIM method for group decision making under bipolar neutrosophic set environment. In F. Smarandache & S. Pramanik (Eds.), New trends in neutrosophic theory and applications, (vol. 2, pp. 140-155). Brussels: Pons Editions.

Pramanik, S., Dalapati, S., Alam, S., & Roy, T. K. (2018). NC-VIKOR based MAGDM strategy under neutrosophic cubic set environment. *Neutrosophic Sets and Systems*, *20*, 95–108. doi:10.5281/zenodo.1235367

Pramanik, S., Dalapati, S., Alam, S., Roy, T. K., & Smarandache, F. (2017). Neutrosophic cubic MCGDM method based on similarity measure. *Neutrosophic Sets and Systems*, *16*, 44–56. doi:10.5281/zenodo.831934

Pramanik, S., Dalapati, S., & Roy, T. K. (2016). Logistics center location selection approach based on neutrosophic multi-criteria decision making. In F. Smarandache & S. Pramanik (Eds.), *New Trends In Neutrosophic Theory And Applications* (pp. 161–174). Brussels: Pons Editions.

Pramanik, S., & Dey, P. P. (2018). Bi-level linear programming problem with neutrosophic numbers. *Neutrosophic Sets and Systems*, *21*, 110–121. doi:10.5281/zenodo.1408669

Pramanik, S., Dey, P. P., & Giri, B. C. (2015). TOPSIS for single valued neutrosophic soft expert set based multi-attribute decision making problems. *Neutrosophic Sets and Systems*, *10*, 88–95. doi:10.5281/zenodo.571238

Pramanik, S., Dey, P. P., & Giri, B. C. (2016). Neutrosophic soft multi-attribute decision making based on grey relational projection method. *Neutrosophic Sets and Systems*, *11*, 98-106. doi.org/10.5281/zenodo.571576

Pramanik, S., Dey, P. P., & Giri, B. C. (2016). Neutrosophic soft multi-attribute group decision making based on grey relational analysis method. *Journal of New Results in Science*, *10*, 25–37. doi:10.5281/zenodo.34869

Pramanik, S., Dey, P. P., & Smarandache, F. (2017). An extended TOPSIS for multi-attribute decision making problems with neutrosophic cubic information. *Neutrosophic Sets and Systems*, *17*, 20–28. doi:10.5281/zenodo.1012217

Pramanik, S., Dey, P. P., & Smarandache, F. (2018). Correlation coefficient measures of interval bipolar neutrosophic sets for solving multi-attribute decision making problems. *Neutrosophic Sets and Systems, 19*, 70–79. doi:10.5281/zenodo.1235151

Pramanik, S., Dey, P. P., Smarandache, F., & Ye, J. (2018). Cross entropy measures of bipolar and interval bipolar neutrosophic sets and their application for multi-attribute decision-making. *Axioms, 7*(21), 1–25. doi:10.3390/axioms7020021

Pramanik, S., & Mallick, R. (2018). VIKOR based MAGDM strategy with trapezoidal neutrosophic number. *Neutrosophic Sets and Systems, 22*, 118–130. doi:10.5281/zenodo.2160840

Pramanik, S., & Mallick, R. (2019). *TODIM strategy for multi attribute group decision making in trapezoidal neutrosophic number environment.* Complex and Intelligent Systems. doi:10.100740747-019-0110-7

Pramanik, S., Mallick, R., & Dasgupta, A. (2018). Contributions of selected Indian researchers to multi-attribute decision making in neutrosophic environment. *Neutrosophic Sets and Systems, 20*, 108–131. doi:10.5281/zenodo.1284870

Pramanik, S., & Mondal, K. (2015). Interval neutrosophic multi-attribute decision-making based on grey relational analysis. *Neutrosophic Sets and Systems, 9*, 13–22.

Pramanik, S., & Mukhopadhyaya, D. (2011). Grey relational analysis based intuitionistic fuzzy multi-criteria group decision-making approach for teacher selection in higher education. *International Journal of Computers and Applications, 34*(10), 21–29.

Pramanik, S., Roy, R., & Roy, T. K. (2016). Teacher selection strategy based on bidirectional projection measure in neutrosophic number environment. In F. Smarandache, M. A. Basset, & V. Chang (Eds.), Neutrosophic Operational Research (vol. 2, pp. 29-53). Brussels: Pons asbl.

Pramanik, S., Roy, R., & Roy, T. K. (2018). Multi criteria decision making based on projection and bidirectional projection measures of rough neutrosophic sets. In F. Smarandache & S. Pramanik (Eds.), *New Trends In Neutrosophic Theory And Applications* (Vol. 2, pp. 175–187). Brussels: Pons Editions.

Pramanik, S., Roy, R., Roy, T. K., & Smarandache, F. (2017). Multi criteria decision making using correlation coefficient under rough neutrosophic environment. *Neutrosophic Sets and Systems, 17*, 29–36. doi:10.5281/zenodo.1012237

Pramanik, S., Roy, R., Roy, T. K., & Smarandache, F. (2018). Multi attribute decision making strategy on projection and bidirectional measures of interval rough neutrosophic sets. *Neutrosophic Sets and Systems*, *19*, 101–109. doi:10.5281/zenodo.1235211

Pramanik, S., Roy, R., Roy, T. K., & Smarandache, F. (2018). Multi-attribute decision making based on several trigonometric Hamming similarity measures under interval rough neutrosophic environment. *Neutrosophic Sets and Systems*, *19*, 110–118. doi:10.5281/zenodo.1235207

Pramanik, S., & Roy, T. K. (2014). Neutrosophic game theoretic approach to Indo-Pak conflict over Jammu-Kashmir. *Neutrosophic Sets and Systems*, *2*, 82-101. doi.org/10.5281/zenodo.571510

Pramanik, S., Dey, P. P., & Giri, B. C. (2015). An extended grey relational analysis based interval neutrosophic multi-attribute decision making for weaver selection. *Journal of New Theory*, *9*, 82-93.

Qiaoyan, Li., Yingcang, Ma., Smarandache, F., & Shauangwu, Z. (2018). Single-valued neutrosophic clustering algorithm based on tsallis entropy maximization. *Axioms*, *7*(57), 1–12.

Rao, R. V., & Singh, D. (2010). An improved grey relational analysis as a decision making method for manufacturing situations. *International Journal of Decision Science Risk Management*, *2*, 1–23.

Sengur, A., & Guo, Y. (2011). Color texture image segmentation based on neutrosophic set and wavelet transformation. *Computer Vision and Image Understanding*, *115*(8), 1134–1144. doi:10.1016/j.cviu.2011.04.001

Smarandache, F. (1998). *A unifying field in logics. Neutrosophy: neutrosophic probability, set and logic*. Rehoboth: American Research Press.

Smarandache, F., & Pramanik, S. (Eds.). (2018). *New trends in neutrosophic theory and applications* (Vol. 2). Brussels: Pons Editions.

Wang, H., Smarandache, F., Zhang, Y., & Sunderraman, R. (2010). Single valued neutrosophic sets. *Rev Air Force Acad,* *1*(16), 10–14. Retrieved from http://213.177.9.66/ro/revista/NR_1_ 2010/Art_Smarandache.pdf

Wei, G. W. (2011). Grey relational analysis method for intuitionistic fuzzy multiple attribute decision making. *Expert Systems with Applications*, *38*(9), 11671–11677. doi:10.1016/j.eswa.2011.03.048

Xu, G., Wang, S., Yang, T., & Jiang, W. (2018). A neutrosophic approach based on TOPSIS method to image segmentation. *International Journal of Computers, Communications & Control, 13*(6), 1047–1061. doi:10.15837/ijccc.2018.6.3268

Ye, J. (2017). Some weighted aggregation operator of trapezoidal neutrosophic number and their multiple attribute decision making method. *Informatica, 28*(2), 387–402. doi:10.15388/Informatica.2017.135

Ye, S., Fu, J., & Ye, J. (2015). Medical Diagnosis Using Distance-Based Similarity Measures of Single Valued Neutrosophic Multisets. *Neutrosophic Sets and Systems, 7*, 47–54.

Zadeh, L. A. (1965). Fuzzy set and systems. In Proceeding of the symposium on system theory. New York Polytechnic Institute of Brooklyn.

Zhang, M., Zhang, L., & Cheng, H. D. (2010). A neutrosophic approach to image segmentation based on watershed method. *Signal Processing, 90*(5), 1510–1517. doi:10.1016/j.sigpro.2009.10.021

Zhang, X., Jin, F., & Liu, P. (2013). A grey relation projection method for multi-attribute decision making based on intuitionistic trapezoidal fuzzy number. *Applied Mathematical Modelling, 37*(5), 3467–3477. doi:10.1016/j.apm.2012.08.012

Chapter 9
Generalised Single–Valued Neutrosophic Number and Its Application to Neutrosophic Linear Programming

Nirmal Kumar Mahapatra
Panskura Banamali College (Autonomous), India

Tuhin Bera
Panskura Banamali College (Autonomous), India

ABSTRACT

In this chapter, the concept of single valued neutrosophic number (SVN-Number) is presented in a generalized way. Using this notion, a crisp linear programming problem (LP-problem) is extended to a neutrosophic linear programming problem (NLP-problem). The coefficients of the objective function of a crisp LP-problem are considered as generalized single valued neutrosophic number (GSVN-Number). This modified form of LP-problem is here called an NLP-problem. An algorithm is developed to solve NLP-problem by simplex method. Finally, this simplex algorithm is applied to a real-life problem. The problem is illustrated and solved numerically.

1 INTRODUCTION

Introduction of fuzzy set by Zadeh (1965) and then intuitionistic fuzzy set by Atanassov (1986) brought a golden opportunity to handle the uncertainty and vagueness in our daily life activities. The fuzzy sets are evaluated by the membership

DOI: 10.4018/978-1-7998-2555-5.ch009

grade of an object only, whereas intuitionistic fuzzy set meets the membership and the non-membership grade of an object simultaneously. To deal with uncertainty more precisely, Smarandache (1998a, 2005b) initiated the notion of neutrosophic set (*NS*, a generalised version of classical set, fuzzy set, intuitionistic fuzzy set etc. In the neutrosophic logic, each proposition is estimated by a triplet *viz* truth grade, indeterminacy grade and falsity grade. The indeterministic part of uncertain data, introduced in *NS* theory, plays an important role to make a proper decision which is not possible by intuitionistic fuzzy set theory. Since indeterminacy always appears in our routine activities, the *NS* theory can analyse the various situations smoothly. But it is too difficult to apply the *NS* theory in real life scenario for it's initial character as pointed out by Smarandache. So to apply in real spectrum, Wang et al. (2011) brought the concept of single valued neutrosophic set (*SVN* set). Ranking of fuzzy number and intuitionistic fuzzy number is an interesting subject needed in decision making, optimization, even in developing of various mathematical structures. From time to time, several ranking methods (Gani et al., 2016; Maleki, 2002; Prabhakaran and Ganesan, 2017; Parvathi and Malathi, 2012; Abbasbandy and Asady, 2006; Nasseri et al., 2005) have been adopted by researchers. Naturally, the ranking of neutrosophic number also was come into consideration from beginning of *NS* theory. Deli and Subas (2016) considered a ranking way of neutrosophic numbers and have used it to a decision making problems. Abdel-Baset (2019a, 2019b) solved group decision making problems based on TOPSIS technique by use of neutrosophic number. To estimate and solve the *NLP* problem in different direction, some respective attempts (Pramanik, 2016; Hussian et al., 2017) by researchers are seen.

This paper introduces the structure of *SVN* number in a different way to opt the notion of generalized single valued trapezoidal neutrosophic number (G_{SVTN} number), generalized single valued triangular neutrosophic number (G_{SVTrN} number) and develops an algorithm to solve *NLP* problem by simplex method. The proposed simplex algorithm is applied to a real life problem. The problem is illustrated and solved numerically.

The organisation of this paper is as follows. Section 2 deals some preliminary definitions. The concept of G_{SVN} number, G_{SVTN} number, G_{SVTrN} number and their respective parametric form are presented in Section 3. The concept of *NLP* problem and it's solution procedure are proposed in Section 4 and Section 5, respectively. In Section 6, the simplex method is illustrated by suitable examples. Finally, the present work is summarised in Section 7.

2 PRELIMINARIES

Some basic definitions are provided to bring the main thought of this paper here.

2.1 Definition (Bera and Mahapatra, 2017)

A continuous t norm $*$ and t conorm $\lozenge$ are two continuous binary operations assigning $[0,1] \times [0,1] \to [0,1]$ and obey the under stated principles:

(i) $*$ and $\lozenge$ are both commutative and associative.

(ii) $x*1 = 1*x = x$ and $x\lozenge 0 = 0\lozenge x = x$, $\forall x \in [0,1]$.

(iii) $x*y \leq p*q$ and $x\lozenge y \leq p\lozenge q$ if $x \leq p$, $y \leq q$ with $x,y,p,q \in [0,1]$.

$x*y = xy$, $x*y = \min\{x,y\}$, $x*y\text{-}\max\{x+y-1,0\}$

are most useful t norms and

$$x\lozenge y = x + y - xy, x\lozenge y = \max\{x,y\}, x\lozenge y = \min\{x+y,1\}$$

are most useful t conorms.

2.2 Definition (Smarandache, 1998a)

An *NS* Q on an initial universe X is presented by three characterisations namely true value T_Q indeterminant value I_Q and false value F_Q so that $T_Q, I_Q, F_Q : X \to]^-0,1^+[$. Thus Q can be designed as:

$$\left\{ \left\langle u, \left(T_Q(u), I_Q(u), F_Q(u) \right) \right\rangle : u \in X \right\}$$

with

$$^-0 \leq \sup T_Q(u) + \sup I_Q(u) + \sup F_Q(u) \leq 3^+.$$

    Here $1^+ = 1 + \delta$ where 1 is standard part and δ is non-standard part. Similarly $^-0 = 0 - \delta$. The non-standard set $]^-0,1^+[$ is basically practiced in philosophical ground and because of the difficulty to adopt it in real field, the standard subset of $]^-0,1^+[$ i.e., $[0,1]$ is applicable in real neutrosophic environment.

2.3 Definition (Wang et al., 2011)

An *SVN* set Q over a universe X is a set

$$Q = \{\langle x, T_Q(x), I_Q(x), F_Q(x)\rangle : x \in X$$

and $T_Q(x), I_Q(x), F_Q(x) \in [0,1]\}$ with

$$0 \leq \sup T_Q(x) + \sup I_Q(x) + \sup F_Q(x) \leq 3.$$

2.4 Definition (Deli and Subas, 2016)

Let $a_i, b_i, c_i, d_i \in R$ (the set of all real numbers) with $a_i \leq b_i \leq c_i \leq d_i (i=1,2,3)$ and $w_{\tilde{p}}, u_{\tilde{p}}, y_{\tilde{p}} \in [0,1] \subset R$. Then an *SVN* number

$$\tilde{p} = \left\langle \left([a_1, b_1, c_1, d_1]; w_{\tilde{p}}\right)\left([a_2, b_2, c_2, d_2]; u_{\tilde{p}}\right)\left([a_3, b_3, c_3, d_3]; y_{\tilde{p}}\right)\right\rangle$$

is a special *SVN* set on R whose true value, indeterminant value, false value are respectively defined by the mappings $T_{\tilde{p}} : R \rightarrow [0, w_{\tilde{p}}]$, $I_{\tilde{p}} : R \rightarrow [u_{\tilde{p}}, 1]$, $F_{\tilde{p}} : R \rightarrow [y_{\tilde{p}}, 1]$ and they are given as:

$$T_{\tilde{p}}(x) = \begin{cases} g_T^l(x), & a_1 \leq x \leq b_1, \\ w_{\tilde{p}}, & b_1 \leq x \leq c_1, \\ g_T^r(x), & c_1 \leq x \leq d_1, \\ 0, & otherwise. \end{cases}$$

$$I_{\tilde{p}}(x) = \begin{cases} g_I^l(x), & a_2 \leq x \leq b_2, \\ u_{\tilde{p}}, & b_2 \leq x \leq c_2, \\ g_I^r(x), & c_2 \leq x \leq d_2, \\ 1, & otherwise. \end{cases}$$

$$F_{\tilde{p}}(x) = \begin{cases} g_F^l(x), & a_3 \leq x \leq b_3, \\ y_{\tilde{p}}, & b_3 \leq x \leq c_3, \\ g_F^r(x), & c_3 \leq x \leq d_3, \\ 1, & otherwise. \end{cases}$$

The functions

$$g_T^l : [a_1, b_1] \rightarrow [0, w_{\tilde{p}}], g_I^r : [c_2, d_2] \rightarrow [u_{\tilde{p}}, 1], g_F^r : [c_3, d_3] \rightarrow [y_{\tilde{p}}, 1]$$

are continuous and non-decreasing functions satisfying:

$$g_T^l (a_1) = 0, g_T^l (b_1) = w_{\tilde{p}}, g_I^r (c_2) = u_{\tilde{p}}, g_I^r (d_2) = 1, g_F^r (c_3) = y_{\tilde{p}}, g_F^r (d_3) = 1.$$

The functions

$$g_T^r : [c_1, d_1] \rightarrow [0, w_{\tilde{p}}], g_I^l : [a_2, b_2] \rightarrow [u_{\tilde{p}}, 1], g_F^l : [a_3, b_3] \rightarrow [y_{\tilde{p}}, 1]$$

are continuous and non-increasing functions satisfying:

$$g_T^r (c_1) = w_{\tilde{p}}, g_T^r (d_1) = 0, g_I^l (a_2) = 1, g_I^l (b_2) = u_{\tilde{p}}, g_F^l (a_3) = 1, g_F^l (b_3) = y_{\tilde{p}}.$$

2.4.1 Definition (Deli and Subas, 2016)

If $[a_1, b_1, c_1, d_1] = [a_2, b_2, c_2, d_2] = [a_3, b_3, c_3, d_3]$ then the *SVN* number $\tilde{p}$ is reduced to a single valued trapezoidal neutrosophic number as:

$$\tilde{p} = \langle ([a_1, b_1, c_1, d_1]; w_{\tilde{p}}, u_{\tilde{p}}, y_{\tilde{p}}) \rangle .$$

$$\tilde{p} = \langle ([a_1, b_1, d_1]; w_{\tilde{p}}, u_{\tilde{p}}, y_{\tilde{p}}) \rangle$$

is called a single valued triangular neutrosophic number if $b_1 = c_1$.

2.5 Definition (Bera and Mahapatra, 2016)

The (α, β, γ) cut of an *NS*. *P* is denoted by $P_{(\alpha, \beta, \gamma)}$ and is defined as:

$$P_{(\alpha, \beta, \gamma)} = \{ x \in X : T_P(x) \geq \alpha, I_P(x) \leq \beta, F_P(x) \leq \gamma \}$$

with $\alpha, \beta, \gamma \in [0,1]$ and $0 \leq \alpha + \beta + \gamma \leq 3$. Clearly, it is a crisp subset X.

2.6 Definition (Abbasbandy and Asady, 2006)

In parametric form, a fuzzy number P is a pair (P_L, P_R) of functions $P_L(r), P_R(r), r \in [0,1]$ satisfying the followings.

(i)   Both are bounded functions.

(ii) P_L is monotone increasing left continuous and P_R is monotone decreasing right continuous function.

(iii) $P_L(r) \leq P_R(r), 0 \leq r \leq 1$.

A trapezoidal fuzzy number is put as $P=(x_0, y_0, \delta, \zeta)$ where $[x_0, y_0]$ is interval defuzzifier and $\delta(>0), \zeta(>0)$ are respectively called left fuzziness, right fuzziness. $(x_0 - \delta, y_0 + \zeta)$ is the support of P and it's membership function is:

$$P(x) = \begin{cases} \dfrac{1}{\delta}(x - x_0 + \delta), & x_0 - \delta \leq x \leq x_0, \\ 1, & x \in [x_0, y_0], \\ \dfrac{1}{\zeta}(y_0 - x + \zeta), & y_0 \leq x \leq y_0 + \zeta, \\ 0, & otherwise. \end{cases}$$

In parametric form

$$P_L(r) = x_0 - \delta + \delta r, \quad P_R(r) = y_0 + \zeta - \zeta r.$$

For arbitrary trapezoidal fuzzy numbers $P=(P_L, P_R)$, $Q=(Q_L, Q_R)$ and scalar $k>0$ the addition and scalar multiplication are $P+Q$, kQ and they are defined by:

$$(P+Q)_L(r) = P_L(r) + Q_L(r) \quad (P+Q)_R(r) = P_R(r) + Q_R(r)$$

and

$$(kQ)_L(r) = kQ_L(r) \quad (kQ)_R(r) = kQ_R(r).$$

3 GENERALISED SINGLE VALUED NEUTROSOPHIC NUMBER

Here, the structure of G_{SVN} number, G_{SVTN} number and G_{SVTrN} number have been presented.

3.1 Definition

The support of three components of an *SVN* set Q over X are given by a triplet $\left(S_{Q_T}, S_{Q_I}, S_{Q_F}\right)$ here

$$S_{Q_T} = \left\{u \in X | T_Q(u) > 0\right\}, \ S_{Q_I} = \left\{u \in X | I_Q(u) < 1\right\}, \ S_{Q_F} = \{u \in X \mid F_Q(u) < 1\}.$$

The height of the components of Q are given by a triplet $\left(H_{Q_T}, H_{Q_I}, H_{Q_F}\right)$ where

$$H_{Q_T} = \max\{T_Q(u) | u \in X\}, H_{Q_I} = \max\{I_Q(u) | u \in X\}, H_{Q_F} = \max\{F_Q(u) | u \in X\}.$$

3.1.1 Example

Define an *SVN* set Q on $\{0, 1, \cdots, 10\} \subset \mathbf{Z}$.(the set of integers) as:

$$\left\{\left\langle u, \left(\frac{u}{1+u}, 1 - \frac{1}{2^u}, \frac{1}{1+u}\right)\right\rangle \mid 0 \le u \le 10\right\}.$$

Then

$$S_{Q_T} = \{1, \cdots, 10\}, \ S_{Q_I} = \{0, \cdots, 10\}, \ S_{Q_F} = \{1, \cdots, 10\}$$

and $H_{Q_T} = 0.909$ at *u*=10; $H_{Q_I} = 0.999$ at *u*=10; $H_{Q_F} = 1$ at *u*=0.

3.2 Definition

A G_{SVN} number

$$\tilde{p} = \left\langle \left([a_1, b_1, \sigma_1, \eta_1]; w_{\tilde{p}} \right) \left([a_2, b_2, \sigma_2, \eta_2]; u_{\tilde{p}} \right), \left([a_3, b_3, \sigma_3, \eta_3]; y_{\tilde{p}} \right) \right\rangle$$

is a special *SVN* set on *R* where $\sigma_i(>0)$, $\eta_i(<0)$ are respectively called left spreads, right spreads and $[a_i, b_i]$ are the modal intervals of truth, indeterminacy and falsity functions for $i=1,2,3$ respectively in $\tilde{p}$ and $w_{\tilde{p}}, u_{\tilde{p}}, y_{\tilde{p}} \in [0,1] \subset R$. The truth, indeterminacy and falsity functions are defined as follows:

$$T_{\tilde{p}}(x) = \begin{cases} \dfrac{1}{\sigma_1} w_{\tilde{p}} \left(x - a_1 + \sigma_1 \right), & a_1 - \sigma_1 \leq x \leq a_1, \\[2mm] w_{\tilde{p}}, & x \in [a_1, b_1], \\[2mm] \dfrac{1}{\eta_1} w_{\tilde{p}} \left(b_1 - x + \eta_1 \right), & b_1 \leq x \leq b_1 + \eta_1, \\[2mm] 0, & otherwise. \end{cases}$$

$$I_{\tilde{p}}(x) = \begin{cases} \dfrac{1}{\sigma_2} \left(a_2 - x + u_{\tilde{p}} \left(x - a_2 + \sigma_2 \right) \right), & a_2 - \sigma_2 \leq x \leq a_2 \\[2mm] u_{\tilde{p}}, & x \in [a_2, b_2], \\[2mm] \dfrac{1}{\eta_2} \left(x - b_2 + u_{\tilde{p}} \left(b_2 - x + \eta_2 \right) \right), & b_2 \leq x \leq b_2 + \eta_2, \\[2mm] 1, & otherwise \end{cases}$$

$$F_{\tilde{p}}(x) = \begin{cases} \dfrac{1}{\sigma_3} \left(a_3 - x + y_{\tilde{p}} \left(x - a_3 + \sigma_3 \right) \right), & a_3 - \sigma_3 \leq x \leq a_3 \\[2mm] y_{\tilde{p}}, & x \in [a_3, b_3], \\[2mm] \dfrac{1}{\eta_3} \left(x - b_3 + y_{\tilde{p}} \left(b_3 - x + \eta_3 \right) \right), & b_3 \leq x \leq b_3 + \eta_3 \\[2mm] 1, & otherwise \end{cases}$$

In parametric form, a G_{SVN} number $\tilde{p}$ consists of three pairs $\left(T_{\tilde{p}}^l, T_{\tilde{p}}^u \right), \left(I_{\tilde{p}}^l, I_{\tilde{p}}^u \right), \left(F_{\tilde{p}}^l, F_{\tilde{p}}^u \right)$ of functions $T_{\tilde{p}}^l(r), T_{\tilde{p}}^u(r)$. $I_{\tilde{p}}^l(r), I_{\tilde{p}}^u(r), F_{\tilde{p}}^l(r), F_{\tilde{p}}^u(r), r \in [0,1]$ satisfying the followings.

1. $T_{\tilde{p}}^{l}, I_{\tilde{p}}^{u}, F_{\tilde{a}}^{u}$ are bounded monotone increasing continuous function.
2. $T_{\tilde{p}}^{u}, I_{\tilde{p}}^{l}, F_{\tilde{a}}^{l}$ are bounded monotone decreasing continuous function.
3. $T_{\tilde{p}}^{l}(r) \leq T_{\tilde{p}}^{u}(r), I_{\tilde{p}}^{l}(r) \geq I_{\tilde{p}}^{u}(r), F_{\tilde{p}}^{l}(r) \geq F_{\tilde{p}}^{u}(r), r \in [0,1]$.

3.2.1 Definition

The support of the components of a G_{SVN} number $\tilde{p}$ are given by a triplet $\left(S_{P_T}, S_{P_I}, S_{P_F} \right)$ where

$$S_{P_T} = \left\{ x \in R \,\middle|\, T_{\tilde{p}}(x) \rangle 0 \right\}, S_{P_I} = \{x \in R \mid I_{\tilde{p}}(x) < 1\}, S_{P_F} = \{x \in R \mid F_{\tilde{p}}(x) < 1\}.$$

The height of the components of $\tilde{p}$ are given by a triplet $\left(H_{P_T}, H_{P_I}, H_{P_F} \right)$ where

$$H\tilde{p}_T = w_{\tilde{p}}, H\tilde{p}_I = 1 - u_{\tilde{p}}, H\tilde{p}_F = 1 - y_{\tilde{p}}.$$

The boundaries of the truth function of $\tilde{p}$ are:

$$LB_{\tilde{p}_T} = \left(a_1 - \sigma_1, a_1 \right) \text{ and } RB_{\tilde{p}_T} = \left(b_1, b_1 + \eta_1 \right)$$

$LB_{\tilde{p}_T}$ and $RB_{\tilde{p}_T}$ are respectively called left boundary and right boundary for truth function of $\tilde{p}$. Similarly,

$$LB_{\tilde{p}_I} = \left(a_2 - \sigma_2, a_2 \right), \; RB_{\tilde{p}_I} = \left(b_2, b_2 + \eta_2 \right)$$

and

$$LB_{\tilde{p}_F} = \left(a_3 - \sigma_3, a_3 \right), \; RB_{\tilde{p}_F} = \left(b_3, b_3 + \eta_3 \right).$$

The core for the truth function of $\tilde{p}$ is a set of points at which it's height is measured. Similarly, the core for other two components are defined.

3.2.2 Example

Consider a G_{SVN} number $\tilde{p}$ on R whose three components are as follows:

$$T_{\tilde{p}}(x) = \begin{cases} \dfrac{0.6(x-11)}{4}, & x \in [11,15] \\ 0.6, & x \in [15,25] \\ \dfrac{0.6(36-x)}{11}, & x \in [25,36] \\ 0, & \text{otherwise.} \end{cases}$$

$$I_{\tilde{p}}(x) = \begin{cases} \dfrac{4.4-0.1x}{4}, & x \in [4,8] \\ 0.9, & x \in [8,13] \\ \dfrac{0.1x+5}{7}, & x \in [13,20] \\ 1, & \text{otherwise.} \end{cases}$$

$$F_{\tilde{p}}(x) = \begin{cases} \dfrac{26-x}{3}, & x \in [23,26] \\ 0, & x \in [26,30] \\ \dfrac{x-30}{8}, & x \in [30,38] \\ 1, & \text{otherwise.} \end{cases}$$

Then $S_{P_T} = (11,36)$, $S_{P_I} = (4,20)$ and $S_{P_F} = (23,38)$. For that $\tilde{p}$

$H\tilde{p}_T = 0.6, H\tilde{p}_I = 0.1, H\tilde{p}_F = 1$.

Here,

$LB_{\tilde{p}_T} = (11,15), RB_{\tilde{p}_T} = (25,36), LB_{\tilde{p}_I} = (4,8), RB_{\tilde{p}_I} = (13,20), LB_{\tilde{p}_F} = (23,26), RB_{\tilde{p}_F} = (30,38).$

The core of truth, indeterminacy and falsity function are [15,25], [8,13], [26,30] respectively.

189

3.3 Definition

Let us assume two G_{SVN} numbers $\tilde{p}$ and $\tilde{q}$ as follows:

$$\tilde{p} = \left\langle \left(\left[a_1, a'_1, \sigma_1, \eta_1 \right]; w_{\tilde{p}} \right), \left(\left[a_2, a'_2, \sigma_2, \eta_2 \right]; u_{\tilde{p}} \right), \left(\left[a_3, a'_3, \sigma_3, \eta_3 \right]; y_{\tilde{p}} \right) \right\rangle$$

$$\tilde{q} = \left\langle \left(\left[b_1, b'_1, \xi_1, \delta_1 \right]; w_{\tilde{q}} \right), \left(\left[b_2, b'_2, \xi_2, \delta_2 \right]; u_{\tilde{q}} \right), \left(\left[b_3, b'_3, \xi_3, \delta_3 \right]; y_{\tilde{q}} \right) \right\rangle .$$

Then for any real number x.

(i)   Addition:

$$\tilde{p} + \tilde{q} = \left\langle \left(\left[a_1 + b_1, a'_1 + b'_1, \sigma_1 + \xi_1, \eta_1 + \delta_1 \right]; w_{\tilde{p}} * w_{\tilde{q}} \right) \right.$$
$$\left. \left(\left[a_2 + b_2, a'_2 + b'_2, \sigma_2 + \xi_2, \eta_2 + \delta_2 \right]; u_{\tilde{p}} \Diamond u_{\tilde{q}} \right) \left(\left[a_3 + b_3, a'_3 + b'_3, \sigma_3 + \xi_3, \eta_3 + \delta_3 \right]; y_{\tilde{p}} \Diamond y_{\tilde{q}} \right) \right\rangle$$

(ii)   Scalar multiplication:

$$x\tilde{p} = \left\langle \left(\left[xa_1, xa'_1, x\sigma_1, x\eta_1 \right]; w_{\tilde{p}} \right) \left(\left[xa_2, xa'_2, x\sigma_2, x\eta_2 \right]; u_{\tilde{p}} \right), \left(\left[xa_3, xa'_3, x\sigma_3, x\eta_3 \right]; y_{\tilde{p}} \right) \right\rangle$$

for $x > 0$

$$x\tilde{p} = \left\langle \left(\left[xa'_1, xa_1, -x\eta_1, -x\sigma_1 \right]; w_{\tilde{p}} \right), \left(\left[xa'_2, xa_2, -x\eta_2, -x\sigma_2 \right]; u_{\tilde{p}} \right), \left(\left[xa'_3, xa_3, -x\eta_3, -x\sigma_3 \right]; y_{\tilde{p}} \right) \right\rangle$$

for $x < 0$.

3.4 Corollary

Let $\tilde{p} = \left\langle \left(\left[a_1, b_1, \sigma_1, \eta_1 \right]; w_{\tilde{p}} \right) \left(\left[a_2, b_2, \sigma_2, \eta_2 \right]; u_{\tilde{p}} \right), \left(\left[a_3, b_3, \sigma_3, \eta_3 \right]; y_{\tilde{p}} \right) \right\rangle$ be an G_{SVN} number.

1.   Any α cut set of the G_{SVN} number $\tilde{p}$ for truth function is denoted by $\tilde{p}_\alpha$ and is given by a closed interval as:

$$\tilde{p}_\alpha = \left[L_{\tilde{p}}(\alpha), R_{\tilde{p}}(\alpha) \right] = \left[a_1 - \sigma_1 + \frac{\sigma_1 \alpha}{w_{\tilde{p}}}, b_1 + \eta_1 - \frac{\eta_1 \alpha}{w_{\tilde{p}}} \right], \ for \ \alpha \in \left[0, w_{\tilde{p}} \right].$$

The value of $\tilde{p}$ corresponding α cut set is denoted by $V_T(\tilde{p})$ and is calculated as:

$$V_T(\tilde{p}) = \int_0^{w_{\tilde{p}}} \left[\left(a_1 - \sigma_1 + \frac{\sigma_1 \alpha}{w_{\tilde{p}}} \right) + \left(b_1 + \eta_1 - \frac{\eta_1 \alpha}{w_{\tilde{p}}} \right) \right] \alpha \, d\alpha$$

$$= \int_0^{w_{\tilde{p}}} \left[a_1 + b_1 + \eta_1 - \sigma_1 - \frac{(\eta_1 - \sigma_1)\alpha}{w_{\tilde{p}}} \right] \alpha \, d\alpha = \frac{1}{6}(3a_1 + 3b_1 - \sigma_1 + \eta_1) w_{\tilde{p}}^2.$$

2. Any β cut set of the G_{SVN} number $\tilde{p}$ for indeterminacy membership function is denoted by $\tilde{p}^\beta$ and is given by a closed interval as:

$$\tilde{p}^\beta = \left[L'_{\tilde{p}}(\beta), R'_{\tilde{p}}(\beta) \right]$$

$$= \left[\frac{(u_{\tilde{p}} - \beta)\sigma_2 + (1 - u_{\tilde{p}})a_2}{1 - u_{\tilde{p}}}, \frac{(\beta - u_{\tilde{p}})\eta_2 + (1 - u_{\tilde{p}})b_2}{1 - u_{\tilde{p}}} \right], \ for \ \beta \in \left[u_{\tilde{p}}, 1 \right].$$

The value of $\tilde{p}$ corresponding β cut set is denoted by $V_I(\tilde{p})$ and is calculated as:

$$V_I(\tilde{p}) = \int_{u_{\tilde{p}}}^1 \left[\frac{(u_{\tilde{p}} - \beta)\sigma_2 + (1 - u_{\tilde{p}})a_2}{1 - u_{\tilde{p}}} + \frac{(\beta - u_{\tilde{p}})\eta_2 + (1 - u_{\tilde{p}})b_2}{1 - u_{\tilde{p}}} \right](1 - \beta) \, d\beta$$

$$= \int_{u_{\tilde{p}}}^1 \left[a_2 + b_2 - \sigma_2 + \eta_2 + \frac{(\sigma_2 - \eta_2)(1 - \beta)}{1 - u_{\tilde{p}}} \right](1 - \beta) \, d\beta = \frac{1}{6}(3a_2 + 3b_2 - \sigma_2 + \eta_2)(1 - u_{\tilde{p}})^2.$$

3. Any γ cut set of the G_{SVN} number $\tilde{p}$ for falsity membership function is denoted by $^\gamma \tilde{p}$ and is given by a closed interval as:

$$^{\gamma}\tilde{p} = \left[L"_{\tilde{p}}(\gamma), R"_{\tilde{p}}(\gamma) \right]$$

$$= \left[\frac{\left(u_{\tilde{p}} - \gamma\right)\sigma_3 + \left(1 - y_{\tilde{p}}\right)a_3}{1 - y_{\tilde{p}}}, \frac{\left(\gamma - y_{\tilde{p}}\right)\eta_3 + \left(1 - y_{\tilde{p}}\right)b_3}{1 - y_{\tilde{p}}} \right], \; for \; \gamma \in \left[y_{\tilde{p}}, 1 \right].$$

The value of $\tilde{p}$ corresponding γ cut set is denoted by $V_F\left(\tilde{p}\right)$ and is calculated as:

$$V_F\left(\tilde{p}\right) = \int\limits_{y_{\tilde{p}}}^{1} \left[\frac{\left(u_{\tilde{p}} - \gamma\right)\sigma_3 + \left(1 - y_{\tilde{p}}\right)a_3}{1 - y_{\tilde{p}}} + \frac{\left(^3 - y_{\tilde{p}}\right)\eta_3 + \left(1 - y_{\tilde{p}}\right)b_3}{1 - y_{\tilde{p}}} \right] (1 - \gamma)d\gamma$$

$$= \int\limits_{y_{\tilde{p}}}^{1} \left[a_3 + b_3 - \sigma_3 + \eta_3 + \frac{\left(\sigma_3 - \eta_3\right)\left(1 - \gamma\right)}{1 - y_{\tilde{p}}} \right] (1 - \gamma)d\gamma = \frac{1}{6}\left(3a_3 + 3b_3 - \sigma_3 + \eta_3\right)\left(1 - y_{\tilde{p}}\right)^2.$$

3.5 Definition

For $\kappa \in [0,1]$ the κ weighted value of an G_{SVN} number $\tilde{b}$ is denoted by $V_\kappa\left(\tilde{b}\right)$ and is defined as:

$$V_\kappa\left(\tilde{b}\right) = \kappa^n V_T\left(\tilde{b}\right) + \left(1 - \kappa^n\right)V_I\left(\tilde{b}\right) + \left(1 - \kappa^n\right)V_F\left(\tilde{b}\right),$$

n being any natural number.

Thus, the κ- weighted value for the G_{SVN} number $\tilde{p}$ defined in Corollary 3.4 is:

$$V_\kappa\left(\tilde{p}\right) = \frac{1}{6}\left[\left(3a_1 + 3b_1 - \sigma_1 + \eta_1\right)\kappa^n w_{\tilde{p}}^2 + \left(3a_2 + 3b_2 - \sigma_2 + \eta_2\right)\left(1 - \kappa^n\right)\left(1 - u_{\tilde{p}}\right)^2 \right.$$
$$\left. + \left(3a_3 + 3b_3 - \sigma_3 + \eta_3\right)\left(1 - \kappa^n\right)\left(1 - y_{\tilde{p}}\right)^2 \right]$$

3.5.1 Property of K (Kappa) Weighted Value Function

The κ weighted value $V_\kappa\left(\tilde{p}\right)$ and $V_\kappa\left(\tilde{q}\right)$ of two G_{SVN} numbers $\tilde{p}, \tilde{q}$ respectively obey the followings.

1. $V_\kappa\left(\tilde{p}\pm\tilde{q}\right)\le V_\kappa\left(\tilde{p}\right)+V_\kappa\left(\tilde{q}\right),\ V_\kappa\left(\tilde{p}+\tilde{q}\right)\ge V_\kappa\left(\tilde{p}\right)\sim V_\kappa\left(\tilde{q}\right)$

    $V_\kappa\left(\tilde{p}-\tilde{p}\right)=V_\kappa\left(\tilde{0}\right)\quad V_\kappa\left(\mu\tilde{p}\right)=\mu V_\kappa\left(\tilde{p}\right)$ for μ being any real number.

2. $V_\kappa\left(\tilde{p}\right)$ is monotone increasing or decreasing or constant according as

    $V_T\left(\tilde{p}\right)>V_I\left(\tilde{p}\right)+V_F\left(\tilde{p}\right)\qquad$ o r $\qquad V_T\left(\tilde{p}\right)<V_I\left(\tilde{p}\right)+V_F\left(\tilde{p}\right)\qquad$ o r

    $V_T\left(\tilde{p}\right)=V_I\left(\tilde{p}\right)+V_F\left(\tilde{p}\right)$ respectively.

Proof. We shall here prove (vi) only. Others can be easily verified by taking any two G_{SVN} numbers. Here,

$$V_\kappa\left(\tilde{p}\right)=\kappa^n V_T\left(\tilde{p}\right)+\left(1-\kappa^n\right)\left(V_I\left(\tilde{p}\right)+V_F\left(\tilde{p}\right)\right)$$

$$\frac{dV_\kappa\left(\tilde{p}\right)}{d\kappa}=n\kappa^{n-1}\left[V_T\left(\tilde{p}\right)-\left(V_I\left(\tilde{p}\right)+V_F\left(\tilde{p}\right)\right)\right].$$

As $\kappa\in[0,1]$ so $\dfrac{dV_\kappa\left(\tilde{p}\right)}{d\kappa}>,<,=0$ for $\left[V_T\left(\tilde{p}\right)-\left(V_I\left(\tilde{p}\right)+V_F\left(\tilde{p}\right)\right)\right]>,<,=0$

respectively. This clears the fact.

3.6 Definition

Let $G_{SVN}(R)$ be the set of all G_{SVN} numbers defined over R. For $\kappa\in[0,1]$ a mapping $\mathfrak{R}_\kappa:G_{SVN}\left(R\right)\to R$ is called a ranking function and it is defined as:

$$\mathfrak{R}_\kappa\left(\tilde{a}\right)=V_\kappa\left(\tilde{a}\right)\text{for } \tilde{a}\in G_{SVN}\left(R\right).$$

For $\tilde{a},\tilde{b}\in G_{SVN}\left(R\right)$ their ranking is defined as:

$$\tilde{a}>_{\mathfrak{R}_\kappa}\tilde{b}\text{ iff }\mathfrak{R}_\kappa\left(\tilde{a}\right)>\mathfrak{R}_\kappa\left(\tilde{b}\right),\ \tilde{a}<_{\mathfrak{R}_\kappa}\tilde{b}\text{ iff }\mathfrak{R}_\kappa\left(\tilde{a}\right)<\mathfrak{R}_\kappa\left(\tilde{b}\right),\ \tilde{a}=_{\mathfrak{R}_\kappa}\tilde{b}\text{ iff }\mathfrak{R}_\kappa\left(\tilde{a}\right)=\mathfrak{R}_\kappa\left(\tilde{b}\right).$$

3.7 Definition

An G_{SVN} number $\tilde{p}$ is called a G_{SVTN} number if three modal intervals in $\tilde{p}$ are equal. Thus

$$\tilde{p} = \left\langle \left([a_0, b_0, \sigma_1, \eta_1]; w_{\tilde{p}} \right) \left([a_0, b_0, \sigma_2, \eta_2]; u_{\tilde{p}} \right) \left([a_0, b_0, \sigma_3, \eta_3]; y_{\tilde{p}} \right) \right\rangle$$

is an G_{SVTN} number whose truth, indeterminacy and falsity functions are as follows:

$$T_{\tilde{p}}(x) = \begin{cases} \dfrac{1}{\sigma_1} w_{\tilde{p}} (x - a_0 + \sigma_1), & a_0 - \sigma_1 \le x \le a_0, \\ w_{\tilde{p}}, & x \in [a_0, b_0], \\ \dfrac{1}{\eta_1} w_{\tilde{p}} (b_0 - x + \eta_1), & b_0 \le x \le b_0 + \eta_1, \\ 0, & otherwise. \end{cases}$$

$$I_{\tilde{p}}(x) = \begin{cases} \dfrac{1}{\sigma_2} \left(a_0 - x + u_{\tilde{p}} (x - a_0 + \sigma_2) \right), & a_0 - \sigma_2 \le x \le a_0, \\ u_{\tilde{p}}, & x \in [a_0, b_0], \\ \dfrac{1}{\eta_2} \left(x - b_0 + u_{\tilde{p}} (b_0 - x + \eta_2) \right), & b_0 \le x \le b_0 + \eta_2, \\ 1, & otherwise. \end{cases}$$

$$F_{\tilde{p}}(x) = \begin{cases} \dfrac{1}{\sigma_3} \left(a_0 - x + y_{\tilde{p}} (x - a_0 + \sigma_3) \right), & a_0 - \sigma_3 \le x \le a_0, \\ y_{\tilde{p}}, & x \in [a_0, b_0], \\ \dfrac{1}{\eta_3} \left(x - b_0 + y_{\tilde{p}} (b_0 - x + \eta_3) \right), & b_0 \le x \le b_0 + \eta_3, \\ 1, & otherwise. \end{cases}$$

In parametric form for $r \in [0,1]$:

$$T_{\tilde{p}}^l (r) = a_0 - \sigma_1 + \frac{\sigma_1 r}{w_{\tilde{p}}}, \quad T_{\tilde{p}}^u (r) = b_0 + \eta_1 - \frac{\eta_1 r}{w_{\tilde{p}}};$$

$$I_{\tilde{p}}^{l}(r) = \frac{\left(1 - u_{\tilde{p}}\right)a_0 + \left(u_{\tilde{p}} - r\right)\sigma_2}{1 - u_{\tilde{p}}}, \quad I_{\tilde{p}}^{u}(r) = \frac{\left(1 - u_{\tilde{p}}\right)b_0 + \left(r - u_{\tilde{p}}\right)\eta_2}{1 - u_{\tilde{p}}};$$

$$F_{\tilde{p}}^{l}(r) = \frac{\left(1 - y_{\tilde{p}}\right)a_0 + \left(y_{\tilde{p}} - r\right)\sigma_3}{1 - y_{\tilde{p}}}, \quad F_{\tilde{p}}^{u}(r) = \frac{\left(1 - y_{\tilde{p}}\right)b_0 + \left(r - y_{\tilde{p}}\right)\eta_3}{1 - y_{\tilde{p}}}$$

3.8 Definition

A G_{SVTN} number $\tilde{p}$ is called a G_{SVTN} number if the modal interval in $\tilde{p}$ is reduced to a modal point. Thus

$$\tilde{p} = \left\langle \left([a_0, \sigma_1, \eta_1]; w_{\tilde{p}}\right)\left([a_0, \sigma_2, \eta_2]; u_{\tilde{p}}\right)\left([a_0, \sigma_3, \eta_3]; y_{\tilde{p}}\right)\right\rangle$$

is a G_{SVTrN} number whose truth, indeterminacy and falsity functions are as follows:

$$T_{\tilde{p}}(x) = \begin{cases} \dfrac{1}{\sigma_1} w_{\tilde{p}}\left(x - a_0 + \sigma_1\right), & a_0 - \sigma_1 \leq x \leq a_0, \\[2mm] w_{\tilde{p}}, & x = a_0, \\[2mm] \dfrac{1}{\eta_1} w_{\tilde{p}}\left(a_0 - x + \eta_1\right), & a_0 \leq x \leq a_0 + \eta_1, \\[2mm] 0, & \text{otherwise.} \end{cases}$$

$$I_{\tilde{p}}(x) = \begin{cases} \dfrac{1}{\sigma_2}\left(a_0 - x + u_{\tilde{p}}\left(x - a_0 + \sigma_2\right)\right), & a_0 - \sigma_2 \leq x \leq a_0, \\[2mm] u_{\tilde{p}}, & x = a_0, \\[2mm] \dfrac{1}{\eta_2}\left(x - a_0 + u_{\tilde{p}}\left(a_0 - x + \eta_2\right)\right), & a_0 \leq x \leq a_0 + \eta_2, \\[2mm] 1, & \text{otherwise.} \end{cases}$$

$$F_{\tilde{p}}(x) = \begin{cases} \dfrac{1}{\sigma_3}\left(a_0 - x + y_{\tilde{p}}\left(x - a_0 + \sigma_3\right)\right), & a_0 - \sigma_3 \le x \le a_0, \\[2mm] y_{\tilde{p}}, & x = a_0, \\[2mm] \dfrac{1}{\eta_3}\left(x - a_0 + y_{\tilde{p}}\left(a_0 - x + \eta_3\right)\right), & a_0 \le x \le a_0 + \eta_3, \\[2mm] 1, & otherwise. \end{cases}$$

3.8.1 Definition

Let $\tilde{a}$ and $\tilde{b}$ be two G_{SVTrN} numbers as follows:

$$\tilde{a} = \left\langle \left([a,\sigma_1,\eta_1]; w_{\tilde{a}}\right)\left([a,\sigma_2,\eta_2]; u_{\tilde{a}}\right), \left([a,\sigma_3,\eta_3]; y_{\tilde{a}}\right) \right\rangle \ldots$$

$$\tilde{b} = \left\langle \left([b,\xi_1,\delta_1]; w_{\tilde{b}}\right), \left([b,\xi_2,\delta_2]; u_{\tilde{b}}\right), \left([b,\xi_3,\delta_3]; y_{\tilde{b}}\right) \right\rangle$$

Then for any real number x.

1.   Addition

$$\tilde{a} + \tilde{b} = \left\langle \left([a+b,\sigma_1+\xi_1,\eta_1+\delta_1]; w_{\tilde{a}} * w_{\tilde{b}}\right) \right.$$
$$\left. \left([a+b,\sigma_2+\xi_2,\eta_2+\delta_2]; u_{\tilde{a}} \Diamond u_{\tilde{b}}\right)\left([a+b,\sigma_3+\xi_3,\eta_3+\delta_3]; y_{\tilde{a}} \Diamond y_{\tilde{b}}\right) \right\rangle$$

2.   Scalar multiplication

$$x\tilde{a} = \left\langle \left([xa,x\sigma_1,x\eta_1]; w_{\tilde{a}}\right)\left([xa,x\sigma_2,x\eta_2]; u_{\tilde{a}}\right), \left([xa,x\sigma_3,x\eta_3]; y_{\tilde{a}}\right) \right\rangle$$

for $x>0$.

$$x\tilde{a} = \left\langle \left([xa,-x\eta_1,-x\sigma_1]; w_{\tilde{a}}\right),\left([xa,-x\eta_2,-x\sigma_2]; u_{\tilde{a}}\right),\left([xa,-x\eta_3,-x\sigma_3]; y_{\tilde{a}}\right) \right\rangle$$

for $x<0$.

3. The κ- weighted value $V_\kappa(\tilde{a})$ of $\tilde{a}$ is given as

$$V_\kappa(\tilde{a}) = \frac{1}{6}\Big[(6a - \sigma_1 + \eta_1)\kappa^n w_{\tilde{a}}^2 + \big\{(6a - \sigma_2 + \eta_2)(1 - u_{\tilde{a}})^2 + (6a - \sigma_3 + \eta_3)(1 - y_{\tilde{a}})^2\big\}(1 - \kappa^n)\Big]$$

3.8.2 Remark

Definition 2.4.1 shows that the supports (i.e. the bases of trapeziums (triangles)) for truth, indeterminacy and falsity function are all same. Then the value of truth, indeterminacy and falsity function (i.e., the area of individual trapezium (triangle)) differs in respect to their corresponding height only. But by Definition 3.7, we consider different supports (i.e. bases of trapeziums (triangles) formed) for truth, indeterminacy and falsity functions. Thus we can allow the supports and heights together to differ the value of truth, indeterminacy and falsity functions in the present study. Briefly, Definition 2.4.1 is a particular case of Definition 3.7. Hence decision maker has a scope of flexibility to choose and compare different G_{SVN} numbers in their study. The facts are shown by the graphical Figure 1 and 2. Figure 1 and Figure 2 represent Definition 2.4.1 and Definition 3.7 respectively.

Figure 1.

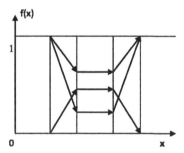

Figure 2.

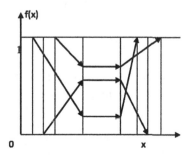

3.9 Definition

1. The zero G_{SVTN} number is denoted by $\tilde{0}$ and is defined as:

$$\tilde{0} = \left\langle \left([0,0,0,0];1\right),\left([0,0,0,0];0\right),\left([0,0,0,0];0\right)\right\rangle.$$

2. The zero G_{SVTrN} number is denoted by $\tilde{0}$ and is defined as:

$$\tilde{0} = \left\langle \left([0,0,0];1\right),\left([0,0,0];0\right),\left([0,0,0];0\right)\right\rangle.$$

4 NEUTROSOPHIC LINEAR PROGRAMMING PROBLEM

Before to discuss the main result, we shall remember the crisp concept of an *LP* problem. The standard form of an *LP* problem is:

Max $z=cx$ such that $Ax=b$, $x \geq 0$

where $c= (c_1,c_2,\ldots,c_n)$, $b= (b_1,b_2,\ldots,b_n)^t$ and $A = [a_{ij}]_{m \times n}$.

In this problem, all the parameters are crisp. we shall now define *NLP* problem.

4.1 Definition

An *LP* problem having some parameters as G_{SVN} number is called an *NLP* problem. Considering the coefficient of the variables in the objective function in an *LP* problem in term of G_{SVN} numbers, an *NLP* problem is designed as follows:

$$Max\ \tilde{z} =_{\mathfrak{R}_\kappa} \tilde{c}x \text{ such that } Mx=b;\ x \geq 0 \tag{4.1}$$

where $b \in R^m, x \in R^n, M \in R^{m \times n}, \tilde{c}^t \in (G_{SVN}(R))^n$ and $\mathfrak{R}_\kappa$ is a ranking function.

4.2 Definition

1. $x \in R^n$ is a feasible solution to equation (4.1) if x satisfies the constraints of that.
2. A feasible solution x^* is an optimal solution if for all solutions x to (4.1), $\tilde{c}x^* \geq_{\mathfrak{R}_\kappa} \tilde{c}x$.

3. For the *NLP* problem (4.1), suppose rank $(M,b) = \text{rank}(M)=m$. M is partitioned as $[B,N]$ where B is a non-singular $m \times m$ matrix i.e., rank(B)=m. A feasible solution $x=(x_B, x_N)^t$ to (4.1) obtained by setting $x_B=B^{-1}b$, $x_N=0$ is called a neutrosophic basic feasible solution (N_{BFS}). Here B and N are respectively called basis and non basis matrix. x_B is called a basic variable and x_N is called a non-basic variable.

4. In an N_{BFS} if all components of $x_B>0$ then x is non-degenerate N_{BFS} and if at least one component of $x_B=0$, then x is degenerate N_{BFS}.

5 SIMPLEX METHOD FOR *NLP* PROBLEM

The NLP-problem (4.1) can be put as follows:

$$Max\ \tilde{z} =_{\Re_\kappa} \tilde{c}_B x_B + \tilde{c}_N x_N$$

such that $Bx_B+Nx_N=b$; $x_B, x_N \geq 0$ where the characters B, N, x_B and x_N are already stated. Then we have,

$$x_B + B^{-1}Nx_N = B^{-1}b \tag{5.1}$$

$$\Rightarrow \tilde{c}_B x_B + \tilde{c}_B B^{-1}Nx_N =_{\Re_\kappa} \tilde{c}_B B^{-1}b$$
$$\Rightarrow \tilde{z} - \tilde{c}_N x_N + \tilde{c}_B B^{-1}Nx_N =_{\Re_\kappa} \tilde{c}_B B^{-1}b \tag{5.2}$$
$$\Rightarrow \tilde{z} + \left(\tilde{c}_B B^{-1}N - \tilde{c}_N\right)x_N =_{\Re_\kappa} \tilde{c}_B B^{-1}b.$$

For an N_{BFS} treating $x_N=0$ we have $x_B=B^{-1}b$ and $\tilde{z} =_{\Re_\kappa} \tilde{c}_B B^{-1}b$ from (5.1) and (5.2), respectively. We can rewrite the *NLP* problem as given in Table 1.

Table 1. Tabular form of an NLP problem

		$\tilde{c}_j$	$\tilde{c}_B$	$\tilde{c}_N$	
		$\tilde{z}$	x_B	x_N	R.H.S
x_B		0	1	$B^{-1}N$	$B^{-1}b$
$\tilde{z}$		1	0	$\tilde{c}_B B^{-1}N - \tilde{c}_N$	$\tilde{c}_B B^{-1}b$

We can get all required initial information to proceed with the simplex method from Table 1. The neutrosophic cost row in the Table 1 is $\tilde{\lambda}_j =_{\Re_\kappa} (\tilde{c}_B B^{-1} a_j - c_j)_{a_j \notin B}$ giving $\tilde{\lambda}_j =_{\Re_\kappa} (\tilde{z}_j - \tilde{c}_j)$ for non-basic variables. The optimality arises if $\tilde{\lambda}_j \geq_{\Re_\kappa} \tilde{0}$, $\forall a_j \notin B$. If $\tilde{\lambda}_l <_{\Re_\kappa} \tilde{0}$ for any $a_l \notin B$ we need to replace x_{B_r} by x_l. We then compute $y_l = B^{-1} a_l$. If $y_l \leq 0$ then x_l can be increased indefinitely and so the problem admits unbounded optimal solution. But if y_l has at least one positive component, then one of the current basic variables blocks that increase, which drops to zero.

5.1 Theorem

In every column a_j of M if $\tilde{z}_j - \tilde{c}_j \geq_{\Re_\kappa} \tilde{0}$ holds for an N_{BFS} x_B of the *NLP* problem (4.1) then it is an optimal solution to that.

Proof. Let $M = [a_{ij}]_{m \times n} = [a_1, a_2, \cdots, a_n]$ where each $a_l = (a_{1l}, a_{2l}, \ldots, a_{ml})^t$ is m component column vector. Suppose $B = [\eta_1, \eta_2, \ldots, \eta_m]$ is the basis matrix and $\tilde{z}_B =_{\Re_\kappa} \tilde{c}_B x_B =_{\Re_\kappa} \sum_{i=1}^{m} \tilde{c}_{B_i} x_{B_i}$ where $\tilde{c}_{B_i}$ is the price corresponding to the basic variable x_{B_i}. Then any column a_l of M may be put as a linear combination of the vectors $\eta_1, \eta_2, \ldots, \eta_m$ of B. Let

$$a_l = y_{1l}\eta_1 + y_{2l}\eta_2 + \cdots + y_{ml}\eta_m = \sum_{i=1}^{m} y_{il}\eta_i = By_l \Rightarrow y_l = B^{-1}a_l.$$

where $y_l = (y_{1l}, y_{2l}, \ldots, y_{ml})^t$ being m component scalars represents a_l the lth vector of M. Assume that

$$\tilde{z}_l =_{\Re_\kappa} \tilde{c}_B y_l =_{\Re_\kappa} \sum_{i=1}^{m} \tilde{c}_{B_i} y_{il}.$$

Let $x = [x_1, x_2, \ldots, x_n]^t$ be any other feasible solution of the *NLP* problem (4.1) and $\tilde{z}$ be the corresponding objective function. Then,

$$Bx_B = b = Mx \Rightarrow x_B = B^{-1}(Mx) = (B^{-1}M)x = yx$$

where $B^{-1}M = y = [y_{ij}]_{m \times n} = [y_1, y_2, \cdots, y_n]$ with y_l defined as above. Thus,

$$\begin{pmatrix} x_{B_1} \\ x_{B_2} \\ \vdots \\ x_{B_m} \end{pmatrix} = \begin{pmatrix} y_{11} & y_{12} & \cdots & y_{1n} \\ y_{21} & y_{22} & \cdots & y_{2n} \\ \vdots & \vdots & \ddots & \vdots \\ y_{m1} & y_{m2} & \cdots & y_{mn} \end{pmatrix} \begin{pmatrix} x_1 \\ x_2 \\ \vdots \\ x_n \end{pmatrix}$$

Equating ith component from both sides, we have $x_{B_i} = \sum_{j=1}^{n} y_{ij} x_j$. Now,

$$\tilde{z}_j - \tilde{c}_j \geq_{\Re_\kappa} \tilde{0} \Rightarrow \left(\tilde{z}_j - \tilde{c}_j \right) x_j \geq_{\Re_\kappa} \tilde{0} \ [as \ x_j > 0] \Rightarrow \sum_{j=1}^{n} \left(\tilde{z}_j - \tilde{c}_j \right) x_j \geq_{\Re_\kappa} \tilde{0}$$

$$\Rightarrow \sum_{j=1}^{n} \tilde{z}_j x_j - \sum_{j=1}^{n} \tilde{c}_j x_j \geq_{\Re_\kappa} \tilde{0} \Rightarrow \sum_{j=1}^{n} x_j \left(\tilde{c}_B y_j \right) - \tilde{z} \geq_{\Re_\kappa} \tilde{0} \Rightarrow \sum_{j=1}^{n} x_j \left(\sum_{i=1}^{m} \tilde{c}_{B_i} y_{ij} \right) - \tilde{z} \geq_{\Re_\kappa} \tilde{0}$$

$$\Rightarrow \sum_{i=1}^{m} \tilde{c}_{B_i} \left(\sum_{j=1}^{n} y_{ij} x_j \right) - \tilde{z} \geq_{\Re_\kappa} \tilde{0} \Rightarrow \sum_{i=1}^{m} \tilde{c}_{B_i} \tilde{x}_{B_i} - \tilde{z} \geq_{\Re_\kappa} \tilde{0} \Rightarrow \tilde{z}_B - \tilde{z} \geq_{\Re_\kappa} \tilde{0}.$$

Thus $\tilde{z}_B$ is the maximum value of the objective function. This optimality criterion holds for all non-basic vectors of M. If a_l be in the basis matrix B say $a_l = \eta_l$ then

$$a_l = \eta_l = 0.\eta_1 + 0.\eta_2 + \cdots + 0.\eta_{l-1} + 1.\eta_l + 0.\eta_{l+1} + \cdots + 0.\eta_m$$

i.e., y_l is a unit vector e_l with lth component unity.

Since $a_l = \eta_l$ we have $\tilde{c}_l = \tilde{c}_{B_l}$ and so

$$\tilde{z}_l - \tilde{c}_l =_{\Re_\kappa} \left(\tilde{c}_B y_l - \tilde{c}_l \right) =_{\Re_\kappa} \left(\tilde{c}_B e_l - \tilde{c}_l \right) =_{\Re_\kappa} \left(\tilde{c}_{B_l} - \tilde{c}_{B_l} \right) =_{\Re_\kappa} \tilde{0}.$$

Thus as a whole $\tilde{z}_j - \tilde{c}_j \geq_{\Re_\kappa} \tilde{0}$ is the necessary condition for optimality.

5.2 Theorem

A non-degenerate N_{BFS}. $x_B = B^{-1}b$, $x_N = 0$ is optimal to *NLP* problem (4.1) iff $\tilde{z}_j - \tilde{c}_j \geq_{\Re_\kappa} \tilde{0}, \forall 1 \leq j \leq n$.

Proof. Suppose $x^* = (x_B^t, x_N^t)^t$ be an N_{BFS} to (4.1) where $x_B = B^{-1}b$, $x_N = 0$. If $\tilde{z}^*$ be the objective function corresponding to x^* then $\tilde{z}^* =_{\Re_\kappa} \tilde{c}_B x_B =_{\Re_\kappa} \tilde{c}_B B^{-1}b$. Let

$x = [x_1, x_2, \ldots, x_n]^t$ be another feasible solution of *NLP* problem (4.1) and $\tilde{z}$ be the corresponding objective function. Then,

$$\tilde{z} =_{\mathfrak{R}_\kappa} \tilde{c}_B x_B + \tilde{c}_N x_N =_{\mathfrak{R}_\kappa} \tilde{c}_B B^{-1} b - \sum_{a_j \notin B} \left(\tilde{c}_B B^{-1} a_j - \tilde{c}_j \right) x_j =_{\mathfrak{R}_\kappa} \tilde{z}^* - \sum_{a_j \notin B} \left(\tilde{z}_j - \tilde{c}_j \right) x_j .$$

This shows that the solution is optimal iff $\tilde{z}_j - \tilde{c}_j \geq_{\mathfrak{R}_\kappa} \tilde{0}$ for all $1 \leq j \leq n$.

5.3 Theorem

For any N_{BFS} to *NLP* problem (4.1), if there is some column not in basis such that $\tilde{z}_l - \tilde{c}_l <_{\mathfrak{R}_\kappa} \tilde{0}$ and $y_{il} \leq 0$, $i = 1, 2, \ldots, m$ then (4.1) admits an unbounded solution.

Proof. Let x_B be a basic solution to the *NLP* problem (4.1). Re-writing the constraints,

$$Bx_B + Nx_N = b \Rightarrow x_B + B^{-1} Nx_N = B^{-1}b \Rightarrow x_B + B^{-1} \sum_j \left(a_j x_j \right) = B^{-1}b, \ a_j \text{s are the columns of } N$$

$$\Rightarrow x_B + \sum_j \left(B^{-1} a_j x_j \right) = B^{-1}b \Rightarrow x_B + \sum_j \left(y_j x_j \right) = y_0, \text{ where } a_j = By_j, a_j \notin B$$

$$\Rightarrow x_{B_i} + \sum_j \left(y_{ij} x_j \right) = y_{i0}, 1 \leq i \leq m, 1 \leq j \leq n \Rightarrow x_{B_i} = y_{i0} - \sum_j \left(y_{ij} x_j \right), 1 \leq i \leq m, 1 \leq j \leq n.$$

If x_l enters into the basis, then $x_l > 0$ and $x_j = 0$ for $j \neq B_i \cup l$. Since $y_{il} \leq 0$, $1 \leq i \leq m$ hence $y_{i0} - y_{il} x_l \geq 0$. So, the basic solution remains feasible and for that, the objective function is:

$$\tilde{z}^* =_{\mathfrak{R}_\kappa} \tilde{c}_B x_B + \tilde{c}_N x_N =_{\mathfrak{R}_\kappa} \sum_{i=1}^{m} \tilde{c}_{B_i} \left(y_{i0} - y_{il} x_l \right) + \tilde{c}_l x_l$$

$$=_{\mathfrak{R}_\kappa} \sum_{i=1}^{m} \tilde{c}_{B_i} y_{i0} - \left(\sum_{i=1}^{m} \tilde{c}_{B_i} y_{il} - \tilde{c}_l \right) x_l =_{\mathfrak{R}_\kappa} \tilde{c}_B y_0 - \left(\tilde{c}_B y_l - \tilde{c}_l \right) x_l =_{\mathfrak{R}_\kappa} \tilde{z} - \left(\tilde{z}_l - \tilde{c}_l \right) x_l .$$

It shows that $\tilde{z}^* >_{\mathfrak{R}_\kappa} \tilde{z}$ as $\tilde{z}_l - \tilde{c}_l <_{\mathfrak{R}_\kappa} \tilde{0}$ and this completes the fact.

5.4 Simplex Algorithm for Solving *NLP* Problem

To solve any *NLP* problem by simplex method, the existence of an initial basic feasible solution is always assumed. This solution will be optimised through some iterations. The required steps are as follows:

Step 1. Check whether the objective function of the given *NLP* problem is to be maximized or minimized. If it is to be minimized, then it is converted into a maximization problem by using the result $Min(\tilde{z}) = -Max(-\tilde{z})$.

Step 2. Convert all the inequations of the constraints ($\leq$ type) into equations by introducing slack variables. Put the costs of the respective variables equal to $\tilde{0}$.

Step 3. Obtain an N_{BFS} to the problem in the form $x_B = B^{-1}b = y_0$ and $x_N = 0$. The corresponding objective function is $\tilde{z} =_{\mathfrak{R}_\kappa} \tilde{c}_B B^{-1}b =_{\mathfrak{R}_\kappa} \tilde{c}_B y_0$.

Step 4. For each basic variable, put $\tilde{\lambda}_B =_{\mathfrak{R}_\kappa} \tilde{z}_B - \tilde{c}_B =_{\mathfrak{R}_\kappa} \tilde{0}$. For each non-basic variable, calculate $\tilde{\lambda}_j =_{\mathfrak{R}_\kappa} \tilde{z}_j - \tilde{c}_j =_{\mathfrak{R}_\kappa} \tilde{c}_B B^{-1}a_j - \tilde{c}_j$ in the current iteration. If all $\tilde{z}_j - \tilde{c}_j \geq_{\mathfrak{R}_\kappa} \tilde{0}$ then the present solution is optimal.

Step 5. If for some non-basic variables, $\tilde{\lambda}_j =_{\mathfrak{R}_\kappa} \tilde{z}_j - \tilde{c}_j <_{\mathfrak{R}_\kappa} \tilde{0}$ then find out $\tilde{\lambda}_l = \min\{\tilde{\lambda}_j\}$. If $y_i < 0$ for all $i = 1, \ldots, m$ then the given problem will have unbounded solution and stop the iteration. Otherwise to determine the index of the variable x_{B_r} that is to be removed from the current basis, compute

$$\frac{y_{r0}}{y_{rl}} = \min\{\frac{y_{i0}}{y_{il}} : y_{il} > 0, 1 \leq i \leq m\}.$$

Step 6. Update y_{i0} by replacing $y_{i0} - \frac{y_{r0}}{y_{rl}} y_{il}$ for $i \neq r$ and y_{r0} by $\frac{y_{r0}}{y_{rl}}$.

Step 7. Construct new basis and repeat the Step 4, Step 5 until the optimality is reached.

Step 8. Find the optimal solution and hence the optimal value of objective function.

6 NUMERICAL EXAMPLE

The *NLP* problems with both G_{SVTN} number and G_{SVTrN} number are solved by the use of proposed algorithm. For simplicity, we define the κ weighted value function for $n=1$ in rest of the paper.

6.1 Example

Two friends F_1 and F_2 wish to invest in a raising share market. They choose two particular shares S_1 and S_2 of two multinational companies. They also decide to purchase equal unit of two shares individually. The maximum investment of F_1 is Rs. 4000 and that of F_2 is Rs. 7000. The price per unit of S_1 and S_2 are Re. 1 and Rs. 3, respectively when F_1 purchases. These are Rs. 2 and Rs. 5 at the time of purchasing of share by F_2. The current value of share S_1 and S_2 per unit is Rs. $\tilde{c}_1$ and Rs. $\tilde{c}_2$ (given in G_{SVN} numbers), respectively. Now if they sell their shares, formulate an *NLP* problem to maximize their returns.

The problem can be summarised as shown in Table 2.

Table 2.

Friends ⇓	Shares S_1	S_2	Purchasing capacity ⇓
F_1	Re. 1	Rs. 3	Rs. 4000
F_2	Rs. 2	Rs. 5	Rs. 7000
Prince per unit ⇒	$\tilde{c}_1 .$	$\tilde{c}_2$	

Let they individually purchase x_1 units of share S_1 and x_2 units of share S_2. The problem is formulated as:

$$Max\ \tilde{z} =_{\Re_{\kappa}} \tilde{c}_1 x_1 + \tilde{c}_2 x_2 .$$

such that $x_1+3x_2 \leq 4000$, $2x_1+5x_2 \leq 7000$; $x_1,x_2 \geq 0$. It is an *NLP* problem where

$$\tilde{c}_1 = \left\langle \left([5,8,1,3];0.2\right),\left([5,8,3,4];0.3\right),\left([5,8,2,1];0.4\right) \right\rangle$$

and

$$\tilde{c}_2 = \left\langle \left([3,7,2,4];0.3\right)\left([3,7,1,3];0.5\right),\left([3,7,2,5];0.6\right)\right\rangle$$

are two G_{SVTN} numbers with a pre-assigned $\kappa = 0.45$.

Rewriting the given constraints by introducing slack variables:

$x_1+3x_2+x_3=4000$, $2x_1+5x_2+x_4=7000$, $x_1,x_2,x_2,x_4 \geq 0$.

We take the t norm and s norm as $p*q = \min\{p,q\}$ and $p \lozenge q = \max\{p,q\}$ respectively. The first feasible simplex table is as shown in Table 3.

Table 3. First iteration

$\tilde{c}_j \Rightarrow$	$\tilde{c}_1$	$\tilde{c}_2$	$\tilde{0}$	$\tilde{0}$	
$x_B \Downarrow$	x_1	x_2	x_3	x_4	R.H.S
x_3	1	3	1	0	4000
x_4	2	5	0	1	7000$\rightarrow$
$\tilde{z} \Rightarrow$	$\tilde{c}_1^{(1)}$	$\tilde{c}_2^{(1)}$	$\tilde{c}_3^{(1)}$	$\tilde{c}_4^{(1)}$	

Here

$$\tilde{c}_1^{(1)} = -\tilde{c}_1 = \left\langle \left([-8,-5,3,1];0.2\right),\left([-8,-5,4,3];0.3\right),\left([-8,-5,1,2];0.4\right)\right\rangle$$

$$\tilde{c}_2^{(1)} = -\tilde{c}_2 = \left\langle \left([-7,-3,4,2];0.3\right),\left([-7,-3,3,1];0.5\right),\left([-7,-3,5,2];0.6\right)\right\rangle$$

and $V_\kappa\left(\tilde{c}_3^{(1)}\right) = V_\kappa\left(\tilde{c}_4^{(1)}\right) = V_\kappa\left(\tilde{0}\right)$.

Then $V_\kappa\left(\tilde{c}_1^{(1)}\right) = \frac{1}{6}(31.64\kappa - 33.28)$ and $V_\kappa\left(\tilde{c}_2^{(1)}\right) = \frac{1}{6}(10.4\kappa - 13.28)$ by Definition 3.5.

Clearly $V_\kappa\left(\tilde{c}_1^{(1)}\right) < 0$, $V_\kappa\left(\tilde{c}_2^{(1)}\right) < 0$ and $V_\kappa\left(\tilde{c}_1^{(1)}\right) - V_\kappa\left(\tilde{c}_2^{(1)}\right) < 0$ for $\kappa = 0.45$.

Then $\tilde{c}_1^{(1)} <_{\mathfrak{R}_\kappa} \tilde{c}_2^{(1)}$. So x_1 enters in the basis and as $\min\{4000/1, 7000/2\} = 3500$ the leaving variable is x_4. The revised table can be seen in Table 4 where $V_\kappa\left(\tilde{c}_1^{(2)}\right) = V_\kappa\left(\tilde{c}_3^{(2)}\right) = V_\kappa\left(\tilde{0}\right)$ and

$$\tilde{c}_2^{(2)} = \frac{5}{2}\tilde{c}_1 - \tilde{c}_2 = \langle([5.5,17,6.5,9.5];0.2),([5.5,17,10.5,11];0.5),([5.5,17,10,4.5];0.6)\rangle.$$

$$\tilde{c}_4^{(2)} = \frac{1}{2}\tilde{c}_1 = \langle([2.5,4,0.5,1.5];0.2),([2.5,4,1.5,2];0.3),([2.5,4,1,0.5];0.4)\rangle.$$

Table 4. Second iteration

$\tilde{c}_j \Rightarrow$	$\tilde{c}_1$	$\tilde{c}_2$	$\tilde{0}$	$\tilde{0}$	
$x_B \Downarrow$	x_1	x_2	x_3	x_4	R.H.S
x_3	0	1/2	1	-1/2	500
x_4	1	5/2	0	1/2	3500
$\tilde{z} \Rightarrow$	$\tilde{c}_1^{(2)}$	$\tilde{c}_2^{(2)}$	$\tilde{c}_3^{(3)}$	$\tilde{c}_4^{(2)}$	$3500\tilde{c}_1$.

Then $V_\kappa\left(\tilde{c}_2^{(2)}\right) = \frac{1}{6}(26.92 - 24.1\kappa)$.and $V_\kappa\left(\tilde{c}_4^{(2)}\right) = \frac{1}{6}(16.64 - 15.82\kappa)$.by Definition 3.5.

Clearly $V_\kappa\left(\tilde{c}_2^{(2)}\right) > 0$ and $V_\kappa\left(\tilde{c}_4^{(2)}\right) > 0$ for $\kappa=0.45$.

Hence the optimality arises and Max $\tilde{z} =_{\mathfrak{R}_\kappa} 3500\tilde{c}_1$, which, using κ- weighted function, becomes Rs. 11107 approximately. Then corresponding return of F_1 and F_2 becomes Rs. 7607 and of Rs. 4107 respectively.

6.1.1 Example

Consider the *NLP* problem defined in Example 6.1 with a pre-assigned $\kappa=0.96$.

The initial simplex table (Table 5) is same as Table 3.

Here $V_\kappa\left(\tilde{c}_3^{(1)}\right) = V_\kappa\left(\tilde{c}_4^{(1)}\right) = V_\kappa\left(\tilde{0}\right)$ and $V_\kappa\left(\tilde{c}_1^{(1)}\right) < 0$, $V_\kappa\left(\tilde{c}_2^{(1)}\right) < 0$ with $V_\kappa\left(\tilde{c}_1^{(1)}\right) - V_\kappa\left(\tilde{c}_2^{(1)}\right) > 0$ for $\kappa=0.96$. Then $\tilde{c}_1^{(1)} >_{\mathfrak{R}_\kappa} \tilde{c}_2^{(1)}$. So x_2 enters in the basis and as $\min\left\{\frac{4000}{3}, \frac{7000}{5}\right\} = \frac{4000}{3}$ the leaving variable is x_3. The revised table is described in Table 6 where $V_\kappa\left(\tilde{c}_2^{(2)}\right) = V_\kappa\left(\tilde{c}_4^{(2)}\right) = V_\kappa\left(\tilde{0}\right)$ and

Table 5. First iteration

$\tilde{c}_j \Rightarrow$	$\tilde{c}_1$	$\tilde{c}_2$	$\tilde{0}$	$\tilde{0}$	
$x_B \Downarrow$	x_1	x_2	x_3	x_4	R.H.S
x_3	1	3	1	0	4000 →
x_4	2	5	0	1	7000
$\tilde{z} \Rightarrow$	$\tilde{c}_1^{(1)}$	$\tilde{c}_2^{(1)} \uparrow$	$\tilde{c}_3^{(1)}$	$\tilde{c}_4^{(1)}$	

$$\tilde{c}_1^{(2)} = \frac{1}{3}\tilde{c}_2 - \tilde{c}_1$$
$$= \langle\left([-7,-8/3,11/3,7/3];0.2\right),\left([-7,-8/3,13/3,4];0.5\right),\left([-7,-8/3,5/3,11/3];0.6\right)\rangle,$$

$$\tilde{c}_3^{(2)} = \frac{1}{3}\tilde{c}_2 = \langle\left([1,7/3,2/3,4/3];0.3\right),\left([1,7/3,1/3,1];0.5\right),\left([1,7/3,2/3,5/3];0.6\right)\rangle.$$

Table 6. Second iteration

$\tilde{c}_j \Rightarrow$	$\tilde{c}_1$	$\tilde{c}_2$	$\tilde{0}$	$\tilde{0}$	
$x_B \Downarrow$	x_1	x_2	x_3	x_4	R.H.S
x_2	1/3	1	1/3	0	4000/3
x_4	1/3	0	-5/3	1	1000/3 →
$\tilde{z} \Rightarrow$	$\tilde{c}_1^{(2)} \uparrow$	$\tilde{c}_2^{(2)}$	$\tilde{c}_3^{(2)}$	$\tilde{c}_4^{(2)}$	$\frac{4000}{3}\tilde{c}_2$.

Then $V_\kappa\left(\tilde{c}_1^{(2)}\right) = \frac{1}{18}(31.32\kappa - 34.96)$ and $V_\kappa\left(\tilde{c}_3^{(2)}\right) = \frac{1}{18}(13.28 - 10.4\kappa)$.

Clearly $V_\kappa\left(\tilde{c}_1^{(2)}\right) < 0$ and $V_\kappa\left(\tilde{c}_3^{(2)}\right) > 0$ for $\kappa=0.96$. So x_1 enters in the basis and as $\min\left\{\frac{4000/3}{1/3}, \frac{1000/3}{1/3}\right\} = 1000$ the leaving variable is x_4. The revised table is shown as Table 7 where $V_\kappa\left(\tilde{c}_1^{(3)}\right) = V_\kappa\left(\tilde{c}_2^{(3)}\right) = V_\kappa\left(\tilde{0}\right)$ and

$$\tilde{c}_3^{(3)} = -5\tilde{c}_1 + 2\tilde{c}_2 = \langle([-34,-11,19,13];0.2),([-34,-11,22,21];0.5),([-34,-11,9,20];0.6)\rangle,$$

$$\tilde{c}_4^{(3)} = 3\tilde{c}_1 - \tilde{c}_2 = \langle([8,21,7,11];0.2),([8,21,12,13];0.5),([8,21,11,5];0.6)\rangle.$$

Table 7. Third iteration

$\tilde{c}_j \Rightarrow$	$\tilde{c}_1$	$\tilde{c}_2$	$\tilde{0}$	$\tilde{0}$	
$x_B \Downarrow$	x_1	x_2	x_3	x_4	R.H.S
x_2	0	1	2	-1	1000 $\rightarrow$
x_1	1	0	-5	3	1000
$\tilde{z} \Rightarrow$	$\tilde{c}_1^{(3)}$	$\tilde{c}_2^{(3)}$	$\tilde{c}_3^{(3)} \uparrow$	$\tilde{c}_4^{(3)}$	$1000(\tilde{c}_1 + \tilde{c}_2)$.

Then $V_\kappa\left(\tilde{c}_3^{(3)}\right) = \dfrac{1}{6}(48.2\kappa - 53.84) < 0$ and $V_\kappa\left(\tilde{c}_4^{(3)}\right) = \dfrac{1}{6}(34.96 - 31.32\kappa) > 0$

for $\kappa = 0.96$. So x_3 enters in the basis and the leaving variable is x_2. The revised table is shown in Table 8 where $V_\kappa\left(\tilde{c}_1^{(4)}\right) = V_\kappa\left(\tilde{c}_3^{(4)}\right) = V_\kappa\left(\tilde{0}\right)$ and $\tilde{c}_2^{(4)} = \dfrac{5}{2}\tilde{c}_1 - \tilde{c}_2$ and

$$\tilde{c}_4^{(4)} = \dfrac{1}{2}\tilde{c}_1.$$

Table 8. Fourth iteration

$\tilde{c}_j \Rightarrow$	$\tilde{c}_1$	$\tilde{c}_2$	$\tilde{0}$	$\tilde{0}$	
$x_B \Downarrow$	x_1	x_2	x_3	x_4	R.H.S
x_3	0	1/2	1	-1/2	500
x_1	1	5/2	0	1/2	3500
$\tilde{z} \Rightarrow$	$\tilde{c}_1^{(4)}$	$\tilde{c}_2^{(4)}$	$\tilde{c}_3^{(4)}$	$\tilde{c}_4^{(4)}$	$3500\tilde{c}_1$.

Then $V_\kappa\left(\tilde{c}_2^{(4)}\right) = \dfrac{1}{6}(26.92 - 24.1\kappa) > 0$

and $V_\kappa\left(\tilde{c}_4^{(4)}\right) = \dfrac{1}{6}(16.64 - 15.82\kappa) > 0$ for $\kappa = 0.96$.

Hence the optimality arises and the optimal solution is $x_1=3500$, $x_2=0$.

6.1.2 Remark

From Example 6.1 and Example 6.1.1, it is seen that the final simplex tables in both cases are same. So, if the optimality exists for an *NLP* problem, the optimal solutions are always unique whatever the value of κ assigned. Depending upon the chosen κ the number of iteration to reach at optimality stage may vary but it does not affect the optimal solutions. However, the character κ plays an important role to assign the optimal value of the objective function in a problem. The fact is shown in Table 9. So, the value of κ is an important factor in any such *NLP* problem. Since the share market depends on so many factors, we claim κ as the degree of political turmoil of the country in the present problem.

6.1.3 Sensitivity Analysis in post Optimality Stage

We shall analyse the results of the problem in Example 6.1 for different values of κ in post optimality stage, shown by the Table 9.

Table 9. Sensitivity analysis

κ	x_1	x_2	$V_\kappa(\tilde{z})$
0	3500	0	19413.33
0.1	3500	0	17567.67
0.2	3500	0	15722
0.3	3500	0	13876.33
0.4	3500	0	12030.67
0.5	3500	0	10185
0.6	3500	0	8339.33
0.7	3500	0	6493.67
0.8	3500	0	4648
0.9	3500	0	2802.33
1	3500	0	956.67

6.2 Example

Max $\tilde{z} =_{\mathfrak{R}_\kappa} \tilde{c}_1 x_1 + \tilde{c}_2 x_2$ s.t. $2x_1 + 3x_2 \leq 4,\ 5x_1 + 4x_2 \leq 15;\ x_1, x_2 \geq$ is an *NLP* problem where

$$\tilde{c}_1 = \langle ([8,1,3];0.6), ([8,3,4];0.2), ([8,2,1];0.5) \rangle$$

and

$$\tilde{c}_2 = \langle ([6,2,6];0.7), ([6,4,3];0.4), ([6,3,5];0.3) \rangle$$

are two G_{SVTrN} numbers with $\kappa=09$.

Rewriting the given constraints by introducing slack variables:

$2x_1 + 3x_2 + x_3 = 4,\ 5x_1 + 4x_2 + x_4 = 15,\ x_1, x_2, x_3, x_4 \geq 0.$

The *t* norm and *s* norm are $p*q = \max\{p+q-1, 0\}$ and $p \Diamond q = \min\{p+q, 1\}$ respectively. The first feasible simplex table is as Table 10.

Table 10. First iteration

$\tilde{c}_j \Rightarrow$	$\tilde{c}_1$	$\tilde{c}_2$	$\tilde{0}$	$\tilde{0}$	
$x_B \Downarrow$	x_1	x_2	x_3	x_4	R.H.S
x_3	2	3	1	0	4 $\rightarrow$
x_4	5	4	0	1	15
$\tilde{z} \Rightarrow$	$\tilde{c}_1^{(1)}$	$\tilde{c}_2^{(1)}\uparrow$	$\tilde{c}_3^{(1)}$	$\tilde{c}_4^{(1)}$	

Here

$$\tilde{c}_1^{(1)} = -\tilde{c}_1 = \langle ([-8,3,1];0.6), ([-8,4,3];0.2), ([-8,1,2];0.5) \rangle .$$

$$\tilde{c}_2^{(1)} = -\tilde{c}_2 = \langle ([-6,6,2];0.7), ([-6,3,4];0.4), ([-6,5,3];0.3) \rangle .$$

and $V_\kappa\left(\tilde{c}_3^{(1)}\right) = V_\kappa\left(\tilde{c}_4^{(1)}\right) = V_\kappa\left(\tilde{0}\right).$

Then $V_\kappa\left(\tilde{c}_1^{(1)}\right)=\dfrac{1}{6}(25.11\kappa-43.11)$ and $V_\kappa\left(\tilde{c}_2^{(1)}\right)=\dfrac{1}{6}(11.62\kappa-31.22)$ by Definition 3.8.1.

Clearly $V_\kappa\left(-\tilde{c}_1\right)<0$, $V_\kappa\left(-\tilde{c}_2\right)<0$ and $V_\kappa\left(-\tilde{c}_1\right)-V_\kappa\left(-\tilde{c}_2\right)>0$ for $\kappa=09$. So x_2 enters in the basis and as $\min\{4/3,\ 15/4\}=4/3$ the leaving variable is x_3. The revised table is Table 11 where $V_\kappa\left(\tilde{c}_2^{(2)}\right)=V_\kappa\left(\tilde{c}_4^{(2)}\right)=V_\kappa\left(\tilde{0}\right)$ and

$$\tilde{c}_1^{(2)}=\frac{2}{3}\tilde{c}_2-\tilde{c}_1=\langle([-4,13/3,5];0.3),([-4,20/3,5];0.6),([-4,3,16/3];0.8)\rangle,$$

$$\tilde{c}_3^{(2)}=\frac{1}{3}\tilde{c}_2=\langle([2,2/3,2];0.7),([2,4/3,1];0.4),([2,1,5/3];0.3)\rangle.$$

Table 11. Second iteration

$\tilde{c}_j\Rightarrow$	$\tilde{c}_1$	$\tilde{c}_2$	$\tilde{0}$	$\tilde{0}$	
$x_B\Downarrow$	x_1	x_2	x_3	x_4	R.H.S
x_2	2/3	1	1/3	0	4/3 $\rightarrow$
x_4	7/3	0	-4/3	1	29/3
$\tilde{z}\Rightarrow$	$\tilde{c}_1^{(2)}\uparrow$	$\tilde{c}_2^{(2)}$	$\tilde{c}_3^{(2)}$	$\tilde{c}_4^{(2)}$	$\dfrac{4}{3}\tilde{c}_2$.

Then $V_\kappa\left(\tilde{c}_1^{(2)}\right)=\dfrac{1}{18}(8.62\kappa-14.92)$ and $V_\kappa\left(\tilde{c}_3^{(2)}\right)=\dfrac{1}{18}(31.22-11.62\kappa)$ by Definition 3.8.1.

Clearly, $V_\kappa\left(\tilde{c}_1^{(2)}\right)<0$ but $V_\kappa\left(\tilde{c}_3^{(2)}\right)>0$ for $\kappa=09$. So x_1 enters in the basis and as $\min\left\{\dfrac{4/3}{2/3},\dfrac{29/3}{7/3}\right\}=2$ the leaving variable is x_2. The revised table is shown as Table 12 where $V_\kappa\left(\tilde{c}_1^{(3)}\right)=V_\kappa\left(\tilde{c}_4^{(3)}\right)=V_\kappa\left(\tilde{0}\right)$ and

$$\tilde{c}_2^{(3)}=\frac{3}{2}\tilde{c}_1-\tilde{c}_2=\langle([6,7.5,6.5];0.3),([6,7.5,10];0.6),([6,8,4.5];0.8)\rangle,$$

$$\tilde{c}_3^{(3)} = \frac{1}{2}\tilde{c}_1 = \langle \left([4, 0.5, 1.5]; 0.6 \right), \left([4, 1.5, 2]; 0.2 \right), \left([4, 1, 0.5]; 0.5 \right) \rangle.$$

Table 12. Third iteration

$\tilde{c}_j \Rightarrow$	$\tilde{c}_1$	$\tilde{c}_2$	$\tilde{0}$	$\tilde{0}$	
$x_B \Downarrow$	x_1	x_2	x_3	x_4	R.H.S
x_1	1	3/2	1/2	0	2
x_4	0	-7/2	-5/2	1	5
$\tilde{z} \Rightarrow$	$\tilde{c}_1^{(3)}$	$\tilde{c}_2^{(3)}$	$\tilde{c}_3^{(3)}$	$\tilde{c}_4^{(3)}$	$2\tilde{c}_1$

Then $V_\kappa\left(\tilde{c}_2^{(3)}\right) = \frac{1}{6}\left(7.46 - 4.31\kappa\right)$ and $V_\kappa\left(\tilde{c}_3^{(3)}\right) = \frac{1}{6}\left(21.555 - 12.555\kappa\right)$ by Definition 3.8.1.

Obviously, $V_\kappa\left(\tilde{c}_2^{(3)}\right) > 0$ and $V_\kappa\left(\tilde{c}_3^{(3)}\right) > 0$ for $\kappa = 09$. Hence the optimality arises. The optimal solution is $x_1 = 2$, $x_2 = 0$ and so Max $\tilde{z} =_{\Re_\kappa} 2\tilde{c}_1$.

7 CONCLUSION

In this paper, the crisp *LP*-problem has been generalised by considering the coefficients of the objective function as G_{SVN}-numbers. This generalised form of crisp *LP*-problem is called *NLP*-problem. Then a simplex algorithm has been proposed to solve such *NLP*-problems. Finally, the newly developed simplex algorithm has been applied to a real life problem. The concept has been illustrated by suitable examples using both G_{SVTN}-numbers and G_{SVTrN}-numbers. In future, the concept of a linear programming problem may be extended in more generalised way by considering some or all of the parameters as G_{SVN}-numbers.

REFERENCES

Abbasbandy, S., & Asady, B. (2006). Ranking of fuzzy numbers by sign distance. *Information Sciences, 176*(16), 2405–2416. doi:10.1016/j.ins.2005.03.013

Abdel-Basset, M. (2019a). An approach of TOPSIS technique for developing supplier selection with group decision making under type-2 neutrosophic number. *Applied Soft Computing*, *77*, 438-452.

Abdel-Basset, M., Manogaran, G., Gamal, A., & Smarandache, F. (2019b). A Group Decision Making Framework Based on Neutrosophic TOPSIS Approach for Smart Medical Device Selection. *Journal of Medical Systems*, *43*(2), 38. doi:10.100710916-019-1156-1 PMID:30627801

Atanassov, K. (1986). Intuitionistic fuzzy sets. *Fuzzy Sets and Systems*, *20*(1), 87–96. doi:10.1016/S0165-0114(86)80034-3

Bera, T., & Mahapatra, N. K. (2016). (α,β,γ) -cut of neutrosophic soft set and it's application to neutrosophic soft groups. *Asian Journal of Math. and Compt. Research*, *12*(3), 160–178.

Bera, T., & Mahapatra, N. K. (2017). On neutrosophic soft linear spaces. *Fuzzy Information and Engineering*, *9*(3), 299–324. doi:10.1016/j.fiae.2017.09.004

Deli, I., & Subas, Y. (2016). A ranking method of single valued neutrosophic numbers and its application to multi-attribute decision making problems. *Int. J. Mach. Learn. and Cyber.* DOI . doi:10.100713042-016-0505-3

Gani, A. N., & Ponnalagu, K. (2016). A method based on intuitionistic fuzzy linear programming for investment strategy. *Int. J. Fuzzy Math. Arch.*, *10*(1), 71–81.

Hussian, A., Mohamed, M., Baset, M., & Smarandache, F. (2017). Neutrosophic linear programming problem. *Mathematical Sciences Letters*, *3*(6), 319–324. doi:10.18576/msl/060315

Maleki, H. R. (2002). Ranking function and their application to fuzzy linear programming. *Far East Journal of Mathematical Sciences*, *4*, 283–301.

Nasseri, S. H., Ardil, E., Yazdani, A., & Zaefarian, R. (2005). Simplex method for solving linear programming problems with fuzzy numbers. *World Academy of Science, Engineering and Technology*, *10*, 284–288.

Parvathi, R., & Malathi, C. (2012). Intuitionistic fuzzy simplex method. *International Journal of Computers and Applications*, *48*(6), 36–48.

Prabakaran, K., & Ganesan, K. (2017). Duality theory for intuitionistic fuzzy linear programming problems. *Int. J. of Civil Eng. and Tech.*, *8*, 546–560.

Pramanik, S. (2016). Neutrosophic multi-objective linear programming. *Global Journal of Engineering Science and Research Management*, *3*(8). doi:10.5281/zenodo.59949

Smarandache, F. (1998a). *Neutrosophy, neutrosophic probability, set and logic.* Amer. Res. Press. Retrieved from http://fs.gallup.unm.edu/eBook-neutrosophics4.pdf

Smarandache, F. (2005b). Neutrosophic set, A generalisation of the intuitionistic fuzzy sets. *International Journal of Pure and Applied Mathematics*, *24*, 287–297.

Wang, H., Zhang, Y., Sunderraman, R., & Smarandache, F. (2011). Single valued neutrosophic sets. *Fuzzy Sets. Rough Sets and Multivalued Operations and Applications*, *3*(1), 33–39.

Zadeh, L. A. (1965). Fuzzy sets. *Information and Control*, *8*(3), 338–353. doi:10.1016/S0019-9958(65)90241-X

Chapter 10
Interval–Valued Neutrosophic Subgroup Based on Interval– Valued Triple T–Norm

Sudipta Gayen

https://orcid.org/0000-0002-6665-7975
National Institute of Technology, Jamshedpur, India

Florentin Smarandache

https://orcid.org/0000-0002-5560-5926
Department of Mathematics, University of New Mexico, USA

Sripati Jha
National Institute of Technology, Jamshedpur, India

Ranjan Kumar
Jain University, Jayanagar, Bengaluru, India

ABSTRACT

Presently, interval-valued neutrosophic set theory has become an important research topic. It is widely used in various pure as well as applied fields. This chapter will provide some essential scopes to study interval-valued neutrosophic subgroup. Here the notion of interval-valued triple T-norm has been introduced, and based on that, interval-valued neutrosophic subgroup has been defined. Furthermore, some homomorphic characteristics of this notion have been studied. Additionally, based on interval-valued triple T-norm, interval-valued neutrosophic normal subgroup has been introduced and some of its homomorphic characteristics have been analyzed.

DOI: 10.4018/978-1-7998-2555-5.ch010

1. INTRODUCTION

In our real physical world, many uncertainties are involved. To tackle these ambiguities, crisp set (CS) theory is not always enough. As a result, researchers needed more capable set theories. Consequently, different set theories have emerged, for instance, fuzzy set (FS) (Zadeh, Fuzzy sets, 1965), intuitionistic fuzzy set (IFS) (Atanassov, 1986), neutrosophic set (NS) (Smarandache, 1999), plithogenic set (PS) (Smarandache, 2018), etc. FS theory is capable of handling real-life uncertainties very well. Still, in some ambiguous situations, researchers need sets that are more general i.e. IFSs or sometimes even more general sets like NSs or PSs, etc. Presently, NS theory has grabbed quite lot attentions of different researchers from various fields. Presently, NS theory has become an important and fruitful research field. Furthermore, Smarandache has also developed neutrosophic measure and probability (Smarandache, 2013), calculus (Smarandache & Khalid, 2015), psychology (Smarandache, 2018), etc. At present, NS theory is used in different applied fields, for instance, in pattern recognition problem (Vlachos & Sergiadis, 2007), image segmentation (Guo & Cheng, 2009), decision making problem (Majumdar, 2015;

Table 1. Some applications of IVNS in various fields

Author & Year	Applications of IVNS in various fields
(Broumi et. al., 2015)	Introduced the concept of n-valued IVNS and mentioned how it can be applied in medical diagnosing.
(Broumi et. al., 2014)	Presented the definition of parameterized soft set in IVNS environment and its application in DMPs.
(Ye, 2014)	Defined Hamming and Euclidean distances between two IVNSs and introduced similarity measures in IVNSs with an application in DMP.
(Ye, 2014)	Introduced a correlation coefficient (improved) of single-valued NSs and extended it to a correlation coefficient between IVNSs. Further, applied it in multiple attribute DMPs.
(Zhang et. al., 2014)	Proposed a technique based on IVNS to solve multi-criteria DMPs.
(Aiwu et. al., 2015)	Proposed an aggregation operation rules (improved) for IVNS and extended the generalized weighted aggregation operator.
(Zhang et. al., 2016)	Illustrated a novel outranking method for multi-criteria DMPs with IVNSs.
(Broumi et. al., 2016)	Extended the notion of neutrosophic graph-based multi-criteria decision-making approach in interval-valued neutrosophic graph theory.
(Deli, 2017)	Proposed the concept of the soft IVNS and investigated its application in DMP.
(Yuan et. al., 2019)	Applied IVNSs in image segmentation.
(Thong et. al., 2019)	Proposed dynamic IVNS for dynamic DMP.

Abdel-Basset et. al., 2017; Abdel-Basset et. al., 2019), mobile-edge computing (Abdel-Basset et. al., 2019), neutrosophic forecasting (Abdel-Basset et. al., 2019), supply chain management (Abdel-Basset et. al., 2019; Abdel-Basset et. al., 2019), supplier selection problems (Abdel-Basset et. al., 2018; Abdel-Basset et. al., 2018), goal programming problem (Abdel-Basset et. al., 2016), multi-objective programming problem (Hezam et. al., 2015), medical diagnosis (Kumar et. al., 2015; Deli et. al., 2015), shortest path problem (Kumar, et al., 2019; Kumar et. al., 2018; Kumar et. al., 2020), transportation problem (Kumar et. al., 2019) etc. Again, gradually some other set theories, like, interval-valued FS (IVFS) (Zadeh, 1975), interval-valued IFS (IVIFS) (Atanassov, 1999) and interval-valued NS (IVNS) (Wang et. al., 2005), etc. have evolved. These notions are generalizations of CS, FS, IFS, and NSs. Presently; these set theories are extensively applied in different fields, mainly in decision-making problems (DMP). In the following Table 1 some applications of IVNSs have been discussed.

Based on FS, Rosenfeld introduced the notion of fuzzy subgroup (FSG) (Rosenfeld, 1971). Gradually, various mathematicians have developed intuitionistic fuzzy subgroup (IFSG) (Biswas, 1989), neutrosophic subgroup (NSG) (Çetkin & Aygün, 2015), etc. Furthermore, they have studied effects of homomorphism on them. Some researchers have analyzed their normal forms also. Furthermore, the notions of interval-valued fuzzy subgroup (IVFSG) (Biswas, 1994), interval-valued intuitionistic fuzzy subgroup (IVIFSG) (Aygünoğlu et. al., 2012), etc. have been defined. In addition, different researchers have studied their normal forms, homomorphic image, homomorphic pre-image, etc. Still, the concept of the interval-valued neutrosophic subgroup is undefined. Also, different algebraic aspects of IVNSGs are needed to be studied.

This Chapter has been arranged as follows: In Segment 2, literature surveys of FS, IFS, INS, FSG, IFSG, and NSG are given. In Segment 3, the notions of IVFS, IVIFS, IVFSG, IVIFSG, etc. have been mentioned. In Segment 4, interval-valued triple T-norm (IVTTN), IVNSG, normal form of IVNSG, etc. are introduced and the effects of homomorphism on these notions are mentioned. Finally, in segment 5, the conclusion has been provided and some scopes of future researches are given.

2. LITERATURE SURVEY

In this segment, some essential notions, like, FS, IFS, NS, FSG, IFSG, NSG, level set, level subgroup, etc., are discussed and also, some of their basic fundamental properties are given. All these notions play vital roles in the development of IVNSG.

Definition 2.1 (Zadeh, 1965) Let $J=[0,1]$. A FS σ of a CS M is a mapping from M to J i.e σ: $M{\to}J$.

Definition 2.2 (Atanassov, 1986) A IFS γ of a CS M is denoted as $\gamma = \{(k,t_\gamma(k), f_\gamma(k))$: $k \in M\}$, where both t_γ and f_γ are FSs of R and $\forall k \in M$ t_γ and f_γ satisfy the criteria $1 \geq t_\gamma(k) + f_\gamma(k) \geq 0$.

Definition 2.3 (Smarandache, 1999) A NS η of a CS M is denoted as $\eta= \{(s,t_\eta(s),i_\eta(s),f_\eta(s))$; s $\in$ M$\}$, where f_η,i_η,t_η: $M{\to}]^-0,1^+[$are the respective degree of falsity, indeterminacy, and truth and of any element k $\in$ R. Here $\forall s \in$ M, f_η, i_η and t_η satisfy the criteria $3+ \geq f_\eta(s) + i_\eta(s) + t_\eta(s) \geq {}^-0$.

Definition 2.4 (Zadeh, 1965) Let α be a FS of M. Then $\forall t \in J$ the sets $\alpha_t= \{k \in M$: $\alpha(k) \geq t\}$ are called level subsets of α.

2.1. Fuzzy Subgroup, Intuitionistic Fuzzy Subgroup and Neutrosophic Subgroup

Definition 2.5 (Rosenfeld, 1971) A FS α of a crisp group M is called a FSG of R iff $\forall k,s{\in}M$, conditions given below are fulfilled:

1. $\alpha(ks) \geq \min\{\alpha(k),\alpha(s)\}$
2. $\alpha(s^{-1}) \geq \alpha(s)$.

Here $\alpha(s^{-1}) = \alpha(s)$ and $\alpha(s) \leq \alpha(e)$ (e is the neutral element of M). Also, in the above definition if only condition (i) is satisfied by α then we call it a fuzzy subgroupoid.

Theorem 2.1 (Rosenfeld, 1971) α is a FSG of M iff $\forall k,\, s \in R$ $\alpha(ks^{-1}) \geq \min\{\alpha(k),\alpha(s)\}$.

Definition 2.6 (Das, 1981) Suppose α is a FSG of a group M. Then $\forall t \in J$ the level subgroups of α are α_t, where $\alpha(e) \geq t$.

Definition 2.7 (Biswas, 1989)An IFS $\gamma= \{(k,t_\gamma(k),f_\gamma(k))$: k $\in$ M$\}$ of a crisp set M is called an IFSG of M iff $\forall k,\, s \in$ M

1. $t_\gamma(ks^{-1}) \geq \min\{t_\gamma(k),\, t_\gamma(s)\}$
2. $f_\gamma(ks^{-1}) \leq \max\{f_\gamma(k),f_\gamma(s)\}$

The collection of all IFSG of M will be denoted as IFSG(M).

Definition 2.8 (Çetkin & Aygün, 2015) Let M be a group and δ be a NS of M. δ is called a NSG of M iff the conditions given below are fulfilled:

1. $\delta(k \bullet s) \geq \min\{\delta(k), \delta(s)\}$, i.e. $t_\delta(k \cdot s) \geq \min\{t_\delta(k), t_\delta(s)\}$, $i_\delta(k \cdot s) \geq \min\{i_\delta(k), i_\delta(s)\}$ and $f_\delta(k \cdot s) \leq \max\{f_\delta(k), f_\delta(s)\}$

2. $\delta(s^{-1}) \geq \delta(s)$ i.e. $t_\delta(s^{-1}) \geq t_\delta(s)$, $i_\delta(s^{-1}) \geq i_\delta(s)$ and $f_\delta(s^{-1}) \leq f_\delta(s)$

The collection of all NSG will be denoted as NSG(R). Here notice that t_δ and i_δ are following Definition 2.5 i.e. both of them are actually FSGs of R.

Example 2.1 (Çetkin & Aygün, 2015) Suppose $M=\{1, -1, i, -i\}$ and δ is a NS of M, where $\delta = \{(1, 0.6, 0.5, 0.4), (-1, 0.7, 0.4, 0.3), (i, 0.8, 0.4, 0.2), (-i, 0.8, 0.4, 0.2)\}$. Notice that $\delta \in$ NSG(M).

Theorem 2.2 (Çetkin & Aygün, 2015) Let M be a group and δ be a NS of M. Then $\delta \in$ NSG(M) iff $\forall k, s \in M$ $\delta(k \cdot s^{-1}) \geq \min\{\delta(k), \delta(s)\}$.

Theorem 2.3 (Çetkin & Aygün, 2015) $\delta \in$ NSG(M) iff $\forall p \in [0,1]$ the p-level sets $(t_\delta)_p$, $(i_\delta)_p$ and p-lower-level set $(\bar{f}_\delta)_p$ are CSGs of M.

Definition 2.9 (Çetkin & Aygün, 2015) Let M be a group and δ be a NS of M. Here δ is called a neutrosophic normal subgroup (NNSG) of M iff $\forall k, s \in M$ $\delta(k \cdot s \cdot k^{-1}) \leq \delta(s)$ i.e. $t_\delta(k \cdot s \cdot k^{-1}) \leq t_\delta(s)$, $i_\delta(k \cdot s \cdot k^{-1}) \leq i_\delta(s)$ and $f_\delta(k \cdot s \cdot k^{-1}) \geq f_\delta(s)$.

The collection of all NNSGs of M will be denoted as NNSG(M).

Definition 2.10 (Anthony & Sherwood, 1979) A FS α of M is said to have supremum property if for any $\alpha' \subseteq \alpha$ $\exists k_0 \in \alpha'$ such that $\alpha(k_0) = \sup_{k \in \alpha'} \alpha(k)$.

Theorem 2.4 (Anthony & Sherwood, 1979) Suppose α is a fuzzy subgroupoid of M based on a continuous TN T and l be a homomorphism on M, then the image (supremum image) of α is a fuzzy subgroupoid on $l(M)$ based on T.

Theorem 2.5 (Rosenfeld, 1971) Homomorphic image or pre-image of any FSG having supremum property is a FSG.

Theorem 2.6 (Sharma, 2011) Let M_1 and M_2 are two crisp groups. Also, suppose l is a homomorphism of M_1 into M_2 then preimage of an IFSG γ of M_2 i.e. $l^{-1}(\gamma)$ is an IFSG of M_1.

Theorem 2.7 (Sharma, 2011) Let l be a surjective homomorphism of a group M_1 to another group M_2, then the image of an IFSG γ of M_1 i.e. $l(\gamma)$ is an IFSG of M_2.

Theorem 2.8 (Çetkin & Aygün, 2015) Homomorphic image or pre-image of any NSG is a NSG.

Theorem 2.9 (Çetkin & Aygün, 2015) Let $\delta \in$ NNSG(M) and l be a homomorphism on M. Then the homomorphic pre-image of δ i.e. $l^{-1}(\delta) \in$ NNSG(M).

Theorem 2.10 (Çetkin & Aygün, 2015) Let $\delta \in$ NNSG(M) and l be a surjective homomorphism on M. Then the homomorphic image of δ i.e. $l(\delta) \in$ NNSG(M).

Table 2. Significance and influences of some authors in FSG, IFSG, and NSG

Author and Year	Different contributions in FSG, IFSG, and NSG
(Rosenfeld, 1971)	Introduced FSG.
(Das, 1981)	Introduced level subgroup.
(Anthony & Sherwood, 1979)	Introduced FSG using general T-norm.
(Anthony & Sherwood, 1982)	Introduced subgroup generated and function generated FSG.
(Sherwood, 1983)	Studied product of FSGs.
(Mukherjee & Bhattacharya, 1984)	Introduced fuzzy normal subgroups and cosets.
(Biswas, 1989)	Introduced IFSG.
(Eroğlu, 1989)	Studied homomorphic image of FSG.
(Hur et. al., 2003)	Investigated some properties of IFSGs and inutionistic fuzzy subrings.
(Hur et. al., 2004)	Defined normal version of IFSG and intuitionistic fuzzy cosets.
(Sharma, 2011)	Studied homomorphism of IFSG.
(Çetkin & Aygün, 2015)	Introduced NSG and NNSG and studied some of their fundamental properties by introducing homomorphism.

In the following Table 2, some sources have been mentioned which have some major contributions in the fields of FSG, IFSG, and NSG.

2.2. A List of Abbreviations

CS signifies "crisp set".
FS signifies "fuzzy set".
IFS signifies "intuitionistic fuzzy set".
NS signifies "neutrosophic set".
FSG signifies "fuzzy subgroup".
IFSG signifies "intuitionistic fuzzy subgroup".
NSG signifies "neutrosophic subgroup".
TN signifies "T-norm".
TC signifies "T-conorm".
IVTN signifies "interval-valued T-norm".
IVTC signifies "interval-valued T-conorm".
IVDTN signifies "interval-valued double T-norm".
IVTTN signifies "interval-valued triple T-norm".
IVFS signifies "interval-valued fuzzy set".
IVIFS signifies "interval-valued intuitionistic fuzzy set".
IVNS signifies "interval-valued neutrosophic set".

IVFSG signifies "interval-valued fuzzy subgroup".
IVIFSG signifies "interval-valued intuitionistic fuzzy subgroup".
IVNSG signifies "interval-valued neutrosophic subgroup".
IVIFNSG signifies "interval-valued intuitionistic fuzzy normal subgroup".
IVNNSG signifies "interval-valued neutrosophic normal subgroup".

2.3. Motivation of the Work

So far, IVFSG and IVIFSG have grabbed a lot of attention and hence, as a result, as a result, it has yielded a lot of promising research fields. Some researchers have introduced functions in the environments of IVFSG and IVIFSG. Furthermore, they have introduced homomorphism in IVFSG and IVIFSG environments and studied some of their fundamental algebraic properties. IVNSG is relatively new and may become fruitful research field in near future. Also, the notion of IVNNSG is needed to be introduced. Furthermore, functions are needed to be introduced in the interval-valued neutrosophic environment and some homomorphic characteristics of IVNSG and IVNNSG are needed to be introduced. In this chapter, the subsequent research gaps are discussed:

- Still, the notion of IVNSG is undefined.
- Homomorphic image and preimage of IVNSG are needed to be studied.
- Still, the notion of IVNNSG is undefined.
- Also, some homomorphic characteristics of IVNNSG are needed to be analyzed.

Therefore, this inspires us to introduce and develop these notions of IVNSG and IVNNSG and analyze some of their algebraic characteristics.

2.4. Contribution of the Work

On the basis of the above gaps, the purpose of this chapter is to give some important definitions, examples and, theories in the field of IVNSG. Also, function has been introduced in interval-valued neutrosophic environment and some homomorphic properties of IVNSG and IVNNSG are discussed properly. The following are some goals that are planned and accomplished during this research work:

- To define IVNSG and study its algebraic properties.
- To define IVNNSG and study its algebraic properties.
- To introduce a function in interval-valued neutrosophic environment.
- To study some properties of homomorphic images and preimages of IVNSG and IVNNSG.

3. DESCRIPTION OF THE WORK

3.1. Research Problem

Until now, several researchers have studied different fundamental properties and algebraic structures of FSG, IFSG, as well as NSG. Again, some researchers have introduced IVFSG, IVIFSG and analyzed their fundamental properties. It is known that homomorphism preserves algebraic structures of any entity. Therefore, it is an essential tool to study some fundamental algebraic properties. Hence, several researchers have introduced and studied homomorphism in the environments of FSG, IFSG, NSG, IVFSG, IVIFSG, etc. In addition, some researchers have introduced the normal forms of FSG, IFSG, NSG, IVFSG, IVIFSG and studied their homomorphic properties. Until now, the notion of IVNSG is undefined and unexplored. Also, the normal form of IVNSG is undefined. Hence, these notions are yet to be introduced. Furthermore, the effects of homomorphism on these notions i.e. fundamental properties of homomorphic images and preimages of these notions are needed to be analyzed.

In this chapter, these essential notions of IVNSG and its normal form have been introduced and analyzed with proper examples. In the following subsection, some important notions have been discussed, which were introduced earlier.

3.1.1. Preliminaries

In this segment, the notions of interval number, IVFS, IVIFS, IVFSG, IVDTN, IVIFSG, IVTTN, etc. have been discussed. These notions are essential for introducing IVNSG.

Definition 3.1 Let $J=[0,1]$. An interval number of J is denoted as $\bar{g}=[g^-,g^+]$, where $0 \le g^- \le g^+ \le 1$.

The set of all the interval numbers of J will be denoted as $\rho(J)$ where $\rho(J) = \{\bar{g}=[g^-,g^+]: g^- \le g^+, g^-, g^+ \in J\}$.

Again, $\forall g \in J$, $g=[g, g] \in \rho(J)$ i.e. interval numbers are more general than ordinary numbers.

Let $\forall i$, $\bar{u}_i = [u_i^-, u_i^+] \in J$. Then supremum and infimum of $\bar{u}_i$ are defined as:

$$\sup(\bar{u}_i) = [\vee u_i^-, \vee u_i^+] \text{ and } \inf(\bar{u}_i) = [\wedge u_i^-, \wedge u_i^+].$$

Also, let

$\bar{g} = [g^-, g^+] \in \rho(J)$ and $\bar{u} = [u^-, u^+] \in \rho(J)$,

then the subsequent are true:

1. $\bar{g} \leq \bar{u}$ iff $g^- \leq u^-$ and $g^+ \leq u^+$.
2. $\bar{g} = \bar{u}$ iff $g^- = u^-$ and $g^+ = u^+$.
3. $\bar{g} < \bar{u}$ iff $g^- \leq u^-$ and $g^{+1} u^+$.

Definition 3.2 (Zadeh, 1975) Let M be crisp set, then the mapping $\bar{\mu} : M \to \rho(J)$ is called an IVFS of M.

A set of all IVFS of M is denoted as IVFS(M). For each $\bar{\mu} \in$ IVFS(M), $\bar{\mu}^-(k) \leq \bar{\mu}^+(k)$ for all $k \in M$. Here, $\bar{\mu}^-(k)$ and $\bar{\mu}^+(k)$ are fuzzy sets of $\bar{\mu}$. Also, Let $(\bar{g}, \bar{u}_i) \in \rho(J) \times \rho(J)$, where $\bar{g}_i = [g_i^-, g_i^+]$ and $\bar{u}_i = [u_i^-, u_i^+]$ with $g_i^+ + u_i^+ \leq 1$, for all i. Then supremum and infimum $(\bar{g}_i, \bar{u}_i)$ are defined as:

(1.) $\bigwedge_{i \in \lambda}(\bar{g}_i, \bar{u}_i) = (\bigwedge_{i \in \lambda} \bar{g}_i, \bigvee_{i \in \lambda} \bar{u}_i) = ([\bigwedge_{i \in \lambda} g_i^-, \bigwedge_{i \in \lambda} g_i^+], [\bigvee_{i \in \lambda} u_i^+, \bigvee_{i \in \lambda} u_i^+])$

(2.) $\bigvee_{i \in \lambda}(\bar{g}_i, \bar{u}_i) = (\bigvee_{i \in \lambda} \bar{g}_i, \bigwedge_{i \in \lambda} \bar{u}_i) = ([\bigvee_{i \in \lambda} g_i^-, \bigvee_{i \in \lambda} g_i^+], [\bigwedge_{i \in \lambda} u_i^+, \bigwedge_{i \in \lambda} u_i^+])$

Again, for all

$(\bar{g}_1, \bar{u}_1), (\bar{g}_2, \bar{u}_2) \in \rho(J) \times \rho(J),$

with

$(\bar{g}_1, \bar{u}_1) = ([g_1^-, g_1^+], [u_1^-, u_1^+]), (\bar{g}_2, \bar{u}_2) = ([g_2^-, g_2^+], [u_2^-, u_2^+]),$

the subsequent are true:

1. $(\bar{g}_1, \bar{u}_1) \leq (\bar{g}_2, \bar{u}_2)$ iff $\bar{g}_1 \leq \bar{g}_2$ and $\bar{u}_1 \geq \bar{u}_2$,
2. $(\bar{g}_1, \bar{u}_1) = (\bar{g}_2, \bar{u}_2)$ iff $\bar{g}_1 = \bar{g}_2$ and $\bar{u}_1 = \bar{u}_2$,
3. $(\bar{g}_1, \bar{u}_1) < (\bar{g}_2, \bar{u}_2)$ iff $\bar{g}_1 \leq \bar{g}_2, \bar{u}_1 \geq \bar{u}_2$ and $\bar{g}_1 \neq \bar{g}_2, \bar{u}_1 \neq \bar{u}_2$.

Definition 3.3 (Atanassov, 1999) Let M be a crisp set, then a mapping $\tilde{\gamma} : M \to \rho(J) \times \rho(J)$ defined as $\tilde{\gamma}(k) = (\bar{t}_{\tilde{\gamma}}(k), \bar{f}_{\tilde{\gamma}}(k))$, with $\bar{t}_{\tilde{\gamma}}^+(k) + \bar{f}_{\tilde{\gamma}}^+(k) \leq 1$, for all $k \in M$ is called an IVIFS of M.

In the above definition, both $\bar{t}_{\tilde{\gamma}}(k)$ and $\bar{f}_{\tilde{\gamma}}(k)$ are IVFSs of M. A set of all IVIFSs of M will be denoted as IVFS(M).

Definition 3.4 (Mondal & Samanta, 2001) Suppose M_1 and M_2 are two crisp sets and $l: M_1 \to M_2$ be a function. Let $\tilde{\gamma}_1 \in$ IVIFS(M_1) and $\tilde{\gamma}_2 \in$ IVIFS(M_2). Then $\forall k \in M_1$ the image of $\tilde{\gamma}_1$ i.e. $l(\tilde{\gamma}_1)$ is denoted as $l(\tilde{\gamma}_1)(s) = (l(\bar{t}_{\tilde{\gamma}_1})(s), l(\bar{f}_{\tilde{\gamma}_1})(s))$ and $\forall s \in M_2$ the preimage of $\tilde{\gamma}_2$ i.e. $l^{-1}(\tilde{\gamma}_2)$ is denoted as $l^{-1}(\tilde{\gamma}_2)(k) = \tilde{\gamma}_2(l(k))$. where

$$l(\tilde{\gamma}_1)(s) = \left[\bigvee_{k \in l^{-1}(s)} (\overline{t}_{\tilde{\gamma}_1})(k), \bigwedge_{k \in l^{-1}(s)} (\overline{f}_{\tilde{\gamma}_1})(k) \right]$$

$$= \left[[l(t^-_{\tilde{\gamma}_1})(s), l(t^+_{\tilde{\gamma}_1})(s)], [l(f^-_{\tilde{\gamma}_1})(s), l(f^+_{\tilde{\gamma}_1})(s)] \right]$$

and

$$l^{-1}(\tilde{\gamma}_2)(k) = \left[[l^{-1}(t^-_{\tilde{\gamma}_2})(k), l^{-1}(t^+_{\tilde{\gamma}_2})(k)], [l^{-1}(f^-_{\tilde{\gamma}_2})(k), l^{-1}(f^+_{\tilde{\gamma}_2})(k)] \right]$$

$$= \left[[t^-_{\tilde{\gamma}_2}(l(k)), t^+_{\tilde{\gamma}_2}(l(k))], [f^-_{\tilde{\gamma}_2}(l(k)), f^+_{\tilde{\gamma}_2}(l(k))] \right]$$

Definition 3.5 (Gupta & Qi, 1991) A function $T: J \to J$ is called a TN iff $\forall k,s,t \in J$, conditions given below are fulfilled:

   (1.) $T(k, 1) = k$

   (2.) $T(k, s) = T(s, k)$

   (3.) $T(k, s) \leq T(t, s)$ if $k \leq t$

   (4.) $T(k, T(s, t)) = T(T(k, s), t)$

Notice that, T is an idempotent TN iff T is minimum TN or $T = \wedge$.

Definition 3.6 (Klement et. al., 2013) Suppose T is a TN, then the function $\overline{T}: \rho(J) \times \rho(J) \to \rho(J)$ defined as $\overline{T}(\overline{g}, \overline{u}) = [T(g^-, u^-), T(g^+, u^+)]$ is called an IVTN.

Notice that, $\overline{T}$ is idempotent if T is idempotent.

Definition 3.7 (Gupta & Qi, 1991) A function $S: J \to J$ is called a TC iff $\forall k,s,t \in J$, subsequent conditions are fulfilled:

   (1.) $S(k,0)=k$

   (2.) $S(k,s)=S(s,k)$

   (3.) $S(k,s) \leq S(t,s)$ if $k \leq t$

   (4.) $S(k,S(s,t))=S(S(k,s),t)$

Note that, S is an idempotent TC iff S is maximum TC or $S=\vee$.

Definition 3.8 (Klement et. al., 2013) Let S be a TC, then the mapping $\overline{S}: \rho(J) \times \rho(J) \to \rho(J)$ defined as $S(\overline{g}, \overline{u}) = [\overline{S}(g^-, u^-), S(g^+, u^+)]$ is called an IVTC.

Note that, $\overline{S}$ is idempotent if S is idempotent.

Definition 3.9 (Aygünoğlu et. al., 2012) Suppose $\overline{T}$ is an IVTN and $\overline{S}$ is an IVTC. Then a mapping $\tilde{T}: (\rho(J) \times \rho(J))^2 \to \rho(J) \times \rho(J)$ denoted as $\tilde{T}((\overline{g}_1, \overline{u}_1), (\overline{g}_2, \overline{u}_2)) = (\overline{T}(\overline{g}_1, \overline{g}_2), \overline{S}(\overline{u}_1, \overline{u}_2))$ is called an IVDTN.

Note that, $\tilde{T}$ is idempotent if both $\overline{T}$ and $\overline{S}$ are idempotent.

Definition 3.10 (Aygünoğlu et. al., 2012) Let M be a crisp group. An IVIFS $\tilde{\gamma} = \{(s, \overline{t}_{\tilde{\gamma}}(s), \overline{f}_{\tilde{\gamma}}(s)) : s \in M\}$ of M is called an IVIFSG of M with respect to IVDTN $\tilde{T}$ if the conditions given below are fullfilled:

1. $\tilde{\gamma}(k \cdot s) \geq \tilde{T}(\tilde{\gamma}(k), \tilde{\gamma}(s))$, $\forall k, s \in M$,
2. $\tilde{\gamma}(s^{-1}) \geq \tilde{\gamma}(s)$, $\forall s \in M$.

Where condition (1.) implies that,

$$\overline{t}_{\tilde{\gamma}}(k \cdot s) \geq \overline{T}(\overline{t}_{\tilde{\gamma}}(k), \overline{t}_{\tilde{\gamma}}(s)), \overline{f}_{\tilde{\gamma}}(k \cdot s) \leq \overline{S}(\overline{f}_{\tilde{\gamma}}(k), \overline{f}_{\tilde{\gamma}}(s))$$

and condition (2.) implies that, $\overline{t}_{\tilde{\gamma}}(s^{-1}) \geq \overline{t}_{\tilde{\gamma}}(s)$, $\overline{f}_{\tilde{\gamma}}(s^{-1}) \leq \overline{f}_{\tilde{\gamma}}(s)$.

The set of all IVIFSG of a group M based on IVDTN $\tilde{T}$ will be mentioned as IVIFSG $(M, \tilde{T})$.

Theorem 3.1 (Aygünoğlu et. al., 2012) Suppose M is a group and $\tilde{\gamma} \in \text{IVIFS}(M)$. Then $\tilde{\gamma} \in \text{IVIFSG}(M, \tilde{T})$ iff $\forall k, s \in M$. $\tilde{\gamma}(k \cdot s^{-1}) \geq \tilde{T}(\tilde{\gamma}(k), \tilde{\gamma}(s))$.

Theorem 3.2 (Aygünoğlu et. al., 2012) Let M_1 and M_2 be two crisp groups with l: $M_1 \rightarrow M_2$ be a homomorphism and $\tilde{T}$ be a continuous IVDTN. If $\tilde{\gamma} \in \text{IVIFSG}(M_1, \tilde{T})$, then $l(\tilde{\gamma}) \in \text{IVIFSG}(M_2, \tilde{T})$.

Theorem 3.3 (Aygünoğlu et. al., 2012) Suppose M_1 and M_2 are two crisp groups and l be a homomorphism from M_1 into M_2. If $\tilde{\gamma}' \in \text{IVIFSG}(M_2, \tilde{T})$, then $l^{-1}(\tilde{\gamma}) \in \text{IVIFSG}(M_1, \tilde{T})$.

Definition 3.11 (Aygünoğlu et. al., 2012) Let M be a crisp group and $\tilde{\gamma} \in \text{IVIFSG}(M, \tilde{T})$. Then $\tilde{\gamma}$ is called an IVIFNSG of M with respect to IVDTN $\tilde{T}$ if $\forall k, s \in M$, $\tilde{\gamma}(k \cdot s) = \tilde{\gamma}(s \cdot k)$.

The set of all IVIFNSG of a crisp group M with respect to $\tilde{T}$ will be denoted as IVIFNSG $(M, \tilde{T})$.

Theorem 3.4 (Aygünoğlu et. al., 2012) Suppose M_1 and M_2 are two crisp groups and l be a homomorphism from M_1 into M_2. If $\tilde{\gamma}' \in \text{IVIFNSG}(M_2, \tilde{T})$, then $l^{-1}(\tilde{\gamma}') \in \text{IVIFNSG}(M_1, \tilde{T})$.

Theorem 3.5 (Aygünoğlu et. al., 2012) Let M_1 and M_2 be two crisp groups and l be a surjective homomorphism from M_1 into M_2. If $\tilde{\gamma} \in \text{IVIFNSG}(M_1, \tilde{T})$, then $l(\tilde{\gamma}) \in \text{IVIFNSG}(M_1, \tilde{T})$.

In the following Table 3, some sources have been mentioned which have some major contributions in the fields of IVFS, IVIFS, IVFSG and IVIFSG.

Table 3. Some important contributions in the fields of IVFS, IVIFS, IVFSG, and IVIFSG

Author and Year	Different contributions in IVFS, IVIFS, IVFSG and IVIFSG
(Zadeh, 1975)	Introduced IVFS
(Biswas, 1994)	Defined IVFSG which is of Rosenfeld's nature.
(Guijun & Xiaoping, 1996)	Introduced IVSGs induced by triangular norms.
(Atanassov, 1999)	Introduced IVIFS.
(Mondal & Samanta, 1999)	Defined topology of IVFSs is and studied some of its properties.
(Davvaz, Interval-valued fuzzy subhypergroups, 1999)	Introduced the concepts of interval-valued fuzzy subhypergroup of a hypergroup.
(Li & Wang, 2000)	Introduced the notion of S_H-IVFSG.
(Mondal & Samanta, 2001)	Defined topology of IVIFSs is and studied some of its properties.
(Davvaz, 2001)	Extended the notion of fuzzy ideal of a near-ring by introducing interval-valued L-fuzzy ideal of a near-ring.
(Jun & Kim, 2002)	Introduced interval-valued fuzzy R-subgroups in near rings.
(Aygünoğlu et. al., 2012)	Defined IVDTN and using that introduced IVIFSG.

In the following section, the notion of IVNSG has been defined, which is based on IVTTN. Also, some essential homomorphic properties of IVNSG has been investigated. Furthermore, the normal form of IVNSG has been defined and its homomorphic characteristics have been studied.

4. PROPOSED NOTION OF INTERVAL-VALUED NEUTROSOPHIC SUBGROUP

Definition 4.1 Suppose $\bar{T}$ and $\bar{I}$ are two IVTNs and $\bar{F}$ be an IVTC. The function

$$\breve{T} : (\rho(J) \times \rho(J) \times \rho(J))^2 \rightarrow \rho(J) \times \rho(J) \times \rho(J)$$

denoted as

$$\breve{T}((\bar{g}_1, \bar{u}_1, \bar{t}_1), (\bar{g}_2, \bar{u}_2, \bar{t}_2)) = (\bar{T}(\bar{g}_1, \bar{g}_2), \bar{I}(\bar{u}_1, \bar{u}_2), \bar{F}(\bar{t}_1, \bar{t}_2))$$

is called an IVTTN.

Definition 4.2 Suppose M is a crisp group. An IVNS $\breve{\delta} = \{(s, \bar{t}_{\breve{\delta}}(s), \bar{i}_{\breve{\delta}}(s), \bar{f}_{\breve{\delta}}(s)) : s \in M\}$ of M is called an IVNSG of M with respect to IVTTN $\breve{T}$ if the conditions given below are fulfilled:

1. $\breve{\delta}(k \cdot s) \geq \breve{T}(\breve{\delta}(k), \breve{\delta}(s))$, $\forall k, s \in M$,
2. $\breve{\delta}(s^{-1}) \geq \breve{\delta}(s)$, $\forall s \in M$.

Now, by condition (1.)

$$\bar{t}_{\breve{\delta}}(k \cdot s) \geq \bar{T}(\bar{t}_{\breve{\delta}}(k), \bar{t}_{\breve{\delta}}(s)), \bar{i}_{\breve{\delta}}(k \cdot s) \geq \bar{I}(\bar{i}_{\breve{\delta}}(k), \bar{i}_{\breve{\delta}}(s)), \bar{f}_{\breve{\delta}}(k \cdot s) \leq \bar{F}(\bar{f}_{\breve{\delta}}(k), \bar{f}_{\breve{\delta}}(s))$$

and by condition (2.) $\bar{t}_{\breve{\delta}}(s^{-1}) \geq \bar{t}_{\breve{\delta}}(s), i_{\breve{\delta}}(s^{-1}) \geq i_{\breve{\delta}}(s)$ and $\bar{f}_{\breve{\delta}}(s^{-1}) \leq \bar{f}_{\breve{\delta}}(s)$.

The set of all IVNSG of a group M with respect to an IVTTN $\breve{T}$ will be denoted as IVNSG $(M, \breve{T})$.

Example 4.1 Let $R = \{e, k, s, ks\}$ be the Klein's four group. Let

$$\breve{\delta} = \{(e, [0.1, 0.3], [0.2, 0.4], [0.1, 0.4]), (k, [0.1, 0.3], [0.2, 0.3], [0.2, 0.4]),$$
$$(s, [0.1, 0.2], [0.2, 0.4], [0.2, 0.5]), (ks, [0.1, 0.2], [0.2, 0.3], [0.2, 0.5])\}$$

be a IVNS of M. Also, let in IVTTN $\breve{T}$, the corresponding IVTNs $\bar{T}$ and $\bar{I}$ consist of minimum TN and corresponding IVTC $\bar{F}$ consists of maximum TC. In Table 4 all possible compositions of elements in $\breve{\delta}$ and their corresponding interval-valued memberships are mentioned.

Clearly, from Table 4, $\breve{\delta}$ satisfies condition (i) of Definition 4.2. Again, each element belonging to $\breve{\delta}$ is its own inverse. Hence, $\breve{\delta}$ satisfies condition (ii) of Definition 4.2. So, $\breve{\delta} \in$ IVNSG $(M, \breve{T})$.

Theorem 4.1 Let M be a group and $\breve{\delta} \in$ IVNSG$(M, \breve{T})$. Then $\forall s \in M$

1. $\breve{\delta}(s^{-1}) = \breve{\delta}(s)$ and
2. $\breve{\delta}(e) \geq \breve{\delta}(s)$, where e is the neutral element of M.

Proof:

1. From Definition 4.2, we have $\breve{\delta}(s^{-1}) \geq \breve{\delta}(s)$, $\forall s \in M$. Again, for any $s \in M$, $\breve{\delta}(s) = \breve{\delta}((s^{-1})^{-1}) \geq \breve{\delta}(s^{-1})$. So, $\breve{\delta}(s^{-1}) = \breve{\delta}(s)$.
2. For any $k \in R$, $\breve{\delta}(e) \geq \breve{\delta}(s \cdot s^{-1}) \geq \breve{T}(\breve{\delta}(s), \breve{\delta}(s^{-1})) = \breve{T}(\breve{\delta}(s), \breve{\delta}(s)) = \breve{\delta}(s)$.

Theorem 4.2 Suppose M is a crisp group and $\breve{\delta} \in$ IVNS(M). Then $\breve{\delta} \in$ IVNSG$(M, \breve{T})$ iff $\forall k, s \in M$, $\breve{\delta}(k \cdot s^{-1}) \geq \breve{T}(\breve{\delta}(k), \breve{\delta}(s))$.

Theorem 4.3 Suppose M is a crisp group and $\breve{\delta}_1, \breve{\delta}_2 \in$ IVNSG$(M, \breve{T})$. Then $\breve{\delta}_1 \cap \breve{\delta}_2 \in$ IVNSG$(M, \breve{T})$.

Proof: Let $\breve{\delta}_1, \breve{\delta}_2 \in$ IVNSG $(M, \breve{T})$. To prove $\breve{\delta}_1 \cap \breve{\delta}_2 \in$ IVNSG $(M, \breve{T})$, it is needed to show that

Table 4. All possible compositions of elements in $\bar{\delta}$ and their interval-valued memberships

$e \cdot e$	$\bar{t}_\delta(e \cdot e) = \bar{t}_\delta(e) \geq \bar{T}(\bar{t}_\delta(e), \bar{t}_\delta(e)),$ $\bar{i}_\delta(e \cdot e) = \bar{i}_\delta(e) \geq \bar{I}(\bar{i}_\delta(e), \bar{i}_\delta(e)), \bar{f}_\delta(e \cdot e) = \bar{f}_\delta(e) \leq \bar{F}(\bar{f}_\delta(e), \bar{f}_\delta(e))$
$e \cdot k$	$\bar{t}_\delta(e \cdot k) = \bar{t}_\delta(k) = [0.1, 0.3] \geq [0.1, 0.3] = \bar{T}([0.1, 0.3], [0.1, 0.3]) = \bar{T}(\bar{t}_\delta(e), \bar{t}_\delta(k)),$ $\bar{i}_\delta(e \cdot k) = \bar{i}_\delta(k) = [0.2, 0.3] \geq [0.2, 0.3] = \bar{I}([0.2, 0.4], [0.2, 0.3]) = \bar{I}(\bar{i}_\delta(e), \bar{i}_\delta(k)),$ $\bar{f}_\delta(e \cdot k) = \bar{f}_\delta(k) = [0.2, 0.4] \leq [0.2, 0.4] = \bar{F}([0.1, 0.4], [0.2, 0.4]) = \bar{F}(\bar{f}_\delta(e), \bar{f}_\delta(k))$
$e \cdot s$	$\bar{t}_\delta(e \cdot s) = \bar{t}_\delta(s) = [0.1, 0.2] \geq [0.1, 0.2] = \bar{T}([0.1, 0.3], [0.1, 0.2]) = \bar{T}(\bar{t}_\delta(e), \bar{t}_\delta(s)),$ $\bar{i}_\delta(e \cdot s) = \bar{i}_\delta(s) = [0.2, 0.4] \geq [0.2, 0.4] = \bar{I}([0.2, 0.4], [0.2, 0.4]) = \bar{I}(\bar{i}_\delta(e), \bar{i}_\delta(s)),$ $\bar{f}_\delta(e \cdot s) = \bar{f}_\delta(s) = [0.2, 0.5] \leq [0.2, 0.5] = \bar{F}([0.1, 0.4], [0.2, 0.5]) = \bar{F}(\bar{f}_\delta(e), \bar{f}_\delta(s))$
$e \cdot ks$	$\bar{t}_\delta(e \cdot ks) = \bar{t}_\delta(ks) = [0.1, 0.2] \geq [0.1, 0.2] = \bar{T}([0.1, 0.3], [0.1, 0.2]) = \bar{T}(\bar{t}_\delta(e), \bar{t}_\delta(ks)),$ $\bar{i}_\delta(e \cdot ks) = \bar{i}_\delta(ks) = [0.2, 0.3] \geq [0.2, 0.3] = \bar{I}([0.2, 0.4], [0.2, 0.3]) = \bar{I}(\bar{i}_\delta(e), \bar{i}_\delta(ks)),$ $\bar{f}_\delta(e \cdot ks) = \bar{f}_\delta(ks) = [0.2, 0.5] \leq [0.2, 0.5] = \bar{F}([0.1, 0.4], [0.2, 0.5]) = \bar{F}(\bar{f}_\delta(e), \bar{f}_\delta(ks))$
$a \cdot a = e$	$\bar{t}_\delta(a \cdot a) = \bar{t}_\delta(e) = [0.1, 0.3] \geq [0.1, 0.3] = \bar{T}([0.1, 0.3], [0.1, 0.3]) = \bar{T}(\bar{t}_\delta(a), \bar{t}_\delta(a)),$ $\bar{i}_\delta(a \cdot a) = \bar{i}_\delta(e) = [0.2, 0.4] \geq [0.2, 0.3] = \bar{I}([0.2, 0.3], [0.2, 0.3]) = \bar{I}(\bar{i}_\delta(a), \bar{i}_\delta(a)),$ $\bar{f}_\delta(a \cdot a) = \bar{f}_\delta(e) = [0.1, 0.4] \leq [0.2, 0.4] = \bar{F}([0.1, 0.4], [0.2, 0.4]) = \bar{F}(\bar{f}_\delta(a), \bar{f}_\delta(a))$
$a \cdot b = b \cdot a$	$\bar{t}_\delta(a \cdot b) = \bar{t}_\delta(b \cdot a) = [0.1, 0.2] \geq [0.1, 0.2] = \bar{T}([0.1, 0.3], [0.1, 0.2]) = \bar{T}(\bar{t}_\delta(a), \bar{t}_\delta(b)),$ $\bar{i}_\delta(a \cdot b) = \bar{i}_\delta(b \cdot a) = [0.2, 0.4] \geq [0.2, 0.3] = \bar{I}([0.2, 0.3], [0.2, 0.3]) = \bar{I}(\bar{i}_\delta(a), \bar{i}_\delta(b)),$ $\bar{f}_\delta(a \cdot b) = \bar{f}_\delta(b \cdot a) = [0.1, 0.4] \leq [0.2, 0.4] = \bar{F}([0.1, 0.4], [0.2, 0.4]) = \bar{F}(\bar{f}_\delta(a), \bar{f}_\delta(b))$
$a \cdot ab = ab \cdot a = b$	$\bar{t}_\delta(a \cdot ab) = \bar{t}_\delta(b) = [0.1, 0.2] \geq [0.1, 0.2] = \bar{T}([0.1, 0.3], [0.1, 0.2]) = \bar{T}(\bar{t}_\delta(a), \bar{t}_\delta(ab)),$ $\bar{i}_\delta(a \cdot ab) = \bar{i}_\delta(b) = [0.2, 0.4] \geq [0.2, 0.3] = \bar{I}([0.2, 0.3], [0.2, 0.3]) = \bar{I}(\bar{i}_\delta(a), \bar{i}_\delta(ab)),$ $\bar{f}_\delta(a \cdot ab) = \bar{f}_\delta(b) = [0.2, 0.5] \leq [0.2, 0.5] = \bar{F}([0.2, 0.4], [0.2, 0.5]) = \bar{F}(\bar{f}_\delta(a), \bar{f}_\delta(ab))$
$b \cdot b = e$	$\bar{t}_\delta(b \cdot b) = \bar{t}_\delta(e) = [0.1, 0.3] \geq [0.1, 0.2] = \bar{T}([0.1, 0.2], [0.1, 0.2]) = \bar{T}(\bar{t}_\delta(b), \bar{t}_\delta(b)),$ $\bar{i}_\delta(b \cdot b) = \bar{i}_\delta(e) = [0.2, 0.4] \geq [0.2, 0.4] = \bar{I}([0.2, 0.4], [0.2, 0.4]) = \bar{I}(\bar{i}_\delta(b), \bar{i}_\delta(b)),$ $\bar{f}_\delta(b \cdot b) = \bar{f}_\delta(e) = [0.1, 0.4] \leq [0.2, 0.5] = \bar{F}([0.2, 0.5], [0.2, 0.5]) = \bar{F}(\bar{f}_\delta(b), \bar{f}_\delta(b))$
$b \cdot ab = ab \cdot b = a$	$\bar{t}_\delta(b \cdot ab) = \bar{t}_\delta(a) = [0.1, 0.3] \geq [0.1, 0.2] = \bar{T}([0.1, 0.2], [0.1, 0.2]) = \bar{T}(\bar{t}_\delta(b), \bar{t}_\delta(ab)),$ $\bar{i}_\delta(b \cdot ab) = \bar{i}_\delta(a) = [0.2, 0.3] \geq [0.2, 0.3] = \bar{I}([0.2, 0.4], [0.2, 0.3]) = \bar{I}(\bar{i}_\delta(b), \bar{i}_\delta(ab)),$ $\bar{f}_\delta(b \cdot ab) = \bar{f}_\delta(a) = [0.2, 0.4] \leq [0.2, 0.5] = \bar{F}([0.2, 0.5], [0.2, 0.5]) = \bar{F}(\bar{f}_\delta(b), \bar{f}_\delta(ab))$
$ab \cdot ab = e$	$\bar{t}_\delta(ab \cdot ab) = \bar{t}_\delta(e) = [0.1, 0.3] \geq [0.1, 0.3] = \bar{T}([0.1, 0.2], [0.1, 0.2]) = \bar{T}(\bar{t}_\delta(ab), \bar{t}_\delta(ab)),$ $\bar{i}_\delta(ab \cdot ab) = \bar{i}_\delta(e) = [0.2, 0.4] \geq [0.2, 0.3] = \bar{I}([0.2, 0.3], [0.2, 0.3]) = \bar{I}(\bar{i}_\delta(ab), \bar{i}_\delta(ab)),$ $\bar{f}_\delta(ab \cdot ab) = \bar{f}_\delta(e) = [0.1, 0.4] \leq [0.2, 0.5] = \bar{F}([0.2, 0.5], [0.2, 0.5]) = \bar{F}(\bar{f}_\delta(ab), \bar{f}_\delta(ab))$

$$(\bar{t}_{\breve{\delta}_1} \wedge \bar{t}_{\breve{\delta}_2})(k \cdot s^{-1}) \geq \bar{T}((\bar{t}_{\breve{\delta}_1} \wedge \bar{t}_{\breve{\delta}_2})(k), (\bar{t}_{\breve{\delta}_1} \wedge \bar{t}_{\breve{\delta}_2})(s)), (\bar{i}_{\breve{\delta}_1} \wedge \bar{i}_{\breve{\delta}_2})(k \cdot q^{-1}) \geq \bar{I}((\bar{i}_{\breve{\delta}_1} \wedge \bar{i}_{\breve{\delta}_2})(k), (\bar{i}_{\breve{\delta}_1} \wedge \bar{i}_{\breve{\delta}_2})(q))$$

and

$$(\bar{f}_{\breve{\delta}_1} \vee \bar{f}_{\breve{\delta}_2})(k \cdot s^{-1}) \leq \bar{F}((\bar{f}_{\breve{\delta}_1} \vee \bar{f}_{\breve{\delta}_2})(k), (\bar{f}_{\breve{\delta}_1} \vee \bar{f}_{\breve{\delta}_2})(s)).$$

As $\breve{\delta}_1, \breve{\delta}_2 \in \mathrm{IVNSG}(M, \breve{T})$, by Theorem 4.2,

$$\breve{\delta}_1(k \cdot s^{-1}) \geq \breve{T}(\breve{\delta}_1(k), \breve{\delta}_1(s)) \text{ and } \breve{\delta}_2(k \cdot s^{-1}) \geq \breve{T}(\breve{\delta}_2(k), \breve{\delta}_2(s)).$$

Which implies,

$$\bar{t}_{\breve{\delta}_1}(k \cdot s^{-1}) \geq \bar{T}(\bar{t}_{\breve{\delta}_1}(k), \bar{t}_{\breve{\delta}_1}(s)), \bar{i}_{\breve{\delta}_1}(k \cdot s^{-1}) \geq \bar{I}(\bar{i}_{\breve{\delta}_1}(k), \bar{i}_{\breve{\delta}_1}(s)), \bar{f}_{\breve{\delta}_1}(k \cdot s^{-1}) \leq \bar{F}(\bar{f}_{\breve{\delta}_1}(k), \bar{f}_{\breve{\delta}_1}(s))$$

and

$$\bar{t}_{\breve{\delta}_2}(k \cdot s^{-1}) \geq \bar{T}(\bar{t}_{\breve{\delta}_2}(k), \bar{t}_{\breve{\delta}_2}(s)), \bar{i}_{\breve{\delta}_2}(k \cdot s^{-1}) \geq \bar{I}(\bar{i}_{\breve{\delta}_2}(k), \bar{i}_{\breve{\delta}_2}(s)), \bar{f}_{\breve{\delta}_2}(k \cdot s^{-1}) \leq \bar{F}(\bar{f}_{\breve{\delta}_2}(k), \bar{f}_{\breve{\delta}_2}(s)).$$

So,

$$\bar{t}_{\breve{\delta}_1}(k \cdot s^{-1}) \wedge \bar{t}_{\breve{\delta}_2}(k \cdot s^{-1}) \geq \bar{T}(\bar{t}_{\breve{\delta}_1}(k), \bar{t}_{\breve{\delta}_1}(s)) \wedge \bar{T}(\bar{t}_{\breve{\delta}_2}(k), \bar{t}_{\breve{\delta}_2}(s)) \Rightarrow (\bar{t}_{\breve{\delta}_1} \wedge \bar{t}_{\breve{\delta}_2})(k \cdot s^{-1}) \geq \bar{T}((\bar{t}_{\breve{\delta}_1} \wedge \bar{t}_{\breve{\delta}_2})(k), (\bar{t}_{\breve{\delta}_1} \wedge \bar{t}_{\breve{\delta}_2})(s)).$$

Similarly, the following can be proved:

$$(\bar{i}_{\breve{\delta}_1} \wedge \bar{i}_{\breve{\delta}_2})(k \cdot s^{-1}) \geq \bar{I}((\bar{i}_{\breve{\delta}_1} \wedge \bar{i}_{\breve{\delta}_2})(k), (\bar{i}_{\breve{\delta}_1} \wedge \bar{i}_{\breve{\delta}_2})(s))$$

and

$$(\bar{f}_{\breve{\delta}_1} \vee \bar{f}_{\breve{\delta}_2})(k \cdot s^{-1}) \leq \bar{F}((\bar{f}_{\breve{\delta}_1} \vee \bar{f}_{\breve{\delta}_2})(k), (\bar{f}_{\breve{\delta}_1} \vee \bar{f}_{\breve{\delta}_2})(s)).$$

Hence, $\breve{\delta}_1 \cap \breve{\delta}_2 \in \mathrm{IVNSG}(M, \breve{T})$.

Theorem 4.4 Suppose M be a group and $\breve{\delta} \in \mathrm{IVNS}(M)$. Then $\breve{\delta} \in \mathrm{IVNSG}(M, \breve{T})$ iff for every $[g_1, u_1]$, $[g_2, u_2]$ and $[g_3, u_3] \in \rho(J)$ with $u_1 + u_2 + u_3 \leq 1$, $(\breve{\delta}_{([g_1, u_1], [g_2, u_2], [g_3, u_3])} \neq \phi)$ $\breve{\delta}_{([g_1, u_1], [g_2, u_2], [g_3, u_3])}$ is a crisp subgroup of M.

Proof: Suppose $\breve{\delta} \in \text{IVNSG}(M, \breve{T})$ and $k, s \in \breve{\delta}_{([g_1,u_1],[g_2,u_2],[g_3,u_3])}$, for arbitrary $[g_1, u_1]$, $[g_2, u_2]$ and $[g_3, u_3] \in \rho(J)$ with $u_1 + u_2 + u_3 \leq 1$. Then we have

$$\bar{t}_{\breve{\delta}}(k) \geq [g_1, u_1], \bar{i}_{\breve{\delta}}(k) \geq [g_2, u_2], \bar{f}_{\breve{\delta}}(k) \leq [g_3, u_3] \text{ and } \bar{t}_{\breve{\delta}}(s) \geq [g_1, u_1], \bar{i}_{\breve{\delta}}(s) \geq [g_2, u_2], \bar{f}_{\breve{\delta}}(s) \leq [g_3, u_3]$$

Now, by Theorem 4.2, we have

$$\begin{aligned}
\breve{\delta}(k \cdot s^{-1}) &\geq \breve{T}(\breve{\delta}(k), \breve{\delta}(s)) \\
&= \breve{T}((\bar{t}_{\breve{\delta}}(k), \bar{i}_{\breve{\delta}}(k), \bar{f}_{\breve{\delta}}(k)), (\bar{t}_{\breve{\delta}}(s), \bar{i}_{\breve{\delta}}(s), \bar{f}_{\breve{\delta}}(s))) \\
&= (\bar{T}(\bar{t}_{\breve{\delta}}(k), \bar{t}_{\breve{\delta}}(s)), \bar{I}(\bar{i}_{\breve{\delta}}(k), \bar{i}_{\breve{\delta}}(s)), \bar{F}(\bar{f}_{\breve{\delta}}(k), \bar{f}_{\breve{\delta}}(s))) \\
&\geq (\bar{T}([g_1, u_1], [g_1, u_1]), \bar{I}([g_2, u_2], [g_2, u_2]), \bar{F}([g_3, u_3], [g_3, u_3])) \\
&= ([g_1, u_1], [g_2, u_2], [g_3, u_3])
\end{aligned}$$

So, from $k \cdot s^{-1} \in \breve{\delta}_{([g_1,u_1],[g_2,u_2],[g_3,u_3])}$. Hence, $\breve{\delta}_{([g_1,u_1],[g_2,u_2],[g_3,u_3])}$ is a crisp subgroup of M.

Conversely, let $\exists k_0, s_0 \in M$ such that $\breve{\delta}(k_0 \cdot s_0^{-1}) \not\geq \breve{T}(\breve{\delta}(k_0), \breve{\delta}(s_0))$ i.e $\bar{t}_{\breve{\delta}}(k_0 \cdot s_0^{-1}) \not\geq \bar{T}(\bar{t}_{\breve{\delta}}(k_0), \bar{t}_{\breve{\delta}}(s_0))$ or $\bar{i}_{\breve{\delta}}(k_0 \cdot s_0^{-1}) \not\geq \bar{I}(\bar{i}_{\breve{\delta}}(k_0), \bar{i}_{\breve{\delta}}(s_0))$ or $\bar{f}_{\breve{\delta}}(k_0 \cdot s_0^{-1}) \not\leq \bar{F}(\bar{f}_{\breve{\delta}}(k_0), \bar{f}_{\breve{\delta}}(s_0))$.

Without losing any generality, let $\bar{t}_{\breve{\delta}}(k_0 \cdot s_0^{-1}) \not\geq \bar{T}(\bar{t}_{\breve{\delta}}(k_0), \bar{t}_{\breve{\delta}}(s_0))$, then

$$\bar{t}_{\breve{\delta}}^-(k_0 \cdot s_0^{-1}) < \bar{T}(\bar{t}_{\breve{\delta}}^-(k_0), \bar{t}_{\breve{\delta}}^-(s_0)) \text{ or } \bar{t}_{\breve{\delta}}^+(k_0 \cdot s_0^{-1}) < \bar{T}(\bar{t}_{\breve{\delta}}^+(k_0), \bar{t}_{\breve{\delta}}^+(s_0)).$$

Let us assume $\bar{t}_{\breve{\delta}}^-(k_0 \cdot s_0^{-1}) < \bar{T}(\bar{t}_{\breve{\delta}}^-(k_0), \bar{t}_{\breve{\delta}}^-(s_0))$.

Again, let $\bar{t}_{\breve{\delta}}(k_0) = [n_1, t_1], \bar{t}_{\breve{\delta}}(s_0) = [n_2, t_2]$. If $[g_1, u_1] = \bar{T}([n_1, t_1], [n_2, t_2])$, then $k_0 \cdot s_0^{-1} \notin \breve{\delta}_{([g_1,u_1],[g_2,u_2],[g_3,u_3])}$ for any $[g_2, u_2], [g_3, u_3] \in \rho(J)$. Again,

$$\bar{t}_{\breve{\delta}}(k_0) = [n_1, t_1] \geq \bar{T}([n_1, t_1], [n_2, t_2]) = [g_1, u_1] \text{ and } \bar{t}_{\breve{\delta}}(k_0) = [n_2, t_2] \geq \bar{T}([n_1, t_1], [n_2, t_2]) = [g_1, u_1].$$

Now, by choosing $[g_2, u_2]$ and $[g_3, u_3]$, satisfying the conditions

$$\bar{i}_{\breve{\delta}}(k_0) \geq [g_2, u_2], \bar{i}_{\breve{\delta}}(k_0) \geq [g_2, u_2], \bar{f}_{\breve{\delta}}(k_0) \leq [g_3, u_3] \text{ and } \bar{f}_{\breve{\delta}}(k_0) \leq [g_3, u_3],$$

it can be proved that, $k_0, s_0^{-1} \in \breve{\delta}_{([g_1,u_1],[g_2,u_2],[g_3,u_3])}$, which contradicts the fact that $\breve{\delta}_{([g_1,u_1],[g_2,u_2],[g_3,u_3])}$ is a crisp subgroup of M.

Similarly, for the cases of $\bar{i}_{\breve{\delta}}(k_0 \cdot s_0^{-1}) \not\geq \bar{I}(\bar{i}_{\breve{\delta}}(k_0), \bar{i}_{\breve{\delta}}(s_0))$ or $\bar{f}_{\breve{\delta}}(k_0 \cdot s_0^{-1}) \not\leq \bar{F}(\bar{f}_{\breve{\delta}}(k_0), \bar{f}_{\breve{\delta}}(s_0))$ the same conclusion as above can be drawn.

4.1. Homomorphism on Interval-valued Neutrosophic Subgroup

In Definition 3.4, image and inverse image of IVNSs under any function has been introduced. Extending Definition 3.4 in neutrosophic environment, the following Definition 4.3 can be given:

Definition 4.3 Suppose M_1 and M_2 are two crisp sets and $l: M_1 \rightarrow M_2$ be a function. Let $\breve{\delta}_1 \in IVNS(M_1)$ and $\breve{\delta}_2 \in IVIFS(M_2)$. Then $\forall k \in M_1$ and $\forall s \in M_2$, the image of $\breve{\delta}_1$ i.e. $l(\breve{\delta}_1)$ is denoted as $l(\breve{\delta}_1)(s) = (l(\overline{t}_{\breve{\delta}_1})(s), l(\overline{f}_{\breve{\delta}_1})(s))$ and the preimage of $\breve{\delta}_2$ i.e. $l^{-1}(\breve{\delta}_2)$ is denoted as $l^{-1}(\breve{\delta}_2)(k) = \breve{\delta}_2(l(k))$, where

$$l(\breve{\delta}_1)(s) = \left[\underset{k \in l^{-1}(s)}{\vee} (\overline{t}_{\breve{\delta}_1})(k), \underset{k \in l^{-1}(s)}{\vee} (\overline{i}_{\breve{\delta}_1})(k), \underset{k \in l^{-1}(s)}{\wedge} (\overline{f}_{\breve{\delta}_1})(k) \right]$$

$$= \left[[l(t_{\breve{\delta}_1}^-)(s), l(t_{\breve{\delta}_1}^+)(s)], [l(i_{\breve{\delta}_1}^-)(s), l(i_{\breve{\delta}_1}^+)(s)], [l(f_{\breve{\delta}_1}^-)(s), l(f_{\breve{\delta}_1}^+)(s)] \right]$$

and

$$l^{-1}(\breve{\delta}_2)(k) = \left[[l^{-1}(t_{\breve{\delta}_2}^-)(k), l^{-1}(t_{\breve{\delta}_2}^+)(k)], [l^{-1}(i_{\breve{\delta}_2}^-)(k), l^{-1}(i_{\breve{\delta}_2}^+)(k)], [l^{-1}(f_{\breve{\delta}_2}^-)(k), l^{-1}(f_{\breve{\delta}_2}^+)(k)] \right]$$

$$= \left[[t_{\breve{\delta}_2}^-(l(k)), t_{\breve{\delta}_2}^+(l(k))], [i_{\breve{\delta}_2}^-(l(k)), i_{\breve{\delta}_2}^+(l(k))], [f_{\breve{\delta}_2}^-(l(k)), f_{\breve{\delta}_2}^+(l(k))] \right]$$

Theorem 4.5 Let M_1 and M_2 be two crisp groups with $l: M_1 \rightarrow M_2$ be a homomorphism and $\breve{T}$ be a continuous IVTTN. If $\breve{\delta} \in IVNSG(M_1, \breve{T})$, then $l(\breve{\delta}) \in IVNSG(M_2, \breve{T})$.
Proof: Let for some $k_1, k_2 \in M_1$, $l(k_1) = s_1$ and $l(k_2) = s_2$. Then

$$l(\breve{\delta})(s_1 \cdot s_2^{-1}) = (l(\overline{t}_{\breve{\delta}})(s_1 \cdot s_2^{-1}), l(\overline{i}_{\breve{\delta}})(s_1 \cdot s_2^{-1}), l(\overline{f}_{\breve{\delta}})(s_1 \cdot s_2^{-1}))$$

$$= \left(\underset{l(p)=s_1 \cdot s_2^{-1}}{\vee} \overline{t}_{\breve{\delta}}(p), \underset{l(p)=s_1 \cdot s_2^{-1}}{\vee} \overline{i}_{\breve{\delta}}(p), \underset{l(p)=s_1 \cdot s_2^{-1}}{\wedge} \overline{f}_{\breve{\delta}}(p) \right)$$

$$\geq (\overline{t}_{\breve{\delta}}(k_1 \cdot k_2^{-1}), \overline{i}_{\breve{\delta}}(k_1 \cdot k_2^{-1}), \overline{f}_{\breve{\delta}}(k_1 \cdot k_2^{-1}))$$

Here,

$$\overline{t}_{\breve{\delta}}(k_1 \cdot k_2^{-1}) \geq \overline{T}(\overline{t}_{\breve{\delta}}(k_1), \overline{t}_{\breve{\delta}}(k_2)), \overline{i}_{\breve{\delta}}(k_1 \cdot k_2^{-1}) \geq \overline{I}(\overline{i}_{\breve{\delta}}(k_1), \overline{i}_{\breve{\delta}}(k_2)), \overline{f}_{\breve{\delta}}(k_1 \cdot k_2^{-1}) \leq \overline{F}(\overline{f}_{\breve{\delta}}(k_1), \overline{f}_{\breve{\delta}}(k_2)).$$

Again, for each $k_1, k_2 \in M_1$ with $l(k_1) = s_1$ and $l(k_2) = s_2$, the following can be obtained:

$$l(\overline{t}_{\breve{\delta}})(s_1 \cdot s_2^{-1}) \geq \overline{T}\left(\underset{l(p)=s_1}{\vee} \overline{t}_{\breve{\delta}}(p), \underset{l(p)=s_2}{\vee} \overline{t}_{\breve{\delta}}(p) \right) = \overline{T}(l(\overline{t}_{\breve{\delta}})(s_1), l(\overline{t}_{\breve{\delta}})(s_2)),$$

$$l(\overline{i}_{\breve{\delta}})(s_1 \cdot s_2^{-1}) \geq \overline{I}\left(\bigvee_{l(p)=s_1} \overline{i}_{\breve{\delta}}(p), \bigvee_{l(p)=s_2} \overline{i}_{\breve{\delta}}(p)\right) = \overline{I}\left(l(\overline{i}_{\breve{\delta}})(s_1), l(\overline{i}_{\breve{\delta}})(s_2)\right)$$

and

$$l(\overline{f}_{\breve{\delta}})(s_1 \cdot s_2^{-1}) \leq \overline{F}\left(\bigwedge_{l(p)=s_1} \overline{f}_{\breve{\delta}}(p), \bigwedge_{l(p)=s_2} \overline{f}_{\breve{\delta}}(p)\right) = \overline{F}\left(l(\overline{f}_{\breve{\delta}})(s_1), l(\overline{f}_{\breve{\delta}})(s_2)\right).$$

Hence, $l(\breve{\delta})(s_1 \cdot s_2^{-1}) \geq \breve{T}\left(l(\breve{\delta})(s_1), l(\breve{\delta})(s_2)\right)$.

Theorem 4.6 Suppose M_1 and M_2 are two crisp groups and l be a homomorphism from M_1 into M_2. If $\breve{\delta}' \in \mathrm{IVSNG}(M_2, \breve{T})$, then $l^{-1}(\breve{\delta}') \in \mathrm{IVNSG}(M_1, \breve{T})$.

Proof: Let $\breve{\delta}' \in \mathrm{IVNSG}(M_2, \breve{T})$ and $k, s \in M_1$. Then

$$\begin{aligned}
l^{-1}(\overline{t}_{\breve{\delta}'})(k \cdot s^{-1}) &= \overline{t}_{\breve{\delta}'}(l(k \cdot s^{-1})) \\
&= \overline{t}_{\breve{\delta}'}(l(k) \cdot l(s)^{-1}) \geq \overline{T}(\overline{t}_{\breve{\delta}'}(l(k)), \overline{t}_{\breve{\delta}'}(l(s))) \\
&= \overline{T}(l^{-1}(\overline{t}_{\breve{\delta}'}(k)), l^{-1}(\overline{t}_{\breve{\delta}'}(s)))
\end{aligned}$$

In a similar way, the followings can be proven:

$$l^{-1}(\overline{i}_{\breve{\delta}'})(k \cdot s^{-1}) \geq \overline{I}(l^{-1}(\overline{i}_{\breve{\delta}'}(k)), l^{-1}(\overline{i}_{\breve{\delta}'}(s))) \text{ and } l^{-1}(\overline{f}_{\breve{\delta}'})(k \cdot s^{-1}) \leq \overline{F}(l^{-1}(\overline{f}_{\breve{\delta}'}(k)), l^{-1}(\overline{f}_{\breve{\delta}'}(s))).$$

So, $l^{-1}(\breve{\delta}')(k \cdot s^{-1}) \geq \breve{T}(l^{-1}(\breve{\delta}')(k), l^{-1}(\breve{\delta}')(s))$.

Corollary 4.1 Suppose M_1 and M_2 are two crisp groups and $l: M_1 \rightarrow M_2$ be an isomorphism. If $\breve{\delta} \in \mathrm{IVNSG}(M_1, \breve{T})$, then $l^{-1}(l(\breve{\delta})) = \breve{\delta}$.

Corollary 4.2 Let M be a crisp group and $l: M \rightarrow M$ be an isomorphism. If $\breve{\delta} \in \mathrm{IVNSG}(M, \breve{T})$, then $l(\breve{\delta}) = \breve{\delta}$ iff $l^{-1}(\breve{\delta}) = \breve{\delta}$.

4.2. Interval-Valued Neutrosophic Normal Subgroup

Definition 4.3 Let M be a crisp group and $\breve{\delta} \in \mathrm{IVNSG}(M, \breve{T})$. Then $\breve{\delta}$ is called an IVNNSG of M with respect to IVTTN $\breve{T}$ if $\forall k, s \in M$, $\breve{\delta}(k \cdot s) = \breve{\delta}(s \cdot k)$.

The set of all IVNNSG of a crisp group U with respect to $\breve{T}$ will be denoted as $\mathrm{IVNNSG}(U, \breve{T})$.

Theorem 4.7 Let M be a group and $\breve{\delta}_1, \breve{\delta}_2 \in \mathrm{IVNNSG}(M, \breve{T})$. Then $\breve{\delta}_1 \cap \breve{\delta}_2 \in \mathrm{IVNNSG}(M, \breve{T})$.

Proof: Let $\breve{\delta}_1, \breve{\delta}_2 \in \mathrm{IVNNSG}(M, \breve{T})$. Then $\forall k, s \in M$, $\breve{\delta}_1(k \cdot s) = \breve{\delta}_1(s \cdot k)$ and $\breve{\delta}_2(k \cdot s) = \breve{\delta}_2(s \cdot k)$. So,

$$\bar{t}_{\check{\delta}_1}(k \cdot s) = \bar{t}_{\check{\delta}_1}(s \cdot k), \bar{i}_{\check{\delta}_1}(k \cdot s) = \bar{i}_{\check{\delta}_1}(s \cdot k), \bar{f}_{\check{\delta}_1}(k \cdot s) = \bar{f}_{\check{\delta}_1}(s \cdot k)$$

and

$$\bar{t}_{\check{\delta}_2}(k \cdot s) = \bar{t}_{\check{\delta}_2}(s \cdot k), \bar{i}_{\check{\delta}_2}(k \cdot s) = \bar{i}_{\check{\delta}_2}(s \cdot k), \bar{f}_{\check{\delta}_2}(k \cdot s) = \bar{f}_{\check{\delta}_2}(s \cdot k).$$

Hence,

$$
\begin{aligned}
(\check{\delta}_1 \cap \check{\delta}_2)(k \cdot s) &= (\bar{t}_{\check{\delta}_1 \cap \check{\delta}_2}(k \cdot s), \bar{i}_{\check{\delta}_1 \cap \check{\delta}_2}(k \cdot s), \bar{f}_{\check{\delta}_1 \cap \check{\delta}_2}(k \cdot s)) \\
&= (\bar{t}_{\check{\delta}_1}(k \cdot s) \wedge \bar{t}_{\check{\delta}_2}(k \cdot s), \bar{i}_{\check{\delta}_1}(k \cdot s) \wedge \bar{i}_{\check{\delta}_2}(k \cdot s), \bar{f}_{\check{\delta}_1}(k \cdot s) \vee \bar{f}_{\check{\delta}_2}(k \cdot s)) \\
&= (\bar{t}_{\check{\delta}_1}(s \cdot k) \wedge \bar{t}_{\check{\delta}_2}(s \cdot k), \bar{i}_{\check{\delta}_1}(s \cdot k) \wedge \bar{i}_{\check{\delta}_2}(s \cdot k), \bar{f}_{\check{\delta}_1}(s \cdot k) \vee \bar{f}_{\check{\delta}_2}(s \cdot k)) \\
&= (\bar{t}_{\check{\delta}_1 \cap \check{\delta}_2}(s \cdot k), \bar{i}_{\check{\delta}_1 \cap \check{\delta}_2}(s \cdot k), \bar{f}_{\check{\delta}_1 \cap \check{\delta}_2}(s \cdot k)) = (\check{\delta}_1 \cap \check{\delta}_2)(s \cdot k)
\end{aligned}
$$

So, $\check{\delta}_1 \cap \check{\delta}_2 \in \text{IVNNSG}(M, \check{T})$.

Proposition 4.1 Suppose M is a crisp group and $\check{\delta} \in \text{IVSG}(M, \check{T})$. Then $\forall k, s \in M$, the subsequent conditions are identical:

1. $\check{\delta}(s \cdot k \cdot s^{-1}) \geq \check{\delta}(k)$
2. $\check{\delta}(s \cdot k \cdot s^{-1}) = \check{\delta}(k)$
3. $\check{\delta} \in \text{IVNNSG}(M, \check{T})$

Proof: $(1) \Rightarrow (2)$: Let $k, s \in M$. As $\check{\delta}(s \cdot k \cdot s^{-1}) \geq \check{\delta}(k)$, it can be shown that

$$\bar{t}_{\check{\delta}}(s \cdot k \cdot s^{-1}) \geq \bar{t}_{\check{\delta}}(k), \bar{i}_{\check{\delta}}(s \cdot k \cdot s^{-1}) \geq \bar{i}_{\check{\delta}}(k) \text{ and } \bar{f}_{\check{\delta}}(s \cdot k \cdot s^{-1}) \leq \bar{f}_{\check{\delta}}(k).$$

Now, replacing s with s^{-1}, $\bar{t}_{\check{\delta}}(s^{-1} \cdot k \cdot s) = \bar{t}_{\check{\delta}}(s^{-1} \cdot k \cdot (s^{-1})^{-1}) \geq \bar{t}_{\check{\delta}}(k)$.
So, $\bar{t}_{\check{\delta}}(k) = \bar{t}_{\check{\delta}}(s^{-1} \cdot (s \cdot k \cdot s^{-1}) \cdot s) \geq \bar{t}_{\check{\delta}}(s \cdot k \cdot s^{-1}) \geq \bar{t}_{\check{\delta}}(k)$ i.e. $\bar{t}_{\check{\delta}}(s \cdot k \cdot s^{-1}) = \bar{t}_{\check{\delta}}(k)$.
In a similar way, $\bar{i}_{\check{\delta}}(s \cdot k \cdot s^{-1}) = \bar{i}_{\check{\delta}}(k)$ and $\bar{f}_{\check{\delta}}(s \cdot k \cdot s^{-1}) = \bar{f}_{\check{\delta}}(k)$. So, $\forall k, s \in M$, $\check{\delta}(s \cdot k \cdot s^{-1}) = \check{\delta}(k)$.

$(2) \Rightarrow (3)$: In (2), replacing k with $k \cdot s$ (3) can be obtained easily.

$(3) \Rightarrow (1)$: Let $k, s \in M$. As, $\check{\delta} \in \text{IVNNSG}(M, \check{T})$, $\check{\delta}(k \cdot s) = \check{\delta}(s \cdot k)$. Replacing k with $k \cdot s^{-1}$ the following can be obtained: $\check{\delta}(s \cdot k \cdot s^{-1}) = \check{\delta}(k \cdot s^{-1} \cdot s) = \check{\delta}(k) \geq \check{\delta}(k)$.

Theorem 4.8 Let M be a group and $\check{\delta} \in \text{IVNS}(M)$. Then $\check{\delta} \in \text{IVNNSG}(M, \check{T})$ iff for every $[g_1, u_1], [g_2, u_2]$ and $[g_3, u_3] \in \rho(J)$ with $u_1 + u_2 + u_3 \leq 1$, $(\check{\delta}_{([g_1, u_1], [g_2, u_2], [g_3, u_3])} \neq \phi)$ $\check{\delta}_{([g_1, u_1], [g_2, u_2], [g_3, u_3])}$ is a crisp normal subgroup of M.

Proof: This can be proved using Theorem 4.4.

Theorem 4.9 Let M be a group and $\breve{\delta} \in$ IVNNSG $(M, \breve{T})$ with respect to an idempotent IVTTN $\breve{T}$. Let $M|_{\breve{\delta}} = \{k \in M : \breve{\delta}(k) = \breve{\delta}(e)\}$, ($e$ is the neutral element of M). Then the crisp set $M|_{\breve{\delta}}$ is a normal subgroup of M.

Proof: Let $\breve{\delta} \in$ IVNNSG $(M, \breve{T})$ and $k, s \in M|_{\breve{\delta}}$. So, $\breve{\delta}(k) = \breve{\delta}(e) = \breve{\delta}(s)$.

Now, $\breve{\delta}(k \cdot s^{-1}) \geq \breve{T}(\breve{\delta}(k), \breve{\delta}(s)) = \breve{T}(\breve{\delta}(e), \breve{\delta}(e)) = \breve{\delta}(e)$. Again, $\breve{\delta}(e) \geq \breve{\delta}(k \cdot s^{-1})$ and hence $\breve{\delta}(k \cdot s^{-1}) = \breve{\delta}(e)$. So, $k \cdot s^{-1} \in M|_{\breve{\delta}}$ i.e. $M|_{\breve{\delta}}$ is a subgroup of M.

Again, let $k \in M|_{\breve{\delta}}$ and $s \in M$. Since, $\breve{\delta} \in$ IVNNSG $(M, \breve{T})$ it can be shown that $\breve{\delta}(s \cdot k \cdot s^{-1}) = \breve{\delta}(k) = \breve{\delta}(e)$. Hence, $s \cdot k \cdot s^{-1} \in M|_{\breve{\delta}}$ i.e. $M|_{\breve{\delta}}$ is a normal subgroup of M.

Note that, Theorem 4.9 is true only when $\breve{T}$ is an idempotent IVTTN. The following (Example 4.2) is a counterexample which will justify current claim.

Example 4.2 Let $M = \{1, i, -1, -i\}$ be a cyclic group and

$$\breve{\delta} = \{(1, [0.8, 0.8], [0.5, 0.5], [0.2, 0.2]), (-1, [0.7, 0.7], [0.5, 0.5], [0.3, 0.3]),$$
$$(i, [0.8, 0.8], [0.5, 0.5], [0.2, 0.2]), (-i, [0.8, 0.8], [0.5, 0.5], [0.2, 0.2])\}.$$

Also, let the corresponding IVTTN $\breve{T}$ is formed by product TNs i.e. $T(k, s) = k \bullet s, I(k, s) = k \bullet s$ and product TC i.e. $F(k, s) = k + s - k \bullet s$. Then, $\breve{\delta} \in$ IVNNSG $(M, \breve{T})$. However, $M|_{\breve{\delta}} = \{1, i, -i\}$ is not a subgroup of M and hence $M|_{\breve{\delta}}$ is not a normal subgroup of M.

4.2.1. Homomorphism on Interval-Valued Neutrosophic Normal Subgroup

Theorem 4.10 Let M_1 and M_2 be two crisp groups and l be a homomorphism from M_1 into M_2. If $\breve{\delta}' \in$ IVNNSG$(M_2, \breve{T})$, then $l^{-1}(\breve{\delta}') \in$ IVNNSG$(M_1, \breve{T})$.

Proof: Let $\breve{\delta}' \in$ IVNNSG$(M_2, \breve{T})$, then $\breve{\delta}' \in$ IVNSG$(M_2, \breve{T})$ and hence from Theorem 4.6, $l^{-1}(\breve{\delta}') \in$ IVNSG$(M_1, \breve{T})$. So, only the normality of $\breve{\delta}'$ is needed to be proved. Let $k, s \in M_1$, then

$$l^{-1}(\breve{\delta}')(k \cdot s) = \breve{\delta}'(l(k \cdot s)) = \breve{\delta}'(l(k) \cdot l(s))$$
$$= \breve{\delta}'(l(s) \cdot l(k))[\text{AS } \breve{\delta}' \in \text{IVNNSG}(M_2, \breve{T})]$$
$$= \breve{\delta}'(l(s \cdot k)) = l^{-1}(\breve{\delta}')(s \cdot k)$$

So, $l^{-1}(\breve{\delta}') \in \text{IVNNSG}(M_1, \breve{T})$.

Theorem 4.11 Suppose M_1 and M_2 be two crisp groups and l be a surjective homomorphism from M_1 into M_2. If $\breve{\delta} \in \text{IVNNSG}(M_1, \breve{T})$, then $l(\breve{\delta}) \in \text{IVNNSG}(M_2, \breve{T})$.

Proof: Let $\breve{\delta} \in \text{IVNNSG}(M_1, \breve{T})$, then $\breve{\delta} \in \text{IVNSG}(M_1, \breve{T})$ and hence by Theorem 4.5, $l(\breve{\delta}) \in \text{IVNSG}(M_2, \breve{T})$. So, only the normality of $\breve{\delta}'$ is needed to be proved.

Now, $\forall k, s \in M_2$, as l is a surjective homomorphism, $l^{-1}(k)^1 \, \phi$, $l^{-1}(s)^1 \phi$ and $l^{-1}(k \cdot s \cdot k^{-1})^1 \phi$. So, $\forall k, s \in M_2$, $l(\overline{t}_{\breve{\delta}})(k \cdot s \cdot k^{-1}) = \bigvee_{r \in l^{-1}(k \cdot s \cdot k^{-1})} (\overline{t}_{\breve{\delta}}(r))$ and $l(\overline{t}_{\breve{\delta}})(s) = \bigvee_{r \in l^{-1}(s)} (\overline{t}_{\breve{\delta}}(r))$.

Let $n \in l^{-1}(k)$, $q \in l^{-1}(s)$ and $n^{-1} \in l^{-1}(k^{-1})$. Now as $\breve{\delta} \in \text{IVNNSG}(M_1, \breve{T})$, the followings can be drawn:

$$\overline{t}_{\breve{\delta}}(n \cdot q \cdot n^{-1}) \geq \overline{t}_{\breve{\delta}}(q), \ \overline{i}_{\breve{\delta}}(n \cdot q \cdot n^{-1}) \geq \overline{i}_{\breve{\delta}}(q) \ \text{and} \ \overline{f}_{\breve{\delta}}(n \cdot q \cdot n^{-1}) \leq \overline{f}_{\breve{\delta}}(q).$$

Since, l is a homomorphism, $l(n \cdot q \cdot n^{-1}) = l(n) \bullet l(q) \bullet l(n^{-1}) = k \cdot s \cdot k^{-1}$ and hence, $n \cdot q \cdot n^{-1} \in l^{-1}(k \cdot s \cdot k^{-1})$. So,

$$
\begin{aligned}
l(\overline{t}_{\breve{\delta}})(k \cdot s \cdot k^{-1}) &= \bigvee_{r \in l^{-1}(k \cdot s \cdot k^{-1})} (\overline{t}_{\breve{\delta}}(r)) \\
&\geq \bigvee_{n \in l^{-1}(k), \, q \in l^{-1}(s), \, n^{-1} \in l^{-1}(k^{-1})} (\overline{t}_{\breve{\delta}}(n \cdot q \cdot n^{-1})) \\
&\geq \bigvee_{q \in l^{-1}(s)} (\overline{t}_{\breve{\delta}}(q)) = l(\overline{t}_{\breve{\delta}})(s)
\end{aligned}
$$

Hence, $\forall k, s \in M_2$, $l(\overline{t}_{\breve{\delta}})(k \cdot s \cdot k^{-1}) \geq l(\overline{t}_{\breve{\delta}})(s)$ and similarly,

$$l(\overline{i}_{\breve{\delta}})(k \cdot s \cdot k^{-1}) \geq l(\overline{i}_{\breve{\delta}})(s), l(\overline{f}_{\breve{\delta}})(k \cdot s \cdot k^{-1}) \leq l(\overline{f}_{\breve{\delta}})(s).$$

So, $l(\breve{\delta})(k \cdot s \cdot k^{-1}) \geq l(\breve{\delta})(s)$ and hence, by Proposition 4.1, $l(\breve{\delta}) \in \text{IVNNSG}(M_2, \breve{T})$.

Corollary 4.3 Let M_1 and M_2 be two crisp groups and $l: M_1 \rightarrow M_2$ be an isomorphism. If $\breve{\delta} \in \text{IVNNSG}(M_1, \breve{T})$, then $l^{-1}(l(\breve{\delta})) = \breve{\delta}$.

Corollary 4.4 Let M be a crisp group and $l: M \rightarrow M$ be an isomorphism on M. If $\breve{\delta} \in \text{IVNNSG}(M_1, \breve{T})$, then $l(\breve{\delta}) = \breve{\delta}$ iff $l^{-1}(\breve{\delta}) = \breve{\delta}$.

5. CONCLUSION

The notion of an IVNSG is nothing but generalization of FSG, IFSG, NSG, IVFSG and IVIFSG. It is known that, to study some fundamental algebraic characteristics of any entity one needs to understand functions, which preserve their algebraic characteristics i.e. one needs to study the effects of homomorphism on them. Hence, in this chapter, IVTTN has been introduced and based on that IVNSG has been introduced. Also, some effects of homomorphism on it have been studied. Furthermore, based on IVTTN, IVNNSG has been defined and some of its homomorphic characteristics have been studied. In future, one can introduce soft set theory in IVNSG and further generalize it.

REFERENCES

Abdel-Basset, M., Atef, A., & Smarandache, F. (2019). A hybrid neutrosophic multiple criteria group decision making approach for project selection. *Cognitive Systems Research*, *57*, 216–227. doi:10.1016/j.cogsys.2018.10.023

Abdel-Basset, M., Chang, V., & Gamal, A. (2019). Evaluation of the green supply chain management practices: A novel neutrosophic approach. *Computers in Industry*, *108*, 210–220. doi:10.1016/j.compind.2019.02.013

Abdel-Basset, M., Hezam, I. M., & Smarandache, F. (2016). Neutrosophic Goal Programming. *Neutrosophic Sets and Systems, 11*, 112-118. Retrieved from http://fs.gallup.unm.edu/NSS/NeutrosophicGoalProgramming.pdf

Abdel-Basset, M., Manogaran, G., Gamal, A., & Smarandache, F. (2018). A hybrid approach of neutrosophic sets and DEMATEL method for developing supplier selection criteria. *Design Automation for Embedded Systems*, *22*(3), 257–278. doi:10.100710617-018-9203-6

Abdel-Basset, M., Manogaran, G., & Mohamed, M. (2019). A neutrosophic theory based security approach for fog and mobile-edge computing. *Computer Networks*, *157*, 122–132. doi:10.1016/j.comnet.2019.04.018

Abdel-Basset, M., Manogaran, G., Mohamed, M., & Smarandache, F. (2019). A novel method for solving the fully neutrosophic linear programming problems. *Neural Computing & Applications*, *31*(5), 1595–1605. doi:10.100700521-018-3404-6

Abdel-Basset, M., Mohamed, M., & Smarandache, F. (2018). A hybrid neutrosophic group ANP-TOPSIS framework for supplier selection problems. *Symmetry*, *10*(6), 226. doi:10.3390ym10060226

Abdel-Basset, M., Mohamed, M., & Smarandache, F. (2019). A aefined approach for forecasting based on neutrosophic time series. *Symmetry*, *11*(4), 457. doi:10.3390ym11040457

Abdel-Basset, M., Mohamed, M., Zhou, Y., & Hezam, I. M. (2017). Multi-criteria group decision making based on neutrosophic analytic hierarchy process. *Journal of Intelligent & Fuzzy Systems*, *33*(6), 4055–4066. doi:10.3233/JIFS-17981

Abdel-Basset, M., Mohamed, R., Zaied, A. N., & Smarandache, F. (2019). A hybrid plithogenic decision-making approach with quality function deployment for selecting supply chain sustainability metrics. *Symmetry*, *11*(7), 903. doi:10.3390ym11070903

Aiwu, Z., Jianguo, D., & Hongjun, G. (2015). Interval valued neutrosophic sets and multi-attribute decision-making based on generalized weighted aggregation operator. *Journal of Intelligent & Fuzzy Systems*, *29*(6), 2697–2706. doi:10.3233/IFS-151973

Anthony, J. M., & Sherwood, H. (1979). Fuzzy groups redefined. *Journal of Mathematical Analysis and Applications*, *69*(1), 124–130. doi:10.1016/0022-247X(79)90182-3

Anthony, J. M., & Sherwood, H. (1982). A characterization of fuzzy subgroups. *Fuzzy Sets and Systems*, *7*(3), 297–305. doi:10.1016/0165-0114(82)90057-4

Atanassov, K. T. (1986). Intuitionistic fuzzy sets. *Fuzzy Sets and Systems*, *20*(1), 87–96. doi:10.1016/S0165-0114(86)80034-3

Atanassov, K. T. (1999). Interval valued intuitionistic fuzzy sets. In *Intuitionistic Fuzzy Sets* (pp. 139–177). Springer. doi:10.1007/978-3-7908-1870-3_2

Atanassov, K. T. (1999). Intuitionistic fuzzy sets. In *Intuitionistic Fuzzy Sets* (pp. 1–137). Springer.

Aygünoğlu, A., Varol, B. P., Çetkin, V., & Aygün, H. (2012). Interval-valued intuitionistic fuzzy subgroups based on interval-valued double t-norm. *Neural Computing & Applications*, *21*(S1), 207–214. doi:10.100700521-011-0773-5

Biswas, R. (1989). Intuitionistic fuzzy subgroups. *Mathematical Forum, 10*, 37-46.

Biswas, R. (1994). Rosenfeld's fuzzy subgroups with interval-valued membership functions. *Fuzzy Sets and Systems*, *63*(1), 87–90. doi:10.1016/0165-0114(94)90148-1

Broumi, S., Bakal, A., Talea, M., Smarandache, F., & Vladareanu, L. (2016). Applying Dijkstra algorithm for solving neutrosophic shortest path problem. In *2016 International Conference on Advanced Mechatronic Systems*, (pp. 412-416). Academic Press. 10.1109/ICAMechS.2016.7813483

Broumi, S., Deli, I., & Smarandache, F. (2014). Interval valued neutrosophic parameterized soft set theory and its decision making. *Journal of New Results in Science*, *3*, 58–71.

Broumi, S., Deli, I., & Smarandache, F. (2015). N-valued interval neutrosophic sets and their application in medical diagnosis. Critical Review, 10, 45-69.

Broumi, S., & Smarandache, F. (2013). Correlation coefficient of interval neutrosophic set. *Applied Mechanics and Materials*, *436*, 511–517. doi:10.4028/www.scientific.net/AMM.436.511

Broumi, S., Smarandache, F., & Dhar, M. (2014). *Rough neutrosophic sets.* Infinite Study.

Broumi, S., Talea, M., Smarandache, F., & Bakali, A. (2016). Decision-making method based on the interval valued neutrosophic graph. In *Future Technologies Conference*, (pp. 44-50). Academic Press. 10.1109/FTC.2016.7821588

Broumi, S., Talea, M., Smarandache, F., & Bakali, A. (2016). Decision-making method based on the interval valued neutrosophic graph. In 2016 Future Technologies Conference, (pp. 44-50). Academic Press.

Çetkin, V., & Aygün, H. (2015). An approach to neutrosophic subgroup and its fundamental properties. *Journal of Intelligent & Fuzzy Systems*, *29*(5), 1941–1947. doi:10.3233/IFS-151672

Das, P. S. (1981). Fuzzy groups and level subgroups. *Journal of Mathematical Analysis and Applications*, *84*(1), 264–269. doi:10.1016/0022-247X(81)90164-5

Davvaz, B. (1999). Interval-valued fuzzy subhypergroups. *Korean Journal of Computational and Applied Mathematics*, *6*, 197–202.

Davvaz, B. (2001). Fuzzy ideals of near-rings with interval valued membership functions. *Journal of Sciences Islamic Republic of Iran*, *12*, 171–176.

Deli, I. (2017). Interval-valued neutrosophic soft sets and its decision making. *International Journal of Machine Learning and Cybernetics*, *8*(2), 665–676. doi:10.100713042-015-0461-3

Deli, I., Ali, M., & Smarandache, F. (2015). Bipolar neutrosophic sets and their application based on multi-criteria decision making problems. In *2015 International Conference on Advanced Mechatronic Systems*, (pp. 249-254). Academic Press. 10.1109/ICAMechS.2015.7287068

Deli, I., Broumi, S., & Smarandache, F. (2015). On Neutrosophic refined sets and their applications in medical diagnosis. *Journal of New Theory*, *6*, 88–98.

Eroğlu, M. S. (1989). The homomorphic image of a fuzzy subgroup is always a fuzzy subgroup. *Fuzzy Sets and Systems*, *33*(2), 255–256. doi:10.1016/0165-0114(89)90246-7

Gayen, S., Jha, S., & Singh, M. (2019). On direct product of a fuzzy subgroup with an anti-fuzzy subgroup. *International Journal of Recent Technology and Engineering*, 8, 1105-1111.

Gayen, S., Jha, S., Singh, M., & Kumar, R. (2019a). On a generalized notion of anti-fuzzy subgroup and some characterizations. *International Journal of Engineering and Advanced Technology*, 8, 385-390.

Gayen, S., Smarandache, F., Jha, S., Singh, M. K., Broumi, S., & Kumar, R. (2019b, 10). Chapter 8: Introduction to plithogenic subgroup. In F. Smarandache, & S. Broumi (Eds.). IGI-Global.

Guijun, W., & Xiaoping, L. (1996). Interval-valued fuzzy subgroups induced by T-triangular norms. *Bulletin Pour Les Sous Ensembles Flous Et Leurs Applicatios*, *65*, 80–84.

Guo, Y., & Cheng, H. D. (2009). New neutrosophic approach to image segmentation. *Pattern Recognition*, *42*(5), 587–595. doi:10.1016/j.patcog.2008.10.002

Gupta, M. M., & Qi, J. (1991). Theory of T-norms and fuzzy inference methods. *Fuzzy Sets and Systems*, *40*(3), 431–450. doi:10.1016/0165-0114(91)90171-L

Haibin, W., Smarandache, F., Zhang, Y., & Sunderraman, R. (2010). *Single valued neutrosophic sets.* Infinite Study.

Hezam, I. M., Abdel-Basset, M., & Smarandache, F. (2015). Taylor series approximation to solve neutrosophic multiobjective programming problem. *Neutrosophic Sets and Systems, 10*, 39-45. Retrieved from http://fs.gallup.unm.edu/NSS/Taylor%20Series%20Approximation.pdf

Hur, K., Jang, S. Y., & Kang, H. W. (2004). Intuitionistic fuzzy normal subgroups and intuitionistic fuzzy cosets. *Honam Mathematical Journal*, *26*, 559–587.

Hur, K., Kang, H. W., & Song, H. K. (2003). Intuitionistic fuzzy subgroups and subrings. *Honam Mathematical Journal*, *25*, 19–41.

Jun, Y. B., & Kim, K. H. (2002). Interval-valued fuzzy R-subgroups of near-rings. *Indian Journal of Pure and Applied Mathematics*, *33*, 71–80.

Klement, E. P., Mesiar, R., & Pap, E. (2013). *Triangular norms* (Vol. 8). Springer Science & Business Media.

Kumar, M., Bhutani, K., Aggarwal, S., & ... (2015). Hybrid model for medical diagnosis using neutrosophic cognitive maps with genetic algorithms. *2015 IEEE International Conference on Fuzzy Systems*, 1-7.

Kumar, R., Edalatpanah, S. A., Jha, S., Broumi, S., Singh, R., & Dey, A. (2019). A Multi objective programming approach to solve integer valued neutrosophic shortest path problems. *Neutrosophic Sets and Systems*, 134.

Kumar, R., Edalatpanah, S. A., Jha, S., Gayen, S., & Singh, R. (2019). Shortest path problems using fuzzy weighted arc length. *International Journal of Innovative Technology and Exploring Engineering*.

Kumar, R., Edalatpanah, S. A., Jha, S., & Singh, R. (2019). A Pythagorean fuzzy approach to the transportation problem. *Complex & Intelligent Systems*, *5*(2), 255–263. doi:10.100740747-019-0108-1

Kumar, R., Edaltpanah, S. A., Jha, S., Broumi, S., & Dey, A. (2018). Neutrosophic shortest path problem. *Neutrosophic Sets and Systems*, *23*, 5–15.

Kumar, R., Jha, S., & Singh, R. (2020). A different appraoch for solving the shortest path problem under mixed fuzzy environment. *International Journal of Fuzzy System Applications*, *9*, 6.

Kumar, R., Edalatpanah, S. A., Jha, S., & Singh, R. (2019). A novel approach to solve gaussian valued neutrosophic shortest path problems. *Int J Eng Adv Technol*, *8*, 347–353.

Li, X., & Wang, G. (2000). The S_H-interval-valued fuzzy subgroup. *Fuzzy Sets and Systems*, *112*(2), 319–325. doi:10.1016/S0165-0114(98)00092-X

Lupiáñez, F. G. (2009). Interval neutrosophic sets and topology. *Kybernetes*, *38*(3/4), 621–624. doi:10.1108/03684920910944849

Majumdar, P. (2015). Neutrosophic sets and its applications to decision making. In *Computational Intelligence for Big Data Analysis* (pp. 97–115). Springer. doi:10.1007/978-3-319-16598-1_4

Mondal, T. K., & Samanta, S. K. (1999). Topology of interval-valued fuzzy sets. *Indian Journal of Pure and Applied Mathematics, 30,* 23–29.

Mondal, T. K., & Samanta, S. K. (2001). Topology of interval-valued intuitionistic fuzzy sets. *Fuzzy Sets and Systems, 119*(3), 483–494. doi:10.1016/S0165-0114(98)00436-9

Mukherjee, N. P., & Bhattacharya, P. (1984). Fuzzy normal subgroups and fuzzy cosets. *Information Sciences, 34*(3), 225–239. doi:10.1016/0020-0255(84)90050-1

Rosenfeld, A. (1971). Fuzzy groups. *Journal of Mathematical Analysis and Applications, 35*(3), 512–517. doi:10.1016/0022-247X(71)90199-5

Sharma, P. K. (2011). Homomorphism of intuitionistic fuzzy groups. *International Mathematical Forum, 6,* 3169-3178.

Sherwood, H. (1983). Products of fuzzy subgroups. *Fuzzy Sets and Systems, 11*(1-3), 79–89. doi:10.1016/S0165-0114(83)80070-0

Smarandache, F. (1999). A unifying field in logics: neutrosophic logic. In Philosophy (pp. 1-141). American Research Press.

Smarandache, F. (2000). An introduction to the neutrosophic probability applied in quantum physics. Infinite Study.

Smarandache, F. (2013). Introduction to neutrosophic measure, neutrosophic integral, and neutrosophic probability. Infinite Study.

Smarandache, F. (2018). Aggregation plithogenic operators in physical fields. *Bulletin of the American Physical Society.*

Smarandache, F. (2018). *Extension of soft set to hypersoft set, and then to plithogenic hypersoft set.* Infinite Study.

Smarandache, F. (2018). Neutropsychic personality: A mathematical approach to psychology. Infinite Study.

Smarandache, F. (2018). *Plithogenic set, an extension of crisp, fuzzy, intuitionistic fuzzy, and neutrosophic sets-revisited.* Infinite Study.

Smarandache, F., & Khalid, H. E. (2015). Neutrosophic precalculus and neutrosophic calculus. Infinite Study.

Thong, N. T., Dat, L. Q., Hoa, N. D., Ali, M., Smarandache, F., & ... (2019). Dynamic interval valued neutrosophic set: Modeling decision making in dynamic environments. *Computers in Industry*, *108*, 45–52. doi:10.1016/j.compind.2019.02.009

Vlachos, I. K., & Sergiadis, G. D. (2007). Intuitionistic fuzzy information-applications to pattern recognition. *Pattern Recognition Letters*, *28*(2), 197–206. doi:10.1016/j.patrec.2006.07.004

Wang, H., Smarandache, F., Sunderraman, R., & Zhang, Y. Q. (2005). Interval neutrosophic sets and logic: theory and applications in computing (Vol. 5). Infinite Study.

Wang, H., Smarandache, F., Sunderraman, R., & Zhang, Y. Q. (2005). *Interval neutrosophic sets and logic: theory and applications in computing: Theory and applications in computing* (Vol. 5). Infinite Study.

Xu, C. Y. (2007). Homomorphism of intuitionistic fuzzy groups. *2007 International Conference on Machine Learning and Cybernetics*, 2, 1178-1183. 10.1109/ICMLC.2007.4370322

Ye, J. (2014). Improved correlation coefficients of single valued neutrosophic sets and interval neutrosophic sets for multiple attribute decision making. *Journal of Intelligent & Fuzzy Systems*, *27*, 2453–2462.

Ye, J. (2014). Similarity measures between interval neutrosophic sets and their applications in multicriteria decision-making. *Journal of Intelligent & Fuzzy Systems*, *26*, 165–172.

Yuan, X., Li, H., & Lee, E. S. (2010). On the definition of the intuitionistic fuzzy subgroups. *Computers & Mathematics with Applications (Oxford, England)*, *59*(9), 3117–3129. doi:10.1016/j.camwa.2010.02.033

Yuan, Y., Ren, Y., Liu, X., & Wang, J. (2019). Approach to image segmentation based on interval neutrosophic set. *Numerical Algebra, Control & Optimization*, 347-353.

Zadeh, L. A. (1965). Fuzzy sets. *Information and Control*, *8*(3), 338–358. doi:10.1016/S0019-9958(65)90241-X

Zadeh, L. A. (1975). The concept of a linguistic variable and its application to approximate reasoning—I. *Information Sciences*, *8*(3), 199–249. doi:10.1016/0020-0255(75)90036-5

Zhang, H., Wang, J., & Chen, X. (2014). Interval neutrosophic sets and their application in multicriteria decision making problems. *The Scientific World Journal*. PMID:24695916

Zhang, H., Wang, J., & Chen, X. (2016). An outranking approach for multi-criteria decision-making problems with interval-valued neutrosophic sets. *Neural Computing & Applications, 27*(3), 615–627. doi:10.100700521-015-1882-3

Chapter 11

New Unconventional Technique to Decipher MOTP in Neutrshopic Environment

Krishna Prabha Sikkannan
PSNA College of Engineering and Technology, India

Vimala Shanmugavel
Mother Terasa Womens University, India

ABSTRACT

Many papers have been proposed so far in the field of fuzzy and intuitionistic fuzzy multi-objective transportation problems. An innovative technique to unravel multi-objective neutroshopic (NS) transportation problem called mean method is proposed in this chapter. The objectives which have different units to membership values are aggregated by finding the mean of the values. A new algorithm is developed in order to solve the problems of this type is explained in this work. A numerical example is instigated to demonstrate the technique and the consequence is compared with VAM's method.

1. INTRODUCTION

The routine actions of our life are primarily allied with shipping and logistics. Transportation pacts with allotment of resources from delivery point to target point. In order to precede with a number of inconsistency and incommensurable goal function the multi-objective transportation problem (MOTP) is structured. To reduce the hauling cost different methods like North West corner, least cost

DOI: 10.4018/978-1-7998-2555-5.ch011

method, Vogel's approximation method are applied. As NS is able to deal indecisive, conflicting and also undefined information, the model of NS is a noteworthy technique to covenant with real methodical and engineering. Single valued neutrosophic acquires extra contemplation and acquire optimized elucidation than other types of fuzzy sets because of accurateness, adoptability and link to a system. Neutrosophic set hypothesis to hold vague, unsure and imprecise problems which cannot be dealt by fuzzy and its assorted kinds was exemplified by Samarandache (2005) in 1995. Smarandache (2005) and Wang et al (2010) projected a subclass of the neutrosophic sets named single-valued neutrosophic sets (SVNS). NS is acquired by three autonomous mapping such as truth (T), indeterminacy (I) and falsity (F) and takes values from $]0^-, 1^+[$. By merging triangular fuzzy numbers (TFNs) and single valued neutrosophic set (SVNS) Biswas et al. (2016) introduced the idea of triangular fuzzy neutrosophic sets (TFNS). Trapezoidal fuzzy neutrosophic set was proposed by Ye (2015) and he urbanized weighted arithmetic and geometric averaging for TFNS. Vogel's approximation technique for solving the Transportation Problem was premeditated by Harvey and Shore (1970). Deshumukh (2012) offered a pioneering technique for unraveling Transportation Problem. Sudhakar, Arunnsankar, and Karpagam (2012) have given a modified approach for solving transportation problem. Transportation Problems with mixed restrictions have been resolved by Pandian and Natarajan (2010). Real life transportation problem in neutrosophic environment is deliberated by Akansha Singh et al (2017). Broumi et al. (2018) proposed an innovative system and technique for the planning of telephone network using NG. Broumi et al. (2019) proposed SPP under interval valued neu- trosophic setting. Defuzzification of triangular neutrosophic numbers by the score function is given by Said Broumi et al (2016). By applying fuzzy linear programming for MOTP Bit et al (1992) arrived with an optimal solution. Trust-region globalization stratagem was offered by Yousria et al (2012).Two different techniques for solving a multi-objective, multi-item solid transportation problem with fuzzy coefficients was proposed by Kundu et al (2013). An alternative method to unravel MOTP by was proposed by Yeola et al (2016).

In this paper, new unconventional technique to decipher MOTP in neutrosophic fuzzy environment is presented to get a basic feasible solution. Mean of the membership functions are estimated and the algorithm is applied to acquire the elucidation. We exhibit the new-fangled approach with a numerical example and compare the result with VAM.

2. PRELIMINARIES

Some important results regarding neutrosophic sets, single valued neutrosophic sets and triangular and trapezoidal fuzzy neutrosophic sets have been referred from the papers, (Singh et al, 2017).

Definition 2.1

Let X be a space of points with generic elements in X denoted by x is the neutrosophic set A is an object having the form, $A = \{x: T_A(X), I_A(X), F_A(X), x \in X\}$, where the functions T,I,F: $X \rightarrow]^-0,1^+[$ define respectively the truth-membership function, indeterminacy- membership function and falsity - membership function of the element $x \in X$ to the set A with the condition $^-0 \leq T_A(X) + I_A(X) + F_A(X) \leq 3^+$. The functions are real standard or non standard subsets of $]^-0,1^+[$.

Definition 2.2 (Wang et al, 2010)

Let $R_N = [R_T, R_I, R_M, R_E]$ (T_R, I_R, F_R) and $S_N = [S_T, S_I, S_M, S_E]$ (T_S, I_S, F_S) be two trapezoidal neutrosophic numbers (TpNNs) and $\theta \geq 0$, then

$$R_N \oplus S_N = [R_T + S_T, R_I + S_I, R_M + S_M, R_E + S_E] \, (T_R + T_S - T_R T_S, \, I_R I_S, \, F_R F_S)$$

$$R_N \otimes S_N = [R_T . S_T, R_I . S_I, R_M . S_M, R_E . S_E] \, (T_R . T_S, \, I_R + I_S - I_R . I_S, \, F_R + F_S - F_R . F_S)$$

$$\theta \, R_N = [\theta R_T, \theta R_I, \theta R_M, \theta R_E] \, (1 - (1 - T_R))^\theta, (I_R)^\theta, (F_R)^\theta)$$

Definition2.3 (Wang et al, 2010)

Let $R = [R_T, R_I, R_M, R_E]$ and $R_T \leq R_I \leq R_M \leq R_E$ then the centre of gravity (COG) in R is

$$
COG(R) = \begin{cases} R \text{ if } R_T = R_I = R_M = R_E \\ \dfrac{1}{3}\left[R_T + R_I + R_M + R_E - \dfrac{R_T R_I - R_M R_E}{R_E + R_M - R_I - R_T} \right] \\ otherwise \end{cases} \quad (1)
$$

Definition 2.4 (Wang et al, 2010)

Let $S_N = [S_T, S_P, S_M, S_E]$ (T_S, I_S, F_S) be a TpNN then the score, accuracy and certainty functions are as follows

$$S(S_N) = COG(R) \times \frac{(2 + T_S - I_S - F_S)}{3} \tag{2}$$

$$a(S_N) = COG(R) \times (T_S - I_S) \tag{3}$$

$$C(S_N) = COG(R) \times (T_S) \tag{4}$$

Definition 2.5 (Biswas et al, 2016)

Let N be a trapezoidal neutrosophic number in the set of real numbers with the truth, indeterminacy and falsity membership functions are defined by

$$T_N(x) = \begin{cases} \dfrac{(x-a)t_N}{b-a} & , \quad a \le x \le b \\ t_N & , \quad b \le x \le c \\ \dfrac{(d-x)t_N}{d-c} & , \quad c \le x \le d \\ 0 & , \quad otherwise \end{cases}$$

$$I_N(x) = \begin{cases} \dfrac{b-x+(x-a)t_N}{b-a} & , \quad a \le x \le b \\ i_N & , \quad b \le x \le c \\ \dfrac{x-c+(d-x)i_N}{d-c} & , \quad c \le x \le d \\ 0 & , \quad otherwise \end{cases}$$

$$T_N(x) = \begin{cases} \dfrac{b-x+(x-a)f_N}{b-a} & , \quad a \le x \le b \\ f_N & , \quad b \le x \le c \\ \dfrac{x-c+(d-x)f_N}{d-c} & , \quad c \le x \le d \\ 0 & , \quad \text{otherwise} \end{cases}$$

where $t_N = [t^L, t^U] \subset [0,1], i_N = [i^L, i^U] \subset [0,1]$, and $f_N = [f^L, f^U] \subset [0,1]$ are interval numbers. Then the number N can be denoted by $([a,b,c,d]: [t^L,t^U], [i^L,i^U], [f^L,f^U])$ called interval valued trapezoidal neutrosophic number.

3. EFFICIENT ALGORITHM VIA MEAN OF MEMBERSHIP VALUES

Step 1: Using the given formulas (1) and (2) transform the given neutrosophic fuzzy numbers into crisp values.

Step 2: Compute the membership value using

$$\mu_k\left(x_{ij}^k\right) = \begin{cases} 0 & x_{ij}^k \ge U_k \\ \dfrac{U_k - x_{ij}}{U_k - L_k} & L_k \le x_{ij}^k \le U_k \\ 1 & x_{ij}^k \ge L_k \end{cases}.$$

where L_k is the smallest crisp value of x_{ij}^k and U_k is the largest crisp value of x_{ij}^k and frame the three penalty tables.

Step 3: Erect a latest table in which each cell is the mean value of all membership values of the subsequent cells in the three penalty tables.

Step 4: Estimate the difference between the highest membership value and subsequent highest membership value for each row / column.

Step 5: Pick the extreme value and seek out the higher membership value in that row / column and allot that cell with the minimum value of a_i or b_j.

Step 6: When making an allocation in a cell if either a row / column is satisfied, then cancel that row / column and exclude that from next calculations.

Step 7: After elimination of the satisfied row / column, calculate again for the remaining row/ column and make allocation of the membership value.

Step 8: Repeat the previous steps until the columns or rows are satisfied.

4. NUMERICAL EXAMPLE

Consider a multi objective transportation problem with neutrosophic fuzzy numbers as the cost values shown in Tables 1, 2, and 3.

Converting the trapezoidal neutrosophic numbers into crisp numbers using the formula,

$$s\ (S_N) = COG\ (R) \times \frac{(2 + T_S - I_S - F_S)}{3} \text{ by eq. 2}$$

$$COG\ (R) = \frac{1}{3}\left[R_T + R_I + R_M + R_E - \frac{R_E R_M - R_I R_T}{R_E + R_M - R_I - R_T} \right] \text{ by eq. 1}$$

(9, 12, 14, 16); 0.6, 0.2, 0.3

$$COG(R) = \frac{1}{3}\left[16 + 14 + 12 + 9 - \frac{16*14 - 12*9}{16 + 14 - 12 - 9} \right] = \frac{1}{3}\left[51 - \frac{224 - 108}{9} \right]$$

$$= \frac{1}{3}\left[51 - \frac{116}{9} \right] = \frac{1}{3}[51 - 12.8] = \frac{38.2}{3} = 12.7$$

$$s\ (S_N) = 12.7 \times \frac{(2 + 0.6 - 0.2 - 0.3)}{3} = 12.7 \times 0.7 = 8.89 = 9$$

According to the first step we evaluate the membership values of the first penalty (p_1) table (Table 4), where $U_K = 12$ and $L_K = 2$ then using the formula, we get Table 6. The membership function used for that is defined as follows

Table 1. Penalty 1

	D1	D2	D3	D4	D5	SUPPLY
O1	(9, 12, 14,16); 0.6, 0.2, 0.3	(15, 18, 21, 26); 0.8, 0.2, 0.6	(12, 15, 14,16); 0.6, 0.2, 0.3	(6, 9, 12,14); 0.6, 0.2, 0.3	(9, 12, 14,16); 0.6, 0.2, 0.3	(5, 9, 14, 19); 0.7, 0.4,0.6
O2	(11, 13, 15, 17); 0.4, 0.6, 0.4	(2, 4, 6, 8); 0.7, 0.3, 0.4	(11, 13, 15, 17); 0.4, 0.6, 0.4	(11, 13, 15, 17); 0.4, 0.6, 0.4	(5, 9, 14, 19); 0.3, 0.7, 0.6	(5, 7, 9, 11); 0.9, 0.7, 0.5
O3	6, 9, 12,14); 0.6, 0.2, 0.3	(5, 9, 14, 19); 0.3, 0.7, 0.6	(9, 12, 14,16); 0.6, 0.2, 0.3	(14, 17, 21,28); 0.8, 0.2, 0.6	(2, 4, 6, 8); 0.7, 0.3, 0.4	(1, 3, 4, 6); 0.6, 0.3, 0.5
O4	6, 9, 12,14); 0.6, 0.2, 0.3	(10, 13, 15, 26); 0.8, 0.2, 0.6	(14, 17, 21,28); 0.8, 0.2, 0.6	(1, 3, 4, 6); 0.6, 0.3, 0.5	(1, 3, 4, 6); 0.6, 0.3, 0.5	(9, 12, 14,16); 0.6, 0.2, 0.3
DEMAND	(4, 8, 11, 15); 0.6, 0.3, 0.2	(4, 8, 11, 15); 0.6, 0.3, 0.2	(9, 11, 14, 16); 0.5, 0.4, 0.7	(1, 3, 4, 6); 0.6, 0.3, 0.5	(4, 8, 11, 15); 0.6, 0.3, 0.2	

Table 2. Penalty 2

	D1	D2	D3	D4	D5	SUPPLY
O1	(1, 3, 4, 6); 0.6, 0.3, 0.5	(9, 12, 14,16); 0.6, 0.2, 0.3	(12, 15, 16, 18); 0.6, 0.4, 0.5	(1, 2, 3,4); 0.2, 0.4, 0.2	(4, 8, 11,15); 0.6, 0.3, 0.2	(5, 9, 14, 19); 0.7, 0.4,0.6
O2	(1, 2, 3,4); 0.2, 0.4, 0.2	(9, 12, 14,16); 0.6, 0.2, 0.3	(9, 12, 14,16); 0.6, 0.2, 0.3	(5, 9, 14, 19); 0.3, 0.7, 0.6	(1, 3, 4, 6); 0.6, 0.3, 0.5	(4, 8, 11,15); 0.6, 0.3, 0.2
O3	(12, 15, 16, 18); 0.6, 0.4, 0.5	(1, 2, 3,4); 0.2, 0.4, 0.2	(12, 15, 16, 18); 0.6, 0.4, 0.5	(4, 8, 11,15); 0.6, 0.3, 0.2	(5, 9, 14, 19); 0.3, 0.7, 0.6	(1, 3, 4, 6); 0.6, 0.3, 0.5
O4	(1, 3, 4, 6); 0.6, 0.3, 0.5	(12, 15, 16, 18); 0.6, 0.4, 0.5	(9, 11, 14, 16); 0.5, 0.4, 0.7	(9, 12, 14,16); 0.6, 0.2, 0.3	(12, 15, 16, 18); 0.6, 0.4, 0.5	(9, 12, 14,16); 0.6, 0.2, 0.3
DEMAND	(4, 8, 11, 15); 0.6, 0.3, 0.2	(4, 8, 11, 15); 0.6, 0.3, 0.2	(9, 11, 14, 16); 0.5, 0.4, 0.7	(1, 3, 4, 6); 0.6, 0.3, 0.5	(4, 8, 11,15); 0.6, 0.3, 0.2	

Table 3. Penalty 3

	D1	D2	D3	D4	D5	SUPPLY
O1	(1, 3, 4, 6); 0.6, 0.3, 0.5	(4, 8, 11, 15); 0.6, 0.3, 0.2	(9, 11, 14, 16); 0.5, 0.4, 0.7	(5, 7, 8,10); 0.5, 0.4, 0.7	(9, 11, 14, 16); 0.5, 0.4, 0.7	(5, 9, 14, 19); 0.7, 0.4,0.6
O2	(4, 8, 11, 15); 0.6, 0.3, 0.2	(12, 15, 16, 18); 0.6, 0.4, 0.5	(4, 8, 11, 15); 0.6, 0.3, 0.2	(9, 12, 14,16); 0.6, 0.2, 0.3	(1, 3, 4, 6); 0.6, 0.3, 0.5	(4, 8, 11,15); 0.6, 0.3, 0.2
O3	(5, 9, 14, 19); 0.7, 0.4,0.6	(5, 7, 8,10); 0.5, 0.4, 0.7	(5, 9, 14, 19); 0.7, 0.4,0.6	(5, 7, 8,10); 0.5, 0.4, 0.7	(9, 11, 14, 16); 0.5, 0.4, 0.7	(1, 3, 4, 6); 0.6, 0.3, 0.5
O4	(9, 11, 14, 16); 0.5, 0.4, 0.7	(9, 12, 14,16); 0.6, 0.2, 0.3	(9, 11, 14, 16); 0.5, 0.4, 0.7	(5, 7, 8,10); 0.5, 0.4, 0.7	(1, 2, 3,4); 0.2, 0.4, 0.2	(9, 12, 14,16); 0.6, 0.2, 0.3
DEMAND	(4, 8, 11, 15); 0.6, 0.3, 0.2	(4, 8, 11, 15); 0.6, 0.3, 0.2	(9, 11, 14, 16); 0.5, 0.4, 0.7	(1, 3, 4, 6); 0.6, 0.3, 0.5	(4, 8, 11, 15); 0.6, 0.3, 0.2	

Table 4. Crisp values for Penalty 1

	D1	D2	D3	D4	D5	SUPPLY
O1	9	12	9	6	9	5
O2	7	3	7	7	5	4
O3	6	5	9	11	3	2
O4	6	8	11	2	2	9
DEMAND	4	4	6	2	4	20

Table 5. Crisp values for penalty 2

	D1	D2	D3	D4	D5	SUPPLY
O1	2	4	6	3	.6	5
O2	4	8	4	9	2	4
O3	5	3	5	3	6	2
O4	6	9	6	3	1	9
DEMAND	4	4	6	2	4	20

Table 6. Crisp values for penalty 3

	D1	D2	D3	D4	D5	SUPPLY
O1	2	9	8	1	4	5
O2	1	9	9	5	2	4
O3	8	1	8	4	5	2
O4	2	8	6	9	8	9
DEMAND	4	4	6	2	4	20

$$\mu_k\left(x_{ij}^k\right) = \begin{cases} 0 & x_{ij}^k \geq U_k \\ \dfrac{U_k - x_{ij}}{U_k - L_k} & L_k \leq x_{ij}^k \leq U_k \\ 1 & x_{ij}^k \geq L_k \end{cases}.$$

L_K is the smallest crisp value of x_{ij}^k and U_k is the largest crisp value of x_{ij}^k.

Now using the second step we calculate the mean of all membership values for the 3 penalties shown in Table 10.

Table 7. Membership values for penalty 1

	D1	D2	D3	D4	D5	SUPPLY
O1	0.3	0	0.3	0.6	0.3	5
O2	0.5	0.9	0.5	0.5	0.7	4
O3	0.6	0.7	0.3	0.1	0.9	2
O4	0.6	0.4	0.1	1	1	9
DEMAND	4	4	6	2	4	20

Table 8. Membership values for penalty 2

	D1	D2	D3	D4	D5	SUPPLY
O1	0.88	0	0.12	1	0.62	5
O2	1	0	0	0.5	0.88	4
O3	0.12	1	0.12	0.62	0.5	2
O4	0.88	0.12	0.38	0	0.12	9
DEMAND	4	4	6	2	4	20

Table 9. Membership values for penalty 3

	D1	**D2**	**D3**	**D4**	**D5**	**SUPPLY**
O1	0.88	0.62	0.38	0.75	0.38	5
O2	0.62	0.12	0.62	0	0.88	4
O3	0.5	0.75	0.5	0.75	0.38	2
O4	0.38	0	0.38	0.75	1	9
DEMAND	4	4	6	2	4	20

Table 10. Mean of membership values

	D1	**D2**	**D3**	**D4**	**D5**	**SUPPLY**
O1	0.68	0.20	0.27	0.78	0.43	5
O2	0.71	0.34	0.37	0.33	0.82	4
O3	0.41	0.81	0.31	0.50	0.59	2
O4	0.62	0.17	0.29	0.58	0.70	9
DEMAND	4	4	6	2	4	20

Now pertaining the remaining steps in our proposed approach we get the results shown in Table 11.

The set of solution is

$$X_{11}=3, X_{14}=2, X_{22}=2, X_{25}=2, X_{32}=2, X_{41}=1, X_{43}=6, X_{45}=2$$

Now optimal solution is given by

$$Z_1(x) = 134, Z_2(x) = 102, Z_3(x) = 90.$$

The optimal solution by VAM's method is given by

$$Z_1(x) = 134, Z_2(x) = 110, Z_3(x) = 120.$$

The mean method gives a better solution than the existing method.

Table 11. Total opportunity cost

	D1	D2	D3	D4	D5	SUPPLY					
O1	0.68 (3)	0.20	0.27	0.78 (2)	0.43	5	(0.10)	(0.10)	(0.25) MAX		
O2	0.71	0.34 (2)	0.37	0.33	0.82 (2)	4	(0.11)	(0.11)	(0.11)	(0.11)	(0.11)
O3	0.41	0.81 (2)	0.31	0.50	0.59	2	(0.22) MAX				
O4	0.62 (1)	0.17	0.29 (6)	0.58	0.70 (2)	9	(0.08)	(0.08)	(0.08)	(0.08)	(0.08)
DEMAND	4	4	6	2	4						
	(0.03)	(0.5)	(0.06)	(0.20)	(0.12)						
	(0.03)	(0.14)	(0.08)	(0.20) MAX	(0.12)						
	(0.03)	(0.14)	(0.08)		(0.12)						
	(0.09)	(0.017) MAX	(0.08)		(0.12)						
	(0.09)		(0.08)		(0.12) MAX						

5. CONCLUSION

In this paper, mean approach is used for solving MONTP. Neutrosophic fuzzy numbers are converted into crisp values and the membership values are calculated and the final cost table is formed by using the mean values of the three penalty tables. Using the proposed method the optimal solution is obtained. The optimum solution by our method gives a better approximation than VAM method.

REFERENCES

Abbasbandy, S., & Hajjari, T. (2009). A new approach for ranking of trapezoidal fuzzy numbers. *Computers & Mathematics with Applications (Oxford, England)*, *57*(3), 413–419. doi:10.1016/j.camwa.2008.10.090

Abo-elnaga, Y., El-sobky, B., & Zahed, H. (2012). Trust Region Algorithm for Multi-objective Transportation, Assignment, and Transshipment Problems. *Life Science Journal*, *9*(3), 1765–1772.

Afwat, A.E., Salama, A.A.M., & Farouk, N. (2018). A New Efficient Approach to Solve Multi-Objective Transportation Problem in the Fuzzy Environment. *International Journal of Applied Engineering Research*, *13*(18), 660-664.

Atanassov, K. (1986). Intuitionistic fuzzy sets. *Fuzzy Sets and Systems*, (20), 87-96.

Basirzadeh, H. (2012). Ones Assignment Method for Solving Assignment Problems. *Applied Mathematical Sciences*, *6*(47), 2345–2355.

Biswas, P., Pramanik, S., & Giri, B.C. (2016). Aggregation of Triangular Fuzzy Neutrosophic Set Information and its Application to Multi attribute Decision Making. *Neutrosophic Sets and Systems*, *12*, 20-40.

Bit, A. K., Biswal, M. P., & Alam, S. S. (1992). Fuzzy programming approach to multicriteria decision making transportation problem. *Fuzzy Sets and Systems*, *50*(2), 135–141. doi:10.1016/0165-0114(92)90212-M

Broumi, S., Bakali, A., Talea, M., & Sarandache, F. (2016). Shortest Path Problem Under Triangular Fuzzy Neutrosophic information. *International Conference on Software, Knowledge, Information Management & Applications (SKIMA)*. 10.1109/SKIMA.2016.7916216

Broumi, S., Bakali, A., Talea, M., Smarandache, F., Kishore, K. K., & Şahin, R. (2019). Shortest path problem under interval valued neutro-sophic setting. *J Fundam Appl Sci*, *10*(4S), 168–174.

Broumi, S., Mohamed, T., Bakali, A., & Smarandache, F. (2016). Single valued neutrosophic graphs. *J New Theory*, *10*, 86–101.

Broumi, S., Ullah, K., Bakali, A., Talea, M., Singh, P. K., Mahmood, T., ... Oliveira, A. D. (2018). Novel system and method for telephone network planing based on neutrosophic graph. *Glob J Comput Sci Technol E Netw Web Secur*, *18*(2), 1–11.

Chen, L.-H., & Lu, H.-W. (2007). An extended assignment problem considering multiple and outputs. *Applied Mathematical Modelling*, *31*(10), 2239–2248. doi:10.1016/j.apm.2006.08.018

Chen, M. S. (1985). On a fuzzy assignment problem. *Tamkang Journal*, *22*, 407–411.

Deshmukh, N. M. (2012). An Innovative Method for Solving Transportation Problem. *International Journal of Physics and Mathematical Sciences*.

Gotmare, D., & Khot, P.G. (2016). Solution of Fuzzy Assignment Problem by using Branch and Bound Technique with application of Lingustic variable. *International Journals of Computer and Technology*, *15*(4).

Huang, L.-S., & Zhang, L. (2006). Solution method for fuzzy assignment problem with Restriction of Qualification. *Proceedings of the Sixth International Conference on Intelligent Systems Design and Applications*. 10.1109/ISDA.2006.247

Kundu, P., Kar, S., & Maiti, M. (2013). Multi-objective multi-item solid transportation problem in fuzzy environment. *Applied Mathematical Modelling*, *37*(4), 2028–2038. doi:10.1016/j.apm.2012.04.026

Lone, M. A., Mir, S. A., Ismail, Y., & Majid, R. (2017). Intustinistic Fuzy Assignment problem: An Application in Agriculture. *Asian Journal of Agricultural Extension, Economics & Socialogy*, *15*(4), 1–6. doi:10.9734/AJAEES/2017/31967

M.C. (2016). Solving Multi-Objective Transportation Problem Using Fuzzy Programming Technique-Parallel Method. *International Journal of Recent Scientific Research*, *7*(1), 8455–8457.

Muruganandam, S., & Hema, K. (2017). Solving Fully Fuzzy Assignment Problem Using Branch and Bound Technique. *Global Journal of Pure and Applied Mathematics*, *13*(9), 4515-4522.

Nagarajan, R., & Solairaju, A. (2010). Assignment Problems with Fuzzy Costs under Robust Ranking Techniques. *International Journal of Computer Applications, 6*(4).

Pandian, P., & Natarajan, G. (2010). A New Approach for Solving Transportation Problems with Mixed Constraints. *Journal of Physical Sciences*, *14*, 53-61.

Shore, H. H. (1970). The Transportation Problem and the Vogel's Approximation Method. *Decision Sciences*, *1*(3-4), 441–457. doi:10.1111/j.1540-5915.1970.tb00792.x

Singh, A., & Kumar, A. (2017). Modified Approach for optimization of real life transportation problem in neutrosophic environment. *Mathematical Problems in Engineering*.

Smarandache, F. (2005). *A unifying field in logic. Neutrosophy: neutrosophic probability, set, logic* (4th ed.). Rehoboth: American Research Press.

Smarandache, F. (1998). Neutrosophic, Neutrosophic Probability set and logic. Amer. Res Press.

Srinivas, B., & Ganesan, G. (2015). Method For Solving Branch-And-Bound Technique For Assignment Problems Using Triangular and Trapezoidal Fuzzy Numbers. *International Journal in Management and Social Science, 3*(3).

Sudhakar, V.J., Arunsankar, N., & Karpagam, T. (2012). A New Approach to find an Optimum Solution of Transportation Problems. *European Journal of Scientific Research*, *68*(2), 254–257.

Thamaraiselvi, A., & Shanthi, R. (2016). A New Approach for Optimization of Real Life Transportation Problem in Neutrosophic Environment. *Mathematical Problems in Engineering*.

Wang, H., Smarandache, F., Zhang, Y., & Sunderraman, R. (2010). Single valued Neutrosophic Sets. *Multisspace and Multistructure*, *4*, 410–413.

Yager, R. R. (1981). A procedure for ordering fuzzy subsets of the unit interval. *Information Sciences*, *24*(2), 143–161. doi:10.1016/0020-0255(81)90017-7

Ye, J. (2015). Trapezoidal fuzzy neutrosophic set and its application to multiple attribute decision making. *Soft Computing*. doi:10.100700500-015-1818-y

Zadeh, L. A. (1965). Fuzzy sets. *Information and Control, 8*(3), 338–353. doi:10.1016/S0019-9958(65)90241-X

Chapter 12
A New LCS–Neutrosophic Similarity Measure for Text Information Retrieval

Misturah Adunni Alaran
Moshood Abiola Polytechnic, Abeokuta, Nigeria

AbdulAkeem Adesina Agboola
Federal University of Agriculture, Nigeria

Adio Taofiki Akinwale
Federal University of Agriculture, Nigeria

Olusegun Folorunso
Federal University of Agriculture, Nigeria

ABSTRACT

The reality of human existence and their interactions with various things that surround them reveal that the world is imprecise, incomplete, vague, and even sometimes indeterminate. Neutrosophic logic is the only theory that attempts to unify all previous logics in the same global theoretical framework. Extracting data from a similar environment is becoming a problem as the volume of data keeps growing day-in and day-out. This chapter proposes a new neutrosophic string similarity measure based on the longest common subsequence (LCS) to address uncertainty in string information search. This new method has been compared with four other existing classical string similarity measure using wordlist as data set. The analyses show the performance of proposed neutrosophic similarity measure to be better than the existing in information retrieval task as the evaluation is based on precision, recall, highest false match, lowest true match, and separation.

DOI: 10.4018/978-1-7998-2555-5.ch012

INTRODUCTION

Proper classification of data which forms the basis of any form of research or reason for solving any research problem has been identified. There are three classes, these are; classical set, fuzzy set and neutrosophic set, each has been identified to be different from the other as the inadequacy of one (in order) gave rise to the emergence of the other. Explanation of how one led to the other, has been given. Also, solving problems relating to human endeavor, the introduction of the neutrosophic set has helped greatly in modeling indeterminacy of which the classical nor the fuzzy sets could handle (Agboola,2016). The process of information searching is assumed to be a means of attempting to resolve some uncertainty in knowledge (Kuhlthau, 1993; 2003). This uncertainty principle can be associated with the ASK (Anomalous State of Knowledge) model. This opined that as the user realizes the inadequacy in his or her state of knowledge, he resorts to information searching to clear the impreciseness. At the initial stage of a problem, it may be impossible for the user to specify precisely what is lacking in his or her knowledge state. In a broad sense, uncertainty describes a situation where a user's knowledge is limited. This uncertainty may be how to express a need, what that need means, or the changing of previously held beliefs (Belkin, Oddy & Brooks, 1982).

An understanding of neutrosophic axioms has been proposed where the difference between the two types of communication has been presented. These are Neutrosophic communication and informational communication. Neutrosophic communication was expressed as the type of communication in which the message consists of incomplete, vague and imprecise elements while informational communication describes a communication whose aim is to share an informational message. Smarandache and Vlăduțescu (2013) affirmed neutrosophic communication as the rule while informational communication as the exception in the ideal sense of communication. In considering a world full of indeterminacy, traditional crisp set with its boundaries of truth and false lacks the ability to reflect the reality. As a result of these claims, neutrosophy is used in recent research as a new representation of the real world as propounded by Florentin Smarandache (Smaradanche,1995). Also, in determining the association between any two entities, distance and similarity measures are very useful techniques (Bhattacharyya, Koli & Majumdar, 2018). To deal with uncertainties in searching or comparing some entities for resemblance, neutrosophic similarity methods will be an appropriate tool to present a realistic situation. This chapter presents the Longest Common Subsequence (LCS) Neutrosophic string similarity measure and its performance is compared with existing classical similarity measures. These results are evaluated to determine the efficiency of the proposed string neutrosophic similarity measure.

Background

Data is a raw fact that when processed becomes information. This information has been described as the most important source in everyday life activities. Information reduces uncertainty and it is transferable. In recent time, information availability is extremely huge in both printed and non-printed format, this in essence results in information overload. The major source of information nowadays is the internet where the abundance of this information confuses some users in differentiating the right information from the wrong one. The task of sourcing information at times is tiresome and this might delay the process of decision-making when there is no effective retrieval method (Bachchhav, 2016). De & Mishra (2017) have applied two different similarity measure formulas to determine the closeness of two neutrosophic data and vague data. They also proposed a similarity measure based α-cut value to generate a SQL command for the imprecise query which could be implemented on both sets. The query returned back different result sets for different α-cut values for checking the closeness between two different sets. Their work established that neutrosophic set gives much more accurate result for any kind of uncertain query rather than vague set. In 2019, De & Mishra also carried out a study on functional dependency in a neutrosophic relational database by extending the classical relational database model using the basic idea of neutrosophic set theory. Their work proposed a new type of neutrosophic functional dependency called *α-nfd* and they further defined the neutrosophic inference rules, partial *α-nfd* and neutrosophic key.

A new method of neutrosophic search with rank and rank neutrosophic set which can be used to answer queries of the lay users from the database of bioinformatics nature has been proposed. This measure proffers a better resource for handling complexities in decision making to provide useful information from a combination of raw data, documents or business models to identify and solve problems as well as make decisions, where a new method of answering queries based on neutrosophic logic was presented (Arora & Ranjit, 2010). Neutrosophic soft sets have been identified to be appropriate and efficient tools to deal with problems involving uncertainty can be seen in social, economic system, medical diagnosis, pattern recognition, coding theory, etc (Mukherjee & Sarkar, 2015). A multi-criteria decision-making (MCDM) problem has been identified in contract services from cloud computing. This becomes an essential need of many organization in the recent time as there is an increase in cloud services available whereas it would be of interest to select the best of these services based on numerous criteria. A framework for this selection has been proposed using a single-valued neutrosophic number, where about five criteria were considered viz; agility, assurance, cost, performance and security. Various activities included in this framework for selection purpose are gathering parameters, eliciting preferences, computing consensus degree, advice generation, rating alternatives and cloud service selection. Illustrative examples were presented for application purpose (Teruel, Cedeño, Gavilanez, Diaz & Vázquez, 2018). Ponce et al (2019) have also presented a new neutrosophic linguistic model where uncertainty in information retrieval has been handled using ordinal neutrosophic linguistic approach.

Three similarity measures for a single-valued neutrosophic set (SVNS) based on Jaccard, Dice and Cosine similarity measures were developed by Ye (2014). These methods when applied, gave a similarity value of a ranking order for all alternatives possible in particular decision criteria. The highest-ranked alternative is chosen to be the best for the decision-maker. These methods were applied to solving problems in investment policymaking. An evaluation of an MCDM problem using SVNS has been proposed where the weight is determined using Step-wise Weight Assessment Ratio Analysis (SWARA) method and SVNS is used to determine the rating of each respondent considering criteria like variety of foods available, quality and taste of the food, to mention a few, this presented an area of application involving selection of suitable restaurant where the application seems appropriate (Stanujkic, Smarandache, Zavadskas, Karabasevic, 2016). A software package has been developed using Excel application to calculate the neutrosophic data and perform analysis on them. These analyses include union, intersection and complement, charts of these analyses are included. This effort also utilized some object-oriented programming languages like c#, .NET and Microsoft Visual Basic to implement the neutrosophic classes (Salama, El-Ghareeb, Manie, & Smarandache, 2014). Single-valued neutrosophic decision-making model has been applied in the choice school for children as determined by their parents. This model is based on hybridization of grey system theory and single-valued neutrosophic set considering a real-life scenario of five criteria in the choice of school. This model has been proved to be helpful in solving a real-life problem in taking the correct and appropriate decision (Mondal & Pramanik, 2015)

PRELIMINARIES

In this section, some definitions of Neutrosophic set, Single-Valued Neutrosophic set (SVNS) and axioms of Neutrosophic Similarity measure are presented.

Neutrosophic Set

A neutrosophic set A on the universe of discourse X is defined as:

$$A = \{\langle x : T_A(x), I_A(x), F_A(x) \rangle, \ x \in X\} \tag{1}$$

where the functions T_A, I_A, F_A: $X \rightarrow$]⁻0, 1⁺[and

$$^-0 \leq T_A(x) + I_A(x) + F_A(x) \leq 3^+ \tag{2}$$

From a philosophical point of view, the neutrosophic set takes the value from real standard or non-standard subsets of]−0, 1+[. Therefore, instead of]−0, 1+[we need to take the interval [0, 1] for technical applications because]−0, 1+[will be difficult to apply in the real applications such as in scientific and engineering problems. For example, suppose a staff (John, from the Administrative Department of XYZ company) has been fired by the Manager for misconduct. But, according to his co-workers, John was not guilty of any wrongdoing. So, John sues the company. At this time, the status of John in the company remains indeterminate.

Single-Valued Neutrosophic Set (SVNS)

A single-valued neutrosophic set A is denoted by $A_{SVNS} = (T_A(x), I_A(x), F_A(x))$ for any x in X (Kanika & Kajal, 2016). For two Single-Valued Neutrosophic sets (SVNSs) A and B, let

$$A_{SVNS} = \{\langle x : T_A(x), I_A(x), F_A(x) \rangle \mid x \in X\} \text{ and}$$
$$B_{SVNS} = \{\langle x : T_B(x), I_B(x), F_B(x) \rangle \mid x \in X\}$$

then two relations are defined in (Wang, Smarandache, Zhang, & Sunderrama, 2010) as follows:

$$A_{SVNS} \subseteq B_{SVNS} \text{ if and only if } T_A(x) \leq T_B(x), I_A(x) \geq I_B(x), F_A(x) \geq F_B(x) \tag{3}$$

$$A_{SVNS} = B_{SVNS} \text{ if and only if } T_A(x) = T_B(x), I_A(x) = I_B(x), F_A(x) = F_B(x) \tag{4}$$

Other properties as presented by Kanika and Kajal (2016) are:

$$A_{SVNS} \cup B_{SVNS} = \left(\max\{T_A(x), T_B(x)\}, \min\{I_A(x), I_B(x)\}, \min\{F_A(x), F_B(x)\} \right) \tag{5}$$

and

$$A_{SVNS} \cap B_{SVNS} = \left(\min\{T_A(x), T_B(x)\}, \max\{I_A(x), I_B(x)\}, \max\{F_A(x), F_B(x)\} \right)$$

(6)

Axioms of Neutrosophic Similarity Measure

A mapping $Sim(A, B)$: $NS(x) \times NS(x) \to [0,1]$, where $NS(x)$ denotes the set of all neutrosophic sets in $x = \{x1, x2,..., xn,\}$, is $_s$aid to $_b$e the degree of similarity between A and B (Ye,2014; Muhkerjee & Sakaar, 2014; Broumi & Smaradanche, 2014) if it satisfies the following conditions:

1) $0 \leq Sim(A,B) \leq 1$ (7)

2) $Sim(A,A)=1$ (Reflexive*)* (8)

3) $Sim(A,B)=1$ if and only if $A=B$, $\forall A,B \in NS$ (Local-Reflexive) (9)

4) $Sim(A,B)=Sim(B,A)$ (Symmetric) (10)

5) $Sim(A,C) \leq Sim(A,B)$ and $Sim(A,C) \leq Sim(B,C)$ if $A \leq B \leq C$ for a SVNS C.

(11)

where all x is in X. (Transitive)

METHODOLOGY

Here, some existing classical similarity measures, viz; Dice, Bi-gram, Trigram and Set-based are presented with the proposed neutrosophic similarity measure and its associated methods.

Existing Classical Similarity Measures

1. **Dice Method:** This measure was originally introduced by Dice (1945) for ecological studies. It is a measure used to evaluate matches between two sets by normalizing the size of their intersection over the average of their sizes. Its usefulness has been greatly expressed in medical image segmentation (Yeghiazaryan & Voiculescu, 2015). For two strings X and Y, the Dice similarity method is expressed in eq(12) (Ismat & Ashraf, 2018).

$$Dice(\text{A}, B) = \frac{2\left(n - gram\left(X \cap Y\right)\right)}{n - gram\left(X\right) + n - gram\left(Y\right)} \qquad (12)$$

2. **Bigram Method:** This describes a fixed length of consecutive and overlapping series of characters called n-gram, where n is equal to 2. Bigram has been greatly applied in cryptography analysis (Adamson & Boreham, 1974). N-gram generally does not care about semantic since it represents only a fragment of processing token (Kowalski, 2011). This method is thus derived from the generalized n-gram method in eq (13) (Niewiadomski & Grzybowski, 2004):

$$\text{Bigram(X, Y)} = \frac{1}{N - n + 1} \sum_{i=0}^{N-n+1} h(i) = \frac{1}{N - 2 + 1} \sum_{i=0}^{N-2+1} h(i) = \frac{1}{N-1} \sum_{i=0}^{N-1} h(i)$$

$$(13)$$

where; h(i) = 1 if n-element subsequence beginning from position i in X appears in Y, otherwise h(i) = 0 and N = max(|X|, |Y|)

3. **Trigram Method:** This is also a derivative of n-gram where n is equal to 3. It is used for text compression and manipulating the length of index terms (Schek, 1978). It is also useful for detecting spelling errors and corrections (Zamora, Pollack, & Zamora, 1981; Angell, Freund, & Willet, 1983). Two string X and Y are determined via the N-gram method as trigram with eq (14) (Niewiadomski & Grzybowski, 2004):

$$\text{Trigram(X, Y)} = \frac{1}{N - n + 1} \sum_{i=0}^{N-n+1} h(i) = \frac{1}{N - 3 + 1} \sum_{i=0}^{N-3+1} h(i) = \frac{1}{N-2} \sum_{i=0}^{N-2} h(i)$$

$$sim\left(X, Y\right) = \frac{1}{N - n + 1} \sum_{i=0}^{N-n+1} h\left(i\right) = \frac{1}{N - 3 + 1} \sum_{i=0}^{N-3+1} h\left(i\right) = \frac{1}{N-2} \sum_{i=0}^{N-2} h\left(i\right) \qquad (14)$$

where; h(i) = 1 if n-element subsequence beginning from position i in X appears in Y, otherwise h(i) = 0 and N = max(|X|, |Y|)

4. **Set-based trigram method:** This method was derived from the theory of set similarity measure. The method measures the similarity between two sets of entities in terms of the number of the common trigram. The weight of string sharing of pattern and text matching is increased by three times. Set-based

trigram is asymmetric because it does not consider (false, false) to be a matched pattern and the definition is as follows (Akinwale & Niewiadomski, 2015):

$$\text{Set-based trigram}(A, B) = \frac{3(trigram(A \cap B))}{trigram(A) + trigram(B) + trigram(A \cap B)}$$

(15)

Proposed LCS-Neutrosophic String Similarity Algorithm

In this section, the algorithm for the new neutrosophic string similarity matching based on the Longest Common Subsequence (LCS) is presented. Consideration for this new approach is majorly based on neighboring identity matches which has a stronger indication of similarity than identity matches that are far apart. The text is an array X[1...n] of length n and that the pattern is an array Y[1...m] of length m, where m ≤ n, thus assumed. Further assumptions are that the elements of X and Y are characters drawn from a finite alphabets $\Sigma = \{0,1\}$ or $\Sigma = \{a,b,...z\}$. The character arrays X and Y are often called strings of characters. Given a sequence X $= x_1 \ldots x_n$, another $Y = y_1 \ldots y_m$, we say that a sequence Z is a common subsequence of X and Y if Z is a subsequence of both X and Y. The algorithm for LCS is as presented in Figure 1.

Figure 1. New Longest common subsequence algorithm for Neutrosophic based Similarity measure

```
LCS_Sim_Matcher(X,Y)

int n= length[X]
int m= length [Y]
string a= compute_max_LCS(X,Y)|

string compute_max_LCS(X,Y){
  j= 0
   LCS[i] = ""
  while(m<>0 or n<> 0){
  for(i=0, i<n-1, i++){
     while (j< m-1){
          if (X[i]==Y[j]{
               LCS[i] = LCS[i] + x[i]
               j++}}
       }}
     a = max(LCS[0,...,i])
  return a
}
```

LCS-Neutrosophic String Similarity Algorithm

The algorithm for the proposed system is presented in Figure 2:

Figure 2. Algorithm for proposed LCS-Neutrosophic string similarity method

Algorithm 2: Neutrosophic string information retrieval method
Input: Text matching X, Pattern matching Y
Output: Similarity value of X and Y, LCS-N-Sim(X,Y) ∈ [0,1]
Procedure
1: Input text as a query for searching
2: Convert each text in the database from the classical domain to Neutrosophic domain.
3: Convert the query text to the Neutrosophic domain.
4: Determine the longest common subsequence of the two texts (input query and each of database text).
5: Using the result of 4, find the neutrosophic similarity between database text value and input query.

Methods for Generating Neutrosophic Values for Each Character in Strings for Comparison

Considering strings A and B for comparison. Let $A = (x_1, x_2, \ldots x_n)$ and $B = (y_1, y_2, \ldots y_m)$, there will be the need to represent each of these character to reflect neutrosophic nature. The existence of a character in a string reflects the true nature of the character in the string where it is found. The more a character exists in a string the more it is reckoned with (truth value), this has a lot effect in its falsity (non-existence) and uncertainty value at every instance. Strings A and B can be written as neutrosophic strings thus presented in equations (16) and (17):

$$A = \{x_1 \langle T_A(x_1), I_A(x_1), F_A(x_1) \rangle, x_2 \langle T_A(x_2), I_A(x_2), F_A(x_2) \rangle, \ldots, x_n \langle T_A(x_n), I_A(x_n), F_A(x_n) \rangle\}$$
(16)

$$B = \{y_1 \langle T_B(y_1), I_B(y_1), F_B(y_1) \rangle, y_2 \langle T_B(y_2), I_B(y_2), F_B(y_2) \rangle, \ldots, y_m \langle T_B(y_m), I_B(y_m), F_B(y_m) \rangle\}$$
(17)

Where,

T's = the truth value
I's = the indeterminacy/ uncertainty value

F's = the falsity value

For each character as a member of the set. These neutrosophic representations are defined thus:

$$T_A(x) = \frac{|x|_A}{|A|} \tag{18}$$

$$I_A(x) = 1 - \frac{|x|_A}{|A| + |B|} \tag{19}$$

$$F_A(x) = 1 - \frac{|x|_A}{|A|} \tag{20}$$

Where;

|A| = length of string A
|B| = length of string B
$|x|_A$ = number of character x in string A

The same works for Text B

Proof: Since $|X|_A \leq |A| \implies T_A(x) \in [0,1]$, conversely $I_A(x)$ and $F_A(x) \in [0,1]$

Then, according to Van Rijsbergen (Rijsbergen, 1986; 2017), that the uncertainty of similarity between two entities can be determined by the extent of information to be added to establish the truth value of the similarity. As proposed here, the extent of similarity is based on the extent of the commonality, represented here as the Longest Common Subsequence (LCS). The higher the commonality, the higher the percentage of certainty that the similarity will exist (truth value) and thus the lower the value of similarity uncertainty and falsity. The difference between the commonality and individual entity compared must determine the level of the uncertainty. Thus, a proposal can be defined as follows:

If $|LCS| = k$ and $|A \cup B| = l$, then

$$LCS-N-Sim_t(A,B) = \frac{\text{mimimum NS values of each character in LCS}}{\text{maximum NS values of each character in } A \cup B} \quad (21)$$

$$LCS-N-Sim_t(A,B) = \frac{\sum_{i=1}^{k} \min\left(T_A(x_i),T_B(x_i)\right) + \min\left(I_A(x_i),I_B(x_i)\right) + \min\left(F_A(x_i),F_B(x_i)\right)}{\sum_{j=1}^{l} \max\left(T_A(x_j),T_B(x_j)\right) + \max\left(I_A(x_j),I_B(x_j)\right) + \max\left(F_A(x_j),F_B(x_j)\right)}$$

$$(22)$$

$$LCS-N-Sim_i(A,B) = \frac{|A-LCS| + |B-LCS|}{|A| + |B|} \quad (23)$$

$$LCS-N-Sim_f(A,B) = 1 - \{LCS-N-Sim_f(A,B)\} \quad (24)$$

Where;

1. LCS-N-Sim$_t$(A, B) be the truth value of Sim(A, B)
2. LCS-N-Sim$_i$(A, B) be indeterminacy of Sim(A, B)
3. LCS-N-Sim$_f$(A, B) be the false value of Sim(A, B)
4. Sim(A, B) means the similarity value between set A and set B

Proposition 1: Suppose the proposed neutrosophic (truth) similarity measure LCS-N-Sim$_t$(A,B) in eq. (22) satisfies the axioms of similarity measure previously defined then:

1. $0 \leq$ LCS-N-Sim$_t$(A,B) ≤ 1
2. LCS-N-Sim$_t$(A,B) $= 1$ iff A $=$ B
3. LCS-N-Sim$_t$(A,B) $=$ LCS-N-Sim$_t$(B, A)
4. If C is a SVNS in X and A⊂B⊂C then LCS-N-Sim$_t$(A,C) $\leq$ LCS-N-Sim$_t$(A,B) and LCS-N-Sim$_t$(A,C) $\leq$ LCS-N-Sim$_t$(B,C)

Proofs:

1. Since $T_A(x)$, $I_A(x)$, $F_A(x) \in [0, 1]$, then LCS-N-Sim$_t$(A,B) $\leq [0, 1]$
2. For any two SNVS A and B if $A_{SVNS} = B_{SVNS}$, this implies that $T_A(x) = T_B(x)$, $I_A(x) = I_B(x)$, $F_A(x) = F_B(x)$, then:

$$\sum_{i=1}^{k} \min(T_A(x_i), T_B(x_i)) + \min(I_A(x_i), I_B(x_i)) + \min(F_A(x_i), F_B(x_i))$$

$$= \sum_{j=1}^{l} \max(T_A(x_j), T_B(x_j)) + \max(I_A(x_j), I_B(x_j)) + \max(F_A(x_j), F_B(x_j))$$

(25)

Thus LCS-N-Sim$_t$(A,B) =1, conversely LCS-N-Sim$_t$(B,A) =1

3. The proof is clear as stated in proof (2)
4. If A⊂B⊂C then $T_A(x) \leq T_B(x) \leq T_C(x)$, $I_A(x) \geq I_B(x) \geq I_C(x)$, $F_A(x) \geq F_B(x) \geq F_C(x)$, then the following inequalities hold:

$$\frac{\sum_{i=1}^{k} \min(T_A(x_i), T_C(x_i)) + \min(I_A(x_i), I_C(x_i)) + \min(F_A(x_i), F_C(x_i))}{\sum_{j=1}^{l} \max(T_A(x_j), T_C(x_j)) + \max(I_A(x_j), I_C(x_j)) + \max(F_A(x_j), F_C(x_j))}$$

$$\leq \frac{\sum_{i=1}^{k} \min(T_A(x_i), T_B(x_i)) + \min(I_A(x_i), I_B(x_i)) + \min(F_A(x_i), F_B(x_i))}{\sum_{j=1}^{l} \max(T_A(x_j), T_B(x_j)) + \max(I_A(x_j), I_B(x_j)) + \max(F_A(x_j), F_B(x_j))}$$

(26)

Thus ; LCS-N-Sim$_t$ **(A, C)** $\leq$ LCS-N-Sim$_t$ **(A, B)**

$$\frac{\sum_{i=1}^{k} \min(T_A(x_i), T_C(x_i)) + \min(I_A(x_i), I_C(x_i)) + \min(F_A(x_i), F_C(x_i))}{\sum_{j=1}^{l} \max(T_A(x_j), T_C(x_j)) + \max(I_A(x_j), I_C(x_j)) + \max(F_A(x_j), F_C(x_j))}$$

$$\leq \frac{\sum_{i=1}^{k} \min(T_B(x_i), T_C(x_i)) + \min(I_B(x_i), I_C(x_i)) + \min(F_B(x_i), F_C(x_i))}{\sum_{j=1}^{l} \max(T_B(x_j), T_C(x_j)) + \max(I_B(x_j), I_C(x_j)) + \max(F_B(x_j), F_C(x_j))}$$

(27)

Thus; LCS-N-Sim$_t$ **(A, C)** $\leq$ LCS-N-Sim$_t$ **(B, C)**

Illustration

In this section, here is an example evaluated to determine the similarity value between any two given set of strings. For neutrosophic similarity, the truth, indeterminacy and false are stated while the classical could only give the true value of similarity measure.

Example 1:

    A = programmer

    B = programming

    LCS = programm

    $A \cup B$ = {p,r,o,g,a,m,e,i,n}

Table 1. Neutrosophic values of text A – PROGRAMMER

Character	T	I	F
P	0.1	0.95	0.9
R	0.3	0.86	0.7
O	0.1	0.95	0.9
G	0.1	0.95	0.9
R	0.3	0.86	0.7
A	0.1	0.95	0.9
M	0.2	0.9	0.8
M	0.2	0.9	0.8
E	0.1	0.95	0.9
R	0.3	0.86	0.7

The values of T, I and F in Tables 1 &2 were generated using equations 18-20.

$$LCS - N - Sim_t(A,B)$$

$$= \frac{\begin{aligned}&(0.09+0.95+0.90)+(0.18+0.86+0.70)+(0.09+0.95+0.90)+(0.10+0.90+0.82)\\&+(0.18+0.86+0.70)+(0.09+0.95+0.90)+(0.18+0.9+0.8)+(0.18+0.9+0.8)\end{aligned}}{\begin{aligned}&(0.1+0.95+0.91)+(0.3+0.9+0.82)+(0.1+0.95+0.91)+(0.18+0.95+0.9)\\&+(0.1+0.95+0.91)+(0.2+0.9+0.82)+(0.1+0.95+0.9)+(0.09+0.95+0.91)+(0.09+0.95+0.91)\end{aligned}}$$

$$= \frac{14.86}{17.70} = 0.84$$

Table 2. Neutrosophic values of text B - PROGRAMMING

Character	T	I	F
P	0.09	0.95	0.91
R	0.18	0.90	0.82
O	0.09	0.95	0.91
G	0.18	0.90	0.82
R	0.18	0.90	0.82
A	0.09	0.95	0.91
M	0.18	0.90	0.82
M	0.18	0.90	0.82
I	0.09	0.95	0.91
N	0.09	0.95	0.91
G	0.18	0.90	0.82

$$LCS - N - Sim_i\left(A, B\right) = \frac{2+3}{10+11} = 0.24$$

$$LCS - N\ Sim_f(\mathbf{A,B}) = 1 - 0.84 = 0.16$$

$$Dice(\mathrm{A}, B) = \frac{2(7)}{9+10} = 0.74$$

$$Bigram(A, B) = \frac{1}{11-1} \times 7 = 0.70$$

$$Trigram(A, B) = \frac{1}{11-2} \times 6 = 0.64$$

$$Set - based\ trigram(A, B) = \frac{3 \times 6}{8+9+6} = 0.78$$

Experiment

In this chapter, wordlist was used as data sets for the experiments. A word list is the set of words that are derived from the same root as a given word (Akinwale & Niawiedomski, 2015). For example, given the word *school*, the similarity measures are to retrieve the other related words such as *schooling, schools and scholar*. The existing classical methods considered here are Dice, Bigram, Trigram and Set-based trigram similarity measures. These existing ones were compared with the new method using data set obtained from WordNet 2.0 to determine the extent of similarity for any two given set of strings as can be experienced while searching words of similar root. The illustration given above shows an example of this calculation manually with existing and new methods.

The effectiveness of several similarity measures was evaluated by calculating how well they are able to distinguish related word pairs from unrelated word pairs. For this experiment, 200 grammatically correct words were used as text matching (database) and users were asked to input a word of similar root to some words in the list into the system which represents the pattern matching. The system is expected to display in descending order of similarity value the list of similar words in the database. Based on the chosen similarity method, the best ten (10) of the retrieved texts were taken for analysis. Ideally, most of the related pairs would occur near the top of a list of pairs arranged by their similarity value (Timothy & Zobel, 2003). This implementation was done with Python 3.7 on HP laptop with an Intel Pentium 2.20GHz dual-core CPU and 2.00GB memory running a 64-bit Windows 10 operating system. A sample is shown in figure 3.

Figure 3. Similarity Measures calculation interface

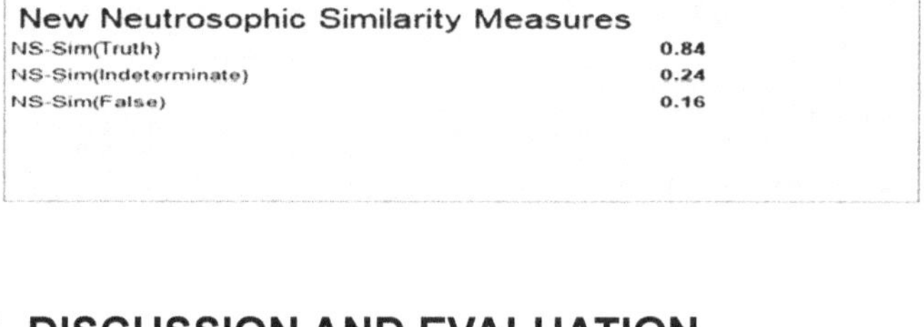

RESULTS, DISCUSSION AND EVALUATION

In practice, most of the related pairs should occur near the top of a list of pairs sorted by their similarity value (Timothy& Zobel, 2003). The evaluation employed the functions of recall, precision to determine to what percentage degree the number of the retrieved and relevant keywords search is proportionally closer to the users' requests. Similarity measure of precision value equals to one (1) would have retrieved relevant documents but misses many useful ones while when recall equals one (1) would have retrieved most relevant documents but includes lots of chunks. A more desirable one is to have a value which is close to 1 (Raymoon, 2001).

$$\text{Precision} = \frac{\text{Relevant retrieved text}}{\text{Retrieved text}} \tag{28}$$

$$\text{Recall} = \frac{\text{Relevant retrieved text}}{\text{Relevant text}} \tag{29}$$

While Recall and Precision have been widely used for estimating similarity measure performance but for more effective evaluation, additional metrics need to be used hence, the need for Highest False Match (HFM) and Separation (Sep) evaluation metrics. HFM is the highest similarity score percentage given to an incorrect result. In order to evaluate separation, the Lowest True Match (LTM) must be known. LTM is the lowest similarity score percentage given to the correct result. Separation (Sep) is, therefore, the difference between LTM and HFM. Sep estimates the distance of a correctly retrieved text with respect to an incorrectly one in the word list search. It is more desirable to consider both together. A high HFM is acceptable if the Sep is high and likewise for a low score. The ratio of the HFM to Sep is a useful indicator of the overall effectiveness of the measures (Timothy & Zobel, 2003).

$$HFM = \frac{\text{Highest ranked irrelevant text similarity value}}{\text{Highest ranked relevant text similarity value}} X\ 100\% \tag{30}$$

$$LTM = \frac{\text{Lowest ranked relevant text similarity value}}{\text{Highest ranked relevant text similarity value}} X\ 100\% \tag{31}$$

$$Sep = LTM - HFM \tag{32}$$

Ten queries were run using all the five methods considered in this chapter and the best ten (10) retrieved data as shown in figure 4 were picked for analyses, sample of which is presented in Table 3 where the similarity value of the query and the text is indicated in the parenthesis (*.**) while the summary of the evaluation result for the experiment is shown in Table 4.

Table 3. Sample of query results for Trigram and LCS-N-simt methods illustrating LTM and HFM: Query = anore

S/No	Trigram	LCS-N-Sim$_t$
1	anorexy (0.60) (HTM=100%)	anorexy (0.94) (HTM=100%)
2	anomie (0.60) (HFM= 0.83%)	anorexia (0.93)
3	anorexia (0.50)	anorectal (0.92)
4	anorexic (0.50)	anorexic (0.92)
5	anorectal (0.43)	anorectic (0.91) (LTM =96.81%)
6	anorectic (0.43) (LTM=71.67%)	anoperineal (0.78) (HFM =82.98%)
7	anorthite (0.43)	anorthite (0.77)
8	absorbed (0.33)	anon (0.64.)
9	absorber (0.33)	afforestation (0.63)
10	accentor (0.33)	anorthopia (0.63)

Figure 4. Information retrieval interface

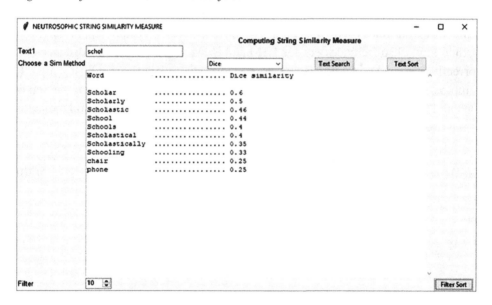

In figure 5, the visualization of the experiment evaluation results summary is thus presented to show the distribution of precision, recall and F-measure on the methods tested. For all the valuation metrics viz; precision, recall and F-measure, LCS-N-Sim$_t$, the truth value of the new similarity measure, has the highest value. This presents the new method better than the existing ones.

Table 4. Summary of evaluation results

Sim measure	Precision	Recall	F-Measure	LTM (%)	HFM (%)	Sep (%)	Sep /HFM
Dice	0.49	0.93	0.64	68.23	78.78	-10.55	-0.13
Bi-gram	0.35	0.67	0.46	70.49	94.85	-24.36	-0.26
Trigram	0.39	0.77	0.52	67.84	85.29	-17.45	-0.20
Set-Based	0.43	0.81	0.56	71.94	83.68	-11.74	-0.14
LCS-N-Sim$_t$	0.53	0.99	0.69	92.76	87.42	5.33	0.06

Figure 5. Graph showing a comparison of new LCS neutrosophic string similarity and other classical similarity measures

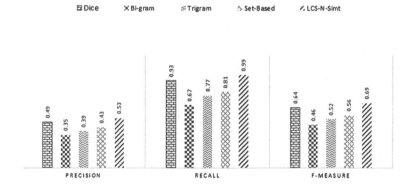

COMPARISON OF LCS-N-SIM SIMILARITY MEASURE
WITH EXISTING ONES

CONCLUSION

This study describes the experiment to present a new method in text information retrieval based on neutrosophic logic. Considering the result in Table 4, only LCS-N-Sim$_t$ could maintain a high value for HFM and Sep while others have high value for HFM and a low value for Sep. A high separation score indicates that the methods could not only rank correct text but could also clearly differentiate from the incorrect text. The new neutrosophic based method could also evaluate truth, indeterminate and false similarity values not previously done in the existing similarity measure.

ACKNOWLEDGMENT

This research received no specific grant from any funding agency in the public, commercial, or not-for-profit sectors.

REFERENCES

Adamson, G., & Boreham, J. (1974). The Use of an Association Measure Based on Character Structure to Identify Semantical Related Pairs of Words and Document Titles. *Information Storage and Retrieval*, *10*(7-8), 253–260. doi:10.1016/0020-0271(74)90020-5

Agboola, A. A. A. (2016). *Fuzzy, Neutrosophic sets, vital to technological advancement*. Seyibabs FUNAAB socio-academic network.

Akinwale, A., & Niewiadomski, A. (2015). Efficient Similarity measures for texts matching. *Journal of Applied Computer Science*, *23*(1), 7–28.

Angell, R., Freund, G., & Willett, P. (1983). Automatic Spelling Correction Using a Trigram Similarity Measure. *Information Processing & Management*, *19*(4), 255–261. doi:10.1016/0306-4573(83)90022-5

Arora, M., & Ranjit, B. (2010). *Deployment of Neutrosophic Technology to Retrieve Answer for Queries Posed in Natural Language*. Academic Press.

Bachchhav, K. P. (2016). Information Retrieval: Search process, Techniques and Strategies. *International Journal of Next Generation Library & Technology*, *2*(1), 1–10.

Belkin, N. J., Oddy, R. N., & Brooks, H. M. (1982). ASK for information retrieval: Part 1 Background and Theory. *The Journal of Documentation*, *38*(2), 61–71. doi:10.1108/eb026722

Bhattacharyya, S., Koli, B., & Majumdar, P. (2018). On Distances and Similarity Measures between two Interval Neutrosophic sets. *Journal of New Theory*, *20*, 27–47.

Broumi, S., & Smarandache, F. (2014). Cosine similarity measure of interval-valued neutrosophic sets. *Neutrosophic Sets and Systems*, *5*, 15–20.

De, S., & Mishra, J. (2017). Inconsistent data processing using vague set and neutrosophic set for justifying better outcome. In *International Conference on Inventive Communication and Computational Technologies (ICICCT)*. IEEE. 10.1109/ICICCT.2017.7975210

De, S., & Mishra, J. (2019). A new approach of Functional Dependency in a Neutrosophic Relational Database Model. *Asian Journal of Computer Science &Technology*, *8*(2), 44–48.

Dice, L. R. (1945). Measure of Amount of Ecological Association between Species. *Ecology*, *26*(3), 297-303.

Ismat, B., & Ashraf, S. (2018). Fuzzy equivalence relations. *Kuwait Journal of Science & Engineering*, *35*, 33–51.

Kanikal, M., & Kajla, B. (2016). Improved similarity measure in a neutrosophic environment and its application in finding a minimum spanning tree. *Journal of Intelligent & Fuzzy Systems*, *31*(3), 1721–1730. doi:10.3233/JIFS-152082

Kondrak, G. (2005). N-gram Similarity and Distance. *SPIRE*, 115-126.

Kowalski, G. (2011). Information Retrieval Architecture and Algorithms. Springer. doi:10.1007/978-1-4419-7716-8

Kuhlthau, C. (1993). A principle of uncertainty for information seeking. *The Journal of Documentation*, *49*(4), 339–355. doi:10.1108/eb026918

Kuhlthau, C. (2003). *Seeking meaning: a process approach to library and information services*. Englewood, CO: Libraries Unlimited.

Mondal, K., & Pramanik, S. (2015). Neutrosophic Decision Making Model of School Choice. *Neutrosophic Sets and Systems*, *7*, 62–68. doi:10.5281/zenodo.571507

Mukherjee, A., & Sarkar, S. (2014). Several similarity measures of neutrosophic soft sets and its application in real-life problems. *Annals of Pure and Applied Mathematics*, *7*, 1–6.

Mukherjee, A., & Sarkar, S. (2015). A new method of measuring similarity between two neutrosophic soft sets and its application in pattern recognition problems. *Neutrosophic Sets and Systems*, *8*, 72–77.

Niewiadomski, A., & Grzybowski, R. (2004). Rozmyte miary podobienstwa tekstow w automatycznej ewaluacji testow egzaminacyjnych. *Informatyka teoretyczna i stosowana*, *4*(6), 75–79.

Ponce, R., Albarracín, M., Jalón, A., Albarracín, Z., Molina, C., Serrano, Q., & Zuñiga, P. (2019). Soft computing In Neutrosophic Linguistic Modeling For The Treatment Of Uncertainty In Information Retrieval. *Neutrosophic Sets and Systems*, *26*, 69–74.

Raymond, M. (2001). *Performance evaluation of information retrieval system.* Academic Press.

Salama, A. A., El-Ghareeb, H. A., & Manie, A. M. (2014). *Smarandache* (Vol. 3). Introduction to Develop Some Software Programs for Dealing with Neutrosophic Sets, Neutrosophic Sets and Systems.

Schek, H. J. (1978). *The Reference String Indexing Method. Research Report.* Heidelberg, Germany: IBM Scientific Center.

Smarandache, F. (1995). *A Unifying Field in Logics. Neutrosophy: Neutrosophic Probability, Set and Logic.* Rehoboth: American Research Press.

Smarandache, F., & Vlăduțescu, S. (2013). Communication vs. Information, an Axiomatic Neutrosophic Solution. *Neutrosophic Sets and Systems*, 1.

Stanujkic, D, Smarandache, F., Zavadskas, E. K., & Karabasevic, D. (2016). Multiple Criteria Evaluation Model Based on the SingleValued Neutrosophic Set. *Neutrosophic Sets and Systems,* 14.

Teruel, K. P., Cedeño, J. C, Gavilanez, H. L., Diaz, C. B., & Vázquez. M. L. (2018). A framework for selecting cloud computing services based on consensus under single-valued neutrosophic numbers. *Neutrosophic Sets and Systems*, 22.

Timothy, C. H., & Zobel, J. (2003). Methods for Identifying Versioned and Plagiarized Documents. *Journal of the American Society for Information Science and Technology*, *54*(3), 203–215. doi:10.1002/asi.10170

Van Rijsbergen, C. J. (1986). A logic for information retrieval. *The Computer Journal*, *29*(6), 481–485. doi:10.1093/comjnl/29.6.481

Van Rijsbergen, C. J. (2017). A New Theoretical Framework for Information Retrieval. *ACM SIGIR Forum*, *51*(2), 44-50. 10.1145/3130348.3130354

Wang, H., Smarandache, F., Zhang, Y. Q., & Sunderrama, R. (2010). Single valued neutrosophic sets. *Multispace and Multistructure*, *4*, 410–413.

Ye, J. (2014). Vector Similarity Measures of Simplified Neutrosophic Sets and Their Application in Multicriteria Decision Making. *International Journal of Fuzzy Systems*, *16*(2), 204–211.

Yeghiazaryan, V., & Voiculescu, I. (2015). *An Overview of Current Evaluation Methods Used in Medical Image Segmentation.* Department of Computer Science, University of Oxford.

Zamora, E. M., Pollack, J. J., & Zamora, A. (1981). Use of Trigram Analysis of Spelling Error Detection. *Information Processing & Management, 17*(6), 305–316. doi:10.1016/0306-4573(81)90044-3

ADDITIONAL READING

Mehmet, A. A., Bart, T., & Wouter, J. (2016). Using character to reference n-gram to match a list of publications to references in bibliographic database. *Scientometrics, 109*(3), 1525–1546. doi:10.100711192-016-2066-3

Singla, N., & Garg, D. (2012). String Matching Algorithms and their Applicability in various Applications. *International Journal of Soft Computing and Engineering, 1*(6), 218–222.

Smarandache, F. (2015). *Symbolic Neutrosophic Theory.* Belgium: EuropaNova asbl.

Sun-Jung, K., Young, J. Y., Jungmin, S., Jeong, G. L., Jin, K., & Young, W. K. (2014). Design & implementation of binary file similarity evaluation system. *International Journal of Multimedia & ubiquitous engineering, 9*(1), 1-10.

Suriana, A., & Daud, M. (2017). A Review on Neutrosophic Set and Its Development. *Menemui Matematik, 39*(2), 61–69.

Syed, M. E., & Nong, Y. (2001). *robustness of Canberra Metric in Computer Intrusion Detection.* West Point: *IEEE Workshop on Information Assurance and Security United State Military Academy.*

Timothy, C. H., & Zobel, J. (2003). Methods for Identifying Versioned and Plagiarized Documents. *Journal of the American Society for Information Science and Technology, 54*(3), 203–215. doi:10.1002/asi.10170

Wael, H. G., & Aly, A. (2014). Arabic short answer scoring with effective feedback for students. *International Journal of Computers and Applications, 86*(2), 35–41. doi:10.5120/14961-3177

Wang, H., Smarandache, F., Zhang, Y. Q., & Sunderraman, R. (2005). *Interval neutrosophic sets and logic: Theory and applications in computing.* Phoenix, AZ: Hexis.

KEY TERMS AND DEFINITIONS

Indeterminate: Neither here nor there.

Neutrosophy: A new study concerning uncertainty phenomenon.

Precision: A measure of ascertaining a fact.

Query: A question for search.

Retrieval: The act of bringing out something from a volume of content.

Similarity: The sense of creating a resemblance or association between two or more entities.

String: A combination of letters, numbers, and/or some special character.

Chapter 13
A Novel Python Toolbox for Single and Interval–Valued Neutrosophic Matrices

Said Broumi
Laboratory of Information Processing, Faculty of Science Ben M'Sik, University Hassan II, Morocco

Selçuk Topal
Faculty of Science and Arts, Bitlis Eren University, Turkey

Assia Bakali
Ecole Royale Navale, Casablanca, Morocco

Mohamed Talea
Laboratory of Information Processing, Faculty of Science Ben M'Sik, University Hassan II, Morocco

Florentin Smarandache
iD https://orcid.org/0000-0002-5560-5926
Department of Mathematics, University of New Mexico, USA

ABSTRACT

Recently, single valued neutrosophic sets and interval valued neutrosophic sets have received great attention among the scholars and have been applied in many applications. These two concepts handle the indeterminacy and consistent information existing in real-life problems. In this chapter, a new Python toolbox is proposed under neutrosophic environment, which consists of some Python code for single valued neutrosophic matrices and interval valued neutrosophic matrices. Some definitions of interval neutrosophic vague set such as union, complement, and intersection are presented. Furthermore, the related examples are included.

DOI: 10.4018/978-1-7998-2555-5.ch013

1. INTRODUCTION

The introduction of the idea of fuzzy set was introduced by (Zadeh, 1965). He proposed that each element in a fuzzy set has a degree of membership. Based on this idea Dr (Atanassov,1986) introduced the concept of intuitionistic fuzzy set on a universe X as a generalization of fuzzy set. His concept is based on two degrees for each element: the degree of membership and degree of non-membership. Later on, Dr (Smarandache,1998) originally gave the definition of a neutrosophic set and neutrosophic logic. The concept of neutrosophic set is based on three degrees for each element totally independent: the degree of membership the degree of indtermination and degree of non-membership. In (Wang et al, 2014) proposed the concept of single valued neytrosophic set which is an extensin of Neutrosophic set. In addition, the author (Zhang et al.,2014) developped a new extension termed as interval valued neutrosophic set.Several scholars have done remarkable achievements in this area (http://fs.gallup.unm.edu/NSS/).

(Biswas et al, 2018)applied the concept of interval trapezoidal neutrosophic numbers for solving MADM Strategy based distance. (Giri et al, 2018) developed TOPSIS Method for MADM based on interval trapezoidal neutrosophic number. (Hazwani et al,2019) introduced the concept of interval neutrosophic vague sets,this concept is acombination of interval valued neutrosophic set and vague sets, the author presented some definitions of interval neutrosophic vague set such as union, complement and intersection with including the basic operations, the derivation of its properties and related examples. (Nagarajan et al., 2019) proposed blockchain single and interval valued neutrosophic graphs and sutdied some of their proprtites with numerical examples.In (Broumi et al., 2019) applied the concept of interval valued neutrosophic graph for solving energy and spectrum analysis using MATLAB software. (Nagarajan et al.,2019) initiated the Dombi interval valued neutrosophic graph and its role in traffic control management. (Kalyan Mondal etal.,2018) applied the interval neutrosophic tangent similarity measure for solving MADM strategy. In (Pramanik et al,2018) applied the concept of interval rough neutrosophic sets for solving multi attribute decision making strategy based on projection and bidirectional projection measures. (Song et al.,2017) applied the interval neutrosophic sets applied to ideals in BCK/BCI-algebras. (Dalapatiet al.,2017) defined the interval neutrosophic -cross entropy for solving MAGDM Strategy. (Dalbinder and Kajla,2017) solved the selection of transportation companies and their mode of transportation under interval valued data. (Mukherjee et al.,2016) defined the restricted interval valued neutrosophic sets and restricted interval valued neutrosophic topological spaces.

(Chunfang and YueSheng,2016) presented a new method to construct entropy of interval-valued neutrosophic set with numerical example. In addition, others hybrid theories can be found in (Rajeswara et al,2016 ; Bausyset al.,2015, Huang et al.,2017,

Şahin,2015, Hong-Xiaaet al.,2015, Ye, 2014 ;20114a ;2015 ;2015a ;2016, Ma et al., Nancy & Garg, 2016, Garg and Nancy,2017, Tian et al.2015, Şahin et al.,2017, Broumi etal.,2016 ;2016a ;2016b ;2017;2019a, Karaşan and Kahraman, 2017, Karaaslan and Khizar, 2018, Kumar et al. 2018;2019;2019a,2019b). In (Broumi et al,2017a,2017b) developped a Matlab Toolbox for computing operational matrices in Neutrosophic Environments.

Recently few researchers (El-Ghareeb, 2019). developed python progamms for solving opoerations on neutrosophic numbers including single valued neutrosophic numbers and interval valued neutrosophic numbers. The weakness of this python progranms cannot deal with neutrosophic matrices, Until now, there has been no study on developping Python code for computing neutrosophic operations. Therefore, the objective of this paper is to developp Python code for neutrosophic matrices.

This paper is structured in the following manner. Section 2 presents some basic mathematical concepts to enhance the understanding of single valued neutrosophic set and interval valued neutrosophic sets. Section 3 describes the python programms for operations on single valued neutrosophic matrices together with numerical examples. Section 4 describes the python programms for operations on interval valued neutrosophic matrices together with numerical examples. Finally, conclusion is stated in section 5.

2. BACKGROUND AND INTERVAL VALUED NEUTROSOPHIC SETS

In this section, we will discuss some definitions regarding neutrosophic sets, single valued neutrosophic sets, interval valued neutrosophic sets, the set-theoretic operators on the interval neutrosophic set and interval valued neutrosophic matrix, which will be used in the rest of the paper. However, for details on the interval valued neutrosophic sets, one can see (Smarandache,1998, Wang et al, 2014, Zhang et al, 2014).

Definition 2.1 (Smarandache,1998): Suppose ξ be an universal set. The neutrosophic set A on the universal set ξ categorized in to three membership functions called the true $T_A(x)$, indeterminate $I_A(x)$ and false $F_A(x)$ contained in real standard or non-standard subset of]-0, 1+[respectively.

$$-0 \leq \sup T_A(x) + \sup I_A(x) + \sup F_A(x) \leq 3+ \tag{1}$$

Definition 2.2 (Wang et al, 2014): Suppose ξ be a universal set. The single valued neutrosophic sets (SVNs) A on the universal ξ is termed as following:

$$A = \{\langle x: T_A(x), I_A(x), F_A(x)\rangle x \in \xi\} \tag{2}$$

The functions $T_A(x) \in [0.\ 1]$, $I_A(x) \in [0.\ 1]$ and $F_A(x) \in [0.\ 1]$ are denoted "the degree of membership the degree of indtermination and degree of non-membership of x in A", with the following condition:

$$0 \leq T_A(x) + I_A(x) + F_A(x) \leq 3 \tag{3}$$

Definition 2.3 (Zhang et al.,2014): Suppose ξ be a space of points (objects)with a generic element in ξ denoted by x. An interval valued neutrosophic set (IVNS) A in ξ is characterized by truth-membership function T_A, indeterminacy-membership function I_A, and falsity-membership function F_A. For each point

$x \in \xi$, $T_A(x), I_A(x), F_A(x) \subseteq [0,1]$.

$$A_{IVNS} = \left\{ \left[T_A^L(x), T_A^U(x) \right], \left[I_A^L(x), I_A^U(x) \right], \left[F_A^L(x), F_A^U(x) \right] : x \in \xi \right\}$$

with

$$0 \leq T_A^U(x) + I_A^U(x) + F_A^U(x) \leq 3 \tag{4}$$

Definition 2.4 (Zhang et al.,2014): Suppose two interval valued neutrosophic sets

$$A_{IVNS} = \left\{ \left[T_A^L(x), T_A^U(x) \right], \left[I_A^L(x), I_A^U(x) \right], \left[F_A^L(x), F_A^U(x) \right] : x \in \xi \right\}$$

and

$$B_{IVNS} = \left\{ \left[T_B^L(x), T_B^U(x) \right], \left[I_B^L(x), I_B^U(x) \right], \left[F_B^L(x), F_B^U(x) \right] : x \in \xi \right\}$$

the set-theoretic operators on the interval neutrosophic set are defined as follow.

1. An interval valued neutrosophic set A is contained in another interval valued neutrosophic set B, $A_{IVNS} \subseteq B_{IVNS}$, if and only if

$$T_A^L(x) \leq T_B^L(x), T_A^U(x) \leq T_B^U(x),$$

$$I_A^L(x) \geq I_B^L(x), I_A^U(x) \geq I_B^U(x),$$

$$F_A^L(x) \geq F_B^L(x), F_A^U(x) \geq F_B^U(x),$$

for all $x \in \xi$.

2. Two interval valued neutrosophic sets A and B are equal, written as $A_{IVNS}=B_{IVNS}$ if and only if $A \subseteq B \, and \, B \subseteq A$, i.e.

$$T_A^L(x) = T_B^L(x), T_A^U(x) = T_B^U(x),$$

$$I_A^L(x) = I_B^L(x), I_A^U(x) = I_B^U(x),$$

$$F_A^L(x) = F_B^L(x), F_A^U(x) = F_B^U(x),$$

for all $x \in \xi$.

3. An interval neutrosophic set A is empty if and only if

$$T_A^L(x) = T_A^U(x) = 0, \; I_A^L(x) = I_A^U(x) = 1, \; \text{and} \; F_A^L(x) = F_A^U(x) = 0$$

for all $x \in \xi$.

4. The complement of an interval neutrosophic set A is denoted by A^c and is defined by

$$A_{IVNS^C} = \left\{ \begin{array}{l} x, \left[F_A^L(x), F_A^U(x)\right], \\ \left[1 - I_A^U(x), 1 - I_A^L(x)\right], : x \in X \\ \left[T_A^L(x), F_A^U(x)\right] \end{array} \right\},$$

for all x in ξ.

5. The intersection of two interval valued neutrosophic sets A and B is an interval valued neutrosophic set $A \cap B$ defined as follow

$$A_{IVNS} \cap B_{IVNS} = \left\{ \begin{array}{l} x, \left[T_A^L(x) \wedge T_B^U(x), T_A^U(x) \wedge T_B^U(x) \right], \\ \left[I_A^L(x) \vee I_B^U(x), I_A^U(x) \vee I_B^U(x) \right], \quad : x \in \xi \\ \left[F_A^L(x) \vee F_B^U(x), F_A^U(x) \vee F_B^U(x) \right] \end{array} \right\},$$

for all *x* in ξ.

6. The union of two interval neutrosophic sets *A* and *B* is an interval neutrosophic set $A_{IVNS} \cup B_{IVNS}$ defined as follow:

$$A_{IVNS} \cup B_{IVNS} = \left\{ \begin{array}{l} x, \left[T_A^L(x) \vee T_B^L(x), T_A^U(x) \vee T_B^U(x) \right], \\ \left[I_A^L(x) \wedge I_B^L(x), I_A^U(x) \wedge I_B^U(x) \right], \quad : x \in \xi \\ \left[F_A^L(x) \wedge F_B^L(x), F_A^U(x) \wedge F_B^U(x) \right] \end{array} \right\},$$

for all *x* in ξ.

7. The difference of two interval neutrosophic sets *A* and *B* is an interval neutrosophic set $A_{\text{IVNS}} \ominus B_{\text{IVNS}}$ defined as follow:

$$A \ominus B = \left\langle \left[T_{A \ominus B}^L, T_{A \ominus B}^U \right], \left[I_{A \ominus B}^L, I_{A \ominus B}^U \right], \left[F_{A \ominus B}^L, F_{A \ominus B}^U \right] \right\rangle \tag{5}$$

where

$$T_{A \ominus B}^L = \min\left(T_A^L(x), F_B^L(x) \right), \quad T_{A \ominus_2 B}^U = \min\left(T_A^U(x), F_B^U(x) \right)$$

$$I_{A \ominus_2 B}^L = \max\left(I_A^L(x), 1 - I_B^U(x) \right), \quad I_{A \ominus_2 B}^U = \max\left(I_A^U(x), 1 - I_B^L(x) \right)$$

$$F_{A \ominus_2 B}^L = \max\left(F_A^L(x), T_B^L(x) \right), \quad F_{A \ominus_2 B}^U = \max\left(F_A^U(x), T_B^U(x) \right)$$

(Karaşan and Cengiz, 2018) introduced a new difference operation for the interval-valued neutrosophic sets as follow:

$$A \ominus_2 B = \left\langle \left[T_{A \ominus_2 B}^L, T_{A \ominus_2 B}^U \right], \left[I_{A \ominus_2 B}^L, I_{A \ominus_2 B}^U \right], \left[F_{A \ominus_2 B}^L, F_{A \ominus_2 B}^U \right] \right\rangle \tag{6}$$

where

$$T_{A \ominus_2 B}^L = T_A^L(x) - F_B^U(x), \quad T_{A \ominus_2 B}^U = T_A^U(x) - F_B^L(x)$$

$$I_{A \ominus_2 B}^L = \max\left(I_A^L(x), I_B^L(x)\right), \quad I_{A \ominus_2 B}^U = \max\left(I_A^U(x), I_B^U(x)\right)$$

$$F_{A \ominus_2 B}^L = F_A^L(x) - T_B^U(x), \quad F_{A \ominus_2 B}^U = F_A^U(x) - T_B^L(x)$$

for all x in ξ.

8. The scalar multiplication of interval neutrosophic set A is $A_{IVNS} \cdot a$, defined as follow

$$A_{IVNS} \cdot a = \left\{ \begin{array}{l} x, \left[\min(T_A^L(x) \cdot a, 1), \min(T_A^U(x) \cdot a, 1)\right], \\ \left[\min(I_A^L(x) \cdot a, 1), \min(I_A^U(x) \cdot a, 1)\right], \quad : x \in \xi \\ \left[\min(F_A^L(x) \cdot a, 1), \min(F_A^U(x) \cdot a, 1)\right] \end{array} \right\}$$

for all $x \in \xi$, $a \in R^+$.

9. The scalar division of interval neutrosophic set A is A_{IVNS}/a defined as follow

$$A_{IVNS} / a == \left\{ \begin{array}{l} x, \left[\min(T_A^L(x) / a, 1), \min(T_A^U(x) / a, 1)\right], \\ \left[\min(I_A^L(x) / a, 1), \min(I_A^U(x) / a, 1)\right], \quad : x \in \xi \\ \left[\min(F_A^L(x) / a, 1), \min(F_A^U(x) / a, 1)\right] \end{array} \right\}$$

for all $x \in \xi$, $a \in R^+$

The convenient method for comparing single valued neutrosophic and interval valued neutrosophic numbers can be done by using score function.

Definition 2.5 (Nancy & Garg, 2016, Garg and Nancy,2017, Şahin, 2015):
Suppose A be an interval neutrosophic number A_{IVNN}, the score function is defined as follow:

$$\tilde{S}_{IVNN}(x) = \frac{T_A^L(x) + T_A^U(x) + 4 - I_A^L(x) - I_A^U(x) - F_A^L(x) - F_A^U(x)}{6} \tag{7}$$

$$\tilde{S}_{SVNN}\left(x\right) = \frac{2 + T_A\left(x\right) - I_A\left(x\right) - F_A\left(x\right)}{3}$$

Definition 2.6 (Deli, 2017): An interval valued neutrosophic matrix(IVNM) of order m×n is defined as

$$A_{IVNM} = \left[\left\langle a_{ij}, [a^L_{ij_T}, a^U_{ij_T}], [a^L_{ij_I}, a^U_{ij_I}], [a^L_{ij_F}, a^U_{ij_F}] \right\rangle\right]_{m\times n}$$

where

$a^L_{ij_T}$ is the lower membership value of element a_{ij} in A.

$a^L_{ij_T}$ is the upper membership value of element a_{ij} in A.

$a^L_{ij_T}$ is the lower indeterminate-membership value of element a_{ij} in A.

$a^L_{ij_T}$ is the upper indeterminate-membership value of element a_{ij} in A.

$a^L_{ij_T}$ is the lower non- membership value of element a_{ij} in A.

$a^L_{ij_T}$ is the upper non-membership value of element a_{ij} in A.

For simplicity, we write A as

$$A_{IVNM} = \left[\left\langle [a^L_{ij_T}, a^U_{ij_T}], [a^L_{ij_I}, a^U_{ij_I}], [a^L_{ij_F}, a^U_{ij_F}] \right\rangle\right]_{m\times n} \tag{8}$$

3. COMPUTING THE SINGLE VALUED NEUTROSOPHIC MATRIX OPERATIONS USING PYTHON LANGUAGE

To generate the Python program for inputting the single valued neutrosophic matrices. The procedure is described as follows:

3.1 Checking the Matrix Is SVNM or Not

To generate the Python program for deciding for a given the matrix is single valued neutrosophic matrix or, simple call of the function **SVNMChecking ()** is defined as follow:

```
# SVNM is represented by 3D Numpy Array ====> row, column and
single valued number with 3 tuples for SVNM Checking
#A1. shape and A2. shape returns (3, 3,3) the dimension of A.
(row, column, numbers of element (Single valued Neutrosophic
Number, 3 elements)
# A.shape[0] = 3 rows
# A.shape[1] = 3 columns
# A.shape[2] = Each single valued neutrosophic number has 3
tuple as usual
#One can use any matrices having arbitrary dimension
import numpy as np
#A1 is a SVNM
A1= np.array([   [[0.000, 0.001, 0.002],   [0.010, 0.011,
0.012], [0.020, 0.021, 0.022]  ],
              [[0.100,0.101,0.102],    [0.110,0.111,0.112],
[0.120,0.121,0.122]   ],
              [[0.200,0.201,0.202],      [0.210, 0.211,0.212],
[0.220,0.221,0.222]    ]
                 ])
#A2 is not SVNM
A2= np.array([   [[0.000, 0.001, 0.002],   [0.010, 0.011,
0.012], [0.020, 0.021, 0.022] ],
              [[0.100,0.101,0.102],    [0.110,0.111,0.112],
[0.120,0.121,0.122]  ],
              [[0.200,0.201,0.202],     [0.210, 0.211,0.212],
[0.220,0.221,0.222]    ]
                 ])
def SVNMChecking (A):
    dimA=A.shape
    control=0
    counter = 0
    for i in range (0,dimA[0]):
        if counter == 1:
            break
        for j in range (0,dimA[0]):
            if counter == 1:
                break
            for  d in range (0, dimA[2]):
                if  counter ==0:
                    if (d==0 or d==1 or d==2):
```

```
                    if  not (0 <=  A[i][j][d] <= 1):
                        counter=1
                        print (A[i][j], ' is not a single
valued neutrosophic number, so the matrix is not a SVNM')
                        control=1
                        break
                    else:
                    print (A[i][j], ' is not a single valued
neutrosophic number, so the matrix is not a SVNM')
                    break
      if control==0:
          print ('The matrix is a SVNM')
```

Example 1. In this example we evaluate the checking the matrix is SVNM or not of the single valued neutrosophic matrix E of order 4X4:

$$E=\begin{pmatrix} \langle.5,.7,.2\rangle & \langle.4,.4,.5\rangle & \langle.7,.7,.5\rangle & \langle.1,.5,.7\rangle \\ \langle.9,.7,.5\rangle & \langle.7,.6,.8\rangle & \langle.9,.4,.6\rangle & \langle.5,.2,.7\rangle \\ \langle.9,.4,.2,\rangle & \langle.2,.2,.2\rangle & \langle.9,.5,.5\rangle & \langle.7,.5,.3\rangle \\ \langle.9,.7,.2\rangle & \langle.3,.5,.2\rangle & \langle.5,.4,.5\rangle & \langle.2,.4,.8\rangle \end{pmatrix}$$

The single valued neutrosophic matrix E can be inputted in Python code like this:

```
E= np.array([ [ [0.5,0.7,0.2], [0.4,0.4,0.5], [0.7,0.7,0.5],
[0.1,0.5,0.7]],
              [[0.9,0.7,0.5], [0.7,0.6,0.8], [0.9,0.4,0.6],
[0.5,0.2,0.7]],
              [[0.9,0.4,0.2], [0.2,0.2,0.2], [0.9,0.5,0.5],
[0.7,0.5,0.3]],
              [[0.9,0.7,0.2], [0.3,0.5,0.2], [0.5,0.4,0.5],
[0.2,0.4,0.8]]
          ])
```

The result of checking the matrix is SVNM or not E can be obtained by the call of the command SVNMChecking () (Figure 1).

Figure 1.

```
35  def SVNMChecking (A):
36      dimA=A.shape
37      control=0
38      counter = 0
39      for i in range (0,dimA[0]):
40          if counter == 1:
41              break
```

```
Shell   AST
            [0.4, 0.4, 0.5],
            [0.7, 0.7, 0.5],
            [0.1, 0.5, 0.7]],

          [[0.9, 0.7, 0.5],
           [0.7, 0.6, 0.8],
           [0.9, 0.4, 0.6],
           [0.5, 0.2, 0.7]],

          [[0.9, 0.4, 0.2],
           [0.2, 0.2, 0.2],
           [0.9, 0.5, 0.5],
           [0.7, 0.5, 0.3]],

          [[0.9, 0.7, 0.2],
           [0.3, 0.5, 0.2],
           [0.5, 0.4, 0.5],
           [0.2, 0.4, 0.8]]]])
>>> SVNMChecking (E)
    The matrix is a SVNM
```

3.2. Determining Complement of Single Valued Neutrosophic Matrix

For a given SVNM $A = \left[\left\langle T_{ij}, I_{ij}, F_{ij} \right\rangle \right]_{m \times n}$, the complement of A is defined as follow:

$$A^c = \left[\{1\} - T_{ij}, \{1\} - I_{ij}, \{-1\} - F_{ij} \right]_{m \times n} \tag{9}$$

$$A^c = \left[F_{ij}, \{1\} - I_{ij}, T_{ij}, \right]_{m \times n} \tag{10}$$

To generate the Python program for finding complement of single valued neutrosophic matrix, simple call of the function **SVNMCompelementOf** () is defined as follow:

The function SVNMCompelementOf(A) the below returns the complement matrix of a given single valued neutrosophic matrix A for (9).

```
# SVNM is represented by 3D Numpy Array ====> row, column and
single valued number with 3 tuples for (9)
import numpy as np
A= np.array([  [        [0.3,0.6,1,-0.2],   [0.1,0.2,0.8]   ],
               [        [0.1,0.12,0,-0.27], [0.5,0.33,0.58]
],
               [        [0.11,0.22,0.6,-0.29],[0.22,0.63,0.88]
```

```
]
                              ])
#A.shape gives (3, 2, 3) the dimension of A. (row, column,
numbers of element (Single valued Neutrosophic Number, 3
elements))
# A.shape[0] = 3 rows
# A.shape[1] = 2 columns
# A.shape[2] = each single valued neutrosophic number with 6
tuple as usual
def SVNMCompelementOf(A):
    global Ac
    dimA=A.shape                              # Dimension of
the matrix
    Ac= []    # Empty matrix with dimension of A to create
complement of A
        for i in range (0,dimA[0]):       # for rows, here 3
        H=[]
        for j in range (0,dimA[1]):  # for columns, here 2
            H.extend([ [ 1-A[i][j][0], 1-A[i][j][1], 1-A[i][j]
[2]] ])
            Ac.append(H)
    print  ('A= ', A)
    print ('***************************************************
*****************')
    print ('***************************************************
*****************')
    print('Ac= ', np.array(Ac))
```

Example 2. Evaluate the complement of matrix E in example 1.

So, the complement of single valued neutrosophic matrix E is portrayed as follow:

$$
E^c = \begin{pmatrix}
\langle.5, .3, .8\rangle & \langle.6, .6, .5\rangle & \langle.3, .3, .5\rangle & \langle.9, .5, .3\rangle \\
\langle.1, .3, .5\rangle & \langle.3, .4, .2\rangle & \langle.1, .6, .4\rangle & \langle.5, .8, .3\rangle \\
\langle.1, .6, .8\rangle & \langle.8, .8, .8\rangle & \langle.1, .5, .5\rangle & \langle.3, .5, .7\rangle \\
\langle.1, .3, .8,\rangle & \langle.7, .5, .8\rangle & \langle.5, .6, .5\rangle & \langle.8, .6, .2\rangle
\end{pmatrix}
$$

The result of the complement of single valued neutrosophic matrix E can be obtained by the call of the command SVNMCompelementOf(E):

```
>>> SVNMCompelementOf(E)
Ac=
[[[0.5 0.3 0.8] [0.6 0.6 0.5] [0.3 0.3 0.5] [0.9 0.5 0.3]]
 [[0.1 0.3 0.5] [0.3 0.4 0.2] [0.1 0.6 0.4] [0.5 0.8 0.3]]
 [[0.1 0.6 0.8] [0.8 0.8 0.8] [0.1 0.5 0.5] [0.3 0.5 0.7]]
 [[0.1 0.3 0.8] [0.7 0.5 0.8] [0.5 0.6 0.5] [0.8 0.6 0.2]]]
```

The function SVNMCompelementOf(A) the below returns the complement matrix of a given single valued neutrosophic matrix A for (10).

```
# SVNM is representable by 3D Numpy Array ====> row, column and
single valued neutrosophic numbers having 3 tuples for (10)
import numpy as np
A= np.array([  [       [0.3,0.6,1], [0.1,0.2,0.8]  ],
               [       [0.1,0.12,0], [0.5,0.33,0.58]          ],
               [       [0.11,0.22,0.6],[0.22,0.63,0.88]    ]
                        ])
#A.shape gives (3, 2, 3) the dimension of A. (row, column,
numbers of element (Single valued Neutrosophic Number,
3elements))
# A.shape[0] = 3 rows
# A.shape[1] = 2 columns
# A.shape[2] = Each single valued neutrosophic number with 3
tuple as usual

def SVNMCompelementOf(A):
    global Ac
    dimA=A.shape                          # Dimension of
the matrix
    Ac= []
    for i in range (0,dimA[0]):      # for rows, here 3
        H=[]
        for j in range (0,dimA[1]):  # for columns, here 2
            H.extend([[ A[i][j][2], 1-A[i][j][1], A[i][j][0]]
])
        Ac.append(H)
    print ('A= ', A)
    print ('****************************************************
****************')
    print ('****************************************************
```

```
****************')
   print('Ac= ', np.array(Ac))
```

The single valued neutrosophic matrix A is a simple example, one can create his/her SVNM and try it into the function **SVNMCompelementOf** ():

3.3. Determining the Score, Accuracy and Certainty Matrices of Single Valued Neutrosophic Matrix

To generate the python program for obtaining the score matrix, accuracy of single valued neutrosophic matrix, simple call of the functions **ScoreMatrix()**, **AccuracyMatrix ()** and **CertaintyMatrix ()** are defined as follow:

```
# SVNM is represented by 3D Numpy Array ====> row, column and
single valued number with 3 tuples for (7)
import numpy as np
A= np.array([ [       [0.3,0.6,1], [0.1,0.2,0.8] ],
              [       [0.1,0.12,0], [0.5,0.33,0.58]          ],
              [       [0.11,0.22,0.6],[0.22,0.63,0.88]    ]
              ])

def ScoreMatrix(A):
    score=[]
    dimA=A.shape                              # Dimension of the
matrix
    for i in range (0,dimA[0]):              # for rows, here 3
        H=[]
        for j in range (0,dimA[1]):         # for columns, here 2
            H.extend([ [ (A[i][j][0] + 1 - A[i][j][1] + 1 -
A[i][j][2])/6 ] ])
        score.append(H)
    print('Score Matrix= ', np.array(score))

def AccuracyMatrix (A):
    accuracy=[]
    dimA=A.shape                              # Dimension of the
matrix
    for i in range (0,dimA[0]):              # for rows, here 3
        H=[]
        for j in range (0,dimA[1]):         # for columns, here 2
```

```
            H.extend([ [  A[i][j][0] - A[i][j][2] + A[i][j][3]
- A[i][j][5]  ] ])
        accuracy.append(H)
    print('Accuracy Matrix= ', np.array(accuracy))
def CertaintyMatrix (A):
    certainty = []
    dimA=A.shape                        # Dimension of the
matrix
    for i in range (0,dimA[0]):         # for rows, here 3
        H=[]
        for j in range (0,dimA[1]):     # for columns, here 2
            H.extend([ [  A[i][j][0] - A[i][j][5]  ] ])
        certainty.append(H)
    print('Certainty Matrix= ', np.array(certainty))
```

3.4. Computing Union of Two Single Valued Neutrosophic Matrices

The union of two single valued neutrosophic matrices A and B is defined as follow:

$$A \cup B = C = \left[\left\langle c_{ij_T}, c_{ij_I}, c_{ij_F} \right\rangle \right]_{m \times n} \tag{11}$$

where

$$c_{ij_T} = a_{ij_T} \vee b_{ij_T}, \ c_{ij_I} = a_{ij_I} \wedge b_{ij_I}, \ c_{ij_F} = a_{ij_F} \wedge b_{ij_F}$$

To generate the python program for finding the union of two single valued neutrosophic matrices, simple call of the following function **Union(A, B)** is defined as follow:

```
# SVNM is represented by 3D Numpy Array ====> row, column and
single valued number with 3 tuples    for (11)
import numpy as np
A= np.array([ [  [0.5,0.7,0.2],  [0.4,0.4,0.5],  [0.7,0.7,0.5],
[0.1,0.5,0.7]],

             [[0.9,0.7,0.5],  [0.7,0.6,0.8],  [0.9,0.4,0.6],
[0.5,0.2,0.7]],

             [[0.9,0.4,0.2],  [0.2,0.2,0.2],  [0.9,0.5,0.5],
```

```
[0.7,0.5,0.3]],
                [[0.9,0.7,0.2], [0.3,0.5,0.2], [0.5,0.4,0.5],
[0.2,0.4,0.8]]
            ])
B= np.array([[[0.3,0.4,0.3], [0.1,0.2,0.7], [0.3,0.2,0.6],
[0.2,0.1,0.3]],
                [[0.2,0.2,0.7], [0.3,0.5,0.6], [0.6,0.5,0.4],
[0.3,0.4,0.4]],
                [[0.5,0.3,0.1], [0.5,0.4,0.3], [0.5,0.8,0.6],
[0.4,0.6,0.5]],
                [[0.6,0.1,0.7], [0.4,0.6,0.4], [0.4,0.9,0.3],
[0.4,0.5,0.4]]
            ])
#A.shape gives (3, 2, 3) the dimension of A. (row, column,
numbers of element (Single valued Neutrosophic Number, 3
elements))
# A.shape[0] = 3 rows
# A.shape[1] = 2 columns
# A.shape[2] = each single valued neutrosophic number with 3
tuple as usual
union=[]
def Union(A, B):
    if A.shape == B.shape:
        dimA=A.shape
        for i in range (0,dimA[0]):      # for rows, here 3
            H=[]
            for j in range (0,dimA[1]):  # for columns, here 2
                H.extend([[ max(A[i][j][0],B[i][j][0]),
min(A[i][j][1], B[i][j][1]), min(A[i][j][2], B[i][j][2])] ])
            union.append(H)
    print('union of two SVN-matrices= ', np.array(union))
```

Example 3. In this example we evaluate the union of the two single valued neutrosophic matrices E and F of order 4X4:

$$E=\begin{pmatrix} \langle.5,.7,.2\rangle & \langle.4,.4,.5\rangle & \langle.7,.7,.5\rangle & \langle.1,.5,.7\rangle \\ \langle.9,.7,.5\rangle & \langle.7,.6,.8\rangle & \langle.9,.4,.6\rangle & \langle.5,.2,.7\rangle \\ \langle.9,.4,.2\rangle & \langle.2,.2,.2\rangle & \langle.9,.5,.5\rangle & \langle.7,.5,.3\rangle \\ \langle.9,.7,.2\rangle & \langle.3,.5,.2\rangle & \langle.5,.4,.5\rangle & \langle.2,.4,.8\rangle \end{pmatrix}$$

The single valued neutrosophic matrix E can be inputted in Python code like this:

```
E= np.array([ [ [0.5,0.7,0.2], [0.4,0.4,0.5], [0.7,0.7,0.5],
[0.1,0.5,0.7]],
              [[0.9,0.7,0.5], [0.7,0.6,0.8], [0.9,0.4,0.6],
[0.5,0.2,0.7]],
              [[0.9,0.4,0.2], [0.2,0.2,0.2], [0.9,0.5,0.5],
[0.7,0.5,0.3]],
              [[0.9,0.7,0.2], [0.3,0.5,0.2], [0.5,0.4,0.5],
[0.2,0.4,0.8]]
          ])
```

$$
F = \begin{pmatrix}
\langle .3,.4,.3 \rangle & \langle .1,.2,.7 \rangle & \langle .3,.2,.6 \rangle & \langle .2,.1,.3 \rangle \\
\langle .2,.2,.7 \rangle & \langle .3,.5,.6 \rangle & \langle .6,.5,.4 \rangle & \langle .3,.4,.4 \rangle \\
\langle .5,.3,.1 \rangle & \langle .5,.4,.3 \rangle & \langle .5,.8,.6 \rangle & \langle .4,.6,.5 \rangle \\
\langle .6,.1,.7 \rangle & \langle .4,.6,.4 \rangle & \langle .4,.9,.3 \rangle & \langle .4,.5,.4 \rangle
\end{pmatrix}
$$

The single valued neutrosophic matrix F can be inputted in Python code like this:

```
F= np.array([[[0.3,0.4,0.3], [0.1,0.2,0.7], [0.3,0.2,0.6],
[0.2,0.1,0.3]],
              [[0.2,0.2,0.7], [0.3,0.5,0.6], [0.6,0.5,0.4],
[0.3,0.4,0.4]],
              [[0.5,0.3,0.1], [0.5,0.4,0.3], [0.5,0.8,0.6],
[0.4,0.6,0.5]],
              [[0.6,0.1,0.7], [0.4,0.6,0.4], [0.4,0.9,0.3],
[0.4,0.5,0.4]]
])
```

So, the union matrix of two single valued neutrosophic matrices is portrayed as follow

$$
E_{SVNM} \cup F_{SVNM} = \begin{pmatrix}
\langle .5, .4, .2 \rangle & \langle .4, .2, .5 \rangle & \langle .7, .2, .5 \rangle & \langle .2, .1, .3 \rangle \\
\langle .9, .2, .5 \rangle & \langle .7, .5, .6 \rangle & \langle .9, .4, .4 \rangle & \langle .5, .2, .4 \rangle \\
\langle .9, .3, .1 \rangle & \langle .5, .2, .2 \rangle & \langle .9, .5, .5 \rangle & \langle .7, .5, .3 \rangle \\
\langle .9, .1, .2 \rangle & \langle .4, .5, .2 \rangle & \langle .5, .4, .3 \rangle & \langle .4, .4, .4 \rangle
\end{pmatrix}
$$

The result of union matrix of two single valued neutrosophic matrices E and F can be obtained by the call of the command Union (E, F):

```
>>> Union(E, F)
Union of two SVN--matrices =
[[[0.5 0.4 0.2] [0.4 0.2 0.5] [0.7 0.2 0.5] [0.2 0.1 0.3]]
 [[0.9 0.2 0.5] [0.7 0.5 0.6] [0.9 0.4 0.4] [0.5 0.2 0.4]]
 [[0.9 0.3 0.1] [0.5 0.2 0.2] [0.9 0.5 0.5] [0.7 0.5 0.3]]
 [[0.9 0.1 0.2] [0.4 0.5 0.2] [0.5 0.4 0.3] [0.4 0.4 0.4]]]]
```

3.5. Computing Intersection of Two Single Valued Neutrosophic Matrices

The union of two single valued neutrosophic matrices A and B is defined as follow:

$$A \cap B = D = \left[\left\langle d_{ij_T}, d_{ij_I}, d_{ij_F} \right\rangle \right]_{m \times n} \tag{12}$$

where

$$d_{ij_T} = a_{ij_T} \wedge b_{ij_T}, \ d_{ij_I} = a_{ij_I} \vee b_{ij_I}, \ d_{ij_F} = a_{ij_F} \vee b_{ij_F}$$

To generate the Python program for finding the intersection of two single valued neutrosophic matrices, simple call of the function Intersection(,) is defined as follow:

```
# SVNM is represented by 3D Numpy Array ====> row, column and
single valued number with 3 tuples    for (12)
import numpy as np
A= np.array([ [       [0.3,0.6,1],  [0.1,0.2,0.8]   ],
              [       [0.1,0.12,0], [0.5,0.33,0.58]  ],
              [       [0.11,0.22,0.6],[0.22,0.63,0.88 ]
              ])
B= np.array([ [       [0.32,0.4,0.1],  [0.13,0.2,0.11]
],
              [       [0.17,0.19,0.66],  [0.25,0.36,0.88]
],
              [       [0.15,0.28,0.67],[0.24,0.73,0.28]   ]
              ])
#A.shape gives (3, 2, 3) the dimension of A. (row, column,
```

```
numbers of element (Single valued Neutrosophic Number, 3
elements))
# A.shape[0] = 3 rows
# A.shape[1] = 2 columns
# A.shape[2] = each single valued neutrosophic number with 3
tuple as usual
intersection=[]
def Intersection(A, B):
    if A.shape == B.shape:
        dimA=A.shape
        for i in range (0,dimA[0]):       # for rows, here 3
            H=[]
            for j in range (0,dimA[1]):  # for columns, here 2
                H.extend([[ min(A[i][j][0],B[i][j][0]),
max(A[i][j][1], B[i][j][1]), max(A[i][j][2], B[i][j][2]) ] ])
                intersection.append(H)
    print('intersection of two SVN-matrices= ',
np.array(intersection))
```

Example 4. In this example we evaluate the intersection of the two single valued neutrosophic matrices E and F of order 4X4 presented in example 3:

So, the intersection matrix of two single valued neutrosophic matrices is portrayed as follow

$$
E_{SVNM} \cap F_{SVNM} = \begin{pmatrix} \langle .3, .7, .3 \rangle & \langle .1, .4, .7 \rangle & \langle .3, .7, .6 \rangle & \langle .1, .5, .7 \rangle \\ \langle .2, .7, .7 \rangle & \langle .3, .6, .8 \rangle & \langle .6, .5, .6 \rangle & \langle .3, .4, .7 \rangle \\ \langle .5, .4, .2 \rangle & \langle .2, .4, .3 \rangle & \langle .5, .8, .6 \rangle & \langle .4, .6, .5 \rangle \\ \langle .6, .7, .7 \rangle & \langle .3, .6, .4 \rangle & \langle .4, .9, .5 \rangle & \langle .2, .5, .8 \rangle \end{pmatrix}
$$

The result of intersection matrix of two single valued neutrosophic matrices E and F can be obtained by the call of the command Intersection (E, F):

```
>>> Intersection (E, F)
intersection of two SVN-matrices=
[[[ 0.3   0.7   0.3] [ 0.1   0.4   0.7] [ 0.3   0.7   0.6] [ 0.1   0.5
0.7]]
  [[ 0.2   0.7   0.7] [ 0.3   0.6   0.8] [ 0.6   0.5   0.6] [ 0.3   0.4
```

```
0.7]]
 [[ 0.5   0.4   0.2]  [ 0.2   0.4   0.3]  [ 0.5   0.8   0.6]  [ 0.4   0.6
0.5]]
 [[ 0.6   0.7   0.7]  [ 0.3   0.6   0.4]  [ 0.4   0.9   0.5]  [ 0.2   0.5
0.8]]]
```

3.6. Computing Addition Operation of Two Single Valued Neutrosophic Matrices

The addition of two single valued neutrosophic matrices A and B is defined as follow:

$$A \oplus B = S = \left[\left\langle s_{ij_T}, s_{ij_I}, s_{ij_F} \right\rangle \right]_{m \times n} \tag{13}$$

where

$$s_{ij_T} = a_{ij_T} + b_{ij_T} - a_{ij_T}.b_{ij_T}, \quad s_{ij_I} = a_{ij_I}.b_{ij_I}, \quad s_{ij_F} = a_{ij_F}.b_{ij_F}$$

To generate the python program for obtaining the addition of two single valued neutrosophic matrices, simple call of the function **Addition (A, B)** is defined as follow:

```
# SVNM is represented by 3D Numpy Array ====> row, column and
single valued number with 3 tuples for (13)
import numpy as np
A= np.array([  [       [0.3,0.6,1],  [0.1,0.2,0.8]],
               [       [0.1,0.12,0], [0.5,0.33,0.58]],
            [          [0.11,0.22,0.6],[0.22,0.63,0.88]]
               ])
B= np.array([  [  [0.32,0.4,0.1],  [0.13,0.2,0.11] ],
               [  [0.17,0.19,0.66], [0.25,0.36,0.88]],
               [  [0.15,0.28,0.67],[0.24,0.73,0.28] ]
               ])
#A.shape gives (3, 2, 3) the dimension of A. (row, column,
numbers of element (Single valued Neutrosophic Number, 3
elements))
# A.shape[0] = 3 rows
# A.shape[1] = 2 columns
# A.shape[2] = each single valued neutrosophic number with 3
```

```
tuple as usual
addition=[]
def Addition(A, B):
    if A.shape == B.shape:
        dimA=A.shape
        for i in range (0,dimA[0]):       # for rows, here 3
            H=[]
            for j in range (0,dimA[1]):  # for columns, here 2
                H.extend([[    A[i][j][0]+B[i][j][0]-A[i][j]
[0]*B[i][j][0],    A[i][j][1]* B[i][j][1],    A[i][j][2]* B[i][j]
[2]    ]])
            addition.append(H)
    print('addition= ', np.array(addition))
```

Example 5. In this example we evaluate the addition of the two single valued neutrosophic matrices E and F of order 4X4 presented in example 3:

So, the addition matrix of two single valued neutrosophic matrices is portrayed as follow

$$
C_{SVNM} \oplus D_{SVNM} = \begin{pmatrix}
\langle .65, .28, .06 \rangle & \langle .46, .08, .35 \rangle & \langle .79, .14, .30 \rangle & \langle .28, .05, .21 \rangle \\
\langle .92, .14, .35 \rangle & \langle .79, .30, .48 \rangle & \langle .96, .20, .24 \rangle & \langle .65, .08, .28 \rangle \\
\langle .65, .12, .02 \rangle & \langle .60, .08, .06 \rangle & \langle .95, .40, .30 \rangle & \langle .82, .30, .15 \rangle \\
\langle .96, .07, .14 \rangle & \langle .58, .30, .08 \rangle & \langle .70, .36, .15 \rangle & \langle .52, .20, .3 \rangle
\end{pmatrix}
$$

The result of addition matrix of two single valued neutrosophic matrices E and F can be obtained by the call of the command addition (E, F):

```
>>> Addition(C, D)
addition=
[[[ 0.65   0.28   0.06] [ 0.46   0.08   0.35] [ 0.79   0.14   0.3] [
0.28   0.05   0.21]]
 [[ 0.92   0.14   0.35] [ 0.79   0.3    0.48] [ 0.96   0.2    0.24] [
0.65   0.08   0.28]]
 [[ 0.95   0.12   0.02] [ 0.6    0.08   0.06] [ 0.95   0.4    0.3 ] [
0.82   0.3    0.15 ]]
 [[ 0.96   0.07   0.14] [ 0.58   0.3    0.08] [ 0.7    0.36   0.15] [
0.52   0.2    0.32]]]
```

3.7. Computing Product of Two Single Valued Neutrosophic Matrices

The product of two single valued neutrosophic matrices A and B is defined as follow:

$$A \odot B = R = \left[\left\langle r_{ij_T}, r_{ij_I}, r_{ij_F} \right\rangle \right]_{m \times n} \tag{14}$$

where

$$r_{ij_T} = a_{ij_T}.b_{ij_T}, \quad r_{ij_I} = a_{ij_I} + b_{ij_I} - a_{ij_I}.b_{ij_I}, \quad r_{ij_F} = a_{ij_F} + b_{ij_F} - a_{ij_F}.b_{ij_F}$$

To generate the python program for finding the product operation of two single valued neutrosophic matrices, simple call of the function **Product (A, B)** is defined as follow:

```
# SVNM is represented by 3D Numpy Array ====> row, column and
single valued number with 3 tuples    for (14)
import numpy as np
A= np.array([  [       [0.3,0.6,1],  [0.1,0.2,0.8]  ],
               [       [0.1,0.12,0], [0.5,0.33,0.58] ],
               [       [0.11,0.22,0.6],[0.22,0.63,0.88]  ]
            ])
B= np.array([  [       [0.32,0.4,0.1],  [0.13,0.2,0.11]  ],
               [       [0.17,0.19,0.66], [0.25,0.36,0.88]  ],
               [       [0.15,0.28,0.67],[0.24,0.73,0.28]   ]
            ])
#A.shape gives (3, 2, 3) the dimension of A. (row, column,
numbers of element (Single valued Neutrosophic Number, 3
elements))
# A.shape[0] = 3 rows
# A.shape[1] = 2 columns
# A.shape[2] = each single valued neutrosophic number with 3
tuple as usual
product=[]
def Product(A, B):
    if A.shape == B.shape:
        dimA=A.shape
        for i in range (0,dimA[0]):      # for rows, here 3
```

```
            H=[]
            for j in range (0,dimA[1]):  # for columns, here 2
                H.extend([[ A[i][j][0]*B[i][j][0]), A[i][j][1]+
B[i][j][1]- (A[i][j][1]*B[i][j][1]), A[i][j][2]+ B[i][j][2]-
(A[i][j][2]*B[i][j][2])] ])
            product.append(H)
    print(' Product = ', np.array(product))
```

Example 6. In this example we evaluate the product of the two single valued neutrosophic matrices E and F of order 4X4 presented in example 3:

So, the product matrix of two single valued neutrosophic matrices is portrayed as follow

$$
E_{SVNM} \odot F_{SVNM} = \begin{pmatrix}
\langle .15, .82, .44 \rangle & \langle .04, .52, .85 \rangle & \langle .21, .76, .80 \rangle & \langle .02, .55, .79 \rangle \\
\langle .18, .76, .85 \rangle & \langle .21, .80, .92 \rangle & \langle .54, .70, .76 \rangle & \langle .15, .52, .82 \rangle \\
\langle .45, .58, .28 \rangle & \langle .10, .52, .44 \rangle & \langle .45, .90, .80 \rangle & \langle .28, .80, .65 \rangle \\
\langle .54, .73, .76 \rangle & \langle .12, .80, .52 \rangle & \langle .20, .94, .65 \rangle & \langle .08, .70, .88 \rangle
\end{pmatrix}
$$

The result of product matrix of two single valued neutrosophic matrices E and F can be obtained by the call of the command Product (E, F):

```
>>> Product(E, F)
Product=
[[[ 0.15  0.82  0.44] [ 0.04  0.52  0.85] [ 0.21  0.76  0.8 ]
 [ 0.02  0.55  0.79]]
  [[ 0.18  0.76  0.85] [ 0.21  0.8   0.92] [ 0.54  0.7   0.76] [
0.15  0.52  0.82]]
  [[ 0.45  0.58  0.28] [ 0.1   0.52  0.44] [ 0.45  0.9   0.8 ]
 [ 0.28  0.8   0.65]]
  [[ 0.54  0.73  0.76] [ 0.12  0.8   0.52] [ 0.2   0.94  0.65] [
0.08  0.7   0.88]]]
```

3.8. Computing Transpose of Single Valued Neutrosophic Matrix

To generate the Python program for finding the transpose of single valued neutrosophic matrix, simple call of the function **Transpose(A)** is defined as follow:

```
# SVNM is represented by 3D Numpy Array ====> row, column and
single valued number with 6 tuples for transpose
import numpy as np
A=np.array([[ [0.3,0.6,1], [0.1,0.2,0.8] ],
             [ [0.1,0.12,0],[0.5,0.33,0.58]],
             [ [0.11,0.22,0.6],[0.22,0.63,0.88]] ])
#A.shape gives (3, 2, 3) the dimension of A. (row, column,
numbers of element (Single valued Neutrosophic Number, 3
elements))
# A.shape[0] = 3 rows
# A.shape[1] = 2 columns
# A.shape[2] = each single valued neutrosophic number with 6
tuple as usual
def Transpose(A):
    DimA= A. shape
    print (' the matrix ', DimA[0],' x ', DimA[1], '
dimension')
    trA = A.transpose()
    DimtrA= trA. shape
    print ('\n')
    print (' its transpose ', DimtrA[1],' x ', DimtrA[2], '
dimension')
    print ('\n')
    print(' transpose = ', trA)
```

Example 7. In this example we evaluate the transpose of the single valued neutrosophic matrix E of order 4X4:

$$
C=\begin{pmatrix}
\langle.5,.7,.2\rangle & \langle.4,.4,.5\rangle & \langle.7,.7,.5\rangle & \langle.1,.5,.7\rangle \\
\langle.9,.7,.5\rangle & \langle.7,.6,.8\rangle & \langle.9,.4,.6\rangle & \langle.5,.2,.7\rangle \\
\langle.9,.4,.2\rangle & \langle.2,.2,.2\rangle & \langle.9,.5,.5\rangle & \langle.7,.5,.3\rangle \\
\langle.9,.7,.2\rangle & \langle.3,.5,.2\rangle & \langle.5,.4,.5\rangle & \langle.2,.4,.8\rangle
\end{pmatrix}
$$

So, the transpose matrix of single valued neutrosophic matrices is portrayed as follow

$$
C^T = \begin{vmatrix}
\langle .5, .7, .2 \rangle & \langle .9, .7, .5 \rangle & \langle .9, .4, .2 \rangle & \langle .9, .7, .2 \rangle \\
\langle .4, .4, .5 \rangle & \langle .7, .6, .8 \rangle & \langle .2, .2, .2 \rangle & \langle .3, .5, .2 \rangle \\
\langle .7, .7, .5 \rangle & \langle .9, .4, .6 \rangle & \langle .9, .5, .5 \rangle & \langle .5, .4, .5 \rangle \\
\langle .1, .5, .7 \rangle & \langle .5, .2, .7 \rangle & \langle .7, .5, .3 \rangle & \langle .2, .4, .8 \rangle
\end{vmatrix}
$$

3.9 Computing Composition of Two Single Valued Neutrosophic Matrices

To generate the python program for finding the composition of two single valued neutrosophic matrices, simple call of the function **Composition (,)** is defined as follow:

```
# SVNM is represented by 3D Numpy Array => row, column and
single valued number with 3 tuples for Composition
#A.shape and B.shape returns (3, 3, 3) the dimension of A.
(row, column, numbers of element (Single valued Neutrosophic
Number, 3 elements))
# A.shape[0] = 3 rows
# A.shape[1] = 3 columns
# A.shape[2] = Each single valued neutrosophic number has 3
tuple as usual
#One can use matrices with any dimensions but dimensions of two
matrices must be the same and nxn
import math
import numpy as np
A= np.array([    [ [0.3, 0.6, 1], [0.1, 0.2, 0.8],
[0.020,0.021,0.022]  ],
                 [ [0.17,0.19,0.66], [0.25,0.36,0.88],
[0.120,0.121,0.122]  ],
                 [ [0.15,0.28,0.67], [0.24,0.73,0.28],
[0.220,0.221,0.222]  ]          ])
B= np.array([    [ [0.11,0.22,0.6], [0.32,0.4,0.1],
[0.13,0.2,0.11]  ],
                 [ [0.100,0.101,0.102], [1,0.111,0.112],
[0.720,0.821,0.152]  ],
                 [ [0,0.73,0.202], [0.22,0.63,0.88],
[0.3,0,0.47]  ]          ])
def Composition(A, B):
```

```
global composition
composition=[]
dimA = A.shape
H=[ ]
if A.shape == B.shape and dimA[0] == dimA[1]:
    for i in range (0,dimA[0]):
        for j in range (0,dimA[0]):
            counter0=0
            for d in range (0, dimA[0]):
                if counter0 ==0:
                    maxtt =     [ A[i][d][0],B[d][j][0] ]
                    maxT = min(maxtt)
                    minii =   [A[i][d][1],B[d][j][1] ]
                    minI =  max(minii)
                    minff = [ A[i][d][2],B[d][j][2]    ]
                    minF = max(minff)
                    counter0  = 1
                else:
                    maxT1        = [  A[i][d][0],B[d][j][0]
]
                    maxT11     = min(maxT1)
                    maxT112   = [  maxT11,  maxT  ]
                    maxT         = max(maxT112)
                    minI1      =  [ A[i][d][1],B[d][j][1]
]
                    minI11    =  max(minI1)
                    minI112  = [ minI11, minI    ]
                    minI        = min(minI112)
                    minF1        =   [ A[i][d][2],B[d][j]
[2]  ]
                    minF11      =  max(minF1)
                    minF112    = [ minF11, minF]
                    minF        = min(minF112)
            H.append([maxT,  minI, minF])
    composition.extend(H)
global nested
nested = [  ]
for k in range(int(math.sqrt(len(composition)))):
            nested.append( composition[k:k+int(math.
sqrt(len(composition))) ]   )
```

```
print('Composition of two SVN-matrices= ',
np.array(nested))
```

Example 8. In this example we evaluate the composition of the two single valued neutrosophic matrices C and D of order 4X4:

So, the composition matrix of two single valued neutrosophic matrices is portrayed as follow

$$E_{SVNM} \odot F_{SVNM} = \begin{vmatrix} \langle.5, .4, .3\rangle & \langle.5, .5, .5\rangle & \langle.5, .5, .5\rangle & \langle.4, .4, .3\rangle \\ \langle.5, .5, .5\rangle & \langle.5, .5 .5\rangle & \langle.4, .4, .3\rangle & \langle.5, .2, .5\rangle \\ \langle.5 .5, .5\rangle & \langle.4, .4, .4\rangle & \langle.5, .2, .5\rangle & \langle.5, .4, .6\rangle \\ \langle.4, .4, .3\rangle & \langle.5, .2, .5\rangle & \langle.5, .4, .6\rangle & \langle.6, .6, .6\rangle \end{vmatrix}$$

The result of composition t matrix of two single valued neutrosophic matrices E and F can be obtained by the call of the command Composition (E, F):

```
>>> Composition (E, F)
Composition of two SVN-matrices=
[[[ 0.5   0.4   0.3]  [ 0.5   0.5   0.5 4]  [ 0.5   0.5   0.5]  [ 0.4
0.4   0.3]]
[[ 0.5   0.5   0.5]  [ 0.5   0.5   0.5]  [ 0.4   0.4   0.3]  [ 0.5   0.2
0.5]]
  [[ 0.5   0.5   0.5]  [ 0.4   0.4   0.3]  [ 0.5   0.2   0.5]  [ 0.5   0.4
0.6]]
  [[ 0.4   0.4   0.3]  [ 0.5   0.2   0.5]  [ 0.5   0.4   0.6]  [ 0.6   0.6
0.6]]]
```

4. COMPUTING THE INTERVAL VALUED NEUTROSOPHIC MATRIX OPERATIONS USING PYTHON LANGUAGE

4.1 Checking the Matrix Is IVNM or Not

To generate the Python program for inputting the interval valued neutrosophic matrices. The procedure is described as follows:

```
import numpy as np
def INMChecking (A):
    dimA=A.shape
    control=0
    counter = 0
    for i in range (0,dimA[0]):
        if counter == 1:
            break
        for j in range (0,dimA[1]):
            if counter == 1:
                break
            for  k in range (0, dimA[2]):
                for  m in range (0, dimA[3]):
                    if  counter ==0:
                        if  not (0 <=  A[i][j][k][m] <= 1
and    A[i][j][k][0] <= A[i][j][k][1] ):
                            counter=1
                            print (A[i][j], ' is not an
interval neutrosophic number, so the matrix is not a INM')
                            control=1
                            break
    if control==0:
        print ('The matrix is a INM')
```

Example 9. Suppose the following interval valued neutrosophic matrix E:

$$
E=\begin{pmatrix}
\langle[.1,.5],[.3,.4],[.2,.5]\rangle & \langle[.3,.4],[.2,.6],[.2,.4]\rangle \\
\langle[.2,.3],[.1,.3],[.4,.7]\rangle & \langle[.1,.7],[.3,.4],[.5,.6]\rangle \\
\langle[.4,.5],[.2,.3],[.1,.3]\rangle & \langle[.5,.8],[.1,.2],[.4,.7]\rangle \\
\langle[.5,.6],[.3,.4],[.4,.5]\rangle & \langle[.2,.5],[.4,.6],[.3,.8]\rangle
\end{pmatrix}
$$

The matrix E is inputted in Python environment (like Thonny) and by calling the function INMChecking (E) we get the result shown in Figure 2.

Figure 2.

```
Thonny - C:\Users\HP\Desktop\broumi\Interval Python by Broumi\INM Checking.py  @ 39 : 1
File  Edit  View  Run  Device  Tools  Help
                                                              Program arguments:
<untitled>    INM Checking.py
   1   import numpy as np
   2
   3   def INMChecking (A):
   4       dimA=A.shape
   5       control=0
   6       counter = 0
   7       for i in range (0,dimA[0]):
   8           if counter == 1:
   9               break
  10           for j in range (0 dimA[1]):
Shell   AST
Python 3.7.2 (bundled)
>>> %cd 'C:\Users\HP\Desktop\broumi\Interval Python by Broumi'
>>> %Run 'INM Checking.py'
>>> E= np.array( [
    [ [  [ 0.1, 0.5], [0.3, 0.4], [ 0.2, 0.5] ], [ [ 0.3, 0.4], [0.2, 0.6], [ 0.2, 0.4]  ]],
    [ [ [ 0.2, 0.3], [0.1, 0.3], [ 0.4, 0.7] ],[  [ 0.1, 0.7], [0.3, 0.4], [ 0.5, 0.6]]],

    [ [ [ 0.4, 0.5], [0.2, 0.3], [ 0.1, 0.3]], [ [ 0.5, 0.8], [0.1, 0.2], [ 0.4, 0.7 ]]],
    [ [ [ 0.5, 0.6], [0.3, 0.4], [ 0.4, 0.5 ]],[  [ 0.2, 0.5], [0.4, 0.6], [ 0.3, 0.8]]] )
>>> INMChecking (E)
  The matrix is a INM
>>> |
```

Example 10. Suppose the non- interval valued neutrosophic matrix E:

$$
E=\begin{pmatrix}
\langle[.5,.1],[.3,.4],[.2,.5]\rangle & \langle[.3,.4],[.2,.6],[.2,.4]\rangle \\
\langle[.2,.3],[.1,.3],[.4,.7]\rangle & \langle[.1,.7],[.3,.4],[.5,.6]\rangle \\
\langle[.4,.5],[.2,.3],[.1,.3]\rangle & \langle[.5,.8],[.1,.2],[.4,.7]\rangle \\
\langle[.5,.6],[.3,.4],[.4,.5]\rangle & \langle[.2,.5],[.4,.6],[.3,.8]\rangle
\end{pmatrix}
$$

The matrix E is inputted in python environment (like Thonny) and by calling the function INMChecking (E) we get the result shown in Figure 3.

Figure 3.

```
Shell   AST
>>> INMChecking (A)
  The matrix is a INM
>>> E= np.array( [  [ [  [ 0.5, 0.1], [0.3, 0.4], [ 0.2, 0.5] ], [ [ 0.3, 0.4], [0.2, 0.6], [ 0.2, 0.4] ]],
    [ [ [ 0.2, 0.3], [0.1, 0.3], [ 0.4, 0.7] ],[  [ 0.1, 0.7], [0.3, 0.4], [ 0.5, 0.6]]],
    [ [ [ 0.4, 0.5], [0.2, 0.3], [ 0.1, 0.3]], [ [ 0.5, 0.8], [0.1, 0.2], [ 0.4, 0.7 ]]],
    [ [ [ 0.5, 0.6], [0.3, 0.4], [ 0.4, 0.5 ]],[  [ 0.2, 0.5], [0.4, 0.6], [ 0.3, 0.8]]] )
>>> INMChecking (E)
  [[0.5 0.1]
   [0.3 0.4]
   [0.2 0.5]]  is not an interval neutrosophic number, so the matrix is not a INM
>>>
```

4.2. Determining Complement of an Interval-Valued Neutrosophic Matrix

The complement of an interval-valued neutrosophic is defined as follow:

$$A^c = \left[\left\langle [a^L_{ij_F}, a^U_{ij_F}], [1 - a^U_{ij_I}, 1 - a^L_{ij_I}], [a^L_{ij_T}, a^U_{ij_T}] \right\rangle \right]_{m \times n} \tag{15}$$

To generate the Python program for finding complement of an interval-valued neutrosophic matrix, simple call of the function named "Complement()" is defined as follow:

```
import numpy as np
#A.shape returns (1, 3, 3, 2)   1 row,  3 columns, and triple
interval values
A=  np.array ([ [ [  [ 0.1, 0.2], [0.3, 0.4], [ 0.5, 0.6]  ],
[  [ 0.4, 0.45], [0.5, 0.53], [ 0.6, 0.66]  ], [  [ 0.7, 0.75],
[0, 1], [ 0.9, 0.98]  ] ]])
#B.shape returns  (3, 3, 3, 2)   3 rows,  3 columns, and triple
interval values
B=  np.array([ [ [  [ 0.1, 0.23], [0.3, 0.45], [ 0.45, 0.6]
], [  [ 0.45, 0.45], [0.5, 0.53], [ 0.6, 0.66]  ], [  [ 0.7,
0.75], [0, 1], [ 0.9, 0.98]  ] ], [ [   [ 0.121, 0.112], [0.22,
0.233], [ 0.331, 0.333]  ], [  [ 0.44, 0.444], [0.55, 0.565], [
0.667, 0.669] ],  [  [ 0.757, 0.778], [0.818, 0.89], [ 0.99,
0.9999]  ]  ], [  [    [ 0, 0.18], [0.213, 0.234], [ 0.34,
0.345]   ], [   [ 0.453, 0.458], [0.56, 0.569], [ 0.637,
0.677]   ], [   [ 0.758, 0.80], [0.879, 0.959], [0.5, 1]  ]
]  ])
def Complement(A):
    global Ac
    dimA=A.shape
    Ac= []
    H=[]
    for i in range (0,dimA[0]):
        H=[]
        for j in range (0,dimA[1]):
            H.extend([  [ A[i][j][2][0],  A[i][j][2][1]  ],
[ 1-A[i][j][1][1],  1-A[i][j][1][0] ],  [  A[i][j][0][0], A[i]
[j][0][1]  ]]  )
```

```
      Ac.append(H)
  print  ('The matrix=  ', A)
  print(' Complement of IVN-matrix t=  ', np.array(Ac))
```

Example 11. Generate the complement of the following the interval valued
neutrosophic matrix E presented in example 9:

So the complement of interval neutrosophic matrix E is

$$
\begin{pmatrix}
\langle [.2,.5],[.6,.7],[.1,.5]\rangle & \langle [.2,.4],[.4,.8],[.3,.4]\rangle \\
\langle [.4,.7],[.7,.9],[.2,.3]\rangle & \langle [.5,.6],[.6,.7],[.1,.7]\rangle \\
\langle [.1,.3],[.7,.8],[.4,.5]\rangle & \langle [.4,.7],[.8,.9],[.5,.8]\rangle \\
\langle [.4,.5],[.6,.7],[.5,.6]\rangle & \langle [.3,.8],[.4,.6],[.2,.5]\rangle
\end{pmatrix}
$$

By calling the function **INMComplementOf(E), we** get the following result:

```
>>> Complement of IVN-matrix=
[[[0.2 0.5]  [0.6 0.7]  [0.1 0.5]  [0.2 0.4]  [0.4 0.8]  [0.3 0.4]]
[[0.4 0.7]  [0.7 0.9]  [0.2 0.3]  [0.5 0.6]  [0.6 0.7]  [0.1 0.7]]
[[0.1 0.3]  [0.7 0.8]  [0.4 0.5]  [0.4 0.7]  [0.8 0.9]  [0.5 0.8]]
 [[0.4 0.5]  [0.6 0.7]  [0.5 0.6]  [0.3 0.8]  [0.4 0.6]  [0.2 0.5]]]
```

4.3. Determining the Score Matrix of an Interval-Valued Neutrosophic Matrix

To generate the Python program for obtaining the score matrix of an interval-valued
neutrosophic matrix, simple call of the function named "ScoreFunction" is defined
as follow:

```
import numpy as np
#A.shape returns (1, 3, 3, 2)   1 row,  3 columns, and triple
interval values
A=   np.array ([ [ [  [ 0.1, 0.2], [0.3, 0.4], [ 0.5, 0.6]  ],
[  [ 0.4, 0.45], [0.5, 0.53], [ 0.6, 0.66]  ], [  [ 0.7, 0.75],
[0, 1], [ 0.9, 0.98]  ]]])
#B.shape returns  (3, 3, 3, 2)   3 rows,  3 columns, and triple
interval values
B= np.array([  [     [  [ 0.1, 0.23], [0.3, 0.45], [
```

```
0.45, 0.6]  ],            [  [ 0.45, 0.45], [0.5, 0.53], [
0.6, 0.66]  ], [  [ 0.7, 0.75], [0, 1], [ 0.9, 0.98]  ]
],[ [ [ 0.121, 0.112], [0.22, 0.233], [ 0.331, 0.333]
],            [  [ 0.44, 0.444], [0.55, 0.565], [ 0.667, 0.669]
], [  [ 0.757, 0.778], [0.818, 0.89], [ 0.99, 0.9999] ]],[ [ [
0, 0.18], [0.213, 0.234], [ 0.34, 0.345]], [ [ 0.453, 0.458],
[0.56, 0.569], [ 0.637, 0.677]], [ [ 0.758, 0.80], [0.879,
0.959], [0.5, 1]]]])
def ScoreFunction(A):
    global Sco
    dimA=A.shape
    Sco= []
    H=[]
    for i in range (0,dimA[0]):
        H=[]
        for j in range (0,dimA[1]):
            H.extend([ [ (4+A[i][j][0][0]+A[i][j][0][1] - (A[i]
[j][1][0] + A[i][j][1][1] +A[i][j][2][0]  + A[i][j][2][1])) /
6  ]])
        Sco.append(H)
    print  ('The matrix= ', A)
    print('Score Matrix= ', np.array(Sco))
```

Example 12. Generate the score matrix of the following the interval valued neutrosophic matrix E presented in example 9:

The score function of matrix E by calling **ScoreFunction(A)** is as follow:

```
Score Matrix = [[[0.53333333] [0.55]]
[[0.5] [0.5]]
[[0.66666667] [0.65]]
[[0.58333333] [0.43333333]]]]
```

Remark 1: the value of score of interval valued neutrosophic matrix is the same as obtained

4.4. Computing Union of Two Interval-Valued Neutrosophic Matrices

The union of two interval valued neutrosophic matrices A and is defined as follow:

$$A \cup B = C = \left[\left\langle [c_{ij_T}^L, c_{ij_T}^U], [c_{ij_I}^L, c_{ij_I}^U], [c_{ij_F}^L, c_{ij_F}^U] \right\rangle \right]_{m \times n} \tag{16}$$

where

$$
\begin{aligned}
c_{ij_T}^L &= a_{ij_T}^L \vee b_{ij_T}^L, & c_{ij_T}^U &= a_{ij_T}^U \vee b_{ij_T}^U \\
c_{ij_I}^L &= a_{ij_I}^L \wedge b_{ij_I}^L, & c_{ij_I}^U &= a_{ij_I}^U \wedge b_{ij_I}^U \\
c_{ij_F}^L &= a_{ij_F}^L \wedge b_{ij_F}^L, & c_{ij_F}^U &= a_{ij_F}^U \wedge b_{ij_F}^U
\end{aligned}
$$

To generate the Python program for finding the union of two interval valued neutrosophic matrices, simple call of the following function named "Union (,)" is defined as follow:

```
import numpy as np
A= np.array([
[ [ [ 0.1, 0.5], [0.3, 0.4], [ 0.2, 0.5] ], [ [ 0.3, 0.4],
[0.2, 0.6], [ 0.2, 0.4] ]],
[ [ [ 0.2, 0.3], [0.1, 0.3], [ 0.4, 0.7] ],[ [ 0.1, 0.7],
[0.3, 0.4], [ 0.5, 0.6]]],
[ [ [ 0.4, 0.5], [0.2, 0.3], [ 0.1, 0.3]], [ [ 0.5, 0.8], [0.1,
0.2], [ 0.4, 0.7 ]]],
[ [ [ 0.5, 0.6], [0.3, 0.4], [ 0.4, 0.5] ],[ [ 0.2, 0.5],
[0.4, 0.6], [ 0.3, 0.8]]]])
B= np.array([
[ [ [ 0.3, 0.4], [0.2, 0.6], [ 0.1, 0.3] ], [ [ 0.4, 0.6],
[0.3, 0.4], [ 0.3, 0.5] ]],
[ [ [ 0.4, 0.7], [0.2, 0.6], [ 0.4, 0.5] ],[ [ 0.2, 0.3],
[0.3, 0.4], [ 0.4, 0.7]]],
[ [ [ 0.1, 0.3], [0.2, 0.4], [ 0.2, 0.3]], [ [ 0.2, 0.6], [0.3,
0.5], [ 0.3, 0.6 ]]],
[ [ [ 0.3, 0.4], [0.2, 0.3], [ 0.3, 0.5] ],[ [ 0.1, 0.2],
[0.1, 0.4], [ 0.2, 0.6]]]])
def Union(A,B):
    if A.shape == B.shape:
        global union
        dimA=A.shape
        union= []
        H=[]
```

```
for i in range (0,dimA[0]):
    H=[]
    for j in range (0,dimA[1]):
        H.extend([  [ [ max(A[i][j][0][0],    B[i][j][0]
[0]), max(A[i][j][0][1],   B[i][j][0][1]) ],[ min(A[i][j][1]
[0],    B[i][j][1][0]), min(A[i][j][1][1],   B[i][j][1][1])], [
min(A[i][j][2][0], B[i][j][2][0]), min(A[i][j][2][1], B[i][j]
[2][1])  ]  ] ])
        union.append(H)
print('Union= ', np.array(union))
```

The union of two interval valued neutrosophic matrices is depicted as follow:

$$
A \cup B = \begin{pmatrix}
\left\langle [.3,\ .5],[.2,.4],[.1,.3] \right\rangle & \left\langle [.4,\ .6],[.2,.4],[.2,.4] \right\rangle \\
\left\langle [.4,\ .7],[.1,.3],[.4,.5] \right\rangle & \left\langle [.2,\ .7],[.3,.4],[.4,.6] \right\rangle \\
\left\langle [.4,\ .5],[.2,.3],[.1,.3] \right\rangle & \left\langle [.5,\ .8],[.1,.2],[.3,.6] \right\rangle \\
\left\langle [.5,\ .6],[.2,.3],[.3,.5] \right\rangle & \left\langle [.2,\ .5],[.1,.4],[.2,.6] \right\rangle
\end{pmatrix}
$$

4.5. Computing Intersection of Two Interval-Valued Neutrosophic Matrices

The union of two interval valued neutrosophic matrices A and B is defined as follow:

$$
A \cap B = D = \left[< [d_{ij_T}^L, d_{ij_T}^U], [d_{ij_I}^L, d_{ij_I}^U], [d_{ij_F}^L, d_{ij_F}^U] > \right]_{m \times n} \tag{17}
$$

where

$$
\begin{aligned}
d_{ij_T}^L &= a_{ij_T}^L \vee b_{ij_T}^L, \ d_{ij_T}^U = a_{ij_T}^U \vee b_{ij_T}^U \\
d_{ij_I}^L &= a_{ij_I}^L \wedge b_{ij_I}^L, \ d_{ij_I}^U = a_{ij_I}^U \wedge b_{ij_I}^U \\
d_{ij_F}^L &= a_{ij_F}^L \wedge b_{ij_F}^L, \ d_{ij_F}^U = a_{ij_F}^U \wedge b_{ij_F}^U
\end{aligned}
$$

To generate the Python program for finding the intersection of two interval-valued neutrosophic matrices, simple call of the function named "Intersection" is defined as follow:

```
import numpy as np
A= np.array([
[ [ [ 0.1, 0.5], [0.3, 0.4], [ 0.2, 0.5] ], [ [ 0.3, 0.4],
[0.2, 0.6], [ 0.2, 0.4] ]],
[ [ [ 0.2, 0.3], [0.1, 0.3], [ 0.4, 0.7] ],[ [ 0.1, 0.7],
[0.3, 0.4], [ 0.5, 0.6]]],
[ [ [ 0.4, 0.5], [0.2, 0.3], [ 0.1, 0.3]], [ [ 0.5, 0.8], [0.1,
0.2], [ 0.4, 0.7 ]]],
[ [ [ 0.5, 0.6], [0.3, 0.4], [ 0.4, 0.5] ],[ [ 0.2, 0.5],
[0.4, 0.6], [ 0.3, 0.8]]]])
 B= np.array([
[ [ [ 0.3, 0.4], [0.2, 0.6], [ 0.1, 0.3] ], [ [ 0.4, 0.6],
[0.3, 0.4], [ 0.3, 0.5] ]],
[ [ [ 0.4, 0.7], [0.2, 0.6], [ 0.4, 0.5] ],[ [ 0.2, 0.3],
[0.3, 0.4], [ 0.4, 0.7]]],
[ [ [ 0.1, 0.3], [0.2, 0.4], [ 0.2, 0.3]], [ [ 0.2, 0.6], [0.3,
0.5], [ 0.3, 0.6 ]]],
[ [ [ 0.3, 0.4], [0.2, 0.3], [ 0.3, 0.5] ],[ [ 0.1, 0.2],
[0.1, 0.4], [ 0.2, 0.6]]]])
def Intersection(A,B):
    if A.shape == B.shape:
        global intersection
        dimA=A.shape
        intersection= []
        H=[]
        for i in range (0,dimA[0]):
            H=[]
            for j in range (0,dimA[1]):
                H.extend([ [    [ min(A[i][j][0][0],   B[i][j]
[0][0]), min(A[i][j][0][1],   B[i][j][0][1]) ],[ max(A[i][j]
[1][0],B[i][j][1][0]), max(A[i][j][1][1],B[i][j][1][1]) ], [
max(A[i][j][2][0], B[i][j][2][0]),  max(A[i][j][2][1],  B[i][j]
[2][1]) ]  ] ] )
            intersection.append(H)
        print('Intersection= ', np.array(intersection))
```

The intersection of two interval valued neutrosophic matrices is depicted as follow:

$$A \cap B = \begin{pmatrix} \left\langle [.1, \ .4], [.3, .6], [.2, .5] \right\rangle & \left\langle [.3, \ .4], [.3, .6], [.3, .5] \right\rangle \\ \left\langle [.2, \ .3], [.2, .6], [.4, .7] \right\rangle & \left\langle [.1, \ .3], [.3, .4], [.5, .7] \right\rangle \\ \left\langle [.1, \ .3], [.2, .4], [.2, .3] \right\rangle & \left\langle [.2, \ .6], [.3, .5], [.4, .7] \right\rangle \\ \left\langle [.3, \ .4], [.3, .4], [.4, .5] \right\rangle & \left\langle [.1, \ .2], [.4, .6], [.3, .8] \right\rangle \end{pmatrix}$$

4.6 Computing Power of an Interval-Valued Neutrosophic Matrix

To generate the Python program for finding the power of interval-valued neutrosophic matrix, simple call of the function named "Power(,)" is defined as follow:

```
import numpy as np
A= np.array ([   [[  [ 0.1, 0.2], [0.3, 0.4], [ 0.5, 0.6]  ],
[  [ 0.4, 0.45], [0.5, 0.53], [ 0.6, 0.66]  ], [  [ 0.7, 0.75],
[0, 1], [ 0.9, 0.98]  ]]  ])
B= np.array([  [[  [ 0.1, 0.23], [0.3, 0.45], [ 0.45, 0.6]
], [  [ 0.45, 0.45], [0.5, 0.53], [ 0.6, 0.66]  ], [  [ 0.7,
0.75], [0, 1], [ 0.9, 0.98]  ]    ], [  [  [ 0.121, 0.112],
[0.22, 0.233], [ 0.331, 0.333]  ],   [  [ 0.44, 0.444], [0.55,
0.565], [ 0.667, 0.669]  ],   [  [ 0.757, 0.778], [0.818, 0.89],
[ 0.99, 0.9999]  ]  ], [ [   [ 0, 0.18], [0.213, 0.234], [
0.34, 0.345]  ], [ [ 0.453, 0.458], [0.56, 0.569], [ 0.637,
0.677]   ], [[ 0.758, 0.80], [0.879, 0.959], [0.5, 1]] ]   ])
def Power(A,k):
    global Pw
    dimA=A.shape
    Pw= []
    H=[]
    for i in range (0,dimA[0]):
        H=[]
        for j in range (0,dimA[1]):
            H.extend(   [     [ A[i][j][0][0]**k,   A[i][j]
[0][1]**k ],    [ A[i][j][1][0]**k,   A[i][j][1][1]**k ],
[  A[i][j][2][0]**k, A[i][j][1][1]**k  ]    ]   )
        Pw.append(H)
    print  ('The matrix= ', A)
    print('Power= ', np.array(Pw))
```

4.7. Computing Addition Operation of Two Interval-Valued Neutrosophic Matrices.

The addition of two interval valued neutrosophic matrices A and B is defined as follow:

$$A \oplus B = S = \left[< [s_{ij_T}^L, s_{ij_T}^U], [s_{ij_I}^L, s_{ij_I}^U], [s_{ij_F}^L, s_{ij_F}^U] > \right]_{m \times n} \quad (18)$$

where

$$s_{ij_T}^L = a_{ij_T}^L + b_{ij_T}^L - a_{ij_T}^L . b_{ij_T}^L \quad s_{ij_T}^U = a_{ij_T}^U + b_{ij_T}^U - a_{ij_T}^U . b_{ij_T}^U$$
$$s_{ij_I}^L = a_{ij_I}^L . b_{ij_I}^L, \quad s_{ij_I}^U = a_{ij_I}^U . b_{ij_I}^U \quad s_{ij_F}^L = a_{ij_F}^L . b_{ij_F}^L, \quad s_{ij_F}^U = a_{ij_F}^U . b_{ij_F}^U$$

To generate the Python program for obtaining the addition of two interval-valued neutrosophic matrices, simple call of the function named "Addition" is defined as follow:

```
import numpy as np
A= np.array([   [ [  [ 0.1, 0.5], [0.3, 0.4], [ 0.2, 0.5]  ],
[  [ 0.3, 0.4], [0.2, 0.6], [ 0.2, 0.4]  ]],
[ [ [ 0.2, 0.3], [0.1, 0.3], [ 0.4, 0.7] ],[  [ 0.1, 0.7],
[0.3, 0.4], [ 0.5, 0.6]]],
[ [ [ 0.4, 0.5], [0.2, 0.3], [ 0.1, 0.3]], [ [ 0.5, 0.8], [0.1,
0.2], [ 0.4, 0.7 ]]],
[ [ [ 0.5, 0.6], [0.3, 0.4], [ 0.4, 0.5] ],[  [ 0.2, 0.5],
[0.4, 0.6], [ 0.3, 0.8]]]])
B= np.array([   [ [  [ 0.3, 0.4], [0.2, 0.6], [ 0.1, 0.3]  ],
[  [ 0.4, 0.6], [0.3, 0.4], [ 0.3, 0.5]  ]],
[ [ [ 0.4, 0.7], [0.2, 0.6], [ 0.4, 0.5] ],[  [ 0.2, 0.3],
[0.3, 0.4], [ 0.4, 0.7]]],
 [ [ [ 0.1, 0.3], [0.2, 0.4], [ 0.2, 0.3]], [ [ 0.2, 0.6],
[0.3, 0.5], [ 0.3, 0.6 ]]],
[ [ [ 0.3, 0.4], [0.2, 0.3], [ 0.3, 0.5] ],[  [ 0.1, 0.2],
[0.1, 0.4], [ 0.2, 0.6]]]])
def Addition(A,B):
    if A.shape == B.shape:
        global addi
        dimA=A.shape
```

```
addi= []
H=[]
for i in range (0,dimA[0]):
    H=[]
    for j in range (0,dimA[1]):
        H.extend([    [    A[i][j][0][0]+    B[i][j][0]
[0] -(A[i][j][0][0]* B[i][j][0][0]), A[i][j][0][1]+    B[i][j]
[0][1] -(A[i][j][0][1]* B[i][j][0][1]) ], [    A[i][j][1][0]*
B[i][j][1][0],  A[i][j][1][1] * B[i][j][1][1]   ],    [    A[i]
[j][2][0]*B[i][j][2][0]),  A[i][j][2][1]* B[i][j][2][1]   ]
])
        if dimA[0]==1:
        print('Addition= ', addi)
    else:
        print('Addition= ', np.asarray(addi))
```

The addition of two interval valued neutrosophic matrices is depicted as follow:

$$
A \oplus B = \begin{pmatrix} \left\langle \left[.37,\ .70\right],\left[.06,.24\right],\left[.02,.15\right]\right\rangle & \left\langle \left[.58,\ .76\right],\left[.06,.24\right],\left[.06,.20\right]\right\rangle \\ \left\langle \left[.52,\ .79\right],\left[.02,.18\right],\left[.16,.35\right]\right\rangle & \left\langle \left[.28,\ .79\right],\left[.09,.16\right],\left[.20,.42\right]\right\rangle \\ \left\langle \left[.46,\ .65\right],\left[.04,.12\right],\left[.02,.09\right]\right\rangle & \left\langle \left[.60,\ .92\right],\left[.03,.10\right],\left[.12,.42\right]\right\rangle \\ \left\langle \left[.65,\ .76\right],\left[.06,.12\right],\left[.12,.25\right]\right\rangle & \left\langle \left[.28,\ .60\right],\left[.04,.24\right],\left[.06,.48\right]\right\rangle \end{pmatrix}
$$

4.8. Computing Product of Two Interval-Valued Neutrosophic Matrices

The product of two interval valued neutrosophic matrices A and B is defined as follow:

$$
A \odot B = R = \left[< [r_{ij_T}^L, r_{ij_T}^U], [r_{ij_I}^L, r_{ij_I}^U], [r_{ij_F}^L, r_{ij_F}^U] > \right]_{m \times n} \tag{19}
$$

where

$$
r_{ij_T}^L = a_{ij_T}^L . b_{ij_T}^L, \ r_{ij_T}^U = a_{ij_T}^U . b_{ij_T}^U
$$
$$
r_{ij_I}^L = a_{ij_I}^L + b_{ij_I}^L - a_{ij_I}^L . b_{ij_I}^L, \ r_{ij_I}^U = a_{ij_I}^U + b_{ij_I}^U - a_{ij_I}^U . b_{ij_I}^U
$$
$$
r_{ij_F}^L = a_{ij_F}^L + b_{ij_F}^L - a_{ij_F}^L . b_{ij_F}^L, \ r_{ij_F}^U = a_{ij_F}^U + b_{ij_F}^U - a_{ij_F}^U . b_{ij_F}^U
$$

To generate the Python program for finding the product operation of two interval-valued neutrosophic matrices, simple call of the function named "Product(,)" is defined as follow:

```
import numpy as np
def Product(A,B):
    if A.shape == B.shape:
        global pro
        dimA=A.shape
        pro= []
        H=[]
        for i in range (0,dimA[0]):
            H=[]
            for j in range (0,dimA[1]):
                H.extend([[A[i][j][0][0]* B[i][j][0][0], A[i]
[j][0][1]* B[i][j][0][1]  ], [  A[i][j][1][0]+  B[i][j][1][0]
-(A[i][j][1][0]*  B[i][j][1][0]), A[i][j][1][1] + B[i][j][1][1]
-(A[i][j][1][1]  * B[i][j][1][1])], [A[i][j][2][0]+B[i][j][2][0]
-(A[i][j][2][0]*B[i][j][2][0]),   A[i][j][2][1]+ B[i][j][2][1]
- (A[i][j][2][1]* B[i][j][2][1])  ]  ])
            pro.append(H)
        print('Production= ', np.array(pro))
```

The product of two interval valued neutrosophic matrices is depicted as follow:

$$
\begin{pmatrix}
\langle[.03, .20],[.44,.76],[.28,.65]\rangle & \langle[.12, .24],[.44,.76],[.44,.70]\rangle \\
\langle[.08, .21],[.28,.72],[.64,.85]\rangle & \langle[.02, .21],[.51,.64],[.70,.88]\rangle \\
\langle[.04, .15],[.36,.58],[.25,.51]\rangle & \langle[.10, .48],[.37,.60],[.58,.88]\rangle \\
\langle[.15, .24],[.44,.58],[.58,.75]\rangle & \langle[.02, .10],[.46,.76],[.44,.92]\rangle
\end{pmatrix}
$$

4.9. Computing Transpose of an Interval-Valued Neutrosophic Matrix

To generate the Python program for finding the transpose of interval-valued neutrosophic matrix, simple call of the function named "Transpose():" is defined as follow:

```
import numpy as np
A=   np.array ([   [     [   [ 0.1, 0.2], [0.3, 0.4], [ 0.5,
0.6]  ],      [   [ 0.4, 0.45], [0.5, 0.53], [ 0.6, 0.66]  ], [
[ 0.7, 0.75], [0, 1], [ 0.9, 0.98]  ] ]   ])
def Transpose(A):
    DimA= A. shape
    print (' the matrix ', DimA[0],' x ', DimA[1], '
dimension')
    trA = A.transpose()
    DimtrA= trA. shape
    print ('\n')
    print (' its transpose ', DimtrA[2],' x ', DimtrA[3], '
dimension')
    print ('\n')
    print('transpose = ', trA)
```

4.10. Computing Difference of Two Interval-Valued Neutrosophic Matrices

The difference of two interval valued neutrosophic matrices A and B is defined as follow:

$$A \ominus_2 B = K = \left[\left\langle [r^L_{ij_T}, r^U_{ij_T}], [r^L_{ij_I}, r^U_{ij_I}], [r^L_{ij_F}, r^U_{ij_F}] \right\rangle \right]_{m \times n} \tag{20}$$

where

$$r^L_{ij_T} = a^L_{ij_T} - b^U_{ij_F}, \ r^U_{ij_T} = a^U_{ij_T} - b^L_{ij_F}$$
$$r^L_{ij_I} = \max\left(a^L_{ij_I}, b^L_{ij_I}\right), \ r^U_{ij_I} = \max\left(a^U_{ij_I}, b^U_{ij_I}\right)$$
$$r^L_{ij_F} = a^L_{ij_F} - b^U_{ij_T}, \ r^U_{ij_F} = a^U_{ij_F} - b^L_{ij_T}$$

To generate the Python program for finding the subtraction operation of two interval-valued neutrosophic matrices, simple call of the function named "Difference1(,)" or "Diffrence2(,)" is defined as follow:

```
import numpy as np
def Difference1(A,B):
    if A.shape == B.shape:
```

```
        global dif1
        dimA=A.shape
        dif1= []
        H=[]
        for i in range (0,dimA[0]):
            H=[]
            for j in range (0,dimA[1]):
                H.extend(  [  [ min(A[i][j][0][0], B[i][j][2]
[0]), min(A[i][j][0][1], B[i][j][2][1])  ],
                            [ max(A[i][j][1][0], 1-B[i][j][1]
[1]), max(A[i][j][1][1], 1- B[i][j][1][0])  ],
                            [ max(A[i][j][2][0],B[i][j][0]
[0]),   max (A[i][j][2][1], B[i][j][0][1])  ]  ])
            dif1.append(H)
        print('Difference1= ', np.array(dif1))
import numpy as np
A=  np.array([
[ [  [ 0.1, 0.5], [0.3, 0.4], [ 0.2, 0.5]  ],  [  [ 0.3, 0.4],
[0.2, 0.6], [ 0.2, 0.4]  ]],
[ [ [ 0.2, 0.3], [0.1, 0.3], [ 0.4, 0.7] ],[  [ 0.1, 0.7],
[0.3, 0.4], [ 0.5, 0.6]]],
[ [ [ 0.4, 0.5], [0.2, 0.3], [ 0.1, 0.3]], [ [ 0.5, 0.8], [0.1,
0.2], [ 0.4, 0.7 ]]],
[ [ [ 0.5, 0.6], [0.3, 0.4], [ 0.4, 0.5] ],[  [ 0.2, 0.5],
[0.4, 0.6], [ 0.3, 0.8]]]])
 B=  np.array([
[ [  [ 0.3, 0.4], [0.2, 0.6], [ 0.1, 0.3]  ],  [  [ 0.4, 0.6],
[0.3, 0.4], [ 0.3, 0.5]  ]],
[ [ [ 0.4, 0.7], [0.2, 0.6], [ 0.4, 0.5] ],[ [ 0.2, 0.3],
[0.3, 0.4], [ 0.4, 0.7]]],
[ [ [ 0.1, 0.3], [0.2, 0.4], [ 0.2, 0.3]], [ [ 0.2, 0.6], [0.3,
0.5], [ 0.3, 0.6 ]]],
[ [ [ 0.3, 0.4], [0.2, 0.3], [ 0.3, 0.5] ],[  [ 0.1, 0.2],
[0.1, 0.4], [ 0.2, 0.6]]]])
def Difference2(A,B):
    if A.shape == B.shape:
        global dif2
        dimA=A.shape
        dif2= []
        H=[]
```

```
        for i in range (0,dimA[0]):
            H=[]
            for j in range (0,dimA[1]):
                H.extend( [  [ A[i][j][0][0]- B[i][j][2][1],
A[i][j][0][1]- B[i][j][2][0]  ],
                            [ max(A[i][j][1][0],  B[i][j][1]
[0]), max(A[i][j][1][1], B[i][j][1][1])  ],
                            [ A[i][j][2][0]-B[i][j][0][1],
A[i][j][2][1]-B[i][j][0][0]  ]  ])
            dif2.append(H)
        print('Difference2= ', np.array(dif2))
```

4.11 Computing Scalar of an Interval-Valued Neutrosophic Matrix

To generate the MATLAB program for obtaining the scalar of interval-valued neutrosophic matrix, simple call of the function named "Scalar(,)" is defined as follow:

```
def Scalar(A,k):
    global S
    dimA=A.shape
    S= []
    H=[]
    for i in range (0,dimA[0]):
        H=[]
        for j in range (0,dimA[1]):
        H.extend([ [ A[i][j][0][0]*k,   A[i][j][0][1]*k ], [
A[i][j][1][0]*k,   A[i][j][1][1]*k ], [  A[i][j][2][0]*k, A[i]
[j][1][1]*k ]])
        S.append(H)
    print  ('The matrix= ', A)
    print('Scalar= ', np.array(S))
```

4.12. Computing Scalar Multiplication of an Interval-Valued Neutrosophic Matrix

The scalar multiplication of an interval neutrosophic matrix A is $A_{IVNM} \cdot z$ is defined as follow:

$$A_{IVNM}.z = Q = \left[\left\langle [q_{ij_T}^L, q_{ij_T}^U], [q_{ij_I}^L, q_{ij_I}^U], [q_{ij_F}^L, q_{ij_F}^U] \right\rangle \right]_{m \times n} \tag{21}$$

where

$$q_{ij_T}^L = \min(a_{ij_T}^L \cdot z, 1), \; q_{ij_T}^U = \min(a_{ij_T}^U \cdot z, 1)$$
$$q_{ij_I}^L = \min\left(a_{ij_I}^L \cdot z, 1\right), \; q_{ij_I}^U = \min\left(a_{ij_I}^U \cdot z, 1\right)$$
$$q_{ij_F}^L = \min(a_{ij_F}^L \cdot z, 1), \; q_{ij_F}^U = \min(a_{ij_F}^U \cdot z, 1)$$

To generate the Python program for obtaining the scalar of interval-valued neutrosophic matrix, simple call of the function named "ScalarMultiplication(,)" is defined as follow:

```python
import numpy as np
def ScalarMultiplication(A,k):
    global SM
    dimA=A.shape
    SM= []
    H=[]
    for i in range (0,dimA[0]):
        H=[]
        for j in range (0,dimA[1]):
            H.extend([[ min(A[i][j][0][0]*k,1),    min(A[i][j]
[0][1]*k,1) ], [ min(A[i][j][1][0]*k,1),    min(A[i][j][1]
[1]*k,1) ],  [   min(A[i][j][2][0]*k,1), min(A[i][j][1][1]*k,1)
] ])
        SM.append(H)
    print   ('The matrix= ', A)
    print('Scalar Multiplication= ', np.array(SM))
```

4.13. Computing Scalar Division of an Interval-Valued Neutrosophic Matrix

The scalar division of an interval neutrosophic matrix A is A_{IVNM}/z is defined as follow:

$$A_{IVNM}.z = P = \left[\left\langle [p_{ij_T}^L, p_{ij_T}^U], [p_{ij_I}^L, p_{ij_I}^U], [p_{ij_F}^L, p_{ij_F}^U] \right\rangle \right]_{m \times n} \tag{22}$$

where

$$p^L_{ij_T} = \min(a^L_{ij_T} / z, 1), \; p^U_{ij_T} = \min(a^U_{ij_T} / z, 1)$$
$$p^L_{ij_I} = \min\left(a^L_{ij_I} / z, 1\right), \; p^U_{ij_I} = \min\left(a^U_{ij_I} / z, 1\right)$$
$$p^L_{ij_F} = \min(a^L_{ij_F} / z, 1), \; p^U_{ij_F} = \min(a^U_{ij_F} / z, 1)$$

To generate the Python program for obtaining the scalar of interval-valued neutrosophic matrix, simple call of the function named "ScalarDivision(,)" is defined as follow:

```
def ScalarDivision(A,k):
    global SM
    dimA=A.shape
    SD= []
    H=[]
    for i in range (0,dimA[0]):
        H=[]
        for j in range (0,dimA[1]):
            H.extend(     [     [ min(A[i][j][0][0]/k,1),
min(A[i][j][0][1]/k,1)   ],
                                [ min(A[i][j][1][0]/k,1),
min(A[i][j][1][1]/k,1)  ],
                                [  min(A[i][j][2][0]/k,1),
min(A[i][j][1][1]/k,1)   ]    ]  )
        SD.append(H)
    print  ('The matrix= ', A)
    print('Scalar Division= ', np.array(SD))
```

$$\left\langle [.05, .25], [.10,.15], [.25,.35] \right\rangle \quad \left\langle [.15, .20], [.10,.30], [.10,.20] \right\rangle$$
$$\left\langle [.10, .15], [.05,.15], [.20,.35] \right\rangle \quad \left\langle [.05, .35], [.15,.20], [.25,.30] \right\rangle$$
$$\left\langle [.20, .25], [.10,.15], [.05,.15] \right\rangle \quad \left\langle [.25, .40], [.05,.10], [.20,.35] \right\rangle$$
$$\left\langle [.25, .30], [.15,.20], [.20,.25] \right\rangle \quad \left\langle [.10, .25], [.20,.30], [.15,.40] \right\rangle$$

5. CONCLUSION

This paper proposed some new Python programs for set-theoretic operations on single valued and interval valued neutrosophic matrices. The package provides some programs such as complement, transpose, scalar multiplication of matrix, scalar division of matrix, computing the union, intersection addition, product, difference and division operations of the proposed neutrosophic matrices. In future work, the interval bipolar neutrosophic matrices can be studied using Python language.

ACKNOWLEDGMENT

S.B. implemented codes of the single valued neutrosophic matrices and their operations and created the scripts on Python 3.7 by using Numpy module. S.T. implemented codes of the interval valued neutrosophic matrices and their operations and created the scripts on Python 3.7 by using Numpy module. S.B. offered the project paper and reviewed the implementations. Conceptualization, S.B. and S.T.; Methodology, S.T.; Validation, S.B., S.T., A.B., M.T and F.S.; Investigation, S.B. and S.T.; Resources, S.B., S.T., A.B., M.T and F.S; Writing-Original Draft Preparation, S.B..; Writing—Review and Editing, S.B., S.T., A.B., M.T and F.S.; Supervision, S.B. and F.S.

The authors are very grateful to the chief editor and reviewers for their comments and suggestions, which is helpful in improving the paper.

REFERENCES

Atanassov, K. (1986). Intuitionistic Fuzzy Sets. *Fuzzy Sets and Systems*, *20*(1), 87–96. doi:10.1016/S0165-0114(86)80034-3

Bausys, E. K., & Zavadskas, E. K. (2015). Multi-criteria decision making approach by VIKOR under interval neutrosophic set environment. *Economic Computation and Economic Cybernetics Studies and Research*, *49*.

Biswas, P., Pramanik, S., & Giri, B. C. (2018). Distance Measure Based MADM Strategy with Interval Trapezoidal Neutrosophic Numbers. *Neutrosophic Sets and Systems*, *19*, 40–46.

Broumi, S., Bakali, A., Talea, M., & Smarandache, F. (2017b). A Matlab Toolbox for interval valued neutrosophic matrices for computer applications. *Uluslararası Yönetim Bilişim Sistemleri ve Bilgisayar Bilimleri Dergisi*, *1*(1), 1–21.

Broumi, S., Bakali, A., Talea, M., Smarandache, F., & Verma, R. (2017). Computing Minimum Spanning Tree in Interval Valued Bipolar Neutrosophic Environment. *International Journal of Modeling and Optimization*, 7(5), 300–304. doi:10.7763/IJMO.2017.V7.602

Broumi, S., Dey, A., Talea, M., Bakali, A., Smarandache, F., Nagarajan, D., ... Kumar, R. (2019). *Shortest Path Problem Using Bellman Algorithm under Neutrosophic Environment*. Complex & Intelligent Systems. doi:10.100740747-019-0101-8

Broumi, S., Smarandache, F., Talea, M., & Bakali, A. (2016). Decision-Making Method Based On the Interval Valued Neutrosophic Graph. Future Technologie, IEEE, 44-50.

Broumi, S., Smarandache, F., Talea, M., & Bakali, A. (2016). Operations on Interval Valued Neutrosophic Graphs. In New Trends in Neutrosophic Theory and Applications. Academic Press.

Broumi, S., Son, L. H., Bakali, A., Talea, M., Smarandache, F., & Selvachandran, G. (2017a). Computing Operational Matrices in Neutrosophic Environments: A Matlab Toolbox. *Neutrosophic Sets and Systems*, 18, 58–66. doi:10.5281/zenodo.1175160

Broumi, S., Talea, M., Bakali, A., Singh, P. K., & Smarandache, F. (2019). Energy and Spectrum Analysis of Interval Valued Neutrosophic Graph Using MATLAB. *Neutrosophic Sets and Systems*, 24, 46–60. doi:10.5281/zenodo.2593919

Broumi, S., Talea, M., Bakali, A., & Smarandache, F. (2016). Interval Valued Neutrosophic Graphs. *Critical Review*, 12, 5–33.

Chunfang, L., & Yue Sheng, L. (2016). A new method to construct entropy of interval-valued Neutrosophic Set. *Neutrosophic Sets and Systems*, 11, 8–11. doi:10.5281/zenodo.571218

Dalapati, S., Pramanik, S., Alam, S., Smarandache, F., & Roy, T. K. (2017). IN-cross Entropy Based MAGDM Strategy under Interval Neutrosophic Set Environment. *Neutrosophic Sets and Systems*, 18, 43–57. doi:10.5281/zenodo.1175162

Dalbinder, K., & Kajla, B. (2017). Selection of Transportation Companies and Their Mode of Transportation for Interval Valued Data. *Neutrosophic Sets and Systems*, 18, 67–79. doi:10.5281/zenodo.1175172

Deli, I. (2017). Interval-valued neutrosophic soft sets and its decision making. *International Journal of Machine Learning and Cybernetics*, 8(2), 665–676. doi:10.100713042-015-0461-3

El-Ghareeb, H. A. (2019). Novel Open Source Python Neutrosophic Package. *Neutrosophic Sets and Systems*, *25*, 136–160. doi:10.5281/zenodo.2631514

Garg, H. (2017). Non-linear programming method for multi-criteria decision making problems under interval neutrosophic set environment. *Applied Intelligence*. doi:10.100710489-017-1070-5

Giri, B. C., Molla, M. U., & Biswas, P. (2018). TOPSIS Method for MADM based on Interval Trapezoidal Neutrosophic Number. *Neutrosophic Sets and Systems*, *22*, 151–167.

Hazwani, H., Lazim, A., & Ashraf, A. Q. (2019). Interval Neutrosophic Vague Sets. *Neutrosophic Sets and Systems*, *25*, 66–75. doi:10.5281/zenodo.2631504

Hong-Xiaa, S., Hao-Xionga, Y., Jian-Zhangb, W., & Yao, O. (2015). Interval neutrosophic numbers Choquet integral operator for multi-criteria decision making. *Journal of Intelligent & Fuzzy Systems*, *28*(6), 2443–2455. doi:10.3233/IFS-141524

Huang, Y. H., Wei, G. W., & Wei, C. (2017). VIKOR Method for Interval Neutrosophic Multiple Attribute Group Decision-Making, information. *Information.*, *8*(4), 144. doi:10.3390/info8040144

Kalyan, M., & Surapati, P., & Bibhas, G. C. (2018). Interval Neutrosophic Tangent Similarity Measure Based MADM strategy and its Application to MADM Problems. *Neutrosophic Sets and Systems*, *19*, 46–56. doi:10.5281/zenodo.1235201

Karaaslan, F., & Hayat, K. (2018). Some new operations on single-valued neutrosophic matrices and their applications in multi-criteria group decision making. *Applied Intelligence*, *48*(12), 4594–4614. doi:10.100710489-018-1226-y

Karaşan, A., & Kahraman, C. (2017). Interval-Valued Neutrosophic Extension of EDAS Method. Advances in Intelligent Systems and Computing, 642. DOI doi:10.1007/978-3-319-66824-6_31

Kumar, R., Edalatpanah, S. A., Jha, S., Broumi, S., & Dey, A. (2018). Neutrosophic shortest path problems. *Neutrosophic Sets and Systems*, *23*, 5–15.

Kumar, R., Edalatpanah, S. A., Jha, S., Broumi, S., Singh, R., & Dey, A. (2019). A multi objective programming approaches to solve integer valued neutrosophic shortest path problems. *Neutrosophic Sets and Systems*, *24*, 134–149.

Kumar, R., Edalatpanah, S. A., Jha, S., & Singh, R. (2019a). A novel approach to solve Gaussian Valued Neutrosophic Shortest Path Problems. *International Journal of Engineering and Advanced Technology*, *8*(3), 347–353.

Kumar, R., Edalatpanah, S. A., Jha, S., & Singh, R. (2019b). A Pythagorean fuzzy approach to the transportation problem. *Complex & Intelligent Systems*, *5*(2), 255–263. doi:10.100740747-019-0108-1

Ma, Y. X., Wang, J. Q., Wang, J., & Wu, X. H. An interval neutrosophic linguistic multi-criteria group decision-making method and its application in selecting medical treatment options. *Neural Computing & Applications*. doi:10.100700521-016-2203-1

Mukherjee, A., Datta, M., & Sarkar, S. (2016). Restricted Interval Valued Neutrosophic Sets and Restricted Interval Valued Neutrosophic Topological Spaces. *Neutrosophic Sets and Systems*, *12*, 45–53. doi:10.5281/zenodo.571145

Nagarajan, D., Lathamaheswari, M., Broumi, S., & Kavikumar, J. (2019). Blockchain Single and Interval Valued Neutrosophic Graphs. *Neutrosophic Sets and Systems*, *24*, 23–35. doi:10.5281/zenodo.2593909

Nagarajan, D., Lathamaheswari, M., Broumi, S., & Kavikumar, J. (2019). Dombi Interval Valued Neutrosophic Graph and its Role in Traffic Control Management. *Neutrosophic Sets and Systems*, *24*, 114–133. doi:10.5281/zenodo.2593948

Nancy, & Garg, H. (2016). An improved score function for ranking neutrosophic sets and its application to decision making process. *International Journal for Uncertainty Quantification*, *6*(5), 377–385. doi:10.1615/Int.J.UncertaintyQuantification.2016018441

Pramanik, S., Roy, R., Roy, T. K., & Smarandache, F. (2018). Multi Attribute Decision Making Strategy on Projection and Bidirectional Projection Measures of Interval Rough Neutrosophic Sets. *Neutrosophic Sets and Systems*, *19*, 101–109. doi:10.5281/zenodo.1235211

Rajeswara, P. R., Naga, I. R., Diwakar, V. R., & Krishnaiah, G. (2016). Lean Supplier selection based on hybrid MCGDM approach using interval valued neutrosophic sets: A case study. *International Journal of Innovative Research and Development*, *5*(6), 291–296.

Şahin, M., Ulucay, V., & Menekşe, M. (2017). (α, β, ϒ) Interval Cut Set of Interval Valued Neutrosophic Sets. In *International Conference on Mathematics and Mathematics Education (ICMME-2017)*. Harran University.

Şahin, R. (2015). Cross-entropy measure on interval neutrosophic sets and its applications in multi-criteria decision making. *Neural Computing & Applications*, 1–11.

Smarandache, F. (1998). *Neutrosophy*. Ann Arbor, MI: Neutrosophic Probability, Set, and Logic. ProQuest Information & Learning.

Song, S.Z., Khan, M., & Smarandache, F., & Jun, Y. B. (2017). Interval neutrosophic sets applied to ideals in BCK/BCI-algebras. *Neutrosophic Sets and Systems*, *18*, 16–26. doi:10.5281/zenodo.1175164

Tian, Z. P., Zhang, H. Y., Wang, J., Wang, J. Q., & Chen, X. H. (2015). Multi-criteria decision-making method based on a cross-entropy with interval neutrosophic sets. *International Journal of Systems Science*, 1–11.

Wang, H., Smarandache, F., Zhang, Y., & Sunderraman, R. (2010). *Single Valued Neutrosophic Sets. Multispace and Multistucture*, *4*, 410–413.

Ye, J. (2014). Similarity measures between interval neutrosophic sets and their applications in multi-criteria decision-making. *Journal of Intelligent & Fuzzy Systems*, *26*(1), 165–172.

Ye, J. (2014a). A multi-criteria decision-making method using aggregation operators for simplified neutrosophic sets. *Journal of Intelligent & Fuzzy Systems*, *26*(5), 2459–2466.

Ye, J. (2015). Interval Neutrosophic Multiple Attribute Decision-Making Method with Credibility Information. *Int. J. Fuzzy Syst*. DOI doi:10.100740815-015-0122-4

Ye, J. (2015a). Multiple attribute decision-making method based on the possibility degree ranking method and ordered weighted aggregation operators of interval neutrosophic numbers. *Journal of Intelligent & Fuzzy Systems*, *28*(3), 1307–1317.

Ye, J. (2016). Exponential operations and aggregation operators of interval neutrosophic sets and their decision making methods. *SpringerPlus*, *5*(1), 1488. doi:10.118640064-016-3143-z PMID:28018779

Zadeh, L. (1965). Fuzzy Sets. *Information and Control*, *8*(3), 338–353. doi:10.1016/S0019-9958(65)90241-X

Zhang, H. Y., Wang, J. Q., & Chen, X. H. (2014). Interval neutrosophic sets and their application in multi-criteria decision making problems. *The Scientific World Journal*. Retrieved from http://fs.gallup.unm.edu/NSS/

KEY TERMS AND DEFINITIONS

Array: A type of ordered series of things.

Implementation: A realization of a technical specification or algorithm as a program.

Interval Valued Neutrosophic Set: Neutrosophic set of element components are intervals.

Matrix Operations: Operations that are defined on matrices.

Python: A programming language which is useful for scientific computations and implementations.

Single Valued Neutrosophic Set: Set of neutrosophic elements dependent to a variable.

Toolbox: Programs or functions accessible from a single menu.

Chapter 14

Improved Correlation Coefficients of Quadripartitioned Single-Valued Neutrosophic Sets and Interval-Quadripartitioned Neutrosophic Sets

Mohanasundari M.
Bannari Amman Institute of Technology, India

Mohana K.
Nirmala College for Women, India

ABSTRACT

A correlation coefficient is one of the statistical measures that helps to find the degree of changes to the value of one variable predict change to the value of another. Quadripartitioned single valued neutrosophic sets is an improvization of Wang's single valued neutrosophic sets. This chapter deals the improved correlation coefficients of quadripartitioned single valued neutrosophic sets, interval quadripartitioned neutrosophic sets, and investigates its properties. And this concept is also applied in multiple-attribute decision-making methods with quadripartitioned single valued neutrosophic environment and interval quadripartitioned neutrosophic environment. Finally an illustrated example is given in the proposed method to the multiple-attribute decision-making problems.

DOI: 10.4018/978-1-7998-2555-5.ch014

1. INTRODUCTION

Fuzzy sets were introduced by Zadeh (1965) which allows the membership function valued in the interval [0,1] and also it is an extension of classical set theory. Fuzzy set helps to deal the concept of uncertainty, vagueness and imprecision which is not possible in the cantorian set. As an extension of Zadeh's fuzzy set theory intuitionstic fuzzy set(IFS) was introduced by Atanassov (1986) which consists of degree of membership and degree of non membership and lies in the interval of [0,1]. IFS theory widely used in the areas of logic programming, decision making problems, medical diagnosis etc.

Smarandache (1995) introduced the concept of Neutrosophic set which provides the knowledge of neutral thought by introducing the new factor called indeterminacy in the set. Therefore neutrosophic set was framed and it includes the components of truth membership function(T), indeterminacy membership function(I), and falsity membership function(F) respectively. Neutrosophic sets deals with non standard interval of]⁻0,1⁺[. Since neutrosophic set deals the indeterminacy effectively it plays an vital role in many applications areas include information technology, decision support system, relational database systems, medical diagnosis, multicriteria decision making problems etc.,

To process the incomplete information or imperfect knowledge to vagueness a new mathematical approach i.e., Rough set was introduced by Pawlak (1991) and it is in terms of a pair of sets include the lower and upper approximations of the original set. A new hybrid model of neutrosophic rough set was introduced by Broumi(2014) by combining the concept of neutrosophic set with rough set. To deal the real world problems, Wang (2010) introduced the concept of single valued neutrosophic sets(SVNS) which is also known as an extension of initutionstic fuzzy sets and it became a very new hot research topic now. Chatterjee.,et al(2016) proposed the concept of Quadripartitioned single valued neutrosophic sets (QSVNS) which is based on Belnap's four valued logic and Smarandache's four numerical valued logic. In (QSVNS) indeterminacy is splitted into two functions known as 'Contradicition' (both true and false) and 'Unknown' (neither true nor false) so that QSVNS has four components T,C,U,F which also lies in the non standard unit interval]⁻0,1⁺[. Further, K Mohana and M Mohanasundari (2018) defined a new hybrid model of Quadripartitioned Single Valued Neutrosophic Rough Sets.

Neutrosophic set has a tremendous applications in various field and many researchers focused in solving real world problems by applying suitable method like similarity measure, correlation coefficient to some important notions of neutrosophic logic, neutrosophic measure, neutrosophic integral, single valued neutrosophic set(SVNS), Quadripartitioned Single Valued Neutrosophic set(QSVNS) etc., In our day-to-day life making correct decision is a challenging task when it involves complex issues like uncertainity, complexity, High risk consequences, alternatives etc., For that multi criteria decision making helps in solving the real world problems including information systems, software engineering, Decision analysis, Economics, Personnel selection, Medical diagnosis, IoT based enterprises for making decisions correctly by analyzing the problem with suitable method. Many methods are available in solving a multi -criteria decision making problems particularly TOPSIS is one of the effective method because of its very good computational efficiency and simplicity.

Similarity measures in neutrosophic sets also has a tremendous application in various fields like decision making, pattern recognition, coding theory, image processing, region extraction, medical diagnosis etc., Similarity measure helps to identify how much alike two data objects are. There are numerous challenges in medical diagnosis where we have identified the diseases under correct symptoms and signs. Similarity measure is one of the effective tool which helps in the field of medical diagnosis to identify the diseases under correct symptoms and signs. Many authors used similarity measure in neutrosophic sets to diagnosis the medical problem under given conditions. Similarity measure is also an important tool in image processing where we can perform operations on an image to get some useful information from it. Guo et al.,(2014) studied a novel image thresholding algorithm based on neutrosophic similarity score which is used in image processing and computer vision.

Correlation coefficient is an effective mathematical tool to measure the strength of the relationship between two variables. So many researchers pay the attention to the concept of various correlation coefficients of the different sets like fuzzy set, IFS, SVNS, QSVNS. D.A Chiang and N.P.Lin(1999) proposed the correlation of fuzzy sets under fuzzy environment. Later D.H.Hong (2006) defined fuzzy measures for a correlation coefficient of fuzzy numbers under Tw (the weakest t-norm) based fuzzy arithmetic operations. Correlation coefficients plays an important role in many real world problems like multiple attribute group decision making clustering analysis, pattern recognition, medical diagnosis etc., Hence many authors focused the concept of defining correlation coefficients to solve the real world problems in particularly multicriteria decision making methods. Ye(2014) defined the improved correlation coefficients of single valued neutrosophic sets and interval neutrosophic sets for multiple attribute decision making to overcome the drawbacks of the correlation coefficients of single valued neutrosophic sets (SVNSs) which is defined by Ye(2013).

In this paper Section 2 provides a detailed literature review for the proposed method. Section 3 gives some basic definitions of Quadripartitioned single valued neutrosophic sets and its complement, union, intersection, interval neutrosophic sets, correlation coefficient of QSVNSs. In Section 4, we introduced the concept of improved correlation coefficient of QSVNSs to overcome the drawbacks of correlation coefficient which is defined in [20] and also discussed some of its properties and decision making method using the improved correlation coefficient of QSVNSs. In Section 5, we introduced the concept of Interval Quadripartitioned Neutrosophic Sets (IQNS) with some basic definitions and defined correlation coefficient of IQNSs. Further we have also discussed some of its properties and decision making method using the improved correlation coefficient with interval quadripartitioned neutrosophic environment. Section 6 an illustrative example is given in above proposed correlation method particularly in multiple criteria decision making problems. Section 7 concludes the paper.

2. LITERATURE REVIEW

Correlation coefficient between two neutrosophic set was first examined by Hanafy et al.,(2012). They defined a correlation coefficient between two neutrosophic sets and studied its properties. Interval neutrosophic set was defined by Wang et al.,(2005) and correlation coefficient, weighted correlation coefficient between two interval neutrosophic sets was first studied by Broumi and Smarandache(2005). Zhang et al.,(2014) covered the definitions of correlation coefficient and weighted correlation coefficient measure, entropy measure of interval neutrosophic sets (INSs), and suggested an objective weight measure which is based on the entropy of INSs. To explain the uses of above defined measures Zhang et al.,(2014) proposed multicriteria decision-making (MCDM) algorithm which is based on the weighted correlation coefficient measure. Wang(2010) defined the single valued neutrosophic set(SVNS) which is an extension of intuitionistic fuzzy sets and correlation coefficient of SVNS set was first studied by Ye and also he illustrated that cosine similarity measure is a special case of the above defined correlation coefficient in SVNS. And also he showed an example in decision making method to calculate alternatives with respect to given conditions using weighted correlation coefficient of SVNSs. Ye(2012) added one more formula for correlation coefficient between two SVNS, and studied its properties. He showed a MCDM method based on the proposed correlation coefficient measure for SVNS.

Based on Smarandache's(2013) refined neutrosophic set to n − components Ye(2016) defined Single-valued neutrosophic multiset (refined) (SVRM) and also correlation coefficient for above defined SVRM set was introduced by Broumi and Deli(2014) and also they applied the proposed correlation measure in medical diagnosis. Recently many researchers, defined the neutrosophic sets with soft set, rough set, refined soft set, single valued neutrosophic rough set, quadripartitioned single valued neutrosophic set which form a new hybrid model of neutrosophic sets and also proposed correlation coefficient for above hybrid models. Many researchers explained the application of correlation coefficient in multi criteria decision making problems with suitable example. J. Ye(2012) defined multicriteria decision-making method using the correlation coefficient under single-valued neutrosophic environment. Because of some drawbacks found in above proposed correlation coefficient in some situations, J.Ye(2014) defined improved correlation coefficients of single valued neutrosophic sets and interval neutrosophic sets for multiple attribute decision making problems to overcome the disadvantages defined by Ye. Rajashi Chatterjee.,et al.,(2016) proposed the concept of Quadripartitioned single valued neutrosophic sets (QSVNS) which is based on Belnap's four valued logic and Smarandache's four numerical valued logic and also defined similarity measures, entropy measure, correlation coefficient measure between two QSVNSs A and B. Due to some drawbacks in calculating the correlation measure defined by Chatterjee(2016) when applied in some real life situations, an improved correlation coefficient of Quadripartitioned Single valued Neutrosophic Sets and Interval Quadripartitioned Neutrosophic Set defined in this chapter and also an example is illustrated in multicriteria decision making problems.

3. PRELIMINARIES

3.1 Quadripartitioned Single Valued Neutrosophic Sets

Definition 3.1. Neutrosophic set is defined over the non-standard unit interval $]^-0,1^+[$ whereas single valued neutrosophic set is defined over standard unit interval [0,1]. It means a single valued neutrosophic set A is defined by

$$A = \left\{ \left\langle x, T_A(x), I_A(x), F_A(x) \right\rangle : x \in X \right\}$$

where

$$T_A(x), I_A(x), F_A(x) : X \to [0,1]$$

such that

$$0 \leq T_A(x) + I_A(x) + F_A(x) \leq 3$$

Definition 3.2. Let X be a non-empty set. A quadripartitioned single valued neutrosophic set (QSVNS) A over X characterizes each element in X by a truth-membership function $T_A(x)$, a contradiction membership function $C_A(x)$, an ignorance membership function $U_A(x)$ and a falsity membership function $F_A(x)$ such that for each $x \in X$, $T_A, C_A, U_A, F_A \in [0,1]$ and

$$0 \le T_A(x) + C_A(x) + U_A(x) + F_A(x) \le 4.$$

When X is discrete, A is represented as

$$A = \sum_{i=1}^{n} \left\langle T_A(x_i), C_A(x_i), U_A(x_i), F_A(x_i) \right\rangle / x_i, x_i \in X.$$

Definition 3.3. The complement of a QSVNS A is denoted by A^c and is defined as,

$$A^C = \sum_{i=1}^{n} \left\langle F_A(x_i), U_A(x_i), C_A(x_i), T_A(x_i) \right\rangle / x_i, x_i \in X$$

i.e.,

$$T_{A^C}(x_i) = F_A(x_i), C_{A^C}(x_i) = U_A(x_i), U_{A^C}(x_i) = C_A(x_i), F_{A^C}(x_i) = T_A(x_i), x_i \in X$$

Definition 3.4. Consider two QSVNS A and B, over X. A is said to be contained in B, denoted by $A \subseteq B$ iff

$$T_A(x) \le T_B(x), C_A(x) \le C_B(x), U_A(x) \ge U_B(x) \, and \, F_A(x) \ge F_B(x)$$

Definition 3.5. The union of two QSVNS A and B is denoted by $A \cup B$ and is defined as,

$$A \cup B = \sum_{i=1}^{n} \left\langle T_A(x_i) \vee T_B(x_i), C_A(x_i) \vee C_B(x_i), U_A(x_i) \wedge U_B(x_i), F_A(x_i) \wedge F_B(x_i) \right\rangle / x_i, x_i \in X$$

Definition 3.6. The intersection of two QSVNS A and B is denoted by $A \cap B$ and is defined as,

$$A \cap B = \sum_{i=1}^{n} \left\langle T_A(x_i) \wedge T_B(x_i), C_A(x_i) \wedge C_B(x_i), U_A(x_i) \vee U_B(x_i), F_A(x_i) \vee F_B(x_i) \right\rangle / x_i, x_i \in X$$

Definition 3.7. Let X be a space of points (objects) with generic elements in X denoted by x. An INS A in X is characterized by a truth-membership function

$T_A(x)$, an indeterminacy – membership function $I_A(x)$ and a falsity membership function $F_A(x)$. For each point x in X, there are

$$T_A(x) = \left[\inf T_A(x), \sup T_A(x)\right] \subseteq [0,1], I_A(x) = \left[\inf I_A(x), \sup I_A(x)\right] \subseteq [0,1]$$

and

$$F_A(x) = \left[\inf F_A(x), \sup F_A(x)\right] \subseteq [0,1].$$

Thus, an INS A can be expressed as,

$$A = \left\{\langle x, T_A(x), I_A(x), F_A(x)\rangle \mid x \in X\right\}$$
$$= \left\{\langle x, \left[\inf T_A(x), \sup T_A(x)\right], \left[\inf I_A(x), \sup I_A(x)\right], \left[\inf F_A(x), \sup F_A(x)\right]\rangle \mid x \in X\right\}$$

Then the sum of $T_A(x), I_A(x), F_A(x)$ satisfies the condition,

$$0 \le \sup T_A(x) + \sup I_A(x) + \sup F_A(x) \le 3.$$

Obviously, when the upper and lower ends of the interval values of $T_A(x)$, $I_A(x)$ and $F_A(x)$ in an INS are equal, the INS reduces to the SVNS. However, SVNSs and INS are all the subclasses of neutrosophic sets.

Definition 3.8. The complement of an INS A is denoted by A^c and is defined as

$$T_{A^c}(x) = F_A(x), \inf I_{A^c}(x) = 1 - \sup I_A(x), \sup I_{A^c}(x) = 1 - \inf I_A(x) \, and \, F_{A^c}(x) = T_A(x)$$

for any x in X.

Definition 3.9. An INS A is contained in the other INS B, $A \subseteq B$ if and only if

$$\inf T_A(x) \le \inf T_B(x), \sup T_A(x) \le \sup T_B(x), \inf I_A(x) \ge \inf I_B(x), \sup I_A(x) \ge \sup I_B(x)$$

and

$\inf F_A(x) \geq \inf F_B(x),\ \sup F_A(x) \geq \sup F_B(x).$

Definition 3.10. Two INSs A and B are equal, written as $A=B$, if and only if $A \subseteq B$ and $B \subseteq A$.

3.2 Correlation Coefficient of QSVNSs

Rajashi Chatterjee (2016) defined the concept of the correlation coefficient of QSVNSs which is based on the correlation coefficient of SVNSs and is defined as follows:

$$K(A,B) = \frac{C(A,B)}{[T(A).T(B)]^{1/2}}$$

$$= \frac{\sum_{i=1}^{n}\left[T_A(x_i).T_B(x_i) + C_A(x_i).C_B(x_i) + U_A(x_i).U_B(x_i) + F_A(x_i).F_B(x_i)\right]}{\sqrt{\sum_{i=1}^{n}\left[T_A^2(x_i) + C_A^2(x_i) + U_A^2(x_i) + F_A^2(x_i)\right]}\sqrt{\sum_{i=1}^{n}\left[T_B^2(x_i) + C_B^2(x_i) + U_B^2(x_i) + F_B^2(x_i)\right]}}$$

$$(3.1)$$

The correlation coefficient $K(A,B)$ satisfies the following properties.

1. $K(A,B)=K(B,A)$;
2. $0 \leq K(A,B) \leq 1$;
3. $K(A,B)=1$ iff $A=B$

There will be some drawbacks in using Equation (3.1) which is given below.

1.   For any two QSVNSs A and B, if

$$T_A(x_i) = C_A(x_i) = U_A(x_i) = F_A(x_i) = 0$$

and /or

$$T_B(x_i) = C_B(x_i) = U_B(x_i) = F_B(x_i) = 0$$

for any x_i in $X(i=1,2,\ldots,n)$, Equation (3.1) is undefined or unmeaningful. In this case it is not possible to use the formula which is given in Equation (3.1).

2. Equation (3.1) satisfies only the necessary condition of the property (3), but not the sufficient condition. That is $A \neq B$, Equation (3.1) may be equal to 1. (detail in the following example)

Example 1 Let A and B be two QSVNSs in X which are given by

$$A = \left\{ \left\langle x, 0.4, 0.2, 0.3, 0.1 \right\rangle \right\}$$

and

$$B = \left\{ \left\langle x, 0.8, 0.4, 0.6, 0.2 \right\rangle \right\}.$$

Here obviously $A \neq B$. Then

$$K(A, B) = \frac{0.4 \times 0.8 + 0.2 \times 0.4 + 0.3 \times 0.6 + 0.1 \times 0.2}{\sqrt{0.4^2 + 0.2^2 + 0.3^2 + 0.1^2} \sqrt{0.8^2 + 0.4^2 + 0.6^2 + 0.2^2}} = 1$$

Hence in this case it is not possible to apply in real life example problems. To overcome these type of disadvantages we shall define an improved correlation coefficient in the following section.

4. IMPROVED CORRELATION COEFFICIENTS

4.1 Improved Correlation Coefficient of QSVNSs

Based on the concept of correlation coefficient of QSVNSs, we have defined the improved correlation coefficient of QSVNSs in the following subsection.

Definition 4.1. Let A and B be any two QSVNSs in the universe of discourse $X = \{x_1, x_2, \ldots, x_n\}$, then the improved correlation coefficient between A and B is defined as follows:

$$M(A, B) = \frac{1}{4n} \sum_{i=1}^{n} \left[\phi_i (1 - \Delta T_i) + \varphi_i (1 - \Delta C_i) + \psi_i (1 - \Delta U_i) + \varsigma_i (1 - \Delta F_i) \right]$$

$$(4.1)$$

where,

$$\phi_i = \frac{4 - \Delta T_i - \Delta T_{max}}{4 - \Delta T_{min} - \Delta T_{max}},$$

$$\varphi_i = \frac{4 - \Delta C_i - \Delta C_{max}}{4 - \Delta C_{min} - \Delta C_{max}},$$

$$\psi_i = \frac{4 - \Delta U_i - \Delta U_{max}}{4 - \Delta U_{min} - \Delta U_{max}},$$

$$\varsigma_i = \frac{4 - \Delta F_i - \Delta F_{max}}{4 - \Delta F_{min} - \Delta F_{max}},$$

$$\Delta T_i = |T_A(x_i) - T_B(x_i)|,$$

$$\Delta C_i = |C_A(x_i) - C_B(x_i)|,$$

$$\Delta U_i = |U_A(x_i) - U_B(x_i)|,$$

$$\Delta F_i = |F_A(x_i) - F_B(x_i)|,$$

$$\Delta T_{min} = \min_i |T_A(x_i) - T_B(x_i)|,$$

$$\Delta C_{min} = \min_i |C_A(x_i) - C_B(x_i)|,$$

$$\Delta U_{min} = \min_i |U_A(x_i) - U_B(x_i)|,$$

$$\Delta F_{min} = \min_i |F_A(x_i) - F_B(x_i)|,$$

$$\Delta T_{\max} = \max_i | T_A(x_i) - T_B(x_i) |,$$

$$\Delta C_{\max} = \max_i | C_A(x_i) - C_B(x_i) |,$$

$$\Delta U_{\max} = \max_i | U_A(x_i) - U_B(x_i) |,$$

$$\Delta F_{\max} = \max_i | F_A(x_i) - F_B(x_i) |,$$

for any $x_i \in X$ and $i=1,2,\ldots,n$.

Theorem 4.1 For any two QSVNSs A and B in the universe of discourse $X= \{x_1, x_2, \ldots, x_n\}$, the improved correlation coefficient $M(A,B)$ satisfies the following properties.

1. $M(A,B) = M(B,A)$;
2. $0 \le M(A,B) \le 1$;
3. $M(A,B) = 1$ *if and only if* $A = B$.

Proof
  1. It is obvious and straightforward.
  2. Here,

$$0 \le \phi_i \le 1, \ 0 \le \varphi_i \le 1, \ 0 \le \psi_i \le 1, \ 0 \le \zeta_i \le 1,$$
$$0 \le 1 - \Delta T_i \le 1, \ 0 \le 1 - \Delta C_i \le 1, \ 0 \le 1 - \Delta U_i \le 1, \ 0 \le 1 - \Delta F_i \le 1.$$

Therefore the following inequation satisfies

$$0 \le \phi_i(1 - \Delta T_i) + \varphi_i(1 - \Delta C_i) + \psi_i(1 - \Delta U_i) + \varsigma_i(1 - \Delta F_i) \le 4 .$$

Hence we have $0 \le M(A.B) \le 1$.

  3. If $M(A,B)=1$, then we get,

$$\phi_i(1 - \Delta T_i) + \varphi_i(1 - \Delta C_i) + \psi_i(1 - \Delta U_i) + \varsigma_i(1 - \Delta F_i) = 4 .$$

Since

$$0 \le \phi_i(1-\Delta T_i) \le 1, 0 \le \varphi_i(1-\Delta C_i) \le 1, 0 \le \psi_i(1-\Delta U_i) \le 1 \, and \, 0 \le \zeta_i(1-\Delta F_i) \le 1,$$

there are

$$\phi_i(1-\Delta T_i) = \varphi_i(1-\Delta C_i) = \psi_i(1-\Delta U_i) = \zeta_i(1-\Delta F_i) = 1.$$

And also since,

$$0 \le \phi_i \le 1, 0 \le \varphi_i \le 1, 0 \le \psi_i \le 1, 0 \le \zeta_i \le 1, 0 \le 1-\Delta T_i \le 1,$$
$$0 \le 1-\Delta C_i \le 1, 0 \le 1-\Delta U_i \le 1, 0 \le 1-\Delta F_i \le 1$$

we get

$$\phi_i = \varphi_i = \psi_i = \zeta_i = 1 \, and \, 1-\Delta T_i = 1-\Delta C_i = 1-\Delta U_i = 1-\Delta F_i = 1.$$

This implies

$$\Delta T_i = \Delta T_{min} = \Delta T_{max} = 0, \Delta C_i = \Delta C_{min} = \Delta C_{max} = 0,$$
$$\Delta U_i = \Delta U_{min} = \Delta U_{max} = 0, \Delta F_i = \Delta F_{min} = \Delta F_{max} = 0$$

$$T_A(x_i) = T_B(x_i), C_A(x_i) = C_B(x_i), U_A(x_i) = U_B(x_i), F_A(x_i) = F_B(x_i)$$

for any $x_i \in X$ and $i=1,2,\ldots,n$. Hence $A=B$.

Now assume that $A=B$. This implies

$$T_A(x_i) = T_B(x_i), C_A(x_i) = C_B(x_i), U_A(x_i) = U_B(x_i), F_A(x_i) = F_B(x_i)$$

for any $x_i \in X$ and $i=1,2,\ldots,n$. Thus,

$$\Delta T_i = \Delta T_{min} = \Delta T_{max} = 0, \Delta C_i = \Delta C_{min} = \Delta C_{max} = 0,$$
$$\Delta U_i = \Delta U_{min} = \Delta U_{max} = 0, \Delta F_i = \Delta F_{min} = \Delta F_{max} = 0$$

Hence we get $M(A,B)=1$.

The improved correlation coefficient formula which is defined in (4.1) is correct and also satisfy the three properties in Theorem 4.1. when we use any constant $\lambda > 3$ in the following expressions,

$$\phi_i = \frac{\lambda - \Delta T_i - \Delta T_{\max}}{\lambda - \Delta T_{\min} - \Delta T_{\max}}, \; \varphi_i = \frac{\lambda - \Delta C_i - \Delta C_{\max}}{\lambda - \Delta C_{\min} - \Delta C_{\max}},$$

$$\psi_i = \frac{\lambda - \Delta U_i - \Delta U_{\max}}{\lambda - \Delta U_{\min} - \Delta U_{\max}}, \varsigma_i = \frac{\lambda - \Delta F_i - \Delta F_{\max}}{\lambda - \Delta F_{\min} - \Delta F_{\max}}$$

When $A \neq B$ consider the same Example 1 we can get $M(A,B)=0.75$ by applying Equation (4.1).

Example 2 Let

$$A = \left\{ \left\langle x, 0, 0, 0, 0 \right\rangle \right\} and \; B = \left\{ \left\langle x, 0.6, 0.5, 0.4, 0.2 \right\rangle \right\}$$

be two QSVNSs in X. Then obviously Equation (3.1) is undefined. Therefore by using Equation (3.1) we get $M(A,B)=0.575$. It shows that the above defined improved correlation coefficient overcome the disadvantages of the correlation coefficient in [20]. In the following we define a weighted correlation coefficient between QSVNS since the differences in the elements are considered into an account.

Let w_i be the weight for each element

$$x_i \, (i = 1, 2, ..., n), w_i \in [0, 1] \, and \sum_{i=1}^{n} w_i = 1,$$

then the weighted correlation coefficient between the QSVNSs A and B be

$$M_w(A, B) = \frac{1}{4} \sum_{i=1}^{n} w_i \left[\phi_i(1 - \Delta T_i) + \varphi_i(1 - \Delta C_i) + \psi_i(1 - \Delta U_i) + \varsigma_i(1 - \Delta F_i) \right]$$

$$(4.2)$$

If $w = (1/n, 1/n, ..., 1/n)^T$ then Equation (4.2) reduces to Equation (4.1). $M_w(A,B)$ also satisfies the three properties in Theorem 4.1

Theorem 4.2 Let w_i be the weight for each element

$$x_i \ (i = 1, 2, ..., n), w_i \in [0,1] \, and \sum_{i=1}^{n} w_i = 1,$$

then the weighted correlation coefficient between the QSVNSs A and B be which is denoted by $M_w(A,B)$ defined in Equation (4.2) also satisfies the following properties.

1. $M_w(A, B) = M_w(B, A)$;
2. $0 \le M_w(A, B) \le 1$;
3. $M_w(A, B) = 1$ *if and only if* $A = B$.

It is similar to prove the properties in Theorem 4.1

4.1 Decision Making Method Using the Improved Correlation Coefficient of QSVNSs

Multiple criteria decision making (MCDM) problems refers to make decisions when several attributes are involved in real-life problem. For example one may buy a car by analysing the attributes which is given in terms of price, style, safety, comfort etc.,

Here we consider a multiple attribute decision making problem with quadripartitioned single valued neutrosophic information, and the characteristic of an alternative $A_i(i=1,2,..,m)$ on an attribute $C_j(j=1,2,...,n)$ is represented by the following QSVNS:

$$A_i = \left\{ \left\langle C_j, T_{A_i}(C_j), \ C_{A_i}(C_j), U_{A_i}(C_j), F_{A_i}(C_j) \right\rangle \mid C_j \in C, j = 1, 2, ..., n \right\}$$

where

$$T_{A_i}(C_j), \ C_{A_i}(C_j), U_{A_i}(C_j), F_{A_i}(C_j) \in [0,1]$$

and

$$0 \le T_{A_i}(C_j) + C_{A_i}(C_j) + U_{A_i}(C_j) + F_{A_i}(C_j) \le 4 \, for \, C_j \in C, j = 1, 2, ..., n \ and \ i = 1, 2, ..., m \, .$$

To make it convenient, we are considering the following four functions,

$$T_{A_i}(C_j), C_{A_i}(C_j), U_{A_i}(C_j), F_{A_i}(C_j)$$

in terms of a quadripartitioned single valued neutrosophic value (QSVNV)

$$d_{ij} = \left\langle t_{ij}, c_{ij}, u_{ij}, f_{ij} \right\rangle (i = 1, 2, ..., m; j = 1, 2, ..., n).$$

Here the values of d_{ij} are usually derived from the evaluation of an alternative A_i with respect to a criterion C_j by the expert or decision maker. Therefore we got a quadripartitioned single valued neutrosophic decision matrix $D = (d_{ij})_{m \times n}$.

In the case of ideal alternative A^* an ideal QSVNV can be defined by,

$$d_j^* = \left\langle t_j^*, c_j^*, u_j^*, f_j^* \right\rangle = \left\langle 1, 1, 0, 0 \right\rangle (j = 1, 2, ..., n)$$

in the decision making method. Hence the weighted correlation coefficient between an alternative $A_i (i=1,2,...,m)$ and the ideal alternative A^* is given by,

$$M_w(A_i, A^*) = \frac{1}{4} \sum_{i=1}^{n} w_j \left[\phi_{ij}(1 - \Delta t_{ij}) + \varphi_{ij}(1 - \Delta c_{ij}) + \psi_{ij}(1 - \Delta u_{ij}) + \varsigma_{ij}(1 - \Delta f_{ij}) \right]$$

$$(4.3)$$

where,

$$\phi_{ij} = \frac{4 - \Delta t_{ij} - \Delta t_{i\max}}{4 - \Delta t_{i\min} - \Delta t_{i\max}},$$

$$\varphi_{ij} = \frac{4 - \Delta c_{ij} - \Delta c_{i\max}}{4 - \Delta c_{i\min} - \Delta c_{i\max}},$$

$$\psi_{ij} = \frac{4 - \Delta u_{ij} - \Delta u_{i\max}}{4 - \Delta u_{i\min} - \Delta u_{i\max}},$$

$$\varsigma_{ij} = \frac{4 - \Delta f_{ij} - \Delta f_{i\max}}{4 - \Delta f_{i\min} - \Delta f_{i\max}},$$

$$\Delta t_{ij} = |\, t_{ij} - t_j^* \,|,$$

$$\Delta c_{ij} = |\, c_{ij} - c_j^* \,|,$$

$$\Delta u_{ij} = |\, u_{ij} - u_j^* \,|,$$

$$\Delta f_{ij} = |\, f_{ij} - f_j^* \,|,$$

$$\Delta t_{i\min} = \min_j |\, t_{ij} - t_j^* \,|,$$

$$\Delta c_{i\min} = \min_j |\, c_{ij} - c_j^* \,|,$$

$$\Delta u_{i\min} = \min_j |\, u_{ij} - u_j^* \,|,$$

$$\Delta f_{i\min} = \min_j |\, f_{ij} - f_j^* \,|,$$

$$\Delta t_{i\max} = \max_j |\, t_{ij} - t_j^* \,|,$$

$$\Delta c_{i\max} = \max_j |\, c_{ij} - c_j^* \,|,$$

$$\Delta u_{i\max} = \max_j |\, u_{ij} - u_j^* \,|,$$

$$\Delta f_{i\max} = \max_j |\, f_{ij} - f_j^* \,|,$$

for any $i=1,2,\ldots,$m and $j=1,2,\ldots,$n.

By using the above weighted correlation coefficient $M_w(A_p A^*)$ ($i=1,2,\ldots,$m) we can derive the ranking order of all alternatives and we can choose the best one among those.

5. INTERVAL QUADRIPARTITIONED NEUTROSOPHIC SETS (IQNS)

Definition 5.1 An IQNS A in X is denoted by truth-membership function $T_A(x)$, an contradiction membership function $C_A(x)$, an unknown membership function $U_A(x)$ and a falsity membership function $F_A(x)$. For each point x in X, there are

$$T_A(x) = \left[\inf T_A(x), \sup T_A(x)\right] \subseteq [0,1], \ C_A(x) = \left[\inf C_A(x), \sup C_A(x)\right] \subseteq [0,1],$$

$$U_A(x) = \left[\inf U_A(x), \sup U_A(x)\right] \subseteq [0,1], \ F_A(x) = \left[\inf F_A(x), \sup F_A(x)\right] \subseteq [0,1].$$

Therefore an IQNS A can be denoted as,

$$
\begin{aligned}
A &= \left\{ \left\langle x, T_A(x), \ C_A(x), U_A(x), F_A(x) \right\rangle \mid x \in X \right\} \\
&= \left\{ \left\langle \begin{array}{l} x, [\inf T_A(x), \ \sup T_A(x)], [\inf C_A(x), \ \sup C_A(x)], \\ [\inf U_A(x), \ \sup U_A(x)], [\inf F_A(x), \ \sup F_A(x)] \end{array} \right\rangle \middle| x \in X \right\}
\end{aligned}
$$

Then the sum of

$$T_A(x), C_A(x), \ U_A(x), F_A(x)$$

satisfies the condition,

$$0 \leq \sup T_A(x) + \sup C_A(x) + \sup U_A(x) + \sup F_A(x) \leq 4.$$

If the upper and lower ends of the interval values of

$$T_A(x), C_A(x), U_A(x) \, and \, F_A(x)$$

in an IQNS are equal then IQNS reduces to the QSVNS. Both QSVNSs and IQNSs are all the subclasses of Quadripartitioned neutrosophic sets (QNS).

Definition 5.2 The complement of an IQNS A is denoted by A^C and is defined as,

$$\inf T_{A^c}(x) = 1 - \sup T_A(x), \sup T_{A^c}(x) = 1 - \inf T_A(x),$$
$$\inf C_{A^c}(x) = 1 - \sup C_A(x), \sup C_{A^c}(x) = 1 - \inf C_A(x),$$
$$\inf U_{A^c}(x) = 1 - \sup U_A(x), \sup U_{A^c}(x) = 1 - \inf U_A(x),$$
$$\inf F_{A^c}(x) = 1 - \sup F_A(x), \sup F_{A^c}(x) = 1 - \inf F_A(x) \quad for\ any\ x\ in\ X$$

Definition 5.3 An IQNS A is contained in the other IQNS B that is $A \subseteq B$ if and only if

$$\inf T_A(x) \le \inf T_B(x), \sup T_A(x) \le \sup T_B(x),$$
$$\inf C_A(x) \le \inf C_B(x), \sup C_A(x) \le \sup C_B(x),$$
$$\inf U_A(x) \ge \inf U_B(x), \sup U_A(x) \ge \sup U_B(x),$$
$$\inf F_A(x) \ge \inf F_B(x), \sup F_A(x) \ge \sup F_B(x) \quad for\ any\ x\ in\ X.$$

Definition 5.4 Two IQNSs A and B are equal i.e.,

$A = B$ *if and only if* $A \subseteq B$ *and* $B \subseteq A.$

5.1 Correlation Coefficient Between IQNSs

In this section we propose a correlation coefficient between IQNSs as a generalization of the improved correlation coefficient of QSVNSs.

Definition 5.5 The correlation coefficient between two IQNSs A and B in the universe of discourse $X = \{x_1, x_2, \dots, x_n\}$ is defined as follows:

$$N(A, B) = \frac{1}{8n} \sum_{i=1}^{n} [\phi_i^{\,L}(1 - \Delta T_i^{\,L}) + \varphi_i^{\,L}(1 - \Delta C_i^{\,L}) + \psi_i^{\,L}(1 - \Delta U_i^{\,L}) + \zeta_i^{\,L}(1 - \Delta F_i^{\,L})$$
$$+ \phi_i^{\,U}(1 - \Delta T_i^{\,U}) + \varphi_i^{\,U}(1 - \Delta C_i^{\,U}) + \psi_i^{\,U}(1 - \Delta U_i^{\,U}) + \zeta_i^{\,U}(1 - \Delta F_i^{\,U})]$$

$$(5.1)$$

where

$$\phi_i^{\,L} = \frac{4 - \Delta T_i^{\,L} - \Delta T_{\max}^{\,L}}{4 - \Delta T_{\min}^{\,L} - \Delta T_{\max}^{\,L}},$$

$$\phi_i^U = \frac{4 - \Delta T_i^U - \Delta T_{\max}^U}{4 - \Delta T_{\min}^U - \Delta T_{\max}^U},$$

$$\varphi_i^L = \frac{4 - \Delta C_i^L - \Delta C_{\max}^L}{4 - \Delta C_{\min}^L - \Delta C_{\max}^L},$$

$$\varphi_i^U = \frac{4 - \Delta C_i^U - \Delta C_{\max}^U}{4 - \Delta C_{\min}^U - \Delta C_{\max}^U},$$

$$\psi_i^L = \frac{4 - \Delta U_i^L - \Delta U_{\max}^L}{4 - \Delta U_{\min}^L - \Delta U_{\max}^L},$$

$$\psi_i^U = \frac{4 - \Delta U_i^U - \Delta U_{\max}^U}{4 - \Delta U_{\min}^U - \Delta U_{\max}^U},$$

$$\varsigma_i^L = \frac{4 - \Delta F_i^L - \Delta F_{\max}^L}{4 - \Delta F_{\min}^L - \Delta F_{\max}^L},$$

$$\varsigma_i^U = \frac{4 - \Delta F_i^U - \Delta F_{\max}^U}{4 - \Delta F_{\min}^U - \Delta F_{\max}^U},$$

$$\Delta T_i^L = |\inf T_A(x_i) - \inf T_B(x_i)|,$$

$$\Delta T_i^U = |\sup T_A(x_i) - \sup T_B(x_i)|,$$

$$\Delta C_i^L = |\inf C_A(x_i) - \inf C_B(x_i)|,$$

$$\Delta C_i^U = |\sup C_A(x_i) - \sup C_B(x_i)|,$$

$$\Delta U_i^L = |\inf U_A(x_i) - \inf U_B(x_i)|,$$

$$\Delta U_i^U = |\sup U_A(x_i) - \sup U_B(x_i)|,$$

$$\Delta F_i^L = |\inf F_A(x_i) - \inf F_B(x_i)|,$$

$$\Delta F_i^U = |\sup F_A(x_i) - \sup F_B(x_i)|,$$

$$\Delta T_{\min}^L = \min_i |\inf T_A(x_i) - \inf T_B(x_i)|,$$

$$\Delta T_{\min}^U = \min_i |\sup T_A(x_i) - \sup T_B(x_i)|,$$

$$\Delta C_{\min}^L = \min_i |\inf C_A(x_i) - \inf C_B(x_i)|,$$

$$\Delta C_{\min}^U = \min_i |\sup C_A(x_i) - \sup C_B(x_i)|,$$

$$\Delta U_{\min}^L = \min_i |\inf U_A(x_i) - \inf U_B(x_i)|,$$

$$\Delta U_{\min}^U = \min_i |\sup U_A(x_i) - \sup U_B(x_i)|,$$

$$\Delta F_{\min}^L = \min_i |\inf F_A(x_i) - \inf F_B(x_i)|,$$

$$\Delta F_{\min}^U = \min_i |\sup F_A(x_i) - \sup F_B(x_i)|,$$

$$\Delta T_{\max}^L = \max_i |\inf T_A(x_i) - \inf T_B(x_i)|,$$

$$\Delta T_{\max}^U = \max_i |\sup T_A(x_i) - \sup T_B(x_i)|,$$

$$\Delta C_{\max}^L = \max_i |\inf C_A(x_i) - \inf C_B(x_i)|,$$

$$\Delta C_{\max}^U = \max_i |\sup C_A(x_i) - \sup C_B(x_i)|,$$

$$\Delta U_{\max}^{L} = \max_{i} |\inf U_{A}(x_{i}) - \inf U_{B}(x_{i})|,$$

$$\Delta U_{\max}^{U} = \max_{i} |\sup U_{A}(x_{i}) - \sup U_{B}(x_{i})|,$$

$$\Delta F_{\max}^{L} = \max_{i} |\inf F_{A}(x_{i}) - \inf F_{B}(x_{i})|,$$

$$\Delta F_{\max}^{U} = \max_{i} |\sup F_{A}(x_{i}) - \sup F_{B}(x_{i})|.$$

Here we introduce a weighted correlation coefficient between IQNSs A and B by consider the weight of the element $x_i(i=1,2,\ldots,n)$ into an account for any $x_i \in X$ and $i=1,2,\ldots,n$.

Let w_i be the weight for each element

$$x_i (i = 1,2,\ldots,n), \ w_i \in [0,1] \text{ and } \sum_{i=1}^{n} w_i = 1,$$

then the weighted correlation coefficient between the IQNSs A and B which is denoted by $N_w(A,B)$ defined in following Equation (5.2)

$$N_w(A,B) = \frac{1}{8} \sum_{i=1}^{n} w_i \ [\phi_i^{L}(1 - \Delta T_i^{L}) + \varphi_i^{L}(1 - \Delta C_i^{L}) + \psi_i^{L}(1 - \Delta U_i^{L}) + \zeta_i^{L}(1 - \Delta F_i^{L})$$
$$+ \phi_i^{U}(1 - \Delta T_i^{U}) + \varphi_i^{U}(1 - \Delta C_i^{U}) + \psi_i^{U}(1 - \Delta U_i^{U}) + \zeta_i^{U}(1 - \Delta F_i^{U})]$$

$$(5.2)$$

If $w = (1/n, 1/n,\ldots, 1/n)^T$ then Equation (5.2) reduces to Equation (5.1). When

$$T_A(x_i) = \inf T_A(x_i) = \sup T_A(x_i), C_A(x_i) = \inf C_A(x_i) = \sup C_A(x_i), U_A(x_i)$$
$$= \inf U_A(x_i) = \sup U_A(x_i), F_A(x_i) = \inf F_A(x_i) = \sup F_A(x_i)$$

in the IQNS A and

$$T_B(x_i) = \inf T_B(x_i) = \sup T_B(x_i), C_B(x_i) = \inf C_B(x_i) = \sup C_B(x_i), U_B(x_i)$$
$$= \inf U_B(x_i) = \sup U_B(x_i), F_B(x_i) = \inf F_B(x_i) = \sup F_B(x_i)$$

in the IQNS B for any x_i in X and $i=1,2,...,n$ then the IQNS A and B reduces to the QSVNSs A and B respectively and also the Equations (4.1) and (4.2) reduces to Equations (4.2) and (4.3). Both $N(A,B)$ and $N_w(A,B)$ also satisfies the three properties of Theorem 3.1 and Theorem 4.2

Theorem 5.1 For any two IQNSs A and B in the universe of discourse $X= \{x_1,x_2,...,x_n\}$, the correlation coefficient $N(A,B)$ satisfies the following properties.

1. $N(A, B) = N(B, A)$;
2. $0 \leq N(A, B) \leq 1$;
3. $N(A, B) = 1$ *if and only if* $A = B$.

It is similar to prove the properties in Theorem 4.1

Theorem 5.2 Let w_i be the weight for each element

$$x_i\,(i = 1,2,...,n),\, w_i \in [0,1]\, and \sum_{i=1}^{n} w_i = 1,$$

then the weighted correlation coefficient between the IQNSs A and B which is denoted by $N_w(A,B)$ defined in Equation (5.2) also satisfies the following properties.

1. $N_w(A, B) = N_w(B, A)$;
2. $0 \leq N_w(A, B) \leq 1$;
3. $N_w(A, B) = 1$ *if and only if* $A = B$.

It is also similar to prove the properties in Theorem 4.1.

5.2 Decision Making Method Using the Improved Correlation Coefficient of IQNSs

Here we consider a multiple attribute decision making problem with interval quadripartitioned neutrosophic information and the characteristic of an alternative $A_i(i=1,2,...,m)$ on an attribute $C_j(j=1,2,...,n)$ is represented by the following IQNS:

$$A_i = \left\{ \left\langle C_j, T_{A_i}(C_j),\ C_{A_i}(C_j), U_{A_i}(C_j), F_{A_i}(C_j) \right\rangle \mid C_j \in C, j = 1, 2, \ldots, n \right\}$$

$$= \left\{ \left\langle \begin{array}{l} C_j, [\inf T_{A_i}(C_j), \sup T_{A_i}(C_j)], [\inf C_{A_i}(C_j), \sup C_{A_i}(C_j)], \\ [\inf U_{A_i}(C_j), \sup U_{A_i}(C_j)], [\inf F_{A_i}(C_j), \sup F_{A_i}(C_j)] \end{array} \right\rangle \mid C_j \in C, j = 1, 2, \ldots, n \right\}$$

where

$$T_{A_i}(C_j),\ C_{A_i}(C_j), U_{A_i}(C_j), F_{A_i}(C_j) \in [0,1]$$

and

$$0 \le \sup T_{A_i}(C_j) + \sup C_{A_i}(C_j) + \sup U_{A_i}(C_j) + \sup F_{A_i}(C_j) \le 4$$
$$\text{for } C_j \in C, j = 1, 2, \ldots, n \text{ and } i = 1, 2, \ldots, m$$

To make it convenient, we are considering the following four functions,

$$T_{A_i}(C_j) = [\inf T_{A_i}(C_j), \sup T_{A_i}(C_j)], C_{A_i}(C_j) = [\inf C_{A_i}(C_j), \sup C_{A_i}(C_j)],$$
$$U_{A_i}(C_j) = [\inf U_{A_i}(C_j), \sup U_{A_i}(C_j)], F_{A_i}(C_j) = [\inf F_{A_i}(C_j), \sup F_{A_i}(C_j)]$$

in terms of a interval quadripartitioned neutrosophic value (IQNV)

$$r_{ij} = \left\langle [t_{ij}^L, t_{ij}^U],\ [c_{ij}^L, c_{ij}^U],\ [u_{ij}^L, u_{ij}^U],\ [f_{ij}^L, f_{ij}^U] \right\rangle \ (i = 1, 2, \ldots, m; j = 1, 2, \ldots, n)$$

Here the values of r_{ij} are usually derived from the evaluation of an alternative A_i with respect to a criterion C_j by the expert or decision maker. Therefore we got a interval quadripartitioned neutrosophic decision matrix $R = (r_{ij})_{m \times n}$.

In this an ideal IQNV can be defined by

$$r_j^* = \left\langle [t_j^{L^*}, t_j^{U^*}],\ [c_j^{L^*}, c_j^{U^*}],\ [u_j^{L^*}, u_j^{U^*}],\ [f_j^{L^*}, f_j^{U^*}] \right\rangle = \left\langle [1,1], [1,1], [0,0], [0,0] \right\rangle (j = 1, 2, \ldots, n)$$

in the ideal alternative A^* is given by,

$$N_w(A_i, A^*) = \frac{1}{8} \sum_{i=1}^{n} w_j [\phi_{ij}{}^L (1 - \Delta T_{ij}{}^L) + \varphi_{ij}{}^L (1 - \Delta C_{ij}{}^L) + \psi_{ij}{}^L (1 - \Delta U_{ij}{}^L) + \zeta_{ij}{}^L (1 - \Delta F_{ij}{}^L)$$
$$+ \phi_{ij}{}^U (1 - \Delta T_{ij}{}^U) + \varphi_{ij}{}^U (1 - \Delta C_{ij}{}^U) + \psi_{ij}{}^U (1 - \Delta U_{ij}{}^U) + \zeta_{ij}{}^U (1 - \Delta F_{ij}{}^U)]$$

$$(5.3)$$

$$\phi_{ij}{}^L = \frac{4 - \Delta t_{ij}{}^L - \Delta t_{i\max}^L}{4 - \Delta t_{i\min}^L - \Delta t_{i\max}^L},$$

$$\phi_{ij}{}^U = \frac{4 - \Delta t_{ij}{}^U - \Delta t_{i\max}^U}{4 - \Delta t_{i\min}^U - \Delta t_{i\max}^U},$$

$$\varphi_{ij}{}^L = \frac{4 - \Delta c_{ij}{}^L - \Delta c_{i\max}^L}{4 - \Delta c_{i\min}^L - \Delta c_{i\max}^L},$$

$$\varphi_{ij}{}^U = \frac{4 - \Delta c_{ij}{}^U - \Delta c_{i\max}^U}{4 - \Delta c_{i\min}^U - \Delta c_{i\max}^U},$$

$$\psi_{ij}{}^L = \frac{4 - \Delta u_{ij}{}^L - \Delta u_{i\max}^L}{4 - \Delta u_{i\min}^L - \Delta u_{i\max}^L},$$

$$\psi_{ij}{}^U = \frac{4 - \Delta u_{ij}{}^U - \Delta u_{i\max}^U}{4 - \Delta u_{i\min}^U - \Delta u_{i\max}^U},$$

$$\varsigma_{ij}{}^L = \frac{4 - \Delta f_{ij}{}^L - \Delta f_{i\max}^L}{4 - \Delta f_{i\min}^L - \Delta f_{i\max}^L},$$

$$\varsigma_{ij}{}^U = \frac{4 - \Delta f_{ij}{}^U - \Delta f_{i\max}^U}{4 - \Delta f_{i\min}^U - \Delta f_{i\max}^U},$$

$$\Delta t_{ij}{}^L = |t_{ij}{}^L - t_j{}^{L^*}|,$$

$$\Delta t_{ij}^{U} = |t_{ij}^{U} - t_{j}^{U^*}|,$$

$$\Delta c_{ij}^{L} = |c_{ij}^{L} - c_{j}^{L^*}|,$$

$$\Delta c_{ij}^{U} = |c_{ij}^{U} - c_{j}^{U^*}|,$$

$$\Delta u_{ij}^{L} = |u_{ij}^{L} - u_{j}^{L^*}|,$$

$$\Delta u_{ij}^{U} = |u_{ij}^{U} - u_{j}^{U^*}|,$$

$$\Delta f_{ij}^{L} = |f_{ij}^{L} - f_{j}^{L^*}|,$$

$$\Delta f_{ij}^{U} = |f_{ij}^{U} - f_{j}^{U^*}|,$$

$$\Delta t_{i\min}^{L} = \min_{j} |t_{ij}^{L} - t_{j}^{L^*}|,$$

$$\Delta t_{i\min}^{U} = \min_{j} |t_{ij}^{U} - t_{j}^{U^*}|,$$

$$\Delta c_{i\min}^{L} = \min_{j} |c_{ij}^{L} - c_{j}^{L^*}|,$$

$$\Delta c_{i\min}^{U} = \min_{j} |c_{ij}^{U} - c_{j}^{U^*}|,$$

$$\Delta u_{i\min}^{L} = \min_{j} |u_{ij}^{L} - u_{j}^{L^*}|,$$

$$\Delta u_{i\min}^{U} = \min_{j} |u_{ij}^{U} - u_{j}^{U^*}|,$$

$$\Delta f_{i\min}^{L} = \min_{j} |f_{ij}^{L} - f_{j}^{L^*}|,$$

$$\Delta f_{i\min}^{U} = \min_{j} |f_{ij}^{U} - f_{j}^{U^{*}}|,$$

$$\Delta t_{i\max}^{L} = \max_{j} |t_{ij}^{L} - t_{j}^{L^{*}}|,$$

$$\Delta t_{i\max}^{U} = \max_{j} |t_{ij}^{U} - t_{j}^{U^{*}}|,$$

$$\Delta c_{i\max}^{L} = \max_{j} |c_{ij}^{L} - c_{j}^{L^{*}}|,$$

$$\Delta c_{i\max}^{U} = \max_{j} |c_{ij}^{U} - c_{j}^{U^{*}}|,$$

$$\Delta u_{i\max}^{L} = \max_{j} |u_{ij}^{L} - u_{j}^{L^{*}}|,$$

$$\Delta u_{i\max}^{U} = \max_{j} |u_{ij}^{U} - u_{j}^{U^{*}}|,$$

$$\Delta f_{i\max}^{L} = \max_{j} |f_{ij}^{L} - f_{j}^{L^{*}}|,$$

$$\Delta f_{i\max}^{U} = \max_{j} |f_{ij}^{U} - f_{j}^{U^{*}}|,$$

for $i=1,2,\ldots,$m and $j=1,2,\ldots,$n.

By using the above weighted correlation coefficient $N_{w}(A_{i}A)$ $(i=1,2,\ldots,m)$ we can derive the ranking order of all alternatives and we can choose the best one among those.

6. ILLUSTRATIVE EXAMPLE

This section deals the example for the multiple attribute decision making problem with the given alternatives corresponds to the criteria allotted under quadripartitioned single valued neutrosophic environment and interval quadripartitioned neutrosophic environment.

6.1 Decision Making Under Quadripartitioned Single Valued Neutrosophic Environment

The example which we will discuss here is about the best mobile phone among all available alternatives based on various criteria. The alternatives A_1, A_2, A_3 respectively denotes the Mobile 1, Mobile 2, Mobile 3. The customer must take a decision according to the following four attributes (1) C_1 is the cost (2) C_2 is the storage space (3) C_3 is the camera quality (4) C_4 is the looks. According to this attributes we will derive the ranking order of all alternatives and based on this ranking order customer will select the best one. The weight vector of the above attributes is given by $w=$ $(0.35, 0.25, 0.20, 0.10)^T$. Here the alternatives are to be evaluated under the above four attributes by the form of QSVNSs. In general the evaluation of an alternative A_i with respect to an attribute $C_j (i=1,2,3; j=1,2,3,4)$ will be done by the questionnaire of a domain expert. In particularly while asking the opinion about an alternative A_1 with respect to an attribute C_1 the possibility he or she say that the statement true is 0.5, the statement both true and false is 0.4, the statement neither true nor false is 0.3 and the statement false is 0.2. It can be denoted in neutrosophic notation as $d_{11}= \langle 0.5, 0.4, 0.3, 0.2 \rangle$. Continuing this procedure for all three alternatives with respect to four attributes we will get the following quadripartitioned single valued neutrosophic decision matrix D.

$$D = \begin{bmatrix} \langle 0.5,0.4,0.3,0.2 \rangle & \langle 0.6,0.7,0.5,0.1 \rangle & \langle 0.3,0.8,0.4,0.2 \rangle & \langle 0.2,0.3,0.1,0.5 \rangle \\ \langle 0.4,0.3,0.2,0.1 \rangle & \langle 0.5,0.1,0.3,0.9 \rangle & \langle 0.1,0.2,0.4,0.7 \rangle & \langle 0.6,0.7,0.5,0.4 \rangle \\ \langle 0.8,0.5,0.4,0.3 \rangle & \langle 0.2,0.1,0.6,0.5 \rangle & \langle 0.7,0.3,0.4,0.1 \rangle & \langle 0.3,0.8,0.1,0.2 \rangle \end{bmatrix}$$

Then by using the proposed method we will obtain the most desirable alternative. We can get the values of the correlation coefficient $M_w(A_i, A^*)$ $(i=1,2,3)$ by using Equation (4.3). Hence

$$M_w(A_1, A^*) = 0.525617, \ M_w(A_2, A^*) = 0.395529, \ M_w(A_3, A^*) = 0.347771.$$

Therefore the ranking order is $A_1 > A_2 > A_3$. The alternative $A_1 (Mobile 1)$ is the best choice among all the three alternatives.

6.2 Decision Making Under Interval Quadripartitioned Neutrosophic Environment

Consider the same example here the three possible alternatives are to be evaluated under the above four attributes by the form of IQNSs. Here the weight vector of the above attributes is given by $w= (0.18, 0.25, 0.37, 0.20)^T$. In general the evaluation of an alternative A_i with respect to an attribute $C_j(i=1,2,3; j=1,2,3,4)$ will be done by the questionnaire of a domain expert. Therefore we get the following interval quadripartitioned neutrosophic decision matrix R.

$$R=\begin{bmatrix} \langle[0.3,0.5]\rangle & \langle[0.1,0.2]\rangle & \langle[0.3,0.6]\rangle & \langle[0.4,0.7]\rangle \langle[0.3,0.5]\rangle & \langle[0.1,0.6]\rangle & \langle[0.4,0.7]\rangle & \langle[0.3,0.7]\rangle \\ \langle[0.1,0.2]\rangle & \langle[0.3,0.4]\rangle & \langle[0.7,0.8]\rangle & \langle[0.4,0.6]\rangle,\langle[0.1,0.5]\rangle & \langle[0.2,0.3]\rangle & \langle[0.5,0.6]\rangle & \langle[0.4,0.6]\rangle, \\ \langle[0.6,0.8]\rangle & \langle[0.6,0.7]\rangle & \langle[0.4,0.6]\rangle & \langle[0.3,0.6]\rangle \langle[0.4,0.5]\rangle & \langle[0.6,0.7]\rangle & \langle[0.4,0.6]\rangle & \langle[0.2,0.8]\rangle \end{bmatrix}$$

$$\begin{bmatrix} \langle[0.3,0.6]\rangle & \langle[0.2,0.6]\rangle & \langle[0.1,0.3]\rangle & \langle[0.4,0.7]\rangle \langle[0.3,0.5]\rangle & \langle[0.1,0.6]\rangle & \langle[0.4,0.7]\rangle & \langle[0.3,0.7]\rangle \\ \langle[0.4,0.5]\rangle & \langle[0.2,0.3]\rangle & \langle[0.4,0.7]\rangle & \langle[0.2,0.5]\rangle,\langle[0.4,0.7]\rangle & \langle[0.1,0.5]\rangle & \langle[0.2,0.8]\rangle & \langle[0.1,0.8]\rangle \\ \langle[0.1,0.3]\rangle & \langle[0.5,0.7]\rangle & \langle[0.2,0.3]\rangle & \langle[0.7,0.8]\rangle \langle[0.2,0.7]\rangle & \langle[0.1,0.6]\rangle & \langle[0.2,0.4]\rangle & \langle[0.2,0.8]\rangle \end{bmatrix}$$

Then by using the proposed method we will obtain the most desirable alternative. We can get the values of the correlation coefficient $N_w(A_i,A^*)$ $(i=1,2,3)$ by using Equation (5.3).

Hence

$$N_w(A_1,A^*)=0.4448, \ N_w(A_2,A^*)=0.4020, N_w(A_3,A^*)=0.47963.$$

Therefore the ranking order is $A_3>A_1>A_2$. The alternative $A_3(Mobile3)$ is the best choice among all the three alternatives with respect to the given criteria under interval quadripartitioned neutrosophic environment.

7. CONCLUSION

In this paper authors have defined the improved correlation coefficient of QSVNSs, IQNSs and this is applicable for some cases when the correlation coefficient of QSVNSs defined in [20] is undefined (or) unmeaningful and also studied its properties. Decision making is a process which plays a vital role in real life problems. The main process in decision making is recognizing the problem (or) opportunity and deciding to address it. Here authors have discussed the decision making method using the improved correlation coefficient of QSVNSs, IQNSs and in particularly an illustrative example is given in multiple attribute decision making problem which involves the several alternatives based on various criteria. Hence the proposed improved correlation coefficient of QSVNSs, IQNSs helps to identify the most suitable alternative to the customer based on the given criteria.

REFERENCES

Abdel-Basset, M., Nabeeh, N. A., El-Ghareeb, H. A., & Aboelfetouh, A. (2019). Utilizing Neutrosophic Theory to Solve Transition Difficulties of IoT-Based Enterprises. *Enterprise Information Systems.*

Atanasov, K. (1986). Intuitionistic Fuzzy Sets. *Fuzzy Sets and Systems, 20*(1), 87–96. doi:10.1016/S0165-0114(86)80034-3

Broumi, S. (2014). Deli, Correlation measure for neutrosophic refined sets and its application in medical diagnosis. *Palestine J. Math., 3*(1), 11–19.

Broumi, S., & Smarandache, F. (2013). Correlation coefficient of interval neutrosophic set. *Applied Mechanics and Materials, 436*, 511–517. doi:10.4028/www.scientific.net/AMM.436.511

Broumi, S., & Smarandache, F. (2014). Rough Neutrosophic sets. *International Journal of Pure and Applied Mathematics, 32*, 493–502.

Chen, L., & Wang, Y. Z. (2003). Research on TOPSIS integrated evaluation and decision method based on entropy coefficient. *Control Decis., 18*, 456–459.

Chiang, D. A., & Lin, N. P. (1999). Correlation of fuzzy sets. *Fuzzy Sets and Systems, 102*(2), 221226. doi:10.1016/S0165-0114(97)00127-9

Deli, I., Broumi, S., & Smarandache, F. (2015). Neutrosophic multi-sets and its application in medical diagnosis. *J. New Theory, 6*, 88–98.

Guo, Y., & Şengür, A. (2014). A novel image segmentation algorithm based on neutrosophic similarity clustering. *Applied Soft Computing, 25*, 391–398. doi:10.1016/j.asoc.2014.08.066

Guo, Y., Sengur, A., & Tian, J. (2016). A novel breast ultrasound image segmentation algorithm based on neutrosophic similarity score and level set. *Computer Methods and Programs in Biomedicine, 123*, 43–53. doi:10.1016/j.cmpb.2015.09.007 PMID:26483304

Guo, Y., Şengür, A., & Ye, J. (2014). A Novel Image Thresholding Algorithm Based on Neutrosophic Similarity Score. *Measurement*, *58*, 175–186. doi:10.1016/j.measurement.2014.08.039

Hanafy, I. M., Salama, A. A., & Mahfouz, K. (2012). Correlation of neutrosophic data. *Int. Refereed J. Eng. Sci.*, *1*(2), 39–43.

Hong, D. H. (2006). Fuzzy measures for a correlation coefficient of fuzzy numbers under Tw (the weakest t norm)-based fuzzy arithmetic operations. *Information Sciences*, *176*(2), 150160. doi:10.1016/j.ins.2004.11.005

Jiang, X., Guo, Y., & Chen, H. (2019). An Adaptive Region Growing Method using Similarity Set Score and Homogeneity Value based on Neutrosophic Set Domain for Ultrasound Image Segmentation. *IEEE Access: Practical Innovations, Open Solutions*, *7*(1), 60584–60593. doi:10.1109/ACCESS.2019.2911560

Karaaslan, F. (2016). Correlation coefficient between possibility neutrosophic soft sets. *Math. Sci. Lett.*, *5*(1), 71–74. doi:10.18576/msl/050109

Karaaslan, F. (2017). Correlation coefficients of single-valued neutrosophic refined soft sets and their applications in clustering analysis. *Neural Computing & Applications*, *28*(2), 2781–2793. doi:10.100700521-016-2209-8

Mohana, K., & Mohanasundari, M. (2018). Quadripartitioned Single Valued Neutrosophic Rough Sets. *Nirmala Annual Research Congress (NARC-2018)*, *3*, 165.

Mohana & Mohanasundari. (2019). On Some Similarity Measures of Single Valued Neutrosophic Rough Sets. *Neutrosophic Sets and Systems, 24*, 10-22.

Nabeeh, N. A., Abdel-Basset, M., El-Ghareeb, H. A., & Aboelfetouh, A. (2019). Neutrosophic Multi-Criteria Decision Making Approach for IoT-Based Enterprises. *IEEE Access: Practical Innovations, Open Solutions*.

Nabeeh, N. A., Smarandache, F., Abdel-Basset, M., El-Ghareeb, H. A., & Aboelfetouh, A. (2019). An Integrated Neutrosophic-TOPSIS Approach and its Application to Personnel Selection: A New Trend in Brain Processing and Analysis. *IEEE Access: Practical Innovations, Open Solutions*.

Pawlak, Z. (1982). Rough sets. *International Journal of Computer and Information Sciences*, *11*(5), 341–356. doi:10.1007/BF01001956

Rajarajeswari, P., & Uma, N. (2014). Correlation measure for intuitionistic fuzzy multi sets. *Int. J. Res. Eng. Technol.*, *1*(3), 611–617.

Rajarajeswari, P., & Uma, N. (2014). Zhang and Fu's similarity measure on intuitionistic fuzzy multi sets. *Int. J. Innov. Res. Sci. Eng. Technol.*, *3*(5), 12309–12317.

Rajashi Chatterjee, P. (2016). Majumdar and S.K.Samanta, On some similarity measures and entropy on quadripartitioned single valued neutrosophic sets. *Journal of Intelligent & Fuzzy Systems*, *30*(4), 2475–2485. doi:10.3233/IFS-152017

Sahin, R., & Liu, P. (2017). Correlation coefficient of single-valued neutrosophic hesitant fuzzy sets and its applications in decision making. *Neural Computing & Applications*, *28*(6), 1387–1395. doi:10.100700521-015-2163-x

Shahin, Guo, Amin, & Sharawi. (2018). A Novel White Blood Cells Segmentation Algorithm Based on Adaptive Neutrosophic Similarity Score. *Health Information Science and Systems, 6*(1).

Shahin, A. I., Amin, K. M., & Amr, A. (2018, May). A Novel Enhancement Technique for Pathological Microscopic Image Using Neutrosophic Similarity Score Scaling. *International Journal for Light and Electron Optics*, *161*, 84–97. doi:10.1016/j.ijleo.2018.02.026

Shi, L. (2016). *Correlation coefficient of simplified neutrosophic sets for bearing fault diagnosis*. Shock Vibr. doi:10.1155/2016/5414361

Shinoj, T.K., & John, S.J. (2012). Intuitionistic fuzzy multi-sets and its application in medical diagnosis. *World Acad. Sci. Eng. Technol., 6*, 1–28.

Smarandache, F. (1999). *A Unifying Field in Logics. Neutrosophy: Neutrosophic Probability, Set and Logic*. Rehoboth: American Research Press.

Smarandache, F. (2005). Neutrosophic set—a generalization of the intuitionistic fuzzy set. *International Journal of Pure and Applied Mathematics*, *24*(3), 287–297.

Smarandache, F. (2013). n-valued refined neutrosophic logic and its applications in physics. *Progr. Phys., 4*, 143–146.

Wang, H., Smarandache, F., Zhang, Y. Q., & Sunderraman, R. (2010). Single valued neutrosophic sets. *Multispace Multistruct, 4*, 410–413.

Wang, H., Smarandache, F., Zhang, Y. Q., & Sunderraman, R. (2005). Interval Neutrosophic Set and Logic: Theory and Applications in Computing. Hexis.

Wang, Z., & Jian, L. (2017). Correlation coefficients of probabilistic hesitant fuzzy elements and their applications to evaluation of the alternatives. *Symmetry*, *9*(11), 2–18. doi:10.3390ym9110259

Wei, G. W., Wang, H. J., & Lin, R. (2011). Application of correlation coefficient to interval-valued intuitionistic fuzzy multiple attribute decision-making with incomplete weight information. *Knowledge and Information Systems*, *26*(2), 337349. doi:10.100710115-009-0276-1

Ye & Smarandache. (2016). Similarity Measure of Refined Single-Valued Neutrosophic Sets and Its Multicriteria Decision Making Method. *Neutrosophic Sets and Systems*, *12*, 41–44. doi:10.5281/zenodo.571146

Ye. (n.d.). Another Form of Correlation Coefficient between Single Valued Neutrosophic Sets and its multiple Attribute Decision Making Method. *Neutrosophic Sets and Systems*, *1*, 8-12. doi:10.5281/zenodo.571265

Ye, J. (2010). Multicriteria fuzzy decision-making method using entropy weights-based correlation coefficients of interval valued intuitionistic fuzzy sets. *Applied Mathematical Modelling*, *34*(12), 38643870. doi:10.1016/j.apm.2010.03.025

Ye, J. (2010). Fuzzy decision-making method based on the weighted correlation coefficient under intuitionistic fuzzy environment. *European Journal of Operational Research*, *205*(1), 202–204. doi:10.1016/j.ejor.2010.01.019

Ye, J. (2012). Multicriteria decision making method using the correlation coefficient under singlevalued neutrosophic environmet. *International Journal of General Systems*, *42*(4), 386–394. doi:10.1080/03081079.2012.761609

Ye, J. (2013). Multicriteria decision-making method using the correlation coefficient under single-valued neutrosophic environment. *International Journal of General Systems*, *42*(4), 386394. doi:10.1080/03081079.2012.761609

Ye, J. (2013). Another form of correlation coefficient between single valued neutrosophic sets and irs multiple attribute decision making method. *Neutrosophic Set Syst.*, *1*, 8–12.

Ye, J. (2014). Similarity measures between interval neutrosophic sets and their application in multicriteria decision-making. *Journal of Intelligent & Fuzzy Systems*, *26*, 165–172.

Ye, J. (2014). Correlation coefficient of dual hesitant fuzzy sets and its application to multiple attribute decision making. *Applied Mathematical Modelling*, *38*(2), 659666. doi:10.1016/j.apm.2013.07.010

Ye, J. (2014). Improved correlation coefficients of single valued neutrosophic sets and interval neutrosophic sets for multiple attribute decision making. *Journal of Intelligent & Fuzzy Systems*, *27*, 24532462.

Ye, J. (2016). Correlation coefficients of interval neutrosophic hesitant fuzzy sets and its application in a multiple attribute decision making method. *Informatica, 27*(1), 179–202. doi:10.15388/Informatica.2016.81

Ye, J. (2017). Multiple attribute decision-making method using correlation coefficients of normal neutrosophic sets. *Symmetry, 9*(80), 2–10.

Ye, J. (2017). Correlation coefficient between dynamic single valued neutrosophic multisets and its multiple attribute decision-making method. *Information, 8*(41), 2–9.

Ye, J., & Zhang, Q. (2014). Single Valued Neutrosophic Similarity Measures for Multiple Attribute Decision-Making. *Neutrosophic Sets and Systems, 2*, 48–54. doi:10.5281/zenodo.571756

Ye, S., & Ye, J. (2014). Dice similarity measure between single valued neutrosophic multisets and its application. *Neutrosophic Sets Syst., 6*, 48–53.

Zadeh, L. (1965). Fuzzy sets. *Information and Control, 8*(3), 87–96. doi:10.1016/S0019-9958(65)90241-X

Zhang, H. Y., Ji, P., Wang, J. Q., & Chen, X. H. (2015). An improved weighted correlation coefficient based on integrated weight for interval neutrosophic set and its application in multi-criteria decision-making problems. *Int. J. Comput. Intell. Syst., 8*(6), 1027–1043. doi:10.1080/18756891.2015.1099917

Zhang, H. Y., Wang, J. Q., & Chen, X. H. (2014). Interval neutrosophic sets and their application in multicriteria decision making problems. *The Scientific World Journal*. PMID:24695916

Chapter 15
Real–Time Neutrosophic Graphs for Communication Networks

Siddhartha Sankar Biswas
Jamia Hamdard (Deemed), India

ABSTRACT

In this century the communication networks are expanding very fast in huge volumes in terms of their nodes and the connecting links. But for a given alive communication network, its complete core topology may not be always available to the concerned communication systems at a given real point of time. Thus, at any real-time instant the complete graph may not be available, but a subgraph of it to the system for executing its communication or transportation activities may be. In this chapter, the author introduces 'real-time neutrosophic graphs' (RTN-graphs) in which all real-time information (being updated every q quantum of time) are incorporated so that the communication/transportation system can serve very efficiently with optimal results. Although the style and philosophy of Dijkstra's algorithm is followed, the approach is completely new in the sense that the neutrosophic shortest path problem (NSPP) is solved with the real-time information of the network where most of the data are neutrosophic numbers.

INTRODUCTION

Many problems of computer science, communication network, transportation systems, etc. can be modeled into graphs and then can be smoothly solved. Graph theory [Bollobas(2002), Harary(1995), Biswas(2012), Balakrishnan(1997)] has

DOI: 10.4018/978-1-7998-2555-5.ch015

wide applications in several branches of Engineering, in particular in Computer Science, Communication systems, Civil Engineering, etc. and also in, Science, Social Science, Optimization, Management Science, Medical Science, Economics, etc. to list a few only out of many.

Besides that, in most of the cases of such directed graphs, the real data about the weights of the arcs are not always crisp but neutrosophic numbers (as a special case could be intuitionistic fuzzy numbers and/or fuzzy numbers). Such type of graphs are known as neutrosophic graphs (Broumi[2016a]). In this Chapter a new type of real time graphs called by 'Real Time Neutrosophic Graphs' (or 'RTN-graphs') is introduced which are a generalized notion of the classical neutrosophic graphs of Broumi. The RTN-graph is a highly flexible and appropriate model as it incorporates the real time information of the network problem to facilitate the decision maker to search for an efficient and optimized results/solutions exactly at the real instant of time. Clearly a RTN-graph is a variable representation of a network with respect to time. Consequently the very popular Dijkstra algorithm is not applicable to solve any SPP in such type of graphs. The very first work on proposing a good algorithm to solve the Neutrosophic Shortest Path Problem (NSPP) was done by Broumi et el in the pioneer work in (Broumi et el [2017a]). However, in this chapter an algorithm is finally developed to solve the Neutrosophic Shortest Path Problem (NSPP) in a RTN-graph. Because of real time property the proposed algorithm may produce different results at different time of initiation, but each time the results will be most efficient for that particular real time only. In this article only those graphs are considered which are without loops.

BACKGROUND

This section recollects some relevant basic preliminaries, and in particular, the work of [Smarandache(1998a,1998b,2002,2005), Salama(2012), Salama et el (2012)] and few other theoretical works [Ansari et el(2013), Ashbacher(2002), Wang et el(2010), Wang et el(2011), Alblowi(2014)], [Ye(2013)]. Smarandache introduced the neutrosophic components T, I, F which represent the membership, indeterminacy, and non-membership values respectively having the domain for each function the non-standard unit interval. $]^-0,1^+[$.

Some Preliminaries of Neutrosophic Theory

In this section, some basic concepts and definitions on neutrosophic sets and single valued neutrosophic sets are reviewed from the existing literature.

Definition 1

Let X be a space of points (objects) with generic elements in X denoted by x. Then the neutrosophic set A (NS A) is an object having the form

$A = \{< x: T_A(x), I_A(x), F_A(x)>, x \in X\},$

where the functions T, I, F: $X \rightarrow$]⁻0,1⁺[define respectively the truth-membership function, indeterminacy-membership function, and falsity-membership function of the element $x \in X$ to the set A with the condition:

$^-0 \leq T_A(x) + I_A(x) + F_A(x) \leq 3^+$.

The trio functions $T_A(x), I_A(x)$ and $F_A(x)$ are real standard or nonstandard subsets of]⁻0,1⁺[.

Since it is difficult to apply NSs to practical problems, the authors [Wang et el(2010), Alblowi(2014)] introduced the concept of a SVNS, which is an instance of a NS and can be used in real scientific and engineering applications.

Definition 2

Let T, I, F be real standard or nonstandard subsets of]⁻0,1⁺[, with

Sup_T=t_sup, inf_T=t_inf

Sup_I=i_sup, inf_I=i_inf

Sup_F=f_sup, inf_F=f_inf

n-sup=t_sup+i_sup+f_sup

n-inf=t_inf+i_inf+f_inf,

T, I, F are called neutrosophic components

Definition 3

The NS 0_N in X is defined as follows:

1. $0_N = \{ <x, (0,0,1)>: x \in X\}$

2. $0_N = \{<x, (0,1,1)>: x \in X\}$
3. $0_N = \{<x, (0,1,0)>: x \in X\}$
4. $0_N = \{<x, (0,0,0)>: x \in X\}$

The NS 1_N in X is defined as follows:

1. $1_N = \{<x, (1,0,0)>: x \in X\}$
2. $1_N = \{<x, (1,0,1)>: x \in X\}$
3. $1_N = \{<x, (1,1,0)>: x \in X\}$
4. $1_N = \{<x, (1,1,1)>: x \in X\}$

Definition 4

Let X be a space of points (objects) with generic elements in X denoted by x. A single valued neutrosophic set A (SVNS A) is characterized by truth-membership function $T_A(x)$, an indeterminacy-membership function $I_A(x)$ and a falsity-membership function $F_A(x)$.

The single valued neutrosophic sets can thus be viewed as subclass of neutrosophic sets. For each point x in X, we have $T_A(x)$, $I_A(x)$, $F_A(x) \in [0,1]$.

Thus a SVNS A can be written as

$$A = \{< x: T_A(x), I_A(x), F_A(x)>, x \in X\} \text{ where } T_A(x), I_A(x), F_A(x) \in [0,1].$$

Definition 5

Let $A_1 = (T_1, I_1, F_1)$ and $A_2 = (T_2, I_2, F_2)$ be two single valued neutrosophic numbers. Then, the operations for SVNNs are defined as below:

1. $A_1 \oplus A_2 = <T_1 + T_2 - T_1 T_2, I_1 I_2, F_1 F_2>$.
2. $A_1 \otimes A_2 = <T_1 T_2, I_1 + I_2 - I_1 I_2, F_1 + F_2 - F_1 F_2>$.
3. $kA_1 = < 1- (1-T_1)^k, I_1^k, F_1^k >$ where k > 0.
4. $A_1^k = < T_1^k, 1- (1-I_1)^k, 1- (1-F_1)^k >$ where k > 0.

Definition 6

The neutrosophic zero 0_N defined as $0_N = \{<x, (0,1,1)>: x \in X\}$ is in fact the absolute neutrosophic zero.

In this chapter wherever the 0_N be used, it is the absolute neutrosophic zero, not the other neutrosophic zeroes.

The works [Ye(2013)], [Chakraborty, A., Mondal, S. P., Ahmadian, Ali, Senu, Norazak, Alam, Shariful and Salahshour, S. (2018)] contain a details of further comprehensive study of various types of neutrosophic numbers and basic operations on them.

Ranking of Neutrosophic Numbers

To solve any SPP in a graph the method involves additions and comparisons of the edge lengths (weights). Since, the addition and comparison between two single valued neutrosophic numbers are not alike those between two precise real numbers, we have used the ranking method proposed by Ye [20]. A convenient method for comparing single valued neutrosophic numbers can be done by using score function as successfully done in the work [Broumi et. el. (2017)].

Definition 7

Let $A_1 = (T_1, I_1, F_1)$ be a single valued neutrosophic number. Then, the score function $s(A_1)$, accuracy function $a(A_1)$ and the certainty function $c(A_1)$ of the SVNN A_1 are defined as below:

1. $s(A_1) = \dfrac{2 + T_1 - I_1 - F_1}{3}$
2. $a(A_1) = T_1 - F_1$
3. $c(A_1) = T_1$

Definition 8

Suppose that $A_1 = (T_1, I_1, F_1)$ and $A_2 = (T_2, I_2, F_2)$ be two single valued neutrosophic numbers. Then a ranking method is defined as follows:

1. if $s(A_1) > s(A_2)$, then the SVNN A_1 is neutrosophic greater than the SVNN A_2 denoted by the notation $A_1 > A_2$.
2. if $s(A_1) = s(A_2)$ but $a(A_1) > a(A_2)$, then the SVNN A_1 is neutrosophic greater than the SVNN A_2 denoted by the notation $A_1 > A_2$.
3. if $s(A_1) = s(A_2)$ but $a(A_1) = a(A_2)$ and $c(A_1) > c(A_2)$, then the SVNN A_1 is neutrosophic greater than the SVNN A_2 denoted by the notation $A_1 > A_2$.
4. if $s(A_1) = s(A_2)$ and $a(A_1) = a(A_2)$ and $c(A_1) > c(A_2)$, then the SVNN A_1 is neutrosophic equal to the SVNN A_2 denoted by the notation $A_1 = A_2$.

However for simple cases, the following ranking method may be followed for easy applications:

1. if $s(A_1) > s(A_2)$, then the SVNN A_1 is neutrosophic greater than the SVNN A_2 denoted by the notation $A_1 \succ A_2$.
2. if $s(A_1) < s(A_2)$, then the SVNN A_1 is neutrosophic less than the SVNN A_2 denoted by the notation $A_1 \prec A_2$.
3. if $s(A_1) = s(A_2)$, then the SVNN A_1 is neutrosophic equal to the SVNN A_2 denoted by the notation $A_1 = A_2$.

For details of the classical notion of neutrosophic set theory of Smarandache, one could see [Smarandache(1998a,1998b,2005a,2005b)]. The concept of a neutrosophic numbers (NNs) is of importance for quantifying an ill-known quantity. In this work throughout, the basic operations like neutrosophic addition $\oplus$, neutrosophic subtraction $\ominus$, and 'ranking' of neutrosophic numbers, etc are used. Using the ranking of n number of neutrosophic numbers, one can soft-compute min and max of these n number of NNs. If A_1, A_2, A_3,...., A_n be n neutrosophic numbers sorted in neutrosophic ascending order i.e. if $A_1 \prec A_2 \prec A_3 \prec .... \prec A_n$, then A_1 and A_n are called respectively the neutrosophic-min and neutrosophic-max of these n neutrosophic numbers.

The concept of neutrosophic numbers is of importance for quantifying an ill-known quantity. In this work here, the operations like neutrosophic addition $\oplus$, neutrosophic subtraction $\ominus$, and 'ranking' of neutrosophic numbers etc are used.

Neutrosophic Sets Are Generalization of Intuitionistic Fuzzy Sets

Theory of Intuitionistic Fuzzy Sets (IFS) was initiated by Atanassov as a generalization of the Theory of Fuzzy Sets. It is needless to mention that vague sets [Gau, W. L. and Buehrer, D. J. (1993)] are intuitionistic fuzzy sets as justified in length in the work [Bustince, H and Burillo, P. (1996)]. The major weakness of fuzzy theory is that if m(x) is the degree of membership of an element x to be in the fuzzy set A of the universe of discourse X, then the rest amount i.e. $1 - m(x)$ is completely and directly assigned to the degree of non-membership of the same x. The value of m(x) is decided by the concerned decision maker by his best possible judgement and credited to the value of membership value, but for the non-membership value of x there is no decision process by the decision maker. It is obtained by a crisp computation with the help of the value of m(x). This issue is overcome by Atanassov in modeling the notion of intuitionistic fuzzy set (IFS). The work [Biswas, Ranjit. (2016a, 2016b, 2019)] is interesting for a detail analysis about the major weakness of fuzzy set theory in soft-computing. In intuitionistic fuzzy set, both the membership value and non-membership value are decided independently by the concerned decision maker. Consequently intuitionistic fuzzy theory is more useful to the analysts in their soft-computing exercises in the quest of better results, as explained very rigorously in the work [Biswas, Ranjit. (2016a, 2016b, 2019)]. But it is now observed that the theory of intuitionistic fuzzy sets too has a sort of limitation. The main drawback of the model of IFS is that the decision maker has to be constrained very seriously to comply with the condition of $m(x) + n(x) + h(x) \leq 1$ every time while proposing the grade values of an element x. This causes a serious biasness into the cognition domain of the concerned decision maker every time for each x. The decision maker is not that much free to decide about the membership values and non-membership values because he must check that the total of $m(x)$ and $n(x)$ does not exceed the value 1 at any cost (i.e. does not exceed 100% in total), even not by a small amount ε (whatever infinitesimal small ε be). This limitation has been very nicely relaxed by a significant amount in the model of Neutrosophic Set (NS) introduced by Smarandache, and thus making the soft model set more appropriate than FS or IFS. The decision maker need not be so tightly constrained before proposing the grade values corresponding to the element x, because 100% or even slightly more span of length are open to propose each of the three grade values $T(x)$, $I(x)$ and $F(x)$ independently in case of NS.

It is now well known [see Smarandache, F. (2005)] to the soft-computing world that neutrosophic set (NS) is a generalization of the intuitionistic fuzzy set (IFS). An intuitionistic fuzzy set can be viewed as a special case of a neutrosophic set, but the converse is not necessarily true. The era of improvement of various models are as below:-

Crisp Set $\rightarrow$ Fuzzy Set (and various types of higher order Fuzzy Sets) $\rightarrow$ IFS$\rightarrow$ NS.

Consequently, by heredity the same is true for the corresponding notion of numbers too, i.e.

Crisp Number $\rightarrow$ Fuzzy Number $\rightarrow$ IFN$\rightarrow$ NN.

However, there are few more models to deal with uncertainty, viz Rough Sets, Soft Sets, etc. But these are not any competitive models of neutrosophic philosophy, rather complimentary models.

WHY NEUTROSOPHIC SHORTEST PATH PROBLEM (NSPP)?

As the title of this chapter "Real Time Neutrosophic Graphs For Communication Networks' says, the flow of the content in this chapter will be mainly as below in this chapter.

1. Introducing 'Real Time Neutrosophic Graph',
2. Optimizing the communication process in a network which is modeled into a Real Time Neutrosophic Graph by optimizing the connectivities between source node and destination node, and for this the important work is
3. How to modify the existing popular Dijkstra's algorithm to make it applicable for solving the Shortest Path Problems in Real Time Neutrosophic Graphs.

First of all it is required to present the importance of 'Graph Theory' in several domains of real life environments. Graph Theory is a very interesting core topic in Discrete Mathematics due to its numerous applications in diverse fields especially in the fields of Computer Engineering, Electrical Engineering, Electronics Engineering, Civil Engineering, Transportation Engineering, etc. Besides several branches of Engineering, Graph theory has wide applications in Natural Science, Social Science, Medical Science, Optimization, Statistics, Decision Science, Management Science, etc. to list a few out of many. In 1736, Swiss mathematician Leonhard Euler presented a general theory that included a solution to a very popular posed problem known as the 'Königsberg Bridge Problem', the very first problem that has ignited this important new branch of discrete mathematics known as "Graph Theory". Since then researchers around the world have attempted and successfully developed various mathematical properties of graphs, various propositions, theorems, and useful results of graphs, and after that scientists and engineers were able to successfully apply the concepts of Graph Theory in their own respective fields to solve many critical and complex problems very easily. Consequently, the application domains of Graph Theory has expanded exponentially in diverse fields. Any situation that has linked-items can be represented using graph theory. For instance, software engineers use graphs as their tools to represent communication networks, data organization, computational devices, the flow of computation etc. Another example of graph theory used by communication / network engineers is the multi-hop cooperative relay communication networks in which the network is comprised of one or more base station and one or more relay stations (nodes) that communicate information to mobile communication devices. Another example is a social network that software engineers are exploiting on sites like Facebook to market products to consumers, be them located at any distance geographically. Software engineers do also use graph theory to represent the structure of a website where the vertices are the available web pages and the edges are the directional connections between pages. The electrical engineers and electronic engineers employ graph theory fluently in the design of integrated circuits (ICs) for electronic devices. The ICs have complex layered microcircuits that can be represented as nodes interconnected by lines or arcs. By applying graph theory, the electrical engineers can optimize the density of components and minimize the connections to optimize processing speed and electrical efficiency. Civil engineers or structural engineers use graph theory to represent the forces in a truss. In their model of graphs the nodes represent the pinned joints in the truss, edges represent the rods in the truss with its end nodes corresponding to the joints that connect the rod to the truss. Edges are also used to represent external forces and reactions. A philosopher or a social scientist/activist exploit graph theory to understand relationships among people, say in a Facebook where an understanding of relationships between people is critical for advertisement and revenue.

A graph G is mathematically defined as an ordered pair (V, E) which consists of two sets V and E, where V is the set of vertices (or, nodes) and E is the set of edges (or, arcs). Here, at most one edge or arc may exist between pair of vertices. Graphs may be of two types: undirected graphs and directed graphs (or digraphs). In an undirected graph the edge (i, j) and the edge (j, i), if exist, are obviously identical unlike in the case of directed graph (digraph). Two graphs $G_1 = (V_1, E_1)$ and $G_2 = (V_2, E_2)$ are identical iff $V_1 = V_2$ and $E_1 = E_2$.

In the real life scenario, while a problem is modeled into a graph then the edges are usually associated with weights (or costs). Thus in a network, the arc length may represent a kind of distance or time or cost, and there might exist a large number of paths from source node to goal node. By the term "Cost of a path p from a node u to a node v" we mean the sum of the costs of the links constituting that path p. The famous Shortest Path Problem (SPP) in Graph Theory is a well defined mathematical problem of optimization, nevertheless it could be re-posed apparently in various engineering problems in various ways subject to network constraints and properties. The Shortest Path Problem (SPP) is the problem to find the path between two vertices of a graph such that the sum of the weights of the edges of the path is minimum. This interesting optimization problem have been and being studied by scientists/ engineers because of its tremendous potential in many important applications in the field of Computer Science, Communications, Optimization, Transportation, Manufacturing, Optimization, Scheduling, Routing, Railway Systems, Airlines Systems, and in fact in the field of any kind of Network Management, etc. While in an active communication process in a network from a source node to a destination node, two highly useful information for the decision makers (which may be a system or a software or any type of intelligent agent) are: shortest path and the corresponding shortest path-length. The very popular algorithm Dijkstra's algorithm conceived by the Dutch computer scientist Edsger Dijkstra in 1959 is a graph search algorithm that solves the single-source shortest path problem for a graph using crisp data. For a given source node (vertex) in the graph, this algorithm finds the path with lowest cost (i.e. the shortest path) between that vertex and every other vertex. It can also be used for finding costs of shortest paths from a single source vertex to a single destination vertex by stopping the algorithm once the shortest path to the destination vertex has been determined. The Dijkstra's algorithm is regarded as a revolutionary contribution for 'Shortest Path Problem (SPP)' towards the Theory of Graph.

Algorithms for SPP

The important existing algorithms for solving the crisp SPP problem are:-

- Dijkstra's algorithm: This algorithm solves the single-source shortest path problem with non-negative edge weight.
- Bellman–Ford algorithm: This algorithm solves the single-source problem where the edge weights may be positive or negative.
- A* search algorithm: This algorithm extracts single pair shortest path using heuristics method in order to speed up the search.
- Floyd–Warshall algorithm: This algorithm solves all pairs shortest paths.
- Johnson's algorithm: This algorithm extracts shortest paths of all pairs of nodes.

Fuzzy Shortest Path Problem (FSPP), Intuitionistic Fuzzy Shortest Path Problem (IFSPP), and Neutrosophic Shortest Path Problem (NSPP)

The concept of crisp graphs is extended to define fuzzy graphs, intuitionistic fuzzy graphs, and the neutrosophic graphs. The Fuzzy Shortest Path Problem (FSPP) and Intuitionistic Fuzzy Shortest Path Problem (IFSPP) are two generalizations of the classical SPP for applications in ill-defined environment and has been found important to many applications such as Communication or Transportation Network, Computational Geometry, Graph Algorithms, Geographical Information Systems (GIS), Network Optimization, etc. In traditional shortest path problems, the arc length of the network takes precise numbers, but in the real-world problem, the arc length may represent transportation time or cost which can be known only approximately due to vagueness of information, and hence it can be considered a fuzzy number or an intuitionistic fuzzy number. The nodes are well precise, but the data about the weights(costs) of the links are sometimes not available as crisp numbers, rather fuzzy numbers or intuitionistic fuzzy numbers or more appropriately neutrosophic numbers. However, the core problem is same as the crisp SPP of Graph Theory, i.e. to find the shortest path from a source vertex S to a single destination vertex D in a directed graph and to compute the corresponding min cost. A FSPP or IFSPP quite naturally to be solved using soft computing technique, where ranking of fuzzy numbers or intuitionistic fuzzy numbers is a key problem to the decision makers dealing with such type of graphs.

One of the first studies on fuzzy shortest path problem (FSPP) in graphs was done by Dubois and Prade [Dubois,D. and Prade,H. (1980)], and then by Klein [Klein, C.M. (1991)]. Though the work of Dubois and Prade was a major break-through, but that paper lacked any practical interpretation as even if fuzzy shortest path is found, but still this may not actually be any of the path in the corresponding network for which it was found. According to their approach, the shortest path length can be obtained, but the corresponding path in the network may not exist. This drawback of their method made it difficult for application in network problems.

There are few methods available in the literature to solve the intuitionistic fuzzy shortest path problem (IFSPP). In the work [Sathi (2012)] the author developed an interesting method to find intuitionistic fuzzy shortest path in a graph. Sathi used a heuristic methodology for solving the IF shortest path problem using the Intuitionistic Fuzzy Hybrid Geometric (IFHG) operator, with the philosophy of Dijkstra's Algorithm. In the work [Karunambigai, M. G., R. Parvathi, K. Atanassov and N. Palaniappan. (2007)], in a team work with Atanassov the researchers present a model based on dynamic programming to find the shortest paths in intuitionistic fuzzy graphs. The author in [Gani, A. Nagoor. (2010)] also developed a method on searching intuitionistic fuzzy shortest path in a network. But all these algorithms have merits and demerits both, none is absolutely best.

Neutrosophic Graph of Broumi et el and NSPP

Broumi et. el. in their work in [Broumi et. el. (2016a, 2016b, 2016c, 2016d, 2016e, 2017a, 2017b, 2017c, 2018)] introduced neutrosophic graph where some(all) of the weights of the edges are neutrosophic numbers instead of real numbers.

In the work [Broumi et. el. (2017)] the authors posed the Neutrosophic Shortest Path Problem (NSPP) and solved the NSPP using the style of Dijkstra's Algorithm. This work addresses for the first time the shortest path in an acyclic neutrosophic directed graph using ranking function. The neutrosophic number is able to represent the indeterminacy in the edge (arc) costs of neutrosophic graph. Broumi et. el. then proposed an algorithm to find the shortest path and the shortest path length from source node to destination node. Finally an illustrative example also included in their work to demonstrate the proposed algorithm in solving the NSPP with single valued neutrosophic arcs.

However, a lot of results on the neutrosophic graphs modeled by Broumi have been now reported by various authors, viz. [Shah(2016a, 2016b), Singh(2017)].

REAL TIME NEUTROSOPHIC GRAPHS (RTN-GRAPHS): A NEUTROSOPHIC MODEL

A graph G is an ordered pair (V, E) which consists of two sets V and E, where V is the set of vertices (or, nodes), and E is the set of edges (or, arcs). Here, such type of graphs are considered where no loop exists. Graphs may be of two types: undirected graphs and directed graphs. In an undirected graph the edge (i, j) and the edge (j, i), if exist, are obviously identical unlike in the case of directed graph.

But in this work here more real situations are considered which are actually and frequently faced by the present day communication systems. For example, consider an Adhoc Network or a MANET where there may exist a path from node u to node v, but because of some reasons this path may be temporarily damaged and hence temporarily unavailable for transmission of packets by the node u to its neighbor node v. This is a very useful information to the communication system if available to the sender node u in advance. Such kind of real time neutrosophic situation are incorporated and are called by Real Time Neutrosophic Graph or RTN-graph. The simple neutrosophic graph introduced by Broumi is a special case of the RTN-graph if all the links/edges are working properly like its original status at the real instant of time under consideration, i.e. if no link is damaged or under repair. The advantage of RTN-graph is that the solution will involve the data of reality and consequently the data/results can be applicable without any risk factors. The disadvantage is that in case all the links are in perfect condition (without any damage) at the real instant of time under consideration, then the Broumi's algorithm will provide faster solution because of the fact that the RTN-graph in such cases too will execute all the steps some of which may be redundant. To analyze further about the RTN-graph, few important terminologies from the work [Biswas(2015)] are borrowed and presented below.

Definition 9: 'Neighbor' Node

For a given node u the node v will be designated as a 'neighbor' node of u if u has a directed link from u to v.

Example

Consider the following directed RTN-graph G (see Figure 1) with neutrosophic weights (NNs). If the node A knows well in advance that the link AC (weight = NN $\tilde{3}$) is temporarily unavailable, then the node A has no other option but to send its packets to its neighbor B via the path AB (weight = NN $\tilde{15}$) only.

Figure 1. A RTN-graph G having one link damaged temporarily.

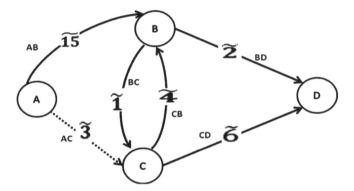

In the proposed mathematical model of graphs, incorporate now the real time data from its platform network to make the graphs more informatics, dynamic, more useful, and hence more efficient to the users. Every node of the graph carries an information vector corresponding to each of its neighbor nodes. If the node u has the node v as a neighbor node then u carries the following information handy with it:-

In real life situation, because of natural phenomenon (flood, earthquake, thunderstorm, solar storm, etc. etc.) or because of some kind of external attack or technical failure or because of an predictable/unpredictable damage of the link, etc. (to list a few only out of many such type of real life problems), it may happen in reality that during a period of time the link uv of the node u to its neighbor v is non-functional. In the proposed model, this is a precious information and is available with the node u here in advance.

Definition 10: Link Status (ls)

Consider a time instant t and a node u of the graph. Corresponding to every neighbor node v of the node u, there exist a Link Status (ls) i_{uv} which takes any of the two values from {0,1} with the following significance:-

$i_{uv} = 0$, if the link uv is non-functional at that time.

$= 1$, if the link uv is functional at that time.

Definition 11: Temporarily Blocked Link (tbl)

Consider a time instant t and a node u of the graph.. If at that real instant of time t, the link status i_{uv} happens to be 0, i.e. if the link uv is non-functional then it is said that the link uv is a temporarily blocked link (tbl) from u.

In a real time graph, the link from u to v may be out of order for some time (till it is repaired by the concerned system). In such a real situation the complete graph thus may not be available due to existence of non-functional status for few links, i.e. due to existence of few tbls; and consequently a sub-graph of it be available for communication (Example: for communication of packets in an Adhoc Network/ MANET, or for a salesman to travel many cities, or for a buss/truck carrying goods/ passengers in a transportation network, etc. one adjacent node of u may become all of a sudden disconnected, but it does not mean than communication will have to become paralysed. Certainly the system should opt for other available links from u to its other neighbourhood nodes which are not temporarily blocked). It is to be noted that a tbl does not mean that this link is permanently blocked. Once it be repaired, it will be well available to the communication system for successful communication process next time.

If a node u has k ($\geq$0) number of neighbor nodes v1, v2, v3,....,vk, then u carries k number of LS: $i_{uv1}, i_{uv2}, i_{uv3}, \ldots\ldots i_{uvk}$. In this mathematical model, it is proposed that there is a system S for the graph which updates all the information of all the nodes after every quantum time τ. This quantum τ is fixed (can be reset) for the system S in a graph but different for different graphs, in general depending upon the various properties of the physical problem for which a graph is modeled.

Definition 12: Link Status Class (LSC) Vector

For a given node u, the collection of all ls are called 'Link Status Class' (LSC) of u denoted by the vector I_u. If a node u has k ($\geq$0) number of neighbor nodes x1, x2, x3,.....,xk, then

$$I_u = \{i_{uv1}, i_{uv2}, i_{uv3}, \ldots\ldots i_{uvk}\}.$$

Definition 13: Temporarily Blocked Neighbor and ReachableNeighbor

If v is a neighbor node of a given node u, and if i_{uv} is 0 at a given instant of time then v is called a temporarily blocked neighbor (tbn) of u for that instant. Figure 2 shows a tbn.

Figure 2. A tbn v of the node u

If a neighbor v is not a tbn, then it is called a reachable neighbor (rn) of u. Figure 3 shows a tbn.

Figure 3. A rn v of the node u

Usually tbn is a temporary phenomenon for a node in a network, and if the concerned link be repaired in due time, then obviously a 'tbn' may regain its 'rn' status at some later stage.

Definition 14: Communicable Node

For a given node u, if $I_u \neq \varphi$ (null vector) then the node u is called a communicable node for that instant of time.

If u does not have any neighbor node then there is no existence of the vector I_u for u, and in that case it is trivial that further communication via u is never possible. However, if I_u exists but equal to φ at some instance of time then it signifies that further communication via u is not possible temporarily.

1. All the real time information mentioned/defined above will get automatically updated at every node of the graph at every q quantum of time (for a quantum q to be pre-fixed depending upon the properties of the network, on what kind of communication/transportation it is performing).

2. The weight w_{uv} corresponding to each link e_{uv} is a neutrosophic number (may be crisp number as a special case for some nodes). In a network, the weight of an arc length may represent time or cost. Let W denotes the set of all neutrosophic weights of the graph G.

Such type of graphs are called by 'Real Time Neutrosophic Graphs' or 'RTN-graphs' as they contain real time information of the networks. Consequently, for a given network the RTN-graph is not a static graph but changes with time.

Consider a communication network represented by the following graph G (in Figure 4) and at some instant its two links are damaged giving the RTN-graph G_1 (in Figure 5).

Figure 4. The original network: Graph G

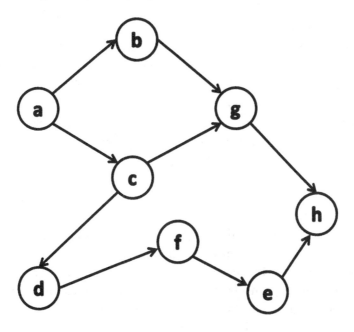

Figure 5. The RTN-graph G_1 of G, where few links are damaged at this point of time.

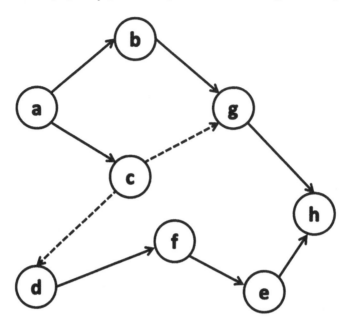

In figure-5, the node c is not a communicable node at the instant of time under consideration. It is because of the reason that c has two neighboring nodes d and g, both being non-rn at this time. For such type of RTN-graphs, none of the existing algorithms for NSPP can be applicable.

In the next section a method is developed to find a neutrosophic shortest path from a source node to a destination node in a RTN-graph.

NEUTROSOPHIC SHORTEST PATH IN A RTN-GRAPH

Graphs are a very important model of network. There are many real life problems of network, transportation, communication, circuit systems, etc. which are modeled into graphs and hence solved. The dynamic model "RTN-graph' is a new concept on the generalization of graphs considering its huge potential for real time applications in communication or transportation systems. In the work of [Broumi(2016a,2016b,2017)] the NSPP is solved, but in this section the NSPP for RTN-graphs is solved.

Consider a directed RTN-graph G where the arcs are of neutrosophic weights (neutrosophic numbers). Suppose that v is a rn of u in G with link status i_{uv}. Suppose that the subalgorithm FW(G) returns the neutrosophic weight set W.

Neutrosophic Shortest path estimate d[v] of a rn vertex v in a directed RTN-graph

The estimate d[v] in RTN-graphs is computed on real time data only. Suppose that s is the source vertex and the currently traversed vertex is u. At this real time, check whether u is a communicable node or not. If yes, then proceed further. If v is not a rn, then d[v] need not be estimated. Otherwise, d[v] of any rn vertex v, in a directed RTN-graph is computed using neutrosophic addition as below (see Figure 6):-

(neutrosophic shortest path estimate of vertex v)

= (neutrosophic shortest path estimate of vertex u)

$\oplus$ (neutrosophic weight corresponding to the arc from the vertex u to the vertex v).

or,

$d[v] = d[u] \oplus w_{uv}$.

Figure 6. Neutrosophic estimation procedure for d[v] in a RTN-graph G

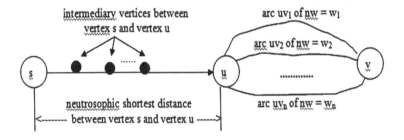

Neutrosophic Relaxation of an Arc in a directed RTN-graph

The classical notion of relaxation is extended here to the case of RTN-graph. At this real time the important deviation from the classical method is that attempt is not made to do relaxation of an arc/link if it is a tbl. By neutrosophic relaxation it is meant here the relaxation process of an arc whose weight is a neutrosophic number (or at best a crisp number). For this, first of all initialize the graph along with its starting vertex and neutrosophic shortest path estimate for each vertices of the graph G. The following 'NEUTROSOPHIC-INITIALIZATION-SINGLE-SOURCE' algorithm NISS will do:

NISS (G, s)

1. For each vertex v ∈ V[G]
2. d[v] = ∞
3. v.π = NIL
4. d[s] = 0

After the neutrosophic initialization, the process of neutrosophic relaxation of each arc begins, but to be applicable at real time only and hence tbl cases are excluded from the execution of relaxation jobs. The sub-algorithm RT-NEUTROSOPHIC-RELAX (see Figure 7) plays the vital role to update d[v] i.e. the neutrosophic shortest distance value between the starting vertex s and the vertex v, which is a rn of the current traversed vertex u. For the step-3 below, ranking of neutrosophic numbers is used, and the notion of the 'neutrosophic shortest distance' is to be understood accordingly.

RT-NEUTROSOPHIC-RELAX (u, v, W)

1. IF u is a communicable node, THEN
2. IF v is a rn, THEN
3. IF d[v] > d[u] ⊕ w_{uv}
4. THEN d[v] ← d[u] ⊕ w_{uv}
5. v.π ← u

where, w_{uv} ∈W is the neutrosophic weight of the arc from the vertex u to the vertex v, and v.π denotes the parent node of vertex v.

Real Time Neutrosophic Shortest Path Algorithm (RT-NSP Algo) in a RTN-Graph

The main algorithm to find single source neutrosophic shortest path in a RTN-graph is presented in this section. Name this by 'Real Time Neutrosophic Shortest Path Algorithm' i.e. in short by the title RT-NSPA. In this algorithm the above subalgorithms are used, and also the subalgorithm RTN-EXTRACT-NEUTROSOPHIC-MIN (Q) which extracts the node u with minimum key using a pre-decided neutrosophic ranking method and updates Q at real time only.

Figure 7. Diagram showing how the RT-NEUTROSOPHIC-RELAX algorithm works in a RTN-graph.

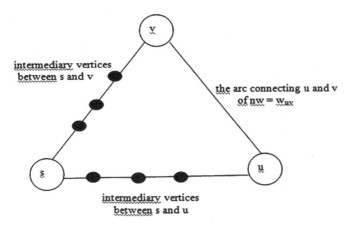

RT-NSPA (G, s)

1. NISS (G, s)
2. W ← NW(G)
3. S ← ∅
4. Q ← V[G]
5. *WHILE* Q ≠ ∅
6. *DO* u ← RT-EXTRACT-NEUTROSOPHIC-MIN (Q)
7. S ← S ∪ {u}
8. *FOR* each rn vertex v ∈ Adj[u]
9. *DO* RT-NEUTROSOPHIC-RELAX (u, v, W)

Example: A Comparison Study

Consider the following directed RTN-Graph G in Figure 8, where the neutrosophic weights (here they are single valued neutrosophic numbers) are shown against each link. The weight of the link AB is the single valued neutrosophic number $1\tilde{5}$ (approximately 15) denoted by w_{AB} (as per the Definition 5, the single valued neutrosophic number $1\tilde{5}$ is to be expressed in the form of (T, I, F) by proposing appropriate values of T, I and F for $1\tilde{5}$ by the concerned decision maker which may be a intelligent neutrosophic system or an intelligent neutrosophic software or any type of intelligent neutrosophic agent) and similarly the weights of all the other links are also neutrosophic numbers here. The objective is to solve the single source neutrosophic shortest paths problem taking the vertex A as the source vertex and the vertex D as the destination vertex, where the LSCs of all the nodes of the RTN-graph G are I_A, I_B, I_C and I_D given by:

$I_A = \{\ i_{AB},\ i_{AC}\ \}$ where $i_{AB} = 1$, $i_{AC} = 0$;

$I_B = \{\ i_{BC},\ i_{BD}\ \}$ where $i_{BC} = 1$, $i_{BD} = 1$;

and

$I_C = \{\ i_{CB},\ i_{CD}\ \}$ where $i_{CB} = 1$, $i_{CD} = 1$;

Figure 8. A RTN-graph G

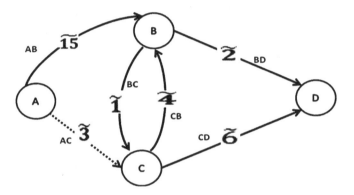

Clearly the RT-NSPA algorithm computes to yield the following result:

1. $w_{AB} = \tilde{15}$, $w_{AC} = \tilde{3}$, $w_{BC} = \tilde{1}$, $w_{CB} = \tilde{4}$, $w_{CD} = \tilde{6}$, and $w_{BD} = \tilde{2}$; and then
2. $S = \{A, B, D\}$, i.e. the RTN neutrosophic shortest path from the source vertex A is:

A→B→D.

3. d–values i.e. RTN neutrosophic shortest distance estimate-values of each vertex from the starting vertex A is:

d[A] = $\tilde{0}$, d[C] = not estimated, d[B] = NN $\tilde{15}$, d[D] = NN $\tilde{17}$,

where all operations are to be carried out using Definition 5. The method of ranking of neutrosophic numbers is already mentioned earlier, and the notion of the 'neutrosophic shortest distance' is to be understood accordingly with the help of this ranking method.

However, if the NSPP algorithm of Broumi, et el [see Broumi, S., Bakali, A., Talea, M. and Smarandache, F. (2016b)] be applied to the original graph G then the result is expected to be as below:-

the neutrosophic shortest path from the source vertex A to the destination vertex D is:

A→C→B→D,

with neutrosophic shortest distance = NN $\tilde{9}$.

This deviation is because of the reason that in Broumi's method it is not considered whether the link AC is damaged or not, and whether it is in working condition or not at real instant of time (by default all the links are considered to be in working status always). This result of Broumi's algorithm is different (mathematically better) from the above result, but surely not useful to the above communication system over RTN-graph. In Step-3 the value of d[C] is not estimated in the above solution, unlike in the Broumi's method. Consequently Broumi's method will cause a delay to traverse this mathematically computed shortest path (without considering the real time scenario of the link AC at the real instant of time under consideration) and surely there will be a wait (halt) at the node A before approaching for the node C till the repair of the link AC be done. Broumi's algorithm will produce best optimal results in all the NSPP problems except in the case of RTN-graphs.

CONCLUSION

There are many real life problems in the networks of transportation, communication, circuit systems, etc. which are initially modeled into graphs and hence solved. But in reality it is very frequent that due to some reason few links may be temporarily unavailable to the communication system at some real instant of time. Consequently, the complete topology of the graph of a network may not be available to the communication system but a subgraph of it is only available. Hence the classical Dijkstra algorithm can not be applicable to solve any SPP in such type of real time graphs for extracting any real solution which could be useful to the communication system. The classical Dijkstra algorithm can provide the mathematically optimal solution without considering whether its optimal path consists of all nodes none of which are not temporarily blocked. Thus in reality this solution is not applicable. The basic difference between the classical Dijkstra algorithm and the modified Dijkstra algorithm proposed in this chapter is that in case any link between two adjacent nodes be not in order temporarily because of certain real issues than too the modified algorithm can provide a real time optimal solution without halting or delaying the communication process. This is the great advantage of the modified Dijkstra algorithm over the classical Dijkstra algorithm. However, if there is no case of tbl in the network at the real time t of the communication under consideration, the modified Dijkstra algorithm and the classical Dijkstra algorithm both will provide identical solution. In this sense the modified Dijkstra algorithm can be viewed as a generalization of the classical Dijkstra algorithm to deal with the real time situation during the communication process over a network.

Besides that, in many of these directed graphs the weights of the arcs are not always crisp but neutrosophic numbers (as a special case could be intuitionistic fuzzy numbers and/or fuzzy numbers). In this Chapter a mathematical modeling of such real time status of a network is done by introducing a generalized structure called by 'RTN-graph'. The real time data/information are updated at each node of a the RTN-graph at every quantum time q. Then a new method called by RT-NSP algorithm is developed to solve the neutrosophic shortest path problem (NSPP) from a source vertex to a destination vertex in a directed RTN-graph. The importance of the proposed method lies in its potential to give solution in real time environment, unlike Broumi's algorithms for NSPP. Obviously because of real time property the proposed algorithm may produce different results at different real instants of time, but every result will surely be most significant for that particular real instant of time; whereas Broumi's algorithms will always produce same results irrespective of the time of the communication concerned.

REFERENCES

Alblowi, S. A., & Salama,, A. A., & Eisa, M. (2014). New Concepts of Neutrosophic Sets. *International Journal of Mathematics and Computer Applications Research*, *4*(1), 59–66.

Ansari, A. Q., Biswas, R., & Aggarwal, S. (2013). Neutrosophic classifier: An extension of fuzzy classifer. *Applied Soft Computing*, *13*(1), 563–573. doi:10.1016/j. asoc.2012.08.002

Ashbacher, C. (2002). *Introduction to Neutrosophic Logic*. American Research Press.

Atanassov, K. T. (1986). Intuitionistic fuzzy sets. *Fuzzy Sets and Systems*, *20*(1), 87–96. doi:10.1016/S0165-0114(86)80034-3

Atanassov, K. T. (1999). *Intuitionistic Fuzzy Sets: Theory and Applications*. Heidelberg, Germany: Springer. doi:10.1007/978-3-7908-1870-3

Atanassov, K. T. (2012). *On Intuitionistic Fuzzy Sets Theory*. Berlin: Springer. doi:10.1007/978-3-642-29127-2

Atanassov, K. T., & Janusz, K. (2016). *Intuitionistic Fuzzy Logic*. Springer.

Balakrishnan, V. K. (1997). *Graph Theory*. McGraw-Hill.

Bhutani, K. R., & Rosenfeld, A. (2003). Fuzzy End Nodes in Fuzzy Graphs. *Information Sciences*, *152*, 323–326. doi:10.1016/S0020-0255(03)00078-1

Biswas, R. (2016). *Is 'Fuzzy Theory' An Appropriate Tool For Large Size Problems?* Heidelberg, Germany: Springer.

Biswas, R. (2019). Intuitionistic Fuzzy Theory for Soft-Computing: More Appropriate Tool Than Fuzzy Theory. *International Journal of Computing and Optimization*, *6*(1), 13–56. doi:10.12988/ijco.2019.955

Biswas, S. S., Alam, B., & Doja, M.N. (2012). A Theoretical Characterization of the Data Structure 'Multigraphs'. *Journal of Contemporary Applied Mathematics*, *2*(2), 88-106.

Biswas, S. S., Alam, B., & Doja, M.N. (2015). Real Time Graphs For Communication Networks: A Fuzzy Mathematical Model. *Advances in Intelligent Systems and Computing*, *1*(379), 463 – 470. Doi:10.1007/978-81-322-2517-1_44

Bollobas, B. (2002). *Modern Graph Theory*. Springer.

Broumi, S., Bakali, A., Talea, M., Smarandache, F., & Rao, V.V. (2018). Interval Complex Neutrosophic Graph of Type 1. Neutrosophic Operational Research, 3, 87-106.

Broumi, S., Bakali, A., Talea, M., & Smarandache, F. (2016b). Applying Dijkstra Algorithm for solving Neutrosophic Shortest Path Problems. *Proceedings of the 2016 International Conference on Advanced Mechatronic Systems*, 412-416. 10.1109/ICAMechS.2016.7813483

Broumi, S., Bakali, A., Talea, M., & Smarandache, F. (2016d). Isolated Single Valued Neutrosophic Graphs. *Neutrosophic Sets and Systems*, *11*, 74–78.

Broumi, S., Bakali, A., Talea, M., Smarandache, F., & Hassan, A. (2017b). Generalized single valued neutrosophic graphs of first type. *SISOM & ACOUSTICS 2017*.

Broumi, S., Dey, A., Bakali, A., Talea, M., Smarandache, F., Son, L. H., & Koley, D. (2017c). Uniform Single Valued Neutrosophic Graphs. *Neutrosophic Sets and Systems*, *17*, 42–49.

Broumi, S., Talea, M., Bakali, A., & Smarandache, F. (2016c). Interval Valued Neutrosophic Graphs. *Critical Review*, *12*, 5–33.

Broumi, S., Talea, M., Bakali, A., & Smarandache, F. (2016e). Single Valued Neutrosophic Graphs. *Journal of New Theory*, *10*, 86-101.

Broumi, S., Talea, M., Bakali, A., Smarandache, F., Bakali, A., & Kishore Kumar, P. K. (2017a). Shortest Path Problem on Single Valued Neutrosophic Graphs. *Int. Symp. On Networks, Computers and Communications (ISNCC-2017)*. 10.1109/ISNCC.2017.8071993

Broumi, S., Talea, M., Smarandache, F., & Bakali, A. (2016a). Single valued neutrosophic graphs: Degree, Order and Size. *Proceedings of the IEEE International Conference on Fuzzy Systems (FUZZ)*, 2444-2451. 10.1109/FUZZ-IEEE.2016.7738000

Bustince, H., & Burillo, P. (1996). Vague sets are intuitionistic fuzzy sets. *Fuzzy Sets and Systems*, *79*(3), 403–405. doi:10.1016/0165-0114(95)00154-9

Chakraborty, A., Mondal, S. P., Ahmadian, A., Senu, N., Alam, S., & Salahshour, S. (2018). Different Forms of Triangular Neutrosophic Numbers, De-Neutrosophication Techniques, and their Applications. *Symmetry*, *10*(8), 327. doi:10.3390ym10080327

Cormen, T. H., Leiserson, C. E., Rivest, R. L., & Stein, C. (2001). *Introduction to Algorithms*. McGraw-Hill.

Dijkstra, E. W. (1959). A note on two problems in connexion with graphs. *Numerische Mathematik*, *1*(1), 269–271. doi:10.1007/BF01386390

Dubois, D., & Prade, H. (1980). *Fuzzy Sets and Systems: Theory and Applications*. New York: Academic Press.

Gani, A. N. (2010). On searching Intuitionistic Fuzzy Shortest Path in a Network. *Applied Mathematical Sciences*, *4*(69), 3447–3454.

Gau, W. L., & Buehrer, D. J. (1993). Vague sets. *IEEE Transactions on Systems, Man, and Cybernetics*, *23*(2), 610–614. doi:10.1109/21.229476

Harary, F. (1995). *Graph Theory*. Addison Wesley Publishing Company.

Karunambigai, M. G., Parvathi, R., Atanassov, K., & Palaniappan, N. (2007). An Intuitionistic Fuzzy Graph Method for Finding the Shortest Paths in Networks. *Advances in Soft Computing*, *42*, 3–10. doi:10.1007/978-3-540-72434-6_1

Klein, C. M. (1991). Fuzzy shortest paths. *Fuzzy Sets and Systems*, *39*(1), 27–41. doi:10.1016/0165-0114(91)90063-V

Mukherjee, S. (2012). Dijkstra's Algorithm for Solving the Shortest Path Problem on Networks Under Intuitionistic Fuzzy Environment. *Journal of Mathematical Modelling and Algorithms*, *11*(4), 345–359. doi:10.100710852-012-9191-7

Salama, A. A. (2012). *The Concept of Neutrosophic Set and Basic Properties of Neutrosophic Set Operations.* Paris: International University of Science, Engineering and Technology.

Salama, A. A., & Alblowi, S. A. (2012). Neutrosophic Set and Neutrosophic Topological Spaces. *IOSR Journal of Math*, *3*(4), 31-35.

Shah, N. (2016a). Some Studies in Neutrosophic Graphs. *Neutrosophic Sets and Systems*, *12*, 54–64.

Shah, N., & Hussain, A. (2016b). Neutrosophic Soft Graphs. *Neutrosophic Sets and Systems*, *11*, 31–44.

Shannon, A., & Atanassov, K. (1994). A First Step to A Theory of The Intuitionistic Fuzzy Graphs. *Proceedings of 1st Workshop on Fuzzy Based Expert Systems* 59–61.

Shannon, A., & Atanassov, K. (2004). On intuitionistic fuzzy multigraphs and their index matrix interpretations. *Proceedings of 2nd International IEEE Conference on Intelligent Systems*, *2*, 440–443. 10.1109/IS.2004.1344788

Singh, P. K. (2017). *Interval-Valued Neutrosophic Graph Representation of Concept Lattice and Its (α,β,γ)-Decomposition.* Arab Jou. Sci. Engg. doi:10.100713369-017- 2718-5

Smarandache, F. (1998a). *Neutrosophy: Neutrosophic Probability, Set, and Logic: Analytic Synthesis & Synthetic Analysis.* Rehoboth, DE: Ameri. Res. Press.

Smarandache, F. (1998b). *A Unifying Field in Logics. Neutrosophy: Neutrosophic Probability, Set and Logic.* Rehoboth, DE: American Research Press.

Smarandache, F. (2002). Neutrosophy and Neutrosophic Logic. In *First International Conference on Neutrosophy, Neutrosophic Logic, Set, Probability, and Statistics.* University of New Mexico.

Smarandache, F. (2005). Neutrosophic set a generalisation of the intuitionistic fuzzy sets. *International Journal of Pure and Applied Mathematics*, *24*, 287–297.

Wang, H. B., Smarandache, F., Zhang, Y. Q., & Sunderraman, R. (2010a). Single valued neutrosophic sets. *Multispace and Multistructure.*, *4*, 410–413.

Wang, H. B., Smarandache, F., Zhang, Y. Q., & Sunderraman, R. (2010b). Single Valucd Neutrosophic Sets. *Tech. Sci. Applications of Mathematics.*

Wang, H. B., Zhang, Y. Q., Sunderraman, R., & And Smarandache, F. (2011). Single valued neutrosophic sets. *Fuzzy Sets. Rough Sets and Multivalued Operations and Applications*, *3*(1), 33–39.

Ye, J. (2013). Another form of correlation coefficient between single valued neutrosophic sets and its multiple attribute decision-making method. *Neutrosophic Sets and Systems*, *1*(1), 8–12.

Chapter 16
Solving Neutrosophic Linear Programming Problems With Two–Phase Approach

Elsayed Metwalli Badr

iD https://orcid.org/0000-0002-7666-1169
Benha University, Egypt

Mustafa Abdul Salam
Benha University, Egypt

Florentin Smarandache

iD https://orcid.org/0000-0002-5560-5926
University of New Mexico, USA

ABSTRACT

The neutrosophic primal simplex algorithm starts from a neutrosophic basic feasible solution. If there is no such a solution, we cannot apply the neutrosophic primal simplex method for solving the neutrosophic linear programming problem. In this chapter, the authors propose a neutrosophic two-phase method involving neutrosophic artificial variables to obtain an initial neutrosophic basic feasible solution to a slightly modified set of constraints. Then the neutrosophic primal simplex method is used to eliminate the neutrosophic artificial variables and to solve the original problem.

DOI: 10.4018/978-1-7998-2555-5.ch016

1. INTRODUCTION

There are many real-world problems (forecasting, population census and petroleum manufacture . . . etc.) contain vague and imprecise information. Dealing with ambiguous information may cost us a lot more and it also affects the optimal solution of such real-world problems. Statistics and probability solve some of such problems and failed to transact with most of these problems. (Zadeh 1965) proposed Fuzzy set theory to handle vague and imprecise information. After then, (Atanassove 1986) proposed the concept of intuitionistic fuzzy set to handle vague and imprecise information, by considering both the truth and falsity function. Later, (Smarandache 1998, 2013, 2014, 2015 & Broumi *et.al.* 2016a, 2016b, 2016c) introduced Neutrosophic set theory to handle vague, imprecise and inconsistent information. Neutrosophic set is a popularization of fuzzy and intuitionistic fuzzy sets; each element of set had a truth, indeterminacy and falsity membership function. So, neutrosophic set can assimilate inaccurate, vague and maladjusted information efficiently and effectively (Brounmi et.al. 2016d)

The first contribution of neutrosophic linear programming theory was suggested by (Abdel-Basset *et al.* 2018). They introduced the neutrosophic linear programming LP models where their parameters are represented with a trapezoidal neutrosophic numbers and presented a technique for solving them. They presented some numerical examples which show their superiority with the state of the art by comparison. On the other hand, they introduced two ranking functions one of them for the maximization neutrosophic linear programs and the other for the minimization neutrosophic linear programs.

In this chapter, we add other new neutrosophic linear programming models and we propose a ranking function for both maximization neutrosophic linear programs and minimization neutrosophic linear programs. On the other hand, we use the same ranking function when we compare between the fuzzy approach and neutrosophic approach which solve the same example so this comparison is fair. Finally, we propose a neutrosophic two-phase method involving neutrosophic artificial variables, to obtain an initial neutrosophic basic feasible solution to a slightly modified set of constraints. Then the neutrosophic primal simplex method is used to eliminate the neutrosophic artificial variables and to solve the original problem.

The remaining part of this research is marshaled as follows: The important concepts of neutrosophic set arithmetic are presented in Sect. 2. The formularization of new NLP models is presented in Sect. 3. Neutrosophic primal simplex algorithm for solving fully neutrosophic linear programming is presented in Sect. 4. The neutrosophic two-phase method is proposed in Sect. 5. The comparison among the proposed approaches and other approaches are introduced in Sect. 6. Finally, conclusions and future trends are clarified in Sect. 7.

2. Preliminaries

In this section, we introduce some basic definitions of the neutrosophic set theory.

Definition 1 [Abdel-Basset *et al.* 2018] A single-valued neutrosophic set N which is a subset of X is defined as follows:

$$N = \{< x, T_N(x), I_N(x), F_N(x) >: x \in X\}$$

where X is a universe of discourse,

$T_N(x)$: $X \rightarrow [0,1]$, $I_N(x)$: $X \rightarrow [0,1]$ and $F_N(x)$: $X \rightarrow [0,1]$

with

$$0 \leq T_N(x) + I_N(x) + F_N(x) \leq 3$$

for all $x \in X$, $T_N(x)$, $I_N(x)$ and $F_N(x)$ represent truth membership, indeterminacy membership and falsity membership degrees of x to N.

Definition 2 [Abdel-Basset *et al.* 2018]: The trapezoidal neutrosophic number $\tilde{A}$ is a neutrosophic set in R with the following truth, indeterminacy and falsity membership functions:

$$T_{\tilde{A}}(x) = \begin{cases} 0 & : x < a_1 \\ \dfrac{\alpha_{\tilde{A}}(x - a_1)}{a_2 - a_1} & : a_1 \leq x \leq a_2 \\ \alpha_{\tilde{A}} & : a_2 \leq x \leq a_3 \\ \alpha_{\tilde{A}}\left(\dfrac{x - a_3}{a_4 - a_3}\right) & : a_3 \leq x \leq a_4 \\ 0 & : x > a_4 \end{cases}$$

$$I_{\tilde{A}}(x) = \begin{cases} 1 & : x < a_1^{'} \\ \dfrac{(a_2 - x + \theta_{\tilde{A}}(x - a_1^{'}))}{a_2 - a_1^{'}} & : a_1^{'} \leq x \leq a_2 \\ \theta_{\tilde{A}} & : a_2 \leq x \leq a_3 \\ \dfrac{(x - a_3 + \theta_{\tilde{A}}(a_4^{'} - x))}{a_4^{'} - a_3} & : a_3 \leq x \leq a_4^{'} \\ 1 & : x > a_4^{'} \end{cases}$$

$$F_{\tilde{A}}(x) = \begin{cases} 1 & : x < a_1^{''} \\ \dfrac{(a_2 - x + \beta_{\tilde{A}}(x - a_1^{''}))}{a_2 - a_1^{''}} & : a_1^{''} \leq x \leq a_2 \\ \beta_{\tilde{A}} & : a_2 \leq x \leq a_3 \\ \dfrac{(x - a_3 + \beta_{\tilde{A}}(a_4^{''} - x))}{a_4^{''} - a_3} & : a_3 \leq x \leq a_4^{''} \\ 1 & : x > a_4^{''} \end{cases}$$

where $\alpha_{\tilde{A}}$, $\theta_{\tilde{A}}$ and $\beta_{\tilde{A}}$ represent the maximum degree of truthiness, minimum degree of indeterminacy, minimum degree of falsity, respectively with $\alpha_{\tilde{A}}$, $\theta_{\tilde{A}}$ and $\beta_{\tilde{A}}$ $\in [0,1]$. The membership functions of trapezoidal neutrosophic number are presented in Fig. 1. It is clear that

$$a_1^{''} \leq a_1 \leq a_1^{'} \leq a_2 \leq a_3 \leq a_4^{'} \leq a_4 \leq a_4^{''}.$$

Remark 1: Here $T_{\tilde{A}}(x)$ increases with a constant rate for $[a_1, a_2]$ and decreases with a constant rate for $[a_3, a_4]$. $F_{\tilde{A}}(x)$ increases with a constant rate for $[a_1^{''}, a_2]$ and decreases with a constant rate for $[a_3, a_4^{''}]$. $I_{\tilde{A}}(x)$ increases with a constant rate for $[a_1^{'}, a_2]$ and decreases with a constant rate for $[a_3, a_4^{'}]$.

Remark 2: If $a_2 - a_1 = a_4 - a_3$ the trapezoidal neutrosophic number is called the symmetric trapezoidal neutrosophic number.

Definition 3 [Abdel-Basset *et al.* 2018]: The mathematical operations on two trapezoidal neutrosophic numbers

$$\tilde{A} = \left\langle a_1, a_2, a_3, a_4; \alpha_{\tilde{A}}, \theta_{\tilde{A}}, \beta_{\tilde{A}} \right\rangle$$

Figure 1. Truth membership, indeterminacy and falsity membership functions of trapezoidal neutrosophic numbers

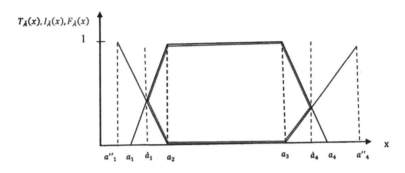

and

$$\tilde{B} = \left\langle b_1, b_2, b_3, b_4; \alpha_{\tilde{B}}, \theta_{\tilde{B}}, \beta_{\tilde{B}} \right\rangle$$

are as follows:

$$\tilde{A} + \tilde{B} = \left\langle (a_1 + b_1, a_2 + b_2, a_3 + b_3, a_4 + b_4); \alpha_{\tilde{A}} \wedge \alpha_{\tilde{A}}, \theta_{\tilde{A}} \vee \theta_{\tilde{A}}, \beta_{\tilde{A}} \vee \beta_{\tilde{A}} \right\rangle$$

$$\tilde{A} - \tilde{B} = \left\langle (a_1 - b_4, a_2 - b_3, a_3 - b_2, a_4 - b_1); \alpha_{\tilde{A}} \wedge \alpha_{\tilde{A}}, \theta_{\tilde{A}} \vee \theta_{\tilde{A}}, \beta_{\tilde{A}} \vee \beta_{\tilde{A}} \right\rangle$$

$$\tilde{A}^{-1} = \left\langle \left(\frac{1}{a_4}, \frac{1}{a_3}, \frac{1}{a_2}, \frac{1}{a_1} \right); \alpha_{\tilde{A}}, \theta_{\tilde{A}}, \beta_{\tilde{A}} \right\rangle \text{ where } (\tilde{A} \neq 0)$$

$$\lambda \tilde{A} = \begin{cases} \left\langle \lambda a_1, \lambda a_2, \lambda a_3, \lambda a_4; \alpha_{\tilde{A}}, \ \theta_{\tilde{A}}, \ \beta_{\tilde{A}} \right\rangle : \lambda > 0 \\ \left\langle \lambda a_4, \lambda a_3, \lambda a_2, \lambda a_1; \alpha_{\tilde{A}}, \ \theta_{\tilde{A}}, \ \beta_{\tilde{A}} \right\rangle : \lambda < 0 \end{cases}$$

$$\tilde{A}\tilde{B} = \begin{cases} \left\langle (a_1 b_1, a_2 b_2, a_3 b_3, a_4 b_4); \alpha_{\tilde{A}} \wedge \alpha_{\tilde{A}}, \theta_{\tilde{A}} \vee \theta_{\tilde{A}}, \beta_{\tilde{A}} \vee \beta_{\tilde{A}} \right\rangle if\ (a_4 > 0, b_4 > 0) \\ \left\langle (a_1 b_4, a_2 b_3, a_3 b_2, a_4 b_1); \alpha_{\tilde{A}} \wedge \alpha_{\tilde{A}}, \theta_{\tilde{A}} \vee \theta_{\tilde{A}}, \beta_{\tilde{A}} \vee \beta_{\tilde{A}} \right\rangle if\ (a_4 < 0, b_4 > 0) \\ \left\langle (a_4 b_4, a_3 b_3, a_2 b_2, a_1 b_1); \alpha_{\tilde{A}} \wedge \alpha_{\tilde{A}}, \theta_{\tilde{A}} \vee \theta_{\tilde{A}}, \beta_{\tilde{A}} \vee \beta_{\tilde{A}} \right\rangle if\ (a_4 < 0, b_4 < 0) \end{cases}$$

$$\frac{\tilde{A}}{\tilde{B}} = \begin{cases} \left\langle \left(\frac{a_1}{b_4}, \frac{a_2}{b_3}, \frac{a_3}{b_2}, \frac{a_4}{b_1}\right); \alpha_{\tilde{A}} \wedge \alpha_{\tilde{A}}, \theta_{\tilde{A}} \vee \theta_{\tilde{A}}, \beta_{\tilde{A}} \vee \beta_{\tilde{A}} \right\rangle if\ (a_4 > 0, b_4 > 0) \\[2mm] \left\langle \left(\frac{a_4}{b_4}, \frac{a_3}{b_3}, \frac{a_2}{b_2}, \frac{a_1}{b_1}\right); \alpha_{\tilde{A}} \wedge \alpha_{\tilde{A}}, \theta_{\tilde{A}} \vee \theta_{\tilde{A}}, \beta_{\tilde{A}} \vee \beta_{\tilde{A}} \right\rangle if\ (a_4 < 0, b_4 > 0) \\[2mm] \left\langle \left(\frac{a_4}{b_1}, \frac{a_3}{b_2}, \frac{a_2}{b_3}, \frac{a_1}{b_4}\right); \alpha_{\tilde{A}} \wedge \alpha_{\tilde{A}}, \theta_{\tilde{A}} \vee \theta_{\tilde{A}}, \beta_{\tilde{A}} \vee \beta_{\tilde{A}} \right\rangle if\ (a_4 < 0, b_4 < 0) \end{cases}$$

Definition 4 Ranking is a viable approach for ordering neutrosophic numbers. Here, we introduce a new rank function which is one convenient approach for solving the *NLP* problems. A ranking function of neutrosophic numbers is a function where $N(R)$ is a set of neutrosophic numbers defined on set of real numbers, which convert each neutrosophic number into the real line. We define orders on $N(R)$ by:

1. If $R(\tilde{a}) > R(\tilde{b})$ then $\tilde{a} \succ \tilde{b}$
2. If $R(\tilde{a}) < R(\tilde{b})$ then $\tilde{a} \prec \tilde{b}$
3. If $R(\tilde{a}) = R(\tilde{b})$ then $\tilde{a} \approx \tilde{b}$

Where

$$\tilde{a} = \left\langle a_1, a_2, a_3, a_4; \alpha_{\tilde{A}}, \theta_{\tilde{A}}, \beta_{\tilde{A}} \right\rangle$$

and

$$\tilde{b} = \left\langle b_1, b_2, b_3, b_4; \alpha_{\tilde{B}}, \theta_{\tilde{B}}, \beta_{\tilde{B}} \right\rangle$$

are two trapezoidal neutrosophic numbers. Also, we write $\tilde{a} \prec \tilde{b}$ if and only if $\tilde{b} \succ \tilde{a}$.

We consider a linear ranking function on

$$\tilde{a} = \left\langle a_1, a_2, a_3, a_4; \alpha_{\tilde{A}}, \theta_{\tilde{A}}, \beta_{\tilde{A}} \right\rangle$$

as:

$$R(\tilde{a}) = \frac{\sum_{i=1}^{4} a_i}{2} + (T_{\tilde{a}} - I_{\tilde{a}} - F_{\tilde{a}}) \tag{1}$$

Which is equivalent to the following function:

$$R(\tilde{a}) = a_1 + a_4 + \frac{a^{m2} - a^{m1}}{2} + (T_{\tilde{a}} - I_{\tilde{a}} - F_{\tilde{a}})$$

where a^{m1} and a^{m2} are first and second median values for trapezoidal neutrosophic number respectively and $(T_{\tilde{a}} - I_{\tilde{a}} - F_{\tilde{a}})$ is the conformation degrees. Also $T_{\tilde{a}}, I_{\tilde{a}}$ and $F_{\tilde{a}}$ are the truth, indeterminacy and falsity degree of trapezoidal number respectively.

Remark 3: We use the above ranking function for the neutrosophic linear programs of type both maximization and minimization.

Remark 4: The decision makers determine the confirmation degrees for each neutrosophic linear programming problem.

3. DIFFERENT MODELS FOR THE NEUTROSOPHIC LINEAR PROGRAMMING (NLP)

(Abdel-Basset *et al.* 2018) proposed four different models for the neutrosophic linear programming (NLP). Here, we add other new models as follows:

Model 1: The NLP problems in this group involve neutrosophic numbers for the *decision variables* and the *right-hand-side* of the constraints

$$Maximize \; \tilde{z} \approx c^T \tilde{x}$$
$$subject \; to : A\tilde{x} \preceq \tilde{b}$$
$$\tilde{x} \succeq \tilde{0}$$

Model 2 [Abdel-Basset *et al.* 2018]: The NLP problems in this group involve neutrosophic numbers for the *coefficients of the decision variables* in the objective function

$$Maxmize\ \tilde{z} \approx \tilde{c}^{T} x$$
$$subject\ to : Ax \le b$$
$$x \ge 0$$

Model 3 [Abdel-Basset *et al*. 2018]: The NLP problems in this group involve neutrosophic numbers for the *coefficients of the decision variables* in the constraints and the *right-hand-side* of the constraints

$$Maxmize\ z = c^{T} x$$
$$subject\ to : \tilde{A}x \tilde{\preceq} \tilde{b}$$
$$x \ge 0$$

Model 4: The NLP problems in this group involve neutrosophic numbers for the *decision variables,* the *coefficients of the decision variables* in the objective function and the *right-hand-side* of the constraints

$$Maxmize\ \tilde{z} \approx \tilde{c}^{T} \tilde{x}$$
$$subject\ to : \tilde{A}x \tilde{\preceq} \tilde{b}$$
$$\tilde{x} \tilde{\succeq} 0$$

Model 5 [Abdel-Basset *et al*. 2018]: The NLP problems in this group involve neutrosophic numbers for the *coefficients of the decision variables in the objective function*, the *coefficients of the decision variables in the constraints* and the *right-hand-side* of the constraints

$$Maxmize\ \tilde{z} \approx \tilde{c}^{T} x$$
$$subject\ to : \tilde{A}x \tilde{\preceq} \tilde{b}$$
$$x \ge 0$$

Model 6 [Abdel-Basset *et al*. 2018]: The NLP problems in this group, the so-called fully neutrosophic linear programming (FNLP) problems, involve neutrosophic numbers for the decision variables, the coefficients of the decision variables in the objective function, the coefficients of the decision variables in the constraints and the right-hand-side of the constraints

$$Maxmize \, \tilde{z} \approx \tilde{c}^T \tilde{x}$$
$$subject \; to : \tilde{A}\tilde{x} \approx \tilde{b}$$
$$\tilde{x} \succeq \tilde{0}$$

4. NEUTROSOPHIC PRIMAL SIMPLEX ALGORITHM FOR SOLVING FULLY NEUTROSOPHIC

Linear Programming

We consider the standard fully neutrosophic linear programming problem FNLP:

$$Maxmize \, \tilde{z} \approx \tilde{c}^T \tilde{x}$$
$$subject \; to : \tilde{A}\tilde{x} \approx \tilde{b} \tag{2}$$
$$\tilde{x} \succeq \tilde{0}$$

where $\tilde{x}$, $\tilde{A}$, $\tilde{b}$, $\tilde{c}$ are $n\times1$, $m\times n$, $m\times1$, $n\times1$, respectively.

A neutrosophic basic feasible solution to this problem corresponds to an extreme point of the feasible region and is characterized mathematically by partitioning matrix $\tilde{A}$ into nonsingular basis matrix $\tilde{B}$ and the matrix of non-basic columns $\tilde{N}$. That is,

$$\tilde{A} = \left(\tilde{B} : \tilde{N} \right) \tag{3}$$

Based on this partition, the linear system $\tilde{A}\tilde{x} = \tilde{b}$ can be rewritten to yield

$$\tilde{B}\tilde{x}_{\tilde{B}} + \tilde{N}\tilde{x}_{\tilde{N}} \tag{4}$$

This simplifies to

$$\tilde{x}_{\tilde{B}} + \tilde{B}^{-1}\tilde{N}\tilde{x}_{\tilde{N}} = \tilde{B}^{-1}\tilde{b} \tag{5}$$

and solving for $\tilde{x}_{\tilde{B}}$ in terms of $\tilde{x}_{\tilde{N}}$ yields

$$\tilde{x}_{\tilde{B}} = \tilde{B}^{-1}\tilde{b} - \tilde{B}^{-1}\tilde{N}\tilde{x}_{\tilde{N}} \tag{6}$$

Now setting $\tilde{x}_{\tilde{N}} = \tilde{0}$, we see that eq. 6 results in $\tilde{x}_{\tilde{B}} = \tilde{B}^{-1}\tilde{b}$. The solution

$$\tilde{x} = \begin{pmatrix} \tilde{x}_{\tilde{B}} \\ \tilde{x}_{\tilde{N}} \end{pmatrix} = \begin{pmatrix} \tilde{B}^{-1}\tilde{b} \\ \tilde{0} \end{pmatrix}$$

is called a basic solution, with vector x_B called the vector of basic variables, and $\tilde{x}_{\tilde{N}}$ is called the vector of non-basic variables. If, in addition, $\tilde{x}_{\tilde{B}} = \tilde{B}^{-1}\tilde{b} \geq \tilde{0}$, then

$$\tilde{x} = \begin{pmatrix} \tilde{B}^{-1}\tilde{b} \\ \tilde{0} \end{pmatrix}$$

is called a basic feasible solution.

Now consider the objective function $\tilde{z} = \tilde{c}\tilde{x}$. Partition the cost vector $\tilde{c}$ into basic and non-basic components i.e. $\tilde{c} = (\tilde{c}_{\tilde{B}}, \tilde{c}_{\tilde{N}})$, the objective function can

$$\tilde{z} = \tilde{c}_{\tilde{B}}\tilde{x}_{\tilde{B}} + \tilde{c}_{\tilde{N}}\tilde{x}_{\tilde{N}} \tag{8}$$

Now, substitution the expression for $\tilde{x}_{\tilde{B}}$ defined 6 into 8 yields

$$\tilde{z} = \tilde{c}_{\tilde{B}}(\tilde{B}^{-1}\tilde{b} - \tilde{B}^{-1}\tilde{N}\tilde{x}_{\tilde{N}}) + \tilde{c}_{\tilde{N}}\tilde{x}_{\tilde{N}} \tag{9}$$

We can rewrite eq. 9 as follows:

$$\tilde{z} = \tilde{c}_{\tilde{B}}\tilde{B}^{-1}\tilde{b} - (\tilde{c}_{\tilde{B}}\tilde{B}^{-1}\tilde{N} - \tilde{c}_{\tilde{N}})\tilde{x}_{\tilde{N}} \tag{10}$$

Thus, we have written z as the constant $c_B B^{-1}b$ less than term $(\tilde{c}_{\tilde{B}}\tilde{B}^{-1}\tilde{N} - \tilde{c}_{\tilde{N}})\tilde{x}_{\tilde{N}}$. And setting $\tilde{x}_N = \tilde{0}$, we see that eq. 10 results in $\tilde{z} = \tilde{c}_{\tilde{B}}\tilde{B}^{-1}\tilde{b}$, which is the objective value corresponding to the current basic feasible solution. Therefore, the current extreme point solution can represent in canonical form:

$$\tilde{z} = \tilde{c}_{\tilde{B}} \tilde{B}^{-1} \tilde{b} - (\tilde{c}_{\tilde{B}} \tilde{B}^{-1} \tilde{N} - \tilde{c}_{\tilde{N}}) \tilde{x}_{\tilde{N}} \tag{11}$$

$$\tilde{x}_{\tilde{B}} = \tilde{B}^{-1} \tilde{b} - \tilde{B}^{-1} \tilde{N} \tilde{x}_{\tilde{N}} \tag{12}$$

with the current basic feasible solution given as

$$\tilde{z} = \tilde{c}_{\tilde{B}} \tilde{B}^{-1} \tilde{b} \tag{13}$$

$$\tilde{x} = \begin{pmatrix} \tilde{x}_{\tilde{B}} \\ \tilde{x}_{\tilde{N}} \end{pmatrix} = \begin{pmatrix} \tilde{B}^{-1} \tilde{b} \\ \tilde{0} \end{pmatrix} \geq \tilde{0} \tag{14}$$

Now, rearranging terms so that all the revised variables are on the left-hand side of the equation, with the constants on the right-hand side, we have

$$\tilde{z} + (\tilde{c}_{\tilde{B}} \tilde{B}^{-1} \tilde{N} - \tilde{c}_{\tilde{N}}) \tilde{x}_{\tilde{N}} = \tilde{c}_{\tilde{B}} \tilde{B}^{-1} \tilde{b} \tag{15}$$

$$\tilde{x}_{\tilde{B}} + \tilde{B}^{-1} \tilde{N} \tilde{x}_{\tilde{N}} = \tilde{B}^{-1} \tilde{b} \tag{16}$$

The simplex tableau is simply a table used to store the coefficients of the algebraic representation in 15 – 16. The top row (row 0) of the tableau consists of the coefficients in the objective equation 15, and the body of the tableau (rows 1 to m) records the coefficients of the constraint equations 16. The general form is as shown in Table 1.Or written more compactly, as shown in Table 2.

Table 1.

	z	$\mathbf{x_B}$	$\mathbf{x_N}$	RHS	
$\tilde{z}$	$\tilde{1}$	$\tilde{0}$	$\tilde{c}_{\tilde{B}} \tilde{B}^{-1} \tilde{N} - \tilde{c}_{\tilde{N}}$	$\tilde{c}_{\tilde{B}} \tilde{B}^{-1} \tilde{b}$	row 0
$\tilde{x}_{\tilde{B}}$	$\tilde{0}$	$\tilde{I}$	$\tilde{B}^{-1} \tilde{N}$	$\tilde{B}^{-1} \tilde{b}$	rows(1 – m)

Table 2.

	z	**x**	**RHS**	
$\tilde{z}$	$\tilde{1}$	$\tilde{c}_{\tilde{B}} \tilde{B}^{-1} \tilde{A} - \tilde{c}$	$\tilde{c}_{\tilde{B}} \tilde{B}^{-1} \tilde{b}$	row 0
$\tilde{x}_{\tilde{B}}$	$\tilde{0}$	$\tilde{B}^{-1} \tilde{A}$	$\tilde{B}^{-1} \tilde{b}$	rows($1 - m$)

Observe that for any basic index $j = Bi$, $1 \leq i \leq m$, we have $B^{-1}a_j = e_i$ where

$e_i = (0, \ldots, 0, 1, 0, \ldots, 0)^T$ is the $i-th$ unit vector, since

$Be_i = [a_{B1}, \ldots, a_{Bi}, \ldots, a_{Bm}] \, ei = a_{Bi} = a_j$, and so we have:

$$\tilde{z}_j - \tilde{c}_j \approx \tilde{c}_B B^{-1} \tilde{a}_j - \tilde{c}_j \approx \tilde{c}_B e_j - \tilde{c}_j \approx \tilde{c}_{B_i} - \tilde{c}_j \approx \tilde{c}_j - \tilde{c}_j \approx \tilde{0} \tag{17}$$

Definition 4 We say that fuzzy vector $\tilde{x} \in (F(R))^n$ is a neutrosophic feasible solution to (1) if $\tilde{x}$ satisfies the constraints of the problem.

Definition 5 A neutrosophic feasible solution $\widetilde{x}^*$ is a fuzzy optimal solution for (2), if for all neutrosophic feasible solution $\tilde{x}$ for (2), we have $\widetilde{cx}^* \succeq \widetilde{cx}$.

Theorem 1 (Optimality conditions.) Assume the neutrosophic linear programming problem (1) is nondegenerate and B is a feasible basis. A neutrosophic basic feasible solution

$$\widetilde{x}^*_B \approx B^{-1}\tilde{b} \succeq \tilde{0}, \widetilde{x}^*_N \approx \tilde{0}$$

is optimal to (2) if and only if $\widetilde{z}^*_j \approx \tilde{c}_B B^{-1} a_j \succeq \tilde{c}_j$ for all j, $1 \leq j \leq n$.

Proof

First, suppose $\widetilde{x}^* \approx (\widetilde{x}^*_B{}^T, \widetilde{x}^*_N{}^T)$ is a neutrosophic basic feasible solution to (2), where

$\widetilde{x}^*_B \approx B^{-1}\tilde{b}, \widetilde{x}^*_N \approx \tilde{0}$.

Then the corresponding fuzzy objective value is:

$$\tilde{z}^* \approx \tilde{c}\tilde{x}^* \approx \tilde{c}_B \tilde{x}^*{}_B \approx \tilde{c}_B B^{-1}\tilde{b} \tag{18}$$

On the other hand, for any fuzzy basic feasible solution $\tilde{x}$ to (2), using the general solution corresponding to basis B, we have $\tilde{x}_B \approx B^{-1}\tilde{b} - B^{-1}N\tilde{x}_N$ for the appropriate $\tilde{x}_N$. Thus, for any fuzzy basic feasible solution to (2), we have

$$\tilde{z} \approx \tilde{c}\tilde{x} \approx \tilde{c}_B \tilde{x}_B + \tilde{c}_N \tilde{x}_N \approx \tilde{c}_B(B^{-1}\tilde{b} - B^{-1}N\tilde{x}_N) \approx$$
$$\tilde{c}_B B^{-1}\tilde{b} - \sum_{j=1}^{n}(\tilde{c}_B B^{-1}a_j - \tilde{c}_j)\tilde{x}_j \approx\approx \tilde{c}_B B^{-1}\tilde{b} - \sum_{j=1}^{n}(\tilde{z}^*_j - \tilde{c}_j)\tilde{x}_j \tag{19}$$

Hence, using (17) and (18) we have

$$\tilde{z} \approx \tilde{z}^* - \sum_{j \neq B_i}(\tilde{z}^*_j - \tilde{c}_j)\tilde{x}_j$$

Now, if for all j, $1 \leq j \leq n$, then for all $\tilde{x}$ we have $(\tilde{z}^*_j - \tilde{c}_j)\tilde{x}_j$ and so we obtain $\sum_{j=1}^{n}(\tilde{z}^*_j - \tilde{c}_j)\tilde{x}_j \succeq \tilde{0}$. Therefore it follows from (18) that $\tilde{z} \preceq \tilde{z}^*$ and thus $\tilde{x}^*$ is optimal solution.

Second, let $\tilde{x}^*$ be a fuzzy optimal basic feasible solution to (2). For $j = B_i; (i = 1, 2...m)$ from (17) we know that $\tilde{z}^*_j - \tilde{c}_j \approx \tilde{0}$. From (19) it is obvious that if corresponding to any nonbasic variable $\tilde{x}_j$ we have $\tilde{z}^*_j \preceq \tilde{c}_j$, then we can enter $\tilde{x}_j$ into the basis and obtain an objective value bigger than $\tilde{z}^*_j$ (because the problem is nondegenerate and $\tilde{x}^*_j \succ \tilde{0}$ in the new basis). This is a contradiction to $\tilde{z}^*$ being optimal. Hence, we must have $\tilde{z}^*_j \succeq \tilde{c}_j, 1 \leq j \leq n$. From first and second, the theorem was proved completely. ■

We are now ready to summarize the steps of the simplex algorithm as applied to the simplex tableau.

Algorithm 1: Neutrosophic Primal Simplex Algorithm

We use the ranking function in Eq. 1 for this algorithm.

Step 0: (Initialization) Start with a neutrosophic feasible basic point and construct the corresponding tableau simplex.

Step 1: (Choice of entering variable) If $\tilde{c}_{0j} \underset{R}{\geq} \tilde{0}$ for j=1, 2, ..., n, STOP. The solution is an optimal. By a certain pivot rule, choose the entering variable with the index s:

$$\tilde{c}_{0s} \underset{R}{<} \tilde{0} \text{, i.e.}$$

$$\tilde{c}_{0s} = min\{ \ \tilde{c}_{0j} : \tilde{c}_{0j} \underset{R}{<} \tilde{0} \text{, for } j = 1,2, ..., n\}$$

Step 2: (Choice of leaving variable) Put I = { i: $\tilde{a}_{is} \underset{R}{>} \tilde{0}$ }. If I=$\varnothing$, STOP. The problem is unbounded. By a certain pivot rule, find the index of pivot column r:

$$\frac{\tilde{b}_r}{\tilde{a}_{rs}} = min\left\{\frac{\tilde{b}_i}{\tilde{a}_{is}} : i \in I\right\}$$

Step 3: (Pivoting) Form the next tableau by the pivoting variable $\tilde{a}_{rs}$ i.e.

Put $\tilde{a}_{rj} \leftarrow \dfrac{\tilde{a}_{rj}}{\tilde{a}_{rs}}$ where $j = 1, 2, ..., n, n+1$

$\tilde{a}_{ij} \leftarrow \tilde{a}_{ij} - \dfrac{\tilde{a}_{rj}}{\tilde{a}_{rs}} \tilde{a}_{is}$ where $i = 0, 1, 2, \ldots$ m ($i \neq r$) and $j = 1, 2, ..., n, n+1$

and go to Step1.

5. THE NEUTROSOPHIC TWO-PHASE METHOD

It is known that the neutrosophic primal simplex method has been designed with the assumption that an initial basic feasible solution is at hand. Otherwise something else must be done. In many applications, the neutrosophic basic feasible solution does not exist. To illustrate, suppose that the constraints are of the form $\tilde{A}\tilde{x} \preceq \tilde{b}, \tilde{x} \succeq \tilde{0}$, such that at least one of the elements of $\tilde{b}$ is negative. In this case, after introducing the fuzzy slack vector $\tilde{x}_s$, we cannot let $\tilde{x} \approx \tilde{0}$, because $\tilde{x}_s \approx \tilde{b}$ violates the nonnegativity conditions.

The main idea of the neutrosophic two-phase method is adding slack, surplus and artificial variables to obtain the identity (neutrosophic basic feasible solution). There are various methods in the literature of linear programming that can be used to eliminate the neutrosophic artificial variables. One of these methods is to minimize the sum of the artificial variables.

The following algorithm describes the neutrosophic Tow-Phase Method:

Algorithm 2: Neutrosophic Two-Phase Method

We use the ranking function in Eq. 1 for this algorithm.

Require: Neutrosophic infeasible basis

Phase I

Use the auxiliary objective function with the original constraints adding the slack and surplus variables to the constraints of type $\preceq$ and the constraints of type $\succeq$ respectively. Adding the artificial variables to the constraints of type $\succeq$ as following:

$$\min \tilde{u} \approx \sum_{j=1}^{t} \tilde{a}_j \tilde{x}_a$$
$$Subject\ to : \tilde{A}\tilde{x} + \tilde{x}_a \approx \tilde{b}$$
$$\tilde{x} \succeq \tilde{0}, \tilde{x}_a$$

where t is the number of artificial variables (number of the constraints of type $\succeq$), $\tilde{a}_j \approx (1,1,...,1)$ is $1 \times t$ constant vector and $(\tilde{x}_a)^T \approx (\tilde{x}_{1a}, \tilde{x}_{2a},...,\tilde{x}_{ta})$. This problem is called a neutrosophic simplex Phase I problem. If at optimality $\tilde{x}_a \not\approx \tilde{0}$, then stop; the original FNLP problem has no feasible solutions. Otherwise, let the neutrosophic basic and nonbasic legitimate variables be $\tilde{x}_B$ and $\tilde{x}_N$.

Phase II

Solve the following linear FNLP problem starting with the neutrosophic basic feasible solution $\tilde{x}_B \approx B^{-1}\tilde{b}$ and $\tilde{x}_N \approx \tilde{0}$

$$\max \tilde{z} \approx \tilde{c}_B \tilde{x}_B + \tilde{c}_N \tilde{x}_N$$
$$Subject\,to : B\tilde{x}_B + N\tilde{x}_N \approx \tilde{b}$$
$$\tilde{x}_B, \tilde{x}_N \succeq \tilde{0}$$

The foregoing linear programming with neutrosophic variables problem is of course equivalent to the original problem. Here, we illustrate our method to solve an FNLP problem.

End

6. COMPARISON AMONG THE PROPOSED MODEL AND OTHER EXISTING MODELS

In this section, we try to prove the applicability and advantages of the proposed method of NLP problems, we solve the same problem (Example 1) which introduced by (Abdel-Basset *et al*. 2018, Ganesan & Veermani 2006, Ebrahimnejad & Tavana 2014). The neutrosophic set takes into consideration the truth, indeterminacy and falsity degree but the fuzzy set takes into consideration the truth degree only. The decision makers always seek to maximize the truth degree and minimize both indeterminacy and falsity degree.

Example 1

$$\max \tilde{z}_{R} = (13,15,2,2)x_1 + (12,14,3,3)x_2 + (15,17,2,2)x_3$$
$$s.t.$$
$$12x_1 + 13x_2 + 12x_3 \leq (475,505,6,6)$$
$$14x_1 + 13x_3 \leq (460,480,8,8)$$
$$12x_1 + 15x_2 \leq (465,495,5,5)$$
$$x_1, x_2, x_3 \geq 0$$

(20)

First: we can transform the problem (20) from the fuzzy representation into the neutrosophic representation as follows:

$$\max_{R} \tilde{z} = (11, 13, 15, 17)x_1 + (9, 12, 14, 17)x_2 + (13, 15, 17, 19)x_3$$

s.t.

$$12x_1 + 13x_2 + 12x_3 \leq (469, 475, 505, 511)$$
$$14x_1 + 13x_3 \leq (452, 460, 480, 488)$$
$$12x_1 + 15x_2 \leq (460, 465, 495, 500)$$
$$x_1, x_2, x_3 \geq 0$$

Now, we can use the ranking function in Eq.(1) to convert each neutrosophic trapezoidal number to its equivalent crisp number with the confirmation degree $(T_{\tilde{a}}, I_{\tilde{a}}, F_{\tilde{a}}) = (1, 0, 0)$. Then the crisp model of above problem will be as follows:

$$\max z = 29x_1 + 27x_2 + 33x_3$$

s.t.

$$12x_1 + 13x_2 + 12x_3 \leq 981$$
$$14x_1 + 13x_3 \leq 941$$
$$12x_1 + 15x_2 \leq 961$$
$$x_1, x_2, x_3 \geq 0$$

Since the conditions of the simplex method are available so we can solve the crisp model by any solver for linear programming say LINGO Solver. The following table shows the comparison among the proposed approach and (Abdel-Basset *et al.* 2018, Ganesan & Veermani 2006, Ebrahimnejad & Tavana 2014).

Table 3. A comparison among the proposed approach

Example 1			
Fuzzy Methods		**Neutrosophic Methods**	
Z	634.6	634.6	868	2622.1
x_1	0	0	0	0
x_2	730/169	730/169	695/169	1729/200
x_3	470/169	470/169	487/13	36193/500

(Abdel-Basset *et al.* 2018, Ganesan & Veermani 2006, Ebrahimnejad & Tavana 2014)

Table 3 show that the proposed method is better than the other method. The objective function of the proposed method is 2622.1 but the objective function of fuzzy method is 634.6 and the objective function in (Abdel-Basset *et al.* 2018) is 868.

The proposed method and the method in (Abdel-Basset *et al.* 2018) have an advantage that it solves a problem with both the symmetric and non-symmetric trapezoidal number but the other methods solve a problem with symmetric trapezoidal number only.

Also, by comparing the proposed method with (Kumar *et. al.* 2011) for solving the same problem we founded some notes. In their model, they convert the fuzzy linear programming problem to its equivalent crisp model. But their model has more variables and constraints. Their models increase the complexity of solving linear programming problem by simplex algorithm. Our model reduces complexity of problem, by reducing the number of constraints and variables. Their model is a time-consuming and complex, but our model is not. Also our model represents reality efficiently and better than their model.

On the other hand, by solving the previous example according to (Saati *et al.* 2015) the proposed method has many constraints so the proposed method is easier than (Saati *et al.* 2015).

Example2: Consider the following NLP:

$$\max_{R} \tilde{z} = 2\tilde{x}_1 - \tilde{x}_2 + \tilde{x}_3$$

s.t.

$$2\tilde{x}_1 + \tilde{x}_2 - 2\tilde{x}_3 \leq (17, 35, 53, 55)$$
$$4\tilde{x}_1 - \tilde{x}_2 + 2\tilde{x}_3 = (7, 9, 11, 13)$$
$$2\tilde{x}_1 + 3\tilde{x}_2 - \tilde{x}_3 \geq (7, 17, 27, 29)$$
$$\tilde{x}_1, \tilde{x}_2, \tilde{x}_3 \geq 0$$

By adding the slake and artificial variables, we obtain the Phase I problem as follows:

$$\min_{R} \tilde{w} = \tilde{R}_1 + \tilde{R}_2$$

s.t.

$$2\tilde{x}_1 + \tilde{x}_2 - 2\tilde{x}_3 + \tilde{x}_4 \approx (17, 35, 53, 55)$$
$$4\tilde{x}_1 - \tilde{x}_2 + 2\tilde{x}_3 + \tilde{R}_1 = (7, 9, 11, 13)$$
$$2\tilde{x}_1 + 3\tilde{x}_2 - \tilde{x}_3 - \tilde{x}_5 + \tilde{R}_2 \approx (7, 17, 27, 29)$$
$$\tilde{x}_1, \tilde{x}_2, \tilde{x}_3, \tilde{x}_4, \tilde{x}_5, \tilde{R}_1, \tilde{R}_2 \geq 0$$

Then the first tableau of Phase I is as shown in Table 4.

Table 4.

	$\tilde{x}_1$	$\tilde{x}_2$	$\tilde{x}_3$	$\tilde{x}_4$	$\tilde{x}_5$	$\widetilde{R}_1$	$\widetilde{R}_2$	R.H.S
				Phase I				
$\tilde{z}$	6	2	1	-1	0	0	0	62
$\tilde{x}_5$	2	1	2	0	1	0	0	(17,35,53,55)
$\widetilde{R}_1$	4	-1	2	0	0	1	0	(7,9,11,13)
$\widetilde{R}_2$	2	3	-1	-1	0	0	1	(7,17,27,29)

It is obvious that $\tilde{x}_1$ is an entering fuzzy variable and $\widetilde{R}_1$ a is a leaving fuzzy variable. Then after pivoting the next tableau is given as shown in Table 5.

So $\tilde{x}_2$ is an entering fuzzy variable and $\widetilde{R}_2$ is a leaving fuzzy variable. The last tableau is given in the below. Now we see all fuzzy artificial variables leaves the basis. So we can remove their columns.

Now consider the first tableau of Phase II which is constructed by the last tableau in the end of the Phase I as shown in Table 7.

Finally as we saw the current fuzzy simplex tableau is optimal based on the optimality condition (Table 8).

Table 8 shows that the proposed two-phase method is better than both fuzzy approach and the method in (Abdel-Basset *et al.* 2018).

Table 5.

	$\tilde{x}_1$	$\tilde{x}_2$	$\tilde{x}_3$	$\tilde{x}_4$	$\tilde{x}_5$	$\widetilde{R}_1$	$\widetilde{R}_2$	R.H.S
				Phase I				
$\tilde{z}$	0	3.5	-2	-1	0	-1.5	0	30.50
$\tilde{x}_5$	0	1.5	1	0	1	-0.50	0	(13,30,47,59)
$\tilde{x}_1$	1	-0.25	0.50	0	0	0.25	0	(82,186,290,292)/100
$\widetilde{R}_2$	0	3.50	-2	-1	0	-0.50	1	(8,13,18,20)

Table 6.

	$\tilde{x}_1$	$\tilde{x}_2$	$\tilde{x}_3$	$\tilde{x}_4$	$\tilde{x}_5$	$\tilde{R}_1$	$\tilde{R}_2$	R.H.S
					Phase I			
z	0	0	0	0	0	-1	-1	0
$\tilde{x}_5$	0	0	1.86	0.43	1	-0.29	-0.43	(1061,2469,3877,3879)/100
$\tilde{x}_1$	1	0	0.36	-0.07	0	0.21	0.07	(121,281,441,443)/100
$\tilde{x}_2$	0	1	-0.57	-0.29	0	-0.14	0.29	(145,337,529,531)/100

Table 7.

	x_1	x_2	x_3	x_4	x_5	R_1	R_2	R.H.S
					Phase II			
z	0	0	0.29	0.14	0	blocked	blocked	6.14
x_5	0	0	1.86	0.43	1	-0.29	-0.43	(1061,2469,3877,3879)/100
x_1	1	0	0.36	-0.07	0	0.21	0.07	(121,281,441,443)/100
x_2	0	1	-0.57	-0.29	0	-0.14	0.29	(145,337,529,531)/100

Table 8. A comparison among the proposed approach, fuzzy approach

	Example 2		
	Fuzzy Approach	**Abdlelbast et al. [13]**	**The Proposed Method Two-Phase**
Z	5.7143	3.5714	6.1429
x_1	7.1429	5.7143	7.4286
x_2	8.5714	7.8571	8.7143
x_3	0	0	0

(Abdel-Basset *et al.* 2018)

7. CONCLUSION

We added other new neutrosophic linear programming models and we proposed a ranking function for both maximization neutrosophic linear programs and minimization neutrosophic linear programs. On the other hand, we used the same ranking function when we compared between the fuzzy approach and neutrosophic approach which solve the same example so this comparison is fair. Finally, we proposed a neutrosophic two-phase method involving neutrosophic artificial variables, to obtain an initial neutrosophic basic feasible solution to a slightly modified set of constraints. Then the neutrosophic primal simplex method is used to eliminate the neutrosophic artificial variables and to solve the original problem.

REFERENCES

Abdel-Basset, Gunasekaran, Mohamed, & Smarandache. (2018). A novel method for solving the fully neutrosophic linear programming problems. *Neural Computing and Applications*. doi:10.100700521-018-3404-6

Atanassov, K. T. (1986). Intuitionistic fuzzy sets. *Fuzzy Sets and Systems, 20*(1), 87–96. doi:10.1016/S0165-0114(86)80034-3

Badr & Moussa. (2019). An upper bound of radio *k*-coloring problem and its integer linear programming model. *Wireless Networks*.

Badr, E. S., Moussa, M., Paparrizos, K., Samaras, N., & Sifaleras, A. (2008). Some computational results on MPI parallel implementation of dense simplex method. *World Academy of Science, Engineering and Technology, 23*, 778–781.

Badr, E. S., Paparrizos, K., Thanasis, B., & Varkas, G. (2006). Some computational results on the efficiency of an exterior point algorithm. *Proc. of the 18th National Conference of Hellenic Operational Research Society (HELORS)*, 1103-1115.

Badr, E. S., Paparrizos, K., Samaras, N., & Sifaleras, A. (2005). On the Basis Inverse of the Exterior Point Simplex Algorithm. *Proc. of the 17th National Conference of Hellenic Operational Research Society (HELORS)*, 677-687.

Broumi, S., Bakali, A., Talea, M., & Smarandache, F. (2016). Isolated single valued neutrosophic graphs. *Neutrosophic Sets and Systems, 11*, 74–78. doi:10.5281/zenodo.571458

Broumi, S., Bakali, A., Talea, M., Smarandache, F., & Vladareanu, L. (2016). Shortest path problem under triangular fuzzy neutrosophic information. *2016 10th international conference on software, knowledge, information management and applications (SKIMA)*, 169–174. 10.1109/SKIMA.2016.7916216

Broumi, S., Smarandache, F., Talea, M., & Bakali, A. (2016). *Single valued neutrosophic graphs: degree, order and size. In 2016 IEEE international conference on fuzzy systems (FUZZ)* (pp. 2444–2451). IEEE. doi:10.1109/FUZZ-IEEE.2016.7738000

Broumi, S., Talea, M., Smarandache, F., & Bakali, A. (2016). Decision making method based on the interval valued neutrosophic graph. In *Future technologies conference* (pp. 44–50). FTC. doi:10.1109/FTC.2016.7821588

Deli, I., & S¸ubas¸, Y. (2017b). Some weighted geometric operators with SVTrN-numbers and their application to multi-criteria decision making problems. *Journal of Intelligent & Fuzzy Systems*, *32*(1), 291–301. doi:10.3233/JIFS-151677

Deli, I. S., & Şubaş, Y. (2017a). A ranking method of single valued neutrosophic numbers and its applications to multi-attribute decision making problems. *International Journal of Machine Learning and Cybernetics*, *8*(4), 1309–1322. doi:10.100713042-016-0505-3

Ebrahimnejad, A., & Tavana, M. (2014). A novel method for solving linear programming problems with symmetric trapezoidal fuzzy numbers. *Applied Mathematical Modelling*, *38*(17-18), 4388–4395. doi:10.1016/j.apm.2014.02.024

Ganesan, K., & Veeramani, P. (2006). Fuzzy linear programs with trapezoidal fuzzy numbers. *Annals of Operations Research*, *143*(1), 305–315. doi:10.100710479-006-7390-1

Kumar, A., Kaur, J., & Singh, P. (2011). A new method for solving fully fuzzy linear programming problems. *Applied Mathematical Modelling*, *35*(2), 817–823. doi:10.1016/j.apm.2010.07.037

Saati, S., Tavana, M., Hatami-Marbini, A., & Hajiakhondi, E. (2015). A fuzzy linear programming model with fuzzy parameters and decision variables. *Int J Inf Decis Sci*, *7*, 312–333.

Smarandache, F. (1998). *Neutrosophy: neutrosophic probability, set, and logic*. Rehoboth: American Research Press.

Smarandache, F. (2013). *Introduction to neutrosophic measure, neutrosophic integral, and neutrosophic probability*. Craiova: Sitech & Education Publisher.

Smarandache, F. (2014). *Introduction to neutrosophic statistics*. Craiova: Sitech & Education Publishing.

Smarandache, F. (2015). *Neutrosophic precalculus and neutrosophic calculus*. Brussels: Europa-Nova.

Zadeh, L. A. (1965). Fuzzy sets. *Information and Control*, *8*(3), 338–353. doi:10.1016/S0019-9958(65)90241-X

Compilation of References

(2016). New Trends. InSmarandache, F., & Pramanik, S. (Eds.), *Neutrosophic Theory And Applications*. Brussels: Pons Editions.

Aal, S. I. A., Ellatif, M. M. A. A., & Hassan, M. M. (2018). Proposed Model for Evaluating Information Systems Quality Based on Single Valued Triangular Neutrosophic Numbers. I.J. *Mathematical Sciences and Computing*, *1*, 1–14.

Abbasbandy, S., & Asady, B. (2006). Ranking of fuzzy numbers by sign distance. *Information Sciences*, *176*(16), 2405–2416. doi:10.1016/j.ins.2005.03.013

Abbasbandy, S., & Hajjari, T. (2009). A new approach for ranking of trapezoidal fuzzy numbers. *Computers & Mathematics with Applications (Oxford, England)*, *57*(3), 413–419. doi:10.1016/j.camwa.2008.10.090

Abdel-Baset, M., Chang, V., & Gamal, A. (2019). Evaluation of the green supply chain management practices: A novel neutrosophic approach. *Computers in Industry*, *108*, 210–220. doi:10.1016/j.compind.2019.02.013

Abdel-Baset, M., Chang, V., Gamal, A., & Smarandache, F. (2019). An integrated neutrosophic ANP and VIKOR method for achieving sustainable supplier selection: A case study in importing field. *Computers in Industry*, *106*, 94–110. doi:10.1016/j.compind.2018.12.017

Abdel-Basset, M. (2019a). An approach of TOPSIS technique for developing supplier selection with group decision making under type-2 neutrosophic number. *Applied Soft Computing*, *77*, 438-452.

Abdel-Basset, M., Hezam, I. M., & Smarandache, F. (2016). Neutrosophic Goal Programming. *Neutrosophic Sets and Systems, 11*, 112-118. Retrieved from http://fs.gallup.unm.edu/NSS/NeutrosophicGoalProgramming.pdf

Abdel-Basset, M., Atef, A., & Smarandache, F. (2019). A hybrid neutrosophic multiple criteria group decision making approach for project selection. *Cognitive Systems Research*, *57*, 216–227. doi:10.1016/j.cogsys.2018.10.023

Abdel-Basset, M., Gamal, A., Manogaran, G., Son, L. H., & Long, H. V. (2019). A novel group decision making model based on neutrosophic sets for heart disease diagnosis. *Multimedia Tools and Applications*, 1–26. doi:10.100711042-019-07742-7

Abdel-Basset, M., Gunasekaran, M., Mohamed, M., & Chilamkurti, N. (2018). Three-way decisions based on neutrosophic sets and AHP-QFD framework for supplier selection problem. *Future Generation Computer Systems*, *89*, 19–30. doi:10.1016/j.future.2018.06.024

Abdel-Basset, M., Manogaran, G., Gamal, A., & Smarandache, F. (2018). A hybrid approach of neutrosophic sets and DEMATEL method for developing supplier selection criteria. *Design Automation for Embedded Systems*, *22*(3), 257–287. doi:10.100710617-018-9203-6

Abdel-Basset, M., Manogaran, G., Gamal, A., & Smarandache, F. (2019). A Group Decision Making Framework Based on Neutrosophic TOPSIS Approach for Smart Medical Device Selection. *Journal of Medical Systems*, *43*(2), 1–13. doi:10.100710916-019-1156-1 PMID:30627801

Abdel-Basset, M., Manogaran, G., & Mohamed, M. (2019). A neutrosophic theory based security approach for fog and mobile-edge computing. *Computer Networks*, *157*, 122–132. doi:10.1016/j.comnet.2019.04.018

Abdel-Basset, M., Manogaran, G., Mohamed, M., & Smarandache, F. (2019). A novel method for solving the fully neutrosophic linear programming problems. *Neural Computing & Applications*, *31*(5), 1595–1605. doi:10.100700521-018-3404-6

Abdel-Basset, M., & Mohamed, M. (2018). The role of single valued neutrosophic sets and rough sets in smart city: Imperfect and incomplete information systems. *Measurement*, *124*, 47–55. doi:10.1016/j.measurement.2018.04.001

Abdel-Basset, M., Mohamed, M., Hussien, A. N., & Sangaiah, A. K. (2018). A novel group decision-making model based on triangular neutrosophic numbers. *Soft Computing*, *22*(20), 6629–6643. doi:10.100700500-017-2758-5

Abdel-Basset, M., Mohamed, M., & Sangaiah, A. K. (2018). Neutrosophic AHP-Delphi Group decision making model based on trapezoidal neutrosophic numbers. *Journal of Ambient Intelligence and Humanized Computing*, *9*(5), 1427–1443. doi:10.100712652-017-0548-7

Abdel-Basset, M., Mohamed, M., Sangaiah, A. K., & Jain, V. (2018). An integrated neutrosophic AHP and SWOT method for strategic planning methodology selection. *Benchmarking: An International Journal*, *25*(7), 2546–2564. doi:10.1108/BIJ-08-2017-0232

Abdel-Basset, M., Mohamed, M., & Smarandache, F. (2018). An extension of neutrosophic AHP–SWOT analysis for strategic planning and decision-making. *Symmetry*, *10*(4), 116. doi:10.3390ym10040116

Abdel-Basset, M., Mohamed, M., & Smarandache, F. (2018b). A Hybrid Neutrosophic Group ANP-TOPSIS Framework for Supplier Selection Problems. *Symmetry*, *10*(6), 226. doi:10.3390ym10060226

Abdel-Basset, M., Mohamed, M., & Smarandache, F. (2019). A aefined approach for forecasting based on neutrosophic time series. *Symmetry*, *11*(4), 457. doi:10.3390ym11040457

Abdel-Basset, M., Mohamed, M., Zhou, Y. M., & Hezam, I. (2017). Multi-criteria group decision making based on neutrosophic analytic hierarchy process. *Journal of Intelligent & Fuzzy Systems, 33*(6), 4055–4066. doi:10.3233/JIFS-17981

Abdel-Basset, M., Mohamed, R., Zaied, A. N., & Smarandache, F. (2019). A hybrid plithogenic decision-making approach with quality function deployment for selecting supply chain sustainability metrics. *Symmetry, 11*(7), 903. doi:10.3390ym11070903

Abdel-Basset, M., Nabeeh, N. A., El-Ghareeb, H. A., & Aboelfetouh, A. (2019). Utilizing Neutrosophic Theory to Solve Transition Difficulties of IoT-Based Enterprises. *Enterprise Information Systems.*

Abdel-Basset, M., Saleh, M., Gamal, A., & Smarandache, F. (2019). An approach of TOPSIS technique for developing supplier selection with group decision making under type-2 neutrosophic number. *Applied Soft Computing, 77*, 438–452. doi:10.1016/j.asoc.2019.01.035

Abdel-Basset, M., Zhou, Y., Mohamed, M., & Chang, V. (2018). A group decision making framework based on neutrosophic VIKOR approach for e-government website evaluation. *Journal of Intelligent & Fuzzy Systems, 34*(6), 4213–4224. doi:10.3233/JIFS-171952

Abo-elnaga, Y., El-sobky, B., & Zahed, H. (2012). Trust Region Algorithm for Multi-objective Transportation, Assignment, and Transshipment Problems. *Life Science Journal, 9*(3), 1765–1772.

Adamson, G., & Boreham, J. (1974). The Use of an Association Measure Based on Character Structure to Identify Semantical Related Pairs of Words and Document Titles. *Information Storage and Retrieval, 10*(7-8), 253–260. doi:10.1016/0020-0271(74)90020-5

Afwat, A.E., Salama, A.A.M., & Farouk, N. (2018). A New Efficient Approach to Solve Multi-Objective Transportation Problem in the Fuzzy Environment. *International Journal of Applied Engineering Research, 13*(18), 660-664.

Agboola, A. A. A. (2016). *Fuzzy, Neutrosophic sets, vital to technological advancement.* Seyibabs FUNAAB socio-academic network.

Aiwu, Z., Jianguo, D., & Hongjun, G. (2015). Interval valued neutrosophic sets and multi-attribute decision-making based on generalized weighted aggregation operator. *Journal of Intelligent & Fuzzy Systems, 29*(6), 2697–2706. doi:10.3233/IFS-151973

Ajitha Priyadharshini, M., & Selvakumari, K. (2017). VIKOR Method For Medical Diagnosis Problem Using Triangular Neutrosophic Soft Matrix. *International Journal of Pure and Applied Mathematics, 114*(16), 169–176.

Akinwale, A., & Niewiadomski, A. (2015). Efficient Similarity measures for texts matching. *Journal of Applied Computer Science, 23*(1), 7–28.

Akram, M., & Davvaz, B. (2012). Strong intuitionistic fuzzy graphs. Faculty of Sciences and Mathematics, University of Nis. *Serbia Filomat, 26*(1), 177–196. doi:10.2298/FIL1201177A

Akram, M., & Dudek, W. A. (2013). Intuitionistic fuzzy hypergraphs with applications. *Information Sciences*, *218*, 182–193. doi:10.1016/j.ins.2012.06.024

Alaca, C., Türkoğlu, D., & Yıldız, C. (2006). Fixed points in intuitionistic fuzzy metric spaces. *Chaos, Solitons, and Fractals*, *29*(5), 1073–1078. doi:10.1016/j.chaos.2005.08.066

Alava,, M.V., Figueroa,, S.P.D., & Alcivar,, H.M.B., & Vã¡zquez, M.L. (2018). Single Valued Neutrosophic Numbers and Analytic Hierarchy Process for Project Selection. *Neutrosophic Sets and Systems*, *21*, 122–130.

Al-Baghdadi, A. Q. (1928). Usul al Din. Istanbul: Academic Press.

Alblowi, S. A., & Salama,, A. A., & Eisa, M. (2014). New Concepts of Neutrosophic Sets. *International Journal of Mathematics and Computer Applications Research*, *4*(1), 59–66.

Alhabib, R., Ranna, M. M., Farah, H., & Salama, A. (2018). Some Neutrosophic Probability Distributions. *Neutrosophic Sets and Systems*, 30.

Alia, M., Delib, I., & Smarandachec, F. (2016). The theory of neutrosophic cubic sets and their applications in pattern recognition. *Journal of Intelligent & Fuzzy Systems*, *16*, 1064–1246.

Altai, M. B. (2016). *God, Nature, and the Cause: Essays on Islam and Science*. John Templeton Foundation.

Angell, R., Freund, G., & Willett, P. (1983). Automatic Spelling Correction Using a Trigram Similarity Measure. *Information Processing & Management*, *19*(4), 255–261. doi:10.1016/0306-4573(83)90022-5

Angelov, P. P. (1997). Optimization in an intuitionistic fuzzy environment. *Fuzzy Sets and Systems*, *86*(3), 299–306. doi:10.1016/S0165-0114(96)00009-7

Ansari, A. Q., Biswas, R., & Aggarwal, S. (2013). Neutrosophic classifier: An extension of fuzzy classifer. *Applied Soft Computing*, *13*(1), 563–573. doi:10.1016/j.asoc.2012.08.002

Anthony, J. M., & Sherwood, H. (1979). Fuzzy groups redefined. *Journal of Mathematical Analysis and Applications*, *69*(1), 124–130. doi:10.1016/0022-247X(79)90182-3

Anthony, J. M., & Sherwood, H. (1982). A characterization of fuzzy subgroups. *Fuzzy Sets and Systems*, *7*(3), 297–305. doi:10.1016/0165-0114(82)90057-4

Arora, M., & Ranjit, B. (2010). *Deployment of Neutrosophic Technology to Retrieve Answer for Queries Posed in Natural Language*. Academic Press.

Ashbacher, C. (2002). *Introduction to Neutrosophic Logic*. American Research Press.

Aslam, M. (2018a). Design of Sampling Plan for Exponential Distribution under Neutrosophic Statistical Interval Method. *IEEE Access: Practical Innovations, Open Solutions*, *6*, 64153–64158. doi:10.1109/ACCESS.2018.2877923

Aslam, M. (2018b). A New Sampling Plan Using Neutrosophic Process Loss Consideration. *Symmetry*, *10*(5), 132. doi:10.3390ym10050132

Aslam, M. (2019a). Attribute Control Chart Using the Repetitive Sampling under Neutrosophic System. *IEEE Access: Practical Innovations, Open Solutions*.

Aslam, M. (2019b). A new failure-censored reliability test using neutrosophic statistical interval method. *International Journal of Fuzzy Systems*, *21*(4), 1214–1220. doi:10.100740815-018-0588-y

Aslam, M., & Arif, O. (2018). Testing of Grouped Product for the Weibull Distribution Using Neutrosophic Statistics. *Symmetry*, *10*(9), 403. doi:10.3390ym10090403

Atanassov, K. (1986). Intuitionistic fuzzy sets. *Fuzzy Sets and Systems*, (20), 87-96.

Atanassov, K. T., & Janusz, K. (2016). *Intuitionistic Fuzzy Logic*. Springer.

Atanassov, K. (1986). Intuitionistic fuzzy sets. *Fuzzy Sets and Systems*, *20*(1), 87–96. doi:10.1016/S0165-0114(86)80034-3

Atanassov, K. T. (1999). Interval valued intuitionistic fuzzy sets. In *Intuitionistic Fuzzy Sets* (pp. 139–177). Springer. doi:10.1007/978-3-7908-1870-3_2

Atanassov, K. T. (1999). Intuitionistic fuzzy sets. In *Intuitionistic Fuzzy Sets* (pp. 1–137). Springer.

Atanassov, K. T. (1999). *Intuitionistic Fuzzy Sets*. New York: Pysica-Verlag A Springer-Verlag Company. doi:10.1007/978-3-7908-1870-3

Atanassov, K. T. (2012). *On Intuitionistic Fuzzy Sets Theory*. Berlin: Springer. doi:10.1007/978-3-642-29127-2

Atanassov, K., & Georgiev, C. (1993). Intuitionistic fuzzy Prolog. *Fuzzy Sets and Systems*, *53*(2), 121–128. doi:10.1016/0165-0114(93)90166-F

Aydoğdu, A. (2015). On Similarity and Entropy of Single Valued Neutrosophic Sets. *Gen. Math. Notes*, *29*(1), 67–74.

Aygünoğlu, A., Varol, B. P., Çetkin, V., & Aygün, H. (2012). Interval-valued intuitionistic fuzzy subgroups based on interval-valued double t-norm. *Neural Computing & Applications*, *21*(S1), 207–214. doi:10.100700521-011-0773-5

Bachchhav, K. P. (2016). Information Retrieval: Search process, Techniques and Strategies. *International Journal of Next Generation Library & Technology*, *2*(1), 1–10.

Badr & Moussa. (2019). An upper bound of radio *k*-coloring problem and its integer linear programming model. *Wireless Networks*.

Badr, E. S., Paparrizos, K., Thanasis, B., & Varkas, G. (2006). Some computational results on the efficiency of an exterior point algorithm. *Proc. of the 18th National Conference of Hellenic Operational Research Society (HELORS)*, 1103-1115.

Badr, E. S., Moussa, M., Paparrizos, K., Samaras, N., & Sifaleras, A. (2008). Some computational results on MPI parallel implementation of dense simplex method. *World Academy of Science, Engineering and Technology, 23*, 778–781.

Badr, E. S., Paparrizos, K., Samaras, N., & Sifaleras, A. (2005). On the Basis Inverse of the Exterior Point Simplex Algorithm. *Proc. of the 17th National Conference of Hellenic Operational Research Society (HELORS)*, 677-687.

Bagis, A. (2007). Determination of the PID controller parameters by modified genetic algorithm for improved performance. *Journal of Information Science and Engineering, 23*, 1469–1480.

Bai, Y., & Roth, Z. S. (2019). Interval Type-2 Fuzzy Logic Controllers. In *Classical and Modern Controls with Microcontrollers* (pp. 549–579). Cham: Springer. doi:10.1007/978-3-030-01382-0_9

Balakrishnan, N. (1989). Approximate MLE of the scale parameter of the Rayleigh distribution with censoring. *IEEE Transactions on Reliability, 38*(3), 355–357. doi:10.1109/24.44181

Balakrishnan, V. K. (1997). *Graph Theory*. McGraw-Hill.

Ban, A. (2008). Trapezoidal approximations of intuitionistic fuzzy numbers expressed by value, ambiguity, width and weighted expected value. *Int. Conf. on IFSs, Sofia, NIFS, 14*(1), 38-47.

Banerjee, D., Pramanik, S., & Giri, B. C. (2017). GRA for multi attribute decision making in neutrosophic cubic set environment. *Neutrosophic Sets and Systems, 15*, 60–69. doi:10.5281/zenodo.570938

Basirzadeh, H. (2012). Ones Assignment Method for Solving Assignment Problems. *Applied Mathematical Sciences, 6*(47), 2345–2355.

Basset, M. A., Nabeeh, N. A., El-Ghareeb, H. A., & Aboelfetouh, A. (2019). *Utilizing Neutrosophic Theory to Solve Transition Difficulties of IoT-Based Enterprises*. Enterprise Information Systems, 2017 Impact Factor: 2.1. doi:10.1080/17517575.2019.1633690

Bausys, E. K., & Zavadskas, E. K. (2015). Multi-criteria decision making approach by VIKOR under interval neutrosophic set environment. *Economic Computation and Economic Cybernetics Studies and Research, 49*.

Beliakov, G., Bustince, H., Goswami, D. P., Mukherjee, U. K., & Pal, N. R. (2011). On averaging operators for Atanassov's intuitionistic fuzzy sets. *Information Sciences, 181*(6), 1116–1124. doi:10.1016/j.ins.2010.11.024

Belkin, N. J., Oddy, R. N., & Brooks, H. M. (1982). ASK for information retrieval: Part 1 Background and Theory. *The Journal of Documentation, 38*(2), 61–71. doi:10.1108/eb026722

Bera, T., & Mahapatra, N. K. (2016). (α,β,γ) -cut of neutrosophic soft set and it's application to neutrosophic soft groups. *Asian Journal of Math. and Compt. Research, 12*(3), 160–178.

Bera, T., & Mahapatra, N. K. (2017). On neutrosophic soft linear spaces. *Fuzzy Information and Engineering, 9*(3), 299–324. doi:10.1016/j.fiae.2017.09.004

Best, D. J., Rayner, J. C., & Thas, O. (2010). Easily applied tests of fit for the Rayleigh distribution. *Sankhya B, 72*(2), 254–263. doi:10.100713571-011-0011-2

Bhattacharyya, S., Koli, B., & Majumdar, P. (2018). On Distances and Similarity Measures between two Interval Neutrosophic sets. *Journal of New Theory, 20,* 27–47.

Bhutani, K. R., & Rosenfeld, A. (2003). Fuzzy End Nodes in Fuzzy Graphs. *Information Sciences, 152,* 323–326. doi:10.1016/S0020-0255(03)00078-1

Biswas, P., Pramanik, S., & Giri, B. C. (2015). Cosine similarity measure based multi-attribute decision-making with trapezoidal fuzzy neutrosophic numbers. *Neutrosophic Sets and Systems, 8,* 46-56. doi.org/10.5281/zenodo.571274

Biswas, P., Pramanik, S., & Giri, B. C. (2016). Value and ambiguity index based ranking method of single-valued trapezoidal neutrosophic numbers and its application to multi-attribute decision making. *Neutrosophic Sets and Systems, 12,* 127–138. doi.org/10.5281/zenodo.571154

Biswas, P., Pramanik, S., & Giri, B. C. (2019). Neutrosophic TOPSIS with group decision making. In C. Kahraman & I. Otay (Eds.), Fuzzy Multicriteria Decision Making Using Neutrosophic Sets, Studies in Fuzziness and Soft Computing (vol. 369, pp. 543-585). Academic Press. doi:10.1007/978-3-030-00045-5_21

Biswas, P., Pramanik, S., & Giri, B.C. (2016). Aggregation of Triangular Fuzzy Neutrosophic Set Information and its Application to Multi attribute Decision Making. *Neutrosophic Sets and Systems, 12,* 20-40.

Biswas, R. (1989). Intuitionistic fuzzy subgroups. *Mathematical Forum, 10,* 37-46.

Biswas, S. S., Alam, B., & Doja, M.N. (2012). A Theoretical Characterization of the Data Structure 'Multigraphs'. *Journal of Contemporary Applied Mathematics, 2*(2), 88-106.

Biswas, S. S., Alam, B., & Doja, M.N. (2015). Real Time Graphs For Communication Networks: A Fuzzy Mathematical Model. *Advances in Intelligent Systems and Computing, 1*(379), 463 – 470. Doi:10.1007/978-81-322-2517-1_44

Biswas. P., Pramanik. S., & Giri, B.C. (2015). Multi-attribute group decision making based on expected value of neutrosophic trapezoidal numbers. *New Math. Natural Comput.*

Biswas, P., Pramanik, S., & Giri, B. C. (2014). A new methodology for neutrosophic multi-attribute decision making with unknown weight information. *Neutrosophic Sets and Systems, 3,* 42–52. doi:10.5281/zenodo.571212

Biswas, P., Pramanik, S., & Giri, B. C. (2014). A new methodology for neutrosophic multi-attribute decision-making with unknown weight information. *Neutrosophic Sets and Systems, 3,* 42–50.

Biswas, P., Pramanik, S., & Giri, B. C. (2014). Cosine Similarity Measure Based Multi-attribute Decision making with Trapezoidal Fuzzy Neutrosophic Numbers. *Neutrosophic Sets and Systems, 8,* 47–57.

Biswas, P., Pramanik, S., & Giri, B. C. (2014). Entropy based grey relational analysis method for multi-attribute decision – making under single valued neutrosophic assessments. *Neutrosophic Sets and Systems, 2*, 102–110.

Biswas, P., Pramanik, S., & Giri, B. C. (2014). Entropy based grey relational analysis method for multi-attribute decision making under single valued neutrosophic assessments. *Neutrosophic Sets and Systems, 2*, 102–110.

Biswas, P., Pramanik, S., & Giri, B. C. (2015). TOPSIS method for multi-attribute group decision-making under single valued neutrosophic environment. *Neural Computing & Applications.* doi:10.100700521-015-1891-2

Biswas, P., Pramanik, S., & Giri, B. C. (2016). Aggregation of triangular fuzzy neutrosophic set information and its application to multi-attribute decision making. *Neutrosophic Sets and Systems, 12*, 20–40.

Biswas, P., Pramanik, S., & Giri, B. C. (2016). Value and ambiguity index based ranking method of single-valued trapezoidal neutrosophic numbers and its application to multi-attribute decision making. *Neutrosophic Sets and Systems, 12*, 127–138.

Biswas, P., Pramanik, S., & Giri, B. C. (2016a). Some distance measures of single valued neutrosophic hesitant fuzzy sets and their applications to multiple attribute decision making. In F. Smarandache & S. Pramanik (Eds.), *New Trends In Neutrosophic Theory And Applications.* Pons Editions.

Biswas, P., Pramanik, S., & Giri, B. C. (2016b). GRA method of multiple attribute decision making with single valued neutrosophic hesitant fuzzy set information. In F. Smarandache & S. Pramanik (Eds.), *New Trends In Neutrosophic Theory And Applications.* Pons Editions.

Biswas, P., Pramanik, S., & Giri, B. C. (2018). Distance Measure Based MADM Strategy with Interval Trapezoidal Neutrosophic Numbers. *Neutrosophic Sets and Systems, 19*, 40–46.

Biswas, P., Pramanik, S., & Giri, B. C. (2018). *Multi-attribute group decision making based on expected value of neutrosophic trapezoidal numbers. In New trends in neutrosophic theory and applications* (vol. 2, pp. 103–124). Pons Editions.

Biswas, P., Pramanik, S., & Giri, B. C. (2018). Multi-attribute group decision making based on expected value of neutrosophic trapezoidal numbers. In F. Smarandache & S. Pramanik (Eds.), *New Trends In Neutrosophic Theory And Applications* (Vol. 2, pp. 103–124). Brussels: Pons Editions.

Biswas, P., Pramanik, S., & Giri, B. C. (2018). Non-linear programming approach for single-valued neutrosophic TOPSIS method. *New Mathematics and Natural Computation.*

Biswas, P., Pramanik, S., & Giri, B. C. (2018a). TOPSIS strategy for multi-attribute decision making with trapezoidal numbers. *Neutrosophic Sets and Systems, 19*, 29–39. doi:10.5281/zenodo.1235335

Biswas, P., Pramanik, S., & Giri, B. C. (2018b). Distance measure based MADM strategy with interval trapezoidal neutrosophic numbers. *Neutrosophic Sets and Systems*, *19*, 40–46. doi:10.5281/zenodo.1235165

Biswas, P., Pramanik, S., & Giri, B. C. (2019). NH-MADM Strategy in neutrosophic hesitant fuzzy set environment based on extended GRA. *Informatica*, *30*(2), 213–242. doi:10.15388/Informatica.2019.204

Biswas, P., Pramanik, S., & Giri, B. C. (2019). *Non-linear programming approach for single-valued neutrosophic TOPSIS method*. New Mathematics and Natural Computation. doi:10.1142/S1793005719500169

Biswas, R. (1994). Rosenfeld's fuzzy subgroups with interval-valued membership functions. *Fuzzy Sets and Systems*, *63*(1), 87–90. doi:10.1016/0165-0114(94)90148-1

Biswas, R. (2016). *Is 'Fuzzy Theory' An Appropriate Tool For Large Size Problems?* Heidelberg, Germany: Springer.

Biswas, R. (2019). Intuitionistic Fuzzy Theory for Soft-Computing: More Appropriate Tool Than Fuzzy Theory. *International Journal of Computing and Optimization*, *6*(1), 13–56. doi:10.12988/ijco.2019.955

Bit, A. K., Biswal, M. P., & Alam, S. S. (1992). Fuzzy programming approach to multicriteria decision making transportation problem. *Fuzzy Sets and Systems*, *50*(2), 135–141. doi:10.1016/0165-0114(92)90212-M

Bollobas, B. (2002). *Modern Graph Theory*. Springer.

Broumi, S., Bakal, A., Talea, M., Smarandache, F., & Vladareanu, L. (2016). Applying Dijkstra algorithm for solving neutrosophic shortest path problem. In *2016 International Conference on Advanced Mechatronic Systems*, (pp. 412-416). Academic Press. 10.1109/ICAMechS.2016.7813483

Broumi, S., Bakali, A., Talea, M., Smarandache, F., & Hassan, A. (2017b). Generalized single valued neutrosophic graphs of first type. *SISOM & ACOUSTICS 2017*.

Broumi, S., Bakali, A., Talea, M., Smarandache, F., & Rao, V.V. (2018). Interval Complex Neutrosophic Graph of Type 1. Neutrosophic Operational Research, 3, 87-106.

Broumi, S., Bakali, A., Talea, M., Smarandache, F., & Vladareanu, L. (2017). Computation of Shortest Path Problem in a Network with SV-Triangular Neutrosophic Numbers. *2017 IEEE International Conference on innovations in Intelligent Systems and Applications (INISTA)*, 426-431.

Broumi, S., Deli, I., & Smarandache, F. (2015). N-valued interval neutrosophic sets and their application in medical diagnosis. Critical Review, 10, 45-69.

Broumi, S., Smarandache, F., & Dhar, M. (2014). *Rough neutrosophic sets*. Infinite Study.

Broumi, S., Smarandache, F., Talea, M., & Bakali, A. (2016). Decision-Making Method Based On the Interval Valued Neutrosophic Graph. Future Technologie, IEEE, 44-50.

Broumi, S., Smarandache, F., Talea, M., & Bakali, A. (2016). Operations on Interval Valued Neutrosophic Graphs. In New Trends in Neutrosophic Theory and Applications. Academic Press.

Broumi, S., Talea, M., Bakali, A., & Smarandache, F. (2016e). Single Valued Neutrosophic Graphs. *Journal of New Theory*, *10*, 86-101.

Broumi, S., Talea, M., Smarandache, F., & Bakali, A. (2016). Decision-making method based on the interval valued neutrosophic graph. In 2016 Future Technologies Conference, (pp. 44-50). Academic Press.

Broumi, S., Talea, M., Smarandache, F., & Bakali, A. (2016). Decision-making method based on the interval valued neutrosophic graph. In *Future Technologies Conference*, (pp. 44-50). Academic Press. 10.1109/FTC.2016.7821588

Broumi, S. (2014). Deli, Correlation measure for neutrosophic refined sets and its application in medical diagnosis. *Palestine J. Math.*, *3*(1), 11–19.

Broumi, S., Bakali, A., Talea, M., & Sarandache, F. (2016). Shortest Path Problem Under Triangular Fuzzy Neutrosophic information. *International Conference on Software, Knowledge, Information Management & Applications (SKIMA)*. 10.1109/SKIMA.2016.7916216

Broumi, S., Bakali, A., Talea, M., & Smarandache, F. (2016). Computation of Shortest Path Problem in a Network with SV-Trapezoidal Neutrosophic Numbers. *Proceedings of the 2016 International Conference on Advanced Mechatronic Systems*, 417-422. 10.1109/ICAMechS.2016.7813484

Broumi, S., Bakali, A., Talea, M., & Smarandache, F. (2016). Isolated single valued neutrosophic graphs. *Neutrosophic Sets and Systems*, *11*, 74–78. doi:10.5281/zenodo.571458

Broumi, S., Bakali, A., Talea, M., & Smarandache, F. (2016d). Isolated Single Valued Neutrosophic Graphs. *Neutrosophic Sets and Systems*, *11*, 74–78.

Broumi, S., Bakali, A., Talea, M., & Smarandache, F. (2017b). A Matlab Toolbox for interval valued neutrosophic matrices for computer applications. *Uluslararası Yönetim Bilişim Sistemleri ve Bilgisayar Bilimleri Dergisi*, *1*(1), 1–21.

Broumi, S., Bakali, A., Talea, M., Smarandache, F., Kishore, K. K., & Şahin, R. (2019). Shortest path problem under interval valued neutro- sophic setting. *J Fundam Appl Sci*, *10*(4S), 168–174.

Broumi, S., Bakali, A., Talea, M., Smarandache, F., & Verma, R. (2017). Computing Minimum Spanning Tree in Interval Valued Bipolar Neutrosophic Environment. *International Journal of Modeling and Optimization*, *7*(5), 300–304. doi:10.7763/IJMO.2017.V7.602

Broumi, S., Deli, I., & Smarandache, F. (2014). Interval valued neutrosophic parameterized soft set theory and its decision making. *Journal of New Results in Science*, *3*, 58–71.

Broumi, S., Dey, A., Bakali, A., Talea, M., Smarandache, F., Son, L. H., & Koley, D. (2017c). Uniform Single Valued Neutrosophic Graphs. *Neutrosophic Sets and Systems*, *17*, 42–49.

Broumi, S., Dey, A., Talea, M., Bakali, A., Smarandache, F., Nagarajan, D., ... Kumar, R. (2019a). *Shortest Path Problem using Bellman Algorithm under Neutrosophic Environment*. Complex & Intelligent Systems. doi:10.100740747-019-0101-8

Broumi, S., Mohamed, T., Bakali, A., & Smarandache, F. (2016). Single valued neutrosophic graphs. *J New Theory*, *10*, 86–101.

Broumi, S., Nagarajan, D., Bakali, A., Talea, M., Smarandache, F., & Lathamaheswari, M. (2019c). *The shortest path problem in interval valued trapezoidal and triangular neutrosophic environment*. Complex & Intelligent Systems. doi:10.100740747-019-0092-5

Broumi, S., & Smarandache, F. (2013). Correlation coeffcient of interval neutrosophic set. *Mechanical Engineering and Manufacturing*, *436*, 511–517.

Broumi, S., & Smarandache, F. (2013). Correlation coefficient of interval neutrosophic set. *Applied Mechanics and Materials*, *436*, 511–517. doi:10.4028/www.scientific.net/AMM.436.511

Broumi, S., & Smarandache, F. (2013). Several similarity measures of neutrosophic sets. *Neutrosophic Sets Syst*, *1*(1), 54–62.

Broumi, S., & Smarandache, F. (2014). Cosine similarity measure of interval-valued neutrosophic sets. *Neutrosophic Sets and Systems*, *5*, 15–20.

Broumi, S., & Smarandache, F. (2014). Rough Neutrosophic sets. *International Journal of Pure and Applied Mathematics*, *32*, 493–502.

Broumi, S., & Smarandache, F. (2015). Interval neutrosophic rough sets. *Neutrosophic Sets and Systems*, *7*, 23–31.

Broumi, S., Smarandache, F., & Dhar, M. (2014a). Rough neutrosophic sets. *International Journal of Pure and Applied Mathematics*, *32*, 493–502.

Broumi, S., Smarandache, F., & Dhar, M. (2014b). Rough neutrosophic sets. *Neutrosophic Sets and Systems*, *3*, 60–66.

Broumi, S., Son, L. H., Bakali, A., Talea, M., Smarandache, F., & Selvachandran, G. (2017a). Computing Operational Matrices in Neutrosophic Environments: A Matlab Toolbox. *Neutrosophic Sets and Systems*, *18*, 58–66. doi:10.5281/zenodo.1175160

Broumi, S., Talea, M., Bakali, A., Singh, P. K., & Smarandache, F. (2019). Energy and Spectrum Analysis of Interval Valued Neutrosophic Graph Using MATLAB. *Neutrosophic Sets and Systems*, *24*, 46–60. doi:10.5281/zenodo.2593919

Broumi, S., Talea, M., Bakali, A., & Smarandache, F. (2016). Interval Valued Neutrosophic Graphs. *Critical Review*, *12*, 5–33.

Broumi, S., Talea, M., Bakali, A., & Smarandache, F. (2016c). Interval Valued Neutrosophic Graphs. *Critical Review*, *12*, 5–33.

Broumi, S., Talea, M., Bakali, A., Smarandache, F., Bakali, A., & Kishore Kumar, P. K. (2017a). Shortest Path Problem on Single Valued Neutrosophic Graphs. *Int. Symp. On Networks, Computers and Communications (ISNCC-2017).* 10.1109/ISNCC.2017.8071993

Broumi, S., Talea, M., Bakali, A., Smarandache, F., Nagarajan, D., Lathamaheswari, M., & Parimala, M. (2019b). *Shortest path problem in fuzzy, intuitionistic fuzzy and neutrosophic environment: an overview.* Complex & Intelligent Systems. doi:10.100740747-019-0098-z

Broumi, S., Talea, M., Smarandache, F., & Bakali, A. (2016a). Single valued neutrosophic graphs: Degree, Order and Size. *Proceedings of the IEEE International Conference on Fuzzy Systems (FUZZ),* 2444-2451. 10.1109/FUZZ-IEEE.2016.7738000

Broumi, S., Ullah, K., Bakali, A., Talea, M., Singh, P. K., Mahmood, T., ... Oliveira, A. D. (2018). Novel system and method for telephone network planing based on neutrosophic graph. *Glob J Comput Sci Technol E Netw Web Secur, 18*(2), 1–11.

Broumi, S., Ye, J., & Smarandache, F. (2015). An extended TOPSIS method for multiple attribute decision making based on interval neutrosophic uncertain linguistic variables. *Neutrosophic Sets and Systems, 8,* 22–31.

Burillo, P., & Bustince, H. (1996). Entropy on intuitionistic fuzzy sets and on interval-valued fuzzy sets. *Fuzzy Sets and Systems, 78*(3), 305–316. doi:10.1016/0165-0114(96)84611-2

Bustince, H., & Burillo, P. (1995). Correlation of interval-valued intuitionistic fuzzy sets. *Fuzzy Sets and Systems, 74*(2), 237–244. doi:10.1016/0165-0114(94)00343-6

Bustince, H., & Burillo, P. (1996). Structures on intuitionistic fuzzy relations. *Fuzzy Sets and Systems, 78*(3), 293–303. doi:10.1016/0165-0114(96)84610-0

Bustince, H., & Burillo, P. (1996). Vague sets are intuitionistic fuzzy sets. *Fuzzy Sets and Systems, 79*(3), 403–405. doi:10.1016/0165-0114(95)00154-9

Can, M. S., & Ozguven, O. F. (2016). Design of the neutronsophic membership valued fuzzy-PID controller and rotation angle control of a permanent magnet direct current motor. *Journal of New Results in Science, 5,* 126–138.

Can, M. S., & Ozguven, O. F. (2017). PID tuning with neutrosophic similarity measure. *International Journal of Fuzzy Systems, 19*(2), 489–503. doi:10.100740815-015-0136-y

Can, M. S., & Ozguven, O. F. (2018). Fuzzy PID Control by Grouping of Membership Functions of Fuzzy Antecedent Variables with Neutrosophic Set Approach and 3-D Position Tracking Control of a Robot Manipulator. *Journal of Electrical Engineering & Technology, 13,* 969–980.

Cao, Y. X., Zhou, H., & Wang, J. Q. (2016). An approach to interval-valued intuitionistic stochastic multicriteria decision-making using set pair analysis. *International Journal of Machine Learning and Cybernetics.* doi:10.100713042-016-0589-9

Çetkin, V., & Aygün, H. (2015). An approach to neutrosophic subgroup and its fundamental properties. *Journal of Intelligent & Fuzzy Systems, 29*(5), 1941–1947. doi:10.3233/IFS-151672

Chakraborty, A., Mondal, S. P., Ahmadian, A., Senu, N., Alam, S., & Salahshour, S. (2018). Ahmadian A., Senu N., Alam S., Salahshour S., Different Forms of Triangular Neutrosophic Numbers, De-Neutrosophication Techniques, and their Applications. *Symmetry, 10*(8), 327. doi:10.3390ym10080327

Chatterjee, R., Majumdar, P., & Samanta, S. K. (2016). On some similarity measures and entropy on quadripartitioned single valued neutrosophic sets. *Journal of Intelligent & Fuzzy Systems, 30*(4), 2475–2485. doi:10.3233/IFS-152017

Chatterjee, R., Majumdar, P., & Samanta, S. K. (2019). *Similarity Measures in Neutrosophic Sets-I. In Fuzzy Multi-criteria Decision-Making Using Neutrosophic Sets* (pp. 249–294). Cham: Springer. doi:10.1007/978-3-030-00045-5_11

Chaturvedi, A., Singh, S. K., & Singh, U. (2018). Statistical Inferences of Type-II Progressively Hybrid Censored Fuzzy Data with Rayleigh Distribution. *Austrian Journal of Statistics, 47*(3), 40–62. doi:10.17713/ajs.v47i3.752

Chen, J., Ye, J., & Du, S. (2017). Scale effect and anisotropy analyzed for neutrosophic numbers of rock joint roughness coefficient based on neutrosophic statistics. *Symmetry, 9*(10), 208. doi:10.3390ym9100208

Chen, J., Ye, J., Du, S., & Yong, R. (2017). Expressions of rock joint roughness coefficient using neutrosophic interval statistical numbers. *Symmetry, 9*(7), 123. doi:10.3390ym9070123

Chen, L.-H., & Lu, H.-W. (2007). An extended assignment problem considering multiple and outputs. *Applied Mathematical Modelling, 31*(10), 2239–2248. doi:10.1016/j.apm.2006.08.018

Chen, L., & Wang, Y. Z. (2003). Research on TOPSIS integrated evaluation and decision method based on entropy coefficient. *Control Decis., 18*, 456–459.

Chen, M. S. (1985). On a fuzzy assignment problem. *Tamkang Journal, 22*, 407–411.

Chen, Y., & Li, B. (2011). Dynamic multi-attribute decision making model based on triangular intuitionistic fuzzy number. *Scientia Iranica B, 18*(2), 268–274. doi:10.1016/j.scient.2011.03.022

Chiang, D. A., & Lin, N. P. (1999). Correlation of fuzzy sets. *Fuzzy Sets and Systems, 102*(2), 221226. doi:10.1016/S0165-0114(97)00127-9

Chi, P., & Liu, P. (2013). An extended TOPSIS method for multi-attribute decision making problems on interval neutrosophic set. *Neutrosophic Sets and Systems, 1*, 63–70.

Chunfang, L., & Yue Sheng, L. (2016). A new method to construct entropy of interval-valued Neutrosophic Set. *Neutrosophic Sets and Systems, 11*, 8–11. doi:10.5281/zenodo.571218

Çoker, D. (1997). An introduction to intuitionistic fuzzy topological spaces. *Fuzzy Sets and Systems, 88*(1), 81–89. doi:10.1016/S0165-0114(96)00076-0

Cormen, T. H., Leiserson, C. E., Rivest, R. L., & Stein, C. (2001). *Introduction to Algorithms.* McGraw-Hill.

Dalapati, S., & Pramanik, S. (2018). A revisit to NC-VIKOR based MAGDM strategy in neutrosophic cubic set environment. *Neutrosophic Sets and Systems, 21*, 131–141. doi:10.5281/zenodo.1408665

Dalapati, S., Pramanik, S., Alam, S., Smarandache, S., & Roy, T. K. (2017). IN-cross entropy based MAGDM strategy under interval neutrosophic set environment. *Neutrosophic Sets and Systems, 18*, 43–57. doi:10.5281/zenodo.1175162

Dalbinder, K., & Kajla, B. (2017). Selection of Transportation Companies and Their Mode of Transportation for Interval Valued Data. *Neutrosophic Sets and Systems, 18*, 67–79. doi:10.5281/zenodo.1175172

Das, P. S. (1981). Fuzzy groups and level subgroups. *Journal of Mathematical Analysis and Applications, 84*(1), 264–269. doi:10.1016/0022-247X(81)90164-5

Das, S., & Guha, D. (2013). Ranking of Intuitionistic Fuzzy Number by Centroid Point. *Journal of Industrial and Intelligent Information, 1*(2), 107–110. doi:10.12720/jiii.1.2.107-110

Davvaz, B. (1999). Interval-valued fuzzy subhypergroups. *Korean Journal of Computational and Applied Mathematics, 6*, 197–202.

Davvaz, B. (2001). Fuzzy ideals of near-rings with interval valued membership functions. *Journal of Sciences Islamic Republic of Iran, 12*, 171–176.

Davvaz, B., Dudek, W. A., & Jun, Y. B. (2006). Intuitionistic fuzzy Hv-submodules. *Information Sciences, 176*(3), 285–300. doi:10.1016/j.ins.2004.10.009

Deli, I. (2016). *A new multi attribute decision making model based on single valued trapezoidal neutrosophic numbers*. International Conference on Mathematics and Mathematics Education (ICMME-2016), Elazıg.

Deli, I., Ali, M., & Smarandache, F. (2015). Bipolar neutrosophic sets and their application based on multi-criteria decision making problems. In *2015 International Conference on Advanced Mechatronic Systems*, (pp. 249-254). Academic Press. 10.1109/ICAMechS.2015.7287068

Deli, I. (2017). Interval-valued neutrosophic soft sets and its decision making. *International Journal of Machine Learning and Cybernetics, 8*(2), 665–676. doi:10.100713042-015-0461-3

Deli, I., & Broumi, S. (2015). Neutrosophic Soft Matrices and NSM-decision Making. *Journal of Intelligent & Fuzzy Systems, 28*(5), 2233–2241. doi:10.3233/IFS-141505

Deli, I., Broumi, S., & Smarandache, F. (2015). Neutrosophic multi-sets and its application in medical diagnosis. *J. New Theory, 6*, 88–98.

Deli, I., Broumi, S., & Smarandache, F. (2015). On Neutrosophic refined sets and their applications in medical diagnosis. *Journal of New Theory, 6*, 88–98.

Deli, I., Simsek, I., & Cagman, N. (2015). A Multiple Criteria Group Decision Making Methods on Single Valued Trapezoidal Neutrosophic Numbers Based on Einstein Operations. In *The 4th Intern. Fuzzy Systems Symp. (FUZZYSS'15)*. Yildiz Technical University.

Deli, I., & Şubaş, Y. (2014). Single valued neutrosophic numbers and their applications to multicriteria decision making problem. *Neutrosophic Sets Syst., 2*, 1–13.

Deli, I., & Şubaş, Y. (2015). Some weighted geometric operators with SVTrN-numbers and their application to multi-criteria decision making problems. *Journal of Intelligent & Fuzzy Systems*. doi:10.3233/jifs-151677

Deli, I., & Şubaş, Y. (2017). A ranking method of single valued neutrosophic numbers and its applications to multi-attribute decision making problems. *International Journal of Machine Learning and Cybernetics, 8*(4), 1309–1322. doi:10.100713042-016-0505-3

Dengfeng, L., & Chuntian, C. (2002). *New Similarity Measures of Intuitionistic Fuzzy Sets and Application to Pattern Recognitions. Pattern Recognition Letters, 23*, 221–225.

Deng, J. L. (1989). Introduction to grey system theory. *Journal of Grey System, 1*(1), 1–24.

Deng, J. L. (2005). *The primary methods of grey system theory*. Wuhan, China: Huazhong University of Science and Technology Press.

De, S., & Mishra, J. (2017). Inconsistent data processing using vague set and neutrosophic set for justifying better outcome. In *International Conference on Inventive Communication and Computational Technologies (ICICCT)*. IEEE. 10.1109/ICICCT.2017.7975210

De, S., & Mishra, J. (2019). A new approach of Functional Dependency in a Neutrosophic Relational Database Model. *Asian Journal of Computer Science &Technology, 8*(2), 44–48.

Deshmukh, N. M. (2012). An Innovative Method for Solving Transportation Problem. *International Journal of Physics and Mathematical Sciences*.

Dettori, S., Iannino, V., Colla, V., & Signorini, A. (2018). An adaptive fuzzy logic-based approach to PID control of steam turbines in solar applications. *Applied Energy, 227*, 655–664. doi:10.1016/j.apenergy.2017.08.145

Dey, P. P., Pramanik, S., Giri, B. C. & Smarandache, F. (2017). Bipolar neutrosophic projection based models for solving multi-attribute decision-making problems. *Neutrosophic Sets and Systems, 15*, 70-79. doi.org/10.5281/zenodo.570936

Dey, P.P., Pramanik, S., & Giri, B.C. (2016). TOPSIS for solving multi-attribute decision making problems under bipolar neutrosophic environment. *New Trends in Neutrosophic Theories and Applications*, 65-77.

Dey, P. P., Pramanik, S., & Giri, B. C. (2015). Generalized neutrosophic soft multi-attribute group decision making basedon TOPSIS. *Critical Review, 11*, 41–55.

Dey, P. P., Pramanik, S., & Giri, B. C. (2015). Multi-criteria group decision making in intuitionistic fuzzy environment based on grey relational analysis for weaver selection in Khadi institution. *Journal of Applied Quantitative Methods*, *10*(4), 1–14.

Dey, P. P., Pramanik, S., & Giri, B. C. (2016). An extended grey relational analysis based multiple attribute decision making in interval neutrosophic uncertain linguistic setting. *Neutrosophic Sets and Systems*, *11*, 21–30.

Dey, P. P., Pramanik, S., & Giri, B. C. (2016). Extended projection based models for solving multiple attribute decision making problems with interval valued neutrosophic information. In F. Smarandache & S. Pramanik (Eds.), *New trends in neutrosophic theory and applications* (pp. 127–140). Brussels: Pons Editions.

Dey, P. P., Pramanik, S., & Giri, B. C. (2016). Extended projection-based models for solving multiple attribute decision making problems with interval –valued neutrosophic information. In F. Smarandache & S. Pramanik (Eds.), *New trends in neutrosophic theory and applications* (pp. 127–140). Brussels: Pons Editions.

Dey, P. P., Pramanik, S., & Giri, B. C. (2016). TOPSIS for solving multi-attribute decision making problems under bi-polar neutrosophic environment. In F. Smarandache & S. Pramanik (Eds.), *New Trends In Neutrosophic Theory And Applications* (pp. 65–77). Brussels: Pons Editions.

Dhaundiyal, A., & Singh, S. B. (2016). Application of Fuzzy Rayleigh Distribution in the Nonisothermal Pyrolysis of Loose Biomass. *Acta Environmentalica Universitatis Comenianae*, *24*(2), 14–22. doi:10.1515/aeuc-2016-0008

Dice, L. R. (1945). Measure of Amount of Ecological Association between Species. *Ecology*, *26*(3), 297-303.

Dijkstra, E. W. (1959). A note on two problems in connexion with graphs. *Numerische Mathematik*, *1*(1), 269–271. doi:10.1007/BF01386390

Dubois, D., & Prade, H. (1980). *Fuzzy Sets and Systems: Theory and Applications*. New York: Academic Press.

Dubois, D., & Prade, H. (1983). Ranking fuzzy numbers in the setting of possibility theory. *Information Sciences*, *30*(3), 183–224. doi:10.1016/0020-0255(83)90025-7

Ebrahimnejad, A., & Tavana, M. (2014). A novel method for solving linear programming problems with symmetric trapezoidal fuzzy numbers. *Applied Mathematical Modelling*, *38*(17-18), 4388–4395. doi:10.1016/j.apm.2014.02.024

Edward Samuel, A., & Narmadhagnanam, R. (2017). Neutrosophic Refined Sets in Medical Diagnosis. *International Journal of Fuzzy Mathematical Archive*, *14*(1), 117-123.

El-Ghareeb, H. A. (2019). Novel Open Source Python Neutrosophic Package. *Neutrosophic Sets and Systems*, *25*, 136–160. doi:10.5281/zenodo.2631514

Elhassouny, A., & Smarandache, F. (2016). Neutrosophic-simplified-TOPSIS multi-criteria decision-making using combined simplified-TOPSIS method and Neutrosophics. *IEEE Int. Conf. Fuzzy Syst.* 10.1109/FUZZ-IEEE.2016.7738003

Eltag, K., Aslamx, M. S., & Ullah, R. (2019). Dynamic Stability Enhancement Using Fuzzy PID Control Technology for Power System. *International Journal of Control, Automation, and Systems*, *17*(1), 234–242. doi:10.100712555-018-0109-7

Eroğlu, M. S. (1989). The homomorphic image of a fuzzy subgroup is always a fuzzy subgroup. *Fuzzy Sets and Systems*, *33*(2), 255–256. doi:10.1016/0165-0114(89)90246-7

Farhadinia, B., & Ban, A. I. (2013). Developing new similarity measures of generalized intuitionistic fuzzy numbers and generalized interval-valued fuzzy numbers from similarity measures of generalized fuzzy numbers. *Mathematical and Computer Modelling*, *57*(3-4), 812–825. doi:10.1016/j.mcm.2012.09.010

Fu, J., & Ye, J. (2017). Simplified neutrosophic exponential similarity measures for the initial evaluation/diagnosis of benign prostatic hyperplasia symptoms. *Symmetry*, *9*(8), 154. doi:10.3390ym9080154

Gaing, Z. L. (2004). A particle swarm optimization approach for optimum design of PID controller in AVR system. *IEEE Transactions on Energy Conversion*, *19*(2), 384–391. doi:10.1109/TEC.2003.821821

Ganesan, K., & Veeramani, P. (2006). Fuzzy linear programs with trapezoidal fuzzy numbers. *Annals of Operations Research*, *143*(1), 305–315. doi:10.100710479-006-7390-1

Gani, A. N. (2010). On searching Intuitionistic Fuzzy Shortest Path in a Network. *Applied Mathematical Sciences*, *4*(69), 3447–3454.

Gani, A. N., & Ponnalagu, K. (2016). A method based on intuitionistic fuzzy linear programming for investment strategy. *Int. J. Fuzzy Math. Arch.*, *10*(1), 71–81.

Garg, H. (2017). Non-linear programming method for multi-criteria decision making problems under interval neutrosophic set environment. *Applied Intelligence*. doi:10.100710489-017-1070-5

Gau, W. L., & Buehrer, D. J. (1993). Vague sets. *IEEE Transactions on Systems, Man, and Cybernetics*, *23*(2), 610–614. doi:10.1109/21.229476

Gayen, S., Jha, S., & Singh, M. (2019). On direct product of a fuzzy subgroup with an anti-fuzzy subgroup. *International Journal of Recent Technology and Engineering,* 8, 1105-1111.

Gayen, S., Jha, S., Singh, M., & Kumar, R. (2019a). On a generalized notion of anti-fuzzy subgroup and some characterizations. *International Journal of Engineering and Advanced Technology*, 8, 385-390.

Gayen, S., Smarandache, F., Jha, S., Singh, M. K., Broumi, S., & Kumar, R. (2019b, 10). Chapter 8: Introduction to plithogenic subgroup. In F. Smarandache, & S. Broumi (Eds.). IGI-Global.

Giri, B. C., Molla, M. U., & Biswas, P. (2018). TOPSIS Method for MADM based on Interval Trapezoidal Neutrosophic Number. *Neutrosophic Sets and Systems*, *22*, 151–167.

Giri, B. C., Molla, M. U., & Biswas, P. (2018). TOPSIS method for MADM based on interval trapezoidal neutrosophic numbers. *Neutrosophic Sets and Systems*, *22*, 151–167. doi:10.5281/zenodo.2160749

Gotmare, D., & Khot, P.G. (2016). Solution of Fuzzy Assignment Problem by using Branch and Bound Technique with application of Lingustic variable. *International Journals of Computer and Technology*, *15*(4).

Grattan-Guiness, I. (1976). Fuzzy membership mapped onto intervals and many-valued quantities. *Mathematical Logic Quarterly*, *22*(1), 149–160. doi:10.1002/malq.19760220120

Grzegorzewski, P. (2002). Nearest interval approximation of a fuzzy number. *Fuzzy Sets and Systems*, *130*(3), 321–330. doi:10.1016/S0165-0114(02)00098-2

Guijun, W., & Xiaoping, L. (1996). Interval-valued fuzzy subgroups induced by T-triangular norms. *Bulletin Pour Les Sous Ensembles Flous Et Leurs Applicatios*, *65*, 80–84.

Gündoğdu, F. K., & Kahraman, C. (2019). Spherical fuzzy sets and spherical fuzzy TOPSIS method. *Journal of Intelligent & Fuzzy Systems*. doi:10.3233/JIFS-181401

Guo, Y., & Cheng, H. D. (2009). New neutrosophic approach to image segmentation. *Pattern Recognition*, *42*(5), 587–595. doi:10.1016/j.patcog.2008.10.002

Guo, Y., & Şengür, A. (2014). A novel image segmentation algorithm based on neutrosophic similarity clustering. *Applied Soft Computing*, *25*, 391–398. doi:10.1016/j.asoc.2014.08.066

Guo, Y., Sengur, A., & Tian, J. (2016). A novel breast ultrasound image segmentation algorithm based on neutrosophic similarity score and level set. *Computer Methods and Programs in Biomedicine*, *123*, 43–53. doi:10.1016/j.cmpb.2015.09.007 PMID:26483304

Guo, Y., Şengür, A., & Ye, J. (2014). A Novel Image Thresholding Algorithm Based on Neutrosophic Similarity Score. *Measurement*, *58*, 175–186. doi:10.1016/j.measurement.2014.08.039

Gupta, A., Goindi, S., Singh, G., Saini, H., & Kumar, R. (2017). Optimal design of PID controllers for time delay systems using genetic algorithm and simulated annealing. *The 2017 International Conference on Innovative Mechanisms for Industry Applications (ICIMIA)*, 66-69. 10.1109/ICIMIA.2017.7975554

Gupta, M. M., & Qi, J. (1991). Theory of T-norms and fuzzy inference methods. *Fuzzy Sets and Systems*, *40*(3), 431–450. doi:10.1016/0165-0114(91)90171-L

Haibin, W., Smarandache, F., Zhang, Y., & Sunderraman, R. (2010). *Single valued neutrosophic sets*. Infinite Study.

Hanafy, I. M., Salama, A. A., & Mahfouz, K. (2012). Correlation of neutrosophic data. *Int. Refereed J. Eng. Sci.*, *1*(2), 39–43.

Hanafy, I. M., Salama, A. A., & Mahfouz, K. M. (2013). Correlation Coeffcients of Neutrosophic Sets by Centroid Method. *International Journal of Probability and Statistics*, 2(1), 9–12.

Hassan, N., Uluçay, V., & Şahin, M. (2018). Q-neutrosophic soft expert set and its application in decision making. *International Journal of Fuzzy System Applications*, 7(4), 37–61. doi:10.4018/IJFSA.2018100103

Hayat, K., Ali, M. I., Cao, B. Y., Karaaslan, F., & Yang, X. P. (2018). Another view of group-based generalized intuitionistic fuzzy soft sets: Aggregation operators and multiattribute decision making. *Symmetry*, 10(12), 25–32. doi:10.3390ym10120753

Hazwani, H., Lazim, A., & Ashraf, A. Q. (2019). Interval Neutrosophic Vague Sets. *Neutrosophic Sets and Systems*, 25, 66–75. doi:10.5281/zenodo.2631504

Heilpern, S. (1992). The expected value of fuzzy number. *Fuzzy Sets and Systems*, 47(1), 81–86. doi:10.1016/0165-0114(92)90062-9

Hezam, I. M., Abdel-Basset, M., & Smarandache, F. (2015). Taylor series approximation to solve neutrosophic multiobjective programming problem. *Neutrosophic Sets and Systems, 10*, 39-45. Retrieved from http://fs.gallup.unm.edu/NSS/Taylor%20Series%20Approximation.pdf

Hong, D. H. (2006). Fuzzy measures for a correlation coefficient of fuzzy numbers under Tw (the weakest t norm)-based fuzzy arithmetic operations. *Information Sciences*, 176(2), 150160. doi:10.1016/j.ins.2004.11.005

Hong, D. H., & Hwang, S. Y. (1995). Correlation of intuitionistic fuzzy sets in probability spaces. *Fuzzy Sets and Systems*, 75(1), 77–81. doi:10.1016/0165-0114(94)00330-A

Hong-Xiaa, S., Hao-Xionga, Y., Jian-Zhangb, W., & Yao, O. (2015). Interval neutrosophic numbers Choquet integral operator for multi-criteria decision making. *Journal of Intelligent & Fuzzy Systems*, 28(6), 2443–2455. doi:10.3233/IFS-141524

Huang, L.-S., & Zhang, L. (2006). Solution method for fuzzy assignment problem with Restriction of Qualification. *Proceedings of the Sixth International Conference on Intelligent Systems Design and Applications*. 10.1109/ISDA.2006.247

Huang, Y. H., Wei, G. W., & Wei, C. (2017). VIKOR Method for Interval Neutrosophic Multiple Attribute Group Decision-Making, information. *Information.*, 8(4), 144. doi:10.3390/info8040144

Hung, W.L., & Yang, M.S. (2006). Fuzzy Entropy on Intuitionistic Fuzzy Sets. *International Journal of Intelligent Systems, 21*, 443-451.

Hung, W. L., & Yang, M. S. (2004). Similarity measures of intuitionistic fuzzy sets based on Hausdorff distance. *Pattern Recognition Letters*, 25(14), 1603–1611. doi:10.1016/j.patrec.2004.06.006

Hur, K., Jang, S. Y., & Kang, H. W. (2004). Intuitionistic fuzzy normal subgroups and intuitionistic fuzzy cosets. *Honam Mathematical Journal*, 26, 559–587.

Hur, K., Kang, H. W., & Song, H. K. (2003). Intuitionistic fuzzy subgroups and subrings. *Honam Mathematical Journal*, *25*, 19–41.

Hussian, A., Mohamed, M., Baset, M., & Smarandache, F. (2017). Neutrosophic linear programming problem. *Mathematical Sciences Letters*, *3*(6), 319–324. doi:10.18576/msl/060315

Hwang, C. L., & Yoon, K. (1981). *Multiple attribute decision making: methods and applications.* New York: Springer. doi:10.1007/978-3-642-48318-9

Ismat, B., & Ashraf, S. (2018). Fuzzy equivalence relations. *Kuwait Journal of Science & Engineering*, *35*, 33–51.

Jana, C., Pal, M., Karaaslan, F., & Wang, J. Q. (2018). Trapezoidal neutrosophic aggregation operators and its application in multiple attribute decision-making process. *Scientia Iranica*, *5*. doi:10.24200/SCI.2018.51136.2024

Jiang, X., Guo, Y., & Chen, H. (2019). An Adaptive Region Growing Method using Similarity Set Score and Homogeneity Value based on Neutrosophic Set Domain for Ultrasound Image Segmentation. *IEEE Access: Practical Innovations, Open Solutions*, *7*(1), 60584–60593. doi:10.1109/ACCESS.2019.2911560

Ji, P., Wang, J. Q., & Zhang, H. Y. (2016). Frank prioritized Bonferroni mean operator with single-valued neutrosophic sets and its application in selecting third-party logistics providers. *Neural Computing & Applications.* doi:10.100700521-016-2660-6

Ji, P., Zhang, H. Y., & Wang, J. Q. (2018). A fuzzy decision support model with sentiment analysis for items comparison in e-commerce: The case study of PConline.com. *IEEE Transactions on Systems, Man, and Cybernetics. Systems.* doi:10.1109/TSMC.2018.2875163

Johnson, N. L., Kotz, S., & Balakrishnan, N. (1994). Continuous univariate distributions (Vol. 1). Academic Press.

Jun, Y. (n.d.). Projection and bidirectional projection measures of singlevalued neutrosophic sets and their decision-making method for mechanical design schemes. *Journal of Experimental & Theoretical Artificial Intelligence*, *29*(4), 731–740.

Jun, Y. B., & Kim, K. H. (2002). Interval-valued fuzzy R-subgroups of near-rings. *Indian Journal of Pure and Applied Mathematics*, *33*, 71–80.

Kalyan, M., & Surapati, P., & Bibhas, G. C. (2018). Interval Neutrosophic Tangent Similarity Measure Based MADM strategy and its Application to MADM Problems. *Neutrosophic Sets and Systems*, *19*, 46–56. doi:10.5281/zenodo.1235201

Kanikal, M., & Kajla, B. (2016). Improved similarity measure in a neutrosophic environment and its application in finding a minimum spanning tree. *Journal of Intelligent & Fuzzy Systems*, *31*(3), 1721–1730. doi:10.3233/JIFS-152082

Karaaslan, F. (2019). Correlation Coefficient of Neutrosophic Sets and Its Applications in Decision-Making. *Springer Nature Switzerland AG*, 369.

Karaaslan, F. (2016). Correlation coefficient between possibility neutrosophic soft sets. *Math. Sci. Lett.*, *5*(1), 71–74. doi:10.18576/msl/050109

Karaaslan, F. (2017). Correlation coefficients of single-valued neutrosophic refined soft sets and their applications in clustering analysis. *Neural Computing & Applications*, *28*(2), 2781–2793. doi:10.100700521-016-2209-8

Karaaslan, F. (2018a). Multi-criteria decision-making method based on similarity measures under single-valued neutrosophic refined and interval neutrosophic refined environments. *International Journal of Intelligent Systems*, *33*(5), 928–952. doi:10.1002/int.21906

Karaaslan, F. (2018b). Gaussian Single-valued neutrosophic number and its application in multi-attribute decision making. *Neutrosophic Sets and Systems*, *22*, 101–117.

Karaaslan, F., & Hayat, K. (2018). Some new operations on single-valued neutrosophic matrices and their applications in multi-criteria group decision making. *Applied Intelligence*, *48*(2), 4594–4614. doi:10.100710489-018-1226-y

Karaşan, A., & Kahraman, C. (2017). Interval-Valued Neutrosophic Extension of EDAS Method. Advances in Intelligent Systems and Computing, 642. DOI doi:10.1007/978-3-319-66824-6_31

Karunambigai, M. G., Parvathi, R., Atanassov, K., & Palaniappan, N. (2007). An Intuitionistic Fuzzy Graph Method for Finding the Shortest Paths in Networks. *Advances in Soft Computing*, *42*, 3–10. doi:10.1007/978-3-540-72434-6_1

Khalid, H. E. (2015). An Original Notion to Find Maximal Solution in the Fuzzy Neutrosophic Relation Equations (FNRE) with Geometric Programming (GP). *Neutrosophic Sets and Systems*, *7*, 3–7.

Khalid, H. E. (2016). The Novel Attempt for Finding Minimum Solution in Fuzzy Neutrosophic Relational Geometric Programming (FNRGP) with (max, min) Composition. *Neutrosophic Sets and Systems*, *11*, 107–111.

Khalid, H. E., Smarandache, F., & Essa, A. K. (2018). The Basic Notions for (over, off, under) Neutrosophic Geometric Programming Problems. *Neutrosophic Sets and Systems*, *22*, 50–62.

Kharal, A. (2014). A neutrosophic multi-criteria decision making method. *New Mathematics and Natural Computation*, *10*(02), 143–162. doi:10.1142/S1793005714500070

Khodadadi, H., & Ghadiri, H. (2018). Self-tuning PID controller design using fuzzy logic for half car active suspension system. *International Journal of Dynamics and Control*, *6*(1), 224–232. doi:10.100740435-016-0291-5

Klein, C. M. (1991). Fuzzy shortest paths. *Fuzzy Sets and Systems*, *39*(1), 27–41. doi:10.1016/0165-0114(91)90063-V

Klement, E. P., Mesiar, R., & Pap, E. (2013). *Triangular norms* (Vol. 8). Springer Science & Business Media.

Kondrak, G. (2005). N-gram Similarity and Distance. *SPIRE*, 115-126.

Koundal, D., Gupta, S., & Singh, S. (2018). Computer aided thyroid nodule detection system using medical ultrasound images. *Biomedical Signal Processing and Control*, *40*, 117–130. doi:10.1016/j.bspc.2017.08.025

Kowalski, G. (2011). Information Retrieval Architecture and Algorithms. Springer. doi:10.1007/978-1-4419-7716-8

Kuhlthau, C. (1993). A principle of uncertainty for information seeking. *The Journal of Documentation*, *49*(4), 339–355. doi:10.1108/eb026918

Kuhlthau, C. (2003). *Seeking meaning: a process approach to library and information services.* Englewood, CO: Libraries Unlimited.

Kumar, R., Edalatpanah, S. A., Jha, S., Broumi, S., Singh, R., & Dey, A. (2019). A Multi objective programming approach to solve integer valued neutrosophic shortest path problems. *Neutrosophic Sets and Systems*, 134.

Kumar, R., Edalatpanah, S. A., Jha, S., Gayen, S., & Singh, R. (2019). Shortest path problems using fuzzy weighted arc length. *International Journal of Innovative Technology and Exploring Engineering*.

Kumar, A., Kaur, J., & Singh, P. (2011). A new method for solving fully fuzzy linear programming problems. *Applied Mathematical Modelling*, *35*(2), 817–823. doi:10.1016/j.apm.2010.07.037

Kumar, A., & Kaur, M. (2013). A Ranking Approach for Intuitionistic Fuzzy Numbers and its Application. *Journal of Applied Research and Technology*, *11*(3), 381–396. doi:10.1016/S1665-6423(13)71548-7

Kumar, M., Bhutani, K., Aggarwal, S., & ... (2015). Hybrid model for medical diagnosis using neutrosophic cognitive maps with genetic algorithms. *2015 IEEE International Conference on Fuzzy Systems*, 1-7.

Kumar, R., Edalatpanah, S. A., Jha, S., Broumi, S., & Dey, A. (2018). Neutrosophic shortest path problems. *Neutrosophic Sets and Systems*, *23*, 5–15.

Kumar, R., Edalatpanah, S. A., Jha, S., Broumi, S., Singh, R., & Dey, A. (2019). A multi objective programming approaches to solve integer valued neutrosophic shortest path problems. *Neutrosophic Sets and Systems*, *24*, 134–149.

Kumar, R., Edalatpanah, S. A., Jha, S., & Singh, R. (2019). A novel approach to solve gaussian valued neutrosophic shortest path problems. *Int J Eng Adv Technol*, *8*, 347–353.

Kumar, R., Edalatpanah, S. A., Jha, S., & Singh, R. (2019). A Pythagorean fuzzy approach to the transportation problem. *Complex & Intelligent Systems*, *5*(2), 255–263. doi:10.100740747-019-0108-1

Kumar, R., Edalatpanah, S. A., Jha, S., & Singh, R. (2019a). A novel approach to solve Gaussian Valued Neutrosophic Shortest Path Problems. *International Journal of Engineering and Advanced Technology, 8*(3), 347–353.

Kumar, R., Edaltpanah, S. A., Jha, S., Broumi, S., & Dey, A. (2018). Neutrosophic shortest path problem. *Neutrosophic Sets and Systems, 23*, 5–15.

Kumar, R., Jha, S., & Singh, R. (2020). A different appraoch for solving the shortest path problem under mixed fuzzy environment. *International Journal of Fuzzy System Applications, 9*, 6.

Kundu, P., Kar, S., & Maiti, M. (2013). Multi-objective multi-item solid transportation problem in fuzzy environment. *Applied Mathematical Modelling, 37*(4), 2028–2038. doi:10.1016/j.apm.2012.04.026

Kwok, D. P., & Sheng, F. (1994). Genetic algorithm and simulated annealing for optimal robot arm PID control. *Proceedings of the First IEEE Conference on Evolutionary Computation*, 707-713. 10.1109/ICEC.1994.349971

Lee, S. J., & Lee, E. P. (2000). The Category Of Intuitionistic Fuzzy Topologcal Spaces. *Bulletin of the Korean Mathematical Society, 37*(1), 63–76.

Liang, R. X., Wang, J. Q., & Li, L. (2018). Multi-criteria group decision making method based on interdependent inputs of single valued trapezoidal neutrosophic information. *Neural Computing & Applications, 30*(1), 241–260. doi:10.100700521-016-2672-2

Liang, R. X., Wang, J. Q., & Zhang, H. Y. (2017). A multi-criteria decision-making method based on single-valued trapezoidal neutrosophic preference relations with complete weight information. *Neural Computing & Applications.* doi:10.100700521-017-2925-8

Liang, R. X., Wang, J. Q., & Zhang, H. Y. (2017). Evaluation of e-commerce websites: An integrated approach under a single-valued trapezoidal neutrosophic environment. *Knowledge-Based Systems, 135*, 44–59. doi:10.1016/j.knosys.2017.08.002

Liang, Z., & Shi, P. (2003). Similarity measures on intuitionistic fuzzy sets. *Pattern Recognition Letters, 24*(15), 2687–2693. doi:10.1016/S0167-8655(03)00111-9

Li, D. F. (2010). A ratio ranking method of triangular intuitionistic fuzzy numbers and its application to MADM problems. *Computers & Mathematics with Applications (Oxford, England), 60*(6), 1557–1570. doi:10.1016/j.camwa.2010.06.039

Li, D. F. (2014). *Decision and Game Theory in Management With Intuitionistic Fuzzy Sets. Studies in Fuzziness and Soft Computing, 308.* Springer. doi:10.1007/978-3-642-40712-3

Li, D. F., Nan, J. X., & Zhang, M. J. (2010). A ranking method of triangular intuitionistic fuzzy numbers and application to decision making. *Int J. Comput. Intell. Syst., 3*(5), 522–530. doi:10.2991/ijcis.2010.3.5.2

Li, P., Zhang, H. Y., & Wang, J. Q. (2016). A projection-based TODIM method under multi-valued neutrosophic environments and its application in personnel selection. *Neural Computing & Applications*. doi:10.100700521-016-2436-z

Liu, B., & Member, S. (2002). Expected Value of Fuzzy Variable and Fuzzy Expected Value Models IEEE. *Transactons on Fuzzy Systems*, *10*(4), 445–450. doi:10.1109/TFUZZ.2002.800692

Liu, P. D., He, L., & Yu, X. C. (2016). Generalized Hybrid Aggregation Operators Based on the 2-Dimension Uncertain Linguistic Information for Multiple Attribute Group Decision Making. *Group Decision and Negotiation*, *25*(1), 103–126. doi:10.100710726-015-9434-x

Liu, P. D., & Li, H. G. (2017). Multiple attribute decision-making method based on some normal neutrosophic Bonferroni mean operators. *Neural Computing & Applications*, *28*(1), 179–194. doi:10.100700521-015-2048-z

Liu, P. D., & Liu, Y. (2014). An approach to multiple attribute group decision making based on intuitionistic trapezoidal fuzzy power generalized aggregation operator. *International Journal of Computational Intelligence Systems*, *7*(2), 291–304. doi:10.1080/18756891.2013.862357

Liu, P. D., & Shi, L. L. (2015). The Generalized Hybrid Weighted Average Operator Based on Interval Neutrosophic Hesitant Set and Its Application to Multiple Attribute Decision Making. *Neural Computing & Applications*, *26*(2), 457–471. doi:10.100700521-014-1736-4

Liu, P., Chu, Y., Li, Y., & Chen, Y. (2014). Some generalized neutrosophic number Hamacher aggregation operators and their application to group decision making. *International Journal of Fuzzy Systems*, *16*(2), 242–255.

Liu, P., Jin, F., Zhang, X., Su, Y., & Wang, M. (2011). Research on the multi-attribute decision-making under risk with interval probability based on prospect theory and the uncertain linguistic variables. *Knowledge-Based Systems*, *24*(4), 554–561. doi:10.1016/j.knosys.2011.01.010

Liu, P., & Tang, G. (2016a). Some power generalized aggregation operators based on the interval neutrosophic numbers and their application to decision making. *Journal of Intelligent & Fuzzy Systems*, *30*(5), 2517–2528. doi:10.3233/IFS-151782

Liu, P., & Wang, Y. (2014). Multiple attribute decision-making method based on single-valued neutrosophic normalized weighted Bonferroni mean. *Neural Computing & Applications*, *25*(7), 2001–2010. doi:10.100700521-014-1688-8

Liu, P., Zhang, X., & Jin, F. (2012). A multi-attribute group decision-making method based on interval valued trapezoidal fuzzy numbers hybrid harmonic averaging operators. *Journal of Intelligent & Fuzzy Systems*, *23*(5), 159–168.

Li, X., & Wang, G. (2000). The S_H-interval-valued fuzzy subgroup. *Fuzzy Sets and Systems*, *112*(2), 319–325. doi:10.1016/S0165-0114(98)00092-X

Li, Y., Liu, P., & Chen, Y. (2016). Some Single Valued Neutrosophic Number Heronian Mean Operators and Their Application in Multiple Attribute Group Decision Making. *INFORMATICA*, *27*(1), 85–110. doi:10.15388/Informatica.2016.78

Li, Y., Olson, D. L., & Qin, Z. (2007). Similarity measures between intuitionistic fuzzy (vague) sets: A comparative analysis. *Pattern Recognition Letters*, *28*(2), 278–285. doi:10.1016/j.patrec.2006.07.009

Lone, M. A., Mir, S. A., Ismail, Y., & Majid, R. (2017). Intustinistic Fuzy Assignment problem: An Application in Agriculture. *Asian Journal of Agricultural Extension,Economics & Socialogy*, *15*(4), 1–6. doi:10.9734/AJAEES/2017/31967

Lupiáñez, F. G. (2009). Interval neutrosophic sets and topology. *Kybernetes*, *38*(3/4), 621–624. doi:10.1108/03684920910944849

M.C. (2016). Solving Multi-Objective Transportation Problem Using Fuzzy Programming Technique-Parallel Method. *International Journal of Recent Scientific Research*, *7*(1), 8455–8457.

Majumdar, P. (2015). Neutrosophic sets and its applications to decision making. In *Computational Intelligence for Big Data Analysis* (pp. 97–115). Springer. doi:10.1007/978-3-319-16598-1_4

Majumdar, P., & Samanta, S. K. (2013). On similarity and entropy of neutrosophic sets. *Journal of Intelligent & Fuzzy Systems*. doi:10.3233/IFS-130810

Maleki, H. R. (2002). Ranking function and their application to fuzzy linear programming. *Far East Journal of Mathematical Sciences*, *4*, 283–301.

Malleham, G., & Rajani, A. (2006). Automatic tuning of PID controller using fuzy logic. *The 8th International Conference on Development and Application Systems*, 120-127.

Ma, Y. X., Wang, J. Q., Wang, J., & Wu, X. H. An interval neutrosophic linguistic multi-criteria group decision-making method and its application in selecting medical treatment options. *Neural Computing & Applications*. doi:10.100700521-016-2203-1

Mohana & Mohanasundari. (2019). On Some Similarity Measures of Single Valued Neutrosophic Rough Sets. *Neutrosophic Sets and Systems, 24*, 10-22.

Mohana, K., & Mohanasundari, M. (2018). Quadripartitioned Single Valued Neutrosophic Rough Sets. *Nirmala Annual Research Congress (NARC-2018), 3*, 165.

Mohana, K., & Mohanasundari, M. (2019). On Some Similarity Measures of Single Valued Neutrosophic Rough Sets. *Neutrosophic Sets and Systems*, *24*, 10–22.

Mondal, K., & Pramanik, S. (2015). Decision making based on some similarity measures under interval rough neutrosophic environment. *Neutrosophic Sets and Systems, 10*, 46-57. doi.org/10.5281/zenodo.571358

Mondal, K., & Pramanik, S. (2015). Neutrosophic refined similarity measure based on cotangent function and its application to multi-attribute decision making. *Global Journal of Advanced Research, 2*(2), 486-494.

Mondal, K., & Pramanik, S. (2015). Neutrosophic tangent similarity measure and its application to multiple attribute decision making. *Neutrosophic Sets and Systems*, *9*, 80-87. doi.org/10.5281/zenodo.571578.

Mondal, K., & Pramanik, S. (2015). Rough neutrosophic multi-attribute decision-making based on grey relational analysis. *Neutrosophic Sets and Systems*, *7*, 8-17. doi.org/10.5281/zenodo.571603

Mondal, K., & Pramanik, S. (2015). Rough neutrosophic multi-attribute decision-making based on rough accuracy score function. *Neutrosophic Sets and Systems*, *8*, 14-21. doi.org/10.5281/zenodo.571604

Mondal, K., Pramanik, S., & Giri, B. C. (2019). Rough neutrosophic aggregation operators for multi-criteria decision-making. In C. Kahraman & I. Otay (Eds.), Fuzzy Multicriteria Decision Making Using Neutrosophic Sets, Studies in Fuzziness and Soft Computing (vol. 369, pp.79-105). Academic Press. doi:10.1007/978-3-030-00045-5_5

Mondal, K., Pramanik, S., & Smarandache F. (2016a). Rough neutrosophic TOPSIS for multi-attribute group decision making. *Neutrosophic Sets and Systems, 13*, 105-117. doi.org/10.5281/zenodo.570866

Mondal, K., Pramanik, S., & Smarandache, F. (2016). Several trigonometric Hamming similarity measures of rough neutrosophic sets and their applications in decision making. *New Trends in Neutrosophic Theory and Applications, 1*, 93-103.

Mondal, K., & Pramanik, S. (2014). Intuitionistic fuzzy multicriteria group decision making approach to quality-brick selection problem. *Journal of Applied Quantitative Methods*, *9*(2), 35–50.

Mondal, K., & Pramanik, S. (2014). Multi-criteria group decision making approach for teacher recruitment in higher education under simplified Neutrosophic environment. *Neutrosophic Sets and Systems*, *6*, 28–34.

Mondal, K., & Pramanik, S. (2015). Cosine similarity measure of rough neutrosophic sets and its application in medical diagnosis. *Global Journal of Advanced Research*, *2*(1), 212–220.

Mondal, K., & Pramanik, S. (2015). Neutrosophic decision making model for clay-brick selection in construction field based on grey relational analysis. *Neutrosophic Sets and Systems*, *9*, 64–71. doi:10.5281/zenodo.34864

Mondal, K., & Pramanik, S. (2015). Neutrosophic decision making model for clay-brick selection in construction field based on grey relational analysis. *Neutrosophic Sets and Systems.*, *9*, 64–71.

Mondal, K., & Pramanik, S. (2015). Neutrosophic decision making model of school choice. *Neutrosophic Sets and Systems*, *7*, 62–68.

Mondal, K., & Pramanik, S. (2015). Neutrosophic Decision Making Model of School Choice. *Neutrosophic Sets and Systems*, *7*, 62–68. doi:10.5281/zenodo.571507

Mondal, K., & Pramanik, S. (2015). Neutrosophic refined similarity measure based on tangent function and its application to multi attribute decision making. *Journal of New Theory, 8*, 41–50. doi:10.5281/zenodo.23176

Mondal, K., & Pramanik, S. (2015). Neutrosophic tangent similarity measure and its application to multiple attribute decision making. *Neutrosophic Sets and Systems, 9*, 85–92.

Mondal, K., & Pramanik, S. (2015). Rough neutrosophic multi-attribute decision-making based on grey relational analysis. *Neutrosophic Sets and Systems, 7*, 8–17.

Mondal, K., & Pramanik, S. (2015). Rough neutrosophic multi-attribute decision-making based on rough accuracy score function. *Neutrosophic Sets and Systems, 8*, 16–22.

Mondal, K., & Pramanik, S. (2015). Tri-complex rough neutrosophic similarity measure and its application in multi-attribute decision making. *Critical Review, 11*, 26–40.

Mondal, K., Pramanik, S., & Giri, B. C. (2018). Hybrid binary logarithm similarity measure for MAGDM problems under SVNS assessments. *Neutrosophic Sets and Systems, 20*, 12–25. doi:10.5281/zenodo.1235365

Mondal, K., Pramanik, S., & Giri, B. C. (2018). Interval neutrosophic tangent similarity measure based MADM strategy and its application to MADM problems. *Neutrosophic Sets and Systems, 19*, 47–56.

Mondal, K., Pramanik, S., & Giri, B. C. (2018). Multi-criteria group decision making based on linguistic refined neutrosophic strategy. In F. Smarandache & S. Pramanik (Eds.), *New trends in neutrosophic theory and applications* (Vol. 2). Pons Editions.

Mondal, K., Pramanik, S., & Giri, B. C. (2018). Single valued neutrosophic hyperbolic sine similarity measure based MADM strategy. *Neutrosophic Sets and Systems, 20*, 3–11. doi:10.5281/zenodo.1235383

Mondal, K., Pramanik, S., & Smarandache, F. (2016). Role of neutrosophic logic in data mining. In F. Smarandache & S. Pramanik (Eds.), *New trends in neutrosophic theory and application* (pp. 15–23). Brussels, Belgium: Pons Editions.

Mondal, K., Pramanik, S., & Smarandache, F. (2016). TOPSIS in rough neutrosophic environment. *Neutrosophic Sets and Systems, 13*, 105–117.

Mondal, K., Pramanik, S., & Smarandache, F. (2016b). Multi-attribute decision making based on rough neutrosophic variational coefficient similarity measure. *Neutrosophic Sets and Systems, 13*, 3–17. doi:10.5281/zenodo.570854

Mondal, K., Pramanik, S., & Smarandache, F. (2016c). Rough neutrosophic hyper-complex set and its application to multiattribute decision making. *Critical Review, 13*, 111–126.

Mondal, K., Pramanik, S., & Smarandache, F. (2018). NN-harmonic mean aggregation operators-based MCGDM strategy in a neutrosophic number environment. *Axioms, 7*(12). doi:10.3390/axioms7010012

Mondal, T. K., & Samanta, S. K. (1999). Topology of interval-valued fuzzy sets. *Indian Journal of Pure and Applied Mathematics, 30*, 23–29.

Mondal, T. K., & Samanta, S. K. (2001). Topology of interval-valued intuitionistic fuzzy sets. *Fuzzy Sets and Systems, 119*(3), 483–494. doi:10.1016/S0165-0114(98)00436-9

Monika, R., Sasireka, M., Prasad, S. S., & Senthilkumar, A. (2019). Multi-objective particle swarm optimization based PID tuning of ball and beam system. *Journal of Control & Instrumentation, 7*, 35–40.

Mukherjee, A., Datta, M., & Sarkar, S. (2016). Restricted Interval Valued Neutrosophic Sets and Restricted Interval Valued Neutrosophic Topological Spaces. *Neutrosophic Sets and Systems, 12*, 45–53. doi:10.5281/zenodo.571145

Mukherjee, A., & Sarkar, S. (2014). Several similarity measures of neutrosophic soft sets and its application in real-life problems. *Annals of Pure and Applied Mathematics, 7*, 1–6.

Mukherjee, A., & Sarkar, S. (2015). A new method of measuring similarity between two neutrosophic soft sets and its application in pattern recognition problems. *Neutrosophic Sets and Systems, 8*, 72–77.

Mukherjee, N. P., & Bhattacharya, P. (1984). Fuzzy normal subgroups and fuzzy cosets. *Information Sciences, 34*(3), 225–239. doi:10.1016/0020-0255(84)90050-1

Mukherjee, S. (2012). Dijkstra's Algorithm for Solving the Shortest Path Problem on Networks Under Intuitionistic Fuzzy Environment. *Journal of Mathematical Modelling and Algorithms, 11*(4), 345–359. doi:10.100710852-012-9191-7

Muruganandam, S., & Hema, K. (2017). Solving Fully Fuzzy Assignment Problem Using Branch and Bound Technique. *Global Journal of Pure and Applied Mathematics, 13*(9), 4515-4522.

Nabeeh, N. A., Basset, M. A., El-Ghareeb, H. A., & Aboelfetouh, A. (2019b). *Neutrosophic Multi-Criteria Decision Making Approach for IoT-Based Enterprises.* IEEE Access. doi:10.1109/ACCESS.2019.2908919

Nabeeh, N. A., Smarandache, F., Basset, M. A., El-Ghareeb, H. A., & Aboelfetouh, A. (2019a). *An Integrated Neutrosophic-TOPSIS Approach and its Application to Personnel Selection: A New Trend in Brain Processing and Analysis.* IEEE Access. doi:10.1109/ACCESS.2019.2899841

Nabeeh, N. A., Abdel-Basset, M., El-Ghareeb, H. A., & Aboelfetouh, A. (2019). Neutrosophic Multi-Criteria Decision Making Approach for IoT-Based Enterprises. *IEEE Access: Practical Innovations, Open Solutions.*

Nabeeh, N. A., Smarandache, F., Abdel-Basset, M., El-Ghareeb, H. A., & Aboelfetouh, A. (2019). An Integrated Neutrosophic-TOPSIS Approach and its Application to Personnel Selection: A New Trend in Brain Processing and Analysis. *IEEE Access: Practical Innovations, Open Solutions.*

Nagarajan, R., & Solairaju, A. (2010). Assignment Problems with Fuzzy Costs under Robust Ranking Techniques. *International Journal of Computer Applications, 6*(4).

Nagarajan, D., Lathamaheswari, M., Broumi, S., & Kavikumar, J. (2019). Blockchain Single and Interval Valued Neutrosophic Graphs. *Neutrosophic Sets and Systems*, *24*, 23–35. doi:10.5281/zenodo.2593909

Nagarajan, D., Lathamaheswari, M., Broumi, S., & Kavikumar, J. (2019). Dombi Interval Valued Neutrosophic Graph and its Role in Traffic Control Management. *Neutrosophic Sets and Systems*, *24*, 114–133. doi:10.5281/zenodo.2593948

Nancy, & Garg, H. (2016). An improved score function for ranking neutrosophic sets and its application to decision making process. *International Journal for Uncertainty Quantification*, *6*(5), 377–385. doi:10.1615/Int.J.UncertaintyQuantification.2016018441

Nasseri, S. H., Ardil, E., Yazdani, A., & Zaefarian, R. (2005). Simplex method for solving linear programming problems with fuzzy numbers. *World Academy of Science, Engineering and Technology*, *10*, 284–288.

Neath, M. J., Swain, A. K., Madawala, U. K., & Thrimawithana, D. J. (2014). An optimal PID controller for a bidirectional inductive power transfer system using multiobjective genetic algorithm. *IEEE Transactions on Power Electronics*, *29*(3), 1523–1531. doi:10.1109/TPEL.2013.2262953

Niewiadomski, A., & Grzybowski, R. (2004). Rozmyte miary podobienstwa tekstow w automatycznej ewaluacji testow egzaminacyjnych. *Informatyka teoretyczna i stosowana*, *4*(6), 75–79.

Olgun, N., & Çelik, M. (2019). Neutrosophic triplet R - module. *Neutrosophic Triplet Research*, *1*, 35–42.

P., & L. (2015b). Some Neutrosophic Uncertain Linguistic Number Heronian Mean Operators and Their Application to Multi-attribute Group Decision making. *Neural Computing & Applications*. doi:10.100700521-015-2122-6

P., & Tang, G. (2016b). Multi-criteria group decision-making based on interval neutrosophic uncertain linguistic variables and Choquet integral. *Cognitive Computation*, *8*(6), 1036-1056.

P., & Teng, F. (2015). Multiple attribute decision making method based on normal neutrosophic generalized weighted power averaging operator. *Internal Journal of Machine Learning and Cybernetics*. doi:10.100713042-015-0385-y

P., & Wang, Y. (2016). Interval neutrosophic prioritized OWA operator and its application to multiple attribute decision making. *Journal of Systems Science & Complexity, 29*(3), 681-697.

P., Zhang, L., Liu, X., & Wang, P. (2016). Multi-valued Neutrosophic Number Bonferroni mean Operators and Their Application in Multiple Attribute Group Decision Making. *Internal Journal of Information Technology & Decision Making, 15*(5), 1181-1210.

Pak, A., Parham, G. A., & Saraj, M. (2014a). Inference for the Rayleigh distribution based on progressive Type-II fuzzy censored data. *Journal of Modern Applied Statistical Methods; JMASM*, *13*(1), 19. doi:10.22237/jmasm/1398917880

Pak, A., Parham, G. A., & Saraj, M. (2014b). Reliability estimation in Rayleigh distribution based on fuzzy lifetime data. *International Journal of System Assurance Engineering and Management, 5*(4), 487–494. doi:10.100713198-013-0190-5

Pandian, P., & Natarajan, G. (2010). A New Approach for Solving Transportation Problems with Mixed Constraints. *Journal of Physical Sciences, 14,* 53-61.

Parvathi, R., & Malathi, C. (2012). Intuitionistic fuzzy simplex method. *International Journal of Computers and Applications, 48*(6), 36–48.

Pawlak, Z. (1982). Rough sets. *International Journal of Information and Computer Sciences, 11*(5), 341–356. doi:10.1007/BF01001956

Peng, J. J., Wang, J. Q., Wu, X. H., Wang, J., & Chen, X. H. (2014). Multi-valued Neutrosophic Sets and Power Aggregation Operators with Their Applications in Multi-criteria Group Decision-making Problems. *International Journal of Computational Intelligence Systems, 8*(2), 345–363. doi:10.1080/18756891.2015.1001957

Peng, J. J., Wang, J. Q., Zhang, H. Y., & Chen, X. H. (2014). An outranking approach for multi-criteria decision-making problems with simplified neutrosophic sets. *Applied Soft Computing, 25,* 336–346. doi:10.1016/j.asoc.2014.08.070

Peng, J. J., Wang, J., & Yang, W. (2016). A multi-valued neutrosophic qualitative exible approach based on likelihood for multi-criteria decision-making problems. *International Journal of Systems Science.* doi:10.1080/00207721.2016.1218975

Ponce, R., Albarracín, M., Jalón, A., Albarracín, Z., Molina, C., Serrano, Q., & Zuñiga, P. (2019). Soft computing In Neutrosophic Linguistic Modeling For The Treatment Of Uncertainty In Information Retrieval. *Neutrosophic Sets and Systems, 26,* 69–74.

Pouresmaeil, H., Shivanian, E., Khorram, E., & Fathabadi, H. S. 2016. An Extended Method Using TOPSIS And Vikor For Multiple Attribute Decision Making With Multiple Decision Makers And Single Valued Neutrosophic Numbers. Advances and Applications in Statistics 2016. Pushpa Publishing House.

Prabakaran, K., & Ganesan, K. (2017). Duality theory for intuitionistic fuzzy linear programming problems. *Int. J. of Civil Eng. and Tech., 8,* 546–560.

Pramanik, S., & Roy, T. K. (2014). Neutrosophic game theoretic approach to Indo-Pak conflict over Jammu-Kashmir. *Neutrosophic Sets and Systems, 2,* 82-101. doi.org/10.5281/zenodo.571510

Pramanik, S., Biswas, P., & Giri, B. C. (2015). Hybrid vector similarity measures and their applications to multi-attribute decision making under neutrosophic environment. *Neural Comput and Applic.* DOI 00521-015-2125-3 doi:10.1007

Pramanik, S., Dalapati, S., & Roy, T. K. (2016). Neutrosophic multi-attribute group decision making strategy for logistics center location selection. In F. Smarandache, M. A. Basset, & V. Chang (Eds), Neutrosophic Operational Research Volume III (pp. 13-32). Brussels: Pons asbl.

Pramanik, S., Dalapati, S., Alam, S., & Roy, T. K. (2018). TODIM method for group decision making under bipolar neutrosophic set environment. In F. Smarandache & S. Pramanik (Eds.), New trends in neutrosophic theory and applications, (vol. 2, pp. 140-155). Brussels: Pons Editions.

Pramanik, S., Dey, P. P., & Giri, B. C. (2015). An extended grey relational analysis based interval neutrosophic multi-attribute decision making for weaver selection. *Journal of New Theory, 9*, 82-93.

Pramanik, S., Dey, P. P., & Giri, B. C. (2016). Neutrosophic soft multi-attribute decision making based on grey relational projection method. *Neutrosophic Sets and Systems, 11*, 98-106. doi. org/10.5281/zenodo.571576

Pramanik, S., Roy, R., & Roy, T. K. (2016). Teacher selection strategy based on bidirectional projection measure in neutrosophic number environment. In F. Smarandache, M. A. Basset, & V. Chang (Eds.), Neutrosophic Operational Research (vol. 2, pp. 29-53). Brussels: Pons asbl.

Pramanik, S. (2016). Neutrosophic multi-objective linear programming. *Global Journal of Engineering Science and Research Management, 3*(8). doi:10.5281/zenodo.59949

Pramanik, S., & Banerjee, D. (2018). Neutrosophic number goal programming for multi-objective linear programming problem in neutrosophic number environment. *MOJ Current Research & Review, 1*(3), 135–141. doi:10.15406/mojcrr.2018.01.00021

Pramanik, S., Banerjee, D., & Giri, B. C. (2016). TOPSIS approach for Multi-Attribute Decision Making in Neutrosophic Environment. In F. Smarandache & S. Pramanik (Eds.), *New trends in neutrosophic theory and applications* (pp. 79–92). Brussels: Pons Editions.

Pramanik, S., Biswas, P., & Giri, B. C. (2017). Hybrid vector similarity measures and their applications to multi-attribute decision making under neutrosophic environment. *Neural Computing & Applications, 28*(5), 1163–1176. doi:10.100700521-015-2125-3

Pramanik, S., & Chackrabarti, S. N. (2013). A study on problems of construction workers in West Bengal based on neutrosophic cognitive maps. *International Journal of Innovative Research in Science. Engineering and Technology, 2*(11), 6387–6394.

Pramanik, S., & Dalapati, S. (2016). GRA based multi criteria decision making in generalized neutrosophic soft set environment. *Global Journal of Engineering Science and Research Management, 3*(5), 153–169. doi:10.5281/zenodo.53753

Pramanik, S., Dalapati, S., Alam, S., & Roy, T. K. (2017). NC-TODIM-based MAGDM under a neutrosophic cubic set environment. *Information, 8*(4), 149. doi:10.3390/info8040149

Pramanik, S., Dalapati, S., Alam, S., & Roy, T. K. (2018). NC-VIKOR based MAGDM strategy under neutrosophic cubic set environment. *Neutrosophic Sets and Systems, 20*, 95–108. doi:10.5281/ zenodo.1235367

Pramanik, S., Dalapati, S., Alam, S., & Roy, T. K. (2018). TODIM method for group decision making under bipolar neutrosophic set environment. In F. Smarandache & S. Pramanik (Eds.), *New Trends In Neutrosophic Theory And Applications* (pp. 140–155). Brussels: Pons Editions.

Pramanik, S., Dalapati, S., Alam, S., & Roy, T. K. (2018). VIKOR based MAGDM strategy under bipolar neutrosophic set environment. *Neutrosophic Sets and Systems*, *19*, 57–69. doi:10.5281/zenodo.1235341

Pramanik, S., Dalapati, S., Alam, S., Roy, T. K., & Smarandache, F. (2017). Neutrosophic cubic MCGDM method based on similarity measure. *Neutrosophic Sets and Systems*, *16*, 44–56. doi:10.5281/zenodo.831934

Pramanik, S., Dalapati, S., Alam, S., Smarandache, S., & Roy, T. K. (2018). NS-cross entropy-based MAGDM under single-valued neutrosophic set environment. *Information*, *9*(2), 37. doi:10.3390/info9020037

Pramanik, S., Dalapati, S., & Roy, T. K. (2016). Logistics center location selection approach based on neutrosophic multi-criteria decision making. In F. Smarandache & S. Pramanik (Eds.), *New trends in neutrosophic theory and applications* (pp. 161–174). Brussels: Pons Editions.

Pramanik, S., Dalapati, S., & Roy, T. K. (2016). Logistics center location selection approach based on neutrosophic multi-criteria decision making. In F. Smarandache & S. Pramanik (Eds.), *New Trends In Neutrosophic Theory And Applications* (pp. 161–174). Brussels: Pons Editions.

Pramanik, S., & Dey, P. P. (2018). Bi-level linear programming problem with neutrosophic numbers. *Neutrosophic Sets and Systems*, *21*, 110–121. doi:10.5281/zenodo.1408669

Pramanik, S., Dey, P. P., & Giri, B. C. (2015). TOPSIS for single valued neutrosophic soft expert set based multi-attribute decision making problems. *Neutrosophic Sets and Systems*, *10*, 88–95. doi:10.5281/zenodo.571238

Pramanik, S., Dey, P. P., & Giri, B. C. (2015). TOPSIS for singled valued soft expert set based multi-attribute decision making problems. *Neutrosophic Sets and Systems*, *10*, 88–95.

Pramanik, S., Dey, P. P., & Giri, B. C. (2016). Neutrosophic soft multi-attribute group decision making based on grey relational analysis method. *Journal of New Results in Science*, *10*, 25–37. doi:10.5281/zenodo.34869

Pramanik, S., Dey, P. P., & Smarandache, F. (2017). An extended TOPSIS for multi-attribute decision making problems with neutrosophic cubic information. *Neutrosophic Sets and Systems*, *17*, 20–28. doi:10.5281/zenodo.1012217

Pramanik, S., Dey, P. P., & Smarandache, F. (2018). Correlation coefficient measures of interval bipolar neutrosophic sets for solving multi-attribute decision making problems. *Neutrosophic Sets and Systems*, *19*, 70–79. doi:10.5281/zenodo.1235151

Pramanik, S., Dey, P. P., Smarandache, F., & Ye, J. (2018). Cross entropy measures of bipolar and interval bipolar neutrosophic sets and their application for multi-attribute decision-making. *Axioms*, *7*(21), 1–25. doi:10.3390/axioms7020021

Pramanik, S., & Mallick, R. (2018). VIKOR based MAGDM strategy with trapezoidal neutrosophic number. *Neutrosophic Sets and Systems*, *22*, 118–130. doi:10.5281/zenodo.2160840

Pramanik, S., & Mallick, R. (2019). *TODIM strategy for multi attribute group decision making in trapezoidal neutrosophic number environment.* Complex and Intelligent Systems. doi:10.100740747-019-0110-7

Pramanik, S., Mallick, R., & Dasgupta, A. (2018). Contributions of selected Indian researchers to multi-attribute decision making in neutrosophic environment. *Neutrosophic Sets and Systems, 20*, 108–131.

Pramanik, S., & Mondal, K. (2015). Cosine similarity measure of rough neutrosophic sets and its application in medical diagnosis. *Global Journal of Advanced Research, 2*(1), 212–220.

Pramanik, S., & Mondal, K. (2015). Cotangent similarity measure of rough neutrosophic sets and its application to medical diagnosis. *Journal of New Theory, 4*, 90–102.

Pramanik, S., & Mondal, K. (2015). Interval neutrosophic multi-attribute decision-making based on grey relational analysis. *Neutrosophic Sets and Systems, 9*, 13–22.

Pramanik, S., & Mondal, K. (2015). Some rough neutrosophic similarity measure and their application to multiattribute decision making. *Global Journal of Engineering Science and Research Management, 2*(7), 61–74.

Pramanik, S., & Mukhopadhyaya, D. (2011). Grey relational analysis based intuitionistic fuzzy multi-criteria group decision-making approach for teacher selection in higher education. *International Journal of Computers and Applications, 34*, 21–29.

Pramanik, S., Roy, R., & Roy, T. K. (2018). Multi criteria decision making based on projection and bidirectional projection measures of rough neutrosophic sets. In F. Smarandache & S. Pramanik (Eds.), *New Trends In Neutrosophic Theory And Applications* (Vol. 2, pp. 175–187). Brussels: Pons Editions.

Pramanik, S., Roy, R., & Roy, T. K. (2018). Multi criteria decision making based on projection and bidirectional projection measures of rough neutrosophic sets. In F. Smarandache & S. Pramanik (Eds.), *New trends in neutrosophic theory and applications-Vol-II* (pp. 175–187). Brussels: Pons Editions.

Pramanik, S., Roy, R., Roy, T. K., & Smarandache, F. (2017). Multi criteria decision making using correlation coefficient under rough neutrosophic environment. *Neutrosophic Sets and Systems, 17*, 29–36. doi:10.5281/zenodo.1012237

Pramanik, S., Roy, R., Roy, T. K., & Smarandache, F. (2018). Multi attribute decision making based on several trigonometric hamming similarity measures under interval rough neutrosophic environment. *Neutrosophic Sets and Systems, 19*, 110–118.

Pramanik, S., Roy, R., Roy, T. K., & Smarandache, F. (2018). Multi attribute decision making strategy on projection and bidirectional measures of interval rough neutrosophic sets. *Neutrosophic Sets and Systems, 19*, 101–109. doi:10.5281/zenodo.1235211

Pramanik, S., Roy, R., Roy, T. K., & Smarandache, F. (2018). Multi attribute decision making strategy on projection and bidirectional projection measures of interval rough neutrosophic sets. *Neutrosophic Sets and Systems*, *19*, 101–109.

Pramanik, S., Roy, R., Roy, T. K., & Smarandache, F. (2018). Multi-attribute decision making based on several trigonometric Hamming similarity measures under interval rough neutrosophic environment. *Neutrosophic Sets and Systems*, *19*, 110–118. doi:10.5281/zenodo.1235207

Qiaoyan, Li., Yingcang, Ma., Smarandache, F., & Shauangwu, Z. (2018). Single-valued neutrosophic clustering algorithm based on tsallis entropy maximization. *Axioms*, *7*(57), 1–12.

Rajarajeswari, P., & Uma, N. (2014). Correlation measure for intuitionistic fuzzy multi sets. *Int. J. Res. Eng. Technol.*, *1*(3), 611–617.

Rajarajeswari, P., & Uma, N. (2014). Zhang and Fu's similarity measure on intuitionistic fuzzy multi sets. *Int. J. Innov. Res. Sci. Eng. Technol.*, *3*(5), 12309–12317.

Rajeswara, P. R., Naga, I. R., Diwakar, V. R., & Krishnaiah, G. (2016). Lean Supplier selection based on hybrid MCGDM approach using interval valued neutrosophic sets: A case study. *International Journal of Innovative Research and Development*, *5*(6), 291–296.

Rao, R. V., & Singh, D. (2010). An improved grey relational analysis as a decision making method for manufacturing situations. *International Journal of Decision Science Risk Management*, *2*, 1–23.

Raymond, M. (2001). *Performance evaluation of information retrieval system*. Academic Press.

Rohan, A., Asghar, F., & Kim, S. H. (2018). Design of fuzzy logic tuned PID controller for electric vehicle based on IPMSM using flux-weakening. *Journal of Electrical Engineering & Technology*, *13*, 451–459.

Rosenfeld, A. (1971). Fuzzy groups. *Journal of Mathematical Analysis and Applications*, *35*(3), 512–517. doi:10.1016/0022-247X(71)90199-5

Saadati, R., & Park, J. H. (2006). On the intuitionistic fuzzy topological spaces. *Chaos, Solitons, and Fractals*, *27*(2), 332–344. doi:10.1016/j.chaos.2005.03.019

Saati, S., Tavana, M., Hatami-Marbini, A., & Hajiakhondi, E. (2015). A fuzzy linear programming model with fuzzy parameters and decision variables. *Int J Inf Decis Sci*, *7*, 312–333.

Şahin, M., & Kargın, A. (2018). Neutrosophic triplet v – generalized metric space. *Axioms – MDPI*, *7*, 67.

Sahin, M., Deli, I., & Ulucay, V. (2016). Similarity measure of bipolar neutrosophic sets and their application to multiple criteria decision making. *Neural Comput & Applic.* DOI 10.1007/S00521

Şahin, M., Kargın, A., & Çoban, M. A. (2018). Fixed point theorem for neutrosophic triplet partial metric space. *Symmetry – MDP*, *10*, 240.

Şahin, M., Kargın, A., & Smarandache, F. (2018). Generalized Single Valued Triangular Neutrosophic Numbers and Aggregation Operators for Application to Multi-attribute Group Decision Making. New Trends in Neutrosophic Theory and Applications. *Quai du Batelage, 2,* 51-84.

Şahin, M., Olgun, N., Uluçay, V., Kargın, A., & Smarandache, F. (2017). A new similarity measure on falsity value between single valued neutrosophic sets based on the centroid points of transformed single valued neutrosophic numbers with applications to pattern recognition. *Neutrosophic Sets and Systems, 15,* 31-48. doi:10.5281/zenodo570934

Şahin, M., Ulucay, V., & Menekşe, M. (2017). (α, β, Υ) Interval Cut Set of Interval Valued Neutrosophic Sets. In *International Conference on Mathematics and Mathematics Education (ICMME-2017)*. Harran University.

Şahin, M., Ecemiş, O., Uluçay, V., & Kargın, A. (2017). Some new generalized aggregation operators based on centroid single valued triangular neutrosophic numbers and their applications in multi-attribute decision making. *Asian Journal of Mathematics and Computer Research., 16*(2), 63–84.

Şahin, M., & Kargın, A. (2017). Neutrosophic triplet inner product space. *Neutrosophic Operational Research, 2,* 193–215.

Şahin, M., & Kargın, A. (2019b). Neutrosophic triplet partial v – generalized metric space. *Neutrosophic Triplet Research, 1,* 22–34.

Şahin, M., & Kargın, A. (2019c). Neutrosophic triplet Lie Algebra. *Neutrosophic Triplet Research, 1,* 68–78.

Şahin, M., Olgun, N., Kargın, A., & Uluçay, V. (2018). *Isomorphism theorems for soft G -modules.* Afrika Matematika; doi:10.100713370-018-0621-1

Şahin, M., Uluçay, V., Olgun, N., & Kilicman, A. (2017). On neutrosophic soft lattices. *Afrika Matematika, 28*(3-4), 379–388. doi:10.100713370-016-0447-7

Şahin, R. (2015). Cross-entropy measure on interval neutrosophic sets and its applications in multi-criteria decision making. *Neural Computing & Applications,* 1–11.

Şahin, R., & Kucuk, A. (2014). Subsethood measure for single valued neutrosophic sets. *Journal of Intelligent & Fuzzy Systems.* doi:10.3233/IFS-141304

Sahin, R., & Liu, P. (2017). Correlation coefficient of single-valued neutrosophic hesitant fuzzy sets and its applications in decision making. *Neural Computing & Applications, 28*(6), 1387–1395. doi:10.100700521-015-2163-x

Sahin, R., & Yigider, M. A. (2016). Multi-Criteria Neutrosophic Group Decision Making Method Based TOPSIS for Supplier Selection. *Applied Mathematics & Information Sciences, 10*(5), 1843–1852. doi:10.18576/amis/100525

Salama, A. A., & Alblowi, S. A. (2012). Neutrosophic Set and Neutrosophic Topological Spaces. *IOSR Journal of Math*, *3*(4), 31-35.

Salama, A. A. (2012). *The Concept of Neutrosophic Set and Basic Properties of Neutrosophic Set Operations*. Paris: International University of Science, Engineering and Technology.

Salama, A. A., El-Ghareeb, H. A., & Manie, A. M. (2014). *Smarandache* (Vol. 3). Introduction to Develop Some Software Programs for Dealing with Neutrosophic Sets, Neutrosophic Sets and Systems.

Sanchez, E. (1976). Resolution of Composite Fuzzy Relation Equations. *Information and Control*, *30*(1), 38–48. doi:10.1016/S0019-9958(76)90446-0

Schek, H. J. (1978). *The Reference String Indexing Method. Research Report*. Heidelberg, Germany: IBM Scientific Center.

Sengur, A., & Guo, Y. (2011). Color texture image segmentation based on neutrosophic set and wavelet transformation. *Computer Vision and Image Understanding*, *115*(8), 1134–1144. doi:10.1016/j.cviu.2011.04.001

Shafiq, M., Atif, M., & Viertl, R. (2017). Parameter and reliability estimation of three-parameter lifetime distributions for fuzzy life times. *Advances in Mechanical Engineering*, *9*(8), 1687814017716887. doi:10.1177/1687814017716887

Shahin, Guo, Amin, & Sharawi. (2018). A Novel White Blood Cells Segmentation Algorithm Based on Adaptive Neutrosophic Similarity Score. *Health Information Science and Systems, 6*(1).

Shahin, A. I., Amin, K. M., & Amr, A. (2018, May). A Novel Enhancement Technique for Pathological Microscopic Image Using Neutrosophic Similarity Score Scaling. *International Journal for Light and Electron Optics*, *161*, 84–97. doi:10.1016/j.ijleo.2018.02.026

Shah, N. (2016a). Some Studies in Neutrosophic Graphs. *Neutrosophic Sets and Systems*, *12*, 54–64.

Shah, N., & Hussain, A. (2016b). Neutrosophic Soft Graphs. *Neutrosophic Sets and Systems*, *11*, 31–44.

Shannon, A., & Atanassov, K. (1994). A First Step to A Theory of The Intuitionistic Fuzzy Graphs. *Proceedings of 1st Workshop on Fuzzy Based Expert Systems* 59–61.

Shannon, A., & Atanassov, K. (2004). On intuitionistic fuzzy multigraphs and their index matrix interpretations. *Proceedings of 2nd International IEEE Conference on Intelligent Systems*, *2*, 440–443. 10.1109/IS.2004.1344788

Sharma, P. K. (2011). Homomorphism of intuitionistic fuzzy groups. *International Mathematical Forum, 6*, 3169-3178.

Shenify, M., & Mazarbhuiya, F. (2015). The Expected Value of a Fuzzy Number. *International Journal of Intelligence Science*, *5*(1), 1–5. doi:10.4236/ijis.2015.51001

Sherwood, H. (1983). Products of fuzzy subgroups. *Fuzzy Sets and Systems, 11*(1-3), 79–89. doi:10.1016/S0165-0114(83)80070-0

Shi, L. (2016). *Correlation coefficient of simplified neutrosophic sets for bearing fault diagnosis.* Shock Vibr. doi:10.1155/2016/5414361

Shinoj, T.K., & John, S.J. (2012). Intuitionistic fuzzy multi-sets and its application in medical diagnosis. *World Acad. Sci. Eng. Technol., 6*, 1–28.

Shore, H. H. (1970). The Transportation Problem and the Vogel's Approximation Method. *Decision Sciences, 1*(3-4), 441–457. doi:10.1111/j.1540-5915.1970.tb00792.x

Simsek, I., & Deli, I. (2015). Expected Value of SV-Trapezoidal Neutrosophic Numbers and its Applications to Multi-Attribute Decision Making Problems. In *The 4th International Fuzzy Systems Symposium (FUZZYSS'15).* Yildiz Technical University.

Singh, A., & Kumar, A. (2017). Modified Approach for optimization of real life transportation problem in neutrosophic environment. *Mathematical Problems in Engineering.*

Singh, P. K. (2017). *Interval-Valued Neutrosophic Graph Representation of Concept Lattice and Its (α,β,γ)-Decomposition.* Arab Jou. Sci. Engg. doi:10.100713369-017- 2718-5

Smarandache, F. (1998). Neutrosophic, Neutrosophic Probability set and logic. Amer. Res Press.

Smarandache, F. (1998a). *Neutrosophy, neutrosophic probability, set and logic.* Amer. Res. Press. Retrieved from http://fs.gallup.unm.edu/eBook-neutrosophics4.pdf

Smarandache, F. (1999). A unifying field in logics: neutrosophic logic. In Philosophy (pp. 1-141). American Research Press.

Smarandache, F. (1999). Neutrosophy: Neutrosophic Probability, Set and Logic. Rehoboth: Amer. Research Press.

Smarandache, F. (2000). An introduction to the neutrosophic probability applied in quantum physics. Infinite Study.

Smarandache, F. (2004). *A Geometric Interpretation of the Neutrosophic Set, A Generalization of the Intuitionistic Fuzzy Set Set.* arXiv preprint math/0404520

Smarandache, F. (2010). Neutrosophic Logic-A Generalization of the Intuitionistic Fuzzy Logic. *Multispace & Multistructure. Neutrosophic Transdisciplinarity, 4*, 396.

Smarandache, F. (2013). Introduction to neutrosophic measure, neutrosophic integral, and neutrosophic probability. Infinite Study.

Smarandache, F. (2014). *Introduction to neutrosophic statistics.* Infinite Study.

Smarandache, F. (2018). *Extension of soft set to hypersoft set, and then to plithogenic hypersoft set.* Infinite Study.

Smarandache, F. (2018). Neutropsychic personality: A mathematical approach to psychology. Infinite Study.

Smarandache, F. (2018). *Plithogenic set, an extension of crisp, fuzzy, intuitionistic fuzzy, and neutrosophic sets-revisited.* Infinite Study.

Smarandache, F., & Khalid, H. E. (2015). Neutrosophic precalculus and neutrosophic calculus. Infinite Study.

Smarandache, F., & Vlăduțescu, S. (2013). Communication vs. Information, an Axiomatic Neutrosophic Solution. *Neutrosophic Sets and Systems*, 1.

Smarandache, F., Khalid, H. E., & Essa, A. K. (2018). Neutrosophic Logic: the Revolutionary Logic in Science and Philosophy. In *Proceedings of the National Symposium.* EuropaNova.

Smarandache, F., Şahin, M., & Kargın, A. (2018). Neutrosophic Triplet G- Module. *Mathematics – MDPI, 6*, 53.

Smarandache, F. (1995). *A Unifying Field in Logics. Neutrosophy: Neutrosophic Probability, Set and Logic.* Rehoboth: American Research Press.

Smarandache, F. (1998). *A Unifying Field in Logics Neutrosophy: Neutrosophic Probability, Set and Logic.* Rehoboth: American Research Press.

Smarandache, F. (1998). *A unifying field in logics, neutrosophy: neutrosophic probability, set and logic.* Rehoboth: AmericanResearch Press.

Smarandache, F. (1998). *A unifying field in logics. Neutrosophy: neutrosophic probability, set and logic.* Rehoboth: American Research Press.

Smarandache, F. (1998). *Neutrosophy, neutrosophic probability, set and logic.* Rehoboth: Amer. Res. Press.

Smarandache, F. (1998). *Neutrosophy.* Rehoboth: Neutrosophic Probability, Set, and Logic, Amer. Res. Press.

Smarandache, F. (1998). *Neutrosophy: neutrosophic probability, set, and logic.* Rehoboth: American Research Press.

Smarandache, F. (1998a). *Neutrosophy: Neutrosophic Probability, Set, and Logic: Analytic Synthesis & Synthetic Analysis.* Rehoboth, DE: Ameri. Res. Press.

Smarandache, F. (2002). Neutrosophy and Neutrosophic Logic. In *First International Conference on Neutrosophy, Neutrosophic Logic, Set, Probability, and Statistics.* University of New Mexico.

Smarandache, F. (2005). *A unifying field in logic. Neutrosophy: neutrosophic probability, set, logic* (4th ed.). Rehoboth: American Research Press.

Smarandache, F. (2005). Neutrosophic set a generalisation of the intuitionistic fuzzy sets. *International Journal of Pure and Applied Mathematics, 24*, 287–297.

Smarandache, F. (2005). Neutrosophic set, a generalisation of the intuitionistic fuzzy sets. *International Journal of Pure and Applied Mathematics*, *24*, 287–297.

Smarandache, F. (2005). Neutrosophic set—a generalization of the intuitionistic fuzzy set. *International Journal of Pure and Applied Mathematics*, *24*(3), 287–297.

Smarandache, F. (2005b). Neutrosophic set, A generalisation of the intuitionistic fuzzy sets. *International Journal of Pure and Applied Mathematics*, *24*, 287–297.

Smarandache, F. (2013). *Introduction to neutrosophic measure, neutrosophic integral, and neutrosophic probability*. Craiova: Sitech & Education Publisher.

Smarandache, F. (2013). n-valued refined neutrosophic logic and its applications in physics. *Progr. Phys.*, *4*, 143–146.

Smarandache, F. (2014). *Introduction to neutrosophic statistics*. Craiova: Sitech & Education Publishing.

Smarandache, F. (2015). *Neutrosophic precalculus and neutrosophic calculus*. Brussels: Europa-Nova.

Smarandache, F. (2018). Aggregation plithogenic operators in physical fields. *Bulletin of the American Physical Society*.

Smarandache, F., & Ali, M. (2016). Neutrosophic triplet group. *Neural Computing & Applications*, *29*(7), 595–601. doi:10.100700521-016-2535-x

Smarandache, F., Colhon, M., Vlăduţescu, Ş., & Negrea, X. (2019). Word-level neutrosophic sentiment similarity. *Applied Soft Computing*, *80*, 167–176. doi:10.1016/j.asoc.2019.03.034

Smarandache, F., Khalid, H. E., Essa, A. K., & Ali, M. (2016). The Concept of Neutrosophic Less Than or Equal To: A New Insight in Unconstrained Geometric Programming. *Critical Review*, *XII*, 72–80.

Smarandache, F., & Pramanik, S. (Eds.). (2018). *New trends in neutrosophic theory and applications* (Vol. 2). Brussels: Pons Editions.

Smarandache, F., Şahin, M., & Kargın, A. (2019a). Neutrosophic triplet partial inner product space. *Neutrosophic Triplet Research*, *1*, 10–21.

Solihin, M. I., Tack, L. F., & Kean, M. L. (2011). Tuning of PID controller using particle swarm optimization (PSO). *Proceeding of the International Conference on Advanced Science, Engineering and Information Technology 2011*, 458-461.

Song, S.Z., Khan, M., & Smarandache, F., & Jun, Y. B. (2017). Interval neutrosophic sets applied to ideals in BCK/BCI-algebras. *Neutrosophic Sets and Systems*, *18*, 16–26. doi:10.5281/zenodo.1175164

Srinivas, B., & Ganesan, G. (2015). Method For Solving Branch-And-Bound Technique For Assignment Problems Using Triangular and Trapezoidal Fuzzy Numbers. *International Journal in Management and Social Science, 3*(3).

Stanujkic, D, Smarandache, F., Zavadskas, E. K., & Karabasevic, D. (2016). Multiple Criteria Evaluation Model Based on the Single Valued Neutrosophic Set. *Neutrosophic Sets and Systems,* 14.

Subas, Y. (2015). *Neutrosophic numbers and their application to Multi-attribute decision making problems* (Masters Thesis). Kilis 7 Aralık University, Graduate School of Natural and Applied Science. (in Turkish)

Sudhakar, V.J., Arunsankar, N., & Karpagam, T. (2012). A New Approach to find an Optimum Solution of Transportation Problems. *European Journal of Scientific Research, 68*(2), 254–257.

Szmidt, E., & Kacprzyk, J. (2003). A Consensus-Reaching Process Under Intuitionistic Fuzzy Preference Relations. *International Journal Of Intelligent Systems, 18*, 837-852.

Szmidt, E., & Kacprzyk, J. (2000). Distances between intuitionistic fuzzy sets. *Fuzzy Sets and Systems, 114*(3), 505–518. doi:10.1016/S0165-0114(98)00244-9

Szmidt, E., & Kacprzyk, J. (2001). Entropy for intuitionistic fuzzy sets. *Fuzzy Sets and Systems, 118*(3), 467–477. doi:10.1016/S0165-0114(98)00402-3

Tan, C. Q. (2011). A multi-criteria interval-valued intuitionistic fuzzy group decision making with Choquet integral-based TOPSIS. *Expert Systems with Applications, 38*(4), 3023–3033. doi:10.1016/j.eswa.2010.08.092

Tan, R., & Zhang, W. (2017). Multiple attribute group decision making methods based on trapezoidal fuzzy neutrosophic numbers. *Journal of Intelligent & Fuzzy Systems, 33*(4), 2547–2564. doi:10.3233/JIFS-161984

Teruel, K. P., Cedeño, J. C, Gavilanez, H. L., Diaz, C. B., & Vázquez. M. L. (2018). A framework for selecting cloud computing services based on consensus under single-valued neutrosophic numbers. *Neutrosophic Sets and Systems,* 22.

Thamaraiselvi, A., & Shanthi, R. (2016). A New Approach for Optimization of Real Life Transportation Problem in Neutrosophic Environment. *Mathematical Problems in Engineering.*

Thong, N. T., Dat, L. Q., Hoa, N. D., Ali, M., Smarandache, F., & … (2019). Dynamic interval valued neutrosophic set: Modeling decision making in dynamic environments. *Computers in Industry, 108*, 45–52. doi:10.1016/j.compind.2019.02.009

Tian, Z. P., Wang, J., Wang, J. Q., & Zhang, H. Y. (2016a). Simplified neutrosophic linguistic multi-criteria group decision-making approach to green product development. *Group Decision and Negotiation.* doi:10.100710726-016-9479-5

Tian, Z. P., Wang, J., Zhang, H. Y., & Wang, J. Q. (2016b). An improved MULTIMOORA approach for multicriteria decision-making based on interdependent inputs of simplified neutrosophic linguistic information. *Neural Computing & Applications.* doi:10.100700521-016-2378-5

Tian, Z. P., Wang, J., Zhang, H. Y., & Wang, J. Q. (2016c). Multi-criteria decision-making based on generalized prioritized aggregation operators under simplified neutrosophic uncertain linguistic environment. *International Journal of Machine Learning and Cybernetics*. doi:10.100713042-016-0552-9

Tian, Z. P., Zhang, H. Y., Wang, J., Wang, J. Q., & Chen, X. H. (2015). Multi-criteria decision-making method based on a cross-entropy with interval neutrosophic sets. *International Journal of Systems Science*, 1–11.

Timothy, C. H., & Zobel, J. (2003). Methods for Identifying Versioned and Plagiarized Documents. *Journal of the American Society for Information Science and Technology, 54*(3), 203–215. doi:10.1002/asi.10170

Tripathy, D., Barik, A. K., Choudhury, N. B. D., & Sahu, B. K. (2019). Performance comparison of SMO-based fuzzy PID controller for load frequency control. In *Soft computing for problem solving* (pp. 879–892). Singapore: Springer. doi:10.1007/978-981-13-1595-4_70

Uluçay, V., Kiliç, A., Yildiz, I., & Sahin, M. (2018). A new approach for multi-attribute decision-making problems in bipolar neutrosophic sets. *Neutrosophic Sets and Systems, 23*(1), 142–159.

Uluçay, V., Şahin, M., & Hassan, N. (2018). Generalized neutrosophic soft expert set for multiple-criteria decision-making. *Symmetry, 10*(10), 437. doi:10.3390ym10100437

Ulucay, V., Şahin, M., & Olgun, N. (2018). Time-Neutrosophic Soft Expert Sets and Its Decision Making Problem. *Afrika Matematika, 34*(2), 246–260.

Van Hecke, T. (2018). Fuzzy parameter estimation of the Rayleigh distribution. *Journal of Statistics and Management Systems, 21*(7), 1391–1400. doi:10.1080/09720510.2018.1519162

Van Rijsbergen, C. J. (2017). A New Theoretical Framework for Information Retrieval. *ACM SIGIR Forum, 51*(2), 44-50. 10.1145/3130348.3130354

Van Rijsbergen, C. J. (1986). A logic for information retrieval. *The Computer Journal, 29*(6), 481–485. doi:10.1093/comjnl/29.6.481

Vlachos, I. K., & Sergiadis, G. D. (2007). Intuitionistic fuzzy information-applications to pattern recognition. *Pattern Recognition Letters, 28*(2), 197–206. doi:10.1016/j.patrec.2006.07.004

Wang, H., Smarandache, F., Sunderraman, R., & Zhang, Y. Q. (2005). Interval neutrosophic sets and logic: theory and applications in computing (Vol. 5). Infinite Study.

Wang, H., Smarandache, F., Sunderraman, R., & Zhang, Y. Q. (2005). *Interval neutrosophic sets and logic: theory and applications in computing: Theory and applications in computing* (Vol. 5). Infinite Study.

Wang, H., Smarandache, F., Zhang, Y. Q., & Sunderraman, R. (2005). Interval Neutrosophic Set and Logic: Theory and Applications in Computing. Hexis.

Wang, H., Smarandache, F., Zhang, Y., & Sunderraman, R. (2010). Single valued neutrosophic sets. *Rev Air Force Acad, 1*(16), 10–14. Retrieved from http://213.177.9.66/ro/revista/NR_1_2010/Art_Smarandache.pdf

Wang, C. H., & Wang, J. Q. (2016). A multi-criteria decision-making method based on triangular intuitionistic fuzzy preference information. *Intelligent Automation and Soft Computing, 22*(3), 473–482. doi:10.1080/10798587.2015.1095418

Wang, H. B., Smarandache, F., Zhang, Y. Q., & Sunderraman, R. (2010a). Single valued neutrosophic sets. *Multispace and Multistructure., 4*, 410–413.

Wang, H. B., Smarandache, F., Zhang, Y. Q., & Sunderraman, R. (2010b). Single Valued Neutrosophic Sets. *Tech. Sci. Applications of Mathematics.*

Wang, H., Smarandache, F., Zhang, Y. Q., & Sunderraman, R. (2005). *Interval neutrosophic sets and logic: theory and applications in computing.* Phoenix, AZ: Hexis.

Wang, H., Smarandache, F., Zhang, Y. Q., & Sunderraman, R. (2010). Single valued neutrosophic sets. *Multispace and Multistructure, 4*, 410–413.

Wang, H., Smarandache, F., Zhang, Y. Q., & Sunderraman, R. (2010). Single valued neutrosophic sets. *Multispace Multistruct, 4*, 410–413.

Wang, H., Smarandache, F., Zhang, Y. Q., & Sunderraman, R. (2010). Single valued neutrosophic sets. *Multispace Multistructure, 4*, 410–413.

Wang, H., Smarandache, F., Zhang, Y., & Sunderraman, R. (2010). Single valued neutrosophic sets. *Multi-space and Multi-structure, 4*, 410–413.

Wang, H., Smarandache, F., Zhang, Y., & Sunderraman, R. (2010). *Single Valued Neutrosophic Sets. Multispace and Multistucture, 4*, 410–413.

Wang, H., Smarandache, F., Zhang, Y., & Sunderraman, R. (2010). Single valued Neutrosophic Sets. *Multisspace and Multistructure, 4*, 410–413.

Wang, H., Zhang, Y., Sunderraman, R., & Smarandache, F. (2011). Single valued neutrosophic sets. *Fuzzy Sets. Rough Sets and Multivalued Operations and Applications, 3*(1), 33–39.

Wang, J. Q., Nie, R. R., Zhang, H. Y., & Chen, X. H. (2013). Intuitionistic fuzzy multi-criteria decision-making method based on evidential reasoning. *Applied Soft Computing, 13*(4), 1823–1831. doi:10.1016/j.asoc.2012.12.019

Wang, J. Q., & Zhang, Z. (2009). Aggregation operators on intuitionistic trapezoidal fuzzy number and its application to multi-criteria decision making problems. *Journal of Systems Engineering and Electronics, 20*(2), 321–326.

Wang, J., Wei, G., & Wei, Y. (2018). Models for Green Supplier Selection with Some 2-Tuple Linguistic Neutrosophic Number Bonferroni Mean Operators. *Symmetry, 10*(5), 131. doi:10.3390ym10050131

Wang, W., & Xin, X. (2005). Distance measure between intuitionistic fuzzy sets. *Pattern Recognition Letters*, *26*(13), 2063–2069. doi:10.1016/j.patrec.2005.03.018

Wang, Z., & Jian, L. (2017). Correlation coefficients of probabilistic hesitant fuzzy elements and their applications to evaluation of the alternatives. *Symmetry*, *9*(11), 2–18. doi:10.3390ym9110259

Wan, S. P. (2013). Power average operators of trapezoidal intuitionistic fuzzy numbers and application to multi-attribute group decision making. *Applied Mathematical Modelling*, *37*(6), 4112–4126. doi:10.1016/j.apm.2012.09.017

Wan, S. P., Wanga, Q. Y., & Dong, J. Y. (2013). The extended VIKOR method for multi-attribute group decision making with triangular intuitionistic fuzzy numbers. *Knowledge-Based Systems*, *52*, 65–77. doi:10.1016/j.knosys.2013.06.019

Wei, G. (2010). Some Arithmetic Aggregation Operators with Intuitionistic Trapezoidal Fuzzy Numbers and Their Application to Group Decision Making. *Journal of Computers*, *5*(3), 345–351. doi:10.4304/jcp.5.3.345-351

Wei, G. W. (2011). Grey relational analysis method for intuitionistic fuzzy multiple attribute decision making. *Expert Systems with Applications*, *38*(9), 11671–11677. doi:10.1016/j.eswa.2011.03.048

Wei, G. W., Wang, H. J., & Lin, R. (2011). Application of correlation coefficient to interval-valued intuitionistic fuzzy multiple attribute decision-making with incomplete weight information. *Knowledge and Information Systems*, *26*(2), 337349. doi:10.100710115-009-0276-1

Wu, J., & Liu, Y. (2013). An approach for multiple attribute group decision making problems with interval valued intuitionistic trapezoidal fuzzy numbers. *Computers & Industrial Engineering*, *66*(2), 311–324. doi:10.1016/j.cie.2013.07.001

Wu, X. H., Wang, J. Q., Peng, J. J., & Chen, X. H. (2016). Cross-entropy and prioritized aggregation operatör with simplified neutrosophic sets and their application in multi-criteria decision-making problems. *International Journal of Fuzzy Systems*, *18*(6), 1104–1116. doi:10.100740815-016-0180-2

Wu, X., Qian, J., Peng, J., & Xue, C. (2018). A Multi-Criteria Group Decision-Making Method with Possibility Degree and Power Aggregation Operators of Single Trapezoidal Neutrosophic Numbers. *Symmetry*, *10*(11), 590. doi:10.3390ym10110590

Xu, Z. (2007). Intuitionistic Fuzzy Aggregation Operators. *IEEE Transactions On Fuzzy Systems*, *15*(6), 1179-1187.

Xu, C. Y. (2007). Homomorphism of intuitionistic fuzzy groups. *2007 International Conference on Machine Learning and Cybernetics*, *2*, 1178-1183. 10.1109/ICMLC.2007.4370322

Xu, G., Wang, S., Yang, T., & Jiang, W. (2018). A neutrosophic approach based on TOPSIS method to image segmentation. *International Journal of Computers, Communications & Control*, *13*(6), 1047–1061. doi:10.15837/ijccc.2018.6.3268

Xu, Z. (2010). Choquet integrals of weighted intuitionistic fuzzy information. *Information Sciences, 180*(5), 726–736. doi:10.1016/j.ins.2009.11.011

Xu, Z. S. (2007). Intuitionistic fuzzy aggregation operators. *IEEE Transactions on Fuzzy Systems, 15*(6), 1179–1187. doi:10.1109/TFUZZ.2006.890678

Xu, Z. S., Chen, J., & Wu, J. (2008). Clustering algorithm for intuitionistic fuzzy sets. *Information Sciences, 178*(19), 3775–3790. doi:10.1016/j.ins.2008.06.008

Xu, Z., & Chen, J. (2007). On Geometric Aggregation Over Interval-Valued Intuitionistic Fuzzy Information. *Fourth International Conference on Fuzzy Systems and Knowledge Discovery (FSKD).* 10.1109/FSKD.2007.427

Xu, Z., & Xia, M. (2011). Induced generalized intuitionistic fuzzy operators. *Knowledge-Based Systems, 24*(2), 197–209. doi:10.1016/j.knosys.2010.04.010

Xu, Z., & Yager, R. R. (2006). Some geometric aggregation operators based on intuitionistic fuzzy sets. *International Journal of General Systems, 35*(4), 417–433. doi:10.1080/03081070600574353

Xu, Z., & Yager, R. R. (2008). Dynamic intuitionistic fuzzy multi-attribute decision making. *International Journal of Approximate Reasoning, 48*(1), 246–262. doi:10.1016/j.ijar.2007.08.008

Yager, R. R. (1981). A procedure for ordering fuzzy subsets of the unit interval. *Information Sciences, 24*(2), 143–161. doi:10.1016/0020-0255(81)90017-7

Yang, J. H., & Cao, B. Y. (2007). Monomial Geometric Programming with Fuzzy Relation Equation Constraints. *Fuzzy Optimization and Decision Making, 6*(4), 337–349. doi:10.100710700-007-9017-7

Ye & Smarandache. (2016). Similarity Measure of Refined Single-Valued Neutrosophic Sets and Its Multicriteria Decision Making Method. *Neutrosophic Sets and Systems, 12*, 41–44. doi:10.5281/zenodo.571146

Ye, J. (2015). Interval Neutrosophic Multiple Attribute Decision-Making Method with Credibility Information. *Int. J. Fuzzy Syst.* DOI doi:10.100740815-015-0122-4

Ye, J. (2016). *Some Weighted Aggregation Operators of Trapezoidal Neutrosophic Numbers and Their Multiple Attribute Decision Making Method.* Retrieved from http://vixra.org/abs/1508.0403

Ye. (n.d.). Another Form of Correlation Coefficient between Single Valued Neutrosophic Sets and its multiple Attribute Decision Making Method. *Neutrosophic Sets and Systems, 1*, 8-12. doi:10.5281/zenodo.571265

Ye, F. (2010). An extended TOPSIS method with interval-valued intuitionistic fuzzy numbers for virtual enterprise partner selection. *Expert Systems with Applications, 37*(10), 7050–7055. doi:10.1016/j.eswa.2010.03.013

Yeghiazaryan, V., & Voiculescu, I. (2015). *An Overview of Current Evaluation Methods Used in Medical Image Segmentation.* Department of Computer Science, University of Oxford.

Ye, J. (2010). Fuzzy decision-making method based on the weighted correlation coefficient under intuitionistic fuzzy environment. *European Journal of Operational Research*, *205*(1), 202–204. doi:10.1016/j.ejor.2010.01.019

Ye, J. (2010). Multicriteria fuzzy decision-making method using entropy weights-based correlation coefficients of interval valued intuitionistic fuzzy sets. *Applied Mathematical Modelling*, *34*(12), 38643870. doi:10.1016/j.apm.2010.03.025

Ye, J. (2011). Expected value method for intuitionistic trapezoidal fuzzy multicriteria decision-making problems. *Expert Systems with Applications*, *38*(9), 11730–11734. doi:10.1016/j.eswa.2011.03.059

Ye, J. (2012). The Dice similarity measure between generalized trapezoidal fuzzy numbers based on the expected interval and its multicriteria group decision-making method. *Journal of the Chinese Institute of Industrial Engineers*, *29*(6), 375–382. doi:10.1080/10170669.2012.710879

Ye, J. (2013). Another form of correlation coefficient between single valued neutrosophic sets and irs multiple attribute decision making method. *Neutrosophic Set Syst.*, *1*, 8–12.

Ye, J. (2013). Another form of correlation coefficient between single valued neutrosophic sets and its multiple attribute decision-making method. *Neutrosophic Sets and Systems*, *1*(1), 8–12.

Ye, J. (2013). Multicriteria decision-making method using the correlation coefficient under single-valued neutrosophic environment. *International Journal of General Systems*, *42*(4), 386–394. doi:10.1080/03081079.2012.761609

Ye, J. (2013). Single valued neutrosophic cross-entropy for multi criteria decision making problems. *Applied Mathematical Modelling*, *38*(3), 1170–1175. doi:10.1016/j.apm.2013.07.020

Ye, J. (2014). Correlation coefficient of dual hesitant fuzzy sets and its application to multiple attribute decision making. *Applied Mathematical Modelling*, *38*(2), 659666. doi:10.1016/j.apm.2013.07.010

Ye, J. (2014). Improved correlation coeffcients of single valued neutrosophic sets and interval neutrosophic sets for multiple attribute decision making. *Journal of Intelligent & Fuzzy Systems*, *27*, 2453–2462.

Ye, J. (2014). Improved correlation coefficients of single valued neutrosophic sets and interval neutrosophic sets for multiple attribute decision making. *Journal of Intelligent & Fuzzy Systems*, *27*, 24532462.

Ye, J. (2014). Improved correlation coefficients of single valued neutrosophic sets and interval neutrosophic sets for multiple attribute decision making. *Journal of Intelligent & Fuzzy Systems*, *27*, 2453–2462.

Ye, J. (2014). Similarity measures between interval neutrosophic sets and their application in multicriteria decision-making. *Journal of Intelligent & Fuzzy Systems*, *26*, 165–172.

Ye, J. (2014). Similarity measures between interval neutrosophic sets and their applications in multicriteria decision – making. *Journal of Intelligent & Fuzzy Systems*, 26(1), 165–172.

Ye, J. (2014). Similarity measures between interval neutrosophic sets and their applications in multi-criteria decision-making. *Journal of Intelligent & Fuzzy Systems*, 26(1), 165–172.

Ye, J. (2014). Similarity measures between interval neutrosophic sets and their applications in multicriteria decision-making. *Journal of Intelligent & Fuzzy Systems*, 26, 165–172.

Ye, J. (2014). Vector similarity measures of simplified neutrosophic sets and their application in multicriteria decision making. *International Journal of Fuzzy Systems*, 16(2), 204–211.

Ye, J. (2014). Vector Similarity Measures of Simplified Neutrosophic Sets and Their Application in Multicriteria Decision Making. *International Journal of Fuzzy Systems*, 16(2), 204–211.

Ye, J. (2014a). A multi-criteria decision-making method using aggregation operators for simplified neutrosophic sets. *Journal of Intelligent & Fuzzy Systems*, 26(5), 2459–2466.

Ye, J. (2014a). A multicriteria decision-making method using aggregation operators for simplified neutrosophic sets. *Journal of Intelligent & Fuzzy Systems*, 26, 2459–2466.

Ye, J. (2014b). Vector Similarity Measures of Simplified Neutrosophic Sets and Their Application in Multicriteria Decision Making. *International Journal of Fuzzy Systems*, 16(2), 204–211.

Ye, J. (2014c). Clustering Methods Using Distance-Based Similarity Measures of Single-Valued Neutrosophic Sets. *Journal of Intelligent Systems*, 23(4), 379–389. doi:10.1515/jisys-2013-0091

Ye, J. (2015). Improved cosine similarity measures of simplified neutrosophic sets for medical diagnoses. *Artificial Intelligence in Medicine*, 63(3), 171–179. doi:10.1016/j.artmed.2014.12.007 PMID:25704111

Ye, J. (2015). Multiple attribute decision-making method based on the possibility degree ranking method and ordered weighted aggregation operators of interval neutrosophic numbers. *Journal of Intelligent & Fuzzy Systems*, 28, 1307–1317.

Ye, J. (2015b). Trapezoidal neutrosophic set and its application to multiple attribute decision-making. *Neural Computing & Applications*, 26(5), 1157–1166. doi:10.100700521-014-1787-6

Ye, J. (2015c). Single-valued neutrosophic similarity measures based on cotangent function and their application in the fault diagnosis of steam turbine. *Soft Computing*. doi:10.100700500-015-1818-y

Ye, J. (2016). Correlation coefficients of interval neutrosophic hesitant fuzzy sets and its application in a multiple attribute decision making method. *Informatica*, 27(1), 179–202. doi:10.15388/Informatica.2016.81

Ye, J. (2016). Exponential operations and aggregation operators of interval neutrosophic sets and their decision making methods. *SpringerPlus*, 5(1), 1488. doi:10.118640064-016-3143-z PMID:28018779

Ye, J. (2016). Projection and bidirectional projection measures of single valued neutrosophic sets and their decision – making method for mechanical design scheme. *Journal of Experimental & Theoretical Artificial Intelligence.* doi:10.1080/0952813X.2016.1259263

Ye, J. (2017). Correlation coefficient between dynamic single valued neutrosophic multisets and its multiple attribute decision-making method. *Information, 8*(41), 2–9.

Ye, J. (2017). Multiple attribute decision-making method using correlation coefficients of normal neutrosophic sets. *Symmetry, 9*(80), 2–10.

Ye, J. (2017). Single valued neutrosophic similarity measures based on cotangent function and their application in the fault diagnosis of steam turbine. *Soft Computing, 21*(3), 817–825. doi:10.100700500-015-1818-y

Ye, J. (2017). Some weighted aggregation operator of trapezoidal neutrosophic number and their multiple attribute decision making method. *Informatica, 28*(2), 387–402. doi:10.15388/Informatica.2017.135

Ye, J. (2018). Fault diagnoses of hydraulic turbine using the dimension root similarity measure of single-valued neutrosophic sets. *Intelligent Automation & Soft Computing, 24*(1), 1–8. doi:10.1080/10798587.2016.1261955

Ye, J. (2019). PID tuning method using single-valued neutrosophic cosine measure and genetic algorithm. *Intelligent Automation & Soft Computing, 25*, 15–23.

Ye, J., & Cui, W. H. (2018). Exponential entropy for simplified neutrosophic sets and its application in decision making. *Entropy (Basel, Switzerland), 20*(5), 357. doi:10.3390/e20050357

Ye, J., & Fu, J. (2016). Multi-period medical diagnosis method using a single valued neutrosophic similarity measure based on tangent function. *Computer Methods and Programs in Biomedicine, 123*, 142–149. doi:10.1016/j.cmpb.2015.10.002 PMID:26506531

Ye, J., & Zhang, Q. (2014). Single Valued Neutrosophic Similarity Measures for Multiple Attribute Decision-Making. *Neutrosophic Sets and Systems, 2*, 48–54. doi:10.5281/zenodo.571756

Ye, S., Fu, J., & Ye, J. (2015). Medical Diagnosis Using Distance-Based Similarity Measures of Single Valued Neutrosophic Multisets. *Neutrosophic Sets and Systems, 7*, 47–54.

Ye, S., & Ye, J. (2014). Dice similarity measure between single valued neutrosophic multisets and its application. *Neutrosophic Sets Syst., 6*, 48–53.

Yuan, Y., Ren, Y., Liu, X., & Wang, J. (2019). Approach to image segmentation based on interval neutrosophic set. *Numerical Algebra, Control & Optimization*, 347-353.

Yuan, X., Li, H., & Lee, E. S. (2010). On the definition of the intuitionistic fuzzy subgroups. *Computers & Mathematics with Applications (Oxford, England), 59*(9), 3117–3129. doi:10.1016/j.camwa.2010.02.033

Zadeh, L. A. (1965). Fuzzy set and systems. In Proceeding of the symposium on system theory. New York Polytechnic Institute of Brooklyn.

Zadeh, L. A. (1965). Fuzzy Sets. *Information and Control*, 8(3), 338–353. doi:10.1016/S0019-9958(65)90241-X

Zadeh, L. A. (1975). The concept of a linguistic variable and its application to approximate reasoning—I. *Information Sciences*, 8(3), 199–249. doi:10.1016/0020-0255(75)90036-5

Zadeh, L. A. (1978). Fuzzy sets as a basis for a theory of possibility. *Fuzzy Sets and Systems*, 1(1), 3–28. doi:10.1016/0165-0114(78)90029-5

Zamora, E. M., Pollack, J. J., & Zamora, A. (1981). Use of Trigram Analysis of Spelling Error Detection. *Information Processing & Management*, 17(6), 305–316. doi:10.1016/0306-4573(81)90044-3

Zavadskas, E. K., Bauiys, R., & Lazauskas, M. (2015). Sustainable Assessment of Alternative Sites for the Construction of aWaste Incineration Plant by Applying WASPAS Method with Single-Valued Neutrosophic Set. *Sustainability*, 7(12), 15923–15936. doi:10.3390u71215792

Zeng, S., & Su, W. (2011). Intuitionistic fuzzy ordered weighted distance operator. *Knowledge-Based Systems*, 24(8), 1224–1232. doi:10.1016/j.knosys.2011.05.013

Zhang, H. Y., Wang, J. Q., & Chen, X. H. (2014). Interval neutrosophic sets and their application in multi-criteria decision making problems. *The Scientific World Journal*. Retrieved from http://fs.gallup.unm.edu/NSS/

Zhang, H., Ji, P., Wang, J., & Chen, X. (2015). Improved Weighted Correlation Coefficient based on Integrated Weight for Interval Neutrosophic Sets and its Application in Multi-criteria Decision Making Problems. *International Journal of Computational Intelligence Systems*, 8(6), 1027–1043. doi:10.1080/18756891.2015.1099917

Zhang, H., Wang, J., & Chen, X. (2014). Interval neutrosophic sets and their application in multicriteria decision making problems. *The Scientific World Journal*. PMID:24695916

Zhang, H., Wang, J., & Chen, X. (2016). An outranking approach for multi-criteria decision-making problems with interval-valued neutrosophic sets. *Neural Computing & Applications*, 27(3), 615–627. doi:10.100700521-015-1882-3

Zhang, M., Zhang, L., & Cheng, H. D. (2010). A neutrosophic approach to image segmentation based on watershed method. *Signal Processing*, 90(5), 1510–1517. doi:10.1016/j.sigpro.2009.10.021

Zhang, X., Jin, F., & Liu, P. (2013). A grey relation projection method for multi-attribute decision making based on intuitionistic trapezoidal fuzzy number. *Applied Mathematical Modelling*, 37(5), 3467–3477. doi:10.1016/j.apm.2012.08.012

Zhou, L., & Wu, W. Z. (2008). On generalized intuitionistic fuzzy rough approximation operators. *Information Sciences*, 178, 2448–2465.

About the Contributors

Mohamed Abdel-Basset received his B.Sc., M.Sc., and the Ph.D. in Operations Research from Faculty of Computers and Informatics, Zagazig University, Egypt. His current research interests are Optimization, Operations Research, Data Mining, Computational Intelligence, Applied Statistics, Decision support systems, Robust Optimization, Engineering Optimization, Multi-objective Optimization, Swarm Intelligence, Evolutionary Algorithms, and Artificial Neural Networks. He is working on the application of multi-objective and robust meta-heuristic optimization techniques. He is also an/a Editor/reviewer in different international journals and conferences. He has published more than 150 articles in international journals and conference proceedings. He holds the program chair in many conferences in the fields of decision making analysis, big data, optimization, complexity and the internet of things, as well as editorial collaboration in some journals of high impact.

Abdullah Kargın was born in Gaziantep, Turkey in 1990, is a PHD student of Gaziantep University, Department of Mathematics, Turkey. He received his M.Sc in Graduate School of Nature and Applied Sciences from Gaziantep University. His search major field is on soft set theory, fuzzy theory, neutrosophic theory, neutrosophic triplet theory, neutrosophic decision making problem, neutrosophic quadruple theory. He published over 20 articles and chapters for books.

Memet Şahin was born in Adıyaman, Turkey in 1965, is a Prof. Dr. of Gaziantep University, Department of Mathematics, Turkey. He received his M.Sc in Graduate School of Nature and Applied Sciences from Hacettepe University, Turkey. Also, he received his PHD in Graduate School of Nature and Applied Sciences from Karadeniz Technical University, Turkey. His search major field is on soft set theory, fuzzy theory, neutrosophic theory, neutrosophic triplet theory, neutrosophic decision making problem, neutrosophic quadruple theory. He published over 60 articles and chapters for books.

* * *

Adio Akinwale studied in Oskar Lange University, Wroclaw, Warsaw University, Warsaw and Technical University, Lodz, Poland where he had M.Sc and Ph.D in Informatics. His area of interest is in Artificial Intelligence in Database Systems.

Misturah Alaran has been teaching Computer Science Courses at Moshood Abiola Polytechnic (MAPOLY), Abeokuta, Ogun State, Nigeria for over a decade, where she has supervised more than fifty Higher National Diploma students in Computing on various applications . She bagged B.Sc. and M.Sc. in Computer Science and currently rounding up her Ph.D programme in Computer Science at Federal University of Agriculture, Abeokuta, Nigeria. Her research interests include Similarity measures, fuzzy logic, Neutrosophic logic, Multi-Criteria Decision Making, Machine Learning, Data Science, Information retrieval, Semantic Analysis. She is the current Head of the Computer Science Department MAPOLY. She is a registered member of many computer professional organisations like Nigeria Computer Society, Computer Professional (Registration Council) of Nigeria, Academia in Information Technology Professional, Nigeria Women in Technology (State Coordinator), Women in Technical Education.

Muhammad Aslam did his M.Sc in Statistics (2004) from GC University Lahore with Chief Minister of the Punjab merit scholarship, M. Phil in Statistics (2006) from GC University Lahore with the Governor of the Punjab merit scholarship, and Ph.D. in Statistics (2010) from National College of Business Administration & Economics Lahore under the kind supervision of Prof. Dr. Munir Ahmad. He worked as a lecturer of Statistics in Edge College System International from 2003-2006. He also worked as Research Assistant in the Department of Statistics, GC University Lahore from 2006 to 2008. Then he joined the Forman Christian College University as a lecturer in August 2009. He worked as Assistant Professor in the same University from June 2010 to April 2012. He worked in the same department as Associate Professor from June 2012 to October 2014. He worked as Associate Professor of Statistics in the Department of Statistics, Faculty of Science, King Abdulaziz University, Jeddah, Saudi Arabia from October 2014 to March 2017. He taught summer course as Visiting Faculty of Statistics at Beijing Jiaotong University, China in 2016. Currently, he is working as a Full Professor of Statistics in department of Statistics, King Abdul-Aziz University Jeddah, Saudi Arabia. He has published more than 340 research papers in national and international well reputed journals including for example, IEEE Access, Journal of Applied Statistics, European Journal of Operation Research, Information Sciences, Journal of Process Control, Journal of the Operational Research Society, Applied Mathematical Modeling, International Journal of Fuzzy Systems, Symmetry, International Journal of Advanced Manufacturer Technology, Communications in Statistics, Journal of Testing and Evaluation and Pakistan Journal of Statistics etc. His papers have been cited more than 2900 times with h-index 29 and i-10 index 87 (Google Scholar). His papers have been cited more than 1700 times with h-index 22 (Web of Science Citations). He is the author of one book published in Germany. He is also HEC approved PhD supervisor since 2011. He supervised 5 PhD theses, more than 25 M.Phil theses and 3 M.Sc theses. Dr. Muhammad Aslam is currently supervising 1 PhD thesis and more than 5 M.Phil theses in Statistics. He is reviewer of more than 50 well reputed international journals. He has reviewed more than 140 research papers for various well reputed international journals. He received meritorious services award in research from National College of Business Administration & Economics Lahore in 2011. He received Research Productivity Award for the year 2012 by Pakistan Council for Science and Technology. His name Listed at 2nd Position among Statistician in the Directory of Productivity Scientists of Pakistan 2013. His name Listed at 1st Position among Statistician in the Directory of Productivity Scientists of Pakistan 2014. He got 371 positions in the list of top 2210 profiles of Scientist of Saudi Institutions 2016. He is selected for "Innovative Academic Research & Dedicated Faculty Award 2017" by SPE, Malaysia. He Received King Abdulaziz University Excellence Awards in Scientific Research for the paper entitled "Aslam, M., Azam, M., Khan, N. and Jun, C.-H. (2015). A New Mixed Control Chart to Monitor the Process, International Journal of Production Research, 53 (15), 4684–4693. He Received King Abdulaziz University citation award for the paper entitled "Azam, M., Aslam, M. and Jun, C.-H. (2015). Designing of a hybrid exponentially weighted moving average control chart using repetitive sampling, International Journal of Advanced Manufacturing Technology, 77:1927–1933 in 2018. Prof. Muhammad Aslam introduced the area of Neutrosophic Statistical Quality Control (NSQC) the first time. His is the founder of neutrosophic inferential statistics (NIS) and NSQC. His contribution is the development of neutrosophic statistics theory for the inspection and process control. He originally developed theory in these areas under the Neutrosophic Statistics. He extended the Classical Statistics theory to Neutrosophic Statistics originally in 2018. He is the member of editorial board of Electronic Journal of Applied Statistical Analysis, Neutrosophic Sets and Systems, Asian Journal of Applied Science and Technology and Pakistan Journal of Commence and Social sciences. He is also member of Islamic Countries Society of Statistical Sciences. He is appointed as an external examiner for 2016/2017-2018/2019 triennium at The University of Dodoma, Tanzania. His areas of interest include reliability, decision trees, Industrial Statistics, acceptance sampling, rank set sampling, neutrosophic statistics and applied Statistics.

Elsayed M. Badr is an associate professor of computer science at Benha Faculty of Computers and Informatics, Benha University in Egypt. He received his Ph.D. in Parallel Algorithms (mainly in parallel graph algorithms) in 2006 from the University of Macedonia, Greece. Dr. Badr holds a Certificate of Quality Assurance from the University of Benha, Egypt and an M.Sc. in Graph Theory and Graph Algorithms applications and a B.Sc. in Mathematics from Benha Faculty of Science in Egypt. In addition to over 8 years of teaching and academic experience in Egypt and Greece, Dr. Badr has accumulated broad practical experiences and developed a solid set of skills in algorithms, graph labeling, wireless networks, distributed systems, parallel programming and linear programming.

Assia Bakali is Professor of Higher Education at the Naval Royal School of Casablanca Morocco. She obtained (Habilitation) at University Hassan II university in 2016 in partnership with University of POITIERS France and a Doctorate of High Graduate Studies degree at the Hassan II University, Mohammedia in 1999.

Tuhin Bera completed both graduate and master's degree in Mathematics from University of Kalyani, WB, India. He is actively engaged in the area of soft set, fuzzy set, intuitionistic fuzzy set and neutrosophic set. More than 20 papers in these areas have been published in different reputed international journals. He has presented his papers in international seminars. He has performed as reviewer in different international journals.

Said Broumi was born in Casablanca, Morocco in 1978, is a PHD of university Hassan II - Casablanca. He received his M.Sc in Industrial Automatic from Hassan II University Ainchok- Casablanca. His search major field is on neutrosophic graph theory, soft set theory, fuzzy theory, intuitionistic fuzzy theory, neutrosophic theory and neutrosophic soft set theory and neutrosophic decision making problem, he published over 150 articles.

Wen-Hua Cui graduated and received her PhD degree in Control Theory and Control Engineering from Shanghai University in China in 2016, and received her M.S. degree in Computer Architecture from the East China Normal University in P.R.China in 2007. Now, she is a lecturer in the Department of Electrical and Automation, Shaoxing University, P.R. China. Her research interests include multicriteria decision making, intelligent control, pattern recognitions, and medical diagnosis. In neutrosophic theory and applications, she has already published more than 10 papers in international journals. The neutrosophic theory includes simplified neutrosophic sets, linguistic neutrosophic uncertain numbers, hesitant linguistic neutrosophic numbers, cubic hesitant fuzzy sets, Q-linguistic neutrosophic variable sets, linguistic cubic hesitant variables, linguistic neutrosophic interval linguistic numbers, neutrosophic numbers, and then their applications include decision making, medical diagnoses, control system design, and so on.

İrfan Deli was born in 1986 Denizli, Turkey. He received his Ph.D. degree from Department of Mathematics, Faculty of Arts and Sciences, Gaziosmanpaşa University, Tokat, Turkey in 2013. At present he is working as Assistant Professor in University of 7 Aralık, Kilis, Turkey. His main interest areas include soft sets, fuzzy sets, intuitionistic fuzzy sets, neutrosophic sets, game theory, decision making, optimization, and so on.

Sudipta Gayen received his M.Sc. degree from Indian Institute of Technology Guwahati, India in 2014. Currently he is a Research Scholar in Department of Mathematics, National Institute of Technology, Jamshedpur, India. His areas of interest are Fuzzy Abstract algebra and its applications, Neutrosophic Abstract algebra and its applications.

Sripati Jha, Associate Professor in the Department of Mathematics, National Institute of Technology, Jamshedpur. He is also serving as Dean, Industry & Alumni Relations which is highly respectable administrative position in the Institution. He has also served as Head of the Department of Mathematics and Dean Student Welfare in the past. He has Published several International and National articles in the fields of Fuzzy and Neutrosophic set theory. Research Interest- Fuzzy logic, mathematical modelling, decision making, operation research, fuzzy and neutrosophic abstract algebra.

Ranjan Kumar has submitted Ph.D. Thesis in 2019 from National Institute of Technology Jamshedpur. He has Completed Masters in Applied Mathematics in 2011 from Birla Institute of Technology, Ranchi. Now, working as an Assistant Professor in The Department of Master of Application, Jain University, Knowledge Campus, Bengaluru, Karnataka. He has Published International and National articles in the field of Fuzzy Logic and Neutrosophic Set. Research Interest- Fuzzy logic, mathematical modeling, decision making, operation research problem, neutrosophic fuzzy, fuzzy Optimization, the multi-objective fuzzy programming problem, linear programming problem, etc.

Nirmal Kumar Mahapatra is acting as an associate professor in Mathematics at Panskura Banamali College (Autonomous), affiliated to Vidyasagar University, WB, India. He obtained B.Sc., M.Sc. and Ph.D. degree from Vidyasagar University. He has performed as reviewer in different international journals. His area of research interest includes inventory control, multi objective optimization, fuzzy optimisation, soft computing, soft set theory, fuzzy set and neutrosophic set theory, etc. He has published more than fifty research papers in different reputed international journals.

Yadigar Polat was born in 1966 Mersin, Turkey. He received his Ph.D. degree from Departman of Animal Science, Faculty of Agriculture, Çukurova University, Adana, Turkey in 2012. At present he is working as Assistant Professor in University of 7 Aralık, Kilis, Turkey. His main interest areas include soft sets, fuzzy sets, intuitionistic fuzzy sets, neutrosophic sets, game theory, decision making, optimization, and so on.

Krishna Prabha Sikkanan is from India, is an Assistant Professor in PSNA College of Engineering and Technology,Dindigul.She have completed her M.Sc,M. Phil in Mathematics and have completed her ME in System Engineering and Operation Research. She has completed her Ph.D in the field of Operation Research. Her research area includes fuzzy theory, intuitionistic theory, neutrosophic theory and operation research. She has published 19 articles and chapters for books.

Rumi Roy was born in 1992 at Kolkata, West Bengal, India. She completed her bachelor's degree in Mathematics from St. Xavier's College, Kolkata in 2013 and Master's degree in Applied Mathematics from Indian School of Mines, Dhanbad in 2015. Now she is a research scholar in the Department of Mathematics at Indian Institute of Engineering Science and Technology, Shibpur.

Sheng-Yi Ruan is an undergraduate in the Department of Electrical and Information Engineering, Shaoxing University, P.R. China. His research interests include intelligent control and decision making.

Siddhartha Sankar Biswas is an Assistant Professor in Computer Science & Engineering in Jamia Hamdard (Deemed University), New Delhi, India. He did his bachelor degree B.Tech. in Information Technology, master degree M.Tech. in Computer Science & Engineering, and Ph.D. in Computer Science & Engineering. His main areas of research are: Neutrosophic Theory, Quantum Computing, Shortest Path Problem, Soft-computing and Multigraph Theory, Graph Theoretic Algorithm. He has about ten years teaching experience, and he has guided a number of M.Tech. scholars in their Project work and thesis.

Vimala Shanmugavel is from India, is an Assistant Professor in Mother Teresa Women's University,Kodaikannal.She have completed her M.Sc,M.Phil in Mathematics .She has completed her Ph.D in the field of Graph Theory. Her research area includes graph theory, fuzzy theory, intuitionistic theory, neutrosophic theory. She have published more than 50 articles and chapters for books.

Mohamed Talea received his Ph.D. degree in physics from Poitiers University, France, in 2001, he obtained a Doctorate of High Graduate Studies degree from the Hassan II University, Morocco, in 1994. Currently, he is a Professor in the department of physics at Hassan II University, Morocco, and he is the Director of Information Treatment Laboratory. He has published over 100 refereed journal and conference papers. His research interest covers Systems engineering, security of system information.

Jun Ye graduated and received his M.S. degree in Automation and Robotics from the Technical University of Koszalin, Poland in 1997. From Feb. 2012 to Aug. 2012, he was a visiting scholar in the School of Engineering of Southern Polytechnic State University in USA. Now, he is a professor in the Department of Electrical and Information Engineering, Shaoxing University, P.R. China. He has more than 30 years of experience in teaching and research. His research interests include soft computing, multicriteria decision making, intelligent control, robotics, pattern recognitions, fault diagnosis, and rock mechanics. He has published more than 260 papers in journals, written few books related to his research work, and finished a few projects sponsored by the government of P.R. China. Especially in neutrosophic theory and applications, he has published more than 70 papers in international journals. The neutrosophic theory includes neutrosophic sets, simplified neutrosophic sets, refined neutrosophic sets, neutrosophic multisets, neutrosophic hesitant fuzzy sets, hesitant neutrosophic sets, trapezoid neutrosophic sets, neutrosophic trapezoid fuzzy sets, neutrosophic linguistic sets, dynamic neutrosophic sets, neutrosophic graph, neutrosophic numbers, neutrosophic linguistic numbers, neutrosophic functions, neutrosophic neural network, and then their applications include decision making, clustering analyses, medical diagnoses, mechanical fault diagnoses, mechanical conceptual design, image processing, control system design, and rock mechanics.

Index

A

C

D

E

F

H

I

T

W

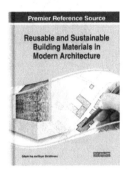
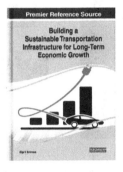
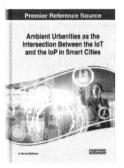
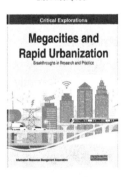
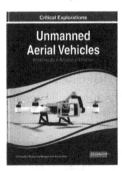
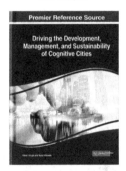

Ensure Quality Research is Introduced to the Academic Community

Become an IGI Global Reviewer for Authored Book Projects

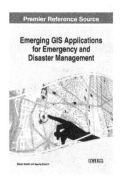
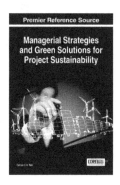

The overall success of an authored book project is dependent on quality and timely reviews.

In this competitive age of scholarly publishing, constructive and timely feedback significantly expedites the turnaround time of manuscripts from submission to acceptance, allowing the publication and discovery of forward-thinking research at a much more expeditious rate. Several IGI Global authored book projects are currently seeking highly-qualified experts in the field to fill vacancies on their respective editorial review boards:

Applications and Inquiries may be sent to:
development@igi-global.com

Applicants must have a doctorate (or an equivalent degree) as well as publishing and reviewing experience. Reviewers are asked to complete the open-ended evaluation questions with as much detail as possible in a timely, collegial, and constructive manner. All reviewers' tenures run for one-year terms on the editorial review boards and are expected to complete at least three reviews per term. Upon successful completion of this term, reviewers can be considered for an additional term.

If you have a colleague that may be interested in this opportunity, we encourage you to share this information with them.

IGI Global's Transformative Open Access (OA) Model:
How to Turn Your University Library's Database Acquisitions Into a Source of OA Funding

In response to the OA movement and well in advance of Plan S, IGI Global, early last year, unveiled their OA Fee Waiver (Offset Model) Initiative.

Under this initiative, librarians who invest in IGI Global's InfoSci-Books (5,300+ reference books) and/or InfoSci-Journals (185+ scholarly journals) databases will be able to subsidize their patron's OA article processing charges (APC) when their work is submitted and accepted (after the peer review process) into an IGI Global journal.*

How Does it Work?

1. When a library subscribes or perpetually purchases IGI Global's InfoSci-Databases including InfoSci-Books (5,300+ e-books), InfoSci-Journals (185+ e-journals), and/or their discipline/subject-focused subsets, IGI Global will match the library's investment with a fund of equal value to go toward subsidizing the OA article processing charges (APCs) for their patrons.

   Researchers: Be sure to recommend the InfoSci-Books and InfoSci-Journals to take advantage of this initiative.

2. When a student, faculty, or staff member submits a paper and it is accepted (following the peer review) into one of IGI Global's 185+ scholarly journals, the author will have the option to have their paper published under a traditional publishing model or as OA.

3. When the author chooses to have their paper published under OA, IGI Global will notify them of the OA Fee Waiver (Offset Model) Initiative. If the author decides they would like to take advantage of this initiative, IGI Global will deduct the US$ 1,500 APC from the created fund.

4. This fund will be offered on an annual basis and will renew as the subscription is renewed for each year thereafter. IGI Global will manage the fund and award the APC waivers unless the librarian has a preference as to how the funds should be managed.

Hear From the Experts on This Initiative:

"I'm very happy to have been able to make one of my recent research contributions, 'Visualizing the Social Media Conversations of a National Information Technology Professional Association' featured in the *International Journal of Human Capital and Information Technology Professionals*, freely available along with having access to the valuable resources found within IGI Global's InfoSci-Journals database."

– **Prof. Stuart Palmer**,
Deakin University, Australia

For More Information, Visit: www.igi-global.com/publish/contributor-resources/open-access or contact IGI Global's Database Team at eresources@igi-global.com

Printed in the United States
By Bookmasters